D1760736

13 MAY 2025

WITHDRAWN

# Reason and Society
## in the
## Middle Ages

# REASON AND SOCIETY
# IN THE
# MIDDLE AGES

*by*
Alexander Murray

CLARENDON PRESS - OXFORD
1978

*Oxford University Press, Walton Street, Oxford* OX2 6DP

OXFORD LONDON GLASGOW
NEW YORK TORONTO MELBOURNE WELLINGTON
IBADAN NAIROBI DAR ES SALAAM LUSAKA CAPE TOWN
KUALA LUMPUR SINGAPORE JAKARTA HONG KONG TOKYO
DELHI BOMBAY CALCUTTA MADRAS KARACHI

© *Alexander Murray 1978*

**British Library Cataloguing in Publication Data**

Murray, Alexander
    Reason and society in the Middle Ages.
    1. Europe—Intellectual life
    I. Title
    189          AZ603          77-30294

ISBN 0-19-822540-7

Printed in Great Britain by
William Clowes & Sons Limited
London, Beccles and Colchester

*to*
*My Parents*

# Preface

In writing this book I have been encouraged, helped, taught, and corrected by many colleagues and friends. I name first one I regret will not see in print those chapters, 6 to 8, which he was the first to read and comment on in draft: the late Dr. Siegurd Zienau, for many years Reader in Theoretical Physics at University College, London. I have a reason all of my own for mourning this polymath: there are few people whose reaction to the book as a whole I would have enjoyed more.

Among the living, my first literary debt is to those who read and criticized drafts: to my sister-in-law Dr. Nancy Uhlar Murray, my Newcastle colleague Miss Claire Lamont, and Dr. Bernard Hamilton, who read single chapters; and to Dr. D. J. A. Matthew and Sir Richard Southern, who generously found time to read and comment on drafts of the whole book. Among critics from whom I have learned I also thank those history societies from universities in Bristol, Dublin, Nottingham, Leeds, Durham, and Newcastle, who let me try out on them constituent ideas—both on 'reason' and on 'society'—as academic papers.

For expert help on specific topics I am indebted to Mrs. Jill Butterworth and Dr. S. V. R. Char, for guidance in the oriental tradition of the *Secretum Secretorum;* to Dr. Janet Cooper, who saved me from an error on medieval Oxford; to Miss A. De la Mare, who found the manuscript calculation pictured in Plate VI (b); to Dr. J. D. North, whose patience withstood a sustained bombardment of questions on medieval astronomy; and to my brother Robin, Fellow of the Institute of Development Studies: if chapter 2 betrays any acquaintance with the economics of poor regions, I owe it to him. I have a long-standing obligation of a slightly different kind also to Miss Helen Beguin, whose faultless typing of an early draft helped me clarify my mind at that stage.

Historians are permanently obliged to librarians. All but one of the libraries which prove that rule in the present case are mentioned in Part I of the bibliography, and in the List of Illustrations. The missing one is that which proves it most conclusively: my own university library in Newcastle, the patient co-operation of whose staff has been a necessary precondition of my researches. I conclude by mentioning two other such preconditions. One is the accommodating sympathy of colleagues and students in Newcastle. If it is not invidious to name one of many, I thank especially my co-medievalist Mrs. Elizabeth Fawcett, who has often volunteered to take on chores threatening work in the next-door study. I owe thanks also to the Margaret Gallagher fund, administered by the History Department in Newcastle, for financial help during a sabbatical year. The final precondition concerns my visits to libraries in London and Oxford. These would have been impossible but for the open-door hospitality I have enjoyed at two houses especially: those of Mr. and Mrs. Isador Caplan in London, and of Sir Richard and Lady Southern in Oxford.

In thanking these, and many other, accessories before the fact, I am far from confident of having produced a book worthy of the learning and kindness they have given me.

A.M.

*Hallbankgate*
*May 1977*

# Note on Translations

Classical Greek prose and verse will be quoted from standard translations by (respectively) Benjamin Jowett and Gilbert Murray. Biblical quotations are taken from any of three versions: the Authorized, the Revised Standard, and the New English Bible—the choice depending on the literary demands of the context. Where no source is indicated for other translations, I am answerable. Translations in epigraphs have occasionally been slightly simplified.

# Contents

# List of Illustrations

Plates

VI    Arithmetical Sophistication: early examples of Arabic numerals in use for calculation.

a) Addition. By courtesy of the Curators of the Bodleian Library, Oxford.

b) Long multiplication: the 'Jalousia' method. By courtesy of the Curators of the Bodleian Library, Oxford.

VII   Ignorant clergy satirized

Carving on south portal, S. Pierre, Aulnay, Charente-Inférieure. Photo: author.

VIII   Inhibitions: Generosity suppresses Avarice

Carving on west door, S. Pierre, Aulnay, Charente-Inférieure. Photo: author.

GRAPHS AND LINE DRAWINGS

MAPS (pp. 508–11)

# CHAPTER 1

# Introduction

On 1st November 1333 the rain began. It poured for
four days and four nights, with fearful lightning and
thunder; and the river rose, and rose, until the water
broke down walls, then buildings, and ended by
carrying away the three main bridges, all this with
inestimable ruin and loss of life. . . . It was agreed
that this flood was the worst catastrophe in the
history of Florence. And in its aftermath a question
arose, and was put both to the learned friars and
theologians, and to the natural philosophers and
astrologers: namely, whether the flood had occurred
through the course of nature or by the judgement of
God.

> Giovanni Villani, *Cronica*, XI, cc. 1–2.

Old families, like men themselves, must die;
  But we don't notice their decline, because
  It takes too long, and human lifetimes fly.
The turning moon lays bare the ceaseless shores
  And covers them again in endless round:
  Thus Fortune works in Florence, without pause.

> Dante, *Paradiso*, XVI, 82–4.

## 1. GREEKS AND HEBREWS

The achievements of science in the last half century are a
matter of both common knowledge and perpetual wonder. A
second matter of such knowledge and wonder is the stubborn
persistence in the same period of a whole range of psychological
and social problems. The juxtaposition is puzzling. It tempts us
to an easy explanation: science, we say, has not yet matched its
triumphs in the physical field with similar ones in the human.
'Not yet': as if the human problems came from a mere

insufficiency of science. The contrary idea scarcely occurs to us—that they may in some way arise *from* science.

Some physical problems do, after all: it is a fashionable truism that applied science, forged as a weapon to defend man in a hostile environment, now itself contributes to the hostility of the environment, in the form of 'pollution' An analogous effect can just as well occur in the mind. A victorious and self-confident institution tends to feed its own peculiarities of thought into the society immediately round it. Theology once did that at the expense of science itself, blocking it for centuries by teaching it to trust authority rather than experiment. Now the case is reversed. Science is on top—put there not only by its achievements, but by the sheer number of its practitioners and their influence as measured by the money they spend, both of which have grown exponentially $(y = X^2)$ for most of this century.[1] The result is that we all tend to think a bit more like scientists than we otherwise would: so much so that we see nothing odd in it—until we compare ourselves with almost any other society that has ever existed.

Such tendencies, flowing from one area of thought to those nearby, are bound to affect views on fundamental questions. These questions may be far removed from the areas where scientific method has won its triumphs, yet they may be of equal or greater practical consequence. Of such questions the most fundamental is one on which, while scientists as such do not appear to have much to say, scientific habits probably influence us all more than we realize. It concerns the nature of our species.

It has always been clear that much is wrong with man. What has not been so clear is *what* is wrong. Two basic answers have been given in western tradition. One is that man's trouble lies ultimately in his mind. He would do what was right if he knew; if he had the right data or drew sounder conclusions from the data he had. The second view finds the trouble in the will: men know what is right well enough (or could find out if they chose), but too often avoid doing it through perversity.

In the last two thousand years these views have intermingled in big and small situations, and sometimes exchanged disguises. But they remain distinct, and as ultimate views on human nature derive from different sides of Europe's cultural ancestry. The first comes from ancient Greeks, like Sophocles:

Of all the perils God has cursed
Mankind with, man's own folly is the worst
(*Antigone* vv. 1243–4).

The second view is on the other hand Hebrew:

Because you have . . . eaten of the tree of which I commanded you
'You shall not eat of it', cursed is the ground because of you.
(Genesis 3 : 17.)

Such is the distinction between the two approaches that a Greek who held the first view would probably not have understood the second.

In medicine all hangs on the diagnosis. So in more general human affairs, what we see as imperfect in ourselves determines what we do about it. If the root of man's trouble is ignorance, then both politics and religion boil down to education. If on the other hand the will is defective, knowledge is not enough: a whole apparatus of restraints and correctives, internal and external, must be expected as a normal part of existence. So the choice between 'Greek' and 'Hebrew' views of the world, in any particular case and in general, is one of practical moment. It is also of infinite complexity, far more than could be put in order in a few sentences, or even a book. Two observations on our modern situation are nevertheless obvious enough. One is that the dominant role of science in our century is likely, on the face of things, to have inclined our culture artificially towards a 'Greek' view of man. The other is that, if it has, then the imbalance thus created must touch every aspect of individual and social life. Conceivable examples of its effects might include, for the individual, what Jung described under the name 'over-differentiated intellect'. For society as a whole, a corresponding hypothetical result might be an intellectualist shift in the dominant élite, damaging the latter's cohesion with those it governs—as when a teacher is ignored and mocked at the back of a class.

These are already daring hypotheses. Even to frame them, it may be said, is to raise awesome questions. If that *is* said, nothing could suit the present purpose better. For it is from questions, rather than from a fixed thesis, that this book begins: twentieth-century questions, of a kind which will go on insisting on answers whatever success or failure a particular writer may

have in contributing to their solution; questions about the mind
and its setting in the rest of the human make-up; questions
about intellectuals in their relation to other kinds of people;
questions, in a word, about reason and society—in the
twentieth century.

I would have liked to write a book offering answers to all these
questions. But my own experience—surely a common one—
suggests that the nearer our human mind gets to reflecting on its
own essence, the harder it finds it to put its discoveries in cogent
and meaningful terms: it wanders off on its own. So I have opted
in this book for a less ambitious approach, but one which I hope
has a better chance of keeping the party together. The approach
is historical. All big psychological and social issues have a
historical dimension, in that knowledge of the past is relevant to
their solution. Of no question is this more palpably true than the
one just outlined, and which stands at the centre of our complex
of questions about reason and society: the comparative
weighing-up of 'Greek' and 'Hebrew' approaches to the world.
These labels themselves betray the antiquity of the tension they
represent. In the familiar centuries of modern European
history, since 1500, the duality of those two ancient attitudes
flaunts itself also in the labels of the great cultural movements of
successive generations. Renaissance and Reformation,
Enlightenment and Puritanism, scientific rationalism and
nonconformity: Greeks and Hebrews have wrestled in different
disguises in each century. Even in our own, the intellectualist
optimism of technology— τεχνολογία —is answered by the
disciples of the Hebrew Marx, for whom the only society they
know is morally rotten at heart.

The polarity between these pairs of opposites—broadly
speaking rationalist and religious—is in fact strikingly obvious
in cultural movements since 1500. Its obviousness reflects one
reason why I shall not be discussing these movements, but
taking the inquiry further back. After the Reformation, Europe
threw to the winds such unity or pretence of unity it had had
before. The first break, between Rome and her opponents, was
followed by others; and the dialectic of ideas, including ideas
peripheral to the main protestant–Catholic rift, came to be
played out in conflicts between states. This coincidence of
ideology and international politics tended to heighten the

identity of ideas. Each became confounded with its appropriate patriotism; and emigrants made the see-saw swing further by changing patriotisms to suit their own philosophies. (For example, protestants and Jews left the Spanish Netherlands for Amsterdam, increasing in that one act both the authoritarian Catholicism of the Spanish Empire and the tolerant prot-estantism of Holland.) But this flight to extremes, while it made for history with sharp outlines, in one sense made the history less significant. For it broke up the ideological interplay which had taken place before the Reformation. In the middle ages the same dialectic had occurred as occurred afterwards. But in the middle ages it occurred as a set of tensions in one society, not, by and large, as a conflict between societies. And it is for that very reason that it eludes the historian. The parties to the medieval dialectic shared one conceptual language. They more often sought to hide their differences than to trumpet them round as battle signals. Yet the tension was there; and if it is harder for us to find, it was proportionately more true to its ideological self. For it existed not in a scattering of military camps, any one of which could jump to arms when pressure grew too high, and thus turn ideological tension into military. It existed in a single social unit, which there was no hope of opposing *en bloc*, or of escaping from physically. The ideological dialectic was in that sense more complete.

That is one reason why I propose to take our problem of Greeks and Hebrews back to the middle ages. There is another. It applies only to the central and late middle ages, the period with which this book in fact deals. It was in the late eleventh century, the time of the first crusade, that Europe first became the *enfant terrible* she still is: a continent whose enduring political vigour is out of proportion to her size and numbers. The threshold of modern history is normally set about the year 1500. But that dating owes something to sixteenth-century polemic, and something more to the mechanics of historical research— matters of language, printed books, and so on. Just how much it owes may be debated. But it owes enough to expose the status of the year 1500 to rival claims. And the year 1000 has in many ways—some to be explored in chapters 2–5—as strong a one. Its claim is sufficiently strong, at least, to assure us that in study-ing Europe in the central middle ages we study the first direct recognizable ancestor of the society we still live in. So it is back to this ancestor we go.

## 2. REASON IN THE MIDDLE AGES[2]

To modern eyes the middle ages have all the appearance of an 'age of faith'. Not only the wealth and influence of the church, but for most of the period the overwhelming bias of literary documents suggests this: with narratives of pilgrimage, crusade, reforms, enthusiasms, and so on, often freely spiced with miraculous happenings and interpretations.

This view of the middle ages, like most oversimplifications of the past, derives from two factors, one objective and one subjective. The objective one is the bias hidden in this mass of evidence. The clerics who wrote most of it had a job to do other, for the most part, than record the religious beliefs of their world accurately for our benefit: a propaganda element is present in much of what they wrote. When we meanwhile reflect that there is little evidence, even in these dubious sources, on religious beliefs among the great mass of people, it must be acknowledged that the notion of the 'age of faith' rests on remarkably slender foundations. The subjective factor is equally significant. The image of a past age of faith, like that of any golden age, performs a psychological function for us: either as a basis for nostalgic criticism of current irreligion, or, in the opposite intent, as a means of disowning both the past and religion at once.

To reflect thus is to be moved to look at the middle ages more closely. A closer look reveals a subtler picture. And it is this subtler picture that the argument in this book starts out from. Faith, the picture shows, was only one element in a dialectic; a dialectic whose working-out forms the complex texture of the history of the period: church and crown, clericalism and anti-clericalism, virtue and vice, certainty and doubt. Our concern will be with one element in the dialectic: reason, as in a certain sense distinct from faith. The so-called disputes of faith and reason are of course a familiar feature of the history of medieval schools. Whether those disputes are rightly so labelled, and indeed the whole question of the conflict (if there is one) of faith and reason in theology, are matters we shall *not* be directly concerned with. The explanation why not, is that the academic disputes were relatively esoteric; and our business is with reason on the broadest-possible social stage.

On this broad stage there will be two kinds of reason in issue. The word 'reason' itself has—and had—two basic connotations. The less strict is ethical. By reasonable conduct we mean conduct that is moderate, fair, and conducive to peaceful order in human communities. Now medieval historiography highlights much that was *un*reasonable in this sense: fanaticism, bloodthirstiness, cruelty, etc. But we can also detect, taking sides in one after another of the great conflicts, a persistent strain of reasonableness: in conflicts about church and monarchy; about clerical discipline (e.g. whether clergy could marry); about lay morals (e.g. whether poverty was essential to Christian perfection, or whether a Christian could rightly accumulate wealth for old age). This is not to say one side in the conflicts was more scholarly or more logically coherent than the other, or right or wrong, or even more consistently reasonable in the ethical sense. It is just to say that, in these conflicts, one party comes nearer than the other to taking its stand on common sense and a wish for smooth social relations.

There is a simple way of putting this 'reasonableness' into relief. It can be juxtaposed with one of its persistent rivals, ascetic monasticism. The tradition of ascetic monasticism included men who were incidentally good scholars, and some who could be masters of judicious compromise. But the tradition as a whole—whether carried by the early Cluniacs, early Cistercians, early friars, or any of their contemporary emulators—does not strike us primarily by its reasonableness. It strikes us by a certain volcanic quality: a force erupting with little or no regard for current social norms as such, and instead raising new norms itself, changing the shape of the countryside. I shall come back to the ascetic–monastic tradition in the last two chapters of this book. But between now, and then, it will be a hidden presence—betrayed only by the occasional appearance of single representatives—setting off the contrasting mentality of the more reasonable people who are our real subject.

The word 'reason' with its derivatives can be used, then, in an ethical sense. But its original meaning is intellectual. It denotes the activity by which the mind gathers information and makes deductions from it. It is the specifically intellectual activity: *inter-lego*—roughly, 'I pick out'. As many medieval theologians were at pains to point out, there was no need at all why this learning and deducing should lead anywhere else than the Catholic faith. Indeed one constant theme among divines was that the world is a book, which if read aright necessarily leads a man to believe in God. However, when the reasoning process did lead to God, it was swallowed into the superior activity of believing. And one result of that is that the word 'reason' on the whole got (and gets) left for the religiously more abortive stages of the process: for anti-religious or non-religious reasoning. In this last sense, too, there was no lack of reasoning in the middle ages.

First: there was a very small amount of rational*ism*. By that modern term I mean a systematic belief in reason alone as the only method of finding truth. Such rationalism was naturally unorthodox. This fact discouraged all but an enthusiastic few from taking up so extreme a position. But the few enthusiasts did take it up, and by the time its philosophical equipment was mature enough to give the position a firm identity, under the inaccurate label 'Averroism',[3] church authorities were ill-placed to stamp it out. From the late thirteenth century onwards authorities certainly protested, and occasionally condemned. But it is clear that serious zealots for reason went on believing in it, and indeed spreading the word among disciples whenever inquisitors were out of earshot.[4]

That sort of rationalism, where it appeared, then, was remarkably hardy. It nevertheless played a very small part on the general intellectual scene, even in the late middle ages. A partial, and much-restricted, rationalism played on the other hand a very large part. This was the kind that took reason as far as to raise questions about religious tenets, and perhaps privately modify them; but without getting to the point of stubborn challenge to orthodoxy. The representatives of this partial rationalism lived, as religious people have often done, in a chronic state of 'double-think'; the logical instability of their condition being buttressed by the fact that many other people lived in it too. We come, with this 'partial rationalism', to the first of the two principal topics of this book. So it will be profitable to pause and draw it into closer focus.

There is one field where this task can be performed better than anywhere else. The field is belief in miracle. Throughout the period from 500 to 1500 ecclesiastical bookshelves were laden with books containing accounts of miraculous happenings. These accounts continued genres older than the middle ages; but they were far from being just a dead relic of the past: they were copied, added to, and imitated. They were there for the purpose of being read out, as the name for the principal type of them declared: *legenda*. The stories in the legends told how this or that saint, living or dead, healed people, raised the dead to life, or did any one of a range of such acts contrary to the observed order of nature. These miracles, largely modelled on those of the Gospel and the Bible generally, formed a more-or-less integral part of medieval Catholic belief. They went on doing so with vigour throughout the middle ages. The fact that the very substantial collection of them known as *The Golden Legend* was made in the late thirteenth century, and copied (and printed) with growing assiduity towards the late fifteenth century, is a reliable indicator of the sustained vitality of this enthusiasm.[5] It was as great in some circles in the fifteenth century as it had been in the tenth.[6]

So people often heard accounts of how Jesus and his saints had raised men to life. Yet the fact remained that not many medieval people had actually *seen* a dead man raised to life. Some thought they had seen it.[7] But yet others, who knew about comas and such things, were not only hesitant about contemporary claims, but ventured even to murmur about the Gospel story of Lazarus.[8] And even a man without expert medical knowledge might reflect that miracles happened less in his own experience than they were said to have happened in others'. Some of the most faithful Catholics confessed they were puzzled by this. Miracles had happened in the past, they said, but did not happen, or not so much, now; and they explained it as if the faith were a tree, which had needed watering with miracles when first planted, but was now sturdy enough to do without.[9]

People in the central middle ages did not, and were aware that they did not, see miracles happening abundantly in their own experience. This was one consideration which created a tension with the church's literature on miracles. What people did see was of equal moment in determining their view. They saw, and learned about, a regular order of nature. With our modern schooling we may imagine that a man only has to open his eyes to see that nature works by constant laws. But on the face of it it is not obvious at all. Water normally flows downwards; yet in a thin glass tube it will rise. Hard substances burn or crack in intense heat; but not asbestos. Nature is full of such apparent anomalies.[10] It takes considerable abstraction, standing on the shoulders of generations of speculation and research, to realize that these apparent breaches of law are only so because we have begun with too particular a law.

The concept of a regular nature therefore needed creating. Its creation appears to have fed on two intellectual tributaries. One was the gamut of sciences which in practice provided the education of the educated, the *litterati*. These sciences were those of language (the *trivium*); theology or 'sacred page'; civil and canon law; and, from the late twelfth century, philosophy. This family of disciplines taught men to think logically about themselves and about how they stood with God and with each other. The disciplines did not, for the most part, directly affect men's view of nature. But indirectly, it is not too much to say they entirely transformed it. For one thing, they opened the door to the influence of Greek and Arabic physics, which took little account of any god who intervened in nature. Equally important, they defined an area where human reason was autonomous. Problems could now be solved by reason which had previously been tackled by a divinatory approach to nature. Among other results of this change was that nature was relieved of a weighty didactic burden. Nature thus became approachable by science. There is no clearer example of this process than the judicial ordeal. The growth of rational judicial procedures threw the ordeal into discredit. Nature—in the form of the instruments of the ordeal (the hot iron, water, etc.)—was now free of this particular obligation to act irregularly, and hence was more accessible to a scientific approach.[11]

The second current feeding the concept of regular nature (and it was a distinct current) was mathematics. At its most practical level this merged with technology. It may be a truism that medieval cathedrals could not have been built without faith. But it is equally true that their fabric would long since have been rubble if their architects had not been closely acquainted with principles of gravity and stress, understood mathematically and known to be constant.[12] On a less technological level, mathematics served, and in its medieval sense included, astronomy. The predictability of astronomical laws stood in contrast with the fortuitous confusion of affairs on earth—despite a hardy penchant for joining the two. This regularity helped make astronomy the most demonstrable medieval ancestor to the mathematical physics of the Renaissance. For closely bound to it was mathematics in our sense, the science of number. By the late middle ages more than one philosopher had a presentiment that number underlay the functioning of the whole physical world, even though none of them quite grasped how that could be turned to scientific account—a step left for Galileo.[13]

Two currents, then, literary and mathematical, combined to feed a more regular concept of nature. The more regular this concept grew, the greater was its tension with inherited notions of miracle. The numerous old exceptions to natural laws, like magnets and eclipses, tended to fade away before the natural philosophy of the twelfth and thirteenth centuries, which showed they were not exceptions at all. Miracle was increasingly left on its own, in tension with an otherwise regular nature. The tension was variously expressed. A principal way was by disbelief in miracles and in other divine interventions. Such disbelief forms an almost perpetual counterpoint to the miraculous literature. Casual disbelief in miracle stories was in the first place virtually as old as the stories themselves; it is mentioned as a literary 'Aunt Sally' from very early on.[14] Then in the central middle ages, while this casual incredulity continued, we hear also of systematic scepticism: like that condemned by the bishop of Paris in 1277, in a long list of current wrong opinions.[15] The interpretation of undisputed events, similarly, admitted conflicting views. The passage quoted from Villani at the head of this chapter, about the flood in Florence in 1333, is one example. A similar discussion followed the Black Death in 1348. Were these calamities directly the work of God, or were there natural causes?[16] We know of other such debates from the thirteenth and fourteenth centuries.

It is unimaginable that European civilization could have developed as it did, as both religious and scientific at once, if no *modus vivendi* had been found between the concepts here in tension: God's direct intervention in nature, and natural laws. Aquinas [† 1274], here as elsewhere, was foremost in finding the resolution.[17] Natural laws operated in all normal circumstances, Aquinas explained, but that did not mean God lost the right to intervene when he saw fit. This view was embodied in a closer definition of miracle, together with the coining in this connection of the word 'supernatural': a thirteenth-century invention, designed to accommodate an old idea of the divine in terms of a new idea of nature.[18] By the end of the thirteenth century the concept of miracle had thus moved into a new conceptual environment. It can be compared to an old church in a modern city: the church itself remains unchanged, but looks quite different because of the buildings which rise round it. In Aquinas' time the age-old belief in miracle, similarly, was hedged round by the rising suburbs of reason.

Miracle may appear from one angle a superficial element in religion. If so, it is surely a narrow angle. For the idea of miracle involves more than the doings of saints in legends. It involves Christ's alleged activities on earth (and hence the credit of the Gospel), together with the supposed resurrection of Christ's body, and of our bodies at the end of time. Our idea of miracle—what it is and whether possible—is indeed bound ultimately to our idea of who or what has power in the universe. Does power lie with inanimate nature as we understand it, and as modified by human applied science? Or does it lie with an invisible being who in the last resort can do just what he likes with nature—for example, reverse time? Here too, Greeks and Hebrews have been in perpetual tension. If nature is at bottom regular, we only have to understand it. If God is in charge, he needs propitiating.

The idea of miracle is thus at the very core of religion. Its modification, or the modification of its terminology, in the context of growing rationalistic currents in the twelfth and thirteenth centuries, is on that ground alone a matter of high intrinsic interest. The interest may be rendered more immediate to some present-day readers by the recollection that, in the confusions which closed the middle ages, Roman Catholic theology anchored itself more firmly to the monumental synthesis of Aquinas. It is hence his concept of miracle, a product not only of his insight but of the circumstances of scholasticism, which governs the definition of miracle among those who still care to define it.

What was new in the two scholastic centuries which culminated with Aquinas was not belief in miracle. It was the rationalistic context through which miracle was seen. Our purpose in this book is to search for the origins of this rationalistic context. We shall search for it not, now, in terms of its intellectual antecedents—Aristotle, Avicenna, etc.—but in terms of men and society. Our question will be a social one. What distinct psychological or social conditions, if any, urged men to think more rationally about nature, and hence generated that tension in their view of God and the world?

This question of course makes an enormous assumption. It assumes that men's way of life in society determines, at least to some extent, how they think. An extreme form of this doctrine is associated with Marxist revolutionary movements. But the core of the doctrine is not revolutionary at all. It is old. It ran right down the middle of medieval theological doctrine. To do so it of course had to start in the Bible itself. Saint Paul, for instance, had put part of the idea in general terms in 2 Tim. 4:3: 'they will heap to themselves teachers after their own lusts, having itching ears'. The lusts, the human passions, came first, the ideas afterwards. The ethical side of this notion was frequently elaborated in the middle ages. Divines pointed out that a man tends to champion, as a matter of principle and on the grounds that they are not sins, sins he habitually commits: usury, fornication, etc. They went further, and saw the impulse from action to thought penetrating even to natural philosophy. Men who habitually follow carnal impulses, the doctrine ran, are thereby obstructed from all comprehension of the objects of faith:

those who occupy themselves with sense-objects, or other things which have nothing to do with faith, and who persistently remain in this state, dwell so far from the truths they should believe that the latter are inaccessible to them.

*Et propter hoc videre non possunt.* Thus went the categorical statement of a sermon on obstacles to faith, written in the thirteenth century and read and repeated subsequently.[19] An Italian vernacular Gospel commentator asked similarly [*c.* 1380]:

> Whence comes this doubt in another life, that makes a man say: 'I see nothing of this God or of this other life'? I will tell you. It comes from his perverse, wicked way of life.[20]

One twelfth-century expression of the same doctrine made the effect of life on philosophy quite specific:

> men given over to the carnal senses, and habituated to corporeal concerns, neither seek reasons [for physical events], nor wait to find out causes, but imagine everything happens unforeseeably and by chance.[21]

The principle was also honoured in its corollary: that a religious view of the world was more likely to be held by someone who normally lived uncontaminated by material preoccupations. An Augustinian canon was in effect saying this when he wrote [*c.* 1200], recommending a student friend to the cloister:

> I think that only they purely and rightly understand the holy writings, who by the purity of their life keep close to that spirit by which the scripture was composed and expounded.[22]

It was thus a commonplace of religious psychology, for most of the middle ages, that habitual action affects a man's philosophy. From the point of view of society and reason, the commonplace fell short in one particular. Except in a few eccentric phases it did not define in social terms what sort of habitual action went with this or that philosophical effect. It is one aspect of this problem that we have to investigate.

It only remains to say how the task of investigating it will be approached.

### 3. THE PLAN OF THE BOOK

It has been customary for European historians to explore social questions in terms of 'class', defined in terms of a relationship to the means of production—as *rentiers*, workers, and so on. Historians exploring the social dimension of thought have understandably been tempted to employ this model. It has yielded striking results. For the study of medieval religion it nevertheless has manifest weaknesses. The most manifest is probably that its results have not been striking enough. For all the discoveries and new interpretations made in the last fifty years by Marxist historians in the field of medieval religion, it remains true that no single historical work of this genre has proved more than half successful as a thesis. Either it has been a case of critics producing evidence to baffle the author's hypothesis;[23] or the author himself proves on scrutiny to have written what Croce called a 'double' history book: where brilliant historical analysis runs side by side with Marxist doctrine, but the two are unconnected.[24]

This consistent half-success, in attempts to link medieval religious allegiances to economic classes, is enough by itself to induce scepticism about the model the attempts start from. There is another reason for being chary about this approach. Contemporary religious writers discourage it. It is not just that medieval writers who do split people up into categories, do so as often as not on quite other criteria than economic (e.g. clerical and lay, young and old, men and women); as if differences in religious approach were woven into a more complex pattern than could be accounted for by an approach in terms of social classes. The writers give more positive testimony even than this. For they frequently aver that such-and-such a religious trait affects all classes equally.

These statements are so frequent, and form such a striking obstacle to too simple a sociological view of medieval religion, that some examples will be in place. From the late Carolingian period, for instance, the best surviving testimony to certain magical beliefs in south-eastern Gaul is that given by Bishop Agobard of Lyons [*c*. 820]. He starts: 'in the regions round here nearly all men, noble and ignoble, townsmen and countrymen, old and young, believe that hail and thunder can be produced at the will of human beings'.[25] In the tenth century the Italian pastors Atto of Vercelli and Ratherius of Verona insist that certain of the canonical abuses they describe are classless: 'multi majores et inferiores' (marry uncanonically);[26] 'from the lowest in the church to the highest, from the most ignorant to him who gives himself out as most learned, from layman to pontiff' (hold canon law in contempt).[27] Radulf Glaber used similar phrases of the craze for pilgrimage in the early eleventh century.[28]

After *c.* 1050 economic classes ramified, and a 'bourgeoisie' began to develop. Yet accounts of religious attitudes still commonly lump all classes together. They do so most conspicuously of all in the thirteenth and fourteenth centuries—the very centuries with most claim to have given birth to a discernible urban proletariat. The mendicant friars made it their business to know how each section of the population stood towards religion, and recorded differences. Yet often, when it came to a special religious practice or belief, they or their friends will say how the feature cuts across classes. An enthusiasm for a miracle-worker will include not only the unschooled populace, but 'many noble women'.[29] A miracle-working statue will attract not only the common folk, but 'some of the best people of Florence'.[30] The apocalyptic prophecies associated with Joachim of Fiore found adherents similarly among educated and uneducated.[31] The flagellant movement which at one time (1260) attached itself to these prophecies had adherents from 'all men from throughout the world, small as well as great, noble knights as well as common people'.[32] The same asseveration occurs often of religious enthusiasms in the thirteenth and fourteenth centuries.[33] It also occurs of irreligion. The Franciscan chronicler Salimbene says the inhabitants of his native city Parma were most 'hard' and 'insolent' to the friars; and this applied to 'clergy and laity, men and women, noble and ignoble'.[34] Moralists echo the same trait. The devil (in a story of a vision granted to a Dominican) lists the types of person he deceives, including all sorts 'down to the ladies' maids who serve in their chamber and flatter them'.[35] Hypocrisy, personified in the *Romance of the Rose*, boasts the same universality: 'I am of all trades, now a prince, now a page . . . now "Robert" now a mere "Robin"'.[36] Even Langland, whose indignation with the rich is a leading motif of *Piers Plowman*, says squarely that the 'pryde' which is destroying his contemporaries' religion is 'waxen . . . amonges riche and pore'.[37] The list of such inclusive assertions could go on.[38]

These assertions are not the whole story. Some have an element of cliché. The fact that any of them was made at all may suggest a presumption the other way. Most, again, echo the view of one observer of one movement or other religious trait; and cases will appear later where class *was* thought to affect religion—at least in degree, and sometimes in kind. Yet none of the assertions quoted can be disproved from other sources, and some can be confirmed. The very frequency of the formula by itself has its lesson. Beliefs, credulities, enthusiasms, hostilities, and vices: all were often said to be common to different social classes—often enough, that is, to obstruct any general, neat equation between class and religious allegiance. So no such neat equation will be attempted. Instead I shall suggest another equation. It will be based on another set of social categories, created from the first set by a simple operation. The operation is that which turns the concept of relative *position* into one of relative *movement* (for mathematicians dy/dt instead of y). Some three centuries before the Renaissance a drawing was in fashion of the Wheel of Fortune, surrounded by four human figures: one going up, one down, and two, at top and bottom, in precarious stability.[39] These are the categories envisaged in this book. They are usually harder to identify in medieval flesh-and-blood than the stationary classes. But they are not so hard that knowledge need perish altogether; and there are reasons for thinking this social calculus the most promising basis for the following investigation.

Social differentiation by movement: this concept, the basis of the following inquiry, will also determine its structure. This structure I shall now describe, beginning with a word on chronology. The focus of this book will be on the 'central' middle ages, *c.* 1100–*c.* 1300: the decisive period, that is, in the creation of that tension in the idea of miracle which it is my purpose to explain. There will be two kinds of exception to this time-bracket. Where an elusive characteristic can be well illustrated from beyond the bracket—by rarely more than a generation or two—I shall make a sortie to get the illustration. The most licentious of these excursions will be to the university of Paris in the fourteenth and early fifteenth centuries, in Part III. Secondly, there will be two historical excursions back into the period 800–1100, for much of Part I, and in chapter 6—each designed to expose a peculiarity in the culture of the central period.

The book is in four parts. The first will describe the social mechanism within which the intellectual 'renaissance' of the twelfth and thirteenth centuries took place. The description has one purpose: to identify an acceleration of up-and-down mobility in society after the millennium, and the path through which this may have affected the intellect. This purpose will be served in four stages covering one chapter each. The first will be purely economic. It will summarize evidence for the view that the one hundred and fifty years 975–1125 witnessed a generic change in the European economy, a change which made the setting for the economy for the rest of the middle ages. The change, it will be argued, represents a lasting shift in the world balance of power. So the scene will be set geographically wider in this chapter than in the rest of the book. And since the shift began in about Charlemagne's time, the story will also be traced back some two centuries earlier.

From 'society', chapters 3 and 4 will start the journey in towards 'reason'. They will trace an effect of the economic shift on men's minds, arguing that the shift intensified up-and-down social mobility by way both of money and of political power: and that this change made significant numbers of men more conscious of the accessibility of power. The journey towards 'reason' will be concluded in chapter 5. The chief instrument to power was the mind. Men recognized this, and cultivated their minds accordingly. Their recognition will be documented from twelfth- and thirteenth-century sources.

Part I, then, will purport to describe the social mechanism within which the rationalistic culture grew. Parts II and III will turn to the rationalistic culture itself, to discern its relation to this structure. The plan of the two Parts corresponds to the twofold current which I identified earlier in this introduction, as affecting the concept of miracle, and establishing the notion of a regular nature: namely, the culture of the educated, the *litterati*; and mathematics. The social mechanism described in Part I will have prepared us to expect that both aspects of the culture would rest on social elements rising in society. That is now argued to have been so. Parts II and III, while from a logical angle symmetrical, will be from a literary angle asymmetrical. The mathematical culture, which will be treated first, largely eluded historical record, and therefore historians. For that reason two of the three chapters devoted to it will try to disinter its history—starting (in chapter 6) with its dark-age prehistory. That done, the last mathematical chapter (chapter 8) will relate that history to the central hypothesis of the book.

The subject of Part III will be the culture of the *litterati*. Unlike mathematics, this stood in an intimate relation to historical record. So it can be portrayed more fully. The four chapters on it will take for granted the chronological history of schools and universities. By dwelling on elements in that history, these chapters will seek to identify a distinct intellectual interest hiding in medieval society, challenging the secular and ecclesiastical authorities in the name of the mind.

Elusive phenomena are put in relief by their opposites. Part IV will therefore explore the reverse side of the culture portrayed in Parts II and III. The rationalistic culture of the risers will there be turned upside-down. Part IV will accordingly study people who could not rise, because they were already at the top, and will describe their association with the ascetic-religious culture which stood in contrast with the rationalistic. The conclusion of the book, which also concludes Part IV, will be presented in the form of a composite portrait: *ecce homo*. Its subject will be the man who, belonging to the ascetic-religious culture and embracing its beliefs in the fullest measure, also, apparently, had sympathies and appeal conspicuously transcending social class.

The questions which this book is meant to answer arose from personal experience: that of someone who grew to adulthood in the ten years after the Second World War. The war witnessed much unreason. One conspicuous sequel to it, all over western Europe, was a swift expansion in universities and other educational institutions: an apotheosis of reason. In those universities, some were content to worry about how to prevent another war. Others were equally concerned with the question—which may come to the same in the end—of what men can do if there is *not* a war: what that is worth doing, that is, and does not mark some kind of moral collapse. The same anxiety, as it happens, had once inspired the doyen of medieval ethical authorities, Cicero: 'fearing lest his son would follow the vices of the Romans, now that the civil wars were over'.[40] It inspired me.

I mention this origin for a more down-to-earth reason than any intrinsic interest it may have: namely, that it may explain how this book stands towards contemporary historical research. I have been in the position of an engineer laying a railway line. The direction of the line is dictated by considerations quite other than the shape of the bumps and swamps it travels over, or of what men have already built on them. My own line has sometimes found firm existing foundations, and in the right places; and then it has gone flat over the top. Elsewhere the foundation had not quite settled, or had settled but seemed likely to shift again, and I have consequently tried there to shore up foundations. In yet other stretches special foundations had to be made; either from materials already put together, and near to hand, which only needed putting in place; or, elsewhere, by pick and shovel. Readers will find from the footnotes which of these operations underlies the text.

The footnotes will also reveal the names of the giants on whose shoulders I stand: all except a few to whom in one respect my debt is biggest of all, since they were accessories before the fact. The history books which made the present thesis seem practicable were about, not the middle ages, but the Italian Renaissance. Alfred von Martin's stimulating but floundering little book *The Sociology of the Renaissance*[41] sent me back to his more solid *Coluccio Salutati*.[42] Something of Von Martin's misgivings as to the values of Renaissance humanism were vindicated by more recent studies, for instance L. Martinez's *The Social World of the Florentine Humanists*.[43] But paradoxically it was Hans Baron's *The Crisis of the Early Italian Renaissance*[44] which actually launched the present medieval enterprise. The author demonstrates the self-conscious role of *ragione* in Florence after 1400; and he, or rather his sources, relate this to the mobility of Florentine society.

The hope of winning public honours and ascending is the same for all [said Chancellor Bruni in 1428], provided they possess industry and natural gifts, and lead a serious-minded and respected way of life . . . it is marvellous to see now powerful this access to public office, once it is offered to a free people, proves to be in awakening the talents of the citizens. For where men are given the hope of attaining honour in the state, they take courage and raise themselves to a higher plane; where they are deprived of that hope, they grow idle and lose their strength.[45]

Others were saying the same thing at the same time. Why the influence of Professor Baron's thesis on the present book is paradoxical is that he seeks to identify a new departure after 1400. In some ways he is successful. But in respect of the mechanism described by Bruni, what Professor Baron succeeds in doing is delineating with exceptional precision a phenomenon which, once identified, must be recognized by the medievalist as his own property. Most of us were taught at school that Florentine Renaissance culture appeared, as if bubbling up from a hole in the ground, just before 1300. What we may not have been taught, though there is now a growing specialist literature on the subject, is that the main tributary to that culture had gone *into* the hole from the scholasticism of the university of Paris, which reached the apogee of its medieval influence just before the Florentine Renaissance began. Traced back, the current leads us to discover some of the features of Florentine Renaissance humanism hiding in the less documented and marginally less articulate culture of the university of Paris and its cousinry; not only intellectual features, but social. Chapters 9 to 13 will be offered in substantiation of that.

The mention of Paris and Florence in one sentence is an occasion to mention one last fact about how this book was written. Its first sketch was a tale of two cities. Florence represented commerce—which made people powerful by making them rich; which was fed by the sin of avarice and in its turn nourished the mathematical culture of accountants. Paris, on the other hand, provided governors for that other great republic, the church; the church, which made people powerful by appointment, was fed by the sin of ambition, and in her turn nourished the literary culture necessary to her role as mistress of communication and record.

It may be pleaded, in extenuation of the half-truths contained in that scheme, that they were encouraged by much of what there was to be read on the subject a few years ago. But as the question led deeper, the distinction between the two cities became confused. The church came to appear both more commercial from one aspect and less republican from another.

Florence, for her part, seemed more and more to have acquired, between the thirteenth and the fifteenth century, some of the role in the universal church which had once distinguished Paris: as supplier of trained manpower. Nor was it as true as everyone seemed to think that mathematics was the child of commercial accounting—as chapter 8 will show. So the tale of two cities fell apart. The pieces have reassembled themselves within a more abstract and general formula. Yet the polarity of the two cities still haunts the subject, and will not go away— surely because there remains something in it. Traces of the polarity will consequently be noticed in this book, for example in the correspondence between 'Avarice' and 'Ambition' in Part I (on one hand), and 'Arithmetic' and 'Reading and Writing' in Parts II and III (on the other).

To the student of it, history can resemble a kaleidoscope: one shake, and the pattern—at one instant sharp, balanced, and all-embracing—vanishes, to be replaced by another. In writing this book I have been victim to this perplexity, but found confidence in the fact that the first pattern kept coming back. It could not have done so, I have reflected, unless it were at least an aspect of the true state of affairs. In that twilight assurance it is offered to the reader.

PART I

ECONOMICS AND THE MIND:
THE MAKING OF WESTERN SOCIETY

# CHAPTER 2

# Money

> When men multiplied and possessions were divided,
> one man had more than he wanted of one com-
> modity, while another had little or none; and of
> another commodity the converse was true. Men
> therefore began to trade by barter. This practice
> persisted in some states till long afterwards. But as
> this exchange and transport of commodities gave rise
> to many inconveniences, men were subtle enough to
> devise the use of money, to be the instrument of
> exchanging the natural riches which of themselves
> minister to human need . . . And it is clear without
> further proof that coin is very useful to the civil
> community, and convenient, or rather necessary, to
> the business of the state.
>
> Nicholas Oresme, *De Moneta* (*The Mint*), c. 1 (*c.*
> 1360).[1]

THE story to be told in this book begins in the eleventh century,
a turning-point in western European history. There have been
other turning-points. As far as the middle ages are concerned
most centuries between the fifth and the fifteenth might stake a
claim. But none of them—except perhaps those two at either
end—could do so as confidently as the eleventh. If we ask when
the great monarchic dynasties of England and France, or the
decentralized dynasties of Germany, effectually took root;
when southern Italy became a separate dominion, or northern
Italy (for practical purposes) a network of separate communes,
the answers all lead back to the eleventh century. The church,
with its reform in Curia, cloister and school, adds to the picture.
Were doubt to remain, the best witness of all would allay it:
Europe's contemporary neighbours, the Muslims. At the start of
the century in the west, at the end of it in the east, Muslims felt

the first buffetings of the western European infant prodigy, whom they had so far, for the most part, disdained as a curiosity for geographers.

Many stories therefore start in the eleventh century. The present one does so for a special reason. From about the millennium, European society began to assume characteristics which distinguish all that came after from all that went before. Some of these characteristics affected psychology; and some of these, in turn, affected culture. The eleventh century, taken with some twenty-five years at either end, witnessed the genesis of a lasting social mechanism which enclosed, and partly shaped, the intellectual development we have to study.

To describe this mechanism is therefore our first task. The task will be eased if we describe the elements in the mechanism one by one. And we start with the most material element. It is money. That short, familiar word sounds a warning bell. 'The Rise of the Money Economy' is so familiar a *deus ex machina* for explaining historical change that it draws discredit on itself: it surely cannot explain everything in every century.[2] Yet the phrase can be used in one sense or another of several centuries, like the sixteenth, or the thirteenth, or even the third century B.C., some of whose eponymous bronze was in fact a crude coinage. But none of this disqualifies the eleventh century for a share in the phrase. This is not only because the creation of today's hypermonetary economy has been a slow and big enough development to accommodate many leaps, each bringing sharp changes to contemporary society. It is also because the speed has varied. The development has occasionally gone into reverse, and occasionally leapt forward. I hope to show that the eleventh century experienced both irregularities: the development had previously gone into reverse and now leapt forward. The result was a change in quantity so big as to count as one in quality.

*Qualitas; qualis;* 'what it is'. We all think we know *what* money is. Most theorists have also carried with them a historical idea of how money was invented. Nicholas Oresme's view, quoted at the head of this chapter, was essentially a commonplace repeated since Aristotle. It is still current. But applied to the two centuries before the millennium, when the monetary genesis began, the commonplace has shortcomings. And before we can understand the qualitative change that took place in the use of money, we must first take a new look both at what money is, and where it fits into a non-monetary economy. We must devise, in other words, a concise new theory of money, tailor-made this time for the early middle ages.[3]

## I. A THEORY OF MONEY FOR THE EARLY MIDDLE AGES

Money is by definition a recognized medium of exchange. An inquiry into its function must therefore go back to exchange. Indeed it must go further: to the distribution of property. For exchange is a way of distributing property. It is only one way.[4] In the early middle ages, much as in our own childhoods, the bulk of property was distributed in other ways. Authority, law, and gift played the biggest parts; and even where violence intruded, law had a way of drawing it in, in codes about combat, booty, and ransom. Exchange played a peripheral role: literally peripheral, on borders (as at Venice), and among separate castes (like the Jews). It only found favour when other means fell short. The question just when this was—that other means of distributing property fell short—is too complex to be answered in a simple generalization. But for reasons not far to seek there was one main occasion. This was when the distribution was between, rather than within, social and political unities (for example, between estates or countries). This inter-group distribution could in turn be set off by either political or economic factors. Two kinds of economic situation above all gave birth to it. Productivity in one or more commodity might rise or fall in one place, creating imbalance between regions. Or contact could be opened up between places where such imbalance already obtained. (The wine and salt trades in the Carolingian empire illustrate the respective situations: wine production on the Rhine grew, encouraging export;[5] salt distribution, once the vast empire was under one government, could be organized on a continental scale, making full use of marine salt.)[6] Alternative means of distribution usually lagged behind such changes in productivity or transit, the more so the larger the geographical scale of operations was. So exchange filled the vacuum.

Money is related to exchange, but through other factors. As a means of exchange, money has the advantage over barter that it can be easily kept, carried, and measured. But that does not automatically mean exchangers will employ it. Two negative factors operate. One is fluidity in the market: if a creditor cannot be sure of finding what he wants on sale tomorrow, he may prefer payment 'in kind' today.[7] This factor is the first of a group—whose significance I shall come to shortly—which vary according to the volume of exchange: the more exchange there is, the more fluid the market will generally be. The second negative factor is the difficulty of getting money. Part of the very idea of money is that it should not 'grow on trees'. If, as a society, you need money to ease exchanges, your choices are few. You can either use other people's money—your neighbours' (if you can get it), or your ancestors' (if it has not worn out)—or you must manufacture some. Manufacturing money calls not only for raw material—usually precious metal—but for skills and labour. The last two items, we happen to know, were commonly priced by early medieval society at rates between 4·5 per cent and 16·6 per cent of the money minted;[8] and if monopolistic overpricing did play a part there, that only hammers the point home—that early medieval Europe had to pay a high price for any money it wanted.

Psychological inertia apart—the friction of the system—the over-all amount of money circulating was the product of the two familiar factors, demand and supply. Demand was broadly a function of the volume of exchange and, combined with it, the inappropriateness of barter for particular kinds of exchange. For example, livestock were constant troublemakers when exchanged outside a district where the owner was known.[9] As to supply, old and foreign coins, and substitute-money (like squirrel-skins or small pieces of cloth,[10] and more particularly ingots) were appropriate for starting a system off, being cheaper than manufactured money. But their quantity, or monetary quality, fell short of what was needed for the longer term. The main long-term requirements were the mining (or buying or stealing) of bullion, together with cheap minting. These called for organization and capital. For these, in turn, early medieval society had normally only one direction to look: an active royal authority.

We come now to the crux of our miniature 'theory of money'. The factors I have identified interacted. Money lubricated exchanges, reducing their cost as against other means of distributing property. A reduction in the cost of exchange increased its volume. That increase in volume not only, as we saw just now, made the market more fluid, reducing the creditor's preference for payment in kind; it also raised the demand for money—for people in a market of growing fluidity tend to find themselves short of cash.[11] A higher demand for money, in turn, lowered the unit-cost of mining and minting, making money cheaper,[12] and thereby available to facilitate even more exchanges, formerly unprofitable without it; and so on. Each factor enhanced the effect of the others. (Conversely: a hold-up in one factor meant a hold-up in the others.) This self-accelerating quality in the process has an important consequence in the study of 'monetarization'. It means explosions will occur in the process. When all the factors come together they can work very fast.

The self-accelerating quality has a further result, finally, in the field of method. It makes the working of the process impossible to describe in a single formula. For example, to describe the process as a 'growth in trade' hardly touches on its complexity. In the economic revival under discussion there is one debate in which this difficulty has been particularly apparent, and which is worth mentioning here because its solution adds yet one more factor to the explosive group just enumerated. This time it is a factor in 'real' economics, not just monetary. The debate is that between the following two contrasting judgments, each from an eminent authority:

The flow of commodities brought in or taken out by the southern trade currents washed over Europe without irrigating the main fields of economic activity outside the Mediterranean world itself, and without greatly accelerating the motion of social change.[13]

And:

The growth of Mediterranean trade in our period undoubtedly affected the way of life of many people ... the activities and organisation which existed to satisfy the demands of the relatively few coloured the whole history of the Middle Ages.[14]

This debate can be put from another angle, in the form of a simple question. Which played the more necessary part in the eleventh-century revival: local exchange, in basic foodstuffs? or

long-distance exchange, mainly in luxuries? Common sense
suggests the former answer. The volume of food trade, both in
bulk and aggregate value, was—it can safely be said—bigger
than that of any other type of commodity. Luxuries which could
afford to venture their way across continents were on the other
hand few, and could only interest a minority of the population.
These considerations lend support to the first of the two views
quoted. However, an equally strong case can be made for the
other view. By smoothing-over trade-routes and trade-prac-
tices, and by putting big sums of gold and silver at the disposal of
small huddles of population, grand commerce stimulated
landowners to organize production for a concentrated market.
That in turn increased efficiency, specialization and the use of
money locally. It is between these points of emphasis that
modern historical scholarship hesitates. For they are, in fact,
only points of emphasis. In reality the two types of trade were
continuous: basic foodstuffs could travel far; and some foreign
luxuries ended by being sold in hamlets. In so far as their centres
of gravity did differ, the ensemble of evidence suggests that
neither type of trade sufficed to cause an economic explosion.
For each is found separately in one or other dark-age society,
without marked dynamic effect.[15] The stimulus of grand
commerce, that seems to say, can only profit an economy
already acquainted with markets. It is the fusion of the two
elements, large and small, not just one or the other, that
provides the main 'real' economic factor in a monetary
explosion.

## 2. THE CAROLINGIAN EMPIRE

It is time to open the history book and read the story of how
these principles came into effect. In medieval Europe the story
starts in the Carolingian empire. The story of money itself does
not begin then: as was said earlier, it is scarcely possible to date
its beginning. But the story of Europe's own hypermonetary
economy begins then. Just as the Carolingian period witnessed
in other fields the first characteristically medieval synthesis of
Roman and barbarian, so in economics it joined fragments of an
old, ex-Roman commercial world with barbarian economies
until recently wholly ignorant of regular coined money (e.g.
Germany east of the Rhine).[16] The fact that the Carolingians

effectively launched the system of pounds, shillings, and pence[17] symbolizes (paradoxically, perhaps, in view of the ending of that system by the E.E.C.) the more substantial one that Pepin and Charlemagne made the first purely European economic community.

Any attempt to quantify how much self-sufficiency, how much barter, and how much monetary exchange there was in the Carolingian world would fail. All three obtained. But not only does evidence forbid any but the most hazardous quantitative estimates (as is clear from attempts to estimate the mass of coinage circulating).[18] A glimpse at the economy at work also shows that in practice each category merged into the next. This second difficulty, the merging, nevertheless proves an accessory in disguise. One merging-process, that of self-sufficiency and barter, is not of direct concern here. But the merging of barter and monetary exchange is. For it is precisely the intermediate character of late dark-age exchange that provides the first explanation for the sharp changes that occurred around the millennium. To see just what that intermediate character was, it will be fitting, without actually telling the long story of money in the dark ages, to spend a few pages picking out the story's main abiding features.

Its first feature is that it was largely a ghost-story. Gibbon noticed that some human inventions are so basic that, whatever the political upheaval, once made they cannot be forgotten. Money in dark-age Europe illustrates this law. After Rome, and still more after Charlemagne, it was hard even for barbarians to be unaware of money. But being aware of it and possessing it were two different things. You might not have much, nor even want much; but still be unable to forget it. The result was a phenomenon which throws a strange sidelight on modern monetary theory. Of the traditional functions of money, its role as a measure of value became uppermost, in a system of payments largely conducted in kind. 'A tapestry worth ten *solidi*', 'a candlestick worth ten *denarii*', are typical phrases in records of payments.[19] In such a system real, hard money was not without a certain role. It had a passive role as 'base' for the imaginary money changing hands as goods. And it had an active role as an adjuster, as if topping up inequalities at the end of a day's bartering. In-kind payments, evaluated as money, are thus very often found accompanied by an element of coinage. 'Fifteen *solidi* with one horse worth thirteen *solidi*' was a typical price paid for a piece of land in Italy in 768.[20] Rents, as well as purchases, frequently appear in the same form: so-much cereal, plus so-much wine, plus so-many *denarii*. It was always useful to have a few coins handy. Such a system—in this one respect like our own—can function on a relatively small coinage; and this was surely one reason why it flourished.

The fact that real coins had a necessary role in the system of 'ghost-money' did not mean they had no other role. Just because people would not or could not use real, hard money, the latter did not lose its absolute theoretical advantages over barter. Where these advantages counted, dark-age payments included more money than the mere 'base' and 'adjustment' principles can account for. This fact introduces a second important feature of the payments system. It was infinitely adjustable. It was adjustable first of all in quantity. Between pure in-kind payment and pure money, there was scarcely a limit to the degrees in which the two could be mixed. The choice between them was frequently left open, for the convenience of one or other party. An annual rent to an Alpine monastery in the middle of the ninth century would be stipulated as 'three *maldri* or six *denarii* or the price of six *denarii* in iron implements, whichever of these is easiest to find'.[21] A tax (in Italy in 799) was to be paid 'in gold and silver or in pieces of cloth to the value of ten *mancusae*'.[22] In any group of prices or payments, the ratio of the two elements could reflect particular local demands, indicative or not of a general rise in a money economy: it could hide share-cropping, or a collusive deal to beat inflation or an irksome law.[23] The system's adjustability is therefore no built-in gauge for historians wishing to measure monetary circulation. But it had a more important consequence: the system was sensitive. The very instant conditions of monetary supply or demand improved, no break with the past was necessary for the payments system to respond. The ratio of money to goods was simply raised.[24]

This sensitivity of the dark-age payments-system was so pregnant a feature that two more of its aspects deserve mentioning. The sensitivity was not, in fact, just a matter of an adjustable goods–money ratio in payments. It was also a matter of the character of money itself: of quality, as well as quantity. Because money did not yet dominate exchange, it was unsure of its own identity. Philosophers had called money, and would call it again, the 'third element in exchange'—*tertium permutationis*—the other two elements being the commodities the respective parties wanted. But in the period in question the distinction between money and other commodities was often blurred. Some dark-age coins, like the gold *solidus* of Uzès, have mystified scholarship for just this reason: they were never money at all, but ornaments.[25] Conversely, some bartered commodities were chosen for monetary qualities. For example, pepper could be more useful as 'money' on a long journey (because of its durability, general acceptability, and ease of transport) than the local coins characteristic of the late Carolingian age.[26] Again, precious metal—in the form of ornaments, ingots, or dust—was often used for payments not only because it was intrinsically cheaper (being unminted) but because for people with weighing-scales it might have more monetary quality than a local coinage of doubtful alloy.[27]

Under the ever-present ghost of money as a measure of value, then, the real thing—in this also like a ghost—hovered on the edge of the payments-system, in both quantity and quality half-in and half-out. This partial, and infinitely variable, role of money had a third aspect. Different social groups and institutions differed in their attitudes to what little money there was. As with other useful devices, a minority had discovered the profitable uses to which this one could be put. But this minority formed only a faint silver or gold fleck in a scene dominated by other colours. This transpires from those records which speak of money in the context of other elements in wealth. The paradox could occur here that the richer you were, the less money you had. In 936 Bishop Ratherius of Verona criticized the conduct of various classes, one by one. Occasionally—notably in a chapter on traders—money gleams in the picture. But when he comes to the 'rich man' (*dives*) this is how he lists his wealth: the *dives* boasts of his 'farms, serfs, serving-maids, horses, oxen and other livestock; of the obsequies of followers, the enjoyment of hounds and hawks; and the abundance of things to wear, implements, corn, wine, oil, and weapons'. Only at the very end come, as if an appendix, 'silver, gold and gems'.[28] In Flanders (where Bishop Ratherius had, as it happens, been born) it is conceivable that monetary conditions were a step ahead of corresponding conditions in the rural Alpine foothills. A contemporary list of possessions from Flanders—its count itemizes his own wealth—puts 'gold and silver' first. Yet even there they are followed by 'clothes, horses, cattle, sheep, produce, corn and cheeses', as if glinting metal, and that again not necessarily coins, was more an adornment to the count's wealth than the substance of it.[29] As in Verona, so in the Low Countries, the rich man's attitude contrasts with that of merchants: some at nearby Tiel, only two generations later (1006), heard of a Viking attack and instantly abandoned all their possessions 'except money, for they were merchants'.[30]

The differences in the evaluation of money as an element in wealth are perhaps best illustrated by the practice of certain church institutions. They might squeeze their monetary hold-ings literally to nothing. A series of incidents relating to the wealthiest Burgundian landlord, Cluny, in the late tenth century, will demonstrate this. The incidents occurred at a time when the Ottonian revival had already begun to send rivulets of money over the western Alps into Burgundy. But Cluny either got none, or got rid of it. In 972 Abbot Majolus of Cluny was captured by Saracen bandits on the Great Saint Bernard Pass. They had taken trouble in selecting their victim and demanded a big ransom. Majolus told them he was personally poor. He would only admit having rich lords under him: and when the 'treasure of infinite weight' was finally assembled for the ransom, the abbey not only had to contribute its part by clearing itself of ornaments, but for the rest had to invoke 'the generosity of good men'.[31] Its need is partly explained by the sequel. Certain knights took revenge on the Saracens by capturing a Saracen lair. They found 'excellent spoils'. But they shared them among themselves, only putting aside for Abbot Majolus 'two beautiful codices'. The abbot's pious biographer does not query the motives of illiterate knights and thinks the gift appropriate.[32] A final incident shows he knew his seniors' tastes. For in 995 the main Saracen redoubt at Fraxinetum was taken, together with armour embellished in gold and silver. This time the knights melted the spoil into a 'huge load of silver talents' and sent them all to Cluny. But what did Cluny do? She made part of the treasure into 'an extremely beautiful silver chalice', and gave the rest to the 'poor', 'to the last penny, as was right'.[33]

In the three centuries preceding the millennium, then, imaginary money measured value; real money changed hands side-by-side with goods—partly as a mere accessory to the conceptual money which measured value, but partly, too, in its own right, as principal medium of exchange. This last role admitted degree. Money could increase its proportion of payments. It could increase its character as money. It could impress its value on a bigger public. The net result of these features was that the system they belonged to, however small the role of money was in it, was capable of responding to any conditions which might arise tending to increase that role.

We can now turn to consider what these conditions were. A view used to be defended that the Carolingian period witnessed, as against its Merovingian predecessor, a general retreat of trade.[34] The more the dark age as a whole is studied, however, and the tricks in its evidence seen through, the more homogeneous its economic character appears. In so far as there was a change between the two dynasties, it is more likely to have been a change in the other direction. Primed in the late seventh century by Frisian traders and their currency, the Frankish empire had by the late eighth century 'nationalized' both that trade and its country of origin;[35] and was moving purposefully towards the making of a vigorous commercial economy. This view, even if no empirical evidence were there to support it, would stand to reason. If those theoretical conditions (of productivity and geographical ease of transit) are recalled, that were needed for a rise in the volume of exchange, it is clear that the Carolingian empire met them. The empire's very creation rested on the mobilization, every year, of an army of some 8,000 men, a quarter of them with horses.[36] This reflected an agricultural surplus on a scale no neighbouring economy shows any sign of having rivalled. The agricultural surplus resulted, in turn, partly from advances in agricultural technique and organization. It is inconceivable that these advances should have been made evenly; and we know that they were not. Both intentionally and unintentionally, estates produced too much of some commodities. While they gave part of their surplus away to the poor or to the government, they also exchanged—and therefore potentially sold—some.[37] Weekly markets, licensed by Pepin and his descendants down to the late ninth century, testify to these conditions.[38] The empire's geographical expansion meanwhile had a similar effect on the larger scale. It created a technological and commercial 'Common Market', whose pooling of economic resources was a replica of the better-known pooling of cultural resources in Charlemagne's court. The new boundaries joined areas with disparate histories of exploitation behind them: old Lombardy and Aquitaine, with new Saxony and Franconia. The Loire, Seine, Rhône, Rhine, and Po river-systems now lay under one government, and that government a keen legislator on routes and weights-and-measures. The historian cannot be astonished in these circumstances to find the actual evidence of long-distance trade which Dopsch and others have presented: corn- and salt-ships plying regularly on the main rivers; specialized market-production of wine, arms, and especially Frisian cloth; towns of well over a thousand inhabitants; and so on.[39]

How much money all this exchange brought into being, within the flexible payments-system described earlier, is nevertheless a harder question. The evidence at first suggests a lot. Capitularies betray the government's concern for coinage; and a fine array of silver pennies survives to show it meant business. Such few records as survive of actual payments (e.g. of rents) often include a monetary element. But a closer look at this evidence reveals gaps and difficulties. Here as elsewhere the capitularies prove little except government intentions. Records of payments, similarly, issue only from a few ecclesiastical estates: the methods of these were certainly avant-garde, and are no sure guide to methods elsewhere. As for the fine array of coins, it is rather *too* fine: most extant coins (except some plainly eroded by conditions in their place of preservation) are in a better state than they would have been if they had been much used.[40] There is one final difficulty. No one can say what coinage was used for small transactions. The silver penny was valuable enough for only twenty-four of them to buy a cow. No hint exists of the minting of bronze after the late sixth century.[41] If old bronze was used it must have been worn beyond formal recognition. Perhaps the much-debased Merovingian silver coinage served these humble functions. Whichever surmise holds, it tells against a deep penetration by coined money of the lower levels of exchange.

In view of the vigour of both exchange and royal authority in Charlemagne's time, it may be asked why no more conspicuous body of money came into being. There are three reasons. The first was psychological inertia, an inertia which commercial demand was too low and too new to conquer. Coins were strange and therefore suspect. This is known from a series of laws, spread right over the central period of the Carolingian economic revival, from 794 to 864, prescribing fines or flogging for persons *refusing* payment in the government's pennies—which were all but pure silver. That the laws were repeated and amended shows they were only partly effective. They suggest those fine pennies were used mainly to pay government contractors, no doubt including soldiers, who then came back complaining they could not get rid of them.[42] Meanwhile the discovery of a certain type of weighing-scale among grave-goods, to the east of the Rhine from the sixth century and in areas to the west of it from the seventh, has suggested to scholars the widespread use in those areas, on the eve of the Carolingian ascendency, of weighed precious metal as a medium of exchange. (The metal included whole or fragmentary old and foreign coins.) This would in turn imply that the popular suspicions referred to in the laws were to marked coins as such, not just the coins of a particular government. Further corroboration lies in the fact that similar laws survive from tenth-century England, when the crown is known to have been active in introducing coinage.[43]

The second obstacle to the creation of a large currency by Charlemagne was one there is no reason to think he noticed, but which became increasingly important as the effects of the first obstacle wore away. It was the problem of bullion. For a living currency, the problem of bullion was more than that of acquiring a given mass of metal, and then reminting it. A living currency is also a dying currency: coins wear out and are lost. A continuing supply is called for. The Carolingians' choice of silver, not gold, for their coinage may have been partly dictated by this problem, since silver was in principle more easily available in the west. But of the three main forms in which it was available, only one offered a permanent supply; and there is little sign that this one was extensively exploited in Charlemagne's time. The three sources were: hoarded silver, mainly in church- and grave-ornaments; older currencies— chiefly Merovingian, Frisian and perhaps some Arabic; and mines. The Franks were committed opponents of iconoclasm, a doctrine which was providing some eastern rulers with an excuse to melt church ornaments. Their export trade, for reasons we shall see in a moment, suffered restrictions too large—in the useful directions at the useful time—to make foreign bullion a sufficient source for a large currency at home. Among sources of new silver, that left mines. References to precious-metal mining in the Carolingian world are extremely thin. They contrast in this with references to iron- and lead-mining, above all with references to salt-extraction.[44] We hear of some silver-mining at the old Roman workings at Melle (Metallum) in Poitou; some in the Harz; and just possibly some in Bohemia.[45] But the Harz was only incorporated into the empire with the reduction of Saxony in 804; and Bohemia, though for a time under Carolingian influence, was never (whatever its mining activities may have been) formally part of the empire. The unimportance of the latter two of these mines (still barely in their infancy) can be judged from Einhard's description, written in the 820s, of his master's eastern campaigns. The Avar treasure (loot from Steppe trade-routes, taken by the Franks on the Danube in 791) dwarfed any other wealth derived from these campaigns, or indeed from any-where else: 'The Franks had appeared almost paupers until that time.'[46]

Suspicion of money and lack of bullion were obstacles that might have been overcome but for a third: shortage of time. The dynasty had interested itself in currency from Pepin the Short onwards. But Charlemagne only settled down to serious currency reform in 794,[47] and he was dead twenty years later, his coinage barely past an experimental stage. By 826 the empire was splitting. By 841 it was in pieces. The Carolingian conditions for creating money collapsed. They were not, it is true, without their legacy. Suspicion of money seems to have subsided with the mere passage of time; so that the paradox appears that acceptance of coin seems actually to have gained ground as Carolingian public authority dwindled. Again, much of the general economic legacy would go on growing: agricultural technology; trade on the Rhine and Po (to which Venetian and Flemish activities gave growing importance from the late ninth century); and the new big church estates in Germany. But one necessary condition had gone: strong royal authority. The rights and duties of coining returned, early in the ninth century, to local authorities. But for all the merits of some of their products, these had neither the care nor the facilities of a strong king for making a good, cheap, and general coinage.

The causes of the Carolingian political collapse need not be rehearsed. But one of its results must be. Charlemagne had partially sealed his frontiers. Laws repeatedly forbade the sale of slaves, or arms and armour, outside the empire. The laws were often ignored, but were not a dead letter. Watchposts to ensure the latter ban, on arms, had been set up in 805 down the east German frontier from the mouth of the Elbe to the Danube.[48] The economic significance of these measures is easy to underestimate. Slaves and arms were not just two of Francia's possible exports. With the possible exception of furs, they were much the most valuable. Charlemagne's ban on the export of these particular products was in effect, therefore, comparable to economic isolationism. Creators of a free-trade area within north-western Europe, Charlemagne sought to stop free trade between his empire and outsiders. Whatever the success of the seals he put on his frontiers in his own day, political collapse nevertheless broke them. The church, main heir to Carolingian public authority, frowned on the slave trade (for humanitarian reasons, now, more than economic). But it could do little. Byzantium, for long the only Christian government worth calling by the name, would have liked to stop European arms-export, except to herself, but was too far away to succeed. There could only be one economic outcome: the ninth century found north-western Europe increasingly exposed to any impulses she might receive from outside. Much has been said of military invasions in this period. But there was another sort. Carolingian frontiers were weak economically. For all her areas of progress, late Carolingian Europe became in this respect a 'backward' area, acted on rather than acting.

## 3. THE EFFECT OF ISLAM: EASTERN ISLAM

To see what may have acted on Carolingian Europe, attention must now be turned from the relatively non-monetary world of the Carolingians to a world in the opposite condition. Before the Franks had made their European 'Common Market', a similar but much bigger one had formed to the east and south. Its claims on the attention of European historians have been doubted. It is hoped that doubts will be dispelled in the course of what follows. But to start the inquiry off, one claim is enough. It is that while Charlemagne was being crowned in Rome in 800, the great southern empire of Islam, little more than 300 miles away, was busy creating, not a small, hesitant, and suspect currency, but the biggest and most vigorous currency the world had ever seen.

Islam's economic success-story, as brilliantly expounded by the late Maurice Lombard, can be sketched here in a few words. In the sixth century, before the Arab conquests, Byzantium and Sassanian Persia had constituted two 'Common Markets', in their separate empires, dividing the east between them. Technology and trade were already on the march in each. But the empires were separate. (When in the sixth century the silkworm had been introduced from the Iranian to the Byzantine empire it had to be smuggled hidden in a walking-stick.)[49] In the seventh century the Muslim conquests—leaving to Byzantium of her Asian possessions only Asia Minor— joined and extended these two free-trade areas. The new empire thus linked the most ancient centres of civilization—north-west India, Mesopotamia, and Egypt—into a vast sub-continent of technological and commercial interchange. Wheat and linen went east from Egypt; the horse and dromedary went north from Arabia; the cultivation of rice, sugar, oranges, and dates came west—to name only a few of the commodities whose production or trade conquered new soil.[50] A measure of the economic explosion caused is the growth of Baghdad. Founded in 762 it had become within fifty years—those of Charlemagne's lifetime—the biggest city in the world, with a population of about two million and an area larger than that of late nineteenth-century Paris.[51]

How and how much this explosion affected Europe has been

much debated. Since most of the relevant concrete elements elude measurement, the debate on the degree of influence will no doubt continue for ever.[52] The nature of what effect there was, however, will become clear from a brief analysis of the forces in Islam's economy. The twin supports of Muslim wealth were industry—mainly agrarian—and commerce. The industry consisted in applying new techniques to wrest more material for food and clothing from a largely uncooperative soil, always ready to return to desert or marsh in the absence of sustained manpower. Manpower: like other industrial revolutions this one called for cheap labour. The Arab warriors who built the empire despised servile work. The privileges of their monotheistic subjects (who soon became monotheists if they were not already) allowed them, too, to resist exploitation. This left Islam's neighbours. The Muslim empire thus created a magnetic field covering half a hemisphere, drawing cheap labour into itself in the form of slaves. That Islam paid for its workers in lump sums, not wages, does not mar the resemblance of its situation to that of most industrial booms. The magnetism worked on a whole medley of peoples whose history would have nothing else in common for centuries: Turks, Slavs, Black Africans, and even (side by side with the latter now) some Anglo-Saxons and Irish.[53]

Commerce, too, had its special needs. Its main one was communication. Once the glories of Arab cavalry were past, the empire's most essential form of communication was by water: that of the Indian ocean and Mediterranean, and their offshoots; and that of rivers and canals. (Baghdad and Cairo were both sited on canals joining major waterways, and their position was typical.) But water needs ships; ships needed wood; and just *because* the centres of Arab commerce were old ones, most of their woodland had been stripped. For the same reason that modern Europe reaches into the Asian and African jungles for her timber needs, Islam sent for hers to her less-worked borders: her own Atlas and Armenia; India; Byzantine Sicily (where raiding parties went and helped themselves) and, last but not least, the European mainland.[54]

The exigencies of the military and of a luxurious upper class redoubled these wants. Armies called for unfastidious recruits, and courts thronged with female slaves and trained eunuchs. As for timber, not only did navies devour it. Metalwork in those days, before serious coalmining, burned huge quantities of wood. So Islam came to use others' timber indirectly, too, by importing iron- and steel-ware: in particular, the Frankish imitation of the Damascus sword (whose steel came actually from Bombay) was esteemed by connoisseurs as effective as the original, and cheaper.[55] Finally, among main imports, Islam's shortage of forest made her short of animals living in forests; and the skins of marten, sable, and their cousins became—as well as sources of comfort in certain areas—status-symbols for a competitive upper class.[56]

The needs of Islam's industry, commerce, and government made her into what is now called a 'metropolitan economy': one which stands to those next to it as town to country, but on a continental scale. The force of such an economy radiates. Others must feel the force in so far as they are unprotected. Western Europe, it has just been shown, now lacked governmental protection. Her other barriers—geographical, linguistic, and religious—may seem formidable. (They seemed so to the historian Henri Pirenne; and contemporary Latin writers thought them so formidable they scarcely thought about Islam at all.) But they could be overcome. Distance, in the eastern sector, might have proved a barrier if the Islamic boom had lasted, like the Carolingian, a mere two generations. But it lasted over three centuries; long enough to find any number of routes, so long as there was profit to be had at the end of them. As for language and religion, the monotheistic world never had to worry long about those as commercial barriers: Alexander and the Caesars had seen to that by scattering over their empires a landless people to whom all settled religions were infidel and who had, by the ninth century A.D., long grown used to learning foreign languages. Jews did not monopolize Islam's external trade in the ninth and tenth centuries. But they guaranteed it, other conditions being right.

For European purposes the centuries of Islam's boom fall into two periods. The first centred in the east. The Muslim economy focused on its cities; and a principal cause of its success had been its speed of conquest, which barely disturbed a flourishing city life. But that city life had been mainly in Mesopotamia, Iran, and Syria; it came no further west than the Nile. The great age

of Roman north Africa had ended more than two centuries
before the Arab conquest; and it had left that region, robbed of
its strong Italian focus, not much more than a thin, east–west
peninsula between land and sea. The rise of Baghdad was in
part a testimony to the same fact: that the centre of gravity of
eighth-century Islam lay in the ex-Sassanian orient.
This fact affected Europe in two ways. Firstly it meant that
Islam's first gift to Europe was in silver, now Europe's own
currency. The east had its gold mines, and a little of its gold even
came (temporarily) north. But the Sassanian currency had been
silver; and the Muslims inherited not only that currency and its
habits, but thriving silver mines. Further conquest brought into
the empire, before the middle of the eighth century, the regions
round Kabul and Tashkent; and with these came silver deposits of legendary fecundity. The maximum annual output of
the *second* biggest of these mines can be roughly calculated as about
thirty tons, or two-thirds of the world production of silver in 1500.[57]
The second outcome for Europe of Islam's early eastern bias
was one which complicated the effect of the first. It was a matter
of geography. The economic impulse Islam sent to Europe went
from Islam's old world; but it came to Europe's new world. The
monetary wave broke, that is to say, not on the remains of
Charlemagne's empire but on the non-Romanized, ill-
developed lands to the north-east, the nearest source of the
imports. It is true there may have been a spell at first when time-
worn routes were tried. 'Rhadanite' Jews, soon to be leading
carriers of Islam's world trade, may originally have got their
name from the Rhône. But the Rhône was now a detour. It was
found that if you were prepared to push your cargo overland for
some fifty miles, you could *sail* from the Baltic to Iran via
Russian rivers; or your cargo could, if you only wished to
operate part of the route yourself. The northern arm of the route
had the added advantage (if you were a Swede, not a multi-
lingual Jew) of lying through the lands of one ethnic group, the
Finns.[58] To slave-traders rivers offered the final attraction that
they could get their slaves by water-borne raids on communities
unused to attack from that quarter.[59] Thus it was over the
steppes to the east of the Frankish empire that Islam first acted
on the European continent.
The extent of its action can only be judged. Costly

commodities flowed south and east, describing the raw terrain they came from. It was probably now, in the ninth century, that the name of Slav—once the terror of eastern Europe's landlubbers—became the Arabic word for slave: *Saqlab*.[60] Forests themselves contributed less directly. Nothing, alas, beyond logic, suggests that these first Volga boatmen sold their boats on reaching the Caspian, to ride back upsteam with full purses. But ships and timber did form one form of invisible export, in the carrying-trade itself.[61] Visible cargo meanwhile comprised mainly such costly, light things as could pay their big fares. Furs excelled: for the hills and cold nights of the northern Iranian region, especially up near the mines, put a high price on mink-coats and their like, even regardless of their value for status. Candle-wax, fish-glue, honey, and bone continued the list.[62] The predatory northern exporters probably also included mercenary service somewhere along the line. The upshot, anyway, of the southward flow of forest-produce was that a wave of silver washed into Europe's tangled back garden. Sixty-two thousand Muslim silver coins have been found in Scandinavian hoards,[63] over 20,000 more in northern Poland, and comparable quantities in Pomerania and northern Russia.[64] Coins preserved and discovered certainly only form a small fraction of what arrived.

The eastern bias of Europe's ninth-century trade with Islam, together with its being paid chiefly in silver, dictated its effect on Europe. The new money was in the latter's native metal, and that of the medium-denomination currency established by the Franks. But the money arrived far outside the Frankish empire. At the time and place it arrived there was not much to spend it on: we can surmise from the content and positioning of the hoards, as well as from other clues, that in most of north-eastern Europe all there was for it to buy was a handful of barbaric luxuries, whose market was too confined, and whose supply too spasmodic, to create substantial monetary circulation.[65] Money that cannot be spent is in one technical sense not money. This one defect needed a remedy before it could become so. The eastern silver could provide a remedy in either of two ways: by creating circulation where it was; or by moving west. The signs are that it did both; but that both processes took time. A glance at each process will explain this.

As Frisian and other foreign coins had once 'primed' the Frankish economy, in the late seventh century, so Muslim silver appears to have done in eastern Europe: lubricating exchanges for long enough, to raise monetary demand high enough, to encourage native production. The possibility that Muslim silver could perform in this way is already suggested by the case of Russia, which lacked minerals, yet where a vigorous currency, partly of Muslim metal and partly of native substitutes (squirrel-skins etc.), was at work from the ninth to the eleventh century.[66] Where appropriate minerals did exist, oriental silver would simply reproduce itself from these. Among regions of east-central Europe, Bohemia was the best equipped for mining. Chronology suggests it was Muslim money that set Bohemians fully exploiting their own resources. Travellers accounts reveal that the Bohemian slave-trade was already attracting Muslim silver in the ninth century, and went on doing so for at least another hundred years. On the 'priming' hypothesis, a rise in demand for currency should be expected to follow in a generation or two. In the middle of the tenth century the signs duly appear: in the use of small-denomination cloth currency (which surprised a Jewish slave-trader in Prague, who had never seen it before)[67] simultaneously with—now, and not earlier—extensive mining. By 969 Bohemia was envied for silver-production as far afield as Russia.[68] A third example of such self-reproduction by foreign silver will be seen in Ottonian Germany in the 970s: with just the same pattern of events—influx of foreign precious metal and then, two or three generations later, intense efforts at native mining.[69] Scholars who look at all the known facts *except* the numismatic find themselves tempted to speak of a stream of 'Transoxanian' silver, flowing through eastern Europe in the late ninth and tenth centuries. The temptation is healthy. But the term should include, by the tenth century anyway, local silver called into currency by exchanges initiated by the imported metal.

The second way Transoxanian silver could cure its defects was by moving west, to England, Germany, and Frankish Gaul. In the early ninth century these were cut from the north-east religiously, linguistically, and by political disturbance. Only from the late ninth century is there much sign that the new silver started coming west; and how it did so is uncertain.

Scandinavian emigrants to the Danelaw, Ireland, and Normandy probably took some in their purses. Trade played a part. Recent tenth-century archaeological finds depict a North Sea emporium much unlike the raw picture familiar from accounts of Viking destruction. Some of the Danegeld and other silver the late tenth-century Vikings took west across the North Sea was making a return journey: the English shopkeeper was being robbed by his Viking ex-customers. Finally, German kings set about laying their hands on the silver directly, by capturing the routes and their nodal points. Hedeby, the Danish commercial capital, fell to Henry I of Saxony in 923.[70] Otto the Great's subjection of the Danes was remembered among his achievements before his subjection of the Magyars.[71] The part played by tribute in both his and his father's wars to subdue the eastern Slavs is explicit in the literary record.[72] The proportion of specifically Transoxanian silver remaining in all this money, at least in such of it as crossed the North Sea, is, it is true, put in doubt by metallic tests so far conducted on tenth-century English and German coinage.[73] But the present hypothesis is unaffected by that doubt. The stream was still 'Transoxanian' in the sense that the man who rolls the first stone causes the avalanche.

Whatever is made of this hypothesis, one fact is clear. Because it came where it did, the effect of Islam's first consignment of silver to Europe was delayed. Either it had to wait until it had generated some monetary circulation in eastern Europe. Or it had to travel to places where it could enter into an existing circulation. Both processes took two or three generations. The impact of Transoxanian silver, direct and indirect, was therefore felt by the ex-Carolingian world in the tenth, rather than the ninth, century. The delay was significant. It meant that the impact of this first monetary wave from Islam coincided in time with that of another, more direct wave, from the south.

## 4. THE EFFECT OF ISLAM: WESTERN ISLAM

North Africa and Spain were Islam's New World. The moment when new worlds come to life is determined by developments in the old. The necessary political and economic overspill in eastern Islam had to await roughly the year 750, when powerful refugees from the new caliphate came west to

start new cities and dynasties.[74] Then, and only then, the revival
of the southern Mediterranean started in earnest. Methods and
skills were imported from the east, and started an agricultural
boom. The boom was yielding fruit by the middle of the ninth
century. Equally important, the new dynasties sprang contacts
with north and south. The conquest of Sicily, between 827 and
872; the simultaneous establishment on the European mainland, at Cordoba, of a western Baghdad; the founding of Fez in
807, as a desert-port for convoys from the Niger; all helped
invigorate the growth.[75] After yet another century (by the
middle of the tenth) the growth would make western Islam at
least the economic rival of eastern. The usurping of the title
'Emir of Believers' by the new Cordoban dynasty of Abd-er
Rahman I in 929, and the buildings of Cairo ('the victorious')
in 975, were two signs of the new ascendancy.[76]

Islam's swing to the west was also a swing from silver to gold.
Western Muslims were never short of silver: Spain, its later role
here again inverted, included silver among its abundant
minerals. But what now distinguished western Islamic wealth
was its new gold, and it made this the golden age for all Islam.
(The Islamic silver–gold ratio, from a peak in about 850,
began a long fall as gold became more abundant.[77] The caliph
of Baghdad's budget, from the early tenth century, was
expressed universally in gold, not gold and silver as hitherto.)[78]
The remote eastern mines would spout silver for another
century (its flow to the Baltic falters from *c.* 970).[79] But the mines
had new, separatist masters now, who sent less of it to the
caliphs.[80] Meanwhile, early in the ninth century, Egypt had
taken Nubia, one of whose ancient gold-mining regions was so
perforated by diggings that it reminded a traveller [*c.* 900] of a
sieve. Egypt's government contractors at the same time
systematically plundered gold from the pharaohs' tombs. Nor
did western Africa fall short. Gold, washed from the rivers south
of the Sahara (near Timbuktu, north of the later 'Gold Coast')
flowed north on camel-routes, battles for whose control engaged
one northern dynasty after another. The legendary splendour
in the tenth century of the Umayyad court in Cordoba and of
the Fatimid at Fustat-Cairo announced the outcome of these
battles.[81]

The late ninth and tenth centuries were, then, not only

Islam's western, but her golden, age. To read the significance of this we must look at a second field where Islam's swing affected Europe. This was in political geography. One result here was direct. The frozen north was now far away; and the north was further discountenanced, in the new economic context, in that the one specifically northern commodity fitted to travel so far, furs, had the damaging flaw now that their use-value sank as they neared the sweltering regions the gold came from. Since Islam's other main needs (slaves, timber, and some types of metal and metalware) could be had near-to-hand, it was Europe's old world, not her new, that felt the impact.

But the impact might never have been felt so powerfully if it had not been for a second, less direct effect of the new geography. The westward move of Islam's centre of gravity had been accompanied by a weakening of the eastern caliphate in Baghdad. This decline in turn strengthened Byzantium. From 842 onwards Byzantium was freed from a struggle for survival that had lasted two centuries.[82] Her loss of Sicily in the west, and the virtual independence of her Italian cities, were minor setbacks in comparison to her relief from Baghdad's military pressure. Anatolia secure, Byzantium was able to turn her attention to rebuilding an empire, together with a useful sphere of influence beyond it, in south-eastern Europe. Despite fluctuations, the new commonwealth went on thriving and expanding into the late eleventh century. Western Europe could not but be affected. Her traders were not only offered rich city markets for corn, easily transportable by ship from the Adriatic.[83] Here—on one condition—was also a source of fine cloth and other manufactures for re-sale in Europe. The condition, of course, was that money could be found to buy them initially from Byzantium. This was where Muslim gold came in. For Byzantium dealt only in gold.

A tripartite circulation of gold thus came into being in the Mediterranean in the tenth century. Muslim gold passed north into Europe, and left again for Byzantium—whence some of it would return to Islam. Goods flowed the other way.[84] With appropriate differences in emphasis the list of goods resembled that for the eastern trade, above all in its principal item. The slave-trade of the Germanic kingdoms was as old as the kingdoms themselves. But as a major inter-continental trade it rose with some abruptness about the middle of the ninth century. Local grumblings were heard about it in France in the 820s, and more general ones in 845.[85] This was just when Carolingian public authority plunged, and when the southern market began its prodigious growth. So the trade grew as an expression of pure economic forces. The victims were now mainly western Slavs, from the middle Elbe, Bohemia, and Dalmatia. Men castrated in Prague were led to Verdun or Lyons, where the Roman road system sped them straight to Cordoba, or to Narbonne, for shipment to Cairo (or Syria).[86] Gangs in Venetian pay meanwhile captured Dalmatians for the same south-easterly shipment. Venice had Christian customers to consider and from time to time felt called to put an official ban on slave export to the infidel, as on the arms and armour she sent to Egypt's arsenals. But the Eldest Child of Liberty was not likely to, nor did she, curtail to any serious degree such a profitable liberty of her own. In Latin—a significant period later than in Arabic—the word for 'Slav', *sclavus*, is found meaning 'slave' in Germany and Spain about the middle of the tenth century, and in northern Italy in the 980s.[87]

One part of the dispute about this period of economic history concerns the amount of gold that entered Europe as a result of this external trade. Coin-hunters have found next to no Arab dinars from this period.[88] But there are references to gold pieces, including *aurei denarii*, from at least the early eleventh century in Latin literature.[89] And the dearth of samples of gold coins circulating within Europe is negative evidence in a period when negative evidence is weak. (But for the single chance discovery of a hoard of Cuerdale in Lancashire we would know either nothing, or next to nothing, of the most important genres of coin from the pre-Conquest Danelaw.)[90] There are clear literary references, too, to the *entry* of large quantities of gold to Europe from western Islam, from about the millennium. And there is an equally clear reason why it should have left no more numismatic trace than it has, in Europe. The gold went out again— just as it is known to have done in Russia, for similar reasons. Gold was harder to come by in Byzantium than at the other end of the cycle in Islam; and gold was therefore unlikely to stay long in poor European hands, when Byzantine artisans had so many ways of tempting it away.

As to the quantity of gold entering, it can be very roughly estimated. Three censuses in Cordoba show that between 921 and 961 the city's population of male slaves rose from 3,750 to 13,750.[91] Of female slaves, near the end of the same time-bracket, the Cordoban caliph's harem alone contained 6,300.[92] Again, that the total slave population of Cordoba (thus well *over* 21,000) was only a fraction of the slave population of western Islam as a whole can be told from a comparable figure for the harem in Cairo: 12,000.[93] At the zenith of Arabic science and government these figures are not to be dismissed as fanciful. Spanish *re*-export of European slaves to the orient should be added to them, if we are to judge total imports. Making allowance for black Africans and Turks, and for Germanic captives taken on the continual slaving raids that marked Spanish history in this period, it is clear that Slav captives of both sexes exported in the tenth century should be estimated in tens of thousands, if not hundreds of thousands. A single consignment of such slaves (Slavs, to judge from their position) bound for Alexandria in 870 was estimated by a Christian monk who saw them at Taranto, at 9,000.[94] An exaggeration, no doubt, this time: but the monk also said the cargo filled six ships, a figure in which he is less likely to have erred. From the fact, meanwhile, that a eunuch (the stricter meaning of *saqlab*)[95] or pretty slave-girl in early tenth-century Cordoba could fetch as much as 1,000 gold dinars,[96] mathematics can easily suggest a figure for the gold value of these imports. There is no proof that all the slaves were bought, but the Slavs must have been bought, by Cordobans, at some stage. Nor is there proof that the prices were all paid in gold, or that the Jewish merchants did not take some of their gold back to Islam. But in view of Islam's gold glut, merchants on both sides must have found the exporting of it from Islam a good bargain. When Saint Adalbert of Prague, himself born a Slav, lamented the slave-trade there *c.* 990, there is every reason to think his expression *infelix aurum* was the appropriate one; nor was he the only imperial subject to think there was a remarkable amount of gold about at that time.

5. THE MONETARY EXPLOSION, *c.* 950–*c.* 1100

It is time to start drawing the lesson of this story, and see how it explains what it has set out to explain: the explosive character of the economic change that took place in the eleventh century. To draw this lesson all we must do is look, from the vantage-point we have arrived at, at the period of the explosion itself.

The first place to look is the Saxon empire, the dominant power in Europe in the year 1000. The economic significance of this empire in the present context is twofold; and this time its geography can be considered first. The Saxon dynasty had originated, about 900, in Merseburg, on the far-eastern frontier of Saxony. The wealth of the first king, Henry I—wealth acquired by marriage with the top local heiress, and by war against Slavs for tribute—would be enough to betray the presence of money in the area even if we had no other reason to suspect it. It lifted Henry to power. It may possibly have played a part in the organization of his army; and his high-handedness with the church might be seen, independently of any questions of church law, as a challenge by 'new world' money to that of the Rhineland, where the metropolitan sees were. Henry's son Otto I took the challenge further. Otto, who spoke Slavonic as his second language to German, had a son by a Slavonic mistress; and in due course imposed the same son on the arch-see of Mainz, former base of Rhineland opposition to his family. Then, largely via the church, the Saxon turned the tables on the other, ex-Roman parts of Germany. When we first hear of Otto's plan to make the north-eastern city of Magdeburg an archbishopric, it is through a complaint by the same archbishop of Mainz (his loyalties now with his Rhineland see) that the king has 'bought' the pope's support, with sums the plaintiff clearly cannot himself afford. Finally, master of the Rhine and upper Danube, Otto turned his attention to the Po, re-created the 'Roman' empire, and spent ten of the last twelve years of his life in Italy—more than any German king before or since, until Barbarossa.[97] Otto's half-Greek grandson Otto III was the apotheosis of the Italian interest.

The telling of a familiar story in this way fits it in with the larger pattern traced so far in this chapter. The rise of the Ottonians brought to its culmination an eastward shift in northern European power, a shift which had begun when Carolingian Aix replaced Merovingian Paris, and which distantly reflected the rise of eastern Islam. Pirenne and his commentators have explored the rationale of the earlier phase of this shift. Our concern is with the later. Eastern Islamic silver, together with the silver it had called into circulation, was filtering through the north-eastern frontier of Charlemagne's Europe just at the end of the ninth century. It raised a dynasty which, once it had achieved political supremacy, discovered a second flow of money, already arriving from south and west, in the Po and Rhine valleys. The two currents met each other.[98] The geography of the Ottonian empire did not represent just any trade revival. It specifically united the two main streams of money impinging on Europe at the start of the tenth century.

The second title of the Ottonian empire to a place in this story concerns the behaviour of the money when it arrived. The other elements for economic expansion were present: land-reclamation, growing population, active public authority, towns, specialization. Both parts of the model obtained: local exchange in food, distant trade in luxury—attested by twenty-nine known licences for major markets and mints, granted by the three Ottos.[99] How necessary new precious metal was to the expansion is shown not only by its absorption (there are practically no hoards from tenth-century Germany), but by the fact that, once expansion gained momentum, the existing supply had to be increased. The efforts of Bohemia in this direction have been indicated. About 970, Otto I 'by his own efforts' (one tradition said) discovered the silver veins at Rammelsberg in the Harz mountains. The Rammelsberg mine, probable home of the seven little miners of legend (if not of Snow White herself: as a folk-tale heroine she had an independent existence long before she met up with the seven dwarfs), became suddenly and long remained Europe's leading native source of silver. Imported silver had multiplied itself many times over.[100]

Otto's empire was only the centre of an economic system stretching beyond it. Its main appendix was England. Over much of England, as earlier in eastern Germany, currency was effectively a newcomer, and its arrival formed part of a new departure.[101] Where under ten mints had existed in the year 900, there were about seventy, all over England, at the millennium. The number of extant coins from tenth-century England is more than that of her coins from all earlier centuries together, and this despite purposeful re-minting. Few were in hoards, except on the periphery of the economy. The laws of Athelstan (Otto I's brother-in-law) and Edgar, particularly after 973, betray a growing concern of monarchy for minting coins and extending their circulation—including laws to coerce creditors who refuse it. The silver is hard to assign exactly to its various sources. Metal analysis so far tends to tell against the presence of much Transoxanian silver, but is inconclusive. The probability that some was from Rammelsberg is more hopeful, particularly in view of the conspicuous quickening of currency developments in 970s, and of the signs of a rising English wool-trade, towards the Ottonian empire. By 970, at all events, south-eastern silver, from far and near, had generated native silver: at least one major royal silver-mine was in operation by that date in England or Wales.[102]

The Anglo-German development reached its peak during the first half of the eleventh century. Under the early Salians and house of Canute, German and English coinage fed a boom in North Sea commerce. In eastern European and Scandinavian hoards (where nearly 10,000 coins have been found from the Cologne mint alone)[103] German and English coinage definitively ousts oriental about the year 1000—without, for all that, showing any signs of failing at home.[104] The boom was accentuated by being joined, by way of the Upper Rhine and Danube, with one in Italy, which in turn profited by the connection.

These conjunctions brought an abruptness to the commercial revival. Each accelerated the other. This effect would probably have been achieved even if Latin Christendom, by some unimaginable hypothesis, had been a continent on its own, with no neighbours. But the effect was sharpened still further by a factor involving her main neighbour; a factor which, though it spans at least a century, is easy to miss in our preoccupation with merchants and trade-routes. Economies are sometimes found in unstable equilibrium to each other: the rich get richer, the poor poorer. When they are, there can be no lasting marginal change from one state to another: any such change translates itself into a leap between extremes. In certain important respects the early Muslim economy stood in this relation to the European. The tenth-century movement was enough to introduce a marginal change in the balance of power.

In the eleventh this turned into a leap, as Christendom and the nearer parts of Islam changed places.

This phenomenon falls naturally into two phases, before and after the tipping-of-the-balance. In ninth- and tenth-century Europe, we read of 'rural stagnation'.[105] Reading further, we find some long-distance trade, and set it off against the stagnation, as a parenthesis, or sign of coming revival. In one way it was. In another it was the opposite: the trade *caused* the stagnation. Let us look at the prime case. The demographic, agrarian, and political upsurge of eastern Europe would play a conspicuous part in the general revival after the millennium, especially in Germany. The causes of the eastern awakening may be largely elusive. But one of them stands out: it was the *ending* of the export trade. For until the late tenth century one part of the population of the area (Slav warriors, as well as Germans and others, joined in the raids)[106] had been engaged in creaming the other of its best young manpower and nubile women. In a region whose first need was muscle and large families this was no recipe for economic growth. Deaths in war and damage to agriculture must be reckoned in with the actual losses of healthy slaves eventually exported. Nor did the dubious effect of foreign money stop with the slave trade. The question might be asked whether trappers, timber-handlers, and even the traders themselves, with their facilities, could not have been employed more profitably for their locality than by serving remote paymasters. Where the money they earned was not positively useful, their work was so much subtracted from the home economy's needs. The most backward regions of Europe were thus put in an impasse by the very existence of Muslim wealth. Their leap after the millennium was partly the outcome of a mere escape from the impasse.

The phenomenon so conspicuous in the case of eastern Europe applied, in smaller degree, to the rest of the continent. Agriculture in ex-Roman Europe suffered a chronic shortage of manpower throughout the dark ages. (The activities of press-gangs, bans on slave-export, and many other such indications, persuade us of that.)[107] It may possibly be fanciful to read significance into the fact that references to *internal* European slave-trading become less frequent, relative to the volume of written sources, after *c.* 800. It may be similarly fanciful to remark on the important technological advances of the later Carolingian period: the water-mill, in particular, and also the crank.[108] What is not at all fanciful—and it may help explain both those apparent trends—is that Franks were heavily outbid by Muslims for any spare labour there was on the market. Only a richer Europe could escape this handicap.

In the ninth and early tenth centuries, then, nothing failed like failure. Complementarily, in the eleventh, nothing succeeded like success. Avoiding any exploration of the explosive effects of eleventh-century Europe's 'real' economic growth, let us concentrate on the matter of bullion. Europeans had so far cajoled a few bags of money out of Islam by trade. But they only sought it that way because, at the time, they could not get it by force—except indirectly by force on Slavs. By the millennium a frontal approach was plausible. The expulsion in 995 of Saracen gangsters at Fraxinetum near Marseilles was a preliminary. The proper onslaught began when Pisa and Genoa set off in 1016 to reconquer Corsica. In the 1040s began the Norman conquest of southern Italy and Sicily. Throughout the middle decades of the century Spanish and French knights hammered the Muslim frontier in Spain. The famous Palestinian crusade of 1095 was only the climax. These adventures gave Latin Christians direct access to Islamic wealth: they now only had to help themselves. A glance at any of these theatres of war shows how richly the blood flowed from Islam's pierced arteries. Genoa began its prodigious capitalistic career on treasure captured from Saracens at the beginning of the eleventh century.[109] When the Norman conquest of southern Italy and Sicily was consolidated, its rulers won, instantly, the reputation of being the richest in western Christendom.[110] Taken by force on Europe's frontiers, bullion meanwhile drifted more peacefully, through innumerable capillaries, into the main European economy. To give one example of many possible: from about 1040 King Ferdinand I of Castile exacted tribute from defeated (but not dispossessed) Spanish emirs. Ferdinand made in turn an annual tribute to Cluny, distant doyen of Spanish monastic colonization, of a thousand gold dinars. His son Alfonso VI doubled that in about 1077. Through Cluny's beneficiaries and creditors that gold sooner or later became generally available.[111]

The tipping-of-the-balance in Europe's favour had one last result, which cemented the process of her recovery. This was the inclusion in the revival of the last major area of ex-Roman Europe still in its dark age. France's relative economic dormancy in the tenth century has not been satisfactorily explained, or even assessed.[112] External raids no doubt played a part. But since raids—as will be explained early in the next chapter—were often a sign of incipient riches, the explanation is incomplete. What is certain is that an invigoration of monetary exchange is detectable there about the middle of the eleventh century; and that it was linked to Europe's *revanche* against Islam.

The link was double. The region in Gaul hit hardest by outside raids in the tenth century was the south. The formation of states in Islam's 'New World' had made the north-western Mediterranean a 'Far West' filled by freebooters. Far from offering Latin Christians a market, these freebooters checked farming, and both land- and sea-trade. Together with the efforts of Provençals themselves, the thrust of Italian and Spanish reconquerors on two flanks robbed the robbers of their lair. Southern France took its opportunity. The building by the abbey of St. Victor of Marseilles, a ruin in the year 1000, of an empire of monasteries across Languedoc and in Spain, serves as one signal of the general rejuvenation; and there are plenty more.[113]

The second strand in the link binding France's revival to the reconquests is Normandy. The leading authority on the duchy in this period has called distant war the Normans' 'national industry'.[114] The industry mulcted both northern and southern streams of money. And it played a big part in redirecting them to the French mainland. Normandy had shared modestly in the English revival of the late tenth century, and her most profitable 'distant war', in 1066, would be in that direction. But the comings-and-goings of race-conscious Normans from Spain, Naples, and later Palermo and Antioch, offered an even richer source of treasure from the south. About the middle of the century there are accordingly signs of a sudden rise in the amount of money circulating. One toll-post, at the neck of the Cherbourg peninsula, multiplied its takings by no less than fourteen between 1049 and 1093.[115] Signs of more minting, and some proto-capitalism, appear about the same time. From Normandy—as well as from the northern Rhineland, Flanders, and Italy—the waves reached northern France a decade or two later. The old Carolingian capital, Laon, got its first regular weekly market in 1071.[116] The first evidence of annual fairs in northern France is from near Paris in 1074. New life on the Rhône link between northern and southern France, although in evidence from about 1030, became conspicuous in the early 1070s.[117]

Europe's economic quickening in the eleventh century represented, then, the swing of a continental pendulum. For neighbouring economies have, besides their tendency to fly to opposite extremes, also, like pendulums, their laws of stable equilibrium. However unintentionally, an empire ends by teaching, equipping, and rousing its backward neighbours, and so putting them in a position to challenge it. The Arabs had done this by the eleventh century. So they yielded their life-blood to others. Turks swept over the eastern Islamic lands. In the west, Latin Christians, better-rooted in their own homeland than those Turkish nomads, contented themselves with avenging their forebears' Mediterranean retreat of the eighth century. The Latin Christians now had a vigorous northern hinterland behind them. On their eastern flank, a slowly dying Byzantium, 'Old Man' of medieval Europe, would both shelter and feed Italy's Levantine merchants. In front—in Spain, north Africa, and the Levant—lay an unprecedented accumulation of treasure. The Germanic world was able to avenge its defeat many-fold.

Europe's revenge on the external front quickened and consolidated her internal monetary development. By 1100 money was established in the nerve-centres, and had begun the long process by which it penetrated every part of the economy. The process would be far from over by 1500. Momentous episodes in the European history of money remained to be enacted, long after the period considered in this chapter. But this period would prove to have been, in this field too, a turning-point, in which the economic language of the central middle ages was first formulated.

That is meant metaphorically. But it is also true literally. The status of the eleventh century as turning-point is witnessed by language. In 1100 and later, the main Latin word for money was *pecunia*. The word had a secondary connotation as 'treasure'. This double meaning was classical. But it had not applied in the dark age. Back in the 750s documents could speak of merchants as a class that 'has no *pecunia*'; or of a man obliged to dwell 'in the *pecunia*' of another.[118] This usage recalled a Latin of long before Cicero, when the word *pecunia* grew up as brother to *pecus* (flock). In the dark age *pecunia* meant lands, buildings, animals, etc., with occasionally some treasure thrown in: roughly, in fact, what the rich man in Bishop Ratherius' polemic listed as his property. As late as the eleventh century, and even later, vestiges of this usage remained in the expression *pecunia viva* for livestock. But that was by then a specialized meaning. From just before the year 1000 the strictly monetary meaning of the word gained ground, to become virtually exclusive by *c.* 1100. A similar shift is traceable in other related words. The Old English word *feoh* changed its connotation similarly in the late tenth and early eleventh centuries. A shift is even noticed—though it is slower and less palpable—in some vernacular words corresponding to 'rich'. At the earlier end of the development the words 'rich', *'riche'*, and *'reich'* meant simply 'powerful'. At latest by the end of the twelfth century all three had a strong secondary meaning which was purely economic. The secondary meaning appears gradually to have pushed forward during the central and late middle ages, until the 'rich man' became, as he is now, the man 'abounding in wealth, especially money'.[119]

But to talk of a rich man is to talk of a person, not a thing; and we must not anticipate.

Dark-age Francia, and Lombardy, and their river-traffic; Baghdad, Cordoba, and their slaves and Jews; Rammelsberg, and the Normans. What these had to do with each other is one question this chapter has tried to answer. There remains a bigger question. What possible connection can, not just any of these, but all of them together, have had with the rationalistic traits which entered European culture during the twelfth and thirteenth centuries? In the next chapter we forge the first link in the causal chain that binds these unlikely companions together.

# CHAPTER 3

# Avarice

*Servit avaritiae ... in hoc aevo scelus omne*
Wrongdoing today all stems from love of money.

Hildebert of Lavardin (*c*. 1055–1133),
*De nummo* (*Of Money*).[1]

MEN usually act for some end-result; for example, planting corn to reap it. Because the environment has its own laws, not all end-results are possible, and people normally aim only at those they know are—most of all when they know it through habit. A radical change, however, in the laws of the environment can create new possibilities. Discovering these, men conceive new goals; and a whole new set of activities and habits ensues.

The entry of money into the European economy was such a radical change in the environment. It brought in new possibilities; and with them new goals, activities, and habits: so many of all of these, in fact, that historians cannot be sure of having spotted them all. There were obvious novelties like a growth in trade and towns. But there were many less obvious: wage–labour, for instance. By enlarging the market from which a worker could claim his livelihood, wages let him specialize more, and so be more expert. One tangible result of that lies in building: travelling gangs spread more sophisticated and uniform styles of architecture. Another novelty stemming from the spread of money was an increase in travel. With a widely-accepted currency travellers no longer had to rely on rights of hospitality. So they could journey more often and more ambitiously. Other examples could be added, equally pregnant. The more we reflect, in fact, the more we realize that money, rather than being a solvent of medieval society as it might first appear, was a prerequisite for its most characteristic achievements—such as cathedrals, pilgrimages, and crusades.[2]

It is the ensemble of these indirect effects of money, taken together, that forms our starting-point now. The ensemble can be characterized in a word: analogy. Among forms of wealth money combines a peculiar group of qualities. By a mechanism as mysterious as its results are unmistakable, analogous qualities appear in societies where money circulates. The qualities of money have been enumerated: it moves freely from hand to hand; it travels; it divides almost anyhow; a lot fits in a small space; it can be left to pile up without suffering natural vicissitudes. These qualities are reflected in societies with money in them. Men's mutual relations shift, as if liquefied by their medium of exchange; *men* travel; social blocks split, like sums of cash, into changeable groupings of individuals; people herd in towns, like coins in a chest; and power, finally, like value, is increasingly abstracted from the perishable to the imperishable, from individuals to institutions. A simple formula captures this whole effect: liquidity in wealth makes for social liquidity; abstraction in wealth makes for an abstraction of power.

This pair of end-products—social liquidity, and the abstraction of power in institutions—are to provide the twin foundations for the thesis of this book. Both were present in some measure before the eleventh century. But both grew in vigour and extent after it; and they remained the double leitmotiv of social history to the end of the middle ages. On one hand, individuals rose and fell; on the other, the institutions of church and state became more comprehensive. They remained, I say, the twin leitmotiv of social history; but also of psychological history. For, to each person in contact with them, the new social conditions spelt new possibilities of action, and hence new goals. From these came new activities and habits. The habits included mental habits. And these mental habits formed, in the twelfth and thirteenth centuries, the psychological matrix of the culture we have to investigate.

Two of the mental habits were especially fundamental. One was the habit of desiring more and more money, a habit which medieval theologians usually called avarice. The other was the habit of desiring that power and dignity which society concentrates in its institutions. Despite some confusion, this usually went under the name of ambition.

The logic by which money could give rise to the first of these habits, money-mindedness, is simple. Money makes wealth mobile. The mind, apprehending that, can start hoping for wealth. The hope breeds actions appropriate for fulfilling it; and after a while, both hope and actions become habitual.

That is the logic. Finding out if and how the logic worked in practice, after the millennium, is not so simple. The task has indeed been approached by more than one historian, from Huizinga on.[3] But the interpretation of evidence in the matter of mentalities abounds with traps, above all at this period, at the threshold of the epoch when documents begin to grow plentiful. Consequently, none of the attempts have been above criticism. Perhaps this one will not be either. A fresh attempt nevertheless has this much to say for it, that any loopholes it leaves will probably themselves be new ones; and if it proves, on its own, to be no less vulnerable than the others, together with them it should help build up the common case towards certainty.

We shall now accordingly examine the evidence for a growth—a *growth*—in money-mindedness in and around the eleventh century. Five areas of evidence will be considered: patterns in crime; trends in appointments to church office; the plight of the Jews; and the literary evidence respectively of satire and homily. These are separate areas. But their evidence points to one result.

### I. ROBBERS

The simplest thing a man can do if he wants money is take it. Other things being equal, theft is therefore likely to be the most cogent historical notice we have of his desire. It is all the more likely to be because theft and money are intrinsically connected: as intrinsically as commerce and money. Among forms of wealth money appeals to merchants because it is portable, acceptable, and storable. The same qualities recommend money also to the thief: he can carry it easily, and exchange it at recognized value without anyone's knowing where the actual coins come from. An extra bonus of a money-economy for the thief is that it goes with mobility in the market (a lot of buying and selling): so that whatever else a thief steals can be speedily sold.

This train of reasoning suggests that the spread of money after the millennium should have made theft easier, hence more tempting, hence more prevalent. Of course social and political factors also operate, both in the tempting and in the prevalence—factors like famine, and lack of strong government. But the economic factor should still be big enough to leave a traceable deposit.

The actual tracing of the deposit would be too complex a task to be attempted *in extenso* here. But I have attempted it elsewhere, and will summarize the result.[4] The problem invites three approaches. The first is by way of the notorious tenth-century pagan invasions. Various explanations of these invasions have been given, in terms of political collapse in Christendom, population-explosion among the invaders, etc. But one explanation lies in the pulling-power of Europe's liquid wealth. Magyars raided the Empire from the 880s to 955. Saracens worked as pirates and highwaymen in Italy and southern Gaul throughout the tenth century. Vikings launched big attacks against England (particularly) in the 990s. All three groups seem to have been attracted especially by money and precious metal, in and near the trade arteries. One example will illustrate the kind of reasoning which tells us this: the Magyars' predecessors on the Danube, the Avars of the eighth century, had raided eastern trade-routes north of Byzantium. The predominant Magyar interest, in the tenth century, was in western Europe. The switch was testimony to, among other things, the economic revival in the Empire, inherited and exploited by the Ottos.[5]

A second line of approach lies by way of native European predators. These appear to have followed the infidels' example. Chronicle-references to cases of robbery and theft suggest a pattern of crime roughly corresponding to the growth in the currency of gold and silver. The counterpoint of the various factors involved in producing crime—social, geographical, and political—is certainly complex, and too complex for a summary. But the drift of the evidence as a whole is in one direction. The places and times of known thefts and robberies are for the most part places and times where we know of revived commercial activity. The sequence is occasionally palpable. For instance, the mention of thieves often occurs in cities we know (sometimes from the same source) to be enjoying an economic boom: such as Prague (*c.* 980), Pavia, Cologne, and Sens (*c.* 1010–30).[6]

A third approach is through hagiography. This was the main literary genre continuous throughout our period, and the vicissitudes of certain motifs in the genre suggest a growth in robbery and theft. The main motif is that a saint miraculously saves a thief from hanging—hanging being *par excellence* a thief's punishment. This motif was dormant before the millennium and increased sharply in *Lives* written just afterwards, as if there were more thieves then.[7]

There were probably also more gallows. For robbery bred its own reaction. On the heels of successive crime waves came a toughening of state authority. The curbing of theft was part of the *raison d'être* of states. It was also part of their livelihood (as judicious and harassed merchants were capable of reminding slack monarchs). While it is true that no medieval state wholly mastered this part of its function, and that there would always be highwaymen, etc., the efforts of all states to curb theft necessarily put limits on it. Infidel Islam remained the only legitimate victim of theft, and that had to be better and better organized. At home, liquid wealth might be desirable. But as a means of getting it, theft, for all its simplicity, did not in the end pay.

So people who wanted money had to find more sophisticated means of getting it. One such means was political venality. We turn next to study one form of this venality, and the study will reveal its growing exploitation during the eleventh century. This growth will provide a second sign that the metal newcomer was having its psychological effect.

## 2. SIMONY: THE GREED OF THOSE WHO SOLD BENEFICES

The reform of the church named after Hildebrand, later Pope Gregory VII, began in earnest in 1049, with the accession of the reforming pope, Leo IX. The reformers directed their attack on a small number of ecclesiastical abuses. One was clerical marriage. Another, later, was lay investiture. But from the earliest days of the reform, one abuse stood out before all others as the target: simony, the buying of church office.

The 'buying' involved in simony had at times been under-stood broadly. In both theory and practice in the eleventh century, it might entail mere exchange, or the handover of land or produce, or even immaterial favours. Pope Gregory I, no doubt wishing to sink as many abuses in one boat as he could, had gone as far as to include favours like flattery in his definition of simony. Theologians went on quoting his definition.[8] However, the original simonist, Simon Magus, had made his offer for the Holy Ghost in hard cash (Acts 8:18–24); and everything suggests that Simon's disciples in the eleventh century usually followed his example. Accounts of this or that simonist, for instance, often mention the sum he is said to have paid: like 100 *solidi*, or £1,000 silver.[9] General deprecations of simony speak of the 'treasure-chests' which finance the simonist's purchase, of 'money-men' who govern the church, or of the 'price' of an office; and so on.[10] These and other indications reveal that in the eleventh century simony normally implied the use of money.

The history of simony in the tenth and eleventh centuries should therefore betray something about men's attitudes to money. For simony represented the impact of money on one sector of the economy, namely the church. Church economics were bound to be affected by the greater use of money.[11] The nature of assets controlled by prelates was such that those assets became, in the new conditions, increasingly a temptation for speculators. This was chiefly because bishops controlled town-centres, but there were other reasons. The reasons obtained especially in northern Italy, not only because Italy as a whole inherited many towns and many bishops, but because the commercial boom struck northern Italy first. On economic grounds alone, therefore, we should expect that the well-chronicled wave of ecclesiastical reform, starting about the middle of the eleventh century, would have been preceded by an equally marked wave of monetary simony.

This hypothetical wave of simony must in the nature of things have been less well chronicled than the wave of reform. For we know of simony mainly because reformers were moved to write about it. Any new impulses in simony before the reform are thus intrinsically elusive. A number of features in the evidence on simony do nevertheless suggest that it had grown worse just before the reformers started complaining about it.

The first feature suggesting this is that few complaints survive from the tenth century, and many from the eleventh. This contrast is sharper than can be explained by the general growth in literature in this period. The German historian Dresdner, who studied the moral climate of the Italian clergy in these centuries minutely, found few witnesses to this particular abuse from the tenth century. The bulk of his sources on simony were from the eleventh.[12] Bishop Ratherius of Verona, a voluminous commentator on the church of the mid-tenth century, is a striking case of a source who hardly mentions simony at all.[13]

Now it could be argued that Ratherius and his contemporaries did not rail against simony because they did not see it as an abuse: that is, simony was so endemic that even the most responsible prelates thought it normal, or at least incurable. Dresdner took that view. However, there is no overwhelming positive evidence for it; and there *is* some positive evidence that simony got worse as the reform approached. One piece of this evidence is that reformers thought it had done. When the time came, the reform would make its start in Italy. But the precocity of Italy in reform was preceded by its precocity in simony. At least, there was a clear tradition to this effect among the reformers. Radulf Glaber, whose Dijon monastery had links with Italy, wrote *c.* 1040 that while simony 'raged far and wide' in his day, and while his own Gaul was affected, the abuse had 'also, much more, taken possession of the whole of Italy'.[14] About 1058 Cardinal Humbert of Silva Candida's *Against the Simonists* said the same more emphatically. A chapter was called 'The especially-bad state of Italy'. It affirmed that 'while a number of provinces are sullied by [simoniacal] ordinations, Italy is worst of all'.[15] The distinction assigned to northern Italy by these writers is confirmed by the distribution of surviving references to cases of simony.[16]

Italy suffered more because it had suffered longer. Cardinal Humbert's own recollection only went back to the early years of the eleventh century. But he had heard tales from older people, and his historical sketch of simony would fit the view that the epidemic had begun in the late Ottonian period (*c.* 970), and in the Empire, whose boundaries included the Po and Rhine valleys:

We need not speak of earlier centuries. But many people still recall how this craze, of buying and selling [churches], struck Germany, the

Gauls, and all Italy, from the time of the Ottos up to Emperor [Henry III, 1035–56]. . . . This last emperor managed to remove the sacrilege in some degree . . . though he wished to stop it altogether. . . . But his contemporary and namesake, the wrecker of western Francia [Henry I of France, 1031–60] and tyrant towards God . . . utterly abuses churches.[17]

Both 'Gauls' included, as it happens, parts of the Empire. It is noticeable that Humbert, a Lorrainer by birth, first alludes specifically to simony in France from the year 1031. That was about the time when Radulf Glaber in Dijon said simony 'raged far and wide'; as it was also about the time when the economic situation would lead us to expect signs of more simony in France.

During the eleventh century simony spread outside northern Italy and Germany. Meanwhile in those areas it got worse. The Pistoian author of the *Life of Saint John Gualbert* spoke of simony as 'pullulating' in Tuscany during the saint's youth (*c.* 1000).[18] Radulf Glaber dated the onslaught of simony on Rome about 1033: the beginning of Benedict IX's pontificate.[19] Conrad II's reign (1024–39) witnessed a heyday for simony in Italy. A bogus prophecy, allegedly by an ancient sibyl but actually written retrospectively between 1084 and 1096, 'prophesied' that after the Emperor Henry II (1002–24) an emperor 'C' would reign, under whom, among other bad customs, would prevail that by which 'evil bishops, tempting God, will sell consecrations, a practice God has forbidden'.[20] Some other contemporary references, general and particular, harmonize with this picture.[21]

The early part of the reign of the emperor 'C' probably witnessed, in or near Rome, the birth of Hildebrand. As in the case of the gallows and robbers, the antidote grew with the disease. Stormily the two grew up together, simony and anti-simoniacal reform, and the very years of Gregory VII's pontificate, 1073–85, marked a new crisis in the epidemic against which he struggled. In Germany, forces curbed by Henry III sprang back after Henry's death in 1056. A chronicler in Constance saw the change coming there in 1056: 'at that time,' he wrote, 'the heresy of simony came to hold sway over those of our diocese, not as once secretly, but blatantly'.[22] It was under the year 1071 that Lampert of Hersfeld, in

Thuringia, chose to put his diatribe on monks who offered big sums of money to get church office. He expressly says things have got worse: such monks, he says, abandon the path of virtue 'which our ancestors followed'.[23] In his entry for 1075 Lampert spoke in the same connection of 'Mammon *in our times* publicly enthroned in the temple of God'.[24] Meanwhile the full force of the epidemic had struck France. In 1073 Gregory VII himself, addressing a French bishop, referred to France's pious past and went on to denounce the present king as having 'attained the very top of the peak' in simony.[25] The same suggestion of a zenith near the end of the eleventh century is given by the nostalgic Sextus Amarcius of Speyer (*c.* 1095). He attacked simony as chief of contemporary ecclesiastical abuses, abuses which made the present age worse than previous ones.[26]

Northern Italy, the Rhineland, finally France; and from about 1070 a fresh impulse all over continental western Europe: the pattern formed by these examples of simony has enough likeness to that of the monetary advance described in chapter 2 to suggest a connection. It is a flexible connection, certainly. Like robbers, simony may reflect other conditions besides economic: especially conditions in canon law and church politics. But money is an accessory. Other things being equal, a general flow of money will make simony easier, and therefore more tempting. The temptation, as far as the receiver of a simoniacal payment was concerned, was to a particular instance of *avaritia:* love of money. Simoniacal acts involved money; and for them to occur, someone must love it.

### 3. THE JEWS

Simony, like robbery, occasioned its own reaction: stricter government, this time in the church. Simony of course survived; but its practitioners, again in this like robbers, no longer had the field to themselves. Yet money remained magnetic for all that. People who wanted it just had to be even *more* sophisticated about getting it. Here was a problem. Not many people in eleventh-century Europe *were* sophisticated, at least in that direction. But there was a defined minority who were; whose traditions, whose esotericism, combined with an international cohesion among themselves, cast them as natural pioneers in the more sophisticated arts of money-making: the Jews.

For the Jews, as for everyone else, the eleventh century was one of change. But for the Jews the change was for the worse. At the start of the century we hear next to nothing of persecution of Jews. Instances survive of Jews living semi-rural agrarian lives side-by-side with Christians, without friction.[27] By 1100 this friendly coexistence had largely gone. The preaching of the first crusade precipitated widespread pogroms, especially in the Rhineland; and these pogroms became for centuries a regular, brutal punctuation-mark of social history.

The deterioration of Jewish–Christian relations in the eleventh century is an unquestioned fact. Where questions start is in explaining it. A penetrating book has been written on the subject by Dr. Lea Dasberg: *Investigations into the Decline in the Status of Jews in the Eleventh Century* (1965).[28] The book also takes full account of previous literature; and, given the complexity of this literature, there can be no better point of departure than Dr. Dasberg's thesis for explaining the place of Jews in our own story.

The outburst against Jews just before 1100 has been given two main explanations. One is that the religious fervour of the crusade, focused as it was on the place of Christ's Passion, naturally entailed a hostility to the race which had supposedly crucified him.[29] An alternative explanation is economic. A non-commercial region entrusts its earliest trade to a foreign caste. Then, once trade is established, native traders oust the foreigners and nationalize their business. The pogroms of the 1090s and later were a case of an indigenous bourgeoisie ousting Europe's commercial pioneers.[30]

The contrasting character of the two explanations will be familiar. If one of them has enjoyed more favour during the last generation it is probably the economic. But Dr. Dasberg annihilates it. Sources close to the pogroms show, for instance, that Europe's native bourgeois generally sought to protect the Jews in the pogroms.[31] On the ruins of this economic theory Dr. Dasberg erects a new ideological one. The Jews, she argues, were victims of the Investiture Contest, the great struggle between Pope and Emperor. The Jews were royal protégés both in law and fact. (The Rhineland bishops who shielded Jews can usually, for example, be shown to have been royal promotions.)

The papalists' quarrel with the king, above all when linked to their Cluniac friends' old, ascetic mistrust of usury, was bound to put their subject laity at loggerheads with the most conspicuous group of royal satellites.[32]

That is a short summary. It is too short to show all the ingenuity and coherence of Dr. Dasberg's thesis. But it is long enough to reveal where a possible loophole lies. Dr. Dasberg has destroyed an economic theory. But is that not because it was the wrong economic theory? A sturdier replacement can be suggested, all the sturdier for being broadly compatible with Dr. Dasberg's own construction. For there is no escaping that the Jews in question *were* economic pioneers, whatever their Christian counterparts may have thought of them. Jewish social structure and traditions, while no doubt barring them from the crude means of getting money reviewed in sections 1 and 2 of this chapter, helped them adapt with exceptional speed to the finer skills of money-making, not least that of finance at interest. The growing circulation of money in the eleventh century thus enabled Jews to become Europe's first *nouveaux riches*. The reaction against them came, not from the ranks of their counterparts and successors, but from the usual enemies of *nouveaux riches:* the old-rich, and the poor. And the resentment against Jews was compounded by their religion. To the blemishes usually attached to the swaggering upstart, Jews added their status as a caste with its own religion. Their new wealth enabled them to enlarge Jewish religious institutions, and consequently self-confidence, to a point where Christians felt threatened. So there was violence, abetted in single instances by the motives of individual debtors.

A construction on these lines would not demolish the theory about papalists and the king. But it may invert the theory. Instead of hating Jews because papalists told them to oppose the king's clients, the laity may equally well have drifted to the papalist side because they already hated the king's Jews. Hatred of Jews could perfectly well extend to their protector without ideological provocation.

This contention could be abundantly illustrated from periods later than the one under consideration—for instance, from the late twelfth century, in Plantagenet England. But three vignettes will show that the same geometry of resentments already obtained in the period treated by Dr. Dasberg. The first is from Sens, within a decade of 1020. Radulf Glaber of Dijon says the count ruling Sens then gloried in the nickname 'king of the Jews' because of his favour to them. Radulf has just told us that Sens as a city had become 'extremely rich'. And he goes on to describe the pitiless government which the same independent ruler exercised on his poorer subjects, a government which clearly earned him widespread fear and loathing.[33]

The second example is from the Speyer poet Sextus Amarcius, writing probably in or before 1095. The worst and biggest of pogroms contemporary with the first crusade began in this selfsame Speyer, in 1096. Sextus Amarcius' copious diatribe against Jews, part of his *Satires*, helps us picture the situation which sparked off the pogrom. A 'poor Christian', complains the poet, is severely punished if he makes an anti-Jewish remark. But at the same time a Jew may violently waylay a Christian with impunity. Sextus Amarcius refers also to the undiscriminating greed of 'certain bishops' for 'profit'.[34] Other sources tell us that the Bishop of Speyer when Sextus Amarcius wrote was a simonist, a friend of the king, and a protector of Jews: it was the bishop who stopped the Speyer pogrom from going further than it did.[35] Once more, the Jews appear to have been hated for their wealth and privilege; and the authorities only to have been hated for protecting them.

A third example of this pattern of resentment comes a generation later, in a famous letter of Peter the Venerable, abbot of Cluny. Peter's works included theological defences of Christian doctrine at points where Jews disagreed, for example, the Incarnation. But Jews were not for Peter mere academic opponents. He passionately resented their status. Just before the second crusade he wrote to King Louis VII, whose inertia made him visibly impatient, to denounce the Jews' faults. Jews scorned honest toil on the land. They tricked money out of Christians. While they should certainly not be killed, their money 'or most of it' should be confiscated. Reversing an opinion widely held in the earlier part of the eleventh century, Peter said Jews were worse than Saracens.[36]

Peter's outburst against the king's inertia is revealing. Its background in Cluny's account-book is equally so. Peter's appointment as abbot had coincided with the first aches and pains felt by Cluny's agrarian empire as it passed into the new conditions of the early twelfth century. These conditions included inflation; for which and other reasons Cluny became short of cash. So she borrowed: during Peter's time in office, the equivalent of some 10,000 silver marks, five times her annual revenue. Peter had apparently done what he could to steer the abbey's debts into Christian waters. But the tide was too strong. From an early stage, gold objects from Cluny's sacristy were in the hands of Jews in nearby Mâcon; and other obligations and gages probably followed them. The stubborn buoyancy of the Jews of Mâcon, as also of Châlon-sur-Saône further up river, struck a distasteful contrast with the flounderings of the great Christian abbey.[37]

At no period does the story of Jews in Christendom yield up all its secrets. But in the short period in question the outline of the situation is surely plain. The theological–eschatological scheme expounded by Dr. Dasberg is one facet of it. Other facets can be identified from the well-known facts of social history: Germany's invidious prominence in twelfth-century persecution, for instance, was largely due to the shortness of her commercial past—the *nouveaux riches* were all the more so there. Equally certainly, however, money as such played a part. It too was a relative newcomer, for most Christians. While not all Jews were wizards with money, nor all wizards with money Jews, enough Jews had enough financial expertise to associate their sect with money in the minds of critics. Jews were associated, in the twelfth century, especially with that sinister self-multiplication of money denounced as usury: the verb *judaizare* could refer to a Christian who became a usurer.[38] Deniers of one Incarnation, the Jews came themselves to be seen as an incarnation of that *avaritia* which was correctly felt to be changing the character of society.

### 4. SATIRE

The following scene is placed in the pontificate of Urban II, the pope who preached the first crusade in 1095.

At this the excellent Gregory, Cardinal of Pavia, who was sitting at the pope's feet, took hold of a book . . . and began to read the following homily, to which pope and cardinals listened attentively.

O how precious are the martyrs Albinus and Rufinus!
How deserving of fame and of praise! Those who
possess their relics are forgiven their sins forthwith, are
turned from earthly beings into heavenly, from impious
to innocent. . . . Who resists when Albinus intercedes?
Who denies when Albinus prays? Who refuses when
Rufinus commands? These are two martyrs who
manfully conquer emperors, dukes, tetrarchs, princes
and all other powers of this world. . . . These are the
precious martyrs whom Rome especially venerates,
whom Latium adores, whom Italy holds dear above all
others . . .

Gregory took a drink . . . and everyone approved what he had said.[39]

*The Translation of the Relics of the Martyrs Rufinus and Albinus*, of
which this is an extract, was probably written in 1099, soon after
the incidents it purports to describe. Its author is agreed to have
been one Garsias, canon of Toledo; and we happen to know
that about 1099 the new and rich archbishopric of Toledo
underwent big administrative changes,[40] which may or may not
have been the occasion of Garsias' visit to Rome in that year.

Accounts of 'translations' (i.e. the moving from one resting-
place to another) of saints' relics had been a favourite literary
genre for over two centuries when Garsias wrote. The translations of relics themselves were similarly a favourite religious
activity; and indeed economic activity, before more stream-
lined ways were found for exchanging the gold and silver that
housed saints' relics. What was new about the *Translation of the
Martyrs Rufinus and Albinus* was that there had never been any
such martyrs; or rather (for that was not new) no one even
believed there had been. The pair were outright imaginary
personifications, representing gold and silver. Their *Translation*
belongs to that subdivision of satire known as parody.

The eleventh century had seen a sporadic increase in money-
satire generally, from Egbert of Liège's *Ship of Plenty* (c. 1025)
down to the *Satires* of Sextus Amarcius, already quoted. In the
generation just before and after the year 1100, money-satire
emerged as a literary sub-category on its own, finding its
literary prototypes in the two western French poets, Hildebert
of Lavardin, Bishop of Tours and Marbod, Bishop of Rennes.
The poems of both were studied and emulated by twelfth- and

thirteenth-century Latinists, so that a whole tradition of money-satire developed in their wake, ramifying and expanding vigorously into the vernaculars.[41]

The money-satire has great variety, not only from a literary point of view (verse, prose, etc.) but also from that of philosophical content. A central theme nevertheless binds it together: the universal appeal of money, and the consequent power money has. The following lines from Marbod of Rennes' poem *De nummo* (*Of the coin*) are typical:

> Monk and senate, prince and prelate,
> Layman, cleric, mistress, man,
> Give them what you like, they'll sell it,
> Get good money if they can.
>
> Money! He's the whole world's master,
> His the voice that makes men run:
> Speak! Be quiet! Slower! Faster!
> Money orders—and it's done.[42]

The list of social functionaries in the first couplet of this quotation was as typical as the rest. The list was sometimes extended, and the power of money elaborated for each type. A poem *De denario* (*Of the penny; c.* 1110) by the Flemish poet Petrus Pictor ('the Painter'; he also painted miniatures) will illustrate this elaboration in respect of women:

> A handsome lover visits his fair whore
> But brings no money—and is shown the door.
> A monster follows, money in his wallet,
> And finds a banquet ready for his palate;[43]

and of wealthy householders:

> A pauper rings upon a rich man's bell
> For love of God; he's told to go to hell.
> But let a penny do the ringing, lo!
> He's shown straight up—while God stays down below.
> With golden guests all soirées are the smarter,
> But without cash you're *persona non grata*.[44]

Petrus Pictor's *De denario* handled a theme with a strong vernacular future before it, burgeoning in the thirteenth century into the personifications Dan Denier and Herr Pfennig, who worked the same wonders with every class of society.[45]

Certain classes dominate these satires—for instance, judges.[46] In the twelfth-century satire, however, one type is most prominent of all: the higher clergy, above all in Rome, special home of Simon Magus and of *avaritia:*

> Radix
>     Omnium
>         Malorum
>             Avaritia[47]

—as one twelfth-century acrostic had it.

The mention of Rome and Simon Magus brings us back to the essential question: the question of what all this satire signifies for the history of thought and manners. The satire follows a clear chronological curve. There had been faint traces of it in the Carolingian renaissance, and then a more-or-less total gap until the eleventh century, whose examples thicken towards 1100. After that examples are legion. The historian of the genre, Professor J. F. Yunck, writes that 'virtually all the poetry to be considered was written between 1100 and 1300'.[48]

The character of the satire, together with the sharp growth in its quantity after 1100, suggests *prima facie* that the fascination with money it depicts became general in society then. This suggestion is nevertheless open to objections which must be met. The first is that, in the twelfth century at least, the bulk of the satire is directed against the Roman Curia, if not that, against the clergy, especially the higher clergy. That is to say, most of the satire suggests, not that *avaritia* was general, but that it was peculiar to the church hierarchy, starting at the top. This first objection is best answered by reflection on the authorship of the satire. It was largely written by clergy. Not only are a clerk's first enemies those of his own household. The middle and higher clergy from which much of the satire came (e.g. Garsias, Walter Map) were those who did most of the paying of the Curia's fees. The bias, in other words, reflects the satire's authorship, rather than the actual state of affairs.

There is a less tractable objection. Money-satire was a literary topos, no more reliable as a description of real manners than a modern 'thriller' would be. Once Hildebert and Marbod had established the theme, it only needed repeating. Furthermore, this topos was not even a medieval invention.

Twelfth-century writers did not speak Latin in early infancy. They had to learn it; and ultimately the teachers they learned it from were Augustans like Horace, Juvenal, and Persius. These had lived in a palpably commercial world. The three named classical poets had left examples of satire which it was the aim of every medieval satirist to emulate. Thus Juvenal's Fourteenth Satire, on money, and Horace's *Regina Pecunia*, were able to flow straight into the medieval literary current. The growth in medieval money-satire, on this view, would reflect, not contemporary conditions, but merely the choice of classical authors admired by the better Latinists. The satire, one could almost say, merely reflected better Latin.

There is no firm answer to this problem. Each author has to be studied on his own for its solution in his case; indeed, each work must be studied, and sometimes each line. But for the satire as a whole, three considerations may incline us to take its social reference seriously. One is that the medieval writers in question could, within limits, choose their models. What drew them to Horace and Juvenal was partly that economic change had created social conditions analogous to those of Augustan Rome: faintly analogous, perhaps, but enough so to make some of the Roman caricatures topical: the *nouveau riche*, the fop, the venal official, etc. In other words, the objection could be turned on its head: Horace's *Regina Pecunia* was taken up *because* of its contemporary reference.

A second consideration is the subjectivity of some of the poems. 'There clings to many of these pieces', writes Professor Yunck, 'the faint residue of sour grapes.'[49] This applies especially to the satire written by clerks who, after sweating at their Latin, were in their own view ill-rewarded. The smart is already palpable in Egbert of Liège, a cathedral schoolmaster who saw Money as the all-conquering Amazon

> Before whose insolent advance
> Little Miss Learning stood no chance
> But when discovered got a 'ho!
> What's this?' a 'whack!' and 'out you go!'[50]

*Cur ultra studeam?* Why should I study any more? asked Petrus Pictor, in the same context.[51] The theme recurs.[52] The cry of hurt interest may make biased social comment; but at least it is social comment, not mere topos.

Medieval money satire rises only to modest literary heights, taken piece by piece. But areas of it, seen as a whole, can claim a profundity of observation at least equal to any achieved by the Augustans. This is the third consideration boosting the historical credit of the satire. The profundity is achieved especially in parody, and namely in that part of parody which apes Christian thought and literature (like the 'Translation' of the two martyrs). Parody is the native genre of schoolboys, and scholars who studied in a Christian milieu might be thought, in choosing Christian material for their parodies, merely to have picked on the material nearest to hand. But this is to underestimate them. For the parodists had observed, as Marx did later, that money exercises a power in very many respects god-like. Elements of the idea may have been inherited, both from the Bible, and from *Regina Pecunia* and her parallels. But the medieval elaboration of the theme is original; and for a good reason. It inverted Christian liturgy and theology, as developed by the twelfth-century renaissance; and put 'Money' where God should have been. Thus there was a money-litany;[53] a Gospel according to the Mark of Silver;[54] and so on,[55] including of course the legend of Rufinus and Albinus. This parody is commonly, and rightly, adduced to illustrate the free familiarity with which clerics could turn on their most sacred texts. But it also illustrates something more specific: a comprehension that what official doctrine predicated of God, Father, Son, and Holy Ghost, was in real life observably true of money. Money could do miracles;[56] overturn human justice;[57] plant and uproot earthly powers;[58] give and take away salvation;[59] and do all the other things God alone was meant to accomplish. Indeed it did more. For Petrus Pictor's *De denario*, which is not a parody, but hides Christian ideas under its fashionable classical disguise, says money is a *greater* god than the Christian Jehovah:

> Cash shares with Jove the throne of emperor,
> For both as gods are worshipped by our race,
> And yet it's cash that really holds first place
> For what the thunderstorm and lightning flash
> Leave *un*moved, can be moved by cash

And insults that great Jove forbears to scold
Would not be spared thus by vindictive gold.[60]
The substitution of money for God in familiar Christian
thought-forms may have had an element of topos, and an
element of meaningless schoolboy merriment; but it also
contained a penetrating truth, and cannot be denied credit for
having observed the same in contemporary life.

### 5. HOMILY

Among surviving weaknesses of my argument so far the most
damaging relates to development. The explosion of money-
satire about 1100 might, in principle, merely reflect the general
literary explosion then—in letter-writing, canon law, history,
government records, and so on. If that is all it reflects it would
not reflect any growth in money-mindedness.

This is again a question that cannot be answered categori-
cally. But one final approach to the problem suggests itself,
which skirts this objection and may ultimately neutralize it.
Even in the darkest parts of the post-Carolingian dark age,
certain literary genres survived, which continued on into the
twelfth century and beyond. These occasionally commented on
contemporary *mores*, usually because the writer wished to
improve them. The main genre in question is the homily or
sermon, but didactic passages of this kind also occur in biblical
exegesis. The emphasis on different vices in these didactic
passages should yield some clue as to their authors' impressions
of contemporary society; and a comparison of these emphases
before and after the eleventh century should, in turn, reveal
whether *avaritia* became a more dominant vice during that
century.

More than one social historian, and notably in recent years
Professor Lester K. Little, has established the preoccupation of
preachers with 'avarice' in the late eleventh century and later.[61]
Whether this preoccupation led theologians to alter their
*psychology* of sin is highly doubtful. Pride had always been
acknowledged as the root of sin.[62] But pride manifests itself
differently in different circumstances. In the circumstances of
the late eleventh century, apparently, it found its most
conspicuous manifestation in love of money. So this was what
homilists worried about. Passages in Cardinal Humbert's

*Against the Simonists;*[63] in Peter Damian's tracts, such as *Philargyria* (a Greek word for 'love of silver');[64] the letters of Gregory VII— for whom Saint Paul's 'Each seeks his own' (Phil. 2:21) was a favourite quotation;[65] these and similar references confirm the message of the satire.[66] They leave us in no doubt that preachers in the late eleventh century were much concerned at contemporary *avaritia*.

But there remains a rub. Here is an instance of it, from a sermon:

The rich themselves, if the whole world could become one man's property, would still yearn to have more of it. As for the poor, they want to be equal in riches with those already wealthy, and suffer an insatiable passion of greed as a result. They go off their heads with their insane desire to possess. The same disease produces different distempers in different people. Yet one and all are so afflicted by a love of *pecunia* that no other affection withstands it: not love of friends or relations, indeed at times not even love of spouses or children.[67]

The difficulty presented by this passage is that it was written around 925, by Saint Odo of Cluny. Homily is one branch of literature which, unlike satire and parody, affords chronological comparison. We turn to it, and find a diatribe against *avaritia* which would be quite at home in the twelfth century. Odo's words, to which contemporary parallels could be found,[68] suggest that a one-sided reading of fragmentary records has created a laborious illusion.

To test this suggestion I have studied a total of seven works by three authors, all from the early or middle part of the tenth century, and all with some didactic intention. The authors are Odo of Cluny, and the two northern Italian bishops, Ratherius of Verona and Atto of Vercelli.[69] What follows is a summary of the result. It is offered to underpin research already undertaken by others.

The word 'avarice' itself is relatively infrequent.[70] Chances to mention or emphasize it are often noticeably missed. For instance, a list of current evils will be given; and avarice and the avaricious are never (literally never, in the works used in the sample) at the head of these lists.[71] Ratherius, in a typical roll-call of contemporary sinners, puts *avari* after adulterers and fornicators;[72] and speaking of clerical vices he puts all 'secular business' firmly after dicing and hunting.[73] Atto, enumerating the sins the devil nourishes in different classes of men—rapine, lust, pride, superstition—gets no nearer to avarice than 'fraud'.[74] Odo makes his three most prominent sins 'pride, lust, and malice',[75] hesitating between 'lust' and 'discord' when it is a question of first place.[76]

Scriptural comment is equally revealing. Some of the Old Testament and all the New were produced in a milieu familiar with money and its attendant vices. Their sentences on the subject called for comment. When Atto came to 1 Tim. 6:10, 'Avarice is the root of all evil', he confined his social comment to the remark that nothing was worse than the avaricious *ecclesiastic* (his book was written for ecclesiastics).[77] For Ratherius, again, 'Mammon' meant only the list of good things in life quoted in chapter 2 as our guide to the non-monetary character of wealth.[78] Some scriptural references to money were brushed aside with a spiritual interpretation. For Odo, Ananias' punishment for withholding money from the apostles (Acts 5:5) was a warning to those who hold part of *themselves* from God.[79] Simon Magus, 'the rich', and 'gold' can be likewise spiritualized.[80] It is true that these glosses were aimed at clerical or monastic audiences. But our authors could have spoken on secular vices if they had wished. They usually did not wish. The surest sign of that is their neglect of a biblical passage which would later be a mainstay of topical preachers who denounced avarice: Jeremiah 6:13, 'from highest to lowest, all are intent on avarice'. It appears once fleetingly in Odo (wrongly attributed to Isaiah); otherwise in none of the seven works used.[81]

Odo often passed through northern Italy, and Ratherius and Atto lived there, in the first phase of the commercial revival. None of the three was ignorant of money, or of the vices it occasioned. But their stresses and silences show it was not their first preoccupation.

Two final circumstances call for mention in corroboration of these findings. Our knowledge of the first comes from Professor Little.[82] Homilies were given in sculpture as well as words. Throughout the tenth and eleventh centuries, as indeed for much longer, vices and virtues were symbolized in art, to warn and encourage. The reference-book *Art Index* records known examples. A count-up of datable examples shows, naturally, a

sharp increase in the number of representations of *avaritia* from
the ninth to the thirteenth century. But the merit of this
particular kind of document is that it also offers a 'control'. The
fortunes of *avaritia* can be measured relatively to those of other
symbolized vices. The following table, calculated from
Professor Little's census, shows the ratio between representations of, on one hand avarice, and on the other pride, over
five centuries:

| Century | 9th | 10th | 11th | 12th | 13th |
|---|---|---|---|---|---|
| Pride: Avarice = 10: | 2 | 4 | 20 | 14 | 15 |

The series of ratios proclaims, more clearly than the absolute
figures, a sharp increase in interest in *avaritia* specifically in the
eleventh century.[83]

The second corroborative circumstance is that the change
suggested in this chapter was noticed by contemporaries. Many
apparently thought *avaritia* was getting worse. This kind of
testimony is not impregnable on its own, since gloomy theories
about a decline of the times may have no objective basis. But the
ensemble of the opinions does lend a certain finish to the rest of
the evidence. Radulf Glaber in Dijon, about 1040, recalled
prophecies that religion would be corrupted in the last days
'through the march of *avaritia*'; and he identified these days
with his own.[84] Towards the end of the century such
historically-defined impressions become more frequent. A lord
near Cluny, charged with attacking Cluny's caravans in about
1074, accused in his apology the '*avaritia* which is creeping upon
secular folk generally'.[85] A man born in 1083, Prior Guigo I of
the Chartreuse, reflected in old age that *avaritia* was a sin which
had got worse in his own lifetime.[86] Some of the satirists at the
turn of the century, notably Sextus Amarcius and Hildebert of
Tours, expressly said that the avarice they attacked was an evil
peculiar to their own day.[87] Most telling of all, because furthest
away in time and most systematic, would be the view of Gerhoh,
Provost of Reichersberg.[88] In 1167 Gerhoh would divide world
history into four periods. The century before the time he wrote,
that is to say the century which began with the career of
Hildebrand, seemed to Gerhoh from the traditions and records
he worked from to have characteristics of its own. Among them
was a dominant sin: avarice.

# CHAPTER 4

# Ambition

The same yearning for power and prestige affects
high and low

John of Salisbury, *Policraticus*, VII, c. 19 (*c.* 1159).

THE temptation to avarice was a direct psychological consequence of the presence of money. Men saw the glittering stuff
and wanted it. But early in the last chapter it was explained that
money also had indirect effects. It facilitated new forms of social
organization; and these new forms had *their* psychological
consequences, which can thus in turn be traced back indirectly
to the metal newcomer. I want in this chapter to consider just
one of these indirect consequences. It was a second mental
habit, an invidious twin to *avaritia;* and can be shown, like
*avaritia*, to have become more general in European society after
the millennium. The twin is *ambitio*, in the sense of a desire to
climb to the top of the social scale.

Ambition can only be linked indirectly with money. So I shall
start by describing the mechanism through which the causation
passed: the social fact, which gave rise to the psychological one.

## I. THE SOCIAL FACT: CLASS MOBILITY

An insistent theme in the money-satire is that money disturbs
social order. It enables men to rise in society. Horace had
already claimed for his *Regina Pecunia* that she could 'give
high birth' to someone without it.[1] Implications of that were
elaborated in the twelfth century. Hildebert of Lavardin's
poem *De nummo* had the bald equation *nummus nobilitas:* 'money
is nobility', as if money were usurping the role of birth[2] in
making men noble. Again, one of Petrus Pictor's long poems on
money said that the man with money 'will rise in honour'.[3]
More circumspectly, their contemporary Marbod of Rennes
said 'money makes honours change hands'.[4] By the late twelfth

century this was a widely-known aphorism. The anonymous verse *De cruce denarii* started with the boast that 'The Penny Cross' (the little star on the English 'sterling' penny) could make a king of a serf and a serf of a king.[5] Vernacular jongleurs made their personifications of money, Dan Denier and Dom Argent, 'raise an ignoble lineage' and 'make a courtier of a peasant'.[6] That these satirists were not merely repeating a cliché is shown by their view's being echoed by more prosaic observers. The Dominican John Bromyard's *Summa* for preachers, for instance, written in the early fourteenth century but from earlier material, repeats that money 'ditat . . . et sublevat'; enriches, and *exalts*.[7]

So money exalted. It remains to inquire how it exalted; or (put in more abstract language) how the presence of money precipitated social mobility. Here the satirists fail. The more careful of them say nothing; and the less careful given an answer which is probably wrong. They suggest that a man piles up money and buys political dignity. That could certainly happen, as it did with those simonists. But as a general picture of social mobility in the eleventh and twelfth centuries this one is almost certainly misleading. The ground for thinking so is that scholarship knows of very few cases in those centuries where a man accumulated enough personal wealth, for long enough, to make much difference to his social status. In the countryside, a peasant who accumulated money seems to have had it as often as not unceremoniously taken away by his lord.[8] After 1100 a few peasant-pioneers and rural industrialists—notably smiths and millers—are occasionally seen cutting out a superior position for themselves; but their superiority remained both modest and precarious.[9] Nor were towns different, for all that town air made you 'free'. Some up-and-down movement in towns, based on private business fortunes, can be detected. But it still had little permanency, and little impact in the big world where politics were made.[10] Italian towns were in this respect probably more advanced than others. But the situation of merchants there is well enough expressed in the epitaph of an archbishop of Milan— probably Latin Europe's most advanced inland city—in 1040. He was a 'protector of orphans, widows, the poor and *merchants*'.[11]

There is very little evidence, therefore, that money changed

honours—*nummus mutat honores*—in any direct sense. Private
business wealth is rarely seen buying a man up the social ladder.
Yet, for all that, there *was* social mobility in the eleventh and
twelfth centuries. And money *was* indirectly behind it. A rarer
theme in the satire can explain the secret. Let us allow it to do so:

> Money, O money! It is thanks to thee
> That Caesar domineers his boundless fee
> And kings contest in fretful war's commotion
> Their wide-flung frontiers of plain and ocean.
> Troy was made ash. 'Twas to *thy* power she bowed,
> As she had by that selfsame power grown proud:
> To crush her thou didst arm the sinews bold
> Of warriors, lusting for her Phrygian gold.
> Tall Rome, the city, rose on thy foundation,
> And paid fine craftsmen for collaboration:
> For what brains started—a great building feat
> Indeed—much cash was needed to complete.[12]

These excursions express a simple truth: the existence and
activities of centralized political authority depend on money.

There is no question, now, of our being in the presence of a
mere poets' conceit. Not only had the father of European
anthropology, Tacitus, noticed precisely the same thing among
first-century Germans.[13] The same truth was put more elaborately in a book that was (unlike Tacitus) read in the twelfth
century: the pseudo-Aristotelian *Secretum Secretorum*. The extraordinary European diffusion of this work, especially in the
thirteenth century and later, will be described in the next
chapter.[14] Here we need only note one reason for its diffusion: the
shrewdness of its observations on politics. One of these
observations was on money. Money, it proclaimed, was part of
the essence of the centralized state. The observation is put most
clearly in the form of a figure, a figure in which the pseudo-
Aristotle claims to summarize the import of his book. It is a
circle, divided into eight segments.

Each element in the circle is causally connected with the next:
'There can be no king without an army'; 'there can be no army
without a state', and so on. The wording and order of the eight
elements vary slightly in different textual traditions, Arabic,
Hewbrew, and Latin. (The present figure is constructed from

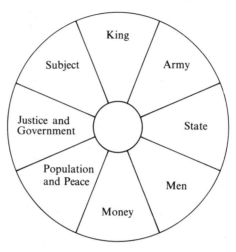

the main Latin text. Plate II shows a slightly different Arabic form.) But the figure remains basically the same in all versions, and can indeed be said to constitute—as the surrounding text in all the versions emphasizes—the kernel and distillation of the whole *Secretum*. The figure may invite improvement. Its symmetry and assurance, like its attribution to Aristotle, carry less conviction today than in the middle ages. But the concept has one great merit. It captures in an easy symbol the essential interdependence of elements in a centralized political structure, a structure which for the first readers of the Latin (and for that matter Arabic) *Secretum* would have been the most palpable of contemporary novelties. Money was integral to the scheme. By making it so the *Secretum* put more soberly the truth uttered with customary licence by the poet: Rome rose on the foundation of money. Put more soberly still it is: because liquid wealth can be concentrated, it facilitates the concentration of public authority.

This concentration of public authority affects both the social status of individuals, and thereby also their attitude towards such status. We look first at the status.

*(i) The risers: social ascent through service.*

The reason why a concentration of authority affects individuals' social status is, at bottom, that such authority is abstract. It needs individuals to exercise it. It draws them in, and they partake of its esteem and wealth. This process, though a Platonistic philosopher might perhaps think it up for himself, is also a matter of cold observation. That includes observation by contemporaries. A servant of one of the earliest of Europe's centralized monarchies, Walter Map, reflected in the 1180s on the odd character of the little society where he had passed his life. He noticed this: the contrast between the intangible permanence of the court itself, and the transience of the flesh-and-blood people who served it.

As Augustine lived in time and spoke of time, yet could not comprehend it, so I live in a court and speak of it, yet can say with the same puzzlement that I cannot comprehend the court. For although a court is a different thing from time, it is *of* time: mutable, variable, never staying in one state. I leave it, knowing the whole court. I return and recognize no one. I feel a stranger. Yet it is only the members who have changed. The court itself stays the same, triumphantly the same; like a giant with a hundred hands, or a hundred-headed hydra, who can lose any number of these members and always replace them, scorning the antics of any Hercules who should threaten it.[15]

Although Walter Map's experience was mainly of one court, the Plantagenet, he had known half-a-dozen others; and he undoubtedly wrote here of the court as such.

The state, then, was abstract. It drew men in. When they were in they partook of its esteem and wealth. Now with merit and luck these latter (the esteem and wealth) might stick to them. A government servant, that is to say, might found a powerful dynasty. Here was, at last, a means of social ascent. It was also a means much employed. For if there is one thing social historians of these centuries are increasingly agreed about, it is that service, not personal wealth, was the key to social ascent.

To be a 'servant' in today's language suggests a drop in social status. But whether it should depends on whom one is a servant to. This is clear from yesterday's language. For many words which by the central middle ages had come to denote high rank can be traced to roots implying servant-status. Examples include: 'knight', 'thegn', and 'vassal' (from two Germanic terms and one Celtic respectively, all meaning 'lad'); 'marshal' (from Germanic 'horse-rascal'); 'ambassador' (from Celtic 'servant'); 'baron' (probably from Celtic 'booby'); 'count' (from the Latin for 'companion'); the German *Ritter* ('knight', related to *Reise*, and meaning originally 'one who goes', e.g. on errands). Some noble surnames, like Stuart and Butler, tell the same story.[16]

It is true that service often presupposed wealth. But the wealth could be granted by the same authority that called for the service. The cost of an armed knight, for instance, could be met by the master who employed him. Rather than riches leading to rank, therefore, it was at this period more normally rank that led to riches. Thus between 1000 and 1150 the German *ministeriales* were deliberately enriched by successive monarchs as counterpoise to the hereditary nobility. In Anglo-Norman feudalism, again, tenure by 'serjeanty' (servantry) gave men rich fiefs for paltry service (e.g. a manor in Suffolk for dancing in front of the king at Christmas).[17] The principle that rank came first, and appropriate wealth was attached to it, can even be found in towns, later strongholds of the opposite idea. For example, after a communal plundering expedition *c.* 1000, the Genoese split the booty up according to the *rank* of participants.[18]

The presence of money helped create nodes of authority, which needed functionaries and could reward them. It is here we must look for the principal means of social ascent in the centuries in question. So let us look here, at the two main categories of riser.

(a) *Businessmen*

The first category was appropriately economic. For centres of political power were also economic centres: with commitments—for food, building, and armament; and with powers—over land and trade. The efficiency with which powers were matched up to commitments could vary. It depended on how well men worked in the context of the changing economy. Those whose skill raised the efficiency were the ones who rose. I take the skilful laity first.

(1) *Laymen.* Such risers among the laity are met with in one after another of the monographs published recently on eleventh- and twelfth-century societies. The successful peasants of the Mâconnais, right on to the thirteenth century, were those

who held office as prévot for count, bishop, or abbot; while of
the burghers of Mâcon itself, the only families anywhere near
attaining nobility by 1200 had chiefs with 'ministerial' office
under count or bishop.[19] In Languedoc, the few rural land-
exploiters who made the leap into the military class were those
who used or misused the comital offices of *vigueier* or *bayle*.[20] A
similar story can be read in Normandy. There, 'rather than
among merchants, it is in the duke's entourage or under the
shadow of churches' that an eleventh-century 'aristocracy of
money' has been found.[21] In the Normans' rich quarry,
England, the same rule applied. The unique surviving guide to
pre-conquest English custom concerning status (datable to
1002–23) envisaged economic mobility within all social levels.
But the key-rank of 'thegn' was kept closely and almost
exclusively attached to royal service.[22] The primary of service as
a means of social rise holds nowhere truer than in Germany.
The *ministerialis* families had often begun as serfs. The favoured
few performed crucial duties for their masters, generation after
generation, and were rewarded; so that some (e.g. the
Hohenstaufen) came to overtop the old nobility.[23]

Among other examples that could be given, thickening in the
twelfth century, one has a special claim to mention: the early
minter. The right to mint was 'regalian'. Like other regalian
rights it was decentralized when the Carolingian empire
declined. As money grew more important in the eleventh
century (and the tenth in Italy), entrepreneurs bid for these
rights, minted public money, and by charging a high 'seig-
neurage' made private fortunes for themselves. By early in the
twelfth century their heyday seems generally to have ended, as
their job was called in to be controlled much more tightly by the
government. But by then we know of at least two minters'
families which had entered the nobility of their respective
kingdoms: the Cancellieri of Milan and the Le Monedier of Le
Puy.[24]

Laymen who did the lord's business efficiently could thus rise
in social status. But the promotion of courtly businessmen
occurred also in a second field. This latter has received less
notice; and deserves notice all the more now for that reason.

(2) *Churchmen (Simony: the ambition of those who bought
benefices)*. Secular magnates had every reason to be close-fisted

in handing out lay fiefs to public servants. They had less reason for jealousy when it came to handing out ecclesiastical fiefs. The church was often too weak to defend herself, even after Gregory VII. It was consequently in the ecclesiastical sphere that the upstart came nearest to being able to buy his way up the social scale. We are back, of course, with simony. But it is now simony seen from below, not above. If the selling of church office betokened money-mindedness in the sellers, the buying of it, in measure as it was not pure financial speculation, could betoken in the buyers a desire to 'get to the top'.

It may be objected that simonists were at the top already. Simony, we are sometimes told, represented a feudal domination of the church, from which a revolutionary papacy freed it. In some regions, some kinds of simony could be accessory to feudal control of the church. But the buying of church office, as such, must in essence have been the reverse of this. It was a solvent of a feudal church, since it put church office up to the highest bidder regardless of legal or hereditary claims. Far from being a prop for dynasties, simony was thus the perfect tool for the opportunist.

If testimony is consulted from the heartland of simony—northern Italy and the Rhineland—it reveals that this was in fact how simony was seen. In Italy, the exploitation of priestly office for social climbing—by ex-serf priests, with sons whom they set up in military careers at their church's expense—was an abuse antedating the eleventh century; and it was coming to its height when a synod in Pavia condemned it in 1022.[25] Careerists were meanwhile climbing higher than the parish level. The rich urban bishoprics had the patronage of enviable diocesan posts: it was these that attracted bolder spirits. The granting of diocesan jobs to persons of 'popular' class had apparently been one factor in the tensions in Milan under Archbishop Landulf II (†998).[26] It was certainly a scandal in the middle of the eleventh century. Humbert of Silva Candida had studied the subject exceptionally closely. His polemic against simonists (*c.* 1058) expressly characterized the latter as low-born. They are, he said, 'not noble and literate persons so much as ignoble and illiterate'.[27] They made their way up to ecclesiastical honours through purely secular—and often frivolously secular—service.[28] The typical bad bishop, Humbert grumbled, builds a retinue from 'middle-class' laity and low-ranking clergy, who pay him in money or service.[29] A few years later Peter Damian echoed these views. In his tract *Courtier-Clergy* he lashed those who climbed to church office, including bishoprics, through either payment or menial service.[30] Peter quoted, as Humbert had done, an ancient decretal against the appointment as bishops of 'strangers and outsiders, and people previously unknown'—in a passage palpably aimed at careerist courtiers.[31]

From the end of the century these Italian observations are matched by some from Germany. In 1069 the gravamen of a charge against a simonist bishop of Constance was that he sold honours 'without acceptance of persons'.[32] At Hirsau in the early 1080s Abbot William spoke of the corrupt motives behind contemporary episcopal appointments: 'abundance of riches' was made a motive distinct from 'vain nobility', as if *nouveaux riches* were involved in the traffic.[33] That simonist bishops and their staff were frequently upstarts also transpires from the *Satires* of Sextus Amarcius, writing probably in Speyer about 1095. In contrast to former days, when the 'vile' man could not get office however much he offered to pay. Amarcius saw his own age as one of moneyed opportunists. His picture is startlingly familiar.

> The man who makes his pile nowadays
> By selling doddery houses, or who lays
> Out tattered, stinking hides for sale, or turns
> A wooden cup or two—can save up what he earns
> And take his savings to the civic hall
> And ask just what he wants. He'll get it all.
> *He* will be tribune; and the craftsman's knife
> And junk that was his father's means of life
> Will not stand in his way: for social class
> And breeding now can be acquired—for brass.[34]

The classical terms of this satire—*atria, tribunus*, etc.—must not stand in *our* way. Such pastiche was his chosen style. What Sextus Amarcius had in mind was contemporary simony. Later in the poem, the discrete disguise is all but dispensed with.

> But certain bishops whom I will not name
> On this score are not innocent of blame,

Promoting as they do ill-bred marauders
To don the dignity of holy orders—
Without inquiring if they thus ordain a
Serf or freeman, drunkard or abstainer.
And why do bishops overlook these data?
—Because they get a handsome cut, *pro rata*.[35]

Sextus Amarcius is thought to have been a cathedral canon, and if so would have shared the high birth of most of that category. One reason why many of his class had turned against their king, Henry IV, was just this: that Henry had actually encouraged this invasion of churches by men of dubious background.[36]

Simony, then, created among other things a ladder: a man otherwise ill-qualified might buy his way into ecclesiastical position. Economically such a man was counterpart to a lay *ministerialis*. The latter, certainly, would normally render most or all of his current profit to his lord, and get some back as a reward. The simonist, by contrast, gave his lord his (the lord's) share of the profit as a sum cash down in advance: i.e. a price, not a rent or return. Otherwise their positions were closely comparable. Both, in different ways and spheres, were men who raised their social status by economic service to public authority.

Now one result of this service was that lords got richer. Economic powers were better employed to match economic commitments. So new commitments could be embraced. This meant better clothes, food, and so on. But the commitment the lord was likely to care most about was the military. It was this that determined his relation with other lords. So it was the military commitment that was likely to absorb most of any improved yield there was. The second main category of discernible social riser in the eleventh and twelfth centuries is, appropriately therefore, the warrior.

(b)  *The military.*

The detection of social ascent among warriors in the late eleventh century is obstructed by two main difficulties. One is that most warriors were illiterate. Though they remembered certain kinds of family history, and these occasionally got written down, the writing normally occurred after memory had had time to play its tricks. The second difficulty was that noble status, which warriors had or aspired to, depended largely on ancestry. So the people who remembered their ancestry might have an interest in remembering it wrong.[37]

In the case I propose to discuss in the next few pages, memories as a result did play tricks. The case is that of the warriors *par excellence* of the first crusading age: the Franks. The trick of memory in their regard has been ingenious enough to impose itself on most historiography in this century, and to establish as canon a view opposite to that so far defended in this chapter. It has taught that up-and-down social movement among the French nobility was fluid *until* the second half of the eleventh century, and *then* became fixed. If that were so the whole purport of my argument would be nonsense. But let us see if it is.[38]

A glance at the narrative evidence is enough to show why the view has prevailed. In the small sector it covers this evidence is almost overwhelming. From the eleventh and early twelfth centuries, accounts survive of the origins of some half a dozen of the great French dynasties, dynasties we can trace as permanencies from just before then. The accounts share a common trait. They tell of an original ancestor, datable to the late ninth or early tenth century, who was an upstart. The Capetian house itself, for instance, was supposed to trace its descent from 'a tiro of no great name' (a tiro was an apprentice-knight), promoted by Charles the Bald for valour. The counts of Anjou, similarly, descended from a 'forester' elevated by the same king. And so on.[39] The bravery of these men-from-nowhere was sometimes contrasted with the sluggardliness of the hereditary nobility of the time. Taken with our knowledge of the same dynasties from the time contemporaries relate their doings in detail, these accounts suggest that the eleventh century was a time of hardening of social classes. The period when tiros could rise and start dynasties, they seem to say, was over. Furthermore, if this was true of the princely families we know about, should it not also apply to elusive families lower down the scale?

This remarkably unanimous evidence comes from narrative sources. But the narrative sources have a weakness. They were not contemporary. The bold tiros were recorded some generations after the time they are meant to have lived. So imagination had had time to affect memory. The suspicion that it did so is turned to a certainty by a test of the narratives. The test involves daunting labour, which is probably why it remained long neglected. But Professor K. F. Werner and others have recently undertaken the labour, working on witness-lists of legal documents. With the help of the established axiom that a dark-age noble family distinguished itself by using a small group of forenames, their research has reconstructed skeleton lines of descent for certain families, including the great eleventh-century princely families in question. The result is startling. There is no sign of the upstarts. Their very names, given sometimes by the narrative sources, are absent from the name-groups of the reconstructed families. The latter appear to be descended, not from bold nobodies, but from ancestors broadly as princely as themselves, going back to Carolingian times, and possibly to Merovingian.[40]

This result cannot be proved in all cases. But it can be proved in enough to throw revealing light on those accounts of valorous foresters. The accounts were fabricated. This should not be too surprising. The late eleventh century was in many respects an age of fabrications, not least in history. Factual history was among forms of literature still establishing its identity, like a new boy at school. It was easily affected by motifs from elsewhere—legend, myth, etc. The motif of the low-born warrior, shooting to fame and honour by his own virtue, could have entered from many quarters. The Roman historian Sallust, for instance, whose hero Marius was just such a warrior, outshining a degenerate patriciate, enjoyed a marked vogue among historians in the eleventh and twelfth centuries.[41] But a more important source for genealogists was probably epic. The *Chansons de Gestes*, after all, were sung in the same lordly milieux which remembered the genealogies. History and epic could easily mingle, as they had when the Greeks had given them the same muse in Clio. Genealogical memory was bound to grow hazy at a certain point. (Surviving genealogies show it often *was* a certain point: the point when a family settled permanently on particular lands.) Beyond the cut-off point was a blank. An ancestor could be invented. A Germanic king might have put in a god. The Franks put in a hero, a hero who was in fact familiar in their *Chansons de Gestes:* a man who, though he might be of high birth, came into a situation where his birth was unknown or scorned, and won knighthood and fair lady by personal prowess. Names given by narrative sources to their original upstarts *do* have an affinity with names in the *Chansons*.[42]

A significant proportion of the top French aristocracy appears, then, to have been older than it pretended. One question remains: why it should pretend. The answer lies with the lower level of nobility, where nobility and non-nobility marched on each other; and in particular with that level which came in the second half of the eleventh century to be defined as the *milites*: the knights. These knights were not always noble to start with. A count or castellan on whom public authority devolved, and who belonged to the high nobility, might owe his position to birth. But where he had to compete, his competitive efficiency depended on his picking warriors for prowess. *Reges ex nobilitate, duces ex virtute sumunt*: Tacitus' adage about the ancient Germans still roughly applied. To pick a warrior for valour did not entail that he would be a poor man. On the contrary, to be effective in war you had to have not only horse and armour, but a lifetime's practice: all of which were very expensive. So the *milites* were usually well-born, and before the year 1000 a gulf appears to have separated all such warriors from even the highest peasantry below them.[43] But eleventh-century conditions allowed the crossing of the gulf. The count or castellan, representative of public authority, was growing richer. Potential recruits might not be able to afford to pay for their own gear and training. But why should not *he* pay?

Evidence shows he often did. Regional and etymological studies accord in identifying two main types of fighting horsemen in the period 1000–1200: those with inherited property or benefices, that is, broadly an old noble or magnate class; and those resident in the lord's castle, or in some other way directly in his service.[44] The latter may be legally indistinguishable from domestic servants (*ministeriales*), but used for war. This was the class that grew with a lord's wealth. They fought and were rewarded. Not least of their rewards was their mixing socially with the hereditary class of *miles*, bound by a common occupation. In the castle they mingled with the sons of noble *milites*, serving apprenticeships under the eye of a lord—like the Norman count of Chester who (says Orderic

Vitalis) 'was always surrounded by a huge household, full of the noise of swarms of youths of both noble and non-noble birth'.[45] In the field they mingled in battle, competing with the better-born for honour, and even for the heiresses which a high male mortality kept throwing on the market.

Shifts in the terminology in sources confirm such a merger. In particular, the term *miles* itself came to comprise both classes;[46] while, as if in haughty reaction to this base alloy, some high nobility began separating themselves off, about the same time: by inflating their own title of *miles* with epithets like *nobilissimus*, *optimus*, etc. Such signs of new distinctions in the upper class, corresponding to the entry to it of new members from below, have been found in Languedoc and Lombardy early in the eleventh century, in various parts of northern France in the second half of the century, and in Germany around the end of it.[47]

To summarize: there survive genealogies, or scraps of genealogical information, about certain high and stable princely houses. At first glance they suggest with their context that access to the nobility was fluid in the late ninth and tenth centuries, and became fixed later. Closely examined, in the context of witness-lists, they say the opposite. They project onto the past a contemporary situation. Far from establishing that their princely dynasties sprang from adventurous knights, they betray a fashion, growing in the eleventh century, for the acquisition of rank by virtue: a fashion based partly, at least, on the experience and ideal of the *milites*. The fashion may have done no more than modify the criterion of an élite of birth. But it did modify it: letting in men recommended more by talent than by high birth. It was these, not any Carolingian adventurers, who were the true 'tiros of no great name'.

### (ii) The observers

By efficiency in business and war, those who served the new centres of power could raise their status. They have been seen doing so in the generations round the year 1100. What must now be shown is whether they did so faster then than before the millennium.

An immediate disclaimer must be made for precocious

northern Italy. That rare lantern of social conditions in tenth-
century Italy, Ratherius of Verona, devoted a chapter of his
*Praeloquia* (*c.* 936) to showing how people rise and fall in society.
His words deserve attention. At first sight they suggest quick
social mobility:

Let me return [writes Ratherius] to what we see happening *every day*.
Do you not see *many people* today, by service or some skill or other, not
merely earn freedom, but even get their masters' inheritance? They
make a noble marriage, inequality notwithstanding; and indeed are
even preferred, despite servile origin, to the lord's own descendants.[48]

As for the lords themselves, Ratherius imagined a supposedly
typical noble dynasty in which a peasant's descendant became a
nobleman.

Now this chapter can be variously interpreted.[49] Some
phrases, like those I have italicized in the quotation, suggest
swift movement. But Ratherius' chapter must be seen as a
whole. Its aim was to dispel noblemen's pride in birth, by
arguing that people rise and fall faster than the well-born
pretend. Given its author's polemical aim and skill the chapter
is weak on facts. Of Ratherius' real-life illustrations all but two
are from scripture or the classics. Of the two remaining, the
longer probably refers anonymously to Ratherius' own
career—whose vicissitudes, up and down and back and forth
between Lombardy and Lorraine, we know anyway to form one
of the wonders of the early Saxon Empire; while the shorter tells
of a serf, who finds a magical cure for epilepsy, cures his master's
son and is made heir to an estate; and Ratherius admits he had
this tale on doubtful hearsay.[50] As for the imaginary illustration
of the peasant's descendant who became noble: the (imaginary)
descendant who did so is the peasant's great-great-great-
grandson. At the end of the thirteenth century, polemic (with
which this passage should be compared) speaks of the
ennoblement of peasants themselves.[51]

Whatever the exact significance of Ratherius' testimony, its
positive side is backed up by a handful of known cases of men
who did grow rich and powerful in tenth-century Italy. Saint
William of Volpiano's grandfather, a Swabian immigrant, had
apparently made himself very wealthy in the second quarter of

the century, perhaps as *miles* to the marquesses of Ivrea.[52] Leading Milanese minters, again, start appearing as land-owners, and as leaders of a Milan patriciate, about 950.[53] At the other end of the Po valley the founder of the great house of Canossa had accumulated a whole network of castles in reclaimed areas, apparently through service to King Hugh, by the time Otto the Great came and made him a count in 962.[54] There are other such cases.[55]

So Italy witnessed some social mobility in the tenth century. At the very end of the century there are signs that England did so too.[56] Outside these regions, direct and cogent evidence of social mobility (or for that matter stability) is elusive and debatable. However, studies of regions with some documentary continuity have suggested to their authors new impulses on social mobility about the millennium (in Languedoc), or in mid-century (in Franconia and the Mâconnais).[57] One such suggestion comes from terminology. Between 1000 and 1200 intermediate terms become more common, especially the term *mediocres*. The term was not unknown in the central Carolingian period. But examples thicken conspicuously from the late tenth century, leaving the impression that some, at least, of the big mass of dark-age *pauperes* had begun to lift themselves from that category.[58]

These remain impressions. A clearer lesson can be read in the careers of two literary themes.

## (a)  *The doctrine of the three orders*

About the year 1026 Bishop Adalbero of Laon wrote in a poem that society was composed of three orders: those who fought, those who worked, and those who prayed.[59] This is the first surviving full statement of a doctrine which would already be a commonplace by the end of the eleventh century, and would reappear constantly for the rest of the middle ages. The appearance of the 'three orders' in the eleventh century may suggest that a new social rigidity came in then, keeping everyone in his place.[60] But we must be careful. It is probably true that social orders were conceptually better defined, for various reasons, after the millennium than before. And there are grounds—chiefly the economic ones already treated—for supposing there was a growing differentiation in wealth between the top and bottom of the social hierarchy. But the rise of the literary doctrine of three orders does not necessarily imply that social mobility declined at the same rate. Closely considered, it may actually imply the opposite.

Like many oft-reiterated doctrines, that of the three social orders was partly propaganda. It was usually uttered by one of the orders, those who prayed; and doubtless won general assent from another, those who fought. But there is no sign that the doctrine attracted widespread enthusiasm from the third order, the great majority who worked. On the contrary, the signs are that the doctrine of the three orders was part of a long campaign to keep low-born people in their places, when they were trying to climb out. Literary references to social order in the eleventh and twelfth centuries can be explicit about this. Just before Adalbero produced his prototype of the doctrine, the chronicler Landulf Senior of Milan can be heard harking back to good old times when merchants, peasants, ploughmen, and herdsmen had each attended to his own business, and therefore lived in harmony; as if they did not now.[61] At about the same time in England the schoolmaster Aelfric adjured (through the mouth of the Master in his *Colloquy* [*c.* 1005]): 'Whatever you are— priest, monk, layman, or *miles*—*be* that! For it is a great ruin and shame for a man to hanker to be other than what he is!'—as if in England, too, there was such hankering.[62] Examples are more numerous in the twelfth century. The Latin jingles composed by clerks in the northern schools and known as 'Goliardic', more than once echoed the theme. A poem on the orders of men lashed the *pauperes elati* of the age, whom not even law could keep down, and who should be held with a firm hand:

> The shepherd, not content to earn his keep,
> Prefers to roam the world and leaves his sheep.
> To help such vagrants is not charity,
> They will not serve, to live; so let them die.[63]

Vernacular verse said the same. On the Danube about 1130 a monk of Melk complained at the uppishness and envy common among peasants, whose dress presumptuously emulated that of their betters: people should stick to their orders.[64] The French *The Villein's Proverbs* (*c.* 1175) adjured:

> Do not believe God does not grieve
>   At poor men's self-elation
> For each man should do what is good
>   Within his proper station;
> Not all can get a coronet
>   Or royal coronation.[65]

In the thirteenth century, the inverted significance of the doctrine of three orders becomes plainer still. The doctrine grew both more widespread and more vigorous during the century, and was never more so than at the end of it.[66] Yet not only do we know from more abundant documents of plenty of actual mobility, between commoner and noble.[67] Moralists' protests reached a new pitch. Thomasin of Zirclaria, writing in Venice *c.* 1215, was ready to say of his time, '*no* one keeps his place'.[68] The travelled Giordano of Pisa, at the beginning of the next century (1305) expatiated on the theme that 'all people worry about now is how to rise in the world'; and he attributed all social ills to people's refusal to stay in their 'squadron'.[69]

The doctrine of the three orders was partly a reaction against, *inter alia*, a threat to the distinction between commoner and noble. The persistence and spread of the doctrine attest the persistence and spread of the threat. The threat of confusion was not only caused by the ascent of individuals, and their attempts to acquire recognized higher social status. But it is safe to assume it was partly that.

A second literary theme teaches a similar lesson from another side.

(b)  *The wheel of Fortune.*

Fortune was a classical goddess, with already a more varied history behind her than most classical goddesses, when the middle ages took her up.[70] Boethius in prison, in the sixth century, had understandably included thoughts on Fortune in his *Consolation of Philosophy*. This treatment alone would have given Fortune the statutory respectability required to admit her to Christian thought. And she had other passports. She accordingly became a regular inhabitant of the medieval world-scheme.

So did her wheel. For Fortune arrived already in possession of this attribute. But her wheel was a peculiar one. In classical and early medieval representations, Fortune's wheel is something she stands on. Of course you cannot *stand* on a wheel. You slip. And that is the point. Fortune slips. This is the meaning of the wheel—or sphere, for it may equally well be that—in the pictures.[71]

The wheel of Fortune that abounds in late medieval illustration is another concept. It is a big wheel *turned by* Fortune. She sometimes has a crank to turn it with. On the most characteristic of late medieval wheels of Fortune are ranged four human figures, frequently kings. These are labelled: 'I reign', 'I have reigned', 'I am without a kingdom', and 'I shall reign'. Their crowns are in appropriate positions—toppling etc. The two types of wheel, early- and late-medieval, are illustrated in Plate III.

The symbol is usually presented in terms of kings, and was sometimes expressly applied to real kings, as for instance in chronicles. But it was envisaged with a wider application. Literary discussions of Fortune, contemporary with the introduction of this wheel, refer (for example) to 'nobility' as a gift of Fortune.[72] Again, one of the earliest of the pictured wheels gives as a variant the non-specific mottoes: 'I am elated in glory', 'I fall diminished', etc., which could apply to anyone, king or beggar.[73] For the thirteenth century, mere private wealth, as for a common citizen, is expressly referred to as material for Fortune's bounty.[74]

The Wheel of Fortune in the central and late middle ages, therefore, represents not just the slipping, but the rotating fortunes of men; and of any men. This image with its implications is today a cliché. Its appropriateness to human situations is too obvious to need comment. But the cliché did not always exist, and we are entitled to ask why this one came into being. Closer dating would be desirable. The rotating wheel of Fortune is known to have spread towards the end of the twelfth century, swiftly becoming general from about 1200.[75] The earliest single drawing of it is an addition, datable to within a decade or two of 1170, in an empty half page of a ninth-century Spanish manuscript of Gregory the Great's *Moralia in Job*. A study of Plate III(a) will show that, except for the artist's clumsy rendering of the cranked handle and its mechanism, the drawing is all but perfect in concept and execution. So it is unlikely to mark the origin of the motif to nearer than a generation. Yet it can be shown from elsewhere that the motif was not much earlier. For the context in which the drawing comes is a commentary on *Job*; and in the long and pregnant tradition of Job commentary before this time it is hard to find any trace of this (slightly unorthodox) association of Fortune with Job's vicissitudes. The same goes for other biblical texts— e.g. texts about wheels, which might have evoked the idea.[76]

The rotating wheel of Fortune was probably not known, therefore, much before the twelfth century. Its appearance then is not explained by the invention of the crank-handled wheel, since that was known at least from the ninth century.[77] The true explanation of its appearance is surely the situation described so far in this chapter: the growing prevalence and vigour, in the eleventh and twelfth centuries, of up-and-down social movement. Men saw this circular movement, and forged an image for it.

Two essentials have been omitted. Nothing has been said of fallers, only of risers. Yet 'where one man rises up, another must fall', as the German Freidank put it [*c.* 1220].[78] Fallers in the period are more elusive than risers; and this chapter is ultimately about a kind of hope, which stems from risers. One kind of faller, or non-riser, will be met in chapter 15. But there *were* visible fallers in the same times and places as the risers. At various stages of the eleventh century we find, for instance, a knight in south-western France who became a poor tramp after being thrown from the marital home;[79] a hut-dweller in Gascony who had come to 'poverty from riches, misery from splendour, leprosy from health';[80] and a magnate's widow in Brittany who was literally penniless.[81] A bishop of Valence, around 1100, was said to have made a practice of discreetly looking out for distressed gentlemen 'who have lived wealthily, but who now, through the fault of the times or of evil men, had fallen to poverty'.[82] In the twelfth century the existence of these unfortunates is more broadly attested. *The Villein's Proverbs*, whose author was keenly aware of the society round him, says he has often seen gentlemen reduced to beggary; and bourgeois families ruined, too, by their children's prodigality.[83] In the thirteenth century the fallen nobleman would be written into the canon of medieval social security, as one of the categories entitled to alms.[84]

So there were fallers, too, to balance the other side of Fortune's wheel. But our picture has lacked a second essential. A simple picture has been drawn of a subject really as complex as life itself. Social mobility has been portrayed, for one thing, as an issue between an individual, and a big society; where in fact men live in a series of Chinese boxes—family, order, nation, etc.—whose mutual relation varies, varying the relations correspondingly of all the individuals within them. Again, social mobility has been drawn as if brought about only by economics and politics. Nature herself, who has no straight lines, in fact sees to it that there is always social mobility. The lotteries of war and plague, opening room at the top; the trends and hazards of family size; and the vagaries of a lover's heart in the confined society of the castle, all put an element of flux into the social pattern.[85] It was as tributary to such natural mobility that our economic and political factors made their impact; not as sole agents.

These aspects of the subject have been ignored as tending to confuse the bolder profile. We need not study every part of a wheel's mechanism to establish that it is accelerating.

### 2. THE PSYCHOLOGICAL FACT: AMBITION

The observation of social movement, I have suggested, gave rise to the philosophical allegory of Fortune's wheel. If men were automatons, no doubt philosophical allegory would have been all it gave rise to. But most people are sensitive to this kind of observation. The sight of someone else winning rank and honour, just like the sight of someone making money, tends to spark off hope and desire in ourselves. It does so infectiously. As a single winning gambler draws a hundred dupes to the roulette-wheel, so one successful careerist in court or castle plants ambition in a hundred young men with no rival aim. 'In wish, if not in fact, there are more rulers than ruled', as one twelfth-century commentator put it.[86] In chapter 3, tests on moralistic literature spanning three centuries were shown to point to a growing emphasis on 'avarice' from the eleventh century. A similar test, applied to similar contemporary literature, points now to a second moral disorder as growing in harmony with the first: ambition.

It will be questioned whether ambition necessarily is a moral

disorder. It was certainly questioned quite keenly in the
thirteenth century, when books by down-to-earth Greeks were
persuading ascetic Christians to come to terms with the hard
realities of social life.[87] But in the eleventh century, and even for
most of the twelfth, the ascetic Christians were innocent of such
worldly wisdom. Ambition was a sin. It was a particular
instance of pride, and often involved vainglory and other vices.
This is to the historian's advantage. For ambition, where
perceived, provoked a sharp reaction; and it is through the
reaction we can discover it.

Does it need discovering? Everything ever written about the
eleventh and twelfth centuries, with the bad barons and
conquering kings, surely attests the growth of ambition. But
'ambition' will be understood here in the more limited sense
used by those who troubled to discuss such words: as the desire,
even in a powerless and obscure person, to rise to power and
renown. It is this kind of ambition that is in question; and the
first question is: was it felt to be worse after the end of the
eleventh century than before the beginning?

### (i)  The prevalence of ambition

The question can be put first to the sample of tenth-century
works used in chapter 3 to supplement existing studies on
'avarice': works of Odo of Cluny, Atto of Vercelli, and
Ratherius of Verona.[88] The same negative result these produced in the case of 'avarice' is more pronounced in that of
'ambition'. Odo uses the word and its kin (*ambire* etc.) very
rarely in the two works studied.[89] He expands on oppression,
greed, ostentation, and vainglory among *magnates;* but says
nothing of any restlessness or place-hunting among persons
lower down the scale.[90] Indeed, he once declares the poor are
rarely proud, and does not add that some of them become so.[91]
Atto leaves the same impression. He again used the word
'ambition' very rarely.[92] He assigns strife and competitiveness
to the upper classes, but expressly states that upper-class sins are
not shared by the great mass of poorer people, whose peculiar
failing is, on the contrary, superstition.[93] In one place Atto
blames serfs for their usurpation of priestly office and property
to serve goals of family aggrandizement.[94] The testimony of
Ratherius keeps its intermediate character. Ratherius lashes

young nobles for their ambition to be bishops.[95] He says much against flattery—a sin of careerist servants.[96] Yet no more than either of the other two does Ratherius allow himself any general outburst against ambition: nothing, for instance, as boisterous as Odo's explosion against avarice quoted on p. 78.

A new note is heard from sources in the same Italian milieu, from the middle of the eleventh century. The word 'ambition' often occurs in the context of simony. For years, writes a hagiographer about 1050, the election of a prelate in Italy has been marred by royal intervention 'or some sort of ambition'.[97] A monk in the 1060s becomes a bishop by 'simony and ambition'; and so on.[98] The most voluble protests are from those smiters of simony, Humbert of Silva Candida and Peter Damian. They often couple 'ambition' to 'avarice' in their denunciations of simonists' vices.[99] Of the two, Peter is more explicit in lashing what he calls the 'madness of wild ambition'.[100] Especially in two long letters *On the Avoiding of Ecclesiastical Dignities* and *Courtier-Clergy*, Peter warns monks not to 'ambire', and denounces clergy who hang round courts, toadying to magnates with rights over church appointments— all through *ambitio* to be bishops.[101]

There is no proof that these two clusters of samples represent a universal trend in social commentary. But the difference between the two is suggestive. In Italy, and especially in the church in Italy, we have seen reason to expect that the eleventh century, with its growth in simony, would witness a growth in what is sometimes called now the 'rat-race mentality'. A look at leading contemporary critics confirms this.

More confirmation is given by comment in the century after the Gregorian reform. 'Ambition' assumed a leading place among vices singled out by critics of the times. The English philosopher Adelard of Bath came back to England from a long voyage abroad about 1135, and recorded his impression of the unwelcome novelties in his homeland: the culminating item in his list was 'almost universal ambition'.[102] The Latin poets also touched on the topic. Petrus Pictor saw ambition as the hallmark of the fallen Rome of his own days, contrasting with its finer original.[103] *The Apocalypse of Bishop Golias* numbered among the six main vices of the clergy not only *fervens ambitio*, but *tumens elatio*.[104] Goliardic verse often returned to this theme.[105] Most telling of all, because in sober prose and by an experienced authority, John of Salisbury's *Policraticus* (*c.* 1158) devoted no less than fifty pages to ambition. 'Huge numbers of people', wrote John, 'are to be seen hunting for positions of power, canvassing for honours. . . . They try to see how they can lift themselves to the top, to be superior to others—or at least, how to *seem* superior, by reason of the company they keep.'[106] Bishoprics were the main prize. Each single bishopric was coveted by many place-hunters, who would slander the incumbent bishop, stress how old he was, consult astrologers about when he would die, etc., 'almost all of them contending like gladiators, each one in the hope that the bishopric will not fall to another'.[107] But it was not only a matter of bishoprics. 'It is not just the bishop's office alone which suffers the onslaught of ambition' he wrote, 'for one and the same thirst for domination and supremacy affects high and low. The man who does not dare aspire to an episcopal throne makes for prefectures, archdeaconries, and other dignities, with the same avidity and the same machinations.'[108]

Among the refinements of John of Salisbury's picture is his austere condemnation of hidden ambition, and the arts contrived by careerist hypocrites to pretend they are not ambitious at all.[109]

Most of the invective I have quoted concerns the church. But this does not mean that churchmen, in the twelfth century, were more ambitious than laymen. The case was the opposite. Not only, as in the case of 'avarice', did clerical critics tend to turn on their own kind. There was a special reason in the case of ambition to confine remarks to the clergy. In lay political life ambition was so endemic as to be ineradicable; indeed John of Salisbury—before his time here—was almost ready to admit it was appropriate in secular politics.[110]

Like avarice, ambition remained at the top of the diabolic pantheon of vices, right through the middle ages. The two vices are to be found closely connected in didactic literature and art.[111] Thirteenth-century preachers who lashed love of money spoke also of social competitiveness as if it were a twin vice of the same milieu.[112] Avarice, after all, could serve ambition; as vice versa.[113] But the connection went deeper. Both tendencies, expressing social competitiveness in different ways, were ultimately facilitated by the same economic and political conditions.

So far we have looked at the extent, only, of 'ambition'. It will be appropriate to finish by looking for a moment at its character. A glance at two features, in particular, of the ambitious man's mental condition, will be found relevant when we come to consider the 'reasoners' in the same society, in Parts II and III of this book.

## *(ii) The character of the ambitious*

### (a) *Industry and shortage of time*

Ambition, firstly, made a man busy, in both senses: externally active, and pressed for time. Humbert of Silva Candida referred to the feverish hard work of his church careerists. They reached their goal only 'after long, painful, and unremitting care, supported day and night by frenetic patience, and at the price of exile, cold, and vigils beyond reckoning'.[114] Bishop Anselm II of Lucca drew the same portrait: 'some simonists,' he said, to win their way to a good position, 'will serve more than ten years in a secular court, bearing every extreme of weather and all other inconveniences with the utmost patience.'[115] Peter Damian spoke the same way in passages arguing that his courtier-clergy paid more dearly in service for their benefactor's favour than if they paid in money. 'To reap their satisfaction at the end,' Peter declared, 'they permit themselves to be crushed by labour.'[116] 'Troubles', 'labours', 'sterile care of business' are expressions typical of his description.[117] Certain monks who wait on princes 'take up Martha's function, flying anxiously hither and thither like swallows'.[118] John of Salisbury, in his turn, noted the toil that went with ambition at court. He might despise the 'laziness' of clerics who treated their jobs as sinecures.[119] Yet he too mocked the labours of courtier-clergy. 'They undertake enormous labours,' he wrote, 'and complete them too; nor feel any shame at buying the flattery they are after by the most assiduous and obsequious services.'[120] John's remarks find an interesting echo a few years later in Walter Map. Walter also despised the lazy. But he warned that the lazy young man would die poor; as if to say, risers should work.[121] And Walter, like John, referred to the 'immense labours' which were the normal condition of an exhausted palace staff.[122]

Servants of government were busy in a second sense: they tended to be short of time. The same sources which recorded the industry of courtiers also reveal that their time was at a premium. Humbert has been heard speaking of the 'vigils' of his ambitious careerists, labouring 'day and night' for their masters. Peter Damian, always the hermit, warns of time-consuming business that attends the abbot of a cenobitic monastery, as he 'prolongs his day of negotiations and general business half-way into the night . . . misses compline with the others, and has to say his mattins before sunrise [i.e. and snatch what sleep he can afterwards]'.[123] John of Salisbury, being a scholar who knew the value of time for practical work, may seem to take the opposite view of simonists: they discover too late that they have wasted time, and can do nothing to remedy their plight.[124] But what he means is that they have spent time on the wrong kind of business: the *labores immensi* and *obsequia* they have employed in rising to high places, and of which John has spoken clearly enough.[125] If John's remarks were not enough to suggest to us the long hours worked by Plantagenet government servants, and if Walter Map's plea that he could hardly find time to write his book[126] failed to convince us of the same, then a lawyers' tradition may perform that task. Bracton records that the assize of *Novel Disseisin* was only produced after 'many thoughtful vigils'.[127]

Man's sense of time has its own history. The history increasingly attracts modern scholars' attention. The attention, however, starts in earnest only from the fourteenth century. The history goes further back, and its eleventh- and twelfth-century phases might repay attention. The assumption that medieval people, whether monks or not, had all the time in the world, would be dangerous even were there no evidence to the contrary. And there *is* evidence to the contrary. The evidence comes partly from the world of courts. But there is other evidence suggesting that shortage of time was also linked to the post-millennium economy as such. 'Avarice', that is to say, may have joined with 'ambition' in putting a higher price on this commodity. For in the economic field, signs of pressure on time occur early. Peasants and artisans near Fleury about the year

1000 ignored feast-days through a need to work in their fields (a complaint which would be endemic in sources from about 1200).[128] Again, a monastic reformer about 1130 resisted his monks' tendency to curtail psalms in favour of manual work; and he changed meal-times instead.[129] Or there was a debtor in London, about 1150, who grew frantically impatient as his prison sentence wore on: 'do they call this a *short* wait?' he asked.[130] And there were merchants and usurers in Lyons in the 1160s 'working night and day' to accumulate money.[131] Perhaps as significant a sign as any, anticipating the specific problem of time and investment, is that from Pisa, in 1117. Pisa had built a fleet to raid Muslim Majorca, but learned that their neighbours in Lucca planned to pillage Pisa while the menfolk were away. 'To *hold back* seemed to dishonour the great expense incurred,' argued leading Pisans; and Florentine soldiers were forthwith hired as Home Guard.[132]

(b) *Dependence on superiors*

Like the sense of pressing time, the topic which finishes this chapter merits more attention that it can have here. Yet it touches from one angle the crux of what I have said so far. The expert Walter Map can describe it. Part-jesting, part-serious, he introduced his book *Courtiers' Trifles* with a comparison of the court to the grammarian's *genus*, as defined by Porphyry: 'a multitude relating in some way to a single principle'. For, explained Walter Map, 'we are certainly an infinite multitude, vying to please just one man'. From that one man, he went on, descends grace, inexplicably and unpredictably, much as from the theologians' God.[133]

The dependence of one man on another was an age-old element of social cohesion, intrinsic to feudalism. The dependence was a legal fact. But it also had its emotional facet, a facet with its own character in each little society where dependence was recognized. It had its own character in the world of the courtiers and *ministeriales* in dynamic centres of government. At its purest their cast of mind can be identified as that 'loyalty' which the great French bailiff and writer, Philippe de Beaumanoir, would make first of the moral qualities in a royal agent.[134] And already in the early twelfth century a single-minded, selfless devotion to one's royal master was both an

ideal, and sometimes an actual attainment. 'My dearest Lord,
in whom after God lies my whole trust . . . I have been yours
while I could, and I have loved you truly and served you most
faithfully. In your service and in my own affairs, I have
committed many great sins and have done few if any good
deeds. . . . I fall at the feet of your majesty in spirit, with tears
and lamentations.'[135] These words, from a begging letter by
King Henry I's agent in northern England, have the ring of
loyalty amounting almost to religion: 'had I but served my God
as I have served my king . . .'

But most government servants were almost certainly content
with more degenerate levels of devotion. Satirists of this
devotion saw only its degenerate side. But like all caricature,
theirs was formed round real-life features. These lines are from
the Goliardic poem *The Flatterer*.

> There, by the prince, the obsequious flatterer stands,
> And leans to adjust, with ever-active hands
> The princely cloak, *already* smooth and clean,
> And plucks at fluff no eyes but his have seen.[136]

He is a 'yes man':

> He imitates the mood of all around him:
> You shiver, for example, and (confound him!)
> He comes out with some cliché like 'cold day!'
> Or else he finds you sweating, and straightway
> Up comes his hanky, to wipe *his* brow and chin.
> Look happy, and he'll be one sunny grin;
> Sad, and he'll make a show of trying to stifle
> *His* sobs . . . Jumping at every trifle
> (Like a salmon) that your lips let spill
> He'd seem a 'do-all'. What he does is: nil.[137]

Twelfth-century courtier-satire still awaits a monograph.[138] But
we do not have to await the monograph to appreciate the
feature aptly caught in the last ten lines quoted: the total
psychological dependence of one man on another. 'As the eyes
of servants look to the hand of their master . . .' The simile
applied as well in the twelfth century A.D. as in the psalmist's
time. In chapter 16 we shall have a chance of putting the
flatterer's obsequiousness in full relief, by contrasting it with its
opposite.

Sociologists have established the word 'charisma' to describe

the power, not wholly subject to our reason, which gives us a
respectful awe of certain people. The charisma a ruler enjoys *ex
officio*—apart from any he may have on his own—derives from
his representing the public at large. His approval gets its
authority from society as a whole. But in the twelfth century as
in others, society's approval could be sought in a hundred other
ways. Like the busy man's shortage of time, this second feature
of 'ambition', its emotional dependence, was one the sycophant
shared with men ambitious in other fields than the court, and
also with the avaricious man. For money, too, becomes a fetish,
or charismatic object, through the derived power of the society
which has faith in it. Both the money-grubber and the social
climber were dependent on society: living denials, that is, of the
αὐτάρκεια self-rule, idealized by the Stoics. In the measure in
which a greedy or ambitious man is dependent on human
approval, in that measure—*tanto, quanto*—his αὐτάρκεια is weakened: or, as the more sophisticated Christian clerics of the
twelfth century would have said, his conscience—that is, God in
his role as inner director of conduct. The clerics in fact did say it:

> Yet others yearn for popular acclaim
> And have no virtue but their public fame
> 'The voice of conscience' is an empty phrase
> To them: they hear but one voice—praise.[139]

Thus spoke satire—impish child of early scholasticism, which
took its parent's features, but dared to say much that its parent
did not.

The scheme drawn in the last three chapters is no doubt
oversimplified. Like most causal systems in history, it could as
well have been drawn the other way round: making men
encourage the spread of money because they were already
thirsty for wealth and power. But history, in this like a physical
object, only presents one side of itself at once; and to refuse to
see it that way is to refuse to see it at all. The scheme, then, can
be offered with that one inevitable proviso. If it is accepted, its
major deficiencies, in the context of the inquiry undertaken in
this book, reduce themselves to one. So far the scheme has
confined itself exclusively to Society in the middle ages. It will be
asked when Reason comes in. The moment has come to start
satisfying that question.

CHAPTER 5

# Reason and Power

It is true that human opinion has sometimes upheld
the value of physical strength, but in truth, physical
strength was never worth so much. For lo, every day
we see strong but stupid men perish, while weak but
wise men thrive.

*Le livre des secrets aux philosophes* (*c.* 1300).[1]

EARLY Muslim philosophers used to repeat a story of a man who
made a camel fall into a pit simply by looking at it and
'thinking'. The story passed westwards with their works to
become part of the bric-à-brac which Latin philosophers used
to drive their points home. In the thirteenth century this class of
incident would be referred to by, among others, Roger Bacon—
with the disarming comment 'and this much is not magic'.[2]

Nor was it magic; or not only that. A story, true or untrue,
rarely lasts more than a couple of generations unless it embodies
an idea with some claim to respect. The idea that a man's
thought can be used to control things in the world outside
him—like camels—is in our own scientific age a commonplace.
But it has not always been a commonplace. We only need recall
our own childhood, with its awe of physical strength (not to
mention ghosts), to see that there are other candidates as
sources of power in the world, besides man's mind. In the
European middle ages, and most tangibly in the central
centuries between 1100 and 1300, today's commonplace was in
fact just beginning to emerge in articulate form. It entered a
field so far divided between two other powers: brute force—that
of nature and of other men; and the imponderable interventions
of what the late middle ages would call the 'supernatural'.
Between these, as a third element, there grew now the
realization that man could control his environment through his
mind.

The first four chapters of this book have charted a connection between economics and psychology. The seven chapters which follow this one will trace another connection, out on the other side of psychology, between psychology and the intellectual renaissance that spread over the twelfth and thirteenth centuries. The present chapter has no such inter-disciplinary ambitions. Its subject is all psychology; and its purpose, that of a bridge. It joins two mental faculties which in history books usually have different habitats. They are Will—the Will that makes its mark most conspicuously in the history of economics and politics; and Reason—normally at home in the so-called history of thought. A moment's reflection tells us that the two faculties cannot really be so separate. And they were in fact closely related in the central middle ages: so pregnantly, in that age of progress, that the more self-conscious intellectuals became aware of the fact.

This awareness is what I hope to demonstrate now: the awareness that reason and its accoutrements were actually useful. From the late eleventh century, it has been argued, certain competitive mental habits became accepted as part of the normal physiology of society. What now has to be discovered is whether reason could play any part in the competition. The best way of showing it did is by showing that men came increasingly to realize that it did. The sources which show this are contemporary with early scholasticism, in the twelfth and thirteenth centuries. But it is not an academic discipline, now, or an author, or master, or text, that will be inquired into. It is a concept, hiding dispersed among them: the concept that the mind, quite apart from any pleasure or edification its exercise may afford, is an efficacious weapon in man's battle with his environment.

The environment we first think of, when it is a question of man's battling with it, is the natural one. So we can treat that first.

### I. REASON IN THE FACE OF NATURE

Since the industrial revolution, men have systematically employed their reason to contend with their natural environment. The history of their doing so is easily traceable back to the sixteenth-century Renaissance. Before that it becomes elusive;

and it is only recently that the term 'technology' has come to feel at home in medieval history at all. But whatever doubts there may be about the achievements of technology itself then, one certainty shines out: its basic principle—that the way to control nature lies through understanding it—was certainly grasped by more perceptive minds throughout the central middle ages. Their recognition of it is apparent in three fields of literature: first, in technology itself; and second and third, in those strange seedbeds of modern science, magic and astrology.

Very few texts from the period deal with real, down-to-earth technology. The only complete medieval treatise on the subject before the thirteenth century was that by 'Theophilus'—a pseudonym for an author who lived in Germany about 1100.[3] Most of Theophilus' book, called *De diversis artibus*, consists of detailed practical directions for making divers church appurtenances: colours for manuscript illumination, stained glass, jugs, bells, etc. What is significant for us now is that Theophilus clearly appreciates his subject's psychological implications. It is the mind that does the work. 'Exert your whole *mind*', he urges the reader approaching the subject.[4] He makes much of the fact that his specialized information is imparted freely, conscious that it is useful.[5] Perhaps most revealing of all, Theophilus is one of the first writers of the medieval renaissance to mention that noticeably intellectualist concept, The Sevenfold Gifts of the Spirit. Four of these Gifts are Wisdom, Understanding, Counsel, and Knowledge. It is worth remarking, furthermore, that Theophilus treats two of the remaining Gifts, Fortitude and Piety, in a manner reminiscent of later Enlightenments, as respectively denoting hard work and fair charges. Traditional religious virtues, for Theophilus, are all packed into the one remaining Gift of 'Fear'. Theophilus saw these seven Gifts as especially apt for the artisan, and a comment on them is the only non-technical passage in the book.[6]

If Theophilus' tract were to leave doubt of technology's self-consciousness so early, casual references to the mechanical arts made by academics in the following century and a half would remove it. Hugh of St. Victor, whose *Didascalicon* (1127–8) became a sort of blueprint for the educational syllabus of the twelfth-century renaissance, could scarcely bring himself to speak of so base a branch of knowledge as 'mechanics'. But he did so for long enough to betray an appreciation that artefacts are a triumph specifically of man's reason.[7] Something of this was implied in the word 'art' itself. By Hugh's time it had gone most of the way to the unpractical connotation it has today. But it had begun in Roman technology, as meaning 'skill', and there were medieval writers who used it that way. We hear an early Italian humanist in 1238 declaring that 'by art heavy weights are lifted; by art fish are caught; by art men are carried dryfoot over sea'.[8] If the liberal arts merged at one side with technology, at the other they were coming to merge, at the same date, with the bulky Greek and Arabic newcomer, philosophy. Philosophy brought with it infinite possibilities in the utilization of knowledge. Roger Bacon's excited imagining of aeroplanes, submarines, and cranes[9] may evoke a smile now. But he had grasped the foundation principle of applied science: if you knew how nature worked there was simply no limit to what you could do with it.

The actual achievements of craftsmen in Roger Bacon's century, for all that there were no submarines, would make a lasting impact in European society. (In speaking of paper and spectacles in chapter 12 we shall touch on only two of many.) But the technological principle—that mind masters matter by understanding it—was not indebted either to these crafts, or to scholars' views on them, for its most forceful literary expression. It was indebted to branches of study which in themselves proved largely abortive.

One was magic. Books of magic enjoyed a growing vogue in the thirteenth century. The vogue was partly just an unexpected result of the growth of literacy. But it also witnessed to the widespread popular penetration of the concept under discussion. Magic promised power through knowledge. The art of the original *magi*, the priestly sages of ancient Persia, was the very type of efficacious natural learning. The degenerate study named after them survived because of the power it offered. Thirteenth-century magical books were frank on this score. When a student has apprehended, announced one, 'all the intelligences and compositions of the things of this world, all things will serve him and he will serve none of them'.[10] Another, equally widely copied, ends: 'so ends the book of the life of the rational soul . . . the book by which every creature can be subjected except the nine orders of angels . . . the book by which all science can be learned'.[11] This bombast, with its 'secrets', and bogus lines of descent for them via ancient eastern kings, characterizes a whole class of books in medieval libraries.[12]

But the ideas in magic were not all bombast. One in particular was shared with more pregnant regions of medieval science. This was the idea of 'properties of things'. Common to natural philosophy as a whole, this idea probably got its main impetus from medicine. Medical use of herbs and rare stones encouraged a view of nature as a vast aggregate of 'things', each with its 'properties'. You only had to learn the 'properties' (or 'natures') of the things, and you could exploit them, for example to heal disease. Demons were also supposed to work their marvels this way.[13] The idea was in form if not content the same as that behind the promises of magic; and of course the idea is still essentially respectable, though its formulation may now appear quaint.

The field which yielded the most express statement of our technological principle was not, however, either magic or medicine. It was astrology. This may seem paradoxical. No field could be further from technology. Quite apart from the question of the soundness of astrological principles, no one can alter the courses of the stars, whether he knows them or not. But paradox or not, astrology was well-fitted to rehearse the principle of applied science. It occupied good minds. Its astral laws prefigured the mathematics of post-Renaissance physics. It was concerned with prediction, and hence with everyday events. Finally, it had to defend itself against criticism, and therefore built itself a strong theoretical basis.

The practical power astrology offered lay entirely in its enabling men to *prepare* for events. The events themselves might be inevitable. But foresight eased their impact. An English astrologer studying in Spain near the end of the twelfth century, put the case thus:

The astronomer, foreseeing how future events are going to turn out, will be able to repel or avoid their harmful effects: e.g. general war, widespread famine, universal earthquake, fires, floods, or plague among men or animals. Even if he cannot entirely escape these evils, a man who foresees the outcome of events can still bear them much more easily than he who knows nothing of them.

Daniel of Morley, who wrote that,[14] was in fact merely putting in his own words what he had read in the works of the ninth-century Baghdad astrologer Albumazar, who in turn had learned it from Ptolemy of Alexandria.[15] In twelfth- and thirteenth-century Europe anyone who studied astrology learned to justify it in this way. It might be objected that this is scarcely justification. The foreknowledge of catastrophe may make it *harder* to bear. But astrologers often turned their supposed foreknowledge to more practical use, in two ways: if you knew a disaster was coming you could either pray to God to avert it, or you could get out of its way. Theologians taught that the stars' influence was limited by God's omnipotence. God was open to prayer. Stellar foreknowledge helped you to pray specifically, and so more effectively. The biblical model for this was Hezekiah in 2 Kings 20, who, warned of his imminent death, successfully prayed to be spared.[16] On the other hand you might effectively ignore the theologians (as most astrologers were perennially suspected of doing), and treat stellar influence as absolute. The events foretold were then sure to happen. Foreknowledge nevertheless told you what precautions to take: farmers could use seasons better; men warned of conflagration could build houses in marshes or caves; warned of flood they could escape to mountains; and so on.[17]

The prospect of practical measures, then, justified the predictive aspect of astrology; and was indeed its chief justification. For what use was the study of the future, astrology could ask rhetorically, if one could not avoid what one foresaw?[18] To preach this idea was for astrology a matter of life and death. It is therefore no surprise to find the idea picked up outside astrology: like magic, astrology shared some principles with less suspect regions of thought. In the later middle ages a much used adage was: 'arrows foreseen wound less'. It justified any sort of prediction. Westerners could have read the phrase in Gregory the Great.[19] But it may have started in eastern astrology, and the service the adage did in western astrologers' apologias in the late twelfth century suggests it was they, quite as much as Gregory, who gave it currency.[20] Its currency was wide. At one moment it will be on the lips of a moralist, recommending the virtue of prudence;[21] at another, it vindicates prophetic speculation by Joachites, based on dates and numbers in the Bible;[22] at yet another, it defends post-mortem examinations designed to prognosticate the course of plague;[23] and so on. In the last instance at least, the plague, the astrologers' principle certainly contributed to a science destined to have tangible results.

The mind, then, offered a man power in the face of nature. Craftsmen, or at least those who watched them at work, were well aware of this fact. So were the more practical of naturalistic disciplines: those which sought to harness nature by knowing its secrets and properties; and, most of all, astrology, which sought to steal a march on nature by prediction. The balance of power between man and nature shifted in the twelfth century. Intellect played a part in the shift; and was aware of doing so.

## 2. REASON IN THE FACE OF OTHER MEN

A man who stole a march on nature put himself in a position to steal a march also on his fellow-men. Why he should wish to, if he did, is not our concern now. At its most immediate a man's confrontation with his fellow-men was a replica of that with nature: floods and plagues broke in on you and killed from time to time; so did other men. A few moralists in the middle ages were ready to take the resemblance further and treat a desire for power over nature as identical with its human equivalent.[24] However that may be, the two fields certainly shared one feature: the key to power in both was the mind. The intellectuals of the twelfth and thirteenth centuries were conscious of this, too: that in the human field, as in the natural, the intellect was a weapon.

They evinced this consciousness in three main ways: in theories of historical development; in views of government, civil and military; and in the evaluations they made of knowledge and intelligence when discussing, on one hand, the value of historical study, and on the other, the virtue of prudence.

### (i) Science in the rise and fall of empires

Among the most striking aspects of the twelfth-century renaissance was its interest in the rise and fall of empires. The agreed outline of this rise and fall was known to anyone with an education. But everyone had his own explanation. Those who came closest to natural determinism, the astrologers, explained the rise and fall according to the intricacies of the astral timetable: give or take a few hundred years, it was not hard to fit the known divisions of history into various astronomical cycles.[25] At the other extreme, theologians explained history in terms of *God's* plan. For reasons known only to himself, God chose first the Jews, then their continuation in the Christian church; and he saw to it that other dominions rose and fell as fitted the salvation of his élite.[26] Between these two, temperamentally as well as philosophically, came a third group: the apologists of learning. And they had *their* explanation for the fortunes of earthly dominions. These fortunes depended on intelligence, and the disciplines that extended it.

The general case was put with varying nuances in the late twelfth century. A trace of it is to be found hiding in the astrologers' determinism. It was the influence of Mercury, some astrologers said, originator of the liberal arts, which had raised the earliest serious civilization above the preceding semi-barbarism.[27] This notion was echoed in circles less committed to astrology, and so better able to give all the credit to the liberal arts themselves. At the very end of the century we find the liberal arts being made *the* key to the rise of ancient dominions. The philosopher Alexander Neckham wrote: 'The glory of any kingdom has always grown vigorously so long as schools of the liberal sciences flourished in it.'[28]

From stating this general rule to reading it in the history of known empires was only a step. The empires whose history most impressed itself on medieval Christian minds were the Greek, the Roman, and the ancient Jewish. Of these the paradigm readiest to hand was Rome. The student who got his Roman history straight from Roman sources was struck by the disparity in forces between early Rome and the numerous peoples she conquered. He naturally surmised that the 'science' and 'doctrine' which formed such a conspicuous part of Rome's legacy to himself, had been the secret of Rome's successes.[29] This interpretation apparently had its literary headquarters in Germany. This too was natural. The Germans had inherited Rome's empire, yet German nobles were peculiarly contemptuous of study. So their schoolmasters employed the Roman example, thus interpreted, as a stick to bludgeon noblemen to their books. In the early eleventh century Wipo, chaplain to the emperor Henry III, put just this argument into a didactic poem.[30] The same argument, in the same context, was still echoing loud in the thirteenth century—fortified by references to the literary accomplishments of Julius Caesar.[31]

For all that the Roman Empire was readiest to hand, it was not the example to leave the deepest mark. The middle ages were after all too involved with the Christian side of ancient Rome to be able to recast its history in terms of the intellect. However, that did not stop academic apologists from searching elsewhere for examples. One obvious place to search was the Bible. A number of passages in the Bible associated strong kingship with wisdom; and that 'wisdom' could be read as technically as one chose, to show (for instance) that learning made a man powerful. One group of passages related to the so-called 'three kings'. They are only 'so-called' kings, because the Three Magi are not kings in the Gospel. The creative exegesis which made the Magi into kings is itself instructive. With the frail support of a seemingly prophetic verse in Psalm 71/2 (v. 10, 'may the kings of Sheba and Seba bring gifts'), the Magi were promoted to royal rank by a slow process beginning in earnest in the late tenth century; as it happens, just when the half-Greek Otto III of Germany was showing how learned kings could be.[32] The intellectual status of the Magi as sages was meanwhile increasingly recognized: they were men of abstruse learning.[33] The final stage in the promotion of the Magi–Kings was reached in the middle of the twelfth century, when Cologne adopted them as patron saints. We may notice once more the association of these learned rulers with Germany. Like Julius Caesar and his Romans, the royal Magi served as a bludgeon for truant noblemen.[34]

Of biblical rulers who prospered through the intellect, none could equal Solomon. Solomon's medieval career as dual representative of wisdom and power had begun with the Carolingian scholars, with their partiality for Old Testament models, and their function (in the ninth century) of trying to civilize their kings.[35] The Solomon tradition they inaugurated nevertheless spread far outside circles of biblical scholarship, and royal milieux. The significance of the tradition is heightened—as was the tradition of the Magi—by the fact of its being swollen by legend. Solomon had two legendary roles, one

respectable, the other not. The former was as the supposed
author of at least three books of scripture—Proverbs, Wisdom,
and Ecclesiastes. These books, written when Israel was subject
to Hellenistic influence, are the principal members of the group
known to scholars as the Wisdom books: they stress the ideal of
the wise man. But there was a second legendary role. Long
before the middle ages, Solomon's reputation for wisdom, and
as author of the Wisdom books, had drawn to itself a less
orthodox stream of literature. It comprised magic, together
with much non-magical worldly-wisdom, all fathered on the
Jewish sovereign. It was in the thirteenth century that the full
impact of this literature struck Europe. We know of the fashion
for it as much from the disgust that graver academics expressed
for it, as from the scores of its own manuscripts that survive. The
second of the two books of magic quoted on pages 113–14 is just
one example (one of its usual titles was 'Book of Solomon').[36]

Medieval legend, stubbornly wrong in detail, could be
remarkably sure-footed when it came to catching the character
of its subject. Of ancient civilizations it was neither the Romans,
nor the Jews, but the Greeks who had set most store by the
power of the mind. It was accordingly in a Greek context that
legend, contemporary with the medieval renaissance, most
ebulliently vindicated the role of cleverness in the achievement
of power. Much the most celebrated of ancient rulers who had
won empires for themselves (and he was a ruler innocent of any
ambivalent relationship with Christianity) was Alexander. It is
true there had been little in Alexander's real career to suggest he
was especially wise or intellectual. But that was soon adjusted.
Alexander had, as a fact, briefly been tutored by Aristotle, the
philosopher who before all others seemed to his medieval
partisans the very embodiment of human reason. Given right
conditions, this kernel was enough for myth to work on. The
work had mostly been done, in fact, in Syria and Persia between
the eighth and eleventh centuries, as native cultures reasserted
themselves against their Arab masters; recalling their great,
earlier conqueror, and at the same time trying to rehabilitate
traditional rationalistic traits against the authoritarian faith of
the conquering Muslims. It was these circumstances which
brought forth the idea that four centuries later so struck the
western imagination: the idea that Alexander's successes—

otherwise baffling explanation—were explained by Aristotle's intellectual genius.

This idea found various means of expression, vague and precise.[37] Among them was a book: that mentioned at the beginning of chapter 4, and known in Latin as *Secretum Secretorum.* The *Secretum* claimed to be the counsel with which Aristotle had equipped the conqueror. The book in its Latin version was itself a conqueror. Between about 1135 and about 1240 the *Secretum* began to circulate in Latin translations from two current Arabic versions; and it circulated prodigiously. At least 250 manuscripts of it still exist, and the advent of printing would in due course bring no fewer than forty editions, in various languages, into being. The distribution and provenance of manuscripts, as well as references in medieval literature, betray that it was read in high as well as low political circles: including those of the princes for whom its twin subject-matter—medicine and politics (for who but a prince would instantly see those two subjects as one?)—made it particularly appropriate.[38]

The *Secretum*'s success, which is its title to our attention, calls for explanation. The reputation of the real Aristotle, whose works were flooding in on the same Arabic tide, is not enough to provide one. For the *Secretum* was copied more often than any of the works of the real Aristotle; and this in turn was because it was read in different circles, and much broader ones. What Aristotle's reputation lent the *Secretum* was a certificate of academic worthiness, which a book with magic in it, as the *Secretum* had, could not well have given itself. Beyond that, the main significance of Aristotle to the *Secretum*'s success was his legend. The supposed origin of the book underlined the message it carried, a message stated repeatedly in the text. The message was this:

Now I will tell you a short maxim which alone would suffice to guide you in all matters temporal and spiritual, even if I had not told you others. O Alexander, the head of policy and judgement is Reason. It is the health of the soul and the mirror of faults. . . . It is the chief of all praiseworthy things, and the fountain-head of all glories.[39]

*Intellectus est capud regiminis, salus anime . . . et radix omnium bonorum.* In the world the Latin *Secretum* entered, the political field was still divided, in many people's minds, between human and superhuman force. In such a field, the *Secretum*'s bold apotheosis of intellect had the attraction of novelty—just the novelty its readers were ready to discover.

The great dominions of the past—Roman, Jewish, and Greek—had risen on the intelligence and learning of their chiefs. So, at least, thought one school of medieval historiography. Since all history is contemporary history, it would be surprising if the lesson thus taught—that intellect is the key to effective political power—had not been conveyed more directly, in the same centuries that read history in this way. There are a number of means of showing that it was.

### (ii) The intellect in government

#### (a) Kings and ministers

However power had been wielded in the past, power in the present, in the twelfth and thirteenth centuries, was wielded from ever-developing structures of centralized government. This government needed trained manpower. And since it often recruited that manpower from among men not born and bred for supreme rule, yet literate, the training called for some written embodiment of rulers' wisdom. In the thirteenth century manuals proliferated on many subjects; so naturally they proliferated also on this. Manuals in the art of government differed from the older genre of 'Mirrors' for princes in being both more practical, and aimed at a wider readership. The pattern of their silences and stresses is all the more telling for that.

This pattern was palpably intellectualist. Three examples will illustrate this. Two of the three manuals in question cover a wider spectrum of topics than merely government. But the group has been chosen because of the wide diffusion of all three works, because of their apparent mutual independence, and because they share a feature which admits comparison between them. The feature is a list of qualities a government chief minister or official should have.

We begin with the *Secretum* itself, one of whose functions—as can be told from both its content and its readership—was that of guide for practical government. One piece of advice in the

*Secretum* tells how to choose a minister. A total of fifteen qualities
are to be sought. The list starts with the demand that the
minister's 'limbs function perfectly'; and goes on to include
hospitality, magnanimity, and other of the virtues later to be
attached to the 'gentleman'. But there is a gap. None of the
fifteen virtues is military. What fills the gap is a whole set—
seven in all, out of the fifteen—of intellectual attainments and
virtues. In second place (after the limbs) comes 'a quick
understanding'; in the third, 'a retentive memory'; in the
fourth, intelligence, 'so that the smallest clue will lead him to
the right conclusion'. The minister, on top of this, must be able
to express himself; must show skill in 'all sciences', and know the
sources of expenditure. Finally, he must be truthful.[40]

We cannot be altogether astonished to learn, as we do from
recent Arabic scholarship, that the list of qualities in the *Secretum*
owes something to Greek models, going back ultimately to that
inventor of the philosopher-king, Plato.[41] Nor should we be
surprised that the promulgators of this tradition, who made its
bias their own, came largely from a class of learned administra-
trators: such men can be expected to recommend learning in an
administrator. But none of this affects the significance, for the
history of twelfth- and thirteenth-century Europe, of the list's
intellectualist bias.

This significance is confirmed by two more examples. They
come from the most dynamic areas of thirteenth-century
government: the French monarchy and the Italian commune.
The French example is Philippe de Beaumanoir's *Coutumes de
Beauvaisis*, written about 1290. The book consists of detailed
working advice for those mobile viceroys, the *baillis*; advice
given by a man who had himself held office as *bailli* for over a
decade. The nineteenth-century editor of the work identified a
minimum number of thirty-four manuscripts, not counting
abridgements.[42] The first chapter of the *Coutumes* lists ten
qualities needed by the *bailli*. In the list, neither loving God nor
loving the king comes higher than second place. The first is held
by that virtue

which is and ought to be lady and mistress of all the others, and
without which the other virtues cannot be employed. This virtue is
called wisdom, which is as much as to say, being wise [*sages*]. Let us
then declare: the man who sets out to hold the *bailli*'s office, and to do

justice, must be wise. Nor will he be able, if he is not, to do what pertains to the office.[43]

*Sapience*, and the *sages*, come first. In the last place on the list, almost as an afterthought, *loyauté* is made wisdom's necessary companion; and others of the mandarin's virtues appear— 'religion', urbanity, patience, boldness, generosity, and obedience. But the space given to each virtue makes the tail of the list confirm the primacy of its first item. For the longest entry (No. 8) states that the *bailli* should be 'tres bien connoisans': able to discriminate, that is, between the loyal and the treacherous, and so on. Entry No. 9, meanwhile, is devoted to the quality of *soutil engieng*: a sort of business astuteness, comprising an ability to do accounts and to swell the king's wealth without actually trespassing on anyone's rights.

A similar result emerges from the study of a third example, an Italian book written in French, for a French-speaking upper class, in 1268. It is Brunetto Latini's *Li Tresors*: 'The Treasure Chest'. Like Philippe de Beaumanoir, the Florentine Latini had held high political office; and like him he attracted a wide readership: at least seventy-three manuscripts of his book survive, while some fifteen more lost manuscripts have been identified.[44] One section of *Li Tresors* treats the office of *podestà* elected chief executive of a commune; and Latini includes here a list of twelve virtues a candidate should have. Faith in God ('and in man': loyalty and religious faith are lumped together under one heading) now comes at the very *end* of the list. And what comes at the head? Once more, it is wisdom: the wisdom of age, or rather of 'long experience', appropriately recommended by Aristotle and 'Solomon' (actually Ecclesiastes 10:16). One synonym used by Latini to denote this wisdom is the French word *sens* ('sense' or 'reason'); which is distinct, he says, from mere intellectual brilliance (*bon engien de savoir*). While wisdom thus described makes the longest, as well as the first, item on Latini's list, it is supported by at least two more of the remaining eleven. No. 4 is Philippe de Beaumanoir's *engieng* again: the ability (here) to understand the matters presented to one, to reach quick decisions, to see the reasons behind cases, and to avoid being deceived through ignorance. No. 8, finally, is the rhetorician author's own forte: the power to speak wisely, as well as to keep quiet when appropriate, and to avoid the damaging word.[45]

The intellectualist bias in these two samples is less over-whelming than that in the *Secretum*. But it is still distinct. It could be explored further. A trace of it is to be found in the ecclesiastical sphere, in advice on the choice of bishops;[46] and more than a trace in the spread and character of books (including 'Mirrors') for the instruction of princes.[47] To fix the exact chronological fortunes of a new emphasis of this kind would be as hard for the thirteenth century as it was (in chapters 3 and 4) for the eleventh, and for the same reason. But even the appearance and multiplication of manuals such as the ones cited, in the thirteenth century, is enough to confirm the impression the examples give: that their insistence on the value of the mind was special to their age and milieu.

## (b) *Warriors*

Great ancient dominions—those of Solomon, Alexander, and the Romans—had achieved effective power by the use of their brains. The executives of civil government in the central middle ages were expected to do the same. But they were not the only ones. For the rising appreciation of brainpower finds testimony also on a second facet of medieval politics: war. The relative absence of military virtues in the new manuals for government did not mean there was less war now: only that government had ramified, and that civil politics and war were on their way to becoming separate specializations. And if attention is turned, now, to the military specialization, we find, there too, signs of a corresponding intellectualist swing, characteristic of the twelfth and thirteenth centuries.

To find an intellectualist military ethos among scholars is no problem. For scholars were often in the position of having to persuade noblemen of the usefulness of the liberal arts; and there was no surer line of approach than this. The arts, they said, helped you win battles. Alexander Neckham was quoted earlier (p. 117), as claiming a political value for the arts. He went on to ask rhetorically:

What enemies could withstand the kingdom that was able to triumph over the sciences? What wiliness of foes would not surrender to the subtlety of those who have tracked down the subtle truths that lurk in the very bosom of nature?[48]

Learning, then, was useful to states which made war. It was also useful to war-making individuals. John of Salisbury emphasized this latter purpose in *Policraticus*,[49] and the educationalist Philip of Harvengt put it in his plan for making princes men of letters.[50] In the thirteenth century, in the hands of Roger Bacon, a similar recommendation of science for warriors would adorn no less a proposal than the defence of Christendom against Islam.[51]

To show that philosophers saw the mind as the key to successful warfare, then, is no problem. It was natural for them to think so. Where problems start is in showing that practical men of war thought the same; and that if they did, they did so any more during and after the intellectual renaissance than before. There are nevertheless two ways the problems can be approached. One lies through a study of the ideal warrior, one through a study of the actual.

(1) *Fortitudo* and *sapientia*. In theory, nobility and warrior-status were normally supposed to be the same; and in tracing the intellectualization of ideal warriors, some progress might be made by a review of 'Mirrors' of nobility throughout the middle ages. In fact, although this approach would not wholly lack profit, it raises too many complications for the present purpose; not least because its starting equation was not equally true in all periods. The ideal warrior will be approached instead by way of the hero; and in particular, through his most celebrated European embodiment, whose literary existence was roughly contemporary with the intellectual renaissance.

The most famous of European heroic epics, the *Chanson de Roland*, was written *c.* 1050, almost certainly by one poet, a clerk called Turoldus; and almost certainly on the basis of legendary material which had accumulated since the ninth century.[52] The popularity of the *Chanson de Roland* is indicated, this time, not by the manuscript tradition (which is meagre), but by references, copies, and not least by the diffusion of its proper names: especially those of Roland (In Italy 'Orlando')[53] and Olivier. It is Olivier's origin and character that call for our attention.

First, Olivier was apparently a crucial element in the success of the Roland story. The prehistory of the *Chanson de Roland* lay among traditions of Charlemagne's Spanish campaign of 778. Olivier was a latecomer in these traditions. He probably entered just before the year 1000, i.e. some fifty years before Turoldus' poem, and a few years before Roland's lady-love Aude. The date of Olivier's entry coincides, as nearly as can be measured, with signs of a rise in the popularity of the Roland theme as a whole. For both names, 'Olivier' and 'Roland', start appearing in charters in the first half of the eleventh century: at first individually (from just before the year 1000), then more and more regularly as a pair, denoting a pair of brothers or cousins. At this stage it is normally Olivier, not Roland, who holds first place—e.g. as the elder brother. Only after the *Chanson*, when the onomastic fashion became general, did Turoldus' tragic hero move into the lead he subsequently kept. This *pas de deux*, whatever else it may mean about the poem's origin, does suggest that Olivier was an important element in the spreading appeal of this group of legends.

This suggestion raises the question of Olivier's character. His very earliest role in the epic was simply as warrior companion to Roland: appropriate enough in the age of the comradely *milites*. But Olivier compounded this role with another. *Olivier* means literally 'olive-tree'. The olive in myth had been created by the goddess Athene;[54] and in the *Iliad* (a Latin translation of which was available to dark-age scholars, and was probably known to Turoldus), Athene patronizes counsel and tactics, as against rash courage—Odysseus as against Achilles. Now in Turoldus' poem Olivier does, in fact, often stand to Roland in just this contrast. Olivier is more *prudent* than Roland. The poem's plot by itself declares this: Roland dies because he proudly refuses to call timely help, against Olivier's advice. The contrast appears in minor episodes too, so much so that the pair almost appear as personifications of the two qualities of courage and wisdom: *fortitudo* and *sapientia*—to use a pair of terms well known in dark-age descriptions of heroes. The poet says all this in a single line

Rollanz est proz et Olivier est sage

(l. 1093)

The contrasting portrayal of wisdom and of rash courage was a motif of classical heroic epic, from Homer onwards. The contrast may even be archetypal in epic as such: for strong traces of it have also been found in *Beowulf*.[55] Turoldus did not invent the motif. But his poem, and the tradition it fostered, gave vivid expression to the motif in terms of French history. And it was this mid-eleventh-century version of it, in the pair Roland and Olivier, that struck the European imagination.

Of the pair it was Olivier who was the newcomer, and apparent prerequisite of the poem's success: Olivier, the hero who added discretion to his valour. An attempt to explain the success of the theme must therefore look partly towards Olivier. It must also look towards contemporary society; and in particular to the hypothesis that in the century of Europe's assault on Islam, the knights who cherished the Roland story were learning to raise the premium they put on prudence: that the *Chanson de Roland*, in other words, was in this respect a swansong for the reckless *fortitudo* of its defeated hero.

Some confirmation for this hypothesis can be had from Latin narrative texts of the period *c*. 1050–*c*. 1125. These naturally made frequent use of the noun *miles* (and its plural *milites*). The noun was often qualified by an adjective. The adjectives have been subjected to analysis, and a significant change is revealed in the last decade of the eleventh century.[56] Over the period covered, 1050–1125, some fourteen main epithets are in issue: 'strong', 'noble', 'active', and so on. Only one of the epithets is intellectual: *prudens* (including derivatives like *prudentissimus*); and this *prudens* has an instructive career. It appears not at all until about 1090. Then it not only appears, but leaps straight to the top of the list, appearing more often than any of its thirteen competitors:[57] in just the years, that is, when Roland and his prudent companion were making their literary conquests. It was Olivier's quality, apparently, rather than Roland's, that was thought flattering in the description of a knight.

From the ideal military hero we pass now to consider some real ones.

(2) *Vegetius.* In 1147 Count Geoffrey Plantagenet, father of England's Henry II, was besieging a castle in the Loire valley. He had been doing so for a fortnight. But his rams had failed to breach the stone walls, backed as they were by tree trunks. An eye-witness pictures Geoffrey sitting down in the middle of the siege to . . . what? To pray? To upbraid his subordinates? No: to study a book in Latin—a language the count did not read easily. A monk fortunately arrived just then on business. He

took the book from the count's hands, and after searching in it for a while, read out a passage, giving detailed instructions how to make a big incendiary bomb, for hurling into fortresses with timber defences. Count Geoffrey said: 'what you have read out today you will see put in action tomorrow'. So it happened, and the castle was taken.[58]

Necessity has always mothered invention. In some circumstances it has also mothered study. It was well able to do so for Count Geoffrey in 1147 because he encouraged scholars and copyists, and habitually had a scholar on call during campaigns.[59] But his situation was in a measure typical, and with time became more typical, of leading men of war. More books were available, and more interpreters of them, and together these could make a learned discipline of that sector of politics where necessity is most pressing. The vignette from Count Geoffrey's *Life* finds no exact parallel in other medieval records. But it gives the key to a range of less vivid documents on the concept of war as a learned art.

The fortune of just one of these documents is especially illustrative. It is the volume which won Count Geoffrey his campaign: a manual on the art of war by the fourth-century Roman Vegetius.[60] Actually it was an augmented Vegetius: that incendiary bomb is not in the original text. But the augmentation only underlines the book's status. For most of the middle ages, Vegetius' *Epitome de re militari* was virtually unique as a military manual, and served as the main vehicle of the living science it taught. Now it is true Vegetius was not markedly intellectualist in bias. His book is not another *Secretum.* He gave straightforward precepts on drill, and on formations and sieges. There are no secret weapons in the original version, and no show of erudition. Yet the author's aim, to capture Roman experience for the dark age he felt to be coming, was essentially scientific in character, not least in that it presumed an ability to read. And there are single counsels in Vegetius' book whose intellectualism is palpable: counsels on foresight,[61] and on judgement of position and geography[62] (the first medieval mention of maps occurs in an augmented Vegetius of *c.* 1280[63]). Vegetius' most characteristic precept, often repeated, is the very essence of the *sapientia* which epic set in contrast with *fortitudo:* the general, says Vegetius, should avoid pitched battle if possible. Manœuvres, diplomacy, victory by starvation: almost anything is better than the putting of men and kingdoms into the hands of that paragon of irrational forces, fortune.[64]

The medieval career of Vegetius' manual is therefore in more than one way a gauge of war's status as a science. The spread of most classical works had begun in the Carolingian renaissance, and Vegetius was no exception. The slight but significant incidence of Vegetius in wills and libraries suggests that, whatever else caused the collapse of the Carolingian empire, it was not a failure by its military experts (*docti ad bellum*: the phrase becomes common in western sources from now on[65]) to study the science of tactics.[66] A few noble dynasties kept their copies of Vegetius through to the eleventh century. The copy Count Geoffrey used in 1147 may have been the same it appears his great-grandfather Count Fulk the Black had possessed in the tenth century; and may indeed have gone on to give Geoffrey's son and grandson, Henry II and Cœur de Lion, the admiration for Vegetius they are said to have felt.[67] If, as seems likely, there was some recopying along the line, that only emphasizes the value the formidable Plantagenet dynasty set on the book. By Geoffrey's time, too, other dynasties had learned the lesson. One was that of the counts of Champagne, the same to whom that utilitarian propagandist for learning, Philip of Harvengt, had addressed his arguments; and whose copy of Vegetius may have been given to them by another of Vegetius' warm admirers, John of Salisbury.[68] The fashion for Vegetius now spread, to a degree probably quite as prodigious as that of the (slightly later) *Secretum*. Fewer manuscripts of Vegetius' own work survive than of the Pseudo-Aristotle's: something short of two hundred, including translations.[69] But the wear-and-tear on a book which went to sieges must be set off as a handicap. And not only that. Vegetius acquired a hidden presence: he was taken up and incorporated *en bloc* in other well-copied books, above all in the political manuals of Alfonso X of Castile and Cardinal Egidius Colonna.[70]

The dates of these two last works (1260, and 1270–85), together with that of Jean de Meung's French translation of Vegetius (1284) (not to mention those of a sizeable proportion of manuscripts of Vegetius himself) hammer the message home.

The dates all fall within a fifty-year bracket. Not only does the same bracket happen to include a marked fashion (in Italy) for the *Chanson de Roland*, with its ambivalent view of precipitate heroes.[71] It includes the two governmental manuals mentioned earlier, by Beaumanoir and Latini, as well as the official and most broadcast translation of the *Secretum* (1259).[72] The half-century which heard intellectual virtues so emphatically recommended in political circles, in other words, was the same which witnessed an explosion of interest in war as a science.

It would be tempting to illustrate further, down into more humdrum levels of government, this awareness of the political power of the mind. One source of illustrations would be the world of abbots, who often ruled small empires of their own. An abbot in the new legal and commercial conditions of the twelfth century might find himself in a lawsuit without lawyers, or near bankruptcy with no one to tell him why; and he would realize with anguished suddenness the very tangible value of brains.[73] Why it would be tempting to illustrate this sort of predicament is that it would be easy. But we shall be glancing again at such predicaments, and the market for specialized brainpower they created, when we come to look at the people who tried to satisfy the market, especially in chapters 8 and 9. Here, we must limit ourselves to more general appreciations of the usefulness of brains.

The most general of all have been left till last. We have considered views on the mind in confrontation with nature; and on the mind as confronting the human environment. Now, lastly, we consider the mind as such.

## 3. THE INHERENT USEFULNESS OF LEARNING AND REASON

The mind, it was understood, was inherently and essentially useful. This usefulness can be illustrated from two complementary fields. The first is learning, and specifically the learning of history.

### (i) The study of history

If one mark of a science is that it knows how to defend its usefulness, then history only reached this status fully in the twelfth century. The perennial taste of the dark ages for history, together with much else that passed as history, was strong enough to dispense with such questions of first principle. But first principles were the special province of the renaissance of Hugh of Saint Victor and his contemporaries; and history, like everything else, had to defend its title to the Christian reader's attention. History could not itself claim to count as a liberal art. And it found only a frail pretext in the fact that the reading of ancient historians was accessory to the liberal art of grammar. It was true that the Bible taught history. But it did not teach the history of Alexander and Caesar, still less that of the heroes of later centuries. What claim had all these on a Christian?[74]

Christian historiography of course had a perfectly good answer. History was useful morally. Roman philosophers had long ago stressed the moral value of history, and twelfth-century Christians who sought to model their lives on a historical Gospel could not shut their ears to this doctrine. On the contrary, the scholastics developed it. The moral value of history became an element in the introductory apologia for almost any standard history book. And it spread further: as a reason, in reformers' polemic, why the literate should behave better than anyone else; and as an excuse for putting little episodes from supposed history into sermons—*exempli gratia*, as preachers used to say: the *exemplum* being the illustrative story from real life.

Beneath this ethical mantle, however, the more perceptive defenders of history saw that it also had what would now be called a prudential value. History helped you avoid mistakes. As an apologia for history this recommendation was much rarer than the moral one. But a few of the more philosophical historians expressly included it: Eadmer,[75] Otto of Freising,[76] and John of Salisbury[77] among them. Their tributes are confirmed by those from persons with less vested interest in the subject. In the thirteenth century a polemicist will be found charging his opponents with ignorance of history, as the source of their misreading of current politics.[78] Again, a teacher will tell his pupils of the practical 'usefulness' of learning history young.[79] A counsellor, similarly, will draw attention to the lessons history teaches in the waging of war.[80] And so on.

These apologists all converged on one principle. It was that the past, in this not unlike the astrologers' stars, revealed the future. This principle was not allowed to go unstated, though it was not the historians who stated it. It emerged in comment on a classical text. Cicero had divided the virtue of Prudence into three 'parts': Memory, Intelligence, and Providence, facing respectively past, present, and future.[81] Now 'Memory' (looking backwards) was not always expressly said to be accessory to 'Providence' (looking forwards). But by at latest the end of the twelfth century moral philosophy was content to take it that way. Providence (wrote Alan of Lille for instance [*c.* 1160] was 'the faculty of forecasting the future according to the past'.[82] This formula harmonized exactly with what some more ambitious dabblers in history had already been claiming;[83] and it remained as a standard support for historical study. The argument might be shaky. Whether the foretelling of the future from the past is a *virtue* may be doubted, and was doubted then.[84] But shaky or not, this accommodation of history in moral theology served to reassure all who henceforward studied the former subject. Theirs might not be a Liberal Art. But it was accessory to a Cardinal Virtue.

It is time, finally, to look more closely at this cardinal virtue, and see if we cannot learn from any other of its dubious interpretations.

### (ii) The virtue of prudence

It was not only knowledge, like knowledge of history, that helped a man fight his battles. It was also plain wit. Some awareness of the usefulness of wit is no doubt primeval—for example, the earliest known European folk tales include themes displaying it.[85] But in the twelfth and thirteenth centuries this awareness was enthroned in an exceptionally high place, and an unexpected one: among the cardinal virtues.

The place was unexpected because virtues are meant to be just *good*, rather than useful; and it is the *usefulness* of intelligence we are considering. As we have just seen, the coherence of medieval ethical language was not absolute. Inconsistencies could creep in unobserved. And the name of one virtue in particular was subject to a *double entendre*, so that different people could mean different things by it. By a subtle merging of the two meanings, some moralists were able to make useful intelligence a supreme virtue.

The virtue was prudence. The literary origin of the *double entendre* about prudence lies in the prehistory of medieval ethics. That prehistory leads back directly to Cicero, and his analysis of the four virtues: prudence, fortitude, temperance, and justice. Indirectly, it leads back to before Cicero. For Cicero, and his near-contemporary Seneca, had inherited their ethics almost complete from middle Stoicism. It was from this ultimate ancestor that medieval theologians got the core of their practical moral doctrine. This derivation had an important result for the virtue of prudence. Stoicism was the most emphatic of western philosophical schools in identifying goodness with wisdom. The Stoic scheme of virtues therefore put prudence firmly at the top. Through Cicero and Seneca, this order of precedence passed to the Christian middle ages.[86]

Medieval theologians were for a long time reserved, as well they might be, towards this piece of their classical inheritance: no substantial theological discussion of the virtue of prudence survives from before the very end of the twelfth century.[87] But resistance could not go on for ever. The ancient moralists were perplexingly good at their trade. The Romans may have fallen short on metaphysics. But their practical cast of mind had left them all the better at ethics. In the patient taking apart of secular moral problems, readers of the Bible—with its mysterious pageant of faltering saints and repentant sinners—and even readers of the ascetic Fathers, had little to set up against Cicero and Seneca. They had still less when, in the early thirteenth century, the complete text of Aristotle's *Nichomachean Ethics* was put in the balance, with its more articulate, pre-Stoic version of the same scheme of four virtues. Eventually, therefore, and above all with the Aristotelians Albert and Aquinas, the Stoic virtue of prudence was dovetailed, after elaborate glossing, into the Christian scheme. It became the first of the four 'moral' virtues—now so called as a lasting reminder of their pre-Christian source.[88] This enthronement of prudence was all the more effective because of the time it occurred. Albert and Aquinas were Dominicans. In their later years their colleagues in the Order of Preachers were inaugurating one of the most prolific literary genres of the later middle ages: moral-penitential handbooks. Through these the scholastic scheme of virtues became the general property of preachers—as also of the artists who preached in paint and stone.[89]

The exaltation of the virtue of prudence gave central importance to the question of what it meant. This was where problems arose. The word 'prudence' could have basically two meanings. One was the Stoic meaning, as heavily elaborated by the scholastics. For them, prudence was the virtue which distinguished aids and obstacles to the love of God. It was the recognition of the moral course of action. Albert, and even Aquinas, could go further, and make prudence include the deliberate *choice* of the moral course.[90] No wonder prudence was 'wagon-driver' to the other virtues! On this interpretation it *was* virtue.

But there was another meaning: another set of presuppositions, that is to say, besides the Christian, for interpreting the chief Stoic virtue. In modern English the word 'prudent' implies worldly-wisdom: locking the front-door at night. So it did commonly in both Latin and the main vernaculars throughout the period when we have testimonies of these languages. According to both vulgate and some medieval vernacular versions (from which the English Authorized Version was partly drawn), Jesus himself had spoken of the *prudence* of the steward who had falsified accounts in his own interest; and had thanked his Father for hiding certain truths 'from the prudent', but revealing them to babes.[91] Saint Augustine had once located prudence in 'the avoidance of traps'; and for a long time this patristic text was the one most reckoned with by scholars.[92] It was also a common literary usage. Odo of Cluny used the word in the tenth century, in a context making it clear it is the pagan virtue he is thinking of, for the policy of a soldier who uses trickery to crush an enemy.[93]

From after the millennium, examples could be multiplied from both Latin and the vernaculars. A close study of them, for which this is not the place, might be revealing. It might show that the theologians' enthronement of prudence as a cardinal virtue slightly discouraged the use of the term for baser worldly wisdom. A whole range of other words seems to have been developed to share the invidious burden of describing this quality: the Latin *sagacitas* as 'trick';[94] the French *engien* and the German *sin*. But they only shared it. *Prudentia* and its equivalents and kindred still mixed freely with these words, and kept their worldly contamination. Examples from dictionaries of ancient vernaculars suggest two common connotations for 'prudence'. One—related to the primitive Latin source of the word, *providentia*—implied foresight. The definition by a commentator on Petrarch ran: 'prudent, i.e. wise, more or less means "seeing for certain"; for the prudent man is so wary that he foresees uncertain events'.[95] We have already seen the philosophers' elaboration of this nuance. The other connotation of 'prudence', which could often combine with the first, is that of the type of wisdom suitable for rulers. A Tuscan proverb ran: 'To the serf, patience; to the master, prudence.'[96] This notion of the ruler's quality was embodied in the traditional term for city counsellors: *prudentes*, which went directly into Italian, and into French as *prud'homes*. Late in the fourteenth century Christine de Pisan exemplified this use of the term in a description of Charles V. No prince equalled him 'in loftiness of reading or speech, and prudent policy in all things generally'.[97] Special expertise can be comprised in this connotation, as in 'jurisprudence'.

Foresight and wise government are no doubt both virtues. But, however they might compare with the old Stoic type of prudence, they are hardly the same as the virtue which thirteenth-century theologians agreed to put at the top of the moral pyramid. Between all these nuances there could be confusion. Occasionally—but only occasionally enough to show there *could* be confusion—we find a distinction expressed, between 'Christian prudence'[98] and 'prudence of the world'.[99] But we also find—and there is no getting away from the fact that the texts where we find it were the ones most widely copied—a tendency to merge the two meanings. The merging had the effect of usurping, for a non-Christian virtue, the Christian virtue's place in the ethical scheme. The non-Christian virtue is often just Stoic, in faintly dressed-up blocks of quotation from the pagan ancients. But it also includes basic worldly wisdom, which bears all the marks of having come straight from daily experience. Thus, in the middle of a disquisition on the excellence of the first virtue, the reader will stumble on some tip for becoming rich, or powerful, or keeping out of a scrape.[100] Among examples is Brunetto Latini's *Li Tresors*. Much of the

ethical section of this book is partially-acknowledged borrow-
ings from Seneca and Cicero. Latini accordingly puts in a long
section on prudence, as first of the moral virtues. In it he
happens to include this advice (not from the ancients, but from
an Italian near-contemporary) : if you are walking beside a man
armed with a dagger, walk on his right; if with a sword, walk on
his left.[101] Equally tell-tale is Gerald of Wales' chapter on
prudence in his book for the instruction of a prince. Having
made prudence the 'polisher of the other virtues', and a *sine qua
non* of the virtuous life (with appropriate quotation from Cicero
and Horace), Gerald leads off on the usefulness of astuteness
and learning in *war*. He lubricates the switch-over with Jesus's
'Be ye prudent [*prudentes*] as serpents'.[102]

Medievalists will be reminded of the military terminology of
swords and battles, incongruously shared by ascetic monks and
by knights, who meant different things by the same words. Like
much in popular religious language, the name of the first moral
virtue lent itself to different interpretations at different levels. At
the highest it could represent the deliberate alignment of a
man's will with God's. That justified the prime status of
prudence among Christian virtues. But at a lower level, as with
the knights and their *militia*, the theologians' emphasis could
serve simply to endorse a policy dictated by not specifically
Christian considerations. At this level, prudence was circumspection. Circumspection, in or out of government, can be used
in God's service. Then it is a virtue. But even then it is not the
virtue which theologians made 'wagon-driver' of the others.
Nor is its virtuous character its essence. Its essence—which it
keeps whether it is virtuous or not—is useful intelligence.

This chapter closes a self-contained section. I have tried in
this section to depict the genesis of a social mechanism: a
mechanism which, starting about the millennium, imparted to
European society a new pattern of impulses, passing from
economics to psychology. This mechanism was fully at work in
just the centuries—the twelfth and thirteenth—when a more
rationalistic view was developing, within European culture, of
the way God worked in nature. It happens to have been at work
then. Nothing so far has shown that the growing dominion of
reason, in the matter of God's dealings with the world, owed

anything to this complex of forces in contemporary society. Yet the foregoing argument invites a surmise. It is that the rationalistic culture was mainly borne by the upward-moving battalions on the Wheel of Fortune; by those who responded— either consciously or unconsciously, either violently or with a gentleness baffling perception—to the pulling power of social rank; by those who knew—perhaps better than King Alfred, who had said it in an earlier renaissance—that 'through wisdom you may come to power, even though you do not yearn for it'.[103]

Here is a big surmise. But it can at least be investigated. The investigation, however, must be broached from the opposite end of the subject to that which has so far been studied: not Society, but Reason. So we go off now to the other end, and take a new look at the whole matter from there.

# PART II

# ARITHMETIC

CHAPTER 6

# The Dark Age of European Arithmetic

DCC    XX 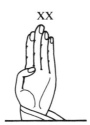   V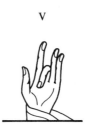

In European tradition, reason has launched itself on the world through two channels: numbers, and words. It was Alcuin or a contemporary, in the eighth century, who effectively drove the division between these channels in the European syllabus, splitting the *quadrivium*—the 'four ways', of arithmetic, geometry, astronomy, and musical theory—from the *trivium*—the 'three ways' of logic, grammar, and rhetoric.[1] But the division was no arbitrary invention of a Carolingian. It lay in the character of knowledge. The histories of numeracy and of literacy, of mathematics and literature, have followed distinct paths—if often roughly parallel ones.

An inquiry into the social origins of our rational concept of nature must follow the same two paths. Parts II and III of this book will therefore be devoted separately to them. The rationale of our inquiry demands that the numerical path be followed first. This is not merely because mathematics has a peculiarly rigorous relationship with reason—though it does have, and was seen to have in the middle ages (as I shall explain in chapter 8). It is because of the character of the natural science that emerged from the middle ages. 'This grand book, the universe . . . cannot be understood unless one first learns to comprehend the language and read the letters in which it is composed. It is written in the language of mathematics.' This remark by Galileo[2] may be said to have inaugurated what is known as 'classical' physics, and with it, the set of presuppositions which from schooldays onwards permeates our modern view of nature. The pursuit of the prehistory of that view must therefore start with mathematics.

For modern mathematics itself had a long prehistory. The very success of Renaissance mathematicians, in establishing their science as the language of the universe, has obscured to us the fact that their discovery was not just the beginning of a development. It was also the end of one, and chronologically a much longer one. Anthropologists report that there are tribes—in California, southern Africa, and elsewhere—whose members cannot count above ten.[3] In Europe's past, precise record of such a disability has been erased. Its vestiges, only, will be seen in this and the next chapter. But the anthropological datum by itself warns us against taking for granted even the most elementary mathematical skills as part of innate human mental equipment. It suggests, set in a European context, that the thousand years before Galileo may have seen in this field an intellectual change as momentous as any that have happened in it since; that the evolution of a mathematical sense, in other words, was one more aspect of the long, creative toil which forms the substance of medieval history.

This evolution of a mathematical sense will be our subject for the next three chapters. Our eyes are turned towards it, we must remember, by the rationale of our inquiry. Why it is important to remember the source of this compulsion is that the latter flouts all emphasis in the historical sources, primary and secondary. Early medieval writers, for reasons to be explained shortly, volunteer next to no information about the numeracy of their ordinary contemporaries. A historian who was content to follow the contours of these sources would largely have to leave mathematics out. That has in fact usually happened. A few histories of the middle ages mention mathematics, and a few histories of mathematics mention the middle ages. But with rare and distinguished exceptions these two streams of research start from points too distant to fructify the common ground between them. Historians who are also mathematicians generally shy from the—from the point of view of sources—daunting task of exploring the primitive concepts behind the earliest deposits of

European mathematics. The further 'histories of mathematics' go back into the middle ages, the more nearly they approximate to sparse catalogues of learned treatises. Seen on their own, from that angle, the treatises have not so far earned the kind of attention that could help us now.

A search for the social origins of mathematics, if it is to go beyond the few memorials of the academic science, therefore calls for more than the mere adding of a dimension to a familiar story. Much of the story has still to be written. There is nothing for it, then, if our search is to go on, but to write the story now— or rather enough of it for our strict purpose. That is what I shall try to do in this and the next chapter. This pair of chapters will between them chart the genesis of what all theoreticians agreed was the most fundamental of mathematical skills, that of arithmetic.[4] Chapter 6 will argue that the four or five centuries before the millennium were a 'dark age' of arithmetic. The task of this chapter is the hard one—hard in many fields of early medieval history—of proving something was not there. So it will highlight every available hint about numeracy or in-numeracy in the early medieval world. Once this darkness is established, the evidence from after the millennium can be better interpreted: what it shows is the *emergence* of an arithmetical sense, and of skills that went with it. This emergence will be the subject of chapter 7.

The aim of chapters 6 and 7 will be to illuminate, not a science *qua* science, but the social orientation of the people who sustained it. The story will be told with this *arrière-pensée*, and should be read with it. If it is, the task of the final chapter in the group will be easier. That task will be to look back swiftly over the development traced, filling in gaps where needed, with the purpose of analysing what social and political forces may have been behind it. By the end of chapter 8 it should be clear enough what the arithmetical sense has to do with the social–psychological mechanism described in Part I.

## I. EARLY GERMANIC EUROPE, *c*. 500–*c*. 800

To recover in early Germanic history the state of those innumerate Californian Indians, we should have to go back further than the middle ages. Tacitus already, though he portrays his Germans as distinctly reckless about land-division, money, voting, and even the calendar (all, as we shall see, potential stimuli to careful counting), still mentions their 'hundreds'—military and judicial units—as if the number meant what it said.[5] When the Germans reappear, in their sixth-century laws, they are already paying murder-fines in money to the tune of several hundreds of *solidi*; while the earliest Germanic verse, from the seventh century, if otherwise bare of number, is acquainted with similar sums.[6]

But dark-age Europe was anyway not just German. Classical influences were present from the beginning. Whatever the truth about the unadulterated Germans, whom no Roman trader or anthropologist ever reached, it is clear that in Gothic and early Frankish Europe not only counting, but a recognizable skill of arithmetic, existed. The obscure prehistory of what we call Arabic numerals hints that numerals like them may have been scratched in sand by illiterates in Gothic Spain before the Arabs arrived.[7] Again, in 725 Bede would describe a system of finger-reckoning whose elements, at least, sound like established practice.[8] In rather clearer focus, school-exercises surviving from the Carolingian period bear traces of an earlier origin—when gold coins circulated, and when even a man with none of those only needed to see his sow bear seven piglets (with the prospect that each of those might bear seven more) to get the idea of geometrical progression.[9]

Nevertheless, the paucity of this evidence about any widespread knowledge of arithmetic in barbarian Europe must leave doubt whether such knowledge existed; and where it did, whether it was more than primitive. Only the odd enthusiast was likely to know any sophisticated arithmetic. He was an exception. Gregory of Tours tells of a slave from Marseilles, for instance, about 570, who was 'fully versed' in 'arithmetical studies' (together with Virgil and the Theodosian Code). The slave travelled north, where his skill was rare enough to earn him a high place in the Frankish royal household.[10]

It is in fact only among the professionally learned that we can look for serious arithmetical knowledge in the early middle ages. This meant, increasingly, in ecclesiastical circles. In theory, the survival of arithmetic as a learned subject was due to Latin educational tradition. Arithmetic was a liberal art, and had been included as such by all those late Latin writers whose business it had been to save culture from the wreck. Cassiodorus had counted it among subjects of 'Secular Letters'. Boethius had written a treatise *De Arithmetica*. Augustine had admitted arithmetic among sciences for which a use could be found in interpreting scripture. Martianus Capella had allegorized arithmetic among his Liberal Arts. In the early middle ages, wherever pretensions to literacy existed, the science of number was thus assured of some measure of acknowledgement.

In practice, however, such modest calculating ability as a literate clerk of the seventh or eighth century possessed was due less to Rome than to Christianity. There were two reasons. The first was that Christianity, too, carried its numerical tradition. Dotted along their length, starting with the Book of Numbers, the old and new testaments bore the stamp of the most numerate cultures of the ancient world—Egyptian, Babylonian, and Greek. The books of Daniel and Revelation, especially, replete as they were with apocalyptic numbers, invited all who pored on the sacred to plunge to any depth they chose into a world of calculation. That invitation was indeed the only flawless excuse—one put by Augustine and repeated by dark-age scholars—a Christian culture had in nourishing the pagan art of arithmetic at all.[11]

But it was only an excuse. The force that first put medieval arithmetic on its feet came, to be sure, from religion; but not straight from the biblical text. It came, ultimately, from a second of Christianity's assets: its peculiarly cosmopolitan and historical character. Impinging on that character, the world-wide political shifts of the seventh and eighth centuries— Muslim conquests, Byzantine decline, and the march of the Roman church northwards—combined to produce, in the north-west, the first major arithmetical enterprise in medieval culture. It is here, in fact, that the story of medieval arithmetic properly begins.

The debates associated with the Christian calendar are nearly as old as Christianity. The earliest of the debates was whether to mark the anniversary of Christ's Resurrection according to the Roman solar, or Jewish lunar, reckoning. It was soon found that the two reckonings could be reconciled; but only with considerable arithmetical juggling. The story of the reconciliation was consequently slow—a fact which illustrates and confirms our strictures on the early phase of mathematics in Europe.[12] From the fifth to the eighth centuries the calendar came to monopolize the attention of the few scholars who knew anything of calculation. The history of the word *computus* testifies to this monopoly: taken from a word for 'to calculate', the meaning of *computus* was restricted, from the fifth to the tenth century, to the art of calendar-reckoning.[13] Despite their pains, when the early computists made what to them were crucial discoveries, it was as often as not by accident.[14] By A.D. 700, although a formidable literary corpus on the subject was in existence, there was still no general agreement about Easter. Even church authority, for all its concern, did not know enough to arbitrate. Meanwhile the cultural pre-eminence of the Irish, rising in the sixth and seventh century *pari passu* with Roman authority, did little to favour the application of practical, critical arithmetic to the calendar-debate.[15]

The calendar-debate was not ended in a day. But it underwent a critical, final phase, among whose results was that Latin Christendom found an acceptable set of principles for determining Easter. The phase passed in England in the late seventh and early eighth centuries. So to that place and period we now turn.

## 2. ENGLAND, *c.* 650–*c.* 750

The Northumbrian Easter dispute which led to the Synod of Whitby forms a well-known episode in Bede's *Ecclesiastical History*. Only a few features of it, however, call for notice here. The first is that the calculation which rained on Northumbria as a result of the dispute fell on virgin ground. For some thirty years, from 627 to the 650s, Bede relates, Northumbrians had contentedly (*patienter*) celebrated two Easters, Celtic and Roman, side by side, without anyone's being seriously moved to reconcile them.[16] The impulse to end the anomaly (which included the queen's fasting on different days from the king) came, not from within Northumbria, but from a group of monks fresh from educations in Italy, Gaul, and Kent.[17] When finally in 664 a meeting was called, neither the Celtic party nor even the king of Northumbria (who was president) disputed the question on any other grounds than those of authority.[18] Only the Romanists—the monks fresh from school—argued from the

PLATES

PLATE I  Avarice and Ambition

(a) Avarice was a favourite subject for pictorial allegory in the central and late middle ages. This example, remarkable for a precocious imaginative vitality, was drawn in the late eleventh century at Moissac, a Cluniac abbey on the route north from Toulouse.

The *avarus*, bent only on the accumulation of money (which he empties from his purse into a vessel), insouciantly treads underfoot the labouring *rusticus*, drawn symbolically small. To the right of this detail the page in the manuscript depicts the contrasting virtue *misericordia*. Other miniatures in the text illustrate the elements of self-interested ambition: *vana gloria, invidia*, and *superbia*. Cf. Katzenellenbogen, 11–13, and Figs. 9, 11, and 12.

Paris, Bibliothèque Nationale, MS Latin 2077, fo. 170r.

(b) The limitless ambition of a promoted courtier, and its just reward, are grimly epitomized here in the person of Haman, the villain of the book of Esther. Above the gallows, Jehovah warns: 'I will break off the horns of the wicked' [Ps. 74/5, v. 10]. The allegorical 'Quest for Honour' [right] comments sardonically: '*this* is how I raise up'. The present drawing is one of an elaborate set of miniatures made in St. Emmeram, Regensburg, in 1165. The next miniature above it on the page illustrates *cupiditas*, whose similarly precarious character is due this time to slippery *fortuna* (reproduced below in Plate III(b)).

Munich, Bayerische Staatsbibliothek, Cod. Lat. 13002, fo. 3v.

(c) 'The lion is ambition'. He is harnessed to the chariot of *Avaritia*, whose hand of coins extends into the upper-left quarter of the detail, and another of whose vicious menagerie displays a scroll top-centre: 'the barking dog is tenacity'. The complex allegory of which this is part was itself part of a collection of similar designs, *The Garden of Delights*, made by Herrad of Hohenbourg in the late twelfth century. The unique manuscript of *Hortus Deliciarum*, formerly in Strasbourg, was a casualty of the Franco-Prussian war; but scholars have been able to reconstruct it in varying degrees of completeness from early-nineteenth-century drawings. The present reproduction is from an edition made by Joseph Walter in 1952. The texts have been checked against the full reconstruction shortly to be published by the Warburg Institute.

(d) Avarice and Vainglory serve as twin attendants on Pride, the source of Bad Government. Avarice, a lean old woman, holds a grappling-hook and a closed treasure-chest. Vainglory, a young woman with jewelled headgear and bare shoulders, admires herself in the traditional mirror. Allegorical virtues and vices could be represented as women without its being implied that they belonged to one sex more than the other.

Detail from Ambrogio Lorenzetti, Allegory of Bad Government (1337–40), fresco in the Council Chamber, Palazzo Pubblico, Siena.

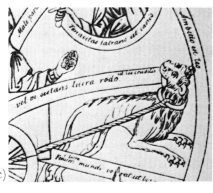

(a)

(b)

(c)

(d)

PLATES II–IV

# Three Late Twelfth-Century 'Wheels'

PLATE II   The 'Circle of the Sphere'
(*see pp. 83–4*)

The king is a shepherd
mustering the army

The army are dragons
fed by money

Law is guidance
governing the
king

Money is food
gathered by the
people

Sovereignty is
lordship exalted
by law

The people are
servants subjected
to justice

The world is a garden
hedged by sovereignty

Justice is happiness
and the establishment
of the world

This figure, showing the interdependence of elements in the centralized state, appears in the Pseudo-Aristotelian *Secretum Secretorum* (*Kitāb Sirr al-Asrār*). The wide diffusion of this work in Europe, from about 1140 to the end of the middle ages, is indicated on p. 120. Latin versions describe the figure in detail and exalt it as 'the substance of this book [*utilitas hujus libri*]'. To find it depicted, however, we must turn to the similarly numerous Arabic and Hebrew texts. (These actually go even further in making the figure a summary of the book—having Aristotle say: 'O Alexander ... if I had not sent to thee anything else except this figure ... it would have sufficed thee;' and so on).

The photograph here is from an Arabic text, probably from the fourteenth century, in Oxford, Bodleian, MS Laud. Or. 210, fo. 90r. I have superimposed on it the English translation by Ismail Ali, from Steele's *Secretum*, pp. 226–7. Further translations of the relevant parts of the Arabic and Hebrew versions can be found respectively there, and in M. Gaster, 'The Hebrew Version of the *Secretum Secretorum*, II: Translation', *Journal of the Royal Asiatic Society*, year 1908, pp. 111–62; pp. 130–1.

PLATE III   The Wheel of Fortune
(*see pp. 98–101*)

(*a*)  *The late-medieval Wheel of Fortune*
Figures rise and fall on a wheel which Fortune turns by hand. The
direction of rotation is anti-clockwise, and the inscriptions read (in
that direction): 'I reign', 'I have reigned', 'I am without a kingdom',
and 'I shall reign'. Although given the language and emblems of
kingship, this image of the rise and fall of personal fortune was
envisaged as applying to all men.

The manuscript in which this drawing appears was mostly written
in the ninth century. The script and style of the drawing itself suggest
it was added in the twelfth century. The artist found a blank space at
the end of a commentary on *Job*, and used it to interject this
comment of his own. If the dating is right, this is the earliest extant
representation of this type of *Rota Fortunae*. (Cf. Pickering [as on p. 441
n. 70], 213).

Manchester, John Rylands Library, MS Latin 83, fo. 66v

(b)  *For comparison: the classical and early-medieval Wheel of Fortune.*
A double-faced Fortuna here balances on her wheel, announcing on a
scroll: 'we turn the wheel in swift revolution'. This version of the older
Wheel of Fortune appears in an elaborate set of miniatures executed in
St. Emmeram, Regensburg, in 1165; and is thus roughly con-
temporary with the newer Wheel depicted in (a). For this and other
versions of the classical Wheel see Katzenellenbogen, 57 and Plate
XXXII; and Pickering, 213 and Plate 32a.

Munich, Bayerische Staatsbibliothek, Cod. Lat. 13002, fo. 3v.

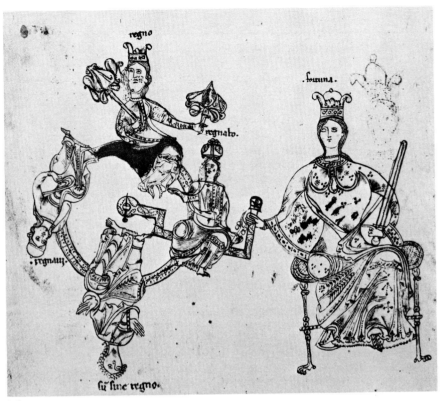

(a)

(b)

PLATE IV   The Wheel of False Religion

An ecclesiastical counterpart of the secular Wheel of Fortune, the Wheel of False Religion depicts the ups and downs of careerism within a wealthy abbey. The figure was devised by the monastic moralist Hugh of Fouilloy ('de Folieto'; †c. 1174), and was widely copied in monastic scriptoria.

The figure takes up several themes discussed in chapters 3–5. The prior 'ascends by money' (Ⓐ; cf. pp. 87–90). The source of the money is indicated on the corresponding *cantus*, or section of the rim (Ⓑ: 'secunda [cantus est] avaritia'), whose spokes—*radii*—are labelled *dīligentia custodie* and *rapacitas* (Ⓒ and Ⓓ). Of ambition, meanwhile, we read (at Ⓔ): 'the circuit of the wheel is the courtliness of ambition'. This *ambitus* (the word can conveniently also mean 'rotation') transforms 'the shame of him who has nothing' (Ⓕ) to 'the honour of the possessor' (Ⓖ). This honour rests on that part of the rim labelled 'pride' (Ⓗ), whose spokes are *tenacitas* and *contemptus* (Ⓙ and Ⓚ). The 'labour' of the go-getter (see pp. 105–7) is included here at Ⓛ; his flattery (pp. 108–9), at Ⓜ—astride the abject *discipulus*: 'the axle is oiled when a master flatters a perverse brother'. As for the role of intellect, it is acknowledged on the very first rising section of the wheel: on the rim (Ⓝ: 'primus cantus est astutia') and on its corresponding spoke (Ⓟ: 'primus radius intelligentia acquirendi').

'This is the wheel of hypocrites', the author announces (Ⓠ). For true monks Hugh devised a *Rota verae religionis*, in every respect the opposite to this. In the present illustration literally, as elsewhere metaphorically, we study only one side of the picture. For both sides and a discussion see Katzenellenbogen, 70–2, and Plates XLIV and XLV.

Heiligenkreuz (Lower Austria), Stiftsbibliothek, Cod. 226, fol. 149v (late twelfth century).

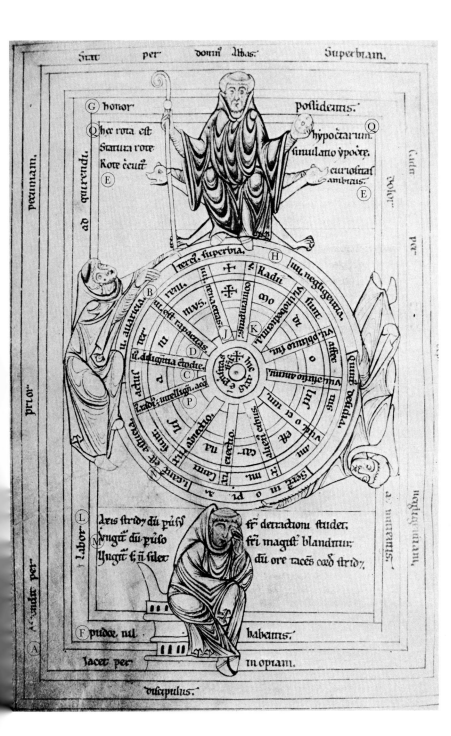

PLATE V   The Dark Age of Arithmetic: finger notation
(*see p. 156*)

From an eleventh-century manuscript of Bede, *De temporum ratione*. The three rows show symbols for units, tens, etc., to 9,000. The legends on the three medallions read:

(left)     *x milia.* [*Manus laeva apponetur*] *pectori supina.*
           ('10,000. [The left hand is placed] palm-forwards on the chest')
(centre)  *xx milia. Pectori expansa.*
           ('20,000 [The left hand is] spread out on the chest')
(right)    *xxx milia. Pectori in cartilagine prona.*
           ('30,000. [The left hand is placed] palm-inwards on the chest [with the thumb] on the breast-bone')

Scrutinies of this and similar tables reveals anomalies, for instance:

1. In the centre medallion here the left hand is *not* 'spread out on the chest'.

2. The symbols for seven hundred here and in the MS illustrated on p. 141 give different positions for the thumb.

3. In the medallions here, the eye-catching iconographical gestures of the *right* hand (not to mention the garb and head-dress) lack any bearing on the purpose of the sketch.

4. The truncated legends (which I have filled out from Bede's text, ed. C. W. Jones, 179–80) would not suffice to describe the gestures.

5. The table may have been incomplete (Bede's account of the symbols goes to a million). We cannot tell, since the next folio of the MS is missing. It was not uncommon, in fact, for such tables to stop at a thousand: see A. Cordoliani, 'À propos du chapitre premier du *De temporum ratione*, de Bède', *Le Moyen Age*, 4$^e$ série, 3 (1948), 209–23; 213.

Taken together, these anomalies suggest that this particular artist, at least, did not take high numbers seriously. Perhaps he agreed with Martianus Capella in dismissing symbols for numbers about 9,000 as 'the gesticulations of a dancer' (see p. 156).

Further examples of these symbols (and their anomalies) can be found in A. Cordoliani, *art. cit.*, and E. Alföldi-Rosenbaum as on p. 451 n. 64.

London, British Library, MS Royal BA XI, fo. 33v.

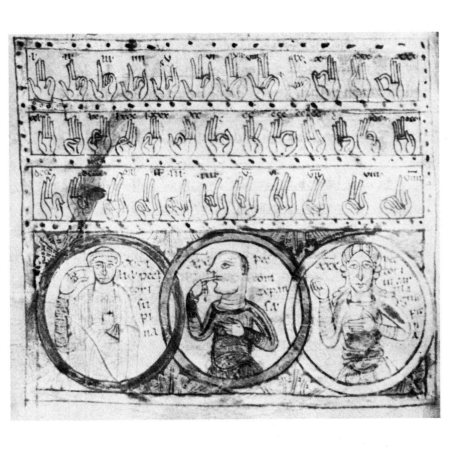

(a) *Addition. Probably 1307–27.*
*The examples read:*

|  |  |  |
|---|---|---|
|  | 12457 | aliud in superius est major numerus et inferius |
| exemplum | 11346 | minor. ('In this example the greater number |
|  | 23803 | is above, the lesser below'). |
|  | 24574 | exemplum in quo minor numerus est superius |
|  | 35685 | et major inferius ('An example in which the |
|  | 60259 | lesser number is above, the greater below') |

(The superscript dots in the MS represent our 'carry one')
John Halifax ('Sacrobosco') [†c. 1250], *Algorismus*.

Oxford, Bodleian, MS Ashmole 1522. fo. 18r. Probably about the time of Edward II, and certainly no later than the middle of the fourteenth century.

(b) *Long Multiplication: the 'Jalousia' Method. About 1300.*
$4569202 \times 502403$ ($= 2,295,570,802,406$)
The numbers to be multiplied are written across, and down the right-hand side of, the 'jalousia' grid. Each digit of the multiplicand is then multiplied separately with each digit of the multiplier, and the answer (of one or two digits) recorded in the appropriate split square. The final addition of the *diagonal* columns (added from top right to bottom left) yields the product, which can be read off down the left-hand side and along the bottom of the grid.

The *jalousia* (jealousy) was a grill placed by Italian householders over their windows, supposedly to stop strangers peering at their wives.

From *A Treatise on Small Measurements, Scientific and General* (*Tractatus de minutis philosophicis et vulgaribus*). Oxford, Bodleian, MS Digby 190, fo. 75r.

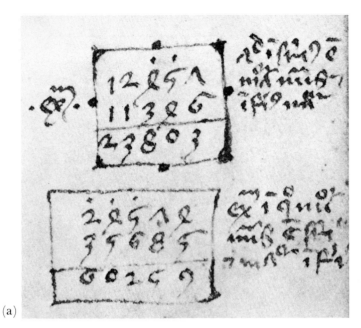

(a)

(b)

PLATE VII   Ignorant clergy satirized
(*see p. 293*)

An asinine priest reads the Gospel.
S. Pierre, Aulnay (Charente-Inférieure), South Portal. About 1150.

PLATE VIII   Inhibitions
(*see p. 354*)

The allegorical Christian knight Generosity suppresses Avarice.
S. Pierre, Aulnay (Charente-Inférieure), West Door. About 1150.

logic of the calendar, citing figures with assurance, and referring to 'the Egyptian method' of calculation.[19] Their leader indeed betrayed visible impatience with opponents who appeared (he said) not even to understand the calculations on which their own wrong dating was based.[20] Bede, who relates all this, shared the impatience.[21]

So, probably, did Bede's earliest readers. For by 731, when the *Ecclesiastical History* was written, people who understood the calendar were no longer a mere foreign-educated spearhead, but a substantial number among the clergy; and it was for this reason, with others, that the Roman Easter was all but universally accepted by then. Already in 710, Abbot Ceolfrid of Monkwearmouth had judged that Easter tables would not be needed any more when the present set (made in the sixth century) ran out, since

today there are so many people able to calculate, that even in our own church in Britain there are many who know the ancient rules of the Egyptians, and can readily extend the cycles of these paschal times for any number of periods of years ahead, even for five hundred and thirty-two years if they so desire.[22]

'Many people', then, in 710, knew 'the rules of the Egyptians'. Much had changed in England since Saint Aidan's time.

These changes, together with the mention by Ceolfrid and others of the Egyptian rules, introduce the second feature of the English Easter-dispute that calls for our attention. The rules were in fact not Egyptian, so much as Babylonian and Greek. Yet by coincidence it appears to have been in Egypt that the English changes of the late seventh century had begun. The year of the defeat of Northumbrian polytheism by missionary preaching, 627, had seen the first military defeat of another polytheism at the opposite corner of the old Roman world: Medina. By 642 Muslims had taken Syria and Egypt. While Saint Aidan charmed his unarithmetical parishioners in Northumbria, Christian refugees from the Levant and North Africa were arriving (from the 640s onwards) in safer parts of the old empire. Well-to-do *émigrés*, for the most part, they brought with them the learning of Hellenistic Alexandria. The Germanic west did not so abound in learned churchmen that it could afford to refuse these men a welcome. Above all, the new church in the north, in England, stood in need of instructed leaders. It was thus—all available evidence suggests—that the Syrian Theodore and the African Hadrian arrived in England in 669 and 670, with a posse of co-refugees.[23]

With Theodore and Hadrian arrived what Bede mysteriously calls 'church arithmetic'. The 'abundant' learning the new-comers imparted to a 'crowd' of pupils comprised, on the secular side, metre, astronomy, musical chant, and 'arithmetica ecclesiastica'.[24] Since Theodore's first measure as archbishop of Canterbury had been to circuit England boosting among other things the Roman Easter, the mysterious new subject doubtless concerned the calendar. But the term does not actually restrict it to that. Indeed the epithet *ecclesiastica* may show an attempt by the pious historian, aware of the suspicion attached to Theodore's Greek past (as a *philosophus*, rapidly made a priest to become archbishop of Canterbury),[25] to justify the presence of a pagan subject in the prelate's curriculum. Anyway, an English scholar of Theodore's time leaves us in no doubt that the science of arithmetic—without restrictions—was taught then, and had the impact of novelty. The scholar was Aldhelm of Malmesbury. He describes the arrival of the new subject in his own curriculum. Nearly forty years old when he wrote, Aldhelm was already a colossus of learning. But arithmetic had made him a boy again.

As for the science of calculation, what shall I say? Why, the near-despair of doing all that reckoning laid so heavy a yoke on my mind that I regarded all past labour spent on study as slight. Nay, to use Saint Jerome's expression (since it seems appropriate) I, who before thought myself a master, began once more to be a pupil. At length, with grace from above, and after incessant study, I have grasped the most difficult of all natural principles, those which lie at the base of reckoning: what they call frāctions.[26]

Allowing for bombast (of which art, too, he was a master), Aldhelm of Malmesbury speaks as a man breaking into undiscovered country. The 'opportunity' he mentions may or may not have been personal tuition by Theodore or Hadrian.[27] But that Aldhelm was also (he relates) studying astronomy, and other subjects of Greek ambience, shows at least that he drank from fountains of which they were then chief custodians.[28]

A double Easter in the north, and political evolution in the south, joined to create in seventh-century England medieval arithmetic's early spring. The effect this all had on minds other than those of arithmeticians should not be undervalued. Anglo-Saxon art, whose early apogee fell just now, at the end of the seventh century, reflects—in the Lindisfarne Gospels, and the crosses of Ruthwell and Bewcastle—a marked mathematical interest. Even the murky *Beowulf* may pay a less sophisticated tribute to the same interest. Though generally shy of any number above fifteen, the poem has a smattering of exceptionally high numbers near the end (one is 100,000).[29] But the arithmetical awakening had an effect even wider and longer-lasting than art and poetry could give it. It was about 700, and in England, that there first came into use what may still prove the most lasting of dark-age cultural achievements: the Christian era. With no effective Roman emperor to reckon dates by, and no secular ruler locally to take his place—only a single, universal church—British calendar-experts took to dating national synods by Christ's 'regnal years'.[30] The idea came actually from one of their Easter tables, and concerned them at the time much less than the fixing of Easter. But the new era may have had a deeper psychological effect. The previous dating-systems had used only the tens and fifteens of reigns and indictions. 'A.D.' dating, as it spread, hung a backcloth of hundreds behind the thought of all who used dates. The hundreds exercised the fascination of novelty. The choice of the year 800 for Charlemagne's coronation was one of the first results of this fascination. The high numbers also gave a new impetus to apocalyptic thought, and the study of the numerical books in the Bible. One revealing result of the fascination with the new dates came when the hundreds reached their first Thousand. The apprehensions of some notorious 'doomsters' testified to the hold which this numerical structure had won even on half-educated minds.[31]

No book played a bigger part in the spread of the Christian era than Bede's *Ecclesiastical History*. Bede's work on the *computus*, similarly, became medieval Europe's standard reading on the subject.[32] Bede was the flower of this vernal numerical consciousness. Without that consciousness indeed, his own fame would be inconceivable. It is true that Bede would be widely venerated as theologian and historian. But specialists who digested his long book on chronology probably put their finger more accurately on Bede's peculiar excellence when they dubbed him 'Beda computator', or 'computator mirabilis', or (in a third case) 'outstanding in book-learning, especially in the calculating art'.[33] Bede's own preoccupations reflect this emphasis. Three of his books (including perhaps his first) were on chronology. The ideas he expounded in them also underlay his books on history.[34] Even the scriptural books singled out for special study (which included Daniel and Revelation) show a predilection for numbers; and as for the way he approached them, modern admirers think fit to excuse Bede as an exegete, for what seems to them an obsession with numbers.[35] Bede's own 'asides' witness the same taste. Carping at bad copyists, he picked out as a matter for special mention their errors in copying numbers, errors made worse (he said) by emenders. One of Bede's rare expressions of sarcasm was against a bad chronologist: 'a fine calculating-teacher!'[36]

*Beda computator* was exceptional, then, and knew it. His character as an exception helps substantiate our thesis that the Germanic world was relatively innumerate. Bede was probably more exceptional, furthermore, at the end of his life in 735 than when he had launched his first, brief essay on chronology in 703. For in 731, at nearly 60, Bede looked back on the days of Theodore and Hadrian (closed by Hadrian's death in 709) as a golden age, in learning as in all else.[37] This was probably no illusion. With Bede's great *De ratione temporum* Minerva's owl had again flown at dusk. The achievements of the *ars calcularia* made in Bede's lifetime would be nourished, but not surpassed before the late tenth century. According to one of its pupils, the archbishop's school in York in the 740s was teaching 'the different kinds of number and the various numerical figures, and how to calculate the Easter cycle.'[38] But not only did the York school stand high above its contemporaries. It was a question there, to judge from the archbishop's conversation, not of pushing mathematical arts forward, but of saving them from extinction.[39] Nor in the event were they saved. Both evidence and lack of evidence suggest decay in all English learning before the first Danish attack in 787. After 787 the arithmetical part of this decay, at least, is certain. When Alfred at length came to revive learning in the 890s, neither arithmetic nor any mathematical art would be mentioned. The subject had indeed grown strange. An Anglo-Saxon version of Bede's *History*, made by or for Alfred, even drops that 'ecclesiastical arithmetic' from the list of subjects taught by Theodore, substituting 'grammar'.[40] The vanguard had retreated from numbers to words.

### 3. THE CAROLINGIAN RENAISSANCE

The English vanguard had retreated, that is to say. For the remnants of English arithmetic had meanwhile migrated to the continent, where the fortunes of early medieval arithmetic pass into a new phase. The credit for this salutary migration, as for much else, goes to Charlemagne's personal interest. The pupil who recalled learning astronomy and arithmetic at York was encountered by Charlemagne in Pavia in 781, to be cajoled at the age of fifty into exile—and as it proved into an illustrious place in history. Alcuin of Tours comes only once into the pages of Einhard, Charlemagne's biographer. His role there points to a specific motive the king had in putting the high price he did on the Englishman's services. Charlemagne (Einhard wrote) studied the liberal arts very keenly. Grammar he learned from Peter of Pisa; the other disciplines from Alcuin:

a man universal in learning, under whose direction the king devoted an enormous amount of time and work to learning rhetoric and dialectic, but above all to astronomy. He learned the art of computation and, in his quest for wisdom, pried deep into the secrets of the stars' courses.[41]

A letter of Alcuin reveals that the mathematical interest he shared with his king extended also to scriptural number-symbolism. In this connection Alcuin once, in a colloquy of scholarly courtiers in the baths at Aix, held forth to Charlemagne on the properties of the number 17.[42] The king who showed such interest in mathematics was one who never learned to write. Indeed, in what may be his earliest capitulary on education, in 789, Charlemagne actually put '*computus*' before 'grammar' among subjects to be taught in episcopal and monastic schools;[43] while the item '*computus*'—if with no more explanation than that—figures more than once in subsequent prescriptions for clerical education under Charlemagne.[44]

A foreign expert; a king's enthusiasm; and some legislative

good intentions: this was the tribute of Charlemagne's renaissance to the art of arithmetic. It was a big tribute from the
point of view of those who gave it. But it was not enough to lift
mathematics out of its dark age, or indeed even to keep for it the
vigour it had had in England. In the act of applauding the
king's own appreciation of the subject, Alcuin lamented in 798
'how few care now about such things!'[45] His lament is borne out
by literary remains. The odd treatise on the calendar, by Bede
or an ancient predecessor, was copied and occasionally glossed.
But in shelf after shelf of literary classics, secular and divine,
such works cut a slim appearance. The monastic library of St.
Riquier in Picardy in 831, for instance, possessed twenty-six
volumes on grammar, one on medicine, and none on arithmetic
or kindred subjects.[46] Writers agreed with librarians. In the
whole body of literary production by the great Carolingian
scholars, down to and including Erigena, one sole treatise
survives in an arithmetical genre. It was by the encyclopedist
Rabanus Maurus, who had studied in Tours soon after Alcuin's
death. And even Rabanus' *De computo*[47] does not in fact disprove
the rule. For despite the eulogy of the science of numbers with
which it opens, its substance is simply another calendar-
computus: competent enough, certainly, but too dependent on
Bede to prove there was any lively pursuit of mathematics in
Carolingian circles.[48]

Rabanus himself, introducing *De computo*, points to one
immediate reason for this arithmetical backwardness. The book
purports to be written for a pupil who had asked that 'being of
mature age' he might have a book to 'rouse his inaction', and
teach him 'a little of the skill of numbers'.[49] It was not a
promising approach. We recall those other two mature
students, Aldhelm and Charlemagne, both about forty when
they began studying mathematics; and recall, too, the 'near-
despair' and 'time and work' which the new subject entailed for
them.[50] The scholar Lupus of Ferrières, similarly, a friend of
Rabanus, was at least thirty years old when he wrote in 836 to
ask Einhard's help in being 'introduced' (as he put it) to the
ready-reckoner.[51] Arithmetic does not appear, then, to have
been a subject for schoolboys: only for a handful of mature
students. The capitularies represented only aspirations, here as
elsewhere. One prescription for clerical education agrees to

limit even its aspirations. If pupils cannot be taught the 'major *computus*', it says, let them be content with the 'minor'—a rigmarole of memorized rules for immediate practical use.[52] It is noticeable, too, among the capitularies, that while syllabuses sometimes include *computus*, prescriptions for the examination of ordinands conspicuously omit it—as if it were too much to ask.[53]

In the arithmetical dearth of Carolingian schooling one exception survives. But it is another of those which helps press home the point. A ninth-century booklet includes a collection of fifty-three arithmetical problems formerly attributed—wrongly but not inappropriately—to Alcuin.[54] The title, 'Propositions for Sharpening Youth', is itself an aspersion on Carolingian arithmetic: it was not an autonomous subject. The problems do nothing to reassure us. Five, jumbled with the others, are riddles only bordering on arithmetic. None of the others is presented in a way suited to identify the procedure it illustrates. The problems certainly show a grasp of basic procedures (subject to limitations to be returned to in a moment); but no more.

The aims and circumstances of Carolingian schools thus barred arithmetic from a regular place in them. These circumstances, together with a few of the schools, lasted for over a century after Charlemagne's death. They alone would account for the poverty of arithmetic before the millennium. But in considering the science's collapse, in this second of dark-age cultures in which it strove for life, another and more radical difficulty it faced must be reckoned with. Latin and Christian traditions, we said, kept arithmetic alive. They also contained elements which blocked its growth.

A second look at both traditions will clarify this. Christian scripture might have its patches of numbers, dense in places. But scripture also had long stretches without numbers. A good example is the Psalms, whose liturgical status gave them a unique psychological influence. Again, a few biblical passages went so far as to be actually hostile to precise number. To read in Genesis 25:7 that the father of the Jewish race had died at 175, or, in 2 Samuel 24, that the greatest of Israel's kings— Charlemagne's own model, David—had been punished for counting his subjects, tended to baffle, not encourage, a dawning sense of arithmetic in the dark-age monk. If scripture had its baffling elements, so did the post-biblical tradition of

Christian spirituality. For all Saint Augustine's vindication of arithmetic as a tool for interpreting scripture, and for all the pious uses calendar-makers had found for what allegorists called their 'stolen Egyptian treasure', the art of arithmetic was never without its enemies in Christian high places. The Benedictine reformers of Charlemagne's time were often among these enemies. The immigrant Alcuin, bewailing the Franks' lack of concern for arithmetic in 798, had added that those few who were keen to learn actually met resistance.[55] Rabanus, thirty years later, was similarly indignant against people who 'condemn numbers'.[56]

Christianity, then, while in part a preserver of the science of number, also obstructed it. The same went for Latin tradition. It was ambivalent. Of leading ancient literate cultures the Latin (the Judaic shortly behind) had been the least numerate. For Rome as for Christianity the science of number was 'stolen treasure': Boethius too used that image.[57] Whatever practical sums Rome's field-measurers and tradesmen had done, the liberal arts remained what a 'free man' needed to know. And the 'free man's' school programme, as bequeathed to the middle ages by Cassiodorus, leaned heavily towards the skills of oratory. The paragon of orators, Cicero, had himself cited the mathematical arts of astrology and geometry as examples of 'vicious' study, which took a man from the pursuit of moral philosophy; and his views on this matter became a commonplace of medieval ethics.[58] Mathematics, in a word, was not respectable. Any gentleman who wished to study it had to cut a lone path. Boethius, one of the few Roman gentlemen to cut such a path, groaned at the 'long toil', 'sleepless nights', and 'sweat' he had spent on what is really quite a modest treatise on numbers.[59] This reserve in Latin literature towards mathematics naturally tended to dampen enthusiasm in medieval 'renaissances'. The more zealous scholars were for all things Latin, the more any propensity they had towards numerical thinking was likely to be dampened.

The dampening effect can actually be seen at work, in an otherwise scarcely significant detail of Carolingian culture. The field most sensitive to arithmetical impulses was dating. The practice of counting days in the month from one to thirty-one started arriving in the west, from Syria and Egypt, in the second half of the sixth century, replacing the numerically more primitive Roman method, which numbered from three points within the month—Kalends, Nones, and Ides. With hesitation the Syriac–Egyptian system spread among the Lombards and Franks, especially (it has been noticed) where vernacular was used. But the Carolingian renaissance was a renaissance specifically of *Latin* tradition. So it reverted to the Roman system, which clung on, as a result, for centuries in the western imperial chancery.[60]

Jerusalem and Rome, then, kept early medieval Europe on a lean arithmetical diet. In one respect it was prohibitively lean. There was a feature in both the Latin and Christian traditions, as they were studied by the literate churchmen of the early middle ages, which put an absolute limit on learned arithmetic. This was Roman numerals. Roman numerals were probably less irrational in their origin than they may appear to us. But taken as they stood, by a culture which looked mainly to the written page for its instruction, the numerals were a poor tool for arithmetic. Our arithmetical sense starts with adding. The science of arithmetic only comes into being with multiplication, and its elaborations.[61] The original sin of Roman numerals was, at bottom, to embalm the primitive principles of addition and subtraction—as in MCMLXXVII ( = 2,000 minus 100, plus 50, etc.)—in such a way as to block the entry, into notation, of that of multiplication—as in our '1977' ( = 1 *times* 1,000, plus 9 *times* 100, etc.) Carolingian culture not only had a respect for writing as such. It was in general attached, to the point of combativeness, to the visible symbols of its abstract thought. This flaw in its notation was therefore bound to cripple numerical exploration.

This effect too can be watched in action. Of treatises mentioned so far one, particularly, involved the sort of solitary exploration which exposed itself to error. This was the 53 'Propositions for Sharpening Youth'. (Calendar-makers, who were responsible for most of the other treatises, could generally check each others' calculations.) The compiler of the 'Propositions' knew the jeopardy he was in. For unlike arithmeticians of the central middle ages he stuck to ready-made problems. Within the problems, similarly, he stuck to safe quantities—the number 100 appears in no fewer than a quarter of the problems as the basic subject of calculation. The caution was wise. For as soon as the compiler's figures ventured as high as tens of thousands (which they did only twice, as it happens—catapulted up by geometrical progression, and then only in powers of two), difficulties began. In one 'Problem'—about pigs bearing piglets—$8^6$ comes out as 262,304, when it should be 262,144. The error enters at $8^5$, so is not merely the copyist's.[62] In another problem, the addition of elements in a progression is abandoned with a craven 'etc.' after $2^{15}$ (32,768). Perhaps it was not so craven. For to see the procedure set out in Latin is to admire the ninth-century computer for having got as far as he did: '. . . In quarta decima [mansione] $\overline{\text{XVI}}$ CCCLXXXIIII. In quinta decima $\overline{\text{XXXII}}$ DCCLXVIII, etc.'[63]

Behind these Roman numerals, it is true, lay other aids to calculation. No one knows for sure how Bede did his sums. But he and Rabanus describe a number-symbolism based on fingers and hands (source of our 'digit'; for illustrations see Plate V and the epigraph to this chapter), and do so in a way suggesting they were not the only ones to know about it.[64] In theory this symbolism went up to a million. Experienced commentators nevertheless complained that the higher numbers (above 9,000) called for 'the gesticulations of dancers'.[65] And actually the system had no over-all advantage over Roman numerals as a help to reckoning. A second aid to calculation, also bequeathed from the Empire, was more to the purpose. This was a multiplication table for products up to 50,000 and down to the smallest Roman fractions. It was known as the *Calculus* of Victorius. In the end however even this ready-reckoner underlines how insurmountable the calculator's problems were. For the manuscripts we have of the *Calculus*, from the ninth century and later, actually contain inaccuracies, religiously repeated by copyists.[66]

Intellectual tradition, Latin and Christian, had held a place open for arithmetic in early barbarian Europe. In England, in the late seventh century, the place was occupied, for long enough to create a *computus* for the few, and a calendar for the many. The ninth century saw a stagnation, to which both circumstance, and the limitations of literary tradition itself, contributed.

The stagnation ended in the last quarter of the tenth century.

It had shown signs of ending before then. The rough line of descent we have traced from Theodore, through Bede and Alcuin, to Rabanus Maurus, never quite died. Auxerre, Paris, Rheims, and Trier show, in turn, signs of a mathematical presence even in the late ninth and early tenth centuries.[67] Nearer the middle of the tenth, it is clear that in both England and Germany practical reckoning was taught to school-children.[68] But it was only in the last three decades of the century that this mathematical interest grew strong enough to come into daylight. About 970—three centuries after Theodore, two after Alcuin—began a third of those spasms of mathematical interest which punctuated dark-age learning. Since this one effectively ended arithmetic's own dark age, a look at its circumstances can conclude this chapter.

### 4. THE AGE OF GERBERT

The mathematical revival of the 970s has always been linked with the name of Gerbert of Aurillac, later Pope Sylvester II. Legend has played a part here, concentrating in one man, as it often does, an evolution which stirred independently of him.[69] But the speed with which legend got to work is one witness to Gerbert's contemporary reputation; and the master himself left enough mathematical writings to vindicate it. Gerbert's full ecclesiastical career will not delay us now. His fame as professor and prelate, and his travels—between Barcelona and Magdeburg, Rome and Rheims—are familiar history. The details even of his mathematical career would take a long time to rehearse at length—with its début in Spain, its climax in Rheims, and its surviving deposit of three treatises and a bundle of letters.[70] Once more, however, certain features of Gerbert's career, and of the milieu it impinged on, invite us to pause and look at them—three features in particular.

The claim of the first of these on our attention is that it confirms the darkness of the age we are leaving. Mathematics struck the tenth century—more even than the seventh and eighth—as novel. For in the first place, contemporaries said it was. Gerbert's pupil Richer claimed that 'music and astronomy were utterly unknown in Italy when Gerbert arrived', while 'Gaul had known nothing of music for a long time'.[71] There is flattery here. But Richer's claims find echoes. Gerbert himself

said, and there are independent reasons for believing him, that
his new method of reckoning was 'unknown, or profoundly
neglected' until his time.[72] An admirer would add that before
Gerbert 'none of the wise men of Italy, Gaul or Germany' had
any idea how to square the circle.[73]

Evidence less direct (and so less open to mistrust) for
mathematics' novelty, lies in the sufferings of its pupils—
reminiscent of earlier martyrdoms to the cause, notably those of
Boethius and Aldhelm. Gerbert himself had studied mathematics 'very hard indeed' in Spain.[74] Yet when asked in 972
what he could teach, Gerbert still, after all that study, only
confessed to a modest ability in this field ('in mathesi se satis
posse').[75] And when in 980 he came to write a booklet on the
new reckoning—a booklet of some four dense pages—he found
the 'toil' so hard as to be 'almost impossible'.[76] Gerbert's
difficulties with mathematics stood in contrast to his facility in
other liberal arts. It appears to have been youthful progress in
grammar that first launched Gerbert on his career. Rhetorical
prowess would crown it. As for logic, Richer says, Gerbert
learned it 'in a fairly short time'.[77] Even the master, then, found
mathematics the hardest branch of learning.

But the master's difficulties were nothing to those of his
pupils. Gerbert's logic-teacher in Rheims, Gerannus, as an
exchange, studied mathematics under Gerbert, 'but was beaten
by the difficulty of the art, and rejected altogether by music'.[78]
As for Richer, who tells us all this, he was still wiping his brow
ten years later at the memory of the 'great sweat we spent on
mathematics'. Arithmetic done, they only got the better of
astronomy, he says, a subject 'scarcely intelligible', with the
help of models, and more 'sweat'. Geometry in its turn cost
them 'labour'.[79] The 'sweat' of Richer and his friends soon
became common currency among chroniclers of the revival,
who claimed that, in spite of it, students of Gerbert's new
reckoning rules 'scarcely understood' them.[80] Indeed we possess
confessions from two of Gerbert's very ablest contemporaries,
Abbo of Fleury and Bernelinus, that their treatises had cost
'tears' and 'mountainous labour'.[81]

For Gerbert's contemporaries, then, mathematics was a new
world. New worlds breed two opposite kinds of reaction: the
despair of exile, and the excitement of exploration. The pattern

of reactions to Gerbert's mathematical new world is the second remarkable feature of its discovery. Richer's uncomfortable reminiscences point to the tepid feelings in one group. In academic society generally, Gerbert had three or four fairly assiduous mathematical correspondents.[82] But, these apart, the only emotion the new science is on record as having aroused here was wonder at the one man who had mastered it. Beyond academic society even this admiration could fail. Precisely what 'popular zeal' it was which—later tradition said—expelled Gerbert from Rheims, is unknown.[83] But his excellence at 'philosophical art' did not generally prejudice the uneducated in his favour.[84] Mathematics in particular was still suspect. Both those contemporaries who wrote, with tears and labour, treatises on reckoning (Abbo and Bernelinus) spoke of the 'envy' of persons who resisted their discoveries.[85] Gerbert and his few fellow-scholars therefore fought largely alone. Doubts can even be raised about the captain's own zeal. When times had changed, mathematics would be remembered as Gerbert's first interest.[86] But the facts of his life tell another story. At one turning-point in it, Gerbert had quitted the only place in Latin Christendom (northern Spain) where mathematics was taught.[87] At another, in 972, he rebuffed a flattering offer of a place as a teacher of mathematics, in order to be a student in logic.[88] In 980, after almost a decade as a professor, Gerbert confessed to not having done practical calculations, or even seen a book on the subject, for many years.[89] Even those dozen of Gerbert's letters which touch mathematics reveal, more often than not, that it is some friend or correspondent, not Gerbert himself, who had volunteered the specifically mathematical interest.[90]

The relatively temperate reaction of scholars, and of the world at large, to the arrival of the new science, puts into relief the enthusiasm of the one man conspicuously to show it. Otto the Great was once blamed for allowing his subjects too much freedom;[91] but in 972, at the height of a power unequalled since Charlemagne, Otto was ready to coerce Gerbert, *qua* mathematician, to stay in his territory. There is reason to believe the emperor had actually spun a web to catch any mathematical fly who flew in. For the very moment (*mox*) Gerbert had appeared in Rome, writes Richer, the pope had sent word to Otto 'that an eager and industrious young man had turned up, who was a great expert in mathematics, and who possessed both the knowledge and the application to instruct members of Otto's entourage'.[92] Otto's answer was equally prompt (*mox etiam*). It 'suggested to the pope that he keep hold of the young man making quite sure no means were allowed him of returning home'.[93] Interviewed, of course, Gerbert showed himself master of a more potent art, rhetoric: he persuaded the emperor to let him go on to Rheims. And before Gerbert returned to imperial territory the old hero was dead. So nothing immediate came of the meeting. But Otto the Great had shown where his interest lay. It was an interest he shared, like his dignity, with Charlemagne. He shared something else too. For this math-ematical enthusiast, like his predecessor, was emphatically no scholar. Otto was thirty-four years old before he started learning to read and write; and the three languages this Roman Emperor could speak by the time of his death did not include Latin.[94]

Some trace of doubt may linger about this mathematical interest in Otto the Great. But any trace has gone when we reach, thirty years later, his half-Greek grandson, Otto III. The first letter written to Gerbert by Otto III, then still in his teens, appears to have refused a demand from Gerbert that the young ruler write some verses: he is not yet competent. At the same time the future scholar-king asks for instruction. As substance for it, he names, not versification, but arithmetic.[95] We know—partly from the survival of his arithmetical text-book—that Otto III would pursue that interest keenly, if not directly under Gerbert.[96] At the apogee of Saxon imperial ambitions, the emperor once more showed a marked penchant for mathematics.

The young Otto III showed again, too, how literary and mathematical interest could diverge. This fact, noticed more than once in our dark-age history, points us towards a third feature of the mathematical revival of Gerbert's time. This, however, is a feature binding Gerbert not with the past—with its blundering exertions of schoolboys, and its *computus* of isolated enthusiasts; it binds him rather with the future, and the central middle ages. For Gerbert's period opened a new phase in the history of mathematics. The time has come, therefore, to move from arithmetic's 'dark age', and, clutching the thread of the story at the point we have reached, to tread into a brighter region: that of the gradual conquest by arithmetic of the educated western mind.

# CHAPTER 7

# The Emergence of the Arithmetical Mentality

WE have been searching, within the bounds of European history, for the origins of arithmetic. Before the millennium there is scarcely anywhere *to* search, except in arithmetic's few academic foyers. A look at those has shown the area round them to have been dark. From the end of the tenth century two developments present themselves. On one hand evidence thickens, if slowly at first, about society generally. On the other, within the academic foyers themselves, mathematics as a science takes wing, to become a recognized element in the scholastic renaissance. For two reasons, then, the focus of our attention can shift from the few to the many, and move a step into the darkness that surrounded the specialists. What is to be seen there from now on is an arithmetical dawn. In the four centuries after Gerbert there emerged, in a significant proportion of society, that familiarity with numbers which was a precondition of Renaissance mathematics.

The growth of this familiarity with numbers began detectably in Gerbert's time. To say that its inception was due to a discovery would be to answer in advance the question underlying this study. Other reasons, too, will be seen in a moment for not saying so. Nevertheless, it is with the discovery that we must start.

Roman numerals manifested and partly occasioned the paralysis of early medieval arithmetic. A hypothesis is bound to suggest itself to our modern minds that our ancestors had to wait for Arabic numerals to break the spell. It happens that a kind of Arabic numerals did in fact start appearing in Latin manuscripts just now (976), not far either from where Gerbert had studied in Spain.[1] But there is a catch. Our book-learning tends to equate culture with written culture. Probably no European century refutes this equation so roundly as the tenth. To understand its mathematical development we must block out this element of our education, and realize that it was precisely their freedom from the proprieties of literary culture which led arithmeticians of this period to their breakthrough. If the dead hand of Roman numerals was to lose its grip, the need was not necessarily for an alternative set. All that was needed was a displacement of writing as a whole from its monopoly in this branch of science. Such a displacement is apparent in fact throughout Gerbert's practice as a teacher of science. Richer and others testify to his free use of 'visual aids'.[2] A more general tendency, away from writing and towards material and symbolic means of expression, helps explain the most pregnant feature of the tenth-century mathematical revival. As in our own time, so in Gerbert's, the drudgery of numerical calculation was being shifted from the written page on to a device: the abacus.

Because the abacus turned its back on writing, little record of its early use in Europe remains to the historian. Nor even to the archaeologist: less than half-a-dozen examples of the medieval European abacus survive. They are late ones, and—since part of the essence (and surely attraction, for some problems) of the abacus was the impermanence of operations done on it[3]—even these examples reveal little. What is known of the instrument's shape, use, and fortunes comes mainly from literary references, in particular from instruction-booklets. These booklets leave gaps. But luckily the gaps are not about the device's basic function, which is what matters to the student of mathematical concepts. After a short period of experiment, the evidence shows, the European abacus settled into one essential form which lasted into the eighteenth century. It was that of a table or board, marked with vertical or horizontal lines, grouped in a manner corresponding to the kind of reckoning to be done: tens, £.*s*.*d*., etc. Numbers were symbolized by what games-players still call 'counters', slid into positions on or between the lines, according to simple rules.[4]

The peculiar status of the abacus in arithmetic's history lay in the principle these simple rules were based on: place-value. A counter on the second line (or column) was worth ten times what it was on the first; in the third, ten times that; and so on. For the dark-age European culture it was now entering, this principle constituted a radical innovation in the representation of number. As if by the turn of a key it opened the path to high numbers. One late Roman writer on arithmetic, Martianus Capella, had once expressly limited the ambitions of arithmetic to low numbers, on the grounds that its symbolism—manual symbolism—foundered above that (i.e. when the 'dancer's contortion of the arms' began, above 9,000).[5] Now, from Gerbert's time onwards, one abacist after another exulted in the limitless recession of their subject's horizons. 'May the last number of the abacus be the length of your majesty's life,' Gerbert himself once rhapsodized to the emperor.[6] His successors alluded more expressly to the new numerical ceiling. 'So it goes on,' wrote one, 'each line exceeding the last by ten times, right into infinity.'[7] Another wrote: 'the columns can proceed three by three, to infinity itself, if desired'.[8] To assess the practical difference the place-system made to reckoning, we only need turn from the 'Propositions for Shapening Youth' of Alcuin's school, to Gerbert's booklet on the abacus. The 'Propositions', like Martianus, call an effective halt at 9,000. Gerbert launches in with multiplication- and division-rules for products up to $10^{10}$ (ten thousand million). This change was one not in degree but in kind.[9]

The abacus's geographical path of conquest can be dimly picked out. A scholar in Auxerre about 900 interpreted the word 'abacus' as meaning a sand-table for drawing geometrical figures.[10] An English school-book from the second half of the tenth century speaks of it similarly.[11] These remarks tend to confirm Gerbert's own later assertion that the reckoning-abacus was 'either unknown or profoundly neglected' until his time.[12]

A claim for Gerbert himself as the rediscoverer of the reckoning-abacus nevertheless has to contend with a reference to it in the Rhineland (Speyer) which may be as early as 970, when Gerbert was in Spain; and with a possibly independent essay on the abacus by Abbo of Fleury.[13] At all events, by soon after Gerbert's death in 1003 the reckoning-abacus was known in various parts of the continent. In the 1020s treatises appeared on it in Tuscany, and Swabia; while Lorraine actually boasted a reputation abroad for the skill of its abacists (*abacistas:* the word was in process of being coined).[14] The human tide that eventually floated the Normans and their allies into England may or may not have brought knowledge of the abacus from Lorraine to England before 1066. It was certainly in England by 1079.[15]

The abacus's swift geographical conquest prepared for its slower conquest through the echelons of society. From between Gerbert's time and 1300 at least eighteen treatises on the abacus are known to have been composed, in various regions.[16] The fullest of the early ones survives in seventeen manuscripts.[17] From the French court in the thirteenth century there spread a fashion for decorating the abacus-counters, or 'reckoning pennies'. Many of these decorated counters remain as witnesses to the virtual ubiquity of the abacus from the fourteenth century to the Renaissance, and indeed long after.[18]

The form and spread of the abacus are subjects which belong immediately to the history of technology. But they have a double bearing on intellectual history. First, the spread of a device for accurate calculation presupposed a preparedness, in the people it spread among, to explore in this direction. The Romans after all had used the abacus, and it had died out after them for no other reason than lack of interest. Secondly, once the device was known, it did not merely, like a mechanism, do the sums put to it. It had to be operated; and it shaped its operators' minds. This effect of matter on mind is endorsed by contemporary recognition. Legend ascribed the origin of the abacus to the father of arithmetic, Pythagoras; but not to help him calculate; it was to fix his purely abstract doctrines into the minds of his pupils.[19] A more frontal reference to the same psychological fact comes from an arithmetician writing in 1202, about the system he was setting up to rival the abacus:

Once, through practice, science has turned into habit, memory and mind come to accord with hands and figures to such a degree that all act in harmony together, as if by one impulse and one breath.[20]

If this delicate observation is collated with what has been shown of the scope and spread of the abacus, the instrument's claim to an effect in intellectual history will be plain. From about the millennium, but above all in the thirteenth and fourteenth centuries, there radiated from this device, wherever it was used, a stimulus towards an accurate concept of numbers.

An attempt will be made later in this chapter to find vestiges of this stimulus in literary sources. But we are not yet done with technology. For the law that what does not grow, fades, applied in this field too. So does the law that the success of an invention can be measured by how far it is surpassed. The abacus prepared its own eclipse. Between the experiments of Gerbert's friends and the early twelfth century, its very virtues had thrown its limitations into relief, and created a demand for something better.

These limitations were two. An abacus-calculation shared with the spoken word confinement to one time and place. The administrator might elude this barrier, since his sum-totals were easily re-frozen into Roman numerals, or tallies. But the calculator was harder hit. Although he liked being able to erase some major stages of his calculations,[21] he had to record major ones. Otherwise (as an arithmetician would explain about 1400) 'if an error occurred the calculator had to start again from his head—granted, too, that the error was not far back'.[22] The abacist needed, then, a quick way of recording stages in his calculation. The abacus's second limitation was slowness. Modern globe-trotters report that, for the sort of sums done in the course of household shopping, the Far-Eastern frame-abacus is faster than their own school arithmetic. The history of the latter might conceivably have been different if the frame-abacus had been used in medieval Europe. But there is no evidence that it was.[23] And the board-abacus was much slower than written arithmetic: perhaps six times slower—if we accept the word of a sixteenth-century zealot for written arithmetic.[24]

The material device, then, was in one respect like those Latin and Christian traditions in the dark age. It helped arithmetic. But at the same time it put limits on it; especially on its sophistication and its speed. We can read as another sign of arithmetic's continuing vigour that, as the abacus had once pushed past the limitations of one sort of writing, it was in turn overtaken by another. In a century when the art of writing was developing anyway—as it was conspicuously doing from the late eleventh century onwards—the next stage in the development followed its own logic. Calculators needed symbols in writing of the abacus-columns, symbols which would include the abacus's special merits: the columns' spatial rendering of powers of ten; and their faculty of being empty. This diagnosis is not just a modern one based on hindsight. It was made at the time, in the course of cogitation and experiment. A mid-twelfth-century mathematician called Ocreatus devised a notation based on the usual numerals, but with a place-value and a sign (O or τ) for 'nothing'. (Our 1089 came out as I.O.VIII.IX.)[25] The notation was of course too clumsy to become general. But not only does it reflect a historic insight in its particular inventor. It reveals the internal evolution which was already starting in Ocreatus' time to bring the solitary reign of the abacus to an end.

It was not only the clumsiness of Ocreatus' project that killed it. By the 1130s Europe was rich enough in minds and money to afford the importation of foreign systems. One of these answered the problems Ocreatus identified. Its distinction was that it was ready-made, and polished.

## 2. THE TOOLS (b) ARABIC NUMERALS

So we come, and from the direction in which contemporaries came, to the subject of Arabic numerals.[26] 'Indian numerals', scholars said then, with a better historical sense for once than ours; or *cifrae*, or *zephirae*, general speech came to call them, from their most peculiar feature: *al-cifr* (in Arabic), 'the vacant one'. Emblems of the most precise of human skills, the Hindu–Arabic numerals defy all precision in their history. But in the European phase of this history, if one certainty stands out, it is its refutation of the idea that inventions by themselves start revolutions. The new numerals were available, complete with

instructions, to any educated persons who wanted them by
1200. It was only *c.* 1400 that they began an effective conquest of
all literate culture. This delay is our opportunity. The pattern of
the numerals' adoption will reflect, not any foreign technological bombardment, but native aspirations and pressures.

Tracing the path of the numerals' advance presents a delicate
problem. A start can be made by looking at surviving examples.
A collection of some two hundred sets of Arabic numerals from
medieval sources was made in 1914 by Mr. G. F. Hill of the
British Museum.[27] Hill's primary purpose was to record, not as
many examples, but as many *types*, as he could. For this purpose
he nevertheless assembled all actual examples he could easily
lay hands on. So their chronological distribution is of some
significance. Omitting those sets of numerals which lack the
specific advantages of proper Arabic numerals for
calculations—especially zero and ease of writing—we find the
following distribution by centuries. Figures are given in dozens
to stress their approximate character.

| | |
|---|---|
| Twelfth century (most–all?—second half) | $\frac{1}{2}$ dozen |
| Thirteenth century | 2–3 dozen |
| Fourteenth century | 3–4 dozen |
| Fifteenth century | 8 dozen |

One scholar, working largely from one library, sixty years ago,
is unlikely to have assembled a complete dossier of samples.
Making all allowance for that, these quantities—set against the
thousands of surviving medieval manuscripts—must seem to
kill outright any notion of an 'Arabic conquest'. Even their
upward curve levels off if seen as a ratio of the general rise in the
production and survival of manuscripts. Furthermore, a look at
numeral forms appears to back up these negative findings. Two
English scribes of the thirteenth century are found not knowing
how to write the numerals properly (one got another scribe to
do it).[28] Again, right into the Renaissance, senseless hybrids can
appear, like '1000.300.80.2' for '1382': the opposite hybrid to
that devised by the shrewd Ocreatus, it will be noticed (and
showing an opposite quality of mind).[29] We know from
elsewhere that plenty of otherwise intelligent and educated
people who knew *about* the Arabic numerals, still saw them

merely as one curiosity among others, without grasping the generic advantage they had over all other systems.[30]

To study Hill's collection of Arabic numerals thus, in isolation, would be to get a thin picture of the numerals' effect before the fifteenth century. It would also be to ignore two prime considerations. The first reintroduces the leitmotiv with which we began: that the paths of numeracy and literacy have been distinct. In the case of specifically Arabic numeracy and specifically Latin literacy, the paths have been more than distinct: they have diverged, consciously and by mutual wish. The literate tradition was for its part hostile to the numerals. In face of them, it added to its innate prejudice against arithmetic a suspicion of all that was not Latin. A witness to this hostility is the fact that our best indirect evidence of the early use of Arabic numerals comes from official attempts to block them.[31] Again, some of the most salient examples of neglect of the numerals stem from those institutions richest in formal record. That former pace-setter for English institutions, the Exchequer, anchored in its own past by an early precocity with the abacus in the twelfth century, would still be writing out its numbers in Roman figures in the sixteenth.[32] The financiers of the Renaissance popes, the Medici, belonged to a city and a profession in the front line of accounting innovations. Yet although Arabic numerals were already in use in less formal areas of their accounts in 1406 (when the extant series of accounts begins) the new system only completed its conquest of all Medici accounts in 1494—a last-minute modernization too late, as it happened, to save the bank from a crash.[33]

Latin official tradition, then, insulated its floor against Arabic numerals: they were a suspect novelty from below, unworthy to be allowed among the hallowed customs of literacy. The numerals meanwhile returned the compliment: their early users appear to have been relatively indifferent to literary education. European writers on Arabic numerals graduated to them from the abacus. If 'literate' at all in our sense, most of them were far from being men of letters. Formal school-teaching in the new arithmetic, where it took place, did so usually at schools separate from those which taught reading and writing.[34] So a man could learn to reckon without ever learning to read and write in the ordinary way. As late as 1387, the university of Florence thought it quite possible its treasurer should be in this predicament.[35] In Italy as a whole the term *abaco* clung on as the normal term for written arithmetic: a lasting token of its descent from outside the main learned tradition.[36]

From the nature of things, therefore, Arabic numerals will not vaunt themselves in the bulk of our literary sources. This is the first caution to be used in reading Hill's tables. The second is related to it. It concerns commerce. Largely because of the time he worked—before the vogue for economic history, and the related vogue for Anglo-Saxon research in Italian archives—Hill scarcely included any items from commercial sources. Fragments of business accounting that have been studied since suggest this is an important lacuna. Some of the more experimental medieval business men saw the merits of Arabic numerals early. Francesco Datini, for instance, the prodigious self-made man of Prato, who died in 1399, and the excellence of whose accounts was certainly a key-element in his success, seems to have used Arabic numerals in those parts of his accounts where he wished to record complete calculations, not just results.[37] Despite the relative dearth of records before Datini, we know that some pathfinders in business methods were accounting in the new numerals at least a century earlier. In its first surviving set of statutes in 1299, the Florentine bankers' guild, the Arte del Cambio, put a clause forbidding the use of Arabic numerals in accounts. It stipulated:

That no member of this guild shall presume to write, or allow to be written by anyone else, in his ledger or account-book, or any part thereof where payments and receipts are recorded, any item in what is known as the style or script of the abacus [=Arabic numerals]. He shall on the contrary write openly [*aperte*] and at length [*extense*], using letters.

The consuls of the guild shall be obliged to impose a fine of twenty small Florentine shillings for each occasion and document wherein the offence is committed. They shall equally be obliged, personally and in their official capacity, to impose a fine as aforesaid, if any document contravening the aforesaid shall come into their hands.

The aforesaid is to have effect from the middle of April in year of our Lord one thousand two hundred and ninety-nine, twelfth of the indiction and thereafter, viz., it shall concern ledgers to be begun from mid-April and thereafter, and accounts written from mid-April and thereafter.[38]

This clause was repeated in at least three subsequent recensions of the statutes, up to 1316 when the extant series ends. This repetition, the clause's tight wording, its penalty, its restriction of the ban to entries of 'payment and receipt', its tacit amnesty for past offences, its context: all combine to tell a story. Money-changers had found it was more convenient to reckon in Arabic numerals by 1299. (The word *extense* in the first paragraph suggests speed as a motive for the use of the new numerals.) They used the numerals at all stages of accounting, including records of payment and receipt. They went on using them despite the ban. Officialdom disapproved, apparently because it did not understand the numerals (cf. the word *aperte* in the first paragraph). It is not hard to divine what sort of officialdom this was. Other clauses in the statutes show that the 'money-changers'—their euphemistic name itself says the same thing—were anxious about slurs on usury. By 1299 Guelf Florence was entering on a big commercial expansion. It did so (temporarily anyway) at the price of close co-operation with the papacy, which correctly suspected the bankers of subterfuge in conceal-ing interest on loans. The bankers who wrote the statute against Arabic numerals almost certainly had ecclesiastical discipli-narians looking over their shoulders.

The strict ecclesiastics had doubtless been to university. That their ignorance of Arabic numerals would not necessarily have been relieved there is clear from another region of evidence. Throughout the late middle ages Italy's universities fought a battle against Arabic numerals as used by the *stationarii*—the booksellers-cum-publishers attached to universities. The first audible shot in the battle came in the (in other respects) worldly-wise university of Padua in 1305. *Stationarii* were to mark books for sale 'on the outside, in an obvious place, in clear letters and not by *cyffras*'.[39] The known wiles of book-markets, and the connotation of our word 'cipher', blur the implications of this clause. It may just mean booksellers put prices in a private code so that they could bargain with gullible customers. But this cannot be the whole explanation. Quire- and page-numberings are very frequent in both Italian and non-Italian manuscripts in the thirteenth century, and even before. This, together with the universities' ban on *cyffras*, suggests that *stationarii*, crossbred as they were from the professions of scholar and merchant, were among the first to grasp the practical advantage of the new numerals.[40]

The entries in Hill's tables must therefore be seen as mere vestiges of a large phenomenon, which lay chiefly outside documents thought worth preserving. One region *where* it lay can be identified by a glance at Hill's list of sources. Most of his numerals come either from handbooks on arithmetic, or from material related to astrology, astronomy, and the calendar: for example (from the mid-thirteenth century), dates. Handbooks on arithmetic were designed to inspire further calculations. That is, for every Arabic numeral surviving in such a handbook thousands more must have been written and lost. For these handbooks were in fact the subject of quite a healthy trade from the thirteenth century onwards. Many manuscripts survive of the 'Popular Algorism' of John Halifax ('Sacrobosco'), the 'Song of Algorism', probably by a certain Alexander of Ville-Dieu, and other works.[41] Astrological handbooks support the same argument. A query could of course be raised as to what all these calculations were written *on*, since paper remained too precious for mere jotting, even after the price dropped *c.* 1300. But here again the divergence of the paths of literacy and numeracy must be remembered. Right up to the fifteenth century, written arithmetic was commonly done on slate.[42]

It is likely on all these grounds that by *c.* 1300 thousands of mathematically-inclined people, in any of the main European monarchies, used Arabic numerals for calculation. 'Thousands' can be said with confidence. The careful Villani in 1345 estimated at 1,000–1,200 the number of children studying '*abaco* and *algorismo*' in Florence alone.[43] Florence was perhaps exceptional. But there can be no question of watertight compartments. If such a question were to be raised, numerous other circumstances would have to be included in the reckoning: the peregrinations of Italian merchants, with their known influence on northern accounting;[44] the visits of northern business men and students to Italy; the nationality of 'Sacrobosco' (he is thought to have been born actually in the 'Holy Wood'—Halifax); the teaching of accounting to boys at some fourteenth-century English schools;[45] the regularity and ease of some surviving Arabic numerals (like those in the early-fourteenth-century calculations in Plate VI); and much else. One of the surest of all testimonies to early familiarity with Arabic numerals comes from the country which from manuscript evidence would seem to have lagged furthest behind: France. About 1236, in Soissons, Walter of Coincy wrote a vernacular poem aimed at a non-learned audience. In it the expression 'a nought without a figure' ('ciffres en augorisme', meaning a vacuous person) began its long literary career.[46] Frankish savants had long debated the character of *nihil*; a wider flock were now credited with an equal familiarity with zero.

From the late tenth century the abacus, from the mid-twelfth century, more slowly, Arabic numerals, began their respective progresses into Europe's culture. Their advance was partly an outcome of arithmetical awakening in the circles they moved into; and partly its cause, as 'memory and mind' came to 'accord with hands and figures'. Both progresses began from small groups of specialists. It should go without saying that while the many introduced themselves to the new skills, the keen few pushed their researches further. The abacists of the eleventh and twelfth centuries were succeeded by the 'algorismists' from the mid-twelfth on, translators and theoreticians of the new arithmetic: Gerard of Cremona, Plato of Tivoli, Robert of Chester, and, laureate of these mathematical pioneers, Adelard of Bath—even if it was not he who introduced to the Latin world the arithmetic of 'Al-Khwarismi', from whom the new science got its medieval name.[47] These scholars and others receive their due in histories of mathematics. There is no need to run through their specialist achievements now. But on such a list of outstanding medieval mathematicians one more name demands a place. Leonardo Fibonacci of Pisa, born about 1170 in North Africa, pursued his researches round the Mediterranean and returned to Pisa to write, in 1202, the most sophisticated general essay on arithmetic that the middle ages produced: the *Liber Abaci*.[48] We will read with reservation Leonardo's claim that the 'Latin race' had so far 'lacked' Arabic arithmetic.[49] But the acceptance of the claim by later Italian historians suggests that for Italy herself it may have been true in 1202, despite her precocity later.[50] At all events, in mastering the science he imported, as well as in his original inventiveness in number theory,[51] Leonardo surpassed all other mathematicians until the high Renaissance. He astonished the imperial court with his skill then, and will do the same now for anyone who approaches him without condescension. For example, Leonardo confidently tackles a quadratic equation involving an irrational number. The confidence is displayed, if by nothing else, by his estimating the irrational number accurately (and without the help of algebraic shorthand) to what would now be nine decimal places.[52]

For the social history of arithmetic, Fibonacci's chief peculiarity was the narrowness of his contemporary influence. The author of *Liber Abaci* saw the book as relatively elementary.[53] Yet it was certainly the book's massive size and high ambitions that has limited our extant copies of *Liber Abaci* to three. Vulgarization was a task left to talents (Sacrobosco's and others) which fell short of genius. These facts must be another warning against allowing the professionals too large a part in the history of arithmetic. That history lies quite as much among the thousands of practical reckoners, readers of Sacrobosco and the *Song of Algorism*. Indeed it lies beyond those thousands: for what were the thousands, in the teeming countryside of Europe before the Black Death? The professionals and reckoners together formed a small minority. But the prehistorian of modern mathematics cannot be content with studying a minority. He must study the science's *i*gnoble line of descent, too. The achievement of this line was less distinguished, but much more widespread, and equally essential as a preparation for the mathematics of the Renaissance. This achievement forms our next subject.

### 3. THE EVOLUTION (a) NUMBERLESSNESS AND EXAGGERATION

The subject lies among the majority, the non-arithmeticians. We have learned where to find non-arithmeticians: in literature. Because literature normally took a different path from mathematics it provides a measure for the influence of mathematics on non-specialist thought. The more deliberately the paths diverged (e.g. because of literary prejudice against numbers), the more telling are the signs of mathematical influence. Literary conventions might resist the infiltration of precise number, but they could not hold out for ever.

Literature, then, is the measure. What the measure shows is that between the millennium and late fourteenth century a slow change took place in the character of European thought about number. The change was not continuous, and taken at random over brief periods the documents can mislead. But over the period as a whole—its beginning roughly contemporary with the introduction of the abacus, its end with the victory of Arabic numerals as a tool for practical arithmetic—a shift can be shown to have occurred in the mental habits of the literate. There emerged among them what can be called an 'arithmetical mentality'.

The meaning of this term will become clearer if we look first at what literary habits were like *before* the emergence of the new mentality. Two particular habits will serve as illustrations. Both were widespread before the thirteenth century, and although present later, grew less intense and less universal. The first of these habits is that of leaving precise numbers out. Large stretches of early medieval literature baffle the modern reader by omitting numbers just when he would hope to find them. One of the most prominent genres with this feature is hagiography. It is perhaps a special case, but still has its significance, and is worth considering for a moment. Students of medieval hagiography often have to search in vain for precise figures, especially dates.[54] For instance, many so-called *Lives* of saints do not give the year when the saint was born or died. They may give the hour or weekday when he died, for liturgical purposes; or for legal purposes the date of gifts to a monastery.[55] Otherwise numbers in hagiography in the central middle ages are as a rule confined to small year-periods ('after twenty years'), small sums of money ('twenty *solidi*'), and very occasionally the achievements of repetitive prayer ('he said the *Paternoster* three hundred times each night': numbers are exceptionally high in this context).[56] It might be objected that this feature does not reflect any general medieval development, only a genre. The datelessness of saints' *Lives* has in fact been shown to vary with the sanctity of the *author* of a *Life*, regardless of chronology.[57] (Saintly hagiographers, even late in the thirteenth century, tend to leave out earthly details like dates.) But the objection has only partial force. Between the millennium and the fourteenth century, hagiography as a whole lost its dominant position in literature. That is to say, the characteristically innumerate genre commanded less of the literary scene.

When we turn away from hagiography to less conservative literary forms the numberlessness of pre-1200 literature is more directly revealing. 'Annals' apart, a shortage of year numbers remained quite a common feature in historiography generally, hardy relic of a time before Bede the *computator* launched his chronology on the world. And year-numbers are only one of many types of number—quantity, distance, price, age—which elude long stretches of early medieval literature.

In lieu of a pilgrimage through this literature, samples can be taken from fields within it where we might most expect to find numbers. The first such field is surely 'technology'. Much the earliest European book with the character of a technological handbook is the *De diversis artibus* written under the pseudonym 'Theophilus' in the Rhineland or central Germany *c.* 1100, and referred to in chapter 5.[58] The book purports to give detailed instructions for such activities as painting and illuminating (including the preparing of materials), making glass, windows, chalices, organs; for setting jewels, and for some blacksmithery. That such a manual would today be full of numbers goes without saying. *De diversis artibus* is remarkable for their dearth. The highest by far is forty (in the measurement of 'forty fingernails').[59] Nails, fingers, hands, arms, feet, thumbs, and straws are the units of measurement—used promiscuously as the author thinks fit.[60] (An eleventh-century source from near Toulouse refers to such measurement by hands, 'thumb-tips touching', as the 'rustics'' method of measurement.[61]) A few weights of precious metal are given, in terms of the equivalent in 'marks' or 'nummi' (up to ten or twelve). And there are a few fractions, which get quite strenuous when it comes to making organ pipes the right length by dividing wax into eighths and thirds).[62] But the general lack of arithmetical ambition in a book otherwise so expert remains striking. Theophilus' quantities are as often as not merely 'a bit more', or 'a medium-sized piece'. The disparity between his subject and his mathematical equipment recalls the same disparity in the ninth-century 'Propositions for Sharpening Youth' mentioned in chapter 6.

My next two examples come from quite a different field, but one equally instructive. Northern France in the twelfth century was the heartland of the intellectual renaissance, and housed, in Chartres, some leading spirits of the mathematical branch of that renaissance. At the centre of French political life in the early twelfth century stood Abbot Suger of St. Denis, administrator of vast estates, even for a time of the kingdom. His celebrated *Life of Louis the Fat*[63] is not shy of details—battle-orders and battle-casualties, political intrigues, etc. Yet in the 140 pages of our printed edition we look in vain for numbers above a hundred given with any serious pretence of accuracy. Twice, only, military forces are assigned a definite figure above that limit: on both occasions as '10,000'.[64] Otherwise it is either an approximation or, much more often, 'quamplures', 'multi', or 'like locusts', which serves as a number.[65] Definite numbers above ten, indeed (such military estimates excluded), appear only once: the value, in ounces of gold or pieces of cloth, of three gifts made by King Louis to the needy.[66] These negative findings take account of dates. Suger the historian never gives the year-number.[67]

Suger stood at the centre of France's political life in the early twelfth century. At the centre of her intellectual life stood Peter Abelard: pioneer in the skills of reason, friend of the Chartres mathematicians, and no slave of tradition. Abelard's autobiography[68] invites the use of numbers: for admirers, fellow-hermits, enemies, assailants, copies of books, dates. But all these are 'many', a 'multitude', or just 'some'.[69] No number above ten—and only one cardinal number above five[70]—appears in the book. Dates are not given, except as 'a few months later', or 'one day'.[71]

The parade of twelfth-century books where we might expect to find numbers, but do not, could continue.[72] It could continue all the longer if books were included which venture above *c.* 100 only in terms of round numbers like 30,000 or 100,000. For such numbers were commonly used by chroniclers as if, rather than numbers, they were names, denoting broad orders of magnitude. Orderic Vitalis's '60,000' is a well-known example. Another writer with a penchant for round thousands (and in multiples of three) is Otto of Freising. Other examples could be found.

The numerical reticence of the twelfth-century renaissance may partly have resulted from the character of the renaissance itself. As in the ninth century, men may have become less numerate as they became more literate, in response to their ancient sources of inspiration. As we saw, Cicero disapproved of mathematics; and we find ethical handbooks of Ciceronian ambience in the twelfth century and later expressly condemning 'the abacus' and 'algorism' as irrelevant to the pursuit of wisdom.[73] Various kinds of Christian influence worked even more strongly. From the beginning of the renaissance it was made clear (and put in Gratian's *Decretum* (*c.* 1140) in case anyone was in doubt) that the *quadrivium* was at best a second-class subject for a Christian to study.[74] In some departments, numeracy may have got worse as a result of these influences. For example, Roman lawyers towards the end of the eleventh century *stopped* using numbers to designate single laws, in favour of verbal titles.[75] In approximately 1130 we find a saintly abbot (Stephen of Obazine) actually *preventing* his subordinates from counting provisions during a crisis, lest—like King David—he seem to be mistrusting God.[76] These counter-trends neverthe-less remained small currents, not affecting the main tide. For innumeracy was not just a result of classical and ascetic influence. (An instance of it wholly free from such influence was the common habit of giving a person's age: 'believed to be nearly 90'; '40 or thereabouts', etc.)[77]

We shall shortly be considering the genre, civic eulogy, in which numbers first invaded literature in force. It is therefore illuminating to realize that an older tradition of civic eulogy was relatively innumerate. A typical example is William FitzStephen's description of London, inserted *c.* 1175 into his biography of Thomas Becket. Fortifications, public buildings, mills, wells, trades, industries, places of sport and acting, noble dwellings, administrative divisions, are all mentioned—but without *any* quantities for these things. A pair of figures for churches, and another pair (unlikely, incidentally) for an army contingent given thirty years before, are all the author supplies.[78] A more extreme example from the same genre comes from much later, from a time when numbers had in other circles already taken up lodgings in this type of literature. John of Jandun wrote his *In Praise of Paris* in 1323. It begins with a critique of the vague generalities which had marred previous books on the topic.[79] The author reviews chapter by chapter the splendours of the Capetian capital; its university and its faculties; its trades and traders, courts, markets, and churches. Yet not a single item deserves an exact figure. Lawyers are 'a numerous multitude'; doctors, 'so many, that if you need one you will easily find one'; churches, so many that 'perhaps none of Christendom's cities holds so many'.[80] As for private houses, to count them would be virtually 'to number stalks in a large field, or the leaves of a huge forest'.[81] The author of this tract was a famous philosopher, noted for *avant-garde* tendencies. He had friends in various branches of government; and although the great French government survey of parishes and hearths was still five years ahead, John could have ascertained some of Paris's statistics if he had tried. He did not try.

In John's case it may have been the very conscientiousness of a philosopher that denuded his work of numbers: he did not want to get them wrong. One literary tradition demanded that he should. This tradition represents the second mental habit illustrative of the innumeracy of early medieval literature. I refer to exaggeration. When medieval writers gave figures they very often inflated them. Critics will ask: 'How do we know?' In the case of gross inaccuracy in no specified direction the figures often betray themselves: scorn for numerical accuracy apparently went together with a similar scorn for consistency. The attaching of different figures by different writers to the same subject; or the attaching of the same figure by the same writer to different subjects (as in the case of Orderic's '60,000') proves an error somewhere. To measure the exaggeration is a finer task. Fortunately the task has been done for a number of cases sufficient to provide all necessary illustration succinctly.

Sir James Ramsay at the beginning of this century checked some English chroniclers' figures against such entries as could be found to correspond to them in the records of the Exchequer.[82] The Exchequer was arithmetically precocious. So it supplies an index for checking items which involved payment or receipt there. Ramsay allowed chroniclers the benefit of every doubt; yet in all the cases he tackled he found exaggeration often between ten- and twentyfold, and at times up to fifty- and sixtyfold. The chronicler Gervase of Canterbury made a tax imposed by Henry II for a war in 1159 yield £180,000. Records for the year show receipts cannot have been above £10,000.[83] Roger of Hoveden made out that between 1194 and 1196 the English government paid more than £730,000 as ransom for Cœur de Lion. Government records suggest one-sixtieth of that figure.[84] The size of the armies led to Scotland by the first two Edwards has recently been investigated. Treasury records suggest a total force of 10–11,000 for Edward I in 1298 and one of nearly 14,000 for Edward II in 1314, the campaign which led to Bannockburn. Both estimates fall far short of those given in contemporary histories. For 1298, Walter of Hemingburgh made the infantry alone number 80,000, an exaggeration of at least tenfold; while contemporary assessments of the English army at Bannockburn varied between 100,000 and 300,000—the last figure being twenty-one times the highest count that can be reached from other records.[85]

Shyness of figures; exaggeration of large numbers: in medieval Europe these features marked most literature in most places at least down to the late thirteenth century. More specimens of both could be assembled from this and even later periods. Psychologically revealing because uncontrived, they show how the antipathy to arithmetic inherited by medieval literature from its forebears struck root deep in medieval soil. The limit of clear numerical consciousness for the bulk of the literate people remained, in effect, roughly that of arithmetic in Roman numerals. Above that, exact quantity was a stranger.

### 4. THE EVOLUTION (b) THE NUMERICAL INVASION

It is impossible to say precisely when the situation just described began to change; it would still be impossible if records were fuller. Like the fingers of dawn, instances of numerical consciousness appear long before culture as a whole began to be illumined. The fact that Ramsay could check English chroniclers' exaggerations itself points to one region, possibly the first, which the fingers of dawn touched early. Both the Norman commissioner who in 1086 put '2½ villeins' down for a

Cambridgeshire village, and the government scribe who rejected the figure with a terse 'inquire quot villani' in Domesday Book, witnessed in different ways to what was probably the first bloom of a statistical sense in medieval Europe—though it should be remarked that nothing shows the Conqueror ever added up the Domesday figures.[86] Domesday was precocious. Perhaps it was even premature. The Anglo-Saxon chronicle, itself relatively numerate, doubtless voiced the average Englishman's opinion in 1085 when it abhorred as 'shameful' that the Conqueror should count England, and in such detail that 'why, not one ox, or cow, or pig, escaped notice!' But if Domesday was precocious it remained an example, which could be remembered in England by political innovators throughout the twelfth century. By the end of the same century we know for a fact that basic arithmetical knowledge existed in much wider circles than those of royal commissioners. In the legal treatise known as 'Glanvill', compiled in 1187, the capacity to count money and measure cloth is said to be the test of legal majority for a burgher's son.[87] There are other indications of fairly widespread basic arithmetic in late twelfth-century England. In France meanwhile the fingers of dawn were probably appearing fractionally more slowly. Since early French treasury records are lost it is hard to say how much more slowly. In Picardy, legal deeds, after a marked anti-numerical phase from 1025 to 1125, pick up their taste for numbers after the later date.[88] Gothic architecture, on whose mathematical prerequisites I shall say more in chapter 8, dates from *c.* 1140, at St. Denis. By the early thirteenth century France had certainly made up for any ground it had lost earlier. In 1223 a French royal official will be found tossing off from his head the annual revenues of the last two kings, to the tune of hundreds of thousands of *livres* (not in round numbers, either)—while a visiting cleric from Lausanne, to whom the boast was made, will be found remembering the figure.[89]

Signs like these of a greater number-consciousness in particular circles and trades can be tracked down in most centres of twelfth-century civilization. They blur the chronology of the metamorphosis we are tracing. But only to a certain degree. The main body of literature still has some title to represent tastes among literate people at large. Here the invasion by numbers is a fact which forces itself on our attention in one time and place.

The time and place are thirteenth-century Italy. The effect can be illustrated by three works, each in its own way psychologically representative of a substantial public. The first is the chronicle of Fra Salimbene of Parma, finished in the late 1280s. Salimbene is unsurpassed by any medieval chronicler as an illuminating gossip about his milieu. He kept in touch. Something about that milieu is therefore revealed by Salimbene's familiarity with numbers. He often mentions them. His ease with dates—year, month, and day—well exceeds what was *de rigueur* for chronicles. Page-references abound.[90] Joachite prophecy fascinates the author, with its computations of the date of Antichrist's arrival. So do more mundane figures. On some nine occasions, speaking of years of famine or plenty, Salimbene appends lists of food prices.[91] He often cites quantities, military, monetary, and spatial: 4,000 were killed, 1·4 million florins were spent on a war; snow was 'five arms' deep; and so on.[92] Besides this partiality for figures, Salimbene clearly reveals—and that in spite of our inability to check them accurately—a fastidiousness for getting numbers right. Military quantities, where they rise above perfectly plausible estimates, invariably (or almost: there is one possible exception) have 'about' or 'it is said' attached.[93] More conclusive is Salimbene's report of a battle in 1284. Genoa had sunk Pisa's navy:

I resolved not to write down the number of killed and wounded, since it is variously reported. The archbishop of Pisa actually gave a precise number in a letter to his brother the bishop of Bologna. But I decided not to write that down either, but rather to wait for the Franciscans of Genoa and Pisa to bring me a more reliable figure.[94]

Salimbene reveals here more than his own fastidiousness. Like the critical Bede, he half-consciously convicts some of his contemporaries of the opposite trait. Salimbene and his fellow-friars were pioneers.

One contemporary Salimbene could not have convicted of carelessness about numbers was the Milanese Bonvesino della Riva. As Salimbene was finishing his chronicle, this younger writer produced a tract which makes the year it was written, 1288, something of a landmark in the history of statistics. A member of the third order of Humiliati (i.e. himself half-way to being a friar), Bonvesino had already established himself as a writer of prose and verse, Latin and Italian. His tract was called *De Magnalibus urbis Mediolani*: 'The Big Things of Milan'.[95] The tract is itself such a big thing. As a literary concentration of numbers it exceeds by some ten times the size of its next medieval competitor. The numbers relate to Milan and its county in 1288: population, buildings, trades, churches, natural and artificial amenities. The city is said to contain 6,000 fountains, 1,000 retail shops, 150 hotels, 10 hospitals, 120 lawyers, 6 trumpeters, 100 armourers, 200 shrines, 200 church bells, 14 monasteries and more than 2,000 burial urns. Each day the city is said to have eaten *inter alia* over 105 tons of corn, 70 cattle (on meat-days), and (on fish-days) over 12 hundred-weight of crustaceans; and so on.[96] The work reads like a stores inventory, or account.

Stores inventories and accounts—government accounts—certainly lay behind Bonvesino's book. Not all the adding had been his own. Nor had he lacked assistants, to buttonhole busy butchers and customs officers, and wring information from them.[97] The relative sophistication of this procedure, together with a broad internal consistency in Bonvesino's figures, lend a measure of credit to his results. It is a measure we must be content with. Bonvesino too has been charged with exaggerating. But thirteenth-century Milan has had less scrutiny from modern demographers than some other urban giants of those days. Until it has more—indeed until modern estimates of medieval city populations themselves settle into some degree of consistency—judgement on Bonvesino's accuracy must wait. The Milanese enumerator must meanwhile be acclaimed for an altogether new degree of literary attention to statistics.[98] The novelty of his enterprise is sufficiently attested by the apologia he starts with: these revelations will not, he says, tempt conquerors (a possible demur against the book), but will rather frighten them away.[99] We know too that *De Magnalibus* still excited amazement in the Milan of Bonvesino's grand-children.[100]

By the time of these grandchildren (members of third orders could have families, and Bonvesino had done so) the statistical laurels had passed to Florence where, in 1347, Giovanni Villani was nearing the end of his life and work. As a document for public psychology Villani's vernacular *Cronica* excels, though in a different way from the garrulous Salimbene. For the *Cronica* was itself a prolific grandfather: it was more widely copied than any other chronicle of the late middle ages. Now Villani may give fewer figures per page than Bonvesino. But there are many more pages. Between the covers of the *Cronica* lies, in fact, the biggest thesaurus of figures in medieval historiography. Connoisseurs can challenge themselves to find in another medieval historian a passage which betrays, so guilelessly, so obsessive a preoccupation with quantity as the following:

On the 18th July 1345 the new bridge over the Arno was finished, replacing the Ponte Vecchio. It consisted of two piers and 3 arches and cost . . . florins [the space left blank and never filled in]. It was raised on solid foundations and was 32 *braccia* wide, with a road in the middle of 16 *braccia*. . . . The shops at either edge of the bridge were each 8 *braccia* wide and eight long, and were raised of stone on the solid arches. There were 43 of these shops, from which the commune drew an annual rental of over 80 gold florins.[101]

not all the *Cronica* is so dense. But it never waits on much of a pretext to break out in a numerical rash—whether for a grain price, a military figure, a rate of tax, or a sum of income or expenditure related to some individual or project. In one section, of four chapters, Villani unites all the statistics he could find about Florence in his day: revenue from toll; the salary of the *podestà*; hospitals with more than a thousand beds; the amount of wine drunk and beef eaten.[102] The items read once more like an account; and once more they acknowledge the influence of accounts. This time economic historians have scrutinized the statistics. One result has been the endorsement of most of Villani's figures as probable.[103] Where he could not discover a number, from communal registers, fugitive mercenaries, or by walking down to the Arno to pace out a bridge, Villani left a blank. That is to say, the numbers he put in were not wild guesses.

Salimbene; Bonvesino; Villani: these three writers alone might suffice to signal a breakthrough. But the sampling could go on with similar results over much of the field of thirteenth-century Italian writing. Students of astronomical records note the first—and for a long time the last—exact record of the measured (as against predicted) duration of an eclipse ('the time taken to walk 250 paces') in a book from Arezzo, relating to 1239.[104] Equally significant of this sudden enthusiasm for numbers was the burst of apocalyptic speculation associated with the works of Joachim of Fiore, speculation of which thirteenth-century Italy was the headquarters. From numbers in Daniel, Revelation, and elsewhere in scripture, the Joachites tried to work out when Antichrist would come, and in what guise. Such numerical speculations on scripture, 'unscientific' as they may appear, had been a concomitant of mathematics in both Bede and Alcuin. They would be again in Newton and Napier. The numerical aspect of Joachimism was thus entirely appropriate to Italy, where Abbot Joachim had died in the very year of Fibonacci's *Liber Abaci*. The link between prophetic and arithmetical interests in thirteenth-century Italy is exemplified best of all (better, even, than in the keen Joachite Salimbene) in Dante. Like Bede's *History*, Dante's *Divine Comedy*, though remembered now as a spring flower of literature, was in an arithmetical context the ripe fruit of a century's enthusiasm. Dante's poem was not merely set in a year determined by the current *arithmetica ecclesiastica*—the papal jubilee year of 1300. Its first line posed a riddle in mental arithmetic. And if its closing analogies came no nearer to that than geometry and mechanics (*Par.* XXXIII, 133 ff. 'Qual' è 'l geometra che tutto s'affige/per misurar lo cerchio . . .' etc.), there remained—as students of its footnotes will know—an almost obtrusive amount of mathematics in between.

The history of the statistical mentality in the Renaissance after Dante was told by Burckhardt; with, as centrepiece, the story of the Venetian Doge who, on his deathbed in 1422, regaled his colleagues from memory with an inventory of their city's revenues and armaments.[105] It has not been my purpose to follow this history beyond its opening. But there remains one respect in which Renaissance evidence can help, with its greater detail. It shows that the metamorphosis in question was no mere switch in literary fashion, but a change in human attitudes. It is true that Latin literature, as it became increasingly a pastime and less a business, in the face of advancing vernaculars, consciously returned to its classical norms—with no arithmetic.

But growing testimony to how people actually thought and spoke (rather than wrote) reveals numerical tastes as an increasingly salient fact of everyday life. The most telling result of this taste, and one which will sufficiently illustrate it, was perhaps the tendency to quantify the value of human beings. This tendency had its strictly commercial side. In the secret accounts of the Bardi and Peruzzi, Villani's contemporaries, these fathers of European banking listed all employees with a note of successive salary-scales, and debts, beside each name.[106] But where bankers wrote out their 'price-tags' for people, others thought them. Already in Dante's time Italian audiences were expected to recognize such expressions as 'a man worth a thousand florins'. The same expression was quite at home in France *c.* 1400, and was normal parlance in fifteenth-century Italy.[107] It is perhaps of interest to note that this expression represents an inverted revival of the Germanic 'wergeld' system, primitive harbinger of numbers: but whereas there a man's status had determined his price, now it was the other way round. This state of affairs even extended to dead people. Bonvesino della Riva, already, in speaking of Milan's burial urns, boasted that 'each cost at least 20,000 silver marks'.[108] As the Italian Renaissance ripened, the ever more solid marble of tombs and monuments yielded increasingly to abstract number, as emblem of dynastic glory. Patrons are to be heard privately registering the cost of all such munificence, to the florin. Nor always privately: the cost of Pius II's tomb would be openly vaunted a lifetime later by the man who paid it.[109] And no modern instance of ostentation can match the almost tasteful *naïveté* of Piero de' Medici's inscription, spotted by Professor Gombrich on the tabernacle in the church of Santissima Annunziata: 'the marble alone cost 4,000 florins'.[110]

The literary change signalled by Salimbene, Bonvesino, and Villani was not, then, a mere writers' fashion. It represented the breakthrough into literature of something more widespread: a growing familiarity with numbers among people in general.

Let us take our stand at the end of the thirteenth century, and reflect on the development that had taken place since the millennium. The abacus was in general use. Arithmetic with Arabic numerals was easily available to those who troubled to find a teacher or popular manual; and was practised by enough people, in some circles, to evoke laws restricting its public use. While specialist mathematics rose far above this common core of arithmetic, there radiated from the core a taste for precise numbers, which affected even those who may not have been able to use an abacus.

It is a long way on every level from the first years of the Northumbrian Easter dispute. Six-and-a-half centuries have seen the evolution of what is virtually a new intellectual faculty. This evolution has been traced in the last two chapters through its darker and lighter phases. It is now time to look back over it, and ask what social or political developments may have sped it on.

# CHAPTER 8

# Men and Mathematics

*Pauperis est numerare pecus*
It is the poor man who counts his sheep

Ovid, *Metamorphoses*, XIII, 824.

THE purpose of the two foregoing chapters has been to write a history so far largely unwritten. That purpose was itself part of a larger one—to examine the social background to the prehistory of modern 'physical laws'. Post-Renaissance physics, it was agreed, depends closely on mathematics. But this latter science did not spring ready-made out of the ground in the late fifteenth century. It emerged from a long medieval development, mostly hidden from familiar historical documents. This is the development whose outline has been traced. We now examine its social dimension.

Both to show what the examination entails and to begin its first stage, here is a current view of the state of knowledge on the subject:

It may seem strange, and even painful [writes Professor Salomon Bochner of Princeton], to contemplate that our present-day mathematics, which is beginning to control both the minutest distances between elementary particles and the intergalactic vastness of the universe, owes its origination to countinghouse needs of 'money changers' of Lombardy and the Levant. But, regrettably, I do not know by what arguments to disagree, when economic determinists, from the right, from the center, and from the left, all in strange unison agree.[1]

The very perplexity of this distinguished writer on mathematics, when it comes to the medieval problem, would be enough to justify the enterprise attempted in these three chapters. Now we are equipped with an outline history, let us try to reduce the perplexity; starting with the 'countinghouse' view of mathematical origins. Since 'money changers' were

only an especially money- and account-conscious type of
merchant, I shall speak not just of them, but of commerce in
general.

## I. COMMERCE

As the main source of European arithmetic, merchants'
accounting presents strong claims. It is true that early
commercial methods form almost as dark a subject as early
arithmetic, and it is dangerously easy to read preconceptions
back into their common darkness. Nevertheless, there are scraps
of evidence from the edge of the darkness which do bind the
two hidden developments together.

The first scrap is nothing other than the common obscurity of
their history. Countinghouses and the art of counting emerge
from dark ages with similar outlines. To state the obvious first:
thirteenth-century Italy saw not only a manifest growth in
mathematical consciousness, among both professionals and
amateurs; but also the most conspicuous urban commercial
boom of the middle ages. The two developments coincide
earlier, and in a more subtle respect. Both histories ran much of
their early course among illiterates, in the days of 'dust'
numerals, and of the abacus. Subsequently, evidence for both
developments often appears in vernacular contexts. It had been
specifically in the vernacular, in seventh-century Lombardy
and Gaul (still just commercial areas then) that our 'arithmetical' way of dating days in the month first began.[2] Again, the
earliest evidence of the learning of the 'times-table' in schools
indicates that vernacular was used for it.[3] Professor Bernhard
Bischoff has found, too, that vernacular intrusions into learned
language not infrequently occur in commercial or numerical
connections. For instance, archbishop Theodore of Canterbury
in the seventh century, who wrote in Latin with a sprinkling of
words from scholars' Greek, employed Anglo-Saxon coin- and
weight-names.[4] Similarly, among Greek words which drifted
into western Latin in the course of the middle ages the only
words from vernacular (as against scholars') Greek were
number-names.[5] A common association of mathematics and
commerce with the vernacular is also found in that heartland of
medieval finance, Tuscany. In the early thirteenth century the
first known documents in Tuscan dialect (*c.* 1211) prove also to

be the first known written commercial accounts of the European middle ages.[6] In Tuscany accounts remained in the vulgar tongue.[7] A crowning example of the association with the vernacular is Dante. Dante, literary prophet of vernacular Italian, was also—as has just been seen—the prophet of literary arithmetic; as well as native to that commercial *enfant terrible*, Florence.

The early histories of commerce and of arithmetic are obscure. So it is dangerous to identify them. But from the edges of the abysses from which both histories emerge there is enough evidence to suggest there was a connection. In particular, both seem to have been associated first with illiteracy, then with the vernacular.

When evidence becomes fuller and more direct the connection between commerce and arithmetic is confirmed. In the twelfth century and later, writers about reckoning will say or suggest that merchants were good reckoners. State accounting, for its part, acknowledged their stimulus: *The Dialogue of the Exchequer* (*c.* 1178) pointed to the facility of 'those who condescend to trade' in 'hiding their wealth', as a motive for stricter accounting by government in dealing with townsmen than when dealing with countrymen.[8] The same stimulus went downwards from traders to the public at large. 'By this method,' promised one handbook on algorism—by Jean de Meurs (1343)—'you will now be able with little outlay to settle all accounts with changers and other people in an advantageous way.'[9] Such tribute by specialists to the link of arithmetic and trade is not always explicit. But it is often implicit. Many of Leonardo Fibonacci's examples, for instance, are drawn from business: 'The man who went to Constantinople to sell three pearls'; 'The two ships which sailed together'; 'Finding the equivalence of bad money and good'; 'The two men who formed a company in Constantinople'. The mere titles of Leonardo's problems point towards commerce as a source for his art.[10]

A common connection with illiterate and vernacular culture; the deliberate statements of writers on accounting and arithmetic: all tend to underline the view that it was in 'counting-houses' that the art of arithmetic was born. Numerous other coincidences between their twin histories further underline the view. The very name of the practical art of algorism echoed, by way of its exponent, 'Al-Khwarismi', the name of the great emporium on the Caspian where Arabs had learned the Indian art of arithmetic. On the eve of the Renaissance in Europe the same geographical coincidence would be repeated in Florence and Nuremberg: both of them leaders in both commerce and mathematics. If seekers for coincidences were not satisfied with that, the work of Luca Pacioli would provide more. The most voluminous writer on pure arithmetic of the Renaissance, Pacioli wrote standard handbooks on both pure, and commercial arithmetic. Finally, the connection between the two currents is corroborated even by those ecclesiastical sources which tried to hold aloof from both. The corroboration can be explicit: a homilist who has occasion to mention the 'beans' and 'little stones' used for arithmetic, also mentions that they 'represent marks of silver'.[11] Or it can be implicit: one conspicuous intrusion of number into ecclesiastical literature concerns sums of money paid for church office by simonists— traders in the sacred.[12] The commercial possibilities offered by corrupt use of church property may indeed have been one stimulus to clerks to study the first art of the *quadrivium*. A thirteenth-century satirist, who thought it was, humorously changed the name of this fundamental art to *aerismetica*: 'the art of money'.[13]

There can be no doubt, then, that the needs of commerce formed one important stimulus to the spread and growth of arithmetic. Money divides and multiplies easily and precisely. Goods can be reduced by it to a common measure; and its use encourages their circulation. The spread of money through a society is a direct invitation to it to calculate with numbers. Especially from the millennium, European commerce accepted that invitation; and the commercial boom of thirteenth-century Italy, we may surmise, contributed so strongly to the impetus towards arithmetical thinking that literature, our main witness, at last dropped its inhibitions and registered the change.

This is the first conclusion. It is a conclusion which, without anticipating what has to be said at the end of this chapter, we can profitably relate to the psychological phenomenon described in chapter 3: the 'avarice' of which preachers complained, in the eleventh century and with new vehemence in the thirteenth. Whatever else could be said for or against a man's concern for money, this concern directly stimulated the growth of an arithmetical sense.

This is the first conclusion; but only the first. As a solitary socio-political explanation of the rise of arithmetic the 'countinghouse' theory has weaknesses. It is time to take stock of them, and with that, to dismiss all idea of reducing the miracles of modern mathematics to a mere commercial origin. The weaknesses are principally two. The first is that no known medieval specialist mathematician can be shown to have been a merchant. The same goes, as it happens, for the writers adduced in the last chapter as peculiarly conscious of numbers—with the exception of Giovanni Villani, whose omnivorous interests made him a freak anyway. The only pure mathematician of the middle ages ever described as a merchant is in fact Leonardo Fibonacci, the greatest of them—though rather more often it is his father who is described as a merchant. However, the only direct authority on Leonardo's life is himself. He says nothing of his own livelihood beyond what is implied by dedications to the emperor, and to a leading imperial courtier. The phrase Leonardo uses to describe Fibonacci senior is that he was 'a [or 'the'] public scribe in the *duana* of Bougie, put in authority for the benefit of Pisan merchants going there'.[14] A clerk of the customs is not a merchant. It might be contended, perhaps, that the son of the customs clerk met a lot of merchants, and therefore might have *learned* his mathematics from one or more of them. But that too appears to be wrong. What Leonardo says of his own study is that it was under a *mirabili magisterio*: an expression implying specialist tuition, undoubtedly—from the circumstances—a Moor.[15] What can be demonstrated in one case can be guessed for others. Nothing suggests that any other major medieval writer on mathematics was directly beholden to a professional trader for the main substance of his knowledge. The only mercantile arithmeticians were writers on mercantile arithmetic. But historians of mathematics are agreed that mercantile arithmetic was a markedly inferior branch of the subject. As for the superior branches, its exponents stood at a distinct distance from practical commerce. Indeed some of them (e.g. Alexander of Ville-Dieu, Jordanus Nemorarius, and

Luca Pacioli) were friars—whose voluntary poverty was a deliberate repudiation of traders' preoccupations.

That is one weakness in the 'countinghouse' theory. The second, similar to it, emerges from arithmetic's literary history. If business had been the main stimulus to Fibonacci's researches the *Liber Abaci* would survive in more than three manuscripts.[16] The paucity of manuscripts of twelfth-century algorisms, similarly, and the primacy in popularity, among thirteenth-century algorisms, of brief, middle-grade manuals like Sacrobosco's suggests that the business public, whatever its practical skills, was decisively behind specialists in mathematical sophistication.[17] As for the vernacular associations of practical reckoning, that reckoning had associations on the other side, too: algorisms in the vulgar tongue were in fact a negligible minority before 1500—among literally hundreds of Latin ones.[18] Far from spurring on arithmetical advance, some otherwise dynamic merchants (in every region of Europe, even Italy) can even appear puzzlingly conservative in the field—accounting—which brought them into contact with arithmetic.[19]

These demurs, biographical and literary, to the 'countinghouse' theory, do not rob commerce of its influence; only of its monopoly. For to make the countinghouse the prime source of European arithmetic is to state only half the truth. It is indeed to simplify even that half to the point of risking distortion. For the truth—or this half of it—was that as money pierced its way further and further into human relationships, it brought its own innate arithmetic into everyone's lives, not just traders'. The problem-examples in Leonardo's *Liber Abaci* include, besides commercial matters about men going to Constantinople to sell pearls etc., puzzles about soldiers' and labourers' wages, about the purchase of relatively small quantities of meat or apples, and about other everyday situations.[20] Because money involved sums, and sums (as Leonardo said) created mental habits, the common transactions of an increasingly liquid economy stimulated numerical thinking generally. The merchant was only a special instance. Thriving in a milieu of competition, he found money a means to success: the more competitive he was the deeper he imbibed its arithmetic. Fra Giordano of Pisa said in 1303—with some exaggeration no doubt—that the Florentine merchant 'did nothing day or night but think and calculate'.[21] Such a man thought arithmetically, in and out of his countinghouse; and when he had children, whether they followed him into trade, or became friars or mathematicians, he would pass on to them a deep familiarity with number. This is surely the merchant's direct role in the rise of mathematics. It was not that of a pioneer, or even a patron of pioneers. It was that of a battler in the world of money, and, as such, the leading recipient of the arithmetical stimulus that issued from it.

## 2. GOVERNMENT

This, then, is half the truth about the social origins of arithmetic. The other half remains to be looked for. A glance back at our miniature history is enough to show where the search must start. In the un-mathematical dark ages, two men, outside a narrow circle of scholars, stood out as enthusiasts for mathematics. Both were kings, the greatest of their respective generations: Charlemagne and Otto the Great. The same lesson can be taught the other way round. If the five chief bearers of medieval mathematical tradition in their respective centuries—Bede, Alcuin, Gerbert, Adelard of Bath, and Leonardo of Pisa—had one salient sociological feature in common, it was that they lived the latter part of their lives as friends of monarchs. Coincidences have been picked out between the histories of trade and arithmetic. These, between the histories of politics and arithmetic, are as significant. They extend further than merely these two sets of names. And they are supported by still other coincidences. Thirteenth-century Italy saw the emergence, it was shown, both of the arithmetical mentality in writers, and of domineering merchant communities. But it also saw the emergence of a third phenomenon: the mature city-state, with its stress on state-sovereignty, underpinned by Roman Law. Roman Law itself may have significance for us. Now that the fortunes of Arabic numerals have been traced it cannot escape notice that the fortunes of Roman Law show curious parallels. Arabic numerals and Roman Law both enjoyed a common bloom in thirteenth-century Italy, and again in late-thirteenth- and early-fourteenth-century France. Both came late, and with the same amount of lateness, into England; which embraced neither with any warmth until the sixteenth century—her central monarchy having been founded before these unlikely twins began their conquests.

Now the association of arithmetic with the growth of centralized government, implied by these coincidences, is partly a mere extension of the 'countinghouse' theory. Authorities needed arithmetic because they, like merchants, had countinghouses. Government arithmetic was still in this measure commercial. It was indeed commercial in more than this measure. Trade was often the ultimate stimulus to government arithmetic. Nearly all the great governmental numbering enterprises of the central middle ages, from Domesday on, owed at least part of their origin to some ruler's desire to sponge up liquidity, created by trade. The same went for the complex taxation arrangements of twelfth- and thirteenth-century Italian communes, with their high demands on the capacity of officials to work out fair shares and proportions.[22] There was yet another sense in which government arithmetic could be analogous to commercial. Certain patterns in organization in the two spheres were shared: for example, internal accounting between ruler and agent resembled in principle that of a big business. Government accountants were for this reason able to learn methods from practitioners lower down the scale, like abbeys. From one angle, then, the encouragement given by kings and communes to arithmetic was the same in essence as that provided by trade.

But this was so only from one angle. From all others, government enters our inquiry in a class of its own. The reasons for its special status are clear even within the same sphere of accountancy. One reason is that a ruler commanded unique intellectual resources. He could cream the merchants themselves: Jews, and later Italians and other professional businessmen, were copiously used as financiers by northern governments. And he could cream scholars: Adelard possibly, and Turchill certainly (a distinguished abacist of the twelfth century) were Exchequer clerks. The second reason why kings in their countinghouses had a special status as breeders of arithmetic was the size of their field of operations. Government revenue in the main states far exceeded that of any one private merchant. The geographical expansion of areas effectively taxed—coming on top of a fairly

steady inflation of the older currencies—had at the same time
the effect of raising the sums administrators had to reckon
with. Thus Siena was spending some 60,000 *lire* p.a. in 1231; a
century later the figure was well over twice that.[23] Louis VII of
France's 228,000 *livres* p.a. of 1180 (already the outcome of one
expansion) had risen to a million in 1328, and would be 4·7
million by the end of the middle ages.[24] Ingredient sums grew
proportionately. As master of the biggest as well as the best
apparatus for counting money, government was thus pre-
eminent in practical reckoning. In England the term 'wardrobe
counter', used from the late middle ages for the more de luxe
type of abacus counter—an acknowledged creation of Louis
IX's treasury, imported to England—would show public
recognition of this fact.[25] The promotion may have extended
even to arithmetical concepts. It happens that the word
'million' (meaning a thousand thousand) came into use—its use
as a sobriquet for Marco Polo being only one of many—at just
the epoch when the revenue of the richest of European
governments, the French, topped a million units.[26]

Governments, like merchants, had countinghouses; but
bigger and better ones. In this respect alone public accountants
excelled as nurses of arithmetic. But the role of government in
our story is not just different in degree. It differed in kind;
necessarily, for the relation of a ruler to everyone else is *not* the
same as that of a merchant, whatever the analogies. A ruler's
function, or one of them, is to take decisions on behalf of many
people, covering long periods, with big resources. His decisions
call for proportionately better conceptual rehearsal of action to
be taken—that is to say, more thought. This at bottom is why
government tends to nourish learning. The principle will
appear again, with special instances, in respect of medieval
literate culture in Part III. It applies now to mathematics, of all
sorts. For it can be shown that, more even than commerce, it was
government, of various kinds and levels, that mainly encouraged
the arithmetical mentality.

'Of various kinds and levels'; the qualification is made at the
outset to ward off any impression that we are dealing only with
governments diplomatically recognized, so to speak; with
Charlemagne and his patronage of Alcuin, or Frederick II
Hohenstaufen and Michael Scot. For government must be

defined here simply by its function of organizing people. And this definition includes bishoprics and the leadership of religious orders. It is as well that it does. For these church rulers shared with communes the laurels for having pioneered, largely in obscurity, some of the most crucial of political techniques later put in monarchies. Among the techniques was that of thinking with numbers. Ascetic and Latin traditions might inhibit arithmetic in the church. But practice here pulled the other way. The two-way pull is sometimes apparent as a tension in one person, much as it had been in King David.[27] Why bishops and religious orders were pioneers in this field was that some of them, usually those dubbed reformers, had religious reasons for taking ordinary governmental duties exceptionally seriously. How seriously, can be told without even leaving the field we have dwelt in so far, accounting. Long before money's age of expansion, bishoprics and abbeys set an example in the measuring and dividing-up of farm produce. After the eleventh century, although bishops as such were largely outrun in this field by the lay governments round them, the precocity of reformed religious orders remained. Bonvesino della Riva (himself a Tertiary of the Humiliati) used a variety of sources for his statistics within Milan; but when it came to assessing the produce of a country estate he spoke only of a Cistercian abbey. We can be sure these were the only accounts available to him.[28] In France in roughly the same epoch the spur given to accounting by a reformed order can be assessed from the visitation-register of the Franciscan archbishop of Rouen, Odo Rigord. The register harps on no fault as often as bad accounting, in monasteries and convents. The pattern of complaints through the book gives grounds for thinking the Franciscan new broom was in fact sweeping this form of negligence clean, in the course of twenty years' visitation.[29] In Germany, for its part, the Teutonic Order is acknowledged to have surpassed even the cities of the Hansa in the excellence of its accounting, in which the north generally lagged behind.[30] Other examples could be given.

The stimulus given to arithmetic by government, thus broadly understood, went beyond accounting. That was indeed fortunate for arithmetic. For rulers in their counting-houses cannot explain, any more than merchants in theirs can, the higher flights of arithmetic. It was Fibonacci *senior* who was the communal customs-clerk, not Leonardo the mathematician. Public accountants (of whom customs-clerks were a subspecies) can sometimes be shown to have been mathematically conservative, no less than some businessmen; for instance, in clinging on to Roman numerals much longer than necessary.[31]

So we have to look beyond the counting of money, and seek out what else governments had to count. The first thing that suggests itself is 'people'. Governments governed individuals—another arithmetical term, as it happens, and appropriately a product of the twelfth century.[32] As rulers' writs ran wider, and European population grew—by some 50 per cent from 1150 to 1300, and by as much as 400 per cent in some urban areas[33]—the numbers of these human units grew. Population-censuses more elaborate than count-ups of abbey-estates, or inquiries like Domesday Book, were still a thing of the future in 1300.[34] But official headcounting still had its part in nourishing the arithmetical mentality; in two ways in particular.

The more important way was in the matter of soldiers. The inaccuracy of medieval writers' military estimates must not obscure for us the merit that lay in their being made at all: armies, in the early middle ages, enticed literary minds into a field they did not otherwise enter. With all the more compulsion they enticed government minds. The very nature of Sir James Ramsay's research, in checking military estimates in chronicles against Exchequer records of payments to soldiers, shows that governments had to be on the scene here long before anyone else. From the monetary point of view mercenaries, and from the strategic point of view infantry (with its higher numbers), fed this compulsion. Infantry began to turn the scale against cavalry from just before 1200. Its effect on public arithmetic came by way of both recruiting and strategy. Thirteenth-century Italian communes, defying both each other and armies from north of the Alps, had to count each able citizen as a soldier. Their need was all the greater in the 1280s, and it is no accident that our statistics from Milan and Florence start appearing then. Both Bonvesino and Villani based their population-figures chiefly on military censuses taken just before.[35] As for the arithmetic of infantry strategy, let us hear that great military authority for the middle ages, the Late Latin author Vegetius:

How to measure the space taken by a formation. 1,000 yards of ground will hold 1,666 foot-soldiers, each soldier taking three feet. If you wish to form six lines on ground 1,000 yards wide you need 9,996 soldiers. If you wish to stretch the same number out in three ranks it will cover 2,000 yards (though it is better to have more lines than stretch out your line). There should be six feet, as I said earlier, from line to line (one foot of which is occupied by the soldiers themselves). So if you form six lines, an army of 10,000 men will cover 42 yards one way and 1,000 the other. By this calculation it is easy to form up 20,000 or 30,000 men, depending on the size of the ground. When a general knows how many a given area can hold, he cannot go wrong.[36]

Can we wonder why Vegetius was the vade-mecum of so many medieval commanders? And as we saw earlier, it happens— whether or not the reasons have anything to do with the present discussion—that Vegetius' appeal became particularly strong in this same epoch, the late thirteenth century.[37]

Governmental head-counting led by a second route towards arithmetical thinking: by way not of military contest this time, but political. For a variety of reasons certain centralized governments ceased to be content with rule by the one, and developed within an oligarchic framework a new means of achieving rule by the many: the majority principle. A vague form of the principle may or may not have been recognized in Italian towns throughout the dark ages.[38] The first clear acceptance of it in a constitution was in 1172, for the election of the Doge of Venice.[39] From there (probably) the church took it up, in 1179, for disputed papal elections.[40] The principle spread during the next century down both channels, communal and ecclesiastical, to find its Promised Land especially in the former, in the Italian cities of the same late thirteenth century. The principle there meant rule by number, precisely counted. It extended in communes in every sphere where it was compatible with the maintenance of oligarchy, and it acquired a whole apparatus of laws about vote-counting, ballots, etc.[41] From communes it went into university constitutions, as at Bologna in the constitutions of 1317–47, where it stood as model for Europe's law students, relentlessly defying any authority but that of the half-plus-one.[42] In the church this political arithmetic held less strict sway. But it was once again through a reformed order, the Dominican, that it probably had what proved its most influential victory. For Dominicans used to provide confessors for kings. They did so in England when parliament was a child; and although post-twelfth-century England was here again an arithmetical laggard, the foundations, at least, of this sort of numbering were laid even here in the late middle ages.[43]

Governments counted people, then, as well as money; and their doing so played a part in fostering a numerical sense in all who came near them. A numerical sense: what of more lofty mathematics? To get nearer to this, let us recall what governments do. They take momentous decisions for big human groups, with proportionately big resources. Their decisions touch not only men's mutual relations, as with war and constitutions; but also men's common relation with nature. But nature is a book written in the language of mathematics. And more than four centuries before Galileo the growth of strong public authority had in fact enabled men to open at least a page or two of that book. It opened, then as later, at two points: where men acted on nature, and vice versa.

Historians will always be in some ignorance about medieval technology. Much of it was a compound of tradition with inspired hit-and-miss. But there were notable exceptions, increasingly from *c.* 1200, for example, in the spheres of navigation, canal-building, and clocks. Some of these exceptions certainly involved a modicum of mathematics. Mathematicians themselves repeated a tradition (first found in Herodotus) that the art of geometry had its origin in the challenge presented by the Nile to the Egyptians, and only later became an abstract science.[44] The consciousness thus expressed, that mathematics served technology, found plenty of contemporary illustration in the thirteenth century. A pre-eminent case was that of building. Architectural historians have patiently measured Gothic cathedrals, and studied and extrapolated from documents; and have established beyond doubt that the building of these big cathedrals presupposed an elaborate understanding both of geometry and—especially through the need to calculate proportions and angles—of its accessory arithmetic. This sophisticated masonic art was profitable to those who professed it. Largely as a result, it remained a more or less well-guarded secret of professionals. This in turn curbed its direct influence on the minds of others. But the same could be said of many esoteric skills, which have still helped shape thought indirectly. To build big buildings, that stayed up and looked right, craftsmen had to open a page of nature's mathematical book; and by doing so eventually made its mysteries available to others.[45]

Whether Gothic architecture deserves a place in connection with government is another question. In many respects it does not. But it does in one respect; and the fact is more worth stating because it is not always the first to be owned by architectural historians. Gothic cathedrals could not have been built without mathematicians. But there was another precondition. The training and feeding of these experts called for a big concentration of capital, deployed in the case of cathedrals by public authority. Chartres's great monument to geometry also commemorates (and was doubtless partly meant to) a bishop's effective control of a wealthy diocese. In 1194 the Bishop of Chartres resolved to channel no less than three years' diocesan revenue into the project; and that was only the start.[46] Any profit and status professional architects had came largely via this and similar sources.

Rulers built big buildings. They also took big decisions, in the light of circumstances which usually were, and were nearly always believed to be, uncontrollable, but which might be exploited if judged correctly. It was perhaps this burden of decision in courtly circles which put a premium on the art which claimed to reduce it to manageable proportions: astrology.

The contribution of so discredited a study as astrology to the rise of modern science greets us as a constant surprise. This may be why astrology, like the arithmetic it involved, has had relatively little historiography of its own—though it is now beginning to get it.[47] One thing already clear is that astrology involved the most complex arithmetic its epoch knew. In this it was in a sense the successor to the calendar *computus*, which had headed the list of mathematics' clients well into the abacus period. In the course of the twelfth century, interest in the skies turned increasingly from calendars to horoscopes, and with new techniques to aid it, brought arithmetic along too. The new technique of Arabic numerals was indeed all but indispensable to the astrology of the twelfth century. Each discipline helped the early success of the other. A sign of their connection is that in twelfth-century literature, handbooks on algorism apart, it is in editions of Albumazar and other astrological authors that the Arabic numerals are most at home.[48] The calculations the numerals were used for, although direct record of them is almost wholly lost, can be partially reconstructed from the known principles of astrology. The reconstruction makes it clear that they were much more ambitious than other known or surmisable medieval calculations. This deduction is confirmed by the words of the Florentine Prosdocimo de' Beldomandi, writing early in the fifteenth century. Introducing his own book on arithmetic he sought to exemplify the kind of problem that tested a system of calculation, and thought at once of 'an astrological calculation'.[49] The peculiar mathematical demands of astrology find further witness in the character of legend and report about some astrologers. Frederick II's astrologer Michael Scot was credited with a specifically mathematical wizardry: such as being able to calculate the height of the sky above the earth to a few inches.[50] More sober testimony to Michael's mathematical reputation is the dedication to him, with the title 'Master', of the second edition of Leonardo Fibonacci's *Liber Abaci*. Again, at the end of the fifteenth century, a list of famous astrologers compiled by the French practitioner Symon de Phares, frequently adds that a named astrologer was also a great calculator, as if the two things were virtually synonymous: 'fut moult expert astrologien ... et moult subtilleur carculleur'; 'subtil carculateur et grant astrologien'; and so on.[51] Padua's chair of astrology certainly had a vigorous, if largely invisible, tradition of mathematical calculation by the time Galileo held it. The intergalactic vastness of the post-Galilean universe, in other words, far from being new colonial territory for serious mathematics, was in effect its medieval breeding-ground.

*Sicque in ceteris ... usque in infinitum progreditur*. Like a calculation on the abacus, the enumeration of stimuli to medieval arithmetic could itself go on to infinity. We cannot go so far, and must be content to have named only the more important areas from which stimulus came. Next to nothing has been said of number-mysticism; partly because plenty has been said on it elsewhere; and partly because number-mysticism, while as esoteric a practice as astrology, fell far short of it as a compulsion to specialist arithmetic. A more damaging neglect has perhaps been that of farming—a world with which the experts themselves must have lived in close contact. (Bernelinus, best of the early writers on the abacus (*c.* 1020) grumbled at the interruption caused in his work by the wine harvest.)[52] The primitive exigencies of land-division, sheep-rearing, and the measurement of arable produce may have coaxed even peasants into elementary arithmetic earlier than records show. Assumptions are hazardous: shepherds (anthropologists report) can know hundreds of sheep as individuals without having any idea 'how many' there are.[53] What is not hazardous is that with the growth of the urban food market (and palpably in the thirteenth century) rural estate managers came to appreciate keenly the value of good measuring and accounting—not only Cistercians and Teutonic knights, but some leading lay estate managers like the Englishman Walter of Henley.

An intellectual development, mathematics; two social developments, commerce and centralized government: without the second pair of developments, the first would be all but inconceivable. In that measure they furnish its 'social dimension'. It remains to see what this signifies for men taken one by one.

### 3. MATHEMATICS AND THE INDIVIDUAL

Trade and government were social facts. Intellectual skills belonged primarily to the individual. Medieval arithmetic has been located in its main social milieux. I shall now suggest how arithmetic related to individual psychology.

As the Wheel of Fortune began to turn, it was argued in Part I, an individual's chance of moving up on it engendered in him an active attraction for power, economic and political. The attraction awoke his reason, whose use offered power. Since some people were more exposed to the attraction than others, it was among these, the more exposed, that we were led to expect the more conspicuously rational forms of activity.

Before any attempt is made to say how this scheme applies to arithmetic, it must be observed that the latter was the purest manifestation of reason. Medieval arithmetic may have had its limitations. But these did not deprive the discipline of its peculiarly rational character; a character which was in fact recognized throughout the middle ages by those who came in contact with it. The character was recognized, first of all, by the learned. Scholars who wrote on the first art of the *quadrivium* showed in various ways their awareness of that art's exceptional logical autonomy; of its consequent distinction from all others, even its junior twin geometry; and of its call for a specifically intellectual power. Boethius, for example, had written: 'arithmetic is a science which needs no other, resting on itself as a foundation', and he observed that the other arts of the *quadrivium* depended on arithmetic, not vice versa.[54] Boethius was echoed in this by the medieval writers whom his classic *De Arithmetica* inspired.[55] Again, the peculiar rigour of arithmetic (this time coupled with geometry) was stressed by the great philosopher of learning John of Salisbury in the twelfth century: in contrast to the uncertainty of natural sciences, 'what mathematics concludes, in regard to such things as numbers, proportions, and figures is indubitably true and cannot be otherwise'.[56] Stories about the origin of the liberal arts meanwhile reflected a similar appreciation of the exceptional rational purity of arithmetic. For instance, arithmetic (with astronomy) had been imparted by Abraham to the Egyptians, who 'as men of the very sharpest *ingenium*' were able to develop the other arts from this beginning.[57] Other such remarks, and legends, could be gleaned from the theorists of learning to show they were perfectly aware of arithmetic's special logical status.

Perhaps more important in our context is that this logical status was also recognized by the less learned. Their recognition is betrayed, not in plain words, but in characteristically indirect ways; and two ways in particular. One is through a game, and two legends about it; the other, through a word.

Chess began its rise to fashion in Europe just before the year 1000. Though there is doubt about the earliest rules of European chess (where dice may have been used), the game soon settled down essentially to the form it still possesses, as a game excluding chance. Its purely rational character was acknowledged. Chess was tolerated by Roman law 'because it resides in natural reason and does not depend on the forces of chance'; and the more genial authorities of the central middle ages here followed Justinian's example.[58] But chess was not only thought of as specially rational. It was also believed to be intimately related to arithmetic. The association may have derived partly from the mere resemblance between the chessboard and the counting-board, as at the Exchequer. But it went deeper. One legend gave chess and arithmetic the same inventor (a Greek, Attalus Asiaticus)—and such genealogies were a normal way of expressing a belief in conceptual kinship.[59] A more graphic expression of the same idea was given in a second legend: that of the 'doubling of the chessboard'. The inventor of chess—an Indian, this time—was begged by the Shah of Persia to name a reward for his invention; and he asked for as many grains of corn as would provide one for the first square, two for the second, four for the third, etc. The total comes to $1 \cdot 8 \times 10^{19}$. The trick is *par excellence* a mathematician's.[60] The assumption that chess, the rational game, came from arithmetic, hid the apparently paradoxical fact that arithmetic was in practice less applied to chess than to games of chance. Dice-throwers were already working towards a simple probability-theory by the late thirteenth century.[61] But the exception again proves the rule. Arithmetic might turn even a game of chance into one of reason. But the arithmetic of chess was innate in it.

Chess and reason; chess and arithmetic: this association already gives one clue to the popular acknowledgement of arithmetic's high intellectual rank. What games and legends show can be shown also by etymology. In the metropolis of medieval reckoning, Italy, from the thirteenth century on, the word *ragione* was normally used, outside the study, to mean 'account'. *Ragionare* meant 'to calculate'; and *Libro della Ragione* not 'Book of Logic', but 'Ledger'.[62] These usages were based on both classical and medieval Latin, where *racio* appeared with other terms—*computus, calculus*, and their derivatives—in references to accounts and calculations. But the near-monopoly of *ragione*, which was also the usual Italian word for 'reason' in our own sense, makes it a particularly telling example. It was

a half-conscious tribute to the bond between the two
meanings.

Arithmetic, then, was a skill in pure reason. In numbers, it
was what the art of dialectic was in the less pure realm of words.
(The statuary in Auxerre's Gothic cathedral actually muddled
the two.)[63] A consequence followed in psychology. If reason led
to power, so also and especially—must arithmetic. This too was
understood. The very word arithmetic was given a bogus
etymology (by Erigena, copied by theorists of learning in the
central middle ages) as deriving from Greek words for 'the *power*
[*virtus*] of number'.[64] The same message can be read elsewhere.
The inclusion of mathematics among the confused enthusiasms
of Roger Bacon will be recalled from chapter 5, and will serve,
in the context of what was said there of astrology, to show that
mathematics' role in the mastery of nature was itself already
dimly recognized.[65] The science of number could also lead to
mastery in a human milieu. Some of the practical uses which
various public and private magnates found for arithmetic have
been indicated. Taken together, these uses suggest a certain
significance of mathematics for the individual. The two areas
where arithmetic most throve, commerce and government,
were, among many other things, society's two main staircases.
In a word: numerical skill could raise a man.

Contemporaries saw this as a commonplace. A burgher's son
had to count and measure to become 'of age' in Henry II's
England. In Villani's competitive Florence pupils flocked in
hundreds to schools for algorism. These, and other such facts
leave no doubt that persons in the commercial world saw the
prudential virtues of arithmetic.[66] The equation of arithmetic
and opportunity held good also on the higher staircase, public
service. The *Secretum Secretorum*, that classic recipe for intelligence in politics, actually put arithmetic at the top of the
sciences kings should seek in a minister. He should be 'skilled in
all sciences; but especially in arithmetic, because it is a true
science, and is a good proof of intellectual sharpness'.[67] The
more pragmatic Philippe de Beaumanoir meanwhile gave
similar advice to his French bailiff: together with 'soutil
engieng', the bailiff should 'bien savoir conter': 'be able to
count well'—or make good deficiencies from his pocket, and be
suspected of disloyalty into the bargain.[68]

This lifting power of arithmetic was not a matter of mere hope, or theory. People actually rose through it. Where the capacity to 'bien savoir conter' was only one of many skills in a servant of commerce or government, its effect cannot be isolated. But the capacity occasionally stood out, and there we can find clues. It is a fact, for example, that a man who was perhaps the most conspicuous shooting star of medieval commerce, Francesco Datini of Prato, left in his accounts proof of excellence in just this regard.[69] In government circles, another fact is that the victorious aristocratic Guelf party of Florence prescribed, in its early-fourteenth-century statutes, that as many as three out of its party treasurers must be *popolani* (commoners): they were clearly the accounting experts, and were co-opted to the party leadership for this reason.[70] A more general lesson is suggested by a reflection on the famous careers we considered earlier. The five successive laureates of medieval mathematics, from Bede to Fibonacci, became acquainted with kings. Four of them shared another biographical feature—not a common one, either, among famous men then. Except for Alcuin, none is known to have been of noble or knightly birth. Bede (the only case of any doubt) was born on a monastic estate, just possibly of a free family. Adelard and Leonardo were common townsmen. (Alcuin too, though noble, may have been born and bred in York itself.) While Gerbert, the founder of medieval arithmetic if anyone was, was also the most prodigious upstart of the early middle ages—whose rise from an 'obscuro loco' to the papacy would have no certainly known imitator until the late thirteenth century.[71]

Such an arbitrary sample of individuals might of course be a freak, and remain so even if it were extended. But the impression it gives can fortunately be corroborated from a very much bigger sample, and one we do not have to choose ourselves. The sample is not one expressly of arithmeticians. It is of astrologers. But the role of arithmetic in astrology has been noted, and the source—which often actually says its astrologers were 'great calculators' etc.[72]—is in fact the nearest thing we have to a contemporary roll of mathematicians. About 1498, an astrologer living in Lyons, Symon de Phares, started writing a huge apologia for his art. His aim was to get himself out of an archbishop's prison and into the favour of King Charles VIII. The first part of the apologia, all that ever got written, purported to be a descriptive list of all the great men who had ever practised astrology. Great men: it aimed to dazzle detractors of the art by showing the worldly greatness of its practitioners: (in the words of the preface) 'patriarchs, prophets, popes, cardinals, archbishops, bishops, emperors, kings, dukes, counts and many other noble men, wise men, grave persons and great doctors, philosophers, and others'.[73]

Symon de Phares' purpose, then, was to show the worldly greatness of astrologers. For students of the social background of medieval mathematics the significance of his book is that this is precisely what it fails to do. A brief scrutiny of the list of astrologers will substantiate this. Most of it (about three-quarters by volume) has no claim to historical reliability: it starts with Adam, Noah, and includes many other names whose connection with astrology is clearly a tendentious fiction. The part of the list which can claim some reliability contains, minus a few repetitions and manifest mistakes or irrelevancies, some 330 names, covering the period *c.* 1180–*c.* 1495.[74] These names fall into two groups. Much the smaller is of people with high rank, but who are not in fact stated or implied to have been more than *patrons* of astrologers, and who therefore would not have had to know professional mathematics.[75] The remainder consists of people who were professional astrologers, but were not of high rank. A closer look at this remainder reveals something else. No less than half of its astrologers are expressly said to have been in service to some high potentate of church or state, or to a town.[76] Of the half who are not said to have been in service, furthermore, the most conspicuous categories are doctors, and members of the less purely contemplative religious orders; both of which categories often supplied attenders at courts.[77] We happen to know that some of these astrologers whom Symon de Phares does not expressly say were in service to the great, were (at least for a time) in such service—like Arnold of Villanuova.[78]

Symon de Phares' list entitles us to suggest that the typical late-medieval lay astrologer was a courtier. This is not to say he was necessarily of ignoble birth. Other features of Symon's book nevertheless show this was usually the case. Despite the author's purpose of puffing up the social rank of his subjects he dares to

give the status of 'chevalier' or 'de cler sang' to no more than
three or four of those three hundred or so of his list clearly in
Group II (i.e. professional astrologers who knew mathematics).[79] And that these were untypical is shown by hints in the
rest of the book. For instance, there is a striking number of
supposed astrologers originating from poor regions: Scotland,
Wales, Brittany, Auvergne.[80] Again, Symon exalts one of his
astrologers as a sort of proto-revolutionary, helping Flemish
rebels to eject 'nobles who oppressed them'.[81] Occasionally
Symon says a man became, or tried to become, rich *through*
astrology.[82] And there is a tell-tale case—tell-tale of both
motives and facts—of a certain Master Dominic who switched
from astrology to medicine because the former had not brought
him a fortune.[83] Finally, the author makes in one place an
admission that virtually scuttles his own case. Discussing a
mythical ancient astrologer who was said to have renounced
worldly wealth, Symon de Phares declares: 'the whole reproach
made nowadays by the calumniators of astrology is that there is
not a single one who is rich'. This assertion, which it is
instructive to hear acknowledged as a contemporary view,
struck at the very thesis which Symon's book was written to
uphold. What does he reply? Simply, 'that the man who is
content is rich'.[84] The author of this lofty pronouncement was in
fact no less of a birth- and class-snob than any of his opponents.
(He is apt, for example, to revile the detractors of astrology as
themselves 'low-born'.)[85] His answer is revealingly weak. His
calculators, it is clear, were for the most part men who had
begun life with little substance of their own.

*Pauperis est numerare pecus.* I suggest that in the middle ages, as
in Ovid's pastoral world, it was primarily the man with room to
rise on fortune's wheel who developed the art of number. The
suggestion may find support from one further reflection. Urban
Italy in the thirteenth century has been identified as a forcing-
ground for medieval arithmetic. It was also a giant upstart,
growing up on the grave of its aristocratic victim, the
Hohenstaufen Empire. Arithmetical Florence, indeed, was the
most conspicuous upstart of all, with its *popolo*, its waves of *nuova
gente*, and its forged Roman genealogies, personal and civic.
Florence in Dante's time was a whole society of successful
*nouveaux riches* traders. The city could even be described as a sort

of collective climber in government service. For the great Tuscan bankers rarely forgot, though historians occasionally do, the identity of their chief client: the pope, head of medieval Christendom. As in the earliest days of medieval arithmetic, when the calendar was being made, the governmental centre of an organized Christendom had, even in the late middle ages, this detectable role in the rearing of arithmeticians.

Here, then, is a suggested conclusion: admitting exceptions, no doubt, but boasting a broad plausibility. What further conclusions follow from this—in respect of reason and religion, of individuals and societies—will unfold in due course, not immediately. For we have studied only one side of the medieval rationalistic culture; and must prepare now for quite a different type of exploration through the other.

# PART III

# READING AND WRITING

# CHAPTER 9

# The University Ladder

Accord some advantage to those who study well, O
Alexander, so that you hold up thereby an example
to other scholars, giving them cause for vigilance.

Pseudo-Aristotle, *Secretum Secretorum* (p. 58.12–14).

OUR rational concept of nature descends on one side of its
ancestry from mathematics, by way of late medieval philosophy
and Galileo. But there is a second side. As a rational assault on
nature, the literate educational tradition of the Latin west, if
less intellectually rigorous than mathematics, is older and has
had wider effect. Despite the tradition's distaste for the hyper-
rationality of number, reason lies near its essence: reason as
applied to human experience. Before Roger Bacon precociously
dreamed of the union of mathematics and physics, men who on
their own confession had skimped or failed in the *quadrivium*
were nourishing disciplines which were in practice more
influential, at that date, in rationalizing the European mentality. The starting-point of these disciplines was the *trivium*:
logic, grammar, and rhetoric—the three arts which most people
really meant when they spoke of the liberal arts. Theology and
law were built on the foundation of these disciplines; and when
Aristotle came with his all-embracing 'philosophy' to expand
academic horizons, it was as an extension to the same three,
more than to the *quadrivium*, that he came. What now has to be
studied, then, from its social angle, is the effectual core of
scholastic education: the 'three ways' with their offshoots; the
*artes sermocinales*, or 'skills of the word'.

In the matter of documentation, to move from numbers to
words is to go from one extreme to another. No region of
medieval life is better documented than scholastic thought.
This wealth poses historiographical problems. One is general:
the wealth of documents derives from a small social group, and

can therefore easily create illusions about how non-academic people thought. A second problem is particular to the present occasion. Partly because of the wealth of documentation, and partly because scholars have looked after their own, the quantity and quality of attention focused during the last century on scholasticism are unique in medieval historiography. This may ease part of our task. The history to be analysed does not have to be written first, as with arithmetic. But the wealth is also an embarrassment: no one can have read all of it. To generalize about scholasticism therefore calls for a special kind of foolhardiness—quite a different kind from that called for by those scattered scraps of evidence about mathematical history.

The exigencies of our inquiry nevertheless impel us on. We move into the heartland of the problem posed in this book. The subject of the next four chapters will be, in effect, universities, and their tributaries. The aim of these chapters is not, now, to rehearse and analyse the main professional utterances of scholastics. It is rather to study their parentheses, and asides; and through that study to try, if at all possible, to identify a single social orientation, characteristic in some measure of the whole university milieu. The task is a long one. So let us begin it without more ado.

## I. THE GREGORIAN REFORM: ITS EFFECT ON THE PLACE OF LEARNING IN THE CHURCH

If one feature of the Gregorian reform had to be chosen as its most characteristic, it would be its basis in canon law. Popes, legates, and councils saw the evils of their age as 'contempt for the canons'. They sought to revive the church's ancient legal framework, with a few surreptitious accretions. This revival sent three distinct impulses into the field of education.

The first impulse arose from the reformers' insistence on canonical appointment to ecclesiastical office. It was shown in chapter 3 that the church, as a big property owner, especially in towns, found itself in the centre of the economic revival of the eleventh century; and one result of its involvement was the exposure of church office, high and low, to intense competition from adventurers. The reformers' onslaught on simony was a reaction to this threat. The onslaught was kept up at full force for two generations—abetted by the self-interest, enlightened and unenlightened, of some lay powers. By 1100 the golden age of simony was consequently over. It would survive, certainly, and from time to time attract new indignation from reformers. But the fact that they used the term 'simony' now increasingly to cover more than straight monetary purchase of office shows, as does much else, that the latter was no longer the norm it had been.[1]

By setting limits to simony, the reform succeeded in identifying one way church offices should *not* be filled. The question how they *should* be filled remained, made only more pressing by the exclusion of purchasers. The reformers' initial answer was that flood of monks, Cluniac and other, which swept over the church's high places in the second half of the eleventh century. But there were two views on the propriety of employing contemplatives in the secular church. By 1100—just as the centralized church began to make itself felt in the world—new orders were appearing whose rules, warned by experience, would immure their members more closely. Those who made appointments were thus thrown back for their choice into the broad, in theory undifferentiated, field of the secular clergy.

This introduces the second respect in which canon law concerns us. The canons included in their province not only the machinery of appointments, but criteria for the choice of candidates. Candidates should be 'suitable', that is, distinguished by various virtues. In practice an unwritten rule existed (whose status and antiquity is to be explored in chapter 12) that church dignities should go only to persons of upper-class birth. The Gregorians normally respected this principle, in the absence of positive contrary considerations.[2] But there was a difficulty. One of the few details the canons filled in about what 'suitability' for church office meant was that dignitaries—indeed all priests—should be 'literate', in the minimum sense current then of being able to read and write Latin. At the time of the early Germanic kingdoms, the two criteria, nobility and literacy, had not clashed: the ex-Roman senatorial aristocracy had excelled in both. But that aristocracy was gradually replaced by the Germanic, for whom literacy was not only not a revered tradition, but commonly an object of scorn. Under the early Carolingians the cosmopolitan element in church appointments helped to hide this difficulty—foreigners being harder to assign to a social category than your own countrymen. But signs of tension between the two criteria had already appeared by the late Carolingian era, before the disorders which closed it threw the canons once more to the winds. When, in the eleventh century, the time came to restore to the secular church the character it had had under Gregory the Great, the shortcomings of the nobility were bound to present a problem. The problem was not that the nobility was *less* literate than other classes. On the whole it was more so, as the Gregorians were well placed to know. The trouble was that it was not literate enough: it could not meet the church's demands in sufficient quantity. This failure weakened, and finally in the thirteenth century would cripple, the nobility's monopoly of high church office. The canons had defended that monopoly from attack by money. But they exposed it to attack by learning.[3]

In the peculiar circumstances of the eleventh century, then, the Gregorians' restriction on simony, and insistence on churchmen's literacy, put a new premium on learning. Economic change had brought an up-and-down social circulation: the church, through purchase of office, had been used as a ladder. The reformers then came and curbed purchase. But by doing so they did not restore social rigidity to the hierarchy. Canon law was egalitarian, and forbade that: office was open to all. Thus the church could still be used as a ladder; but from a new direction. A stress on literacy, in other words, merely gave a new and finer channel to the zeal of ambition.

The part played by canon law in the revival of learning did not end here. It had a third, direct effect. The decretals demanded that priests be 'literate'. It was a minimal demand. Literacy was the 'foundation of learning'.[4] But it was only that: not enough, by itself, to make a good priest—or for that matter to call up elaborate schools. A priest must be literate for a purpose: an illiterate (to use an expression from Gregory VII himself) 'can neither teach others nor defend himself'.[5] What a man taught and defended: that was what gave point to his literacy.

In the first instance, for a clerk, this was the 'sacred writings':

the body of doctrine soon to be systematized as theology. But even the proper study of God entailed, the Fathers taught, some acquaintance with man and his world. On top of this, the political dimension of the Hildebrandine church made secular knowledge a practical necessity. Grammar was needed for letter-writing; rhetoric for polemic; dialectic for disputation. Last and not least, all three arts were called for in the service of the sacred writings and of canon law itself—with its nearly limitless ramifications in spheres of family, politics, commerce, and property; not to mention religion, public and private. Recent study has stressed how in the twelfth century, as the reformed church gathered momentum, it was canon law more than anything else whose lack was felt most painfully by educational sluggards.[6]

Changes in the church, not the state, have provided this overture to a study of the scholastic renewal. There are two reasons. It is a question of literate learning, and for a century after Gregory VII, the 'clergy' (who held the hegemony in such learning) were still a distinct body-politic, under church law: the term had not yet come into its own as an amorphous designation for the educated. This first fact reflects a second one of more consequence. Legal self-consciousness, of the kind won for the church by canonists, was a grace largely denied to the lay state until the burgeoning of Roman Law studies in the late twelfth century. States as such thus played no direct part in launching scholasticism.

Their indirect part however was all the greater. One paradoxical result of the canonical revival and the burst of education that followed it, was that kings could now lay their hands on learned officials. In the century between Henry IV of Germany and Henry II of England, bitter lessons would teach kings the dangers of allowing the church its monopoly of the supply of these officials, and they would act to undermine it. But even before then the figure of the monarch stood behind what appeared as a clerical education. The monarch was always a potential employer of scholars, and a rich one. The mechanisms that created the schools might come from canon law. But among forces that worked the mechanisms, state wealth and power were added to ecclesiastical, as another magnet, drawing careerists to school.

Consideration has been given here to the period, lasting about half a century, when the foundations were laid for the church of the central middle ages. Account has been taken of the stimulus the innovations of that period gave to study. The conquests Gregory VII and his contemporaries won, however, were defended and expanded by following generations. The Gregorian church lasted in outward essentials to the end of the fourteenth century: the lifetime of scholasticism. The mechanism whose origin we have just sketched therefore endured for more than a half-century. It would operate during the entire history of the medieval schools: like one of those concentric spheres which, in medieval cosmology, encased the busy human world, disposing its activities, and without a consideration of whose influence the world's workings could not be understood.

Having acquainted ourselves with the mechanism, we now descend to see its effect in the world of scholars.

## 2. UNIVERSITY CAREERISM: THE 'LUCRATIVE SCIENCES'

In 1179 the third Lateran council put cathedral schools on a regular economic basis. Its decree on the matter would not be uniformly observed straightaway, and had to be repeated in 1215; nor was its impact on the main stream of education as direct as it was meant to be. The decree's wording reflects none the less clearly for that the intention of the most influential legislators in medieval education. It has merited more than any other statement the status of economic charter for medieval education. The decree ran:

Lest the poor, who have no family wealth to help them, be deprived of the opportunity of studying and making progress, a benefice of suitable size in each cathedral church is to be assigned to a master, so that he can teach the poor for nothing. The teacher will thus be protected from want, and the road to learning lie open to his pupils.[7]

The council fathers were unequivocal, then, about whom they meant to help: those without wealth. Here was a charter not only for education, but for the 'poor'; or some of them. In thus taking thought for moneyless boys, the Lateran council was following an old church tradition. Great dark-age patrons of learning—Charlemagne, and Alfred the Great—had seen to it that children from lower social levels mixed with those from higher in their schools;[8] while the more purposeful monastic and episcopal schools of the eleventh centuries had won the same reputation.[9] The council of 1179 inscribed the principle into the law of the twelfth-century academic revival. Benefactors throughout the middle ages would carry it from there into the foundation of a whole constellation of universities and colleges.[10]

Flinging school doors wide was in the church's interest. She needed recruits. Declarations survive from long before the twelfth century, as well as from after it, that law-makers acted in consciousness of this need.[11] Yet we cannot read the decree of 1179 without sensing a second motive. The church, as universal mother, sought fair play. Not only prudence; justice, too, made its plea: 'ne pauperibus ... proficiendi opportunitas subtrahatur'. 'Proficior' is our 'get on'. It need not, it is true, mean 'getting on' in relation to anyone else, or at his expense. But it may. The phraseology of later university founders, in the fourteenth century, with their inclusion of *privata res* as one object served by universities, gives every support to such an interpretation.[12] In seeking fair play the church at the very outset of university history was led into sanctioning what could easily be understood as private interest.

How easily, can be seen better at ground level. About 1200 an idealistic young Burgundian was kneeling one evening after Vespers in a small Paris church, uncertain what to do with his life, when an inquiring parish priest approached him. Apprised of the newcomer's doubts the priest, a 'simple and honest man', had this to say of the great university:

There are many, many students in this city who fill every available moment of the period they have devoted to acquiring knowledge, with study. Night runs into day with it, in a welter of work, exhausting and burdensome. Yet they have one target only: the pomp of Satan. For this is what they say to themselves:

'When I have acquired enough book-learning in Paris and got my doctorate I shall return home. There my merits will be rewarded with high honour. Who knows? My learning may eventually raise me to the highest honour in the city.'

What is all that but the pomp of Satan?[13]

Any exaggeration there may have been in the priest's outburst would have lost nothing in the reporting. The anecdote by itself would prove little. But it is not by itself. A perusal of sources from both before and after this particular incident shows it for what it is: a vivid parody of what many observers saw as the most hardy social characteristic of the scholar.

That love of office was a motive for study is revealed by sources which begin, not in the twelfth-century renaissance, but in the Carolingian; whence they dog the footsteps of such dark-age education as there was. A contemporary of Louis the Pious had lashed the jobbery of bishops who raised low-born kinsmen from 'the servitude that is their due' by giving them—an act of 'the utmost peril to both teachers and pupils'—'instruction in the liberal arts'.[14] Alfred the Great for his part had consciously exploited love-of-office as a motive for study: he threatened dismissal of functionaries who neglected their books, so that 'thoroughly alarmed [*perterriti*]' they obeyed.[15] Perhaps late Anglo-Saxon law followed his example, too, when it allowed a thegn's status to a scholar who 'throve'.[16] Under Otto the Great, meanwhile, a church-politician of wide experience remarked that when sons of nobles went to school—which was rare enough—they 'everywhere seem to do so more from ambition to be bishops, than from a wish to fight for the Lord'.[17]

The golden age for careerism via the schools nevertheless began with the twelfth century. In a sermon given to students and teachers about 1140, Bernard of Clairvaux put avarice and ambition first among the vices to which such 'clerks' made themselves slaves.[18] A few years later John of Salisbury, from his experience in Paris and Chartres, could put the same two vices (as 'elatio' and 'cupiditas'), together with 'curiosity', as the main inducements for philosophical study in his time. 'It is all done', he added, 'for the sake of some folly—either of an improper self-indulgence, or of an empty notion of utility.'[19] A few years later still, at the end of the century, Walter Map wrote of learning in his native England that it was mainly supported, not by the upper class, but by 'slaves, which we call peasants' who were 'eager to nourish their low-born and degenerate children in the arts unfitted to them, not so that they may divest themselves of their vices, but so that they may win great riches'.[20]

In the thirteenth century, as schools partook in the general demographic 'explosion', this motif went some way towards being a moralists' commonplace. The satirists got hold of it, and could endow it with considerable humour. A German satirist at the end of the century, for instance, a schoolmaster in Bamberg called Hugo of Trimberg, wrote in his own vernacular:

> You want the wealthy man to greet
> You, and the poor to kiss your feet?
> To have great potentates defer,
> And say 'professor', call you 'sir'?
> Then dress up well, and tell it far
> You're twice as learned as you are
> *And* twice as rich!—In half a year
> They'll make you a privy counsellor!
> Yes! If you know no better stunt,
> Then turn your collar back-to-front!
> Hey presto! You'll be twice the man
> Your father was when you began.[21]

The advice caricatured in satire could nevertheless be given in deadly earnest in soberer walks of literature. One of the shrewdest thirteenth-century purveyors of practical wisdom was the French septuagenarian knight Philippe de Novare. Philippe counselled youth starting out in life to consider carefully the career of 'clergie', on the grounds that

through *clergie* it has often happened, and can happen again, that the son of a poor man becomes a great prelate; and enjoys riches and honours, and is father and lord over the man formerly lord over him and his family; and can govern and rule everyone in the region; nay, he may become pope, and be father and lord of all Christendom.[22]

No prevarication now on what 'opportunitas proficiendi' meant.

Neither Hugo nor Philippe de Novare had actually been to university. Viewed from afar, the opportunities offered by education and the careerism they engendered seemed evenly spread over the whole academic world. But from close to, it was clear that in the university, at least, some faculties were affected more than others. Social forces impinged unevenly on university disciplines. They caused what would now be called a 'brain-drain', between faculties. Already in the twelfth century theology had begun to feel itself the loser. Concern for the church's health, as well as moral disapproval, made theologians cry out against what they called the *scientiae lucrativae*.

Foremost of these lucrative sciences was law: civil law primarily, but also canon law. It is well known that in the twelfth and thirteenth centuries doctors 'of both laws' multiplied on the top levels of church government. Glimmers from more elusive layers of lay society suggested that this multiplication was only the tip of a pyramid. We know, for instance, that the notarial profession—the humblest of those demanding legal knowledge—was very popular among rural immigrants into thirteenth-century Florence, seeking a niche for themselves in the competitive society they were entering.[23] That their choice was shrewd is suggested by the case of Padua, where notaries have been found conspicuous among social risers (one low-born notary, just after 1300, was actually able to launch his children into the nobility).[24] On a higher level, a full academic legal training, for those who could afford it, was correspondingly richer in its promises. Advocates and judges who 'made good' are again best-documented in Italy.[25] But their traces can in fact be found in any of the more vigorous European monarchies. There is the striking case of a peasant-boy in Burgundy, who attained to nobility by way of the Bologna law-school and ducal service.[26] Less spectacular, but more telling, is the result of a computer-analysis of the careers of some fifteen thousand recorded ex-scholars of Oxford, from the thirteenth century to the fifteenth. The analysis shows it was Oxford's lawyers (especially civil lawyers) who were more likely than other graduates, other things being equal, to win positions in the various echelons of courts, secular and ecclesiastical.[27]

What we learn from the study of particular societies is confirmed by more general literature. Wealth and honours attract satire; and it is in satire that we find some of the clearest evidence for lawyers' worldly success. 'If you want wealth, be a lawyer'; 'Justinian is the distributor of honours'; 'follow the decretalists and fill—not purses, but—*chests*'; are saws of a type well-rooted in school talk by the early thirteenth century.[28] Such slogans not only betray, they also explain, the brain-drain towards law. Graver minds meanwhile worried about more than mere numbers. They did not mind that people should study law. Far from it: lawyers were needed. What they minded was that law was studied for the wrong motive, making the study contemptible. Another of the German vernacular satirists, Thomasin of Zirclaria, writing *c.* 1215, declared:

> We study edict, papal letter
> Only so that we may better
> Ape the folly of our day.
> You cavil, do you, and shout 'hey!
> That is not so!'? Then tell me why
> We pass the gate of wisdom by
> —I mean of course the Sacred Page,
> Which at one time was all the rage—
> If not because we've let our brains
> Go crazy, in pursuit of gains.[29]

The reason for these misgivings was that lawyers' greed ended, not by guaranteeing justice, but by perverting it. About the time that jingle was written, a more prosaic critic noticed how it was precisely 'the people who blush to follow the Crucified' who 'have the incredible front to usurp His patrimony'; while 'the more learned such people are in the law, the readier they are in practice to compromise it'.[30]

Examples of all these kinds of invective could be multiplied. But it is not in the end the volatile moralists who most surely describe their target. It is the less indignant observers, nearer the swing of the times. Two such were Pierre Dubois and John of Jandun. They wrote after a university boom in legal studies at the end of the thirteenth century, a boom of which lawyer Dubois was one beneficiary. Of civil-law studies Dubois noted drily, in 1306, how

Young scholars . . . nearly all go into the study of civil law in quest, not only of rich livings therein and thereby, but of greater prelacies too— hoping to follow in the steps of those who have acquired such prelacies in the past, through civil law and its practice.[31]

Of canon law, similarly, John of Jandun remarked in 1323 that

those who busy themselves with handling and arbitrating in the business of chapters and courts weigh up pretty well what chance decretalists enjoy nowadays for acquiring rule of churches.[32]

Not just moralists and monks, but dispassionate men of the

world who had themselves climbed the university ladder, acknowledged the career-consciousness that hung especially round the law-schools.

At the top of the list of lucrative sciences stood law. But it had a strange companion: medicine. There were two main reasons for medicine's status. Linked as it was with astrology, medicine was almost alone in the scientific field as an academic discipline with practical application: the doctor focused in himself all the aura of today's university-trained scientist. Second, he was a natural guest round those fountains of office, courts. Doctors are accordingly found rising on the ladder of office from the earliest days of the Gregorian reform. Cardinal Humbert allowed them as the only type of 'simonist' for whose cause something could be said (he omits lawyers altogether): at least (he says) they have *some* learning.[33] With the twelfth century, medicine came to be regularly coupled with law when lucrative sciences were spoken of. 'Many scholars say: I shall go to medicine or the laws; since only chaff is to be gathered from other sciences, from these, grain';[34] 'Many students transfer to physic [i.e. medicine] for financial reasons, and abandon theology';[35] 'students are on the hunt for money, like legists, or medics...';[36] 'if you want rewards, be a lawyer or doctor';[37] are typical observations, made with or without irony, in the years around 1200. Twelfth-century church councils could speak the same sort of language, forbidding those in religious orders from studying 'secular law and medicine, for the sake of lucre'.[38]

Some critics appeared to limit medicine's gifts to mere private wealth: for example, while 'Justinian' distributed 'honours', 'Galienus' distributed 'riches'.[39] What evidence there is of medical earnings, from the late middle ages, bears out that they could be large.[40] But—no doubt for the second of the two reasons given at the beginning of the last paragraph—honours were to be had too. Even when straight monetary simony was curbed, after Cardinal Humbert's complaint, medical men still made successful church careers. They played a noticeable part in the first big invasion of the German episcopate by non-nobles, in the thirteenth century.[41] The most widely-read medical writer of the same century, Peter of Spain, became pope as John XXI. Two generations later, 'the best physician in the whole world' (according to one manuscript containing his work), John Grise of Montpellier, was made bishop of Verdun, then of Freising.[42] The mysterious junction of medical knowledge with political power, seen in chapter 5 in the myth of the Pseudo-Aristotle, thus also appeared in the flesh and blood of men's careers.

Aspersions on the lucrative sciences came chiefly from devotees of the less lucrative. They stressed the contrast. Satirists of lawyers' and doctors' greed were the same who epitomized arts scholars—their own colleagues—as barefooted beggars. Similarly, theologians who equated worldly motives with the desertion of theology left the impression that theology was studied for God's sake alone. In fact the contrast was not absolute. The liberal arts as such might promise big rewards only to the few. And unemployment occasionally struck at the unluckier arts men. But the fact remained that both philosophy and theology *could* lead to high place. 'Inane philosophy' was one subject the theologian Alan of Lille spoke of as enticing worldly students from scripture; and if he did not actually name honours or riches as the motive, the link can be traced elsewhere.[43] One side of philosophy was joined to medicine, itself sometimes just given the broad title *physica*; and both could be put together among 'the lucrative sciences studied by the Greeks'.[44] Philosophers' own remarks can suggest the same. Those of Michael Scot, court philosopher of Frederick II, are an example. He opened his astrological *Liber Introductorius* (*c.* 1230) with the following bombastic allurement:

One who wishes to have honour among the peoples of the world will gain it either by divine providence such as becoming bishop, abbot or patriarch by perfect election; or by perfect work, which is had by genius of nature, such as being an approved master in some faculty.... It behoves one who desires to have in this world gain of much utility and honour first to have grace from above, by which he may wisely regulate his genius and capacity of apprehending art.[45]

By 'faculty' and 'art' Michael almost certainly here envisaged the ensemble of disciplines in which he himself excelled— roughly those 'studied by the Greeks'—which together con- stituted philosophy. Its study promised utility and honour.

It is inconceivable that where promotion was so often conceived of as via church office, theology itself should not have had its lucrative side. That the depreciation of other sciences came often from theologians meant that less was said of their own faculty. But enough was said to show that, like law, medicine, and philosophy, it too exposed its charges to temptations of careerism. Lawyers themselves could envy theologian-priests the honour in which they were held.[46] 'Divines who speak learnedly' could be ironically cast, along with lawyers, among models for youngsters who yearned to fill chests with money.[47] A doyen of theology will mention, as guilty of 'mental simony', a teacher of theology who 'mentally desires a prelacy, or favour, or temporal reward, and not God above all'.[48] An anonymous German sermon, possibly from as early as the late thirteenth century, attacks the priest who studies scripture just so that people say, 'That is a good priest. He is worth a good church.' 'They study for no other reason [the preacher continues] than that they should win the title of "Master", and use the degree to attain high office'.[49]

Careerism through theology is perhaps best seen, however, less as the perquisite of one isolated discipline, than as attaching to a churchman's education as a whole; which would include the *trivium*, chant, and some canon law as well. It was excellence in these studies altogether—plus luck and diligence later—that made the standard churchman's ladder. Acknowledgement of this fact can be heard, once more, from opposite parties: those who climbed the ladder and those who refused to. In the thirteenth century the most signal of the former was Pope Urban IV. Son of a Troyes shoemaker, he was not only the first French pope since the Cluniacs, but the first pope since Gerbert of indubitably low birth. The first rung in his rise had been Laon cathedral chapter. After election as pope in 1261, Urban thanked the chapter with a privilege. He enumerated the succession of ecclesiastical grades to which it had secured his promotion; and went on:

There [in Laon] my studies had their first successes [*profectus*], there I received the first-fruits of my fortune, from there I proceeded to other churches, gradually rising by such steps, with God's favour, to a higher place in each.[50]

Urban's dispassionate rehearsal of the ecclesiastical *cursus* echoes that of Philippe de Novare, explaining how *clergie* can even make a poor boy pope. And it is indeed possible, from the dates, that it was Urban's recent election that Philippe had in mind.[51]

Being French-speakers, neither Urban nor Philippe de Novare had any quarrel with a system which was opening such wide doors to their countrymen. It was a system which would soon create a whole curia of learned Frenchmen at Avignon. But an equally telling acknowledgement of theology's lifting-power can be heard from the opposite camp: from one of the system's loudest critics, in a university whose novelty and geographical position largely closed to it the routes to high church office. In other respects than this Prague became in the fourteenth century the Paris of the imperial east. There, another shooting star of humble origin like Urban IV would guiltily declare:

When I was a young student, I confess to have entertained an evil desire, for I had thought to become a priest quickly in order to secure a good livelihood and dress well and to be held in esteem of men.[52]

John Hus, who said this, ended with more esteem than he had bargained for. But it was by rebound from, not by grace of, priestly careerism that he did so: a careerism he never ceased to denounce as endemic in papalist circles.[53]

Most people who passed through any faculty of a medieval school, then, nourished some expectation of a better job afterwards. But the people who passed through a school were not its core. The core was the masters, who spent most or all their lives there. Theirs was scholarship for its own sake; not training for an outside career. It may be asked whether the affective atmosphere of the mobile student-sector extended here too. A consideration of this question will close the present chapter.

### 3. THE STATUS OF LEARNING

The answer to the question was bound to be yes. In so far as learning helped careerists, purveyors of it were creditors to the successful. Not much knowledge of life, though perhaps some generosity, was needed to recognize that

> Many a swell in church and state
> Who went to school and then grew great
> Would still count as an unknown dunce
> But for the men who taught him once.[54]

Teachers might complain (as Hugo of Trimberg, who wrote
that, was doing) about the world's ingratitude to them: a
literary class was well placed to do so. But their profession would
not have survived all those centuries if its precious services had
in fact been had for nothing. Nor were they.

Taken on even the simplest level, teaching was a living. A
traditional portrait of any scholar's life stressed its poverty. But
the portrait applied more to scholars who learnt than to those
who taught; and one reason why the former were poor was
because some of the latter grew relatively rich out of them. The
ethics of buying and selling knowledge was the subject of a long
debate. But by 1300 even the most other-worldly theologian
could admit not only that teachers must be paid, but that
theology itself, the most sacred of sciences, could be taught for
money—even (though this was highly undesirable) when there
was no other motive.[55] The presence of the money-motive in the
main scholastic centres is not in question. Victims of masters'
'avarice' were vocal about it; and if their squeals make frail
indictments we can still reflect that the *lucra* of which Abelard
boasted—and whose copiousness he expected his readers to be
able to reckon from his prodigious success as a lecturer—can be
translated 'profits'.[56] From Peter Damian in the eleventh
century, with his 'piles of riches' made as a young teacher,[57]
down to Walter the Teuton in the thirteenth, with his 'large
salary',[58] and other professors who entered the mendicant
orders, we hear of famous teachers being converted to lives of
poverty as if they had been rich merchants. Any precise
questions about academic remuneration, where answerable at
all, would call for special answers according to time and place.
For all the talk of avarice and profit, the depths of the
profession—say a visiting children's tutor in a city—are known
to have been very ill paid.[59] But equally it remains a general
truth that from an economic angle a teacher, with or without
scruples of conscience, was retailer to a greedy market, whose
funds he was thus in some position to lay hands on.

The precise way he laid hands on them varied according to
discipline, talent, and temperament. Market-place conditions,
though they could obtain quite literally, normally held only in
the abstract. The more a branch of study was conceived of as in
the public rather than the private interest, the more likely a

teacher's living was to come in the form of a permanent post. This type of post existed long before the decree of 1179 came to regularize it. The attraction of better jobs, and what governed the amount of income attached to them, was rank. Authority often saw to it that this was high. Before the rise of the universities the main post was that of cathedral *scholasticus*. The *scholasticus* was often the only non-noble member of an otherwise purely noble cathedral chapter.[60] He had 'nobility of learning'—like that which had earned Gerbert his place in the Rheims chapter in 972.[61] In the hierarchy of early eleventh-century Milan the cathedral-school headmaster actually enjoyed top precedence after the archbishop, shared with the viscount.[62] Many noble chapters, it is true, begrudged any true equality to their learned colleagues. But others made up for it, with or without government prodding, by picking on the *scholasticus* when it came to electing a bishop.[63] In the later middle ages, others still did so by simply extending their conditions of admission to say 'nobles *or* graduates'.[64]

The services that teachers rendered their fellow-men were rewarded, then, by various levels of payment, and by official dignities. In the most vigorous areas of academic life a third type of worldly reward was coveted: glory. Those who criticized the moral side of the teaching trade coupled 'vainglory' with 'lucre' as the most likely alternative alloy for a teacher's motives. The temptation was not lacking. Not only were swarms of impressionable young, the *turba studentium*, there to turn the head of an unwary professor. A further trap lay in friendship with the great, which some famous teachers are known to have had. The charge of vainglory anyway tended to cling to the learned. There is a kind of teacher, wrote one critic in Paris about 1200, who 'thinks how marvellous it is for people to point at him with their finger, and say "that is the man"'.[65] The anonymous German sermon quoted earlier about ambitious priests goes on to speak of academic vainglory. Those who work to obtain their master's degree and the right to teach, find in the end that their attainments give them no peace:

For they scratch their heads night and day to see how they can hatch up some new, rare, unheard-of theory, confounding God's goodness with their words, prying and probing into every single thing in creation—and all for vainglory, not God.[66]

One rumour had it that even the great theologian and philosopher Hugh of St. Victor had had to spend a while in purgatory for this failing.[67]

To speak of academic vainglory as a failing is to adopt the language of one party to the case. The best evidence of the strength of this feature in academic circles is that another party did not think vainglory really *was* a failing. Unabashed relish of professional success, long a norm among the military aristocracy, extended to scholarship centuries before the Italian Renaissance with which it is associated. This unabashed relish can sometimes raise the eyebrows of readers not used to it. I cite as one illustration the description of a lecture on canon law given by Master Gerald of Wales in Paris in 1177.

On the day the city knew he had chosen to speak, such a crowd— almost all the professors with their students—collected to hear his charming voice that the largest hall could scarcely hold the audience. The speaker supported his apt citations from civil and canon law with such forceful arguments, and embellished his points with such structured and colourful prose, together with interpretations of such substance—fitting in quotations from philosophers and legal authorities to the right places with wonderful skill—that the more learned and experienced the members of the audience were, the more keenly and attentively they applied their ears and souls to marking and remembering it. So soothed and entranced were they, indeed, by the sweetness of his language, that despite the length and prolixity of his lecture—a length that usually bores many people—the audience, far from tiring, could not have enough of it.

The embellishment, structure, colour and prolixity of the description themselves go far to give its author away: Gerald himself;[68] and with him, a not uncommon mentality among such fashionable Paris teachers.

For masters, then, as for their pupils, the martyrdoms of scholarship could be offset by rewards: at worst a pittance; at best near-episcopal dignity; for those who could and would, fame. The *trivium*, with the disciplines that led out of it, taught a man to think and communicate the skills needed by growing institutions. In whatever capacity a man studied these arts, he partook of their mysterious power.

That the mysterious power lay in all the arts as such, not in any one of them, or in an institution, can be demonstrated by a simple consideration. Anyone who had watched warriors at work, or read of them in epic, knew that strength was an occasion for boasting. This rule transferred itself to the intellectual field. Not just the vainglorious master or worldly lawyer: anyone, young or old, who came into the smallest contact with school learning, met the temptation. Scholar's swagger as an image follows the footsteps of medieval education like a stage zany. The image is sometimes satirical, sometimes not. In it the scholar betrays crudely his consciousness of superiority to his neighbour. 'Away with you, peasant,' a schoolboy says to his shepherd-brother in one old, often-read story: 'your job is to feed sheep, mine to work at books. The function my office gives me makes me nobler. Your job as shepherd makes you a mere serf.'[69] That particular speech had the eventual good result of presenting the world with Saint Patroclus of Troyes—the insulted party, who took the point, went to school, and eventually became a bishop. But the writer of the story viewed the first scholar's arrogance none the less critically for that. As uppish intellectuals became more of a blight on the social scene, satire became livelier. About 1030, the same period when a schoolmaster held the second dignity below the viscount in Milan, a Lombard scholar was thus parodied by an opponent in Aquitaine:

My uncle [says the Lombard] has taken me all over the place to study grammar. My knowledge has already cost him two thousand *solidi*, paid to my professors. I have studied for nine years, and am still studying. . . . I have reached the very perfection of knowledge. I own two large houses full of books. Although I have not read them all yet, every day I pore over them. There is no book in the whole country which I do not possess. When I leave school there will be no one under heaven as learned as I.[70]

'Standing, sitting, walking, lying down—wherever he is,' add the friends of the pompous Lombard, 'words flow from his mouth like water from the Tigris.' 'In our land,' they explain, 'no one is accounted learned unless he is a great talker.'[71]

This was caricature. But caricatures are drawn to be recognized, and the type, its contours changing as wandering scholars settled into schools, became increasingly familiar when universities grew. In the heyday of scholasticism it will turn up in the most surprising places and forms.

> Distinctions have I three:
> Two laws; philosophy.
> Fiddle-di-dee.

Something like the Latin equivalent of that was said, again by enemies, to have been chalked by a bishop of St. Andrews on his own church gate in 1254 (a rhymed riposte to which boast 'did so gall him as taking to bed he died within a few days').[72] We read of a Dominican with the reputation for thinking none of his colleagues 'were to be compared with him in literary knowledge or learning in the scriptures'.[73] Indeed, such a Dominican became the subject of one of the sharpest medieval parodies: the mendicant 'False Seeming' in *The Romance of the Rose*:

> The world, if I may claim this prize,
> Contains no prelate half as wise
> Or half as literate as me
> With my theology degree;
> I've even taught it, ages since;
> And been confessor to a prince
> And other lords, who know their stuff
> And found none other wise enough.[74]

'False Seeming' lay around in the libraries of enough lords in the late middle ages to assure us that they knew the type well, and enjoyed a laugh at its expense.

The intellectual revival of the central middle ages came in the wake of political and economic changes, which it in turn accelerated. The changes created a magnetic field for scholars, relating them to the new foci of power. In many ways and degrees scholars felt this relationship, and it beset their whole culture with a potential 'original sin', of a kind common in the vicinity of power. Keener eyes even than those which noticed the day-to-day sins of universities—their violence, intemperance, and so on—acknowledged the presence of this original sin. *Scientia inflat*, Saint Paul had taught; and observation confirmed it. One of the most cogent contemporary impressions in this sense was that of Alexander Neckham. Himself a well-known philosopher, Neckham knew both great and small, both in and out of schools. Under the heading 'knowledge' in his encyclopedia *De naturis rerum* (*c.* 1200), Neckham admitted the toil and expense needed to get knowledge. He then added:

> But when the potentiality of a gifted mind has become a habit (by virtue of an academic discipline, and practice), and when that power has been stored up in the treasure-house of memory, then—I know not for what reason—it sometimes begets an ill-omened child. I refer to arrogance.... Why should it be that the very man who explores nature's subtleties most diligently, succumbs in the principles of the very craft he professes, thrown back by a tiny obstacle? For how can anyone fail to read in the researches he undertakes the message of his own mortality?... Knowledge reads this message; yet at the same time it thirsts insatiably for human praise, seeking glory, following a shadow—for what after all is the favour of the windy populace but itself wind?[75]

By talking of arrogance, Neckham still echoes the language of moral diatribe. A limitation of any study of moral climate in the schools is its need to rely on such language. Diatribe and satire overstate. They also have a tantalizing minimum range: fine moral measurements in the heart of their target are beyond their competence. So this chapter has not been a substitute for a Last Judgement on medieval scholars. It has been an impressionist portrait, drawn from a new angle, depicting one perennial, characteristic expression on the social face of medieval universities.

Neckham's 'arrogance' also marks the end of this chapter. For this chapter has been about people looking up, as they climbed up a ladder. 'Arrogance' means looking down. Intellectuals looking down are a subject on their own.

# CHAPTER 10

# The Intellectual Élite

*Ergo deos dicamus eos vitaque fruentes*
*Qui scribunt artesque bibunt ratione vigentes*
We call them gods, and say they live for ever
Who study, write, and struggle to be clever.

Lambert of St. Bertin (*c.* 1100).

(Curtius, *Eur. Lit.* 523.)

A LOVE of knowledge was understood by the Greeks, who made
a discipline of it, to lift a man out of himself and make him a
lover of all men. This notion had a distinguished career in the
European middle ages. It was incorporated into Christian
mysticism, with and without Greek trappings. In a more
ostensibly classical garb it made a lasting home among scholars;
thanks on one side to Aristotle and his ethics, and on the other to
Latin Stoical authors from Seneca to Boethius. Peace with all
men was these philosophers' ideal. 'All men generally and
universally are to be loved.'[1] Against this ideal, combativeness
for private interest—*privata res*—was an affront. It turned a man
into a beast.

If such ideals worked perfectly there would be no history. The
philosophical–stoical ideal of the middle ages, like other ideals,
ran into difficulties in practice. My purpose now is to identify
one particular difficulty it ran into: to trace, where possible, the
vestiges of a kind of private interest, in the opinions and
activities of those who called themselves, or were called,
philosophers.

Students of the Renaissance humanists are familiar with the
verbal ferocity their disputes sometimes employed: even over
the meaning of a line in Latin verse, or a word's derivation. The
humanists fought like knights at a tournament, aiming deadly
blows—but on paper. That the fighting was in both cases for a
cause did not make it any the less fighting. Now at a number of

places in this book we have found that features commonly attributed to the Italian Renaissance were present far back in the middle ages. More such features will be identified in this chapter; and this is one: the latent or open combativeness of philosophers.[2] Since combativeness presents itself falsely or truly as the opposite of universal love, it makes a suitable starting-point to a sketch of the difficulties of that ideal.

Aggressive noises have already been heard from one type or other of medieval scholar. But the opprobrium they uttered was mostly moral. The characteristic testiness of the philosopher was based on intellectual grounds. Those he did not suffer gladly were *fools*. Culling examples of this sentiment in the middle ages is not difficult. Single words denoting folly or madness—*insanire, insipientes, stulti, vesania*—were a fairly common form of literary ammunition, fired off in the course of an argument by almost any writer with intellectual pretensions and a temper.[3] Such words were not a monopoly of 'philosophers' of the scholastic period. The depreciation of opponents as fools does, however, seem to have been a motif to which these philosophers lent themselves with special ease. It appears with striking regularity either in the works of natural philosophers, or in the more philosophic works of writers who wrote other kinds of book as well.

I give a few examples from the twelfth century onwards. The Chartrean William of Conches was an early defender of certain Aristotelian views, and concluded his defence with: 'I would not be bothering to expound Aristotle's views on the subject but for certain people among us who pretend to be sons of Aristotle when they are unfit to work in his kitchen.'[4] (To equate someone with a cook was particularly rude in medieval literary circles.) Similar combative phrases are found elsewhere in William's work. William's contemporary Adelard of Bath will write likewise: 'every day now we find Platos and Aristotles born to us who hold forth without a blush both on what they know and what they do not know, trusting in extreme verbosity.'[5] That again is a mere sample. With the progress of natural philosophy around the end of the twelfth century the trait became more marked. Some of William of Auvergne's aspersions from *De Universo* will be quoted in a moment. The combativeness of the unfortunate Roger Bacon is perhaps too

idiosyncratic to serve as a general example. But there is no lack
of others. Albert the Great, perhaps the greatest of medieval
natural philosophers, can astonish the reader with his testiness.
'Certain persons who know nothing', he explodes in one place,
'are trying as hard as they can to impugn the study of
philosophy. . . . They blaspheme like brute beasts against things
of which they know nothing.'[6] Even the lofty equanimity of that
other scholastic saint, Aquinas, stirs when it is a case of
defending the idea of natural causation: to deny which is
*absurdum, ridiculum, stultitia.*[7] The next great prince of philosophers, Ockham, had the most combative pen of all. He
would lash (for instance) the 'detestable presumption' of
contemporaries who 'arrogate to themselves' the title of master,
enviously 'tearing to pieces, like barking dogs, every view
dissenting from their own dogmas'.[8] A field even richer than
philosophy in this trait is probably astrology. Indignation at the
insolent folly of critics of the science forms a regular feature of
prefaces and other apologiae for it. For instance, the critics of
astrology are 'hypocrites, as detestable as those popular
deceivers who usurp the title of astrologer';[9] or 'low-born',
'dim-wits', and 'asses and dim-wits, worse than ignorant, and
uneducated'; etc.[10]

Ockham's outburst did the service just now of mentioning
*other* scholars who bark like dogs. In other words the trait was
endemic. Those in a position to observe philosophy from outside
remarked on the aggressiveness with which it was frequently
pursued. It could be noticed of ancient philosophers that they
had disputed 'bitterly'.[11] And here too scholastics stood on the
shoulders of the ancients. No one was better placed to comment
on the matter than the chancellor of the university of Paris,
above the mêlée. Haimeric de Vari, chancellor in the middle of
the thirteenth century, compared the disputes of his professors
to a great cock-fight. Claws, beaks, and spurs were replaced by
words, but the same *amour propre* was there; making the
university ridiculous in the eyes of outsiders.[12]

Learned combativeness was merely the friction of any system
with moving parts. An investigator cared for the truths he
defended, and custom allowed for the exchange of such
aspersions without hard feelings. The barking dogs did not
usually bite. The barking of dogs nevertheless commonly

performs a useful didactic function. It alerts us to the presence of an interest. Endemic testiness among medieval philosophers does the same. For behind their particular barkings, a distinct interest can be discovered, as having formed itself in the heart of the medieval community. I shall call it the intellectual interest. Not all adherents of the interest were university men, nor were all university men its adherents. But the interest throve round schools, and that is chiefly where it must be studied.

The studying will involve a short essay in detection. For the intellectual interest was invisible to many contemporaries, most of all to those best placed professionally to describe it. Yet it can be detected, as a natural force can be detected, by a study of its action. For it did act: like most interests, it fought for itself. Its fight can be traced in two directions, downwards and upwards. The interest fought persons below it in the social hierarchy, to rise above them. And it fought those above, to replace them. It was to this extent a body-politic on its own, pushing its way up, almost invisibly, through the *societas Christiana*. Its two battle-fronts, below and above, will be the subjects respectively of this chapter, and the next pair.

## I. 'RUSTICS' AND 'THE CROWD'

Saint Patroclus' brother was heard at the end of the last chapter putting the pastoral profession to scorn. The swaggering Lombard of the eleventh century likewise dismissed his opponents as 'rustics'. These gibes are a preliminary signal of the battle intellectuals fought below them. Beyond any bragging caricature, and often enough for it to rank as a *déformation de métier*, our intellectuals expressed disdain for peasantry.

The disdain can be seen most immediately through the literary usage of a word: *rusticus*. The word's basic meaning was 'countryman'. In Domesday book and contemporary legal documents it was often used in that sense, or as synonym to *operarius* or 'farmworker'.[13] But the literary revival gave it subtler connotations. In writings where classes of society were contrasted, 'rustic' was used for 'low-class'; so that the 'rustics' even of a town could be contrasted with its nobles.[14] At the same time a usage gathered force whereby the word meant 'stupid', 'coarse', or 'ill-mannered'. One dignitary will commit a

'rusticity' by insulting another.[15] Wicked nobles are 'rusticis-
simi'.[16] This conjunction of meanings was in fact classical, and
echoes of the classical usage can be heard in the dark ages.[17] It
might therefore be argued to have no special significance in the
central middle ages. A look at the contexts in which the term
was used disposes of this doubt. The term and its relations
occupy too much intermediate ground between the literal and
transferred meanings. For example: a flesh-and-blood compatriot of the swaggering Lombard, in the same decade, reviled
his archbishop as a man 'illiterate and of rural provenance'.[18] A
combative philosopher in the twelfth century (it is William of
Conches again) taunted his critics with wishing 'that we should
believe like *rustici*, so that they may have company in their
ignorance'.[19] Near the end of the twelfth century a scholarly
count of Flanders and his chief schoolmaster Philip of Harvengt
agreed in condemning any prince who could not read and write
as 'not a little degenerate, like a *rusticus*, and in a certain way
like a beast'.[20] Academic devotees of courtly love, similarly,
depreciated the love of a rustic as no better than that of a mule.[21]
Even the devotee of homosexual love employs a corresponding
comparison, in a verse parody on that subject: rational man,
says the parodied cleric, should not emulate the sexual life of
animals, for 'only *rustici* ... who can be called beasts, should
properly ... filthy themselves with women'.[22] 'Country-
dwelling', 'low-class', and 'coarse', while remaining distinct
connotations, were thus deliberately associated. The meanings
can be found side-by-side in successive sentences. In thirteenth-
century Italy, which saw an unprecedented degree of urbani-
zation, the phrase 'rural and bestial men' could slip from a
townsman's pen without the slightest pause for reservations.[23]

Etymological usage, because not consciously controlled, is a
revealing index of social attitudes. But social attitudes as
important as this one—the evaluation by educated people of
peasantry—naturally came in for more expansive expression.
Treatment of the countryside and countrymen in medieval
literature is a subject with almost infinite nuances. Traces are
found remarkably early in the writings and lives of townsmen of
those rural fancies which have grown *pari passu* with man's move
into towns. Weightier than fancy, too, in the middle ages, was
the conviction of some moralists—a conviction usually stronger

the nearer an author was to the ascetic-monastic tradition—
that the peasant's life was essentially more virtuous than any
other: being laborious, close to nature and productive of food.[24]

These tributes to country life nevertheless throw into relief a
contrary tradition, bitterly hostile to peasantry. Typical of this
tradition is a parody-prayer, recorded in some dozen surviving
versions from the twelfth to the fifteenth centuries. It starts: 'O
God, who hast sown discord between clergy and peasant,
permit us by Thy Grace to live from their work, enjoy their
wives, cohabit with their daughters and delight in their
death.'[25] Other satire in verse or prose presents the peasant as
characteristically vicious, filthy, and dishonest.[26] The theme
even extends to certain motifs in courtly and troubadour
poetry.[27] Its variations combine to show it expressed a real
sentiment. It was not a mere literary flourish. Dante did not
speak only for himself when he wished the 'stinking' peasants
would leave Florence and go back to their wretched villages.[28]
In what was probably his most widely-read book, Petrarch, too,
took up the theme. He answered an imaginary complaint by a
landowner that his farm-foreman was dishonest, by explaining
that any farmworker not in the last degree idle and fraudulent
was to be counted a blessing.[29]

The literary depreciation of peasantry, with its references to
the 'envy' of rustics and to standing conflict between them and
clergy, may suggest we are in the presence of medieval class
conflict. There may have been conflict. But fine distinctions are
necessary in deciding what classes were involved. In chapter 11
something will be said about variations in the meaning of the
term 'clergy': it did not always mean what we would mean by
it.[30] Other considerations, too, suggest that it was the educated
man as such, not the churchman as such, who was most tempted
to cry down the peasant. One is that in the twelfth and
thirteenth centuries the homeland of this literary motif was
France, whose schools and universities made it by general
consent a conspicuously well-educated country.[31] Again, when
the motif gathered strength outside France, in the fourteenth
century, it would be found not only in the new universities (one
particularly sharp parody in the late middle ages is signed by its
author 'B. A. Vienna'),[32] but in Italian humanistic circles
represented by Dante and Petrarch. Finally, the same lesson

can be learned from the content of the attack. The peasant, besides being stinking, greedy, etc., is often an 'ass' and a 'fool'.[33] That is intellectual contempt. The 'fool' of drama in fact owes part of his ancestry to this image of the peasant bumpkin, victim of the humour of ingenious townsmen scarcely his social superiors, in the fourteenth and fifteenth centuries.[34]

The satirists and their audiences did not object to the country-dweller just because he happened to live out of town. It was only that *rustici* in the first sense, of 'countrymen', happened also to be *rustici* in the other senses, base and brutish. The true target of the educated man's disdain was the mass of the base and brutish. This fact is betrayed by another common pejorative usage: that of the term *vulgus* (crowd), with its near synonyms. Professor Thorndike, in his marathon study of texts in the history of magic and experimental science, has noticed the frequency with which terms like *vulgus* and *plebs* occur in pejorative contexts in medieval Latin scientific writers.[35] Typical expressions are: the 'grossness and turbidity of the mind of the masses, and of uneducated people';[36] or (from Neckham, the scholar who has told us of learning's innate tendency to arrogance) the 'windy populace' (*ventosa plebs*).[37] Our combative William of Conches and Roger Bacon often let slip such aspersions on the *vulgaris* and the *vulgus*.[38] Similar aspersions occur in writings which, while having less claim to be called scientific, still have some to be called philosophic, and which in one way or another represented a substantial literate public. The *Secretum Secretorum* is not without its elitist traits. For instance 'Aristotle' urges 'Alexander' in one place: 'do not be like the ignorant people of the temples who follow the letter without understanding the meaning.'[39] Fra Salimbene, spokesman for third-generation, well-bred Franciscans, does not hesitate to revile certain religious enthusiasts as good-for-nothing 'swineherds and cowherds'; as a 'ribald, swineherding, foolish and ignoble crowd' of persons 'no use' for anything.[40] (That idea of a person 'no use for anything' occurs also in the widely-copied *Moralium Dogma Philosophorum*, which borrowed it from Cicero.)[41] Here again the middle ages foreshadow the Italian Renaissance. The two cultures, if they really were two, meet in the much-read Petrarch. Petrarch uses with great regularity a figure of speech which contrasts the 'wise'—who are 'rare' or 'few', with the *volgar gente, turba*, or *vulgus*—the last characterized by 'raving' and the pursuit of pleasure.[42]

A trend sympathetic to these uncomplimentary remarks about low-class persons can be traced in a negative view of poverty in the abstract, prevalent in some of the same circles in the thirteenth century. Saint Francis apotheosized Lady Poverty. But there was another view. It is best expressed in *The Romance of the Rose*, a document which can claim in this particular to have struck quite as deep a chord in the minds of educated contemporaries as Saint Francis's allegory. In the *Romance* Poverty is not a lady. She is an ogress 'worse than death'. She is wife of Faint Heart and mother of Theft.[43] Hating poverty like this did not mean hating the poor. It might even be said to mean the opposite, in the sense that to make poverty the source of pusillanimity and dishonesty is to excuse any poor persons guilty of those defects. What is certain, about the allegory in the *Romance*, is that it lacked the character of a positive compliment to the poor *as they are*, implied by the Franciscan exaltation of poverty.

A frequent pejorative use of the term 'rustic'; occasional aspersions on the brutality of country-dwellers and on the *vulgus*: these traits, occurring here and there in academically respectable literature, suggest a distinct social attitude. The educated were an élite, set above the herd of ordinary men.

'Herd' is the right word. For this interpretation is corroborated, not now by mere literary 'asides', but by two distinct philosophical concepts, found in the same literature. The first of these concepts was that the uneducated man was sub-human. The argument had a concise form and some more elaborate ones. Philip of Harvengt, who was heard a moment ago comparing an illiterate prince to a beast, expounded the concise form. The *Carmina Burana*, those revealing songs of students in off-duty mood, were a degree more expansive:

> The illiterate man is like a brute
> Since he to art is deaf and mute.[44]

Others could go further and make the illiterate man actually dead. The essence of the idea was the same. For it *was* an idea, and at bottom quite a sophisticated one. Boethius had taught that the essential difference between men and animals was that man knew himself.[45] Self-knowledge only had to be confounded with education for the uneducated to come out as theoretical animals. 'It is an old proverb', wrote an enthusiast for learning *c.* 1160, 'and one celebrated by the ancients, that as far as men are removed from beasts, so far are the educated removed from the illiterate.'[46] The very widely-read ethical manual of Guillaume Peyraut, written about 1240, actually cited Boethius for its contention that 'the uneducated are wretched in this life. They are in a certain way lower than the brutes.'[47] Like other ideas in its family this equation of humanity with education reached its most confident expression in the Italian Renaissance, for instance in Petrarch and Salutati.[48] But it has a clear medieval ancestry.

The equation of the uneducated man with a beast was at home mainly among humanists. The other, scientific wing of the intellectual élite, represented by astrologers, used a second argument. The chief scholastic problem relating to astrology was that of free will. Did the stars infringe human free will or not? If they did, what was left of Christianity? If they did not, what was left of astrology's claim to predict human affairs, on which a large part of its title to attention rested? Astrology would not have survived if there had been no device for resolving this problem. There were in fact several devices. One is tell-tale in the present connection. For in reconciling two inimical sides of the paradox, what it succeeded in doing was splitting human society—along the same lines, wise and unwise, few and many, as in the case of the humanists.

The whole procedure comes out well in William of Auvergne's *De Universo*, written *c.* 1230.

The common crowd, because of its multitude and paucity of intellect, as well as because of other evil dispositions, lives almost like brute animals. This crowd for the most part therefore follows its inborn natures. . . . It is swept into committing robberies, thefts, murders, and into fighting wars. In the same way wolves driven by hunger attack and eat men whom they at other times avoid. . . . Once the causes of such events are understood, the disorders which follow in the world of man can be predicted. A prediction can be made with certainty, and as a rule for the whole. But the same prediction cannot be made for the particular. For no one can foreknow anything of this sort about a single human being. This is because the wise, and those who dominate their passions, know that human passions are not to be obeyed. Through the virtuous use of free will the wise avoid following their passions. Indeed, they suppress and extinguish them in their own persons.[49]

To exhaust the questions leading out of this passage would be to write another *De Universo*. But one question poses itself immediately. Can free will logically be denied to a collective when granted to its members? William of Auvergne, one of the most intelligent as well as one of the most historically illuminating of medieval philosophers, ignores this question; and for a transparent reason. Those who make any use of free will are the wise few. They are so few as to allow an amicable political settlement with astrology, on the basis of a blithe, Stoical carve-up of the *societas Christiana*.

William's solution to this point was not just his own. Put more or less elaborately, it was standard material for those who ran up against this question. How deep it lodged in scholastic thought can be judged from its presence in Aquinas. In one place, Aquinas allowed himself to write as follows on the subject:

[The?] many follow their passions, i.e. the motions of the sensitive appetite. This is where the celestial bodies can play their part. The wise, on the contrary, who resist these passions, are few. Therefore astrologers can predict truly about the many, above all about the whole. But they cannot predict about the particular. For nothing prevents any man resisting his passions by free will. Whence the astrologers themselves say: 'the wise man dominates the stars'—in as far, that is, as he governs his passions.[50]

The contrast between the raging many and the wise few is less graphic in Aquinas than in William. But the logic of the two arguments is the same. And they give the same impression of political compromise. Turning straight from his Aristotle and his Ptolemy, the angelic doctor solves an imponderable theological question with a stroke of the pen. His élite here is the Stoic élite of the wise.

Academics, then, sometimes depreciated the rustic, brute-like multitude. To read their depreciation out of its context is to risk distorting their portrait. Their remarks were not made as sneers after a good dinner. They were side-blows in a struggle against ignorance, a struggle whose earnestness will not necessarily be clear to us after seven more centuries of cultural development. Yet even before the Italian Renaissance such intellectualist outlooks had won some victories. People in high places held them, and the outlooks were often embodied in substantial political privileges, of a sort to be discussed in chapter 12. So they have been worth gathering together. They portray a shaded, but still distinct, facet of the medieval university soul.

We are discussing in this chapter the relationship of the intellectual élite with those below it. Two further elements in this relationship need exploring.

## 2. POPULAR REACTIONS

It may be asked, if education really did encourage elitism of the sort that rained abuse on rustics, and if the élite really did get into positions where rustics might feel the weight of this contempt, why the rustics should rarely be heard complaining. The answer is that medieval rustics are rarely heard saying anything. They generally had to revolt to be heard even in their own time. It is only the greater of their revolts that can be heard by us at six centuries' distance. Nevertheless, if a historian listens carefully to these great medieval peasant revolts he will, in the appropriate milieux, hear an expressly anti-academic note in some of them.

In the appropriate milieux: the great age of French university expansion was the thirteenth century; that of English, the fourteenth. Both expansions coincided with the most notorious medieval peasant revolts of their respective countries. The rising of the *Pastoureaux*, cow-herds, struck France in 1251, the year before Aquinas settled in Paris. The English peasants rose in 1381, Wyclif's heyday. Each of these famous revolts had its own political and economic causes, independent of academic history. They nevertheless shared one element which connects both with the schools: a general hostility to 'clerks' in the special sense of those who had benefited by education.

The fullest account of the *Pastoureaux* is that by Matthew Paris. The details he gives of its outbreak add together to give a consistent message. He tells how the rebels saw their foremost target in the Dominican and Franciscan orders (orders just then establishing themselves in universities); how the peasants marched first to Orleans 'where a university of scholars flourished'; how they answered words (from a scholars' spokesman) with brute force; how it was the 'clerks' rather than anyone else, who thought fit to lock themselves behind closed doors, and yet saw twenty-five of their number killed; how the peasants, after smashing windows to get in, seized priceless books and burned them; how it was particularly the university that suffered, while the townsmen either looked on or actually helped the rebels; and finally how the bishop of Orleans and his episcopal clergy only involved themselves tardily on the university's behalf, to avoid seeming feeble.[51]

The same note is heard later in the tumult of the English Peasants' Revolt. The English rebels in their turn included Dominicans and Franciscans among their leading victims, together with other highly-placed clerics. The fact that some of the lower priesthood joined in the revolt, and that the rebels had no quarrel with the purely religious functions of clergy, makes their objection to the 'clergy' in an academic sense stand out all the more. This objection is not a mere inference. Rural unease about the drain of farm-labour through schools is in evidence from the years before and after the revolt. A Commons petition of 1376 had warned against villeins' sons who 'seek advancement by clergy'. In the 1390s an anti-clerical vernacular poem, *Pierce the Ploughmans Crede*, would specifically revile the 'beggar's brat' who is sent to school, so that he can 'dwell with a lord' or even 'become a bishop'. In the revolt of 1381 antipathy to the scholar was occasionally explicit. Some of the rebels in the eastern counties burned the privileges of Cambridge university. Nor was that entirely a matter of tenant fighting landlord: for at the bonfire an old woman is said to have cried, 'Away with the learning of the clerks, away with it!' Thomas of Walsingham, the fullest if not always the most reliable narrative source for the revolt in the eastern counties, says 'it was dangerous to be seen with an inkhorn at one's side'.[52]

The anti-academic elements in the French rising of 1251, and in the English of 1381, are notable enough in themselves, attaching as they do to two of the most violent medieval peasant revolts. But they also serve to alert us to the possibility that the feature may have attached to less well-documented revolts. We know that clergy were a common target of these revolts. The 'clergy' in question may—according to the circumstances of each case—have been the specifically academic kind. Again, what has been learned of the revolts of 1251 and 1381 may urge us to search for the anti-academic motif outside the well-trodden annals of a revolt, in contemporary records of schools and universities. One pointer to the possible fruitfulness of this procedure touches a third famous peasant rising, the *Jacquerie* of 1358. We open the cartulary of the university of Paris for that year, and what do we find? A request by the arts faculty, in May, for government permission to block the two ends of its street at night. The reason is that lecturers and students have recently been coming into their classrooms in the morning to find 'filth' spread on their seats and elsewhere. The filth had been deliberately brought in from the streets by 'lewd men' and 'common whores', moved by the devil to 'impede the flower and pearl of learning'.[53] Plebeian disgruntlement at the airs and privileges of Paris scholars is apparent at various points in the late fourteenth century, but at no other point was it as explicitly plebeian, or as explicitly anti-scholar, as this.[54] Our document says this filthying of lecture-rooms is a recent scourge. This chronology, chiming in with that of the famous rising in the same year, suggests that we are once more in the presence of a popular discontent, one face of which was consciously turned against academics.

Rustics, when heard at all, are heard directly, talking the un-academic language of brutal revolt. Although the main victims of learned disdain, however, illiterate rustics were not the only ones. Depreciation of learned for ignorant might be felt further up the scale, by people themselves partly educated. At this point in the scale, too, some counter-resentment shows itself. It does so, appropriately, in a less physically extrovert way than the peasants': namely by myth and tale, in the half-legendary margin of academic history. For some medieval philosophers, especially those concerned with natural science, left along this margin a wake of rumour which suggests blemishes in their social relations.

The first rumour was a categorical one: intellectual curiosity as such, it said, endangered a man's social relations. 'If you exercise the virtue of prudence to excess,' warned *The Four Virtues*, an ancient ethical manual very popular in the twelfth century and later, 'you will be thought deviously clever; and your investigation of secrets will bring you a reputation for awesome subtlety. Your wish to know every little thing will cast you as envious, suspicious, solicitous and full of fear and cogitations. ... People will point at you and say you are wily and malicious, an enemy of simplicity. You will be universally condemned.'[55] That passage was one of those picked out for inclusion by that great exponent of the virtue of prudence, the Florentine Brunetto Latini, in his own manual *Li Tresors* (*c.* 1268).

One way the public expressed its antipathy to the curious was in the belief, true or false, that the culprits came to a bad end, or in some way suffered misfortune. John of Salisbury expressed this belief in relation both to 'diviners' and to astrologers. The long attack on *mathematici* in John's *Policraticus* (1159) concludes triumphantly:

I have attended the lectures of a very large number of astrologers, and known quite a few personally; yet I recall none who persisted long in this error, but that in the Lord's hand brought some condign punishment on him.[56]

This belief was a hardy one. It was echoed by Fra Giordano of Pisa, preaching in 1304. Giordano referred to 'those who wish to pry deeply into the secrets of God'. These 'want to understand by reason what they should hold by faith, and attain to things not granted to them'. Such people, said Giordano, 'break their necks, and go blind and mad'.[57]

What actual over-curious philosophers or astrologers John and Giordano were referring to, no one knows. There happen to be ominous blanks—possibly concealing 'bad ends'—in the biographies of at least two Chartrean philosophers (William of Conches and Adelard of Bath), if not astrologers, to which John's remark might in a general way have applied. He might also have had in mind the story told with some embarrassment by William of Malmesbury, of the learned bishop Gerard of York, found dead in 1108 with a book of 'curious arts' under his pillow.[58] Fra Giordano too may have been thinking of famous contemporaries. For the story was told in his Dominican circles, not without glee, of how that paragon of medieval medical writers, Peter of Spain, latterly Pope John XXI, had been crushed to death by a falling roof in 1277 while laughing at monks *quasi glorians in seipso*.[59] Or Giordano may have been thinking obliquely of the most controversial Paris philosopher of his day, Siger of Brabant, murdered in Orvieto in 1282 by his secretary who had 'gone mad'.[60] Perhaps the secretary too was an over-curious philosopher.

Whether or not these celebrities really were the ones envisaged, both John and Giordano could have found plenty of meat for their generalizations in periods outside their own. It had long been told of Erigena, the morning star of medieval philosophy in the ninth century, that he had been stabbed to death by his pupils with their pens. William of Malmesbury, who records this story,[61] gives it a degree more likelihood by saying in another place that Erigena was 'quick-tempered'.[62] Again, at the turn of the millennium the greatest northern French master of the *quadrivium*, 'who excelled all his contemporaries in extent of wisdom', Abbo of Fleury, was murdered. The motive of his murder is unclear. It occurred during a riot in and round a monastery he was visiting in a wild part of Aquitaine in 1004, and we only know that one party of the monks had some grievance against Abbo. But two facts, even if they are quite irrelevant, deserve recording in the present context. Immediately before he was called out to cope with the riot, Abbo had been sitting in the cloister 'dictating certain arithmetical calculations'. And long before, it is once revealed that Abbo's learning had aroused 'envy'.[63]

This police-court list may be fortuitous. Bad ends were not confined to philosophers. But there is just enough eerie concurrence of opinion and fact here to hint that natural science was not, as it might first have appeared, the safest of medieval pursuits. Similar evidence from Islam, for what it is worth, backs up the surmise: there too, a famous philosopher might meet his end by murder.[64] That some of the danger came from disaffected subordinates is corroborated by the existence of hostile legends about some philosophers. These included legends about less lethal 'bad ends': e.g. that the philosopher Simon of Tournai had (according to Gerald of Wales) expressed

such impious thoughts that he was punished finally by paralysis
and madness.[65] Again, some notable medieval men of science
acquired reputations for magic. Gerbert (known anyway to
have had a rough passage from his Rheims parishioners) won
such a name. Bacon, and above all Albert the Great, got it in the
thirteenth century. Even Grosseteste was believed by some
people to be a magician. There were others.[66] These legends
cannot but give us food for thought. They contrast symmetri-
cally with legends about saints: magic in one case, miracle in
the other. The difference points to a real divergence in popular
assessment of the two corresponding types of celebrity.

By the time of Albert the Great's death in 1270 the European
educated stratum was big enough to house a wide measure of
scepticism towards all these legends. Just as it became so, along
the same margin of academic history which the legends
occupied, better biographical data offer clearer evidence of
what the legends revealed only indirectly: coolness between the
sage and his subordinates. At the beginning of the fourteenth
century the first literary colossus of the Italian Renaissance,
Dante, was remembered in Florence as having had one fault
only: 'Because of his knowledge he was somewhat supercilious,
haughty, and disdainful, and, rather in the manner of an
ungracious philosopher, could not converse with unlearned
persons.[67] *Quasi nel modo di filosafo mal grazioso:* Villani, who
recorded this view, spoke as if the type would be recognized.
Indeed, it might have been recognized from Dante's own friend
Guido Cavalcanti ('one of the finest logicians the world
possessed', according to Boccaccio),[68] who was also remembered as *isdegnoso* (disdainful).[69] At the end of the same century
its most signal intellectual upstart, another Italian, Pope Urban
VI, whose studious tastes and asceticism had won him
widespread regard at the time of his election, was nevertheless
stigmatized even then for a single fault: 'he trusted too much in
his own prudence'.[70] A single fault: yet enough, in the view of
some contemporaries, to being the whole house of the church
tumbling down after 1378.

One element in the anticlericalism of some popular revolts
was reaction to the rise of an élite based on 'clergy', *alias*
educational qualification. On a higher level, the memories of
certain intellectual giants were hedged by unflattering legend

and report, suggestive of coolness between them and their subordinates. This much of a riposte can be detected, then, to those aspersions on rustics and cooks which punctuated philosophical tradition. Some of the intellectual giants, it is true, made up any quarrel they had with the multitude. Abbo and Albert in particular, far from suffering bad ends, had in an other-worldly sense the best ends imaginable. For both eventually passed through scrutiny into the church's canon as saints. Their progresses form one complication to the picture drawn. But they do not destroy it. The evidence presented shows that in the same measure that the intellectual bruised the head of his inferiors, they bruised his heel.

The progress of those intellectual giants to sainthood calls to mind, too, another group of personal histories, lending even further confirmation to our picture. To pass an eye over the scholastic roll of honour is to be struck by the number of its entries whose careers split in two, as they turned in some measure against their philosophical studies. Pierre Mandonnet noticed that certain thirteenth-century mendicants (most notably Vincent of Beauvais, Robert Kilwardby, and Thomas of Chantimpré, all three Dominicans), ended by veering more or less sharply away from the Aristotelianism they had begun with: towards less naturalistic, Augustinian paths of thought.[71] Similar bifurcation in scholars' personal careers can be traced more widely: above all in the same Dominican order—the order which made the knitting of piety and learning its peculiar province. Those scholars who entered the order in mid-career (like Alexander of Hales, or Roland of Cremona—who asked for the habit halfway through a lecture) were at a different stage on the same road as the philosophers who wearied of Aristotle. Even Aquinas, who put down his pen at forty-seven, calling his writings 'straw', went that way. Furthermore, the drift of part of the order at and after the end of the thirteenth century—especially in the Germany of Eckhart and Tauler—towards mysticism, may be seen as a corporate expression of the same trend.

Such bifurcation in personal careers was not, however, peculiar to Dominicans, or even to mendicants in general. It was a scholastic phenomenon. A number of prominent scholars over the twelfth and thirteenth centuries had evinced increasingly contemplative leanings towards the end of their lives. The poet-laureate of Aristotelianism, Alan of Lille, died in 1202 as a Cistercian monk. Few careers had been more boldly split in two in this way (though it was split more than once) than that of the arch-logician Abelard, stretching as it did from the rowdy *quartier latin* to his quiet monastic deathbed. If to these pilgrim scholars are added those bright youths (of whom Bruno of Cologne, head of the Rheims school at twenty-five, later founder of the Carthusians, is prototype) whose early conversion robbed them of mention in academic annals; and to those, others, in turn, who made no ceremony of their retreat (like ex-chancellor Gerson in the fifteenth century, exchanging letters with Carthusians from Lyons) we face something like a deserting army. In so far as the ruffian peasants of 1251 and 1381 were voicing a critique of the moral facet of the world of education, they found support from inside it. At its very heart that world was restive.

The intellectual interest, it was said earlier, was largely invisible. An attempt has been made to trace its physiognomy by observing its action, and reactions to it, in various spheres. There remains one sphere of these actions and reactions still to be looked at—a very big sphere.

3. NATIONAL PRIDE IN INTELLECT: FRANCE AND FLORENCE

Men of cultivated intelligence could look out on the world as the few looking on the many. But added up, the few were no so few. Their merits and circumstances, too, gave whatever numbers they had peculiar force. At their strongest they formed a vigorous and self-confident educated class. It might be expected that the ethos of such a group would exert influence on that of its body-politic. It did; and the influence can be traced. Indirect influences, elusively shaping the value-judgements of citizens by thousands, will appear from time to time in the following two chapters. But our tracing, now, of the moral physiognomy of an élite would be incomplete unless we paused at this point to remark on its direct extension, into national character. In those medieval societies most noted for rearing intellectuals, the pride in intellect noticed just now among individuals can be found transferred *en bloc* to national consciousness. Two societies in particular illustrate this.

Whatever other ancient dignities may have descended to her easterly neighbours, it was clear already in the twelfth century that France had inherited Athenian intellectual pre-eminence—France in the stricter sense, meaning the region round Paris. Paris might be a political and trading city of the first importance. Yet from about 1200 the first thing a visitor remarked on was the city's university: as likely as not it was what he had come for. Now in close co-operation with this academic growth grew political power: in effect a French colonial expansion, first to her own south, then to the Mediterranean. By 1300 France was known for more than her studies. She was the leading power in continental politics.

As an individual's success within his own nation affected his soul, so France's success in the consort of nations affected hers. The idea that the French were peculiarly proud was not entirely an invention of the late thirteenth century. Traces of it are to be found much earlier.[72] But now, in the age of Charles of Anjou and Philip the Fair, *superbia Gallica* became a watchword among all who felt their status threatened by it. 'They love themselves and despise everyone else. ... They think they have a right to first place in the world', wrote a Rhinelander in 1288.[73] 'Superbissimi . . . sunt Gallici,' wrote Parma's Fra Salimbene [*c.* 1280]: 'they scorn all the nations of the world, and especially the English and Italians.'[74] At the start of the fourteenth century Pope Boniface VIII was said to have staked his soul on crushing *superbia Gallicana*,[75] and Villani records the Flemings as having fought the battle of Courtrai in the same cause.[76] From the North Sea to Palermo the self-confidence of the new imperial power ruffled feelings. Even the Frenchman, John of Jandun, praising his capital in 1323, had to admit that when its inhabitants did depart from the golden mean, it was to be 'somewhat boastful'.[77]

While the cry of hurt susceptibilities makes imperfect historical testimony, this one is widely enough heard, and well enough corroborated from within France, to deserve attention. Why *superbia Gallica* deserves special attention now is because of one peculiarity it had. It was largely an intellectual pride: the French were best because they were more intelligent. We can perhaps read this message in the exultation of Jean de Meung [*c.* 1277] that Duke Charles of Anjou, a mere 'pawn' in the international game of chess being played in southern Italy, had conquered through out-playing his rivals.[78] We can perhaps read it in the plea of one of France's most redoubtable foes, the contentious Italian pope Urban VI, to the young emperor-to-be Wenzel in 1382: Wenzel must not be 'outwitted' by the 'traps and snares' that lay in the smooth words of the French, who hide ambitions of world-rule under an unmilitary manner.[79] But the message does not have to be sought out in oblique phrases. It was stated explicitly by France's own literary patriots, from the mid-thirteenth to the early fourteenth century.

They expressed it through the familiar devices for expressing opinion. The first of the patriots in question used the device of ancient prophecy. He was the author of the 'Fountain of all Sciences', attributed to the apocryphal ancient 'philosopher Sidrach'.[80] Written probably about 1243 in Lyons, the book gained a wide circulation in French and some other vernaculars during the fourteenth and fifteenth centuries. Not only did the author have a high view of the role of the French in the world. ('They will be the best people in both God's eyes and the world's,' prophesies 'Sidrach'.)[81] That role depended to a notable degree on the mind. As world leaders the French replaced the ancient Greeks, masters of science and astronomy.[82] The French will be 'the most honoured people of this world,' says 'Sidrach', 'and the most wise'.[83] The author also mentions France's religion and courage among her titles to hegemony.[84] But the 'philosopher Sidrach' puts wisdom first.

Another way, besides 'prophecy', in which new opinions were expressed was through the reinterpretation of old ones. One familiar opinion was that stars influenced character. Stellar influence did not just affect individuals. The stars' aspect was bound to be broadly the same, it could be argued, over a whole region. So it affected national character too. This astrological reasoning lent itself to the rationalization of views on national orders of precedence. It also built into such rationalization an intellectualist cast, characteristic of all astrology. Both tendencies are illustrated in the employment of this idea by the ideologue Pierre Dubois, writing in 1306:

Through . . . the benevolence of heavenly harmony, those men born and reared in the kingdom of the French, especially near Paris, far excel in nature those born in other regions: in how they behave; in constancy, fortitude, and good looks. This is taught by experience, the supreme mistress of practical knowledge.[85]

In a more private memoir Dubois explained precisely what this French excellence consisted in. It was above all a matter of 'reason'. For

the Gauls use the true judgement of reason much more surely than any other nation in the world. They are not moved otherwise than in due order. They hardly ever or never at all, impugn right reason. We do not see this in other nations.[86]

Among old ideas on the formation of national character, the thirteenth century possessed a more down-to-earth one than any provided by astrology. It related to climate. The idea came in Aristotle. In the *Politics* (vii, vii, 1–3), Aristotle had explained how climate affected temperament: the hot Asians were intelligent but spiritless; the cold northern Europeans were courageous but stupid; only the Greeks, whose climate stood half-way, combined intelligence with spirit, and consequently deserved to rule the world. This passage had a lively medieval career. Part of the career took it to France. In 1323 John of Jandun employed it in his encomium of Paris. But the Aristotelian passage called for changes. Divine bounty, pitying human frailty, has put—not Greece, now, but—France under a temperate aspect of the stars. Its inhabitants neither freeze, nor lose 'blood and spirit' through pores opened by heat. Heat inclines man to such brutal rages that 'it stops patient, thoughtful inquiry, and the exercise of prudent judgement'. Cold meanwhile paralyses men into a state of permanent apprehension.

But the third quality, the one pertaining to Gaul, stands between these two, enjoying a fit proportion of each. From one extreme her nature wins the manly vigour of the spirit to rule; from the other, meanwhile, the talent of divine prudence. Consequently—and it is truth, not adulation that moves me to say this—the most illustrious and excellent kings of France deserve to be kings of the whole world—so far, that is, as it is a question of an inborn preference for the good.[87]

France's claim to first place in the world rested on, besides manly vigour, 'divine prudence'. In adapting Aristotle's model John had in fact used some of the intelligence he claimed for his nation. He had made a deft change in the climatic map in his model: for John, heat produced ferocity; for Aristotle, down in the hot Aegean, it had produced intelligence. So small was the change needed to make Greek self-confidence at home in Paris.

As an example of the irrational behaviour of other nations Pierre Dubois had cited the danger pilgrims ran in Italy, where they could be knocked down by the crowd and killed by a horse without anyone's bothering.[88] But while Pierre Dubois wrote, Fra Giordano of Pisa was astonishing Florentines with tales of his travels in France. He had seen corpses, up to four hundred at a time, left hanging on gallows until they rotted—a horrible sight, he said.[89] So there were two views about who the ferocious barbarians were. There were conversely two views on the identity of the most rational nation. Next to France, Italy was chief contestant. The region of Italy that contested most bravely was the region where Giordano thus scandalized his listeners: Tuscany, with its own political *enfant terrible*, Florence. Like France, Florence had a reputation for pride. The wounded Dante often levelled this charge against the city which had expelled him. But the charge was not only his. Florence's most sober inhabitants could recall later that in Dante's time 'Florence was *fat*, full of citizens, puffed up with pride'.[90] The chroniclers of the decades of Dante's exile, just after the year 1300, return again and again to their city's *rigoglio* or *superbia*.[91] Nor do we lack occasional first-hand illustrations. It was fairly standard Florentine rhetoric in Dante's time, for example, to say in Florence that her glory was such that 'no splendour could sufficiently express' it.[92]

Though there was nothing extraordinary in civic pride as such, the degree of it in Florence appears to have been egregious, and it might deserve attention for that reason alone. But there is another reason. Like French pride, Florentine had an intellectual cast, which it shared to some extent with a general Tuscan feeling of the same kind. Professor Baron has shown, with abundant quotation, that in the crisis of 1400 Florence would start putting about how she was the most 'reasonable' (*ragionevole*) of cities.[93] Now there is no doubt that Florence did put that view about after 1400. Bernardino of Siena, himself a Tuscan, and the greatest preacher of the age, began his Florentine preaching career in 1424 with the words:

'Italy is the most intelligent country in Europe. Tuscany is the most intelligent region in Italy. Florence is the most intelligent town in Tuscany.'[94] There is every reason to think this compliment only confirmed the audience's estimate of itself.

The one adjustment that needs making in Professor Baron's view is that traces of Tuscan intellectual self-confidence are detectable long before 1400. Northern Italians in general could think themselves, and be thought, especially clever from as early as the eleventh century.[95] The signs thicken in the thirteenth. Bartholomaeus Anglicus, who like many northerners did not distinguish the different provinces of Italy very clearly, puts the 'Venetians', though not the Lombards or Tuscans in his dictionary (*c.* 1240); and includes 'providentia' among the outstanding virtues of that race.[96] Even Alexander of Roes (*c.* 1284), despite his attribution of intellectual hegemony to the French, included 'prudentia' among Italian national virtues.[97] In the thirteenth century the signs gather round Florence. In the 1260s a rout of Florence's army had been followed by a prophecy that the city would, despite the defeat, live for ever 'by means of dissimulation'.[98] Soon after 1300 Florence's most famous son, bitter in his exile, would address his native city sarcastically as *tu con senno:* 'thou so wise'.[99] Boccaccio, similarly, would criticize his compatriots for the habit of 'offering an opinion on everything in the world'.[100] The Italian usage of calling Germans 'barbarians' is supposed to have been launched by Petrarch.[101] But statesmen who saw the world with Italian eyes had called the Germans barbarians from at least the beginning of the fourteenth century: for example, Robert of Anjou, in recommending there should be no more German emperors after the death of Henry VII in 1311.[102] The term 'barbarian' did not simply mean 'stupid'. But it had that connotation among others: Roger Bacon had characterized irrationality as the essence of barbarism.[103]

The intellectual self-confidence of Tuscans is nevertheless best illustrated once more in the posthumous career of Aristotle's passage on climate. The Italian climate was manifestly nearer to the Greek than the French climate was. So the adaptation of Aristotle's idea was easier. Already in *c.* 1270, the Florentine Dominican Remigio de' Girolami, in a prologue to Aristotle's *Ethics*, repeated that climatic view of history which gave the inhabitants of Mediterranean countries normally a 'better brain and ingenuity than those who live in cold regions'.[104] Others had more precise climatic ideas. In Arezzo the belief was already well-established when recorded just after 1300 that the town's air and site produced *sottilissimi uomini*.[105] About the turn of the century another Dominican, Ptolemy of Lucca, gave a full-scale elaboration of Aristotle's theory of climate, for Tuscan benefit. In Ptolemy's eyes Africa, Asia, and even southern Italy were too hot, northern Europe too cold, to produce people with the right mixture of courage, and 'reliance on their intelligence'. The right mixture was to be found pre-eminently in the northern half of the writer's own peninsula, whose cities were consequently—the familiar conclusion— justified in their political claims.[106]

Pride in intellect, then, penetrated to a national level. Through *superbia gallica* and *lo rigoglio dei Fiorentini*, it played its part in international politics. Its appearance there helps teach us its force and character. The intellectual élite could identify itself with a nation.

Our proper subject remains, nevertheless, the operation of intellectual 'pride' within societies, rather than between them. For it is only inside a social hierarchy that the slow growth of the intellectual élite can be measured. The élite's efforts to distinguish itself from those below it have been described. But distinguishing itself from those below was only the lesser of its difficulties. The greater one was clearing a path above. The human layer that now, in the central middle ages, separated itself from the rustics in a bid to make an élite of the mind, must sooner or later touch up against the underside of the existing top stratum, the ruling powers in church and state. The story of what happened when it did is one of new battles, on new fields.

CHAPTER 11

# The Assault on the Citadel: Theory

Men of vigorous intellect are the natural rulers and
lords of others.

Pierre Dubois, *De recuperatione Terrae Sanctae* (1306)
p. 112, (paraphrasing Aristotle, *Politics*, I, 2, §2).

BEFORE educated persons, as such, came to play any substantial
role in the European political scene, two types of élite had been
acknowledged there: one ecclesiastical, one secular. The new
intellectual élite had an impact on both. As often when social
forces advance—especially if they command pen and paper—
direct impact was preceded by an artillery barrage of theory.
To be more precise there were two barrages. For they were
distinct: the doctrine of each of the two existing élites, church
and lay, needed its own approach. This chapter will consider
the attack on each in turn.

### I. THE THEORETICAL ASSAULT ON PRIESTLY AUTHORITY

Medieval Europe was theoretically a *societas Christiana*. By the
same theory its top stratum was the clergy, in particular the
priesthood. One aspect of the Gregorian envigoration of canon
law had been the sharper division of clergy and laity. Within the
clergy the Gregorians had also emphasized the special rank of
the priest, the man through whom the eucharistic bread was
miraculously changed to flesh. These distinctions were in
practice challenged at all levels by political and economic
forces. But the canonical supremacy of the priesthood as such
over everyone else remained the most consistent theory of
hierarchy the middle ages knew. It was an integral part of the
doctrine which the schools, at least their theological and legal
faculties, existed to expound. As a theory it outlived most of a
succession of violent attempts to reduce it.

In view of this resilience and the learned support it drew on, it must seem all the more surprising that this theory should even come into question as a possible target for the rising intellectual estate. Most medieval learned men, after all, are supposed to have been clergy. Not a few had priest's orders—which were open to most of those who took the necessary trouble. Where theology crowned a school career, and priesthood clerical status, the claims of learning and ecclesiastical orders were from one angle identical; and they were frequently spoken of as such.

But the symmetry was only from one angle. Theology itself separated by crucial distinctions the essence of philosopher from the essence of priest. The former was marked out by moral and intellectual qualities, the latter by appointment and function. Canonically—it never came to this in practice—the wisest layman yielded place to the most ignorant priest. For all their tendency to coalesce in the middle ages, the two notions of 'wise man' and 'priest' thus remained in theoretical tension. Now relationships established in theory have generally, so far in this book, been found reflected in the everyday world. This tension was no exception. We only have to search in the right places to find, in either acute or chronic form, a challenge made by the intellectual estate to the priesthood.

## (*i*) *Intellectualist heresy*

'A challenge to the priesthood': that sounds like heresy. The field of formal and recognized heresy, accordingly, is an appropriate place for the search to begin. On an abstract plane the status of heresy as a specifically intellectual challenge to authority is so clear as to be scarcely worth pointing out. 'Heresy' meant 'choice' in Greek. Although you had yourself to be fairly high in the intellectual élite to know that fact, the term 'heresy' throughout its medieval vicissitudes kept this connotation. A man 'chose' his own path of thought or action, independently of authority. What he chose *by*, naturally, was his intellect. (The word had almost the same root in Latin as 'heresy' had in Greek: *lego*, 'I choose'.) Any heresy at all, that is to say, because it involved conscious decision in defiance of authority, was by definition an intellectual challenge to the priesthood.

In terms of concrete history things were not so simple. Let us look at out-of-school heresies first. Peasant enthusiasms ignited by will-o'-the-wisp visions; Cathars who thought the wicked world not worth rationalizing about; heady anchoresses seduced by supernatural embraces; anti-scholastic Spiritual Franciscans, whose mistrust of reason as a threat to faith was so great as to call their own faith in question: none of these propose themselves as having been particularly rational in standpoint. In appearance at least, much popular heresy was pronouncedly *un*intellectual. It could even be anti-intellectual, as it was with those book-burning cow-herds of Orleans.

Yet these unintellectual manifestations remained secondary, even among heresies which had nothing or little to do with universities. Behind such manifestations the broad, perennial core of dissent vindicated the Greek etymology of the word 'heresy'. For this core included the most widespread and hardy movements: Waldensians, Joachites, Wyclifites—to name the main groups. And these movements shared certain rationalistic features, which form a constant counter-motif to orthodox church history from at least the twelfth century on. The rationalistic features can be brought down to three. All the movements just named showed a 'common-sense' antipathy to popular practices they saw as superstitious, for example, profuse veneration of relics and saints. All, secondly, implicitly defended the right of devotees to interpret scripture inde-pendently of church authority: one man's understanding was above the authority of the hierarchy. (The extra prominence sometimes given to the Holy Ghost within the Trinity was one sign of this stress on the role of individual understanding.) Thirdly, all these movements set a high value on the duty of preaching. It was superior to the duty of obedience, in a believer; and in a priest, according to one approach, it was superior even to that of celebrating the sacraments—as if the words of mortals were the only means God had of illuminating men's minds.

Holding aloof from popular superstition; making up one's own mind; then telling everyone else about it—these three practices, characteristically rational, were also characteristic of a broad core in medieval popular heresy. The core was in that measure intellectualist.

What of heresies within the universities? Appearances can

also be confusing there. Yet there too the intellectualist connotation of the word 'heresy' was vindicated. To demonstrate this thoroughly would take far longer than is now appropriate. But one well-known and representative case will serve as an illustration. The most palpably heterodox current in thirteenth-century Paris was the one labelled by historiography 'Averroism'. Among the elusive strands of thought behind this label one was—and others were related to—gnosticism. The name of that ancient doctrine signals its emphasis. It stressed knowledge—not grace, faith, sacraments, charity, or any of the other elements in Christian schemes of salvation—as the path to God. Through neo-Platonist channels, some just charitable, gnostic influence was invading Christian philosophy during Aquinas' lifetime. Its best-known figurehead, Siger of Brabant, was said to have preached *inter alia* the ascent of man to God by way of the mind alone. Man's intellect came by its own efforts to participate in God's. Siger was and is harder to pin down in writing. But writings by others make it clear that a doctrine of this sort was common talk in the philosophy faculty where he taught.[1]

So the intellectualist challenge to priestly authority can, as was to be expected, partly be sought in the history of medieval heresies. Despite the apparently anti-rational character of some popular heretical movements, the perennial core of popular heresy, represented by Waldensians and other sects with wide influence, had certain intellectualist traits. Meanwhile the universities' 'Averroism' presented a related challenge in a more philosophical form. Knowledge, not any external institution or its officers, was the supreme authority.

Elaborations of this principle could be multiplied from histories of heresy, academic and non-academic. To seek our intellectualist challenge to the priesthood simply in histories of formal heresy would however be to miss at least half the quarry. For the corpus of surviving records on heresy does not, in fact, give a true or complete replica of the vagaries of medieval religious opinion. There are two reasons why not. The first is that most of the corpus is made up of documents belonging primarily not to the history of heresy but to the history of persecution. The two histories obey different impulses. Not only do persecutors tend to paint the difference of heresy and orthodoxy as black and white, when really there were shades of grey. The records only exist where circumstances were such as to set moving the cumbersome machinery of persecution: like outraged popular devotion, or a threat to social order. These circumstances apart, recorded cases of heresy in fact dwindle to a few squabbles amongst monks. Outside such restricted circles, people in practice got away with thinking and saying all sorts of unorthodox things which never got labelled as heresy.

The second reason why we cannot be content to search sources on 'heresy' is one which immediately concerns the matter of intellectuals. The intellectuals *par excellence* were scholars. When it came to charges of unorthodox belief scholars had an advantage. For all its exposure to publicity, and the academic in-fighting which made accusations the order of the day, the academic body as such was virtually immune from charges of heresy. It held the key posts. From at least the early thirteenth century, when Dominicans replaced Cistercians as chief persecutors, the authorities whose job it was to distribute labels of heresy were usually university *alumni*. Quite apart from that, Christendom's main centre of higher education, Paris, actually came to see *herself*, as an institution, as principal arbiter of Catholic doctrine. Whether or not there was heresy in that very claim, the fact that it was made, more or less unchallenged, both illustrates and indicates the privileged status of the body of scholars it favoured. The profession of learning had often enjoyed this privilege. The ethics of the Roman learned, Stoic ethics, had been accepted as good Christianity for centuries by the early church, for the simple reason that the only people intellectually qualified to decide otherwise had been reared in the classical tradition: it took the threat of Manicheism to make the Fathers realize that the ethics of their classical masters were not only incomplete, but distorted.[2] That lesson had to be learned more than once. Now, in the late middle ages (after 1277) it was a fact that learned persons usually had to throw the gauntlet down *outside* the schools before dangerous fulminations of heresy were launched at them. The arch-heretics of the fourteenth century, Marsilius and Wyclif, were revered and unmolested while they remained merely academic figures (as Pope Gregory XI complained when he finally condemned Wyclif).[3] The University of Paris's biggest *cause célèbre* in that century was on a matter (the Immaculate Conception) which had troubled ordinary authorities for years before the university took it up.[4] Conversely, in the fifteenth century, the most vigorous prosecution at the university's instigation was that of—not any Averroist or unbeliever, though plenty were available, but—the one type most conspicuously foreign to university sympathy: an illiterate girl, Joan of Arc, later canonized. Specifically intellectual assault on church authority meanwhile came only rarely and slowly to figure as heresy, even when it flaunted itself in the high politics of conciliarism.

In our search for the intellectuals' challenge to priestly authority, then, there are two reasons why heresy cannot tell the whole story. One is that the sources for heresy follow contours dictated by the politics of persecution. The other is that the milieu from which the challenge mostly came, the universities, was also the milieu which defined orthodoxy. There are other reasons; but these are the main ones.

## (ii) The 'clergy' of the educated

It is not, then, in inquisitorial records that the intellectuals' challenge to the priesthood must primarily be sought. The challenge was too broad and too subtle. Its spearhead acted indeed almost invisibly—invisibly even to the eyes of the challengers. The man qualified by intellect did not charge at the priesthood full tilt. He merely usurped its place.

Such tacit usurpations reflect themselves nowhere better than in linguistic usage. In the usage of the central middle ages a word immediately suggests itself in this context for consideration: 'clerk'. The 'clerk' had originally, in Greek, been a person chosen by lot. The very word 'clergy' had meant 'élite'. The meaning 'élite' remained when the word entered Latin. But how was the élite distinguished? In canon law, which was responsible for its entry, *clericus* meant someone in ecclesiastical orders, that is, who had been ceremoniously tonsured and (probably) also invested with at least the minor order of 'doorkeeper'. But by the twelfth century a second meaning had come into being, and this second meaning established itself in common language as a rival to the first. In the thirteenth century, Aristotle, or that scourge of the papacy and its clergy Frederick II, could be said without any sense of anomaly to be great 'clerks'. In the fourteenth century Wyclif, for all the body-blows he levelled at the doctrine of clerical supremacy over the laity, was once praised as 'the greatest clerk that ever was at Oxford'. In short, the word also meant 'scholar'. It had the same connotations as 'scholar' has now, that is, a learned person, in or out of school. An intellectual distinction had slipped in beside a sacramental.

Of course if these two meanings had been kept distinct in medieval minds no special psychological conclusion could be drawn. But they were not. An occasional thoughtful observer might see what was happening to his language.[5] But he was exceptional. In some regions the two meanings of 'clerk' were confounded so deeply as to defy modern efforts to separate them. How far students at Paris, Oxford, and other northern universities in the thirteenth century were in the canonical sense clergy is much harder to establish then we might imagine. A *Sermo ad clericos* can be understood as addressed to university students and masters. But whether all were tonsured is doubtful: scarcely a trace of any enactment has been found, in volumes of university legislation, compelling laggards to take tonsures. If tonsures had been the norm such enactments would surely have survived.[6] Again, when, from the thirteenth century, kings' officers came seeking criminous clerks, efforts would be made by all parties to define who was and who was not under church privilege; as if the answer was not always clear from the start. Such doubt was in fact chronic to the exercise of a scholar's jurisdictional privilege as a whole.[7] In the fourteenth century, when there are more documents and more universities to study, and when legal distinctions may have been more fastidious, we can measure the proportion of *tonsured* clergy among students at some new universities. The answer comes out astonishingly low—for instance, 35 per cent at Cologne, and 20 per cent at Heidelberg.[8] Yet 'clerk', for all that, went on being generally understood as 'scholar'. Nor, whatever the exact prescriptions of canon law on the subject, was this kind of clerk any more clearly distinguished by celibacy; as a common group of English and French surnames testifies.

The same story could be told upside-down about 'lay', and it would have the same moral.[9] The equivocal use of these two terms has done mischief in historiography. It has encouraged a tendency to exaggerate the ecclesiastical character of medieval education; and it has at the same time obscured the real character. For, once the equivocation is detected, it points diametrically the other way. 'It is precisely the breaking-down and blurring of these ecclesiastical distinctions between orders', the late Herbert Grundmann wrote, 'that make one of the university's most noteworthy effects.'[10] But this is only half the truth. Distinctions were not merely broken down. They were rebuilt on a new criterion. The boundary between clerk and lay, rather than vanishing, made a subtle shift. From a distinction defined by sacrament and function it came in day-to-day thinking to cover one of intellect and achievement: between educated, and uneducated.

### (iii) The priesthood of the wise

The quiet usurpation of an ecclesiastical category by an intellectual can thus be discovered hidden in ordinary parlance. But the same usurpation can be sensed on more explicit levels of expression. I refer firstly to certain remarks thrown out by respectable theologians, in the course of some discussion, which imply that learning is in some way the essence of Christian perfection. Even the aphorism of Philip of Harvengt, the twelfth-century Flemish Benedictine abbot, might be included in this group: that the school is 'another monastery'; and that scarcely anything better befits the tonsured state than constant study, book in hand.[11] More telling is a passage in the *Summae* of the distinguished Paris theologian Henry of Ghent (†1293), who treats the illiteracy of the first apostles as a puzzle. Why should God have picked *un*educated persons to lead the church? The only answer that suggested itself to Henry of Ghent was that the special circumstances of Christ's time must have demanded it. Now the circumstances were inverted, and graduates alone should direct Christ's flock.[12] Again, those schemes which split the world into *docti* and *indocti* breathed the same sentiment. Guillaume Peyraut's manual on virtues and vices set special store by this distinction. And to the two classes of *docti* and *indocti* Peyraut added a third class at the top: not priests; not *docti* who were also priests; but *doctores*. The learning of a doctor, Peyraut said, yielded more than that of a thousand others.[13] Peyraut was a member of the

Dominican Order of Preachers; and quite as suggestive as this remark are certain utterances by other contemporary enthusiasts for preaching. Made more enthusiastic by the relative novelty of the art, some of these were ready to give preaching top place among Christian works. 'He sent me not to baptize but to preach,' said Saint Paul (1 Cor. 1:17). The Franciscan Thomas Docking (*c.* 1260) read in this text the lesson that preaching was 'more excellent' than that sacrament by which—according to an old doctrine—souls were brought within the ark of salvation.[14]

Even at this more explicit level, then, intellectual categories tended to impose themselves sometimes on sacramental. In the four writers just quoted this was only a tendency, a stress on one side of their orthodoxy. Philip of Harvengt with his 'other monastery' hastened to add (if in parenthesis) how of course it was not study and books but grace and sacraments, and so on, that made the real guarantees of salvation. Henry of Ghent, while he wanted only graduates promoted, in defiance of the apostles' example, meant exclusively theology graduates—that is, those who had studied scripture intensively, under guidance. Peyraut and his fellow-mendicants, in their zeal for teaching and preaching, were thinking likewise exclusively of divinity. This was no careless university elitism. Nor did the bias of such remarks put them outside the limits of safe traditional doctrine.

But other hierarchical notions could venture further. Outside the narrow enclosure of the theologians can be heard views in which the church's own élite, of priesthood and clergy, was actually replaced, by the theologically dubious category of 'philosophers' or 'the wise'. Three examples will show this, one by innuendo, two in so many words.

Michael Scot was in some respects untypical of scholasticism. But he was enough part of it to be praised by a pope in 1225 as 'singularly gifted in science among men of learning'.[15] To encourage beginners in tackling his huge *Introduction to Astrology* (*c.* 1232), Michael pointed to the heavenly reward of the *sapiens*, or 'wise man'. In Michael's time theologians acknowledged that a man could be placed after his death among one or other of the several angelic orders, according to his specific merits while on earth. In unanimous obedience to Pseudo-Denys they put the first three angelic orders in the series, from the top down,

Seraphim, Cherubim, and Thrones. Knowledge, the property Michael Scot exalted in his *Introduction*, belonged peculiarly to the Cherubim, the second order. The first place in the orthodox scheme then went to those who 'burned', that is, loved: the Seraphim. But Michael changed the order of precedence. A *sapiens*, or philosopher, who dies in the Lord will go to the order of Cherubim, now placed at the head of the series. Next in the list came hermits and persons in religious orders, who went among the Seraphim, if they had loved the Lord while on earth. Finally came pope, emperor, cardinals, and prelates, who went among the Thrones.[16] No new dogma was stated by Michael's change in order. But it betrayed a private sense of priorities. As with Dante, whose *Paradiso* embodied the traditional series, Michael's sense of heavenly priorities reflected his view on this world, too: philosophers with their wisdom preceded the ardour of friars and the authority of popes and bishops. Michael's own political career did not belie this interpretation of his remarks.

The second example has its hierarchy squarely in this world. It comes in a book recommended to our attention not in any degree by its author's distinction, but by its popularity in the late middle ages: 'Sidrach'. The imaginary philosopher explains in one place the 'four manners of person who maintain the world'. Typical in this of many writers we have met in the *demi-monde* between orthodoxy and heresy, the anonymous author describes the first 'manner of person' in conveniently ambiguous terms:

The first are those who demonstrate the sciences, and teach people what is good, and [teach] belief in God the omnipotent father [and] how they should conduct themselves in this world.[17]

The idosyncrasies of the rest of the series—cultivators in second place, lords and warriors in third, and merchants in fourth— have their own interest. But our interest here can rest with the opening phrase: 'Primiers sont cil qui les sciences mostrent . . .'. The philosopher 'Sidrach's' felicitous confusion of scientist and priest allows him, without actually flaunting any un-Christian leanings, to give first rank in the world to his own kind.

The last and most explicit of our three examples is from the work of the Paris philosopher John of Jandun. A demur may be raised that his thought was untypical. He died under a papal curse. But that was because, late in life, he had developed his views into a positive and dangerous anti-papal programme. Until 1325 he had enjoyed the highest respectability as—in an enemy's words—a 'pretty famous' professor of philosophy; as head of a college; and as protégé of high church potentates, including a cardinal.[18] For most of John's working life he was among Paris's most favoured *alumni*.

John's ideas of hierarchy therefore deserve attention. They appear by innuendo even in his encomium of Paris. Not only is this encomium mostly about the university; that was not abnormal. More significantly, John treated as first of the Paris faculties that of 'philosophy or arts' (in that order). The preference is betrayed repeatedly in the course of the book. As for the 'quiet' theology faculty, John spoke politely of their ingenious disputations, but added: 'what use such gymnastics are to the Catholic religion, God knows'.[19]

These were innuendoes. In his philosophical works John endorses and elaborates them. A passage in his Aristotelian commentary, *Questions on the 'Metaphysics'*, discusses the 'orders' of mankind. Highest were the men who contemplated the 'separate substances' and God. These were philosophers, alias 'speculatives'. They formed a small élite. Because 'men in the multitude are prone to evil', and are 'rude, gross, and undisciplined', the philosopher's task was to reduce the multitude to virtue by the art of persuasion, namely rhetoric.[20] It followed that all other powers in the state must depend on philosophers; and 'all' included priests. 'Priests depend on speculatives, . . . because priests must know God, and ought indeed to *be* speculatives.' Priests must obey either what speculatives told them, or, if they were themselves speculatives, their own speculation. The sacramental claims of priesthood gave no authority: 'priests have no quality that speculatives do not have, except exterior acts.'[21]

If John's *Questions on the 'Metaphysics'* left us in doubt about his philosophers' claim to supremacy, the doubt is removed in a second commentary on Aristotle, the *Exposition on the Third Book of 'De Anima'*. There John elaborated a fourfold scheme for human hierarchy, based on an obscure passage in Averroës. Because the passage is so far unprinted I quote it at length. It does not allude to priests as such, but mentions other classes purposefully enough to make the exclusion of priests meaningful. Society, said John, had two extremes:

There are some who only use their senses and imagination. Or if they do use their other powers, they do so in such small degree that it can be counted as nothing. The profoundly ignorant common people and peasantry are of this sort: aware of nothing but what they individually, or as men, perceive through the senses. . . . Others transcend the objects of sense and imagination, distinguishing abstract meanings from concrete impressions, general and particular: for example, goodness, evil, wickedness, the filial relation, fame, fear, etc.[22]

Between these extremes were two 'middle' grades, spaced respectively nearer the bottom, and nearer the top. John elaborated all these divisions in everyday terms.

By the lowest class I understand men purely practical, whose grasp of higher things is either slight or non-existent. In this class are the bulk of those engaged in trade and industry; and if I may make bold to say so, almost all jurists nowadays are in it too. By the top class I understand metaphysicians, who attain to contemplation of the quiddities of abstract forms, and of the supreme God himself. . . . By the class next above the lowest I understand—saving their reverence—mathematicians, who consider numbers, magnitudes, and soluble problems. . . . These things are still *sensibilia*, though *sensibilia* common to all men, not just to this or that individual; and this puts mathematicians above the lowest class. . . . By the other middle grade I understand those perfect and excellent in natural science, who elicit abstract qualities from the objects of sense, by careful thought, and who extract hidden truths from the natural phenomena with which they have such thorough acquaintance.

It should be added that each of these orders or grades has much latitude and diversity, because of the diversity of individual characters. All, nevertheless can reasonably be reduced to these four. The bottom grade is that of most of mankind. The top grade contains only outstanding and very distinguished people. All studious persons reach the second grade, while the third is reserved for those who are exceptionally learned.[23]

It can be seen that John's four-tier social order disregarded any but an intellectual criterion. He says as much: 'the diversity of these grades can be reduced to unity; they all depend on the power of cognition. He who has the lowest measure of that power is in the lowest grade; he who has the highest, is in the highest; and so for the middling grades, as aforesaid.'[24]

While John of Jandun wrote these commentaries, shelves in Bologna, Rome, and even Paris itself were filling with volumes by canonists on the same subject: hierarchy. They defined more and more closely the relations within the church hierarchy: popes, bishops, and ecclesiastical judges; clergy and laity, and so on. For John, and no doubt for many of those who heard him during his more than ten years of Paris teaching, these volumes were a foreign land—the province of benighted 'jurists'. The jurists, canon and civil, might reach high office. Yet John and his pupils in the arts faculty represented at least as large a proportion of university populations. Here a different, non-canonical view of human stratification was preached. John's view corresponded on the philosophical plane to that linguistic usage which made 'clerk' mean 'scholar'. For John took account, not of sacraments, miracle-working functions, and the other accoutrements of church law, but of the largely intellectual qualities that made a man a metaphysician. Not God's anointed, as such, but the wise, as such, were Christendom's chief estate.

Certain heresies, with rationalistic traits; the scholar's unconscious usurpation of the name 'clerk'; the philosopher's claim to quasi-priestly supremacy: these three phenomena betray in different ways the upward thrust of Mind, within the polity defined by canon law.

But canon law was not the only law that applied in Christendom. Outside the clergy, in the strict canonical sense, another élite was in effective power: the nobility. In the second half of this chapter we consider how the theories of the intellectual estate challenged this other obstacle to its ascent.

### 2. THE THEORETICAL ASSAULT ON THE NOBILITY

The growth of technical knowledge and of government had by the thirteenth century begun to clear tracks up and down society. At least a few of the irrational obstructions were gone which had blocked social aspirations in the low-born. Intelligence and hard work could now offer rewards. Of course new obstacles had appeared in the form of law and its enforcers.

But law was rational, relating to the *bonum commune*. A man ready to give his efforts to the service of that common good could hope for personal advantage from the new institutions.

One *irr*ational obstruction nevertheless remained. It was the claim to authority, on all society's commanding heights, of a hereditary class. The class was less purely hereditary than it liked to pretend. Noble pedigrees usually called for a leap of faith at some point. But even such pretences betray the force of the prejudice they appealed to: that a man's title to nobility, and hence to rule, rested not in the first instance on his own virtues, but on 'excellency of race and ancient riches' (as Aristotle had defined it); that is to say, on qualities far beyond the reach of the will of any individual, however diligent and however learned.

The arguing, job-hunting scholars of the twelfth- and thirteenth-century schools were bound to question this principle. Not only was it *prima facie* unreasonable. Noble claims, after all, were an affront to the natural union between authority and merit—a union every reasonable man must desire. In so far as scholars aimed at government office, the principle was also a threat to their hopes of livelihood. Professional rationalism and private interest thus merged to cast the growing ranks of the literate as critics of the hereditary ideal. Nor did they fail this role. Literature and philosophy had scarcely entered their medieval renaissance before both were engaged in a campaign, to swell with them and ultimately to outlive the middle ages, against the social rights of birth. The campaign's character and intensity varied from age to age and place to place. But viewed as a whole it reveals enough about the social orientation of our literate class to deserve a few moments' attention.

The literary campaign against nobility of birth itself had a long pedigree. As far as the middle ages are concerned the pedigree began in ancient Rome. Rome's philosophers and poets had insisted that 'true' nobility was not a matter of birth. It lay solely in 'virtue'. Juvenal's satire on the Roman nobility, the eighth, had expressed the principle in the terse declaration (in line 20) that

*Nobilitas sola est atque unica virtus.*

Sallust, in *The War Against Jugurtha* (chapter 85), had expanded on the idea in a speech he put in the mouth of the plebeian general Marius. Marius derides the claims of his degenerate rivals in the Roman nobility, and exalts the merits of the man who has struggled to prominence by his own 'virtue'. To these pre-Christian expressions of the theme Christian writers in due course added fresh nuances. Saint Ambrose, when Italy's nobility was half in and half out of Catholicism, stressed 'faith, not ancestors' as the only true mark of distinction among men;[25] while his pupil Augustine thirty years later insisted that God judged by 'conduct, not family'.[26] In the sixth century Boethius gave a place in his *Consolation* to another and more pregnant criticism of the idea of hereditary nobility: the human race stemmed from one home and one Father.[27]

These classical passages were all known in the middle ages, and became the source of a formidable literary current.[28] In particular, Juvenal's line became one of those commonplaces cited even by authors with only superficial knowledge of the classics. The line's career as a quotation, in Latin poetry and in philosophical and didactic treatises, began in earnest in the twelfth-century renaissance and outlasted that of the fifteenth century. Paraphrases of the idea it embodied, that nobility consisted exclusively in virtue, meanwhile appeared in verse, Latin and vernacular, in proverbs, and even in mottoes. (One well-known form of it was the motto of the successful commoner Wykeham: *manners makyth man.*) For all its lively career in literature the motif was nevertheless far from being a mere literary cliché. It turns up with equal assurance in everyday talk: in a papal letter, for example, reproving a cathedral chapter for excluding non-nobles from its midst; in a reformer's critique of certain religious ladies who have grown too idle; or in the proud answer the self-made churchman Jacques Pantaléon made to a jibe on his birth, that 'nobility sprang from virtue, and he had made up by diligence what he lacked in birth'.[29]

The equation of nobility with virtue was a widespread idea. Exactly who believed it and in what sense cannot be gauged, certainly not as medieval studies now stand. For the fortunes of the motif have never been thoroughly charted. It has actually been queried whether the charting of so general a theme could serve any purpose beyond mere cataloguing. Some literary historians have nevertheless thought it worthwhile to draft small areas of the chart; enough to permit generalizations on some of the motif's peculiarities. They tell us that it was originally more a Roman than a barbarian idea, and correspondingly in the middle ages more Romance than German;[30] that its literary headquarters was as much in vernacular as in Latin;[31] that it was 'bourgeois', and received special impetus in Guelf Florence;[32] yet that it could on occasion be employed by the nobility itself, to ward off rivalry from *nouveaux riches* who lacked aristocratic virtues.[33] A comprehensive study if it ever does appear might serve not only to set these opinions in proper relation to each other, but to answer other questions: for instance, how much the idea owed to Christian modes of thought as distinct from classical; and what force, if any, it lent to the scholastic analysis of virtue being hammered out in the same centuries.

Only one aspect of this unwritten history concerns us now. The scholastics were hammering out an analysis of virtue. They may or may not have been influenced by the motif under discussion. What is certain is that the motif, on its side, was influenced by them. It was influenced in a direction set by the background and circumstances of the ethical speculation. When so much of the literary material for this speculation descended from Stoics, it was inevitable that features of Stoic ethics should be perpetuated. Among these features was an emphasis on mind: right *reason* was the source of all virtue. The absolute primacy of prudence in the system of virtues inherited from the Stoics is one manifestation of this emphasis. It was echoed especially by those medieval writers most obviously beholden to Cicero and Seneca for their ethical views. And this Stoic rationalism had an influence on the notion of 'true nobility'. For true nobility was virtue. Virtue came from the mind. The two equations only needed adding together to produce a new formula:

*Nobilitas hominis mens est, deitatis imago.*

Man's nobility is mind, image of the deity.

This was the first line of one of the *Carmina Burana*.[34] The copious notes to this poem in Otto Schumann's edition makes clear that the idea was not the monopoly of one thirteenth-century poet.

To say that true nobility lies in the mind is not perhaps to say anything startling. The idea could be housed in more than one religious scheme, Christian or non-Christian. However, in the hands of a socially-conscious educated class the formula lent itself to a specialized interpretation. It could be read as meaning that virtue, and hence nobility, rested in the man who particularly cultivated his mind, *alias* the educated man. There was another useful corollary. The opposite of 'mind' was surely 'flesh'. So the opposite of mental nobility was carnal nobility. The application of this term to the actual hereditary nobility made good polemic. The concept it embodied was of course dubious, since mental qualities can also be inherited (a fact which was in practice recognized then).[35] But that was no obstacle. Nothing was easier for an educated man than to apply this concept, with the other, to the relation of himself and the actual nobility. *He* was a true, mental noble. *They* were a false, 'carnal' nobility. Read this way, the formula of mental nobility provided the last stage in a process of conceptual ju-jitsu. The claims of born nobility were first impugned, in the name of natural equality. Then a side-door was opened to let inequality back in. *If* any distinction was to be made it should be one of virtue. But virtue stemmed from the mind. The mind was cultivated by education. *Ergo*, if there was to be a nobleman, it was not the 'carnally' noble man but the educated one.

This process of reasoning was not spelt out fully before the fifteenth century, in authors I shall refer to in a moment. But its rudiments are present earlier. This is not just a matter of the easy verbal juxtapositions we overhear of 'the learned and virtuous', as if the two were the same. (As for instance in Matteo Villani, who says (*c.* 1350) that Florence founded a university so that her citizens could become 'scenziati e virtudiosi'.)[36] The evidence is a degree more elaborate. It starts from the period when we should expect on other grounds to find it: the middle and late thirteenth, and early fourteenth centuries. A brief parade of passages in four writers will substantiate this. Each of the four approached the topic in a way distinct from the others. Each represented a significant block of contemporary opinion.

### (i) Peyraut

Probably the most widely-read of thirteenth-century ethical treatises was Guillaume Peyraut's *Summa, On Virtues and Vices*, written *c.* 1240, apparently in Lyons, and already mentioned

more than once in this book.[37] Just then and there it was
probably especially easy for a scholar, as heir of the city's old
educational tradition, to think ill of the local hereditary
nobility. Peyraut anyway did so. The theory behind nobility
was worthless. Nobility of the body was a 'corporal thing'. It
was therefore a 'sack full of filth', deriving from 'an unclean and
shameful act' of the parents.[38] (Theological dualism was
another local tradition. That Peyraut was a Dominican,
pledged to fight heresy, need not mean he was unaffected by
some of its notions.) Peyraut's onslaught on the rights of birth
did not however kill the idea that some men should have special
honour. For another fault in the honour of born nobles was that
it was not 'personally earned'.[39] The implication that earned
honour was permissible naturally attaches itself to Peyraut's
concept of 'nobility of mind', which he sometimes set over
against that of the body.[40] The final sophistication, that the
nobility of the mind is a nobility of the educated, is also
suggested. Denouncing noble monopolies in cathedral chapters, and specifically the argument used in their defence that
nobles were needed to protect cathedral property, Peyraut
retorted: 'it is much more important for learned and holy men
to be made canons, to defend the cathedral's spiritual
domain.'[41] *Litteratos et sanctos*: the two were jumbled together as
if there was scarcely a distinction. Elsewhere Peyraut could
drop the *sanctos*: noble exclusiveness turned church-
government upside-down, he said, so that the feet were where
the head should be—the head being 'those who have to rule the
church, namely the learned (*litterati*)'.[42] When not thinking
about nobles Peyraut could be a scourge of intellectual pride, as
of other sorts. He had no use for choppers of logic, and saw the
sons of Adam as essentially equal.[43] Yet the heat of his anti-
noble polemic imprinted on his mind, as polemic often does to
its practitioners, the thought-structures of his opponents. He
attacked the 'carnal' nobility. But in the attack can be read the
faint suggestion that the nobles' superior position be merely
transferred: to the educated.

### (ii) Jean de Meung

Similar innuendoes can be heard from Peyraut's younger
contemporary Jean de Meung. *The Romance of The Rose* was

verse, not prose; an allegory, not a treatise; by, not a Dominican, but a professed foe of the order. Its moral values differ from Peyraut's, and as far as can be judged it was aimed at a different sector of the reading public. Two fat, eclectic, widely-read books from the same milieu could scarcely have been more different. For social and intellectual history this fact highlights the similarity between their two views on nobility.

In a long digression on this topic, put in the mouth of 'Nature', Jean denied that birth could raise anyone above the ordinary level of men who lived by their labour.[44] Nature had given to all men their *naturel franchise*—inborn liberty—together with the Reason which God had granted men to perfect them in his image.[45] These depreciations of nobility were no mere 'asides' from Jean de Meung; nor are the allegorical figures in his poem consistent enough to suggest these were not the poet's own private opinions.[46] They were deeply felt. The mere mention of nobles was often enough to touch off a burst of Jean's egalitarian indignation.

Yet Jean's egalitarianism allowed the familiar exception. 'No man is a gentleman,' a typical declaration ran, 'if he is not intent on virtue. Nor is any man a villein but on account of his vices, such as to show him to be a foolish ruffian.'[47] With a looser tongue than Peyraut's Jean also came nearer to revealing what he understood by virtue in this context. For he sometimes replaced it by an alternative word: *proeces*—a term which combined connotations from our 'talents', 'accomplishments', and 'guts'. It was these 'prowesses' which gave a man true social rank. 'If anyone wants gentility', the allegorical Nature declared, 'other than that excellent gentility which I bestow, called *naturel franchise* ... let them win new gentility, if they have in them the necessary *proeces*. For if they don't achieve it by themselves they will never be gentle through anyone else.'[48]

In this scheme of honour, finally, relying as it did on *vertu* and *proeces*, Jean de Meung made even clearer than Peyraut the role he envisaged for education. In a general way the use of reason was usually equated with virtue: *nices* (stupid) was a common pejorative—more than once a rhyme for the *vices* of noblemen;[49] while *sen* (intelligence) was similarly bonded with virtue and *proece*.[50] Consequently, in the social extension, it was *reason* which conferred true nobility. It was 'Reason' herself—Jean de

Meung's allegorical character with that name—who said so. She promised to make her wooer 'so great a lord that none greater will ever have been heard of'.[51] Jean was more specific still. The man who developed his reason was, we have seen, the 'clerk'. It was the clerk's occupation which Jean saw as the best road to true nobility. It was not the only road, it is true: soldiering could be set beside it (as when a man in quest of gentility was given the alternative recommendations of going 'to arms or to his studies').[52] But it was the clerk's pursuit, study, whose claims against the nobility Jean most cordially defended. Through acquaintance with ancient moral example the clerk 'is far better placed to be gentle, courteous, and wise, than those who hunt wild deer'.[53] Looking round at the barefooted ex-scholars in his own day Jean lamented the golden age when great clerks were given their due, and made real lords, as Virgil was of Naples, 'a fairer city than Paris'.[54] (That Augustus had made Virgil lord of Naples was an old and tenacious myth, itself perhaps a clue about the ambitions of those who nurtured it.) Jean rapped modern princes, by contrast, for not prizing scholars 'so much as an apple', when the scholars 'are more gentle than those who go hunting hares, and those whose life is spent tending their inherited dunghills'.[55]

### (iii) Dante

In the course of this rapping, Jean de Meung said scholars in his day were having to wander off to foreign lands.[56] We know from other sources that some Paris scholars wandered to Italy. The scholar's critique of nobility went with them. About 1308, in Verona, it was given what became its classic expression in Dante's *Convivio*. Like many intelligent Florentines Dante was fascinated by the subject of nobility, and dealt with it with varying nuances in several works. But Book IV of the *Convivio* contained his longest essay on the subject, and the one that became best known. The essay was devoted to an attack on the dominant concept of nobility, as the author saw it. True nobility clung neither to birth nor to ancient riches. It belonged only to virtue.[57] Dante borrowed his list of virtues from the contemporary ethical canon, with its strong Aristotelian element. If he made no freakish changes, perhaps even here Dante betrayed a meritocratic cast of thought. For he seems to have inclined, against Aristotle, towards putting the rational virtue of prudence among the 'moral' group:[58] that group which formed the path to true nobility 'because [he says in another place in the same book] they are from every angle within our power'.[59]

It was less the content of the argument in the *Convivio*, however, than its con*text*, that revealed Dante's leaning for a kind of meritocracy. The occasion for the debate had been a conservative utterance on nobility from the emperor Frederick II. (In fact it was ultimately from Aristotle's *Politics* (IV, 3), but Dante did not know that in 1308, and it would have spoiled half the point of his argument if he had.) Characteristic of his age in this, Dante was not content to take issue with what his opponent said. He challenged his right to say it. It was not for emperors to arbitrate on philosophical questions. Saying so, the author gave a clue to an idiosyncratic view he held of Christian polity. Scholarship has to thank Étienne Gilson for having followed up this clue, and others in Dante's works, and for having identified this idiosyncrasy at the cost of some pious misconceptions about the great Catholic poet.[60] Like other Catholic thinkers Dante acknowledged the authority of the spiritual and temporal hierarchies. But he envisaged also, for some matters, a third authority: that of philosophers. Within a broadly Catholic framework Dante granted to the tiny group he recognized as true philosophers a practically autonomous status. His view shared traits and some ancestry with John of Jandun's. The Frenchman's philosophical élite turned its rougher edge to the church, the Florentine's to the nobility. Dante's adjustment to Catholic tradition was very much the milder. Yet each of the two thinkers in his own way and degree conjured up the same challenge to authority: to all constituted authority, sacramental and hereditary—in so far, that is, as it did not depend on pure 'wisdom'.

### (iv) Cecco of Ascoli

Although he never won a circle of readers comparable in size to those of Peyraut, Jean de Meung, or Dante, a fourth scholar who wrote on nobility in these decades deserves to be set beside them. His views were more typical than theirs of one category of schoolman: the man of science, or *matematico*. Cecco of Ascoli's excursion into moral philosophy (part of *L'Acerba*,[61] or 'The Heap': it was an encyclopedia) was written in 1326. Cecco endorsed the anti-noble sentiments of Dante, the only contemporary author on the subject he knew of. But Cecco's approach was peculiar to himself. Peyraut, Jean de Meung, and Dante had impugned hereditary nobility as partisans of human free will. Against the inexorable dictates of descent they had offered rewards of honour 'personally earned' through virtues 'within our power'. The emancipating character of this philosophy doubtless contributed to the huge appeal of these three writers. Its absence in Cecco, conversely, must have helped rob him of such appeal—as it did of life, too, since he was executed in 1327 on the pretext of excessive determinism. For Cecco approached the question of nobility as an astrologer. He rejected the constraint imposed by descent. But he replaced it with one imposed by stars.[62] The reason why merit, the essence of true nobility, could not (according to Cecco) be passed from father to son was simply that father and son were born under different constellations.[63] Thus the son's merit, for Cecco, was still largely preordained for him from birth. This astrological scheme approached, in fact, more nearly even than Jean de Meung with his *proeces*, the theory of an aristocracy of talent. It was an aristocracy from which a man born without virtuous disposition was absolutely debarred, as surely as serfs' sons were debarred from dynastic aristocracies.

Now Cecco's 'virtue' was not, it is true, identified in this passage with reason, much less with mere education. But Cecco's astrological preoccupation itself signalled an intensely rationalistic temperament. And the fact that his ethical concepts corresponded to it is clear from other passages in *L'Acerba*. 'There is no virtue where there is little wit'; 'knowledge is worth more than any treasure'; 'he who does nought but despise knowledge loses this life and the next'.[64] It was prudence, or discretion, with its probing of past and future, that opened the way to other virtues.[65] Again, a disposition to virtue was imparted by the planet Mercury: the same Mercury who in one tradition had once invented the liberal arts.[66] Cecco stopped short of positing a nobility of science, just as he stopped short (in his written work) of absolute astral determinism. But to stop short is to have gone some way. It may be that Cecco, a poor, gifted boy who became counsellor to a duke (and whom Villani charges with a certain vanity),[67] unconsciously framed a doctrine of nobility which favoured a case like his own.

If he did he was not the only one. In Italy, in particular, the ladder which had raised Cecco to his dangerous eminence served a growing number of careers during the fourteenth century. Partly as a result the theme of mental nobility boomed as the Renaissance advanced. Dante's treatment of it in the *Convivio* became classic. In the middle of the century Petrarch, and at the end Salutati, were its cordial exponents.[68] After 1400, and Florence's soul-searching crisis, the theme came of age. The alignment of virtue and education became explicit. The alignment is best revealed in a dialogue by Buonaccorso da Montemagno.[69] The dialogue is between rival contestants, noble and low-born, for the hand of a young lady. To furnish the low-born contestant with an argument Buonaccorso borrowed the classic speech by Marius from Sallust: a man who had risen by his own merits was more worthy, the suitor declared, than one who had inherited his position. But in borrowing this speech Buonaccorso changed it. He transferred one quality from the account of the effete nobleman, to that of the dynamic plebeian: education. Literary accomplishments, attached by Sallust's Marius to the degenerate aristocrat whose claims were under fire, were shifted by Buonaccorso to the other side of the equation, to become the poor man's main claim to true nobility. The literary success of Buonaccorso's dialogue, which went into the main vernaculars and on to the stage, witnesses to the theme's appeal. So did the continuing series of essays 'Of Nobility'. Not all were as precise as Buonaccorso's *Dialogue* in their apotheosis of education. But some were even more so. The apogee was reached about 1500 with a tract by the Neapolitan humanist Galateo, called *Of Nobility, and Distinction within the Human Race*.[70] It proposed a scheme of social distinction wherein the actual nobility came out as 'plebs', their place taken by the 'boni' and 'docti', who Galateo in many places implies, and in one place actually says, are the same.[71]

The chronicling of the heyday of this theme in the Italian Renaissance would be a long task. It is not our business. But the bare fact of the heyday is. It helps interpret the sparser medieval evidence. A hallmark of Renaissance culture was its stress on literary skills. That the equation of virtue and nobility was so at home in it suggests that the theme was the *idée fixe* predominantly of one intellectual type: those who wrote and spoke professionally. This conjunction makes our discoveries in medieval writers less surprising. Conversely, the medieval prehistory of the theme throws light on its Renaissance phase. The theme was not the sudden discovery by one republic with revolutionary ideas. It was a challenge, innate in schools as such, and more or less coeval with them, to a criterion of power which took no account of what scholars had to offer, and at the same time thwarted their social aspirations.

Two challenges have been considered which the intellectual estate made to the theories of those above it. Its challenge to the clergy was manifested, heresy apart, chiefly in the usurpation of a canonical distinction; and in the erection of a rival magisterial authority in 'philosophers'. The idea of nobility was more directly bombarded. True rank was not based on birth or wealth, but on 'virtue'—a term which could be read, by those who wished, as meaning the virtues of an educated man.

This was all mere theory. To become the ruling class in practice was a different matter. Our study of the literate culture of the middle ages, seen in its social dimension, would not be complete without an allusion to practice: without a consideration, that is to say, of the culture's tangible advances in the field of power politics. The last chapter in this section of the book is accordingly devoted to that subject.

# CHAPTER 12

# The Assault on the Citadel: Practice

> Letter from the University of Paris to King Henry
> VI of England and France, concerning Joan the
> Maid (21 November 1430):
>> It pertains singularly to us, by virtue of our
>> profession, to extirpate such manifest iniquities,
>> above all in cases touching our common Catholic ·
>> faith. We cannot close our eyes, therefore, to the
>> long delay there has been in the prosecution of this
>> case. . . .[1]

To use the term 'clerk' to mean 'scholar' was not in the slightest
degree to change the rules concerning ordination. Similarly,
schemes to make the wise as such high priests of a new social
order produced no sympathetic effect in canon law. Any effect
they had was actually the other way. The same two late
medieval centuries which saw the spread, among same laity, of
a philosophical view of society, based on reason and the
common good, saw in the church the opposite: an elaboration
of conservative, hierarchical authoritarianism, theoretical and
practical. While philosophers read Aristotle, lawyers read
Justinian; and it was the lawyers who did the ruling.

The theory that true nobility lay in virtue was similarly
thwarted. For in practice the born nobility remained; and it is
clear, if only from the choler of polemics against it, that a
widespread belief in the value of high birth was far from being
exorcized by all those words. The very cultures that nourished
the 'virtue' theory of nobility provide, behind literature's
façade, proof of the hardiness in real life of birth-snobbery.
'Republican' Florence is itself the best example: despite the
theories of the city's great writers, 'nobility' went on in practice
meaning the hereditary kind, and being valued by most
individuals with any claim to it.[2] Into this hereditary élite,
whatever its waxing and waning fortunes, scholars as a class

gained no access. Nor could they ever do. The studies of an individual scholar might make him a lord: like the peasant's son I mentioned earlier in thirteenth-century Burgundy, who passed through the university of Bologna into ducal service, and ended with a knighthood and a castle;[3] or the famous Jean Jouvenal, who went the same sort of way in the fourteenth century;[4] and more, of whom critics of ambition in law-schools certainly had longer tallies than could be reconstructed now. But the ennoblement of a graduate was not the ennoblement of scholars as such. On the contrary, the new noble was a deserter, whose sons might or might not return to their father's college, but who would not owe their rank to it. They had passed from the intellectual to the born élite. Loyal schoolmen meanwhile, with their built-in ideal of individual virtue, were necessarily barred from dynastic rank: like Dante's philosophers in Limbo, never able to grasp the beatitude they beheld.

Theoretical assaults by intellectuals on ruling powers did not, then, have the effects they envisaged. The historian might be tempted to treat them therefore as vapour, of no concrete significance. But they have significance. The theories betray to us the constant pressure of an interest. It was unlikely that so articulate a pressure should have no political effect of any sort. When the effect is looked for, it is duly there: dispersed, and half-hidden, through several areas of late medieval life, both ecclesiastical and secular. This time the secular sphere will be considered first.

## I  THE ASSAULT IN SECULAR POLITICS

### (i)  *The university as an autonomous power*

The best way for any broad interest to make itself felt was by associating and becoming an institution. The main institution representing the intellect was the university. Conceived in the late twelfth century as a shell to protect the embryo of the studious life, this privileged corporation developed with the centuries into a self-ruling political force, offensive as well as defensive. It is easy—university propaganda meant it to be easy—to miss seeing its autonomous character. The same mistake is made about universities as about clerks, making them one and the same with the church. But plenty of considerations teach otherwise. Since we shall have much to say in this chapter about the university's political dimension, it will be appropriate to begin by looking at two of these considerations in particular.

One was geographical. After the earliest age, that of monastic and cathedral schools, the main intellectual centres, far from clinging to centres of church authority, avoided them with striking consistency. Canonist Bologna was as far from Rome—nearly 200 miles—as it could be without exchanging mild papal overlordship for imperial. Oxford's bishop was 120 miles away, in Lincoln. Strong, tolerant Venice shielded the university of Padua from the inquisitorial Dominicans, away in Genoa. Prague, within two generations of its foundation, was notorious for the insolent freedom it enjoyed, far from ancient ecclesiastical centres. Even Paris, the most theological of universities, clung to the commercial and political centre of northern France, not its ecclesiastical; which was a convenient sixty-four miles to the south-east, at Sens. The famous university would think nothing, in the fourteenth century, of claiming it had been there before the bishops of Paris were heard of.[5]

This geographical fact reflects a second, more abstract, legal one. Universities' privileges carefully insulated them from both the secular and church hierarchies. Whatever the niceties of their constitutions—which can still puzzle scholars as they puzzled lawyers then—the universities' corporate status gave them virtual internal self-rule. This, in turn, with their near-monopoly in some types of useful expertise, gave them an autonomous role in public politics. The universities came to form in effect a third public force, standing beside the ecclesiastical and secular hierarchies. Dante's philosopher, independently judging popes and emperors, was thus clothed in the flesh and blood of an institution. If the great poet-philosopher had belonged to Paris and not Florence (which had no university) he might well have expressed his claims for philosophy in institutional terms. As it was, his cast of mind was too individualistic; and it was left to other writers to describe things as they really were. These writers, contemporaries of Dante, augmented the two familiar authorities of medieval polity, *sacerdotium* and *regnum*, with a third: not any individual 'philosopher', now, but the institutional 'learning', or *studium*. For instance, William of Nangis [who flourished *c.* 1270–

*c.* 1300] in describing the political structure of his native France, used the three points of the fleur-de-lys to symbolize this trinity: priesthood, monarchy, and 'learning'. The intruder, *studium*, was spoken of as if it had always been there: a fact which only emphasizes the completeness of its intrusion.[6]

The autonomous university, geographically and legally insulated from its political seniors, was in practice the main institutional expression the intellect had. Since the subject of this chapter is practice rather than theory, it will be instructive to look now at an actual example of such an autonomous university, in a particular place and time; so that the political vitality of the intellectual interest can be assessed *in situ*.

The place and time choose themselves. No epitome suggests itself as readily as Paris. Nor does any short period in the university's history suggest itself in this context more strongly than the second half of the fourteenth century. For the self-assertiveness of the queen of universities was then sharpened by competition from new rivals abroad. And the Capetian–Valois crown, wounded by the Hundred Years War, left enough of a power-vacuum at the centre of French affairs to invite contestants to expand into it—the university among others. This place and time have the extra merit that their dossier is ready-to-hand, in the third volume of Denifle and Chatelain's *Cartulary of Paris University*.

On the subject of the university as an autonomous political power this dossier reveals a great deal. First, it reveals perennial wrangles over ceremonial precedence, in which the university (according to its own documents at least) generally came out well. For instance at royal funerals academic chiefs sought pride of place over the episcopal chapter of Paris; and after disputes and even fights the university finally—two years after the strong Charles V was dead—won a definitive judgement of its precedence, even over the bishop himself.[7] Nearer to everyday business meanwhile was a struggle between the chancellor and the rector—i.e. between the chief appointed from outside the university, and the rival chief elected internally. The old contest between these two officers was basically about rank. It reached a crisis in 1384, ending once again in considerable measure of victory for the scholars when the leader of their campaign was himself made chancellor.[8]

These victories in the sphere of precedence were substantiated in the more concrete sphere of jurisdiction. Here the university had a peculiar advantage. Not only did everyone matriculating have to swear to defend its privileges. A clause added that he must do so 'whatever rank he shall attain to'.[9] What this additional clause did was to create, in effect, a huge sworn society, a *commune juratum*, bound together for protection and discipline. It reached far beyond school walls, into the furthest recesses of church and state. The university was thus given grounds to intervene in cases with little apparent pertinence to academic concerns. It is found, for example, protecting a monk against his archbishop, the monk being seventy years old, the archbishop no less a prelate than he of Rouen. The university brushed impatiently aside the archbishop's demur that 'it is hardly likely the man is a scholar, considering his age'.[10] Such intervention could reach almost anywhere. With the growth of bureaucracies many ex-university men held high rank in church or lay government. The existence of this sworn freemasonry allowed the university to tackle even the highest political authorities, in the knowledge that many of the men who staffed those authorities were its own subjects. The chancellor, for example, when defending his rights against the university, in the famous case just referred to, failed to find a lawyer: the ruling group on the other side had banned all *alumni* of the law faculty from appearing for their adversary.[11] This weapon could even be turned against the pope and king. In the chancellor's case a cardinal was sent by the pope to settle matters and, on pain of excommunication, he *commanded* a certain lawyer to defend the chancellor. The lawyer made his obedience conditional on the university's express consent.[12] As for the king: a case of 1353 hinged on the vital matter of whether a man's oath to the university prejudiced his obedience to the crown, a question on which Saint Louis's royalist lawyers a century before would not have hesitated. Now the royal court of appeal left it open 'for each man's conscience' to decide.[13]

These examples are a few of dozens of similar ones teaching roughly the same lesson, from Paris in the years 1350–94. They reveal the private law, *privi-legium*, of the university pushing outwards into neighbouring jurisdictions, even those of pope and monarch. Of course there was an abundant pressure in the other direction: lecturers flung into prison by city police, ex-scholars in the countryside bullied by barons, and so on. The documents are not complete enough to allow an exact comparative assessment of these pressures. What they do show, for the extent of the sample, is that the university had both a will and a way to inch out its frontiers, whenever there was a vacuum on the other side.

*Sacerdotium, regnum, studium:* the threefold division could be a juridical reality.

### (ii)   The privileges of the faculty of arts

Now it may be objected that this expansion of university inflence had nothing specifically to do with intellectuals. It may have been just another case of the native wickedness of all institutions with rights, and with a lively community behind them: they tend to expand. This objection can be met in a number of ways; but best of all if the inquiry is extended vertically. Below, and above, university level institutional expansions are found whose intellectual character is less equivocal.

We look first below university level. There, analogous tendencies to those just described are present in the history of the so-called arts faculties. These faculties were the peculiar home of such academic rationalism as there was in the middle ages. The reason was historical. With the raising of theology and canon law as academic disciplines in the twelfth century, the seven 'arts' of classical education had been relegated to the level of preliminaries. Simultaneously, the works of Aristotle and other non-Christian philosophers had started arriving, posing among other problems the one of where in the curriculum they should be put. Since these philosophers would not go away, as the authorities would have preferred; and since they were pagan and the liberal arts were pagan and also since Aristotle had first been known as a logician, it was gradually settled that they should go among the arts. By the middle of the thirteenth century the faculty was commonly called that of 'philosophy or arts' without anyone's remarking there was any difference.[14]

Before the end of the thirteenth century, then, the term 'arts faculty' had become a subtle misnomer. The curriculum of the

*Reading and Writing*

faculty was dominated by philosophy, chiefly Aristotelian. This fact both helps explain, and gives significance to, the remarkable constitutional adventures of that faculty within the university. These adventures mainly consisted, from the middle of the thirteenth century, in a slow assumption of effectual leadership in university government. The story was in some degree common to all northern universities. But once again it can best be watched in Paris. The story is that of the 'rector'. This official had begun as a mere keeper-of-order among 'arts' students of different nations. Long before the end of the thirteenth century the faculty had made him its leader, in a campaign to steal precedence over theology and canon law. Despite rearguard action by the latter two, the rector had more or less won this campaign by the middle of the fourteenth century. The attack on the chancellor, already referred to, was its *coup de grâce*.[15]

Now the perennial pretext for the arts faculty's high status was that arts made the *fundamentum* for the learning of other faculties.[16] There was just a kernel of truth here. For the status of 'foundation' had long been agreed on for grammar, logic, rhetoric, etc. But the pretext was in fact something of a fraud. For the seven arts were no longer in command. What *was* in command were books like Aristotle's *Physics*, or *De generatione*, or *De celo et mundo*, all of which were compulsory reading for arts men,[17] and which could hardly be described as *foundations* for further learning. Such works *were* learning. The faculty's claim was in fact deftly equivocal. The real reason for its *putsch* was distinct from the pretext. The reason was political. Arts was much the biggest faculty. It was biggest even without counting its ex-members in other faculties, over whom it claimed to keep jurisdiction. Comparative numerical estimates only become possible from 1349. The arts faculty then appears to have represented about 84 per cent of the university. The figures rise unevenly to about 90 per cent in 1403.[18] There is reason to believe this was a late stage in a process begun long before, and that arts men had accounted for the bulk of university growth even in the thirteenth century. It is true that the preponderance is partly explained by the arts' status as a preliminary—since only the persistent stayed on for higher degrees. But the philosophical character of the course also played a part. For the

Aristotelian reading list was a magnet, as we learn for instance from its prominence in the advertisement for a new university (in Toulouse) in 1229, seeking to win students.[19] We learn the same from complaints by theologians that their own charges (now senior students in the *theology* faculty) are perpetually wanting to turn back to their Aristotle.[20]

While the university advanced within society generally, then, philosophy advanced within the arts faculty, and the arts faculty advanced within the university. The second, dual, development was as significant as the first. And it was less ambivalent. What it reflected was not merely institutional expansionism, but the conquest of the university by persons whose training and sympathy were not primarily, in the strictest sense, ecclesiastical. Theology might claim in theory to be queen of the sciences. Practical politics were different.

The political advance of an intellectual interest was apparent on the level of the university, and below it on that of the university's philosophical faculty. It is also apparent, finally, on a level far above the university. This is to be expected. For if the social forces emanating from the mind were really so vital, they must have had some effect, however slight, in the high politics of states. It can be shown that they did.

### (iii) The intellectual aspect of French colonialism

It is well known to medievalists that in the course of the thirteenth century Germany declined as an international power, while France rose. The replacement of Hohenstaufen authority in Italy by that of Angevins and other French noblemen was among the central facts of that century. So was the growth of Saint Louis's monarchy, and the slow volte-face of the papacy from the Empire to France. These changes were interconnected. But they were also all connected with a further one: the rapid growth of the university of Paris. The fortunes of monarchy and university were bound together. The university might be in principle international. Some of its most famous teachers might come from Italy, Germany, Britain, and elsewhere, as well as from France. But in the student population there was a bias towards France. This is not surprising. Not to mention such questions as language, mere travel expense made Paris more accessible to the French than to anyone else.[21] A study of the university's 'nations' confirms that, even before the pronounced nationalization of the university in the fourteenth century, subjects of the French crown were numerically preponderant.[22] The growth of the university of Paris must consequently be seen in a French political context. Their country's political expansion offered students jobs. They in their turn backed up the political conquerors with an army of intellectual colonists. French ascendancy can be seen from this aspect as that of a Paris-trained national élite.

A small but crucial section of France's success-story will illustrate this. The thirteenth century, as will be more fully explained in chapter 13, saw the first general breakthrough to the episcopate of non-nobles who had risen by mental ability. The papacy did not escape this effect. The century had begun with the appointment, by Innocent III, of two non-noble associates from Paris—a fellow-student (Langton) and a teacher (Peter of Corbeil)—as primates respectively of England and France. Not only such appointments, but the direct way they were made—signalling a growth in centralized bureaucracy in the Curia—omened well for talented graduates. A golden age for them accordingly followed. Its essence is caught in its most meteoric career. Jacques Pantaléon was a shoemaker's son from Troyes. He had probably been a student in Paris at the time Innocent III died. Graduating in arts and canon law, he was soon distinguishing himself as chief administrator of Liège cathedral. He held this post in 1245 when Innocent IV, chased from the Empire, held a general council in Lyons, and chanced to meet him. Pantaléon impressed the pope and was made a papal chaplain. Later he was made a cardinal. Finally in 1261 he became pope, as Urban IV.[23]

That meeting of Jacques Pantaléon and Innocent in 1245 proved a historical turning-point. For Urban IV was not only the first French pope since the Cluniacs. Nor was he only the first conspicuous case since Sylvester II (another Frenchman) of a pope born humbly, raised by learning and service. He was in both respects the beginning of a new development in papal history. Directly and indirectly, Urban launched on to the political scene a whole host of clever compatriots. Twelve weeks after his election he gave cardinals' hats to (in a whole group of

Frenchmen) the future popes Clement IV and Martin IV, both ex-Paris scholars (the first possibly Urban's friend there).[24] And by the time these three popes together had done with the cardinals' college, in 1285, it was well on the way to becoming that fortress of French bureaucrats it would be at Avignon. Nor were Urban IV's acts in secular politics any less consequential for his ambitious compatriots. It was he who recruited Charles of Anjou to rule southern Italy, thereby opening the way for intelligent Frenchmen to yet another source of office.

The expansion of France in the thirteenth century, to fill Germany's place in Mediterranean politics, was not, therefore, just one more European changing-of-the-guard. It spelt the replacement of one type of government by another: by one which drew on a rising university élite. Now this interpretation of thirteenth-century politics is not new. It was made in almost the same terms at the same time. The man who made it was Alexander of Roes, a canon of Cologne. Between 1281 and 1288 Alexander wrote three pamphlets which, despite their polemical tone, form together one of the most sophisticated of contemporary political comments.[25] Alexander had been indignant to find that the new French popes, while amending the missal used in the papal chapel, had had the effrontery to drop the German king's name from the pope's regular prayers. This was more than a national insult. It violated the order of things. So Alexander set out to explain what this latter was. He was among those contemporary commentators, referred to just now, who allowed authority to three powers, *sacerdotium*, *regnum*, and *studium*. Alexander's peculiarity was that he attached each of the three powers to a European nation. The Germans, with their martial qualities, should provide the emperor, to defend the church against violence. Theirs was *regnum*. The Italians, with their steadfastness in the Catholic faith, made the best popes. Theirs was *sacerdotium*. The French, being (when uncorrupt) naturally 'circumspect, watchful, and ... clear-thinking',[26] found their national excellence in learning. Theirs was *studium*. The office of the French in Christendom was to 'prove and demonstrate by invincible argument why the truths of faith should be held'.[27] Alexander's ingenious doctrine was set out far more elaborately than this. But through all its elaborations, not without their occasional contradictions,[28] the message was simple. France's proper excellence was *studium*. She should leave both the papacy, and the task of protecting it, to others. Hidden in the French ascendancy of the late thirteenth century, that is to say, Alexander discerned what we have discerned: Christendom's intellectuals invading high politics. This view of course reflected, more specifically and in the opposite polemical context, that French pride in rationality we heard flaunted by Pierre Dubois and others in the same period. This was the same national characteristic, identified from a different angle. Nor was the identification in Alexander's case the quirk of one man. The manuscript history of his tracts shows his view found plenty of sympathy, particularly (and not surprisingly) in Germany during the conciliar period.[29]

The university in society; within the university, its 'arts' faculty; beyond the university, France and its nationalism: in each of these spheres the intellect, *qua* intellect, manifested its cutting power in the context of pure politics.

It is time now to move away from pure politics, in the secular sense. For learning was *clergie*. Its proper home was the church. It is its cutting power here, its bids to take over its ecclesiastical home, that will occupy us for the second half of this chapter.

## 2. THE ASSAULT IN ECCLESIASTICAL POLITICS

Most of the evidence about medieval ecclesiastical politics comes naturally from the *litterati*: the 'educated'. But it is precisely the role of the *litterati* within the church that now has to be assessed. Their direct evidence may not always be trustworthy. So the evidence will now be approached obliquely, to see what it reveals indirectly.

### (i) *'Illiteracy' in the church: the crescendo of protest*

It is common knowledge that many of the people holding office in the medieval church were inadequate. The fact might perhaps be arrived at analytically. But there is evidence of it, too, coming in some shape and degree from every medieval century. This evidence, like other medieval evidence, thickens from the twelfth century. From then on can be picked out with growing assurance the single failings attributed to one or other area of the hierarchy: episcopal greed, priestly concubinage, monastic instability, and so on.

Among these criticisms one took on special clarity during the thirteenth century. It was that office-holders, especially the higher ones, were insufficiently *educated*. They were not, or not enough, *litterati*, in the more exacting sense the word acquired in this very century.

Now the kernel of this objection was certainly old. Traces of it can be found from the millennium, not to speak of earlier centuries.[30] The Gregorian reform is perhaps a natural place to look for it; and it is occasionally there, as in Humbert of Silva Candida's *Against the Simonists*,[31] and in Peter Damian.[32] Similar vestiges of the criticism can indeed be found at almost any point in the twelfth century: in some satire, for instance, light-heartedly victimizing the unlettered priest or prelate, like the priestly 'ass' at Aulnay pictured in Plate VII.[33]

Until the end of the twelfth century, nevertheless, and even into the thirteenth, this motif—that clergy were inadequately educated—remains remarkable for its timidity. Not only does it escape prominence in those lists of abuses where it does appear. In sources where we should expect to find it, it is often not there at all. An example is the letters of the great reformer himself, Gregory VII. They do not include any general complaint on this score.[34] There is hardly a word of it, either, from those reforming councils which sat in Rome and elsewhere in the early twelfth century; so far, that is, as we have records of their enactments.[35] Examples equally telling are available even from later in the century. One is the so-called 'Goliardic' poetry. The authors of this topical, satirical Latin verse often sing the song of the disappointed clerk: 'learning gets you nowhere nowadays'; and they rail against criteria by which appointments are made. But among the many charges the fictional 'Golias' brings against successful churchmen—greed, fraud, sensual indulgence, and so on—lack of learning is notable for its almost total absence.[36] From roughly the same period another significant instance is heresy. As critics of the church hierarchy, heretics left 'Golias' far behind. We will never know all the heretics said. But in the corpus of what we do know, from the decades just before and after 1200, scarcely a word remains about low educational standards in the Catholic priesthood.[37] A final example of this reticence takes us into the thirteenth century. The Franciscan order came into being as in some ways a reaction to the church hierarchy. At least in its early years it was ideally placed to criticize, and it did. Yet Franciscan criticism from these years has very little to say on poor clerical education. Saint Anthony of Padua's diatribes on the upper clergy, for instance, pronounced in the 1220s, say absolutely nothing on this fault.[38] The most remarkable case of all is that of Odo Rigord, Franciscan Archbishop of Rouen. Odo compiled a register of visitations from 1248 to 1268. It is a systematic record of abuses and shortcomings in a large archdiocese. It runs to thousands of entries and hundreds of pages. Four times Odo records examinations he has made (in obedience to a law of 1215) of the Latin of parish priests, with poor results; five times he notes the presence of idiots or alcoholics in convents; and very occasionally he mentions someone's 'simplicity', or ignorance on a particular matter. But the term *insufficientia litterarum*, or anything like it, comes only once, as barring a man's promotion. That is all. The silence was striking enough to have been noticed by the register's nineteenth-century editor.[39]

The silences of these Franciscans partly reflect the reservations their order had about the value of scholarship. In this particular the order was conservative. Other contemporaries were becoming more vocal. In 1179, Alexander III's Lateran Council had already, in two of its twenty-seven canons, drawn attention to this subject of clerical education.[40] Innocent III's Lateran Council in 1215 took the matter further, in three or four of its seventy canons. We already hear in these the theme that would grow so loud later: that 'carnal and illiterate' persons, and 'the ignorant and rude', are too often given church appointments.[41] French provincial councils and reformers echoed the complaint.[42] Yet even now it remained moderate. A French council in 1289, for instance, listed qualities to be sought in ordinands. 'Literacy' was one; but there were nineteen others, nothing to do with learning.[43] Again, in 1281 we find Archbishop Pecham of Canterbury upset that simple priests are sometimes made fools of in archdeacons' courts; but it is the *archdeacons* he finds fault with, not the priests.[44]

In one area, however, the complaint that clergy are too unlettered does become more prominent in the thirteenth century. This is among the more academic mendicants. About 1240 the Dominican Guillaume Peyraut, in a disquisition on promotions in the church, identified those whom he saw as the most useful sort of Christian. They were the *doctissimi*. Consequently, in place of all the nobles who get promoted, *litterati et sancti* (in that order) should be preferred.[45] About 1265 another influential Dominican, Humbert de Romans, protested that some cardinals scarcely ever opened a book; that too many bishops were 'simple'; and that the parish clergy generally were poorly educated.[46] About the same time Archbishop Federigo Visconti, pupil of Dominicans and their tireless ally, put a similar preoccupation explicitly. *Scientia*, he told the clergy of his Pisan province, should in these days be the priest's most active concern, even before zeal and good works.[47] A few years later this chorus would be joined by a Franciscan, in an order now mellowed towards scholarship. Fra Salimbene of Parma inveighed against papal nepotism in appointments to the cardinals' college. What was his argument? There were, he said, 'a thousand Franciscan friars more suited to the cardinalate by reason of their learning and holy life'. *Ratione scientie et sancte vite:* like Peyraut before him, Salimbene chose the order of his words unconsciously.[48]

In friars' criticism of other clergy the educational motif now found a permanent place, and a prominent one. But by the fourteenth century the friars too had found such a place, as all but part of the church 'establishment'. So their role as chief critic passed largely to other groups. It was these that gave our theme its fullest development. I do not mean primarily those elusive authors, themselves largely from the lower and middle clergy, who gave birth to the vernacular 'satire and complaint' which G. R. Owst analysed; though this and its kindred-genres were, as Owst showed, certainly prolific of attacks on priestly ignorance.[49] I mean above all that literate quasi-laity, which about the year 1300 was coming to demand radical readjustments of the church's place in society. Their criticism contains a new note. Two spokesmen will help us identify it.

In 1308, probably at royal behest, the Norman lawyer Pierre Dubois wrote a polemic called 'Remonstrance of the People of France'. In the context of the campaign of the French crown to dissolve the order of Knights Templar, the 'Remonstrance' sought to intimidate Pope Clement V by exposing scandals in the church hierarchy. Dubois spoke of a number of canonical abuses. But he returned to none so warmly as the appointment to high office of unlearned men. Clement's nepotism had bypassed 'two hundred or more masters in theology and canon law, and doctors of civil law . . . each one of whom is four times the clerk his nephew is, or ever could be'. Clement had handed great bishoprics to unworthy kinsmen or servants 'when there are many more learned persons unable to have so much'. Clement's successor would depose his protégés as 'too little lettered for such an estate . . . and he will replace them with great masters in divinity . . . each greater, if he chooses, than anyone to be found in the Roman *Curia* today'. Here and elsewhere the 'Remonstrance' implied that learning was the main claim to high church office. It once said so plainly: donors of benefices should use the bigger and better part of them to honour *persones plus letrés*.[50]

Dubois wrote expressly to woo public opinion, and his feelings were not his alone. His outbursts at high-level ignorance were echoed, and indeed surpassed by a second writer, sixteen years later, Marsilius of Padua. Marsilius' *Defender of the Peace* attacked, not current abuses in the church, but its essence as normally understood. But abuses played their part. Marsilius came back again and again to one particular abuse. 'Because of the corruption of the ecclesiastical regime, the greatest part of the priests and bishops are only slightly, and if one may say so insufficiently, versed in holy Scripture.'[51] 'Invoking as witnesses God and the multitude of the faithful, I swear that I have seen and heard very many priests, abbots, and other church prelates who were so inferior that they could not even speak grammatically.'[52] He found the fault on every level of the church: in the pope; among cardinals; bishops; electoral chapters; abbots, priors, and even curates. The pope bestowed most church offices 'from the highest to the lowest, upon uneducated persons ignorant of divine letters'.[53]

Political and intellectual conditions made Paris in Philip the Fair's reign an appropriate platform for criticism of the church. New conditions soon prevailed: the end of the Capetians; the Hundred Years War; a French papacy at Avignon. After mid-century Marsilius and his views were more or less forgotten.[54] It was only in the last decades of the century that grumbles about church abuses again grew loud in Paris. When they did, it was as part of a larger grumble, heard all over northern Europe. In most places this gradually identified itself as the conciliar movement.

It was the conciliar movement which in effect brought the word 'reform' into common Christian usage.[55] Among the abuses it sought to reform, low educational standards among leading ecclesiastics took a prominent place. When in 1394 the university of Paris first mooted the idea of an autonomous council, it claimed equal representation with the hierarchy in such a council on the grounds (chiefly) that 'rather a large number of prelates in our times are unfortunately unlettered'.[56] The reformist writer Nicholas of Clamanges made it the first fault of bishoprics *c.* 1400 that they were held by 'ignorant and illiterate men', or at least by men without qualifications in theology.[57] Pierre d'Ailly was more emphatic: searching for suitable subject-matter for a reforming council, he lighted first on the fact that *fatui* and *ignari* were given the best benefices.[58] The university of Paris agreed: not literates and graduates, but the unqualified—cooks, stewards and ostlers—were given benefices, to the great hurt of the faith.[59] In a French debate whether the pope or national bishops made the better appointments, the one thing tacitly understood by all parties was that a good appointment was one involving a 'clerk' or 'notable person', not one 'unlettered'.[60] When the Council of Constance finally met, it expressed this view both in debates and legislation.[61] The Council of Basle in the 1430s went even further.[62]

Nothing better illustrates the depth to which this pre-occupation took root in the early fifteenth century than the fact that it was nourished not only by the councils, but by their most influential victim. It has sometimes been noticed that John Hus—paradoxically—shared some of his persecutors' peculiar biases and sensitivities. He shared this one. His sermons, comments, and letters cast frequent aspersions on the ignorance of holders of high church office. Once, for instance, he was recommending that the pope should read the story of Jesus's humble entry to Jerusalem on an ass; and interjected 'if he *can*'.[63]

Taken over the central and late middle ages as a whole, complaints on ignorance in ecclesiastical places, especially high ones, form an audible crescendo. No generation had been entirely without these complaints. But the isolated aspersions of some mendicants, followed in the fourteenth century both by satire and by the more studied outbursts of French polemicists, followed, again, after a lull, by uproar in the conciliar period; these successive phases of complaint form three distinct upward steps in surviving criticism on this subject. They were steps not only in its volume, but in its degree of emphasis.

Now there is plenty of particular evidence in the late middle ages to confirm the general criticism that grew so loud then. From the thirteenth century we have anecdotes, passed around among preachers and other story-mongers, of all sorts of ignorant clergy: from the country curate who cannot tell a Parisian street-cry from the Latin office; up to the bishop who stumbles in reading his Latin consecration oath.[64] Fourteenth-century and later visitation diaries contain brief but sober notices such as: 'the curate reads badly'; 'the curate is ignorant and knows nothing'; 'the curate does not know the office', etc.[65] Modern studies of pre-Reformation national churches have revealed enough of this type of evidence to leave us in no doubt that those reformers, from *c.* 1300 on, were not simply imagining the abuses they decried.

The protest at church illiteracy forms a crescendo. The protest finds corroboration in particular evidence. These two facts, taken together in the context of inquiries into the background to Luther and Calvin, have sometimes fed the idea—perhaps implicit in the word 'Reformation'—that the late medieval church was decadent. It may have been, in this or that sphere. But in the sphere of literacy the case is unproven. The mere bulk of evidence on the church's shortcomings, graphic as it is, and abysmal as the shortcomings may be, does not prove decadence. It may prove the opposite. In fact, in the present case, a few simple considerations will show that it does.

*(ii) 'Illiteracy' in the church: the reality*

The simple considerations are three. The first is the *bulk* of evidence. The fourteenth-century church produced more documents to its own illiteracy because it produced more documents. Regular records of episcopal visitations do not start until the late thirteenth century (Odo Rigord was a pioneer); nor parish registers until the second quarter of the fourteenth. These novelties were the outcome of a familiarity with documents which had been gradually spreading since the eleventh century. The spread is shown by a glance at the centre of the church's written business, also its paragon in the matter of records: the papal Curia. I mean literally a glance. Most of the medieval registers still stand in rows on their shelves in the Vatican archive, and the mere sight of the volumes shows the growth in correspondence during the thirteenth and fourteenth centuries. The same lesson can be read a little more precisely in the graph opposite. It shows the average number of volumes of registered papal correspondence per year, in each major pontificate. (The volumes are roughly the same size.)[66]

Circumstances relating to the making and survival of these volumes vary too much for this measure of papal correspondence to be taken as absolute. But the trend is too strong to allow such doubts much importance. Even before the move to Avignon, the rise of the average under the French popes (Urban IV, Clement IV, and Martin IV) is conspicuous. As for the deluge of documentation in the fourteenth century, it exceeded even the estimate shown in the graph. For the Vatican archive contains not only more registers in the fourteenth century, but wholly new series' of records—for example, tax-collectors' reports (beginning c. 1275). The significance of these estimates from the Curia is not confined to the history of one writing-office. They represent a growth in the number of literate experts all over Christendom, with whom the Curia corresponded.

That is the first simple consideration about the evidence for church illiteracy after c. 1300. The second is that much of the evidence, when read carefully, testifies to rising standards. About the year 1040 a Cluniac historian in France had averred, with hyperbole but without indignation, that forty years before the art of reading was almost wholly lacking throughout the entire parish clergy of his kingdom.[67] Indignation in the fourteenth century was greater, the delinquency less. The rise in standards is illustrated by two particular circumstances. The term *litteratus*, together with its contrary *illiteratus*, shifted its meaning. A study of the context this pair of terms was used in shows that roughly down to the mid-thirteenth century *litteratus* meant 'able to read and write Latin'. From then on it implied the acquaintance with Latin literature which a student might expect to acquire at a serious school or at university. It became much like our 'lettered', or even our 'educated'.[68] The second circumstance to betray rising standards is the attitudes of religious orders towards institutional learning. In just these same years, the late thirteenth century, the older orders began to follow the mendicants in force into the universities. In the case of the Benedictines this was simply a late acknowledgement that the order had changed from being an exporter of

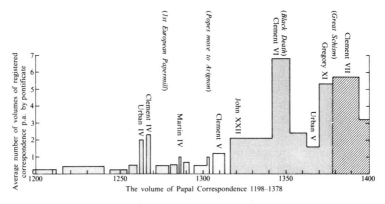

The volume of Papal Correspondence 1198–1378

*Source.* Calendar of Entries in the Papal Registers relating to Great Britain and Ireland (1893– ); K. A. Fink, *Das Vatikanische Archiv* (Rome 1951[2]); Ross Fund Report, by Ian B. Cowan, (Glasgow University, (1967 and 1968; a duplicated report on sources for medieval Scottish history in Vatican Archives).

knowledge to being an importer. For other orders, who had never professionally dealt with this kind of knowledge, the rush to universities represented a new set of values. By the late fourteenth century, for instance, the Cistercian order was quite as keen to establish its recruits in the schools of Paris[69] as the order's founder-father Saint Bernard had been in the twelfth to drag them out. Again, in 1356, the Knights Hospitaller were anxious that their brotherhood lacked lawyers[70]—when barely two generations before the chiefs of their sister order the

Templars had gone to the stake without reflecting for a moment that this was where their weakness lay.[71]

A third simple consideration suggests itself about the evidence for illiteracy in the late medieval church. It is the simplest of all. It is technical. The printing revolution of the fifteenth century has robbed of publicity a quieter revolution of the late thirteenth and early fourteenth century: the paper revolution. In that century-and-a-half paper was widely substituted for parchment as the favourite writing material. It thereafter cost less, in absolute terms, to write something down: square inch for square inch, French royal accounts of the fourteenth century, for example, show that paper cost about half parchment. Paper's price-advantage partly reflected a change in the organization of its manufacture. Paper had been known in Sicily (and also in Genoa) in the early twelfth century, and in parts of the Empire and France in the thirteenth. But this paper had been imported from Islam, and thereby damaged in its first recommendation of cheapness. The earliest European paper-mill to be mentioned was working in 1276, the second in 1293. Significantly both were in the papal states. (Those voluminous Avignon registers represented on the graph on page 300 were all on paper.) France had its first mill in 1348 (near Troyes). Germany followed in 1390, Flanders probably in 1405. An increasing *use* of paper is in evidence outside these regions from the early fourteenth century, for example, in England by 1309, and in Holland by 1346.[72]

Like printing later, the relatively cheap writing material came in with a whole complex of sympathetic changes in neighbouring branches of technology and economics. Parchment itself got some rarity value in the face of rising demand in the late thirteenth century: a fact surely in the minds of the early investors in papermaking—eager to exploit a market starved of writing material—as we know it to have been in the minds of parchment dealers.[73] The profession of scribe gained momentum, too, both in numbers and professionalism. The number of professional scribes in Milan, excluding the religious orders, apparently rose from two to forty in the thirteenth century, and there are signs from elsewhere that this heralded a more general trend.[74] Fourteenth-century manuscripts betray quickened activity. Many more of them survive than from earlier centuries. The number of distinct scripts grows, suggesting ramification in the activity of scriptoria.[75] Most of the scripts share, among other characteristics, a new impetus towards abbreviation: as if scribes felt growing pressure on their time and raw materials.[76] The related trade of book-dealing gained similarly in momentum. In the last decade of the thirteenth century the Paris book-dealers rose to the class of those listed for tax-purposes, and a whole series of them is known by name from then on.[77] The trade spread meanwhile to new centres, and was international. (A bishop of Durham said in 1345 he had no difficulty in getting books sent from France, Germany, or Italy, if he sent money in advance.)[78] Even the reading, finally, of all this material underwent a technical revolution. For the 1290s witnessed the invention of spectacles. Originating from Venice, spectacles were a familiar novelty to the average educated man anywhere in Europe by about 1300. In the following generations they would be helping many mature thoughts on to paper that would not otherwise have got there: Petrarch's, for instance.[79]

Our three simple considerations, each weighed on its own, prove to be not so simple. They pose a new range of questions on pre-Renaissance history. But they remain simple in one respect. A mere instant's reflection on them is enough to raise a caution against any impression that the fourteenth-century church, outside its disastrous middle years, was specially illiterate. Neither in the church nor anywhere else can literacy in any sense have been declining. Reformers' feelings apart, positive evidence points the other way: products, standards, and even the equipment of reading and writing were more (or better) at the end of the century than at the beginning.

A logical hiatus therefore gapes in front of us. The evil criticized got less. The criticism got more intense. To bridge the hiatus, one more consideration must be invoked. This time it is quite a complicated one. But its complications will bring us, I hope, to a clearer understanding of our subject.

### (iii) *The paradox resolved: graduates and jobs*

Often in the middle ages the church felt herself short of properly educated recruits. Most of the aspersions on churchmen's illiteracy in early centuries—roughly up to 1250—were made in the context of this feeling. Pontiffs and councils noted clerical ignorance; and they blamed, not bad choice in appointments, but lack of choice: sources of supply were lacking. Endowment of schools was the outcome. It was an act not just of philanthropy but of long-term administrative planning. But long-term plans can run into unforseen difficulties. This one did. The rise of an ambitious intellectual élite, much of it expert in everything *but* theology, had not been part of the fathers' scheme. The quality of their source of supply, that is to say, baffled expectations. So, for related reasons, did its quantity. The history of education parades statutes which founded schools. Outside monasticism it seldom records schools' closure. Yet where there is variable demand and supply the chances are that each will take its turn in exceeding the other. Medieval education was no exception. There are signs that at some periods the schools turned out more graduates than the church knew what to do with. Supply exceeded demand.

Many of these signs relate to the period immediately under discussion, *c.* 1250–*c.* 1450. We can begin by looking at the signs that relate to supply.

(a) *The supply of graduates in the later middle ages*

The question of the size of medieval university populations has exercised, and is exercising, some distinguished scholars.[80] We need not review their estimates now. This is partly because big unresolved doubts remain—which alone would show how unhelpful the evidence on this subject is. But it is also because absolute numbers are not what concerns us. What do concern us are trends, up and down. Although absolute numbers, where known over a period, are a good way of gauging these trends, other ways exist, for example, symptoms of pressure on resources, cries for help, and so on. Since the question of trends has not so far been in the forefront of discussion, it will be useful to set out what the evidence suggests when seen from this angle.

The university of Paris is agreed probably to have reached a high water-mark about the year 1300 or a year or two later, apparently after a particularly brisk expansion in the previous twenty years.[81] This phase coincides broadly with the energetic reign of Philip the Fair (1285–1314), who lavished privileges on the university. Just afterwards, however, in 1316–17, contemporaries spoke of a slump: teachers in arts were reduced to a tenth of their former numbers (it was said) and the faculty feared closure. By the 1320s, however, signs of the slump had gone; though the level of Philip the Fair's reign does not seem to have been reached again. The full force of the Black Death of 1348 did not hit Paris until the long vacation had begun, and—surely for that reason—the catastrophe has left relatively few surviving traces on a university otherwise vulnerable.[82] But a second plague in 1363 hit Paris hard. Complaints at lack of masters and empty schools betray a deep depression, perhaps one compounded with the effects of the first outbreak.[83] Symptoms of recovery, nevertheless, multiply from *c.* 1370 to 1400: talk of 'thousands', 'multitudes', and classes of up to three hundred.[84] The numbers on the promotion-rolls seem to confirm this trend in the same years, and suggest a new peak near the end of the century. Only in 1425 do we hear of a new decline, followed by rather better figures from the mid-fifteenth century, suggesting a recovery to a level, with only slight variations now above and below.

There is less agreement as yet about the curve at Oxford. But there are reasons for believing it to have been broadly similar, without about half the numbers.[85] The known and conjectural dates of the establishments of student halls (and the earliest colleges) suggest a build-up in numbers between the 1240s and 1280s. Intermittent though it may have been, the build-up probably continued for most of the reign of Edward I (1274–1307). H. E. Salter found cases of emergency requisition of classrooms around 1276, and again from 1303 to 1306.[86] In at least one parish with university connections, St. Peter's in the East, the surviving rent-roll of a big landlord shows a sharp rise in the number of clerical lessees between *c.* 1290 and the beginning of the fourteenth century.[87] In 1298, after a big clash of town and gown, the town authorities dared to speak of 'thousands' of students.[88] These facts, though far from conclusive, would be consistent with a demographic increase contemporary with that in Paris. In the early fourteenth century we are back in the dark. Salter argued for a continuous fall in numbers throughout the century. His view has until recently been accepted as canon; but that has been *faute de mieux*, and in its bald form it is unlikely to survive much longer. The establishment of some apparently new academic halls in 1324,[89] not to mention that of some colleges, is enough to show that in the early decades of the century any fall there was in Oxford's student population was not catastrophic. It probably *was* more catastrophic at the Black Death. It is true that in Oxford, as in Paris, scholars were better placed than townsmen to disperse (or not convene) at the onset of plague. But plague could strike at the university indirectly. One pointer to its having done so is a tradition, repeated from 1350 to the 1440s, that the university had been much bigger before 1348 than after.[90] Another is that later college statutes speak of plague as having reduced numbers.[91] At all events, hints of a new build-up in population come in the 1370s: not least of them being the foundation of 'New' College in 1379 (on a site left vacant since the Black Death)—an act which at a stroke nearly doubled the university's college population.[92] Another such hint of a build-up (and a build-up, incidentally, despite the growing vigour of Cambridge, which would have drawn off recruits) is that we start finding signs of a *new* decline early in the fifteenth century. There survive mild complaints on the subject from a year or two after 1400, and from 1415; and an anguished complaint, of a grave collapse in population, from 1438. Measures taken to heal this last crisis led to a healthy recovery.[93]

These conjectural population trends in the two leading northern universities suggest summits at the very beginning, and very end, of the fourteenth century; with a common, long trough after mid-century. This pattern, for all the uncertain elements in it, takes on both sharpness and a new significance when seen in the context of European universities more generally. Trends in these were analysed by Miss Anna Campbell in *The Black Death and Men of Learning*.[94] To the twenty or so universities existing in 1300, Miss Campbell finds, nine more were added in the first half of the fourteenth century. A depression followed, in which (over the '40s and '50s) five universities disappeared from historical record. The period 1350–70 saw an attempt at revival, with the foundation of seven new universities. But Miss Campbell remarked that these seven were either stillborn, or only successful after 1370.[95] The real revival only came after the latter date, between when and 1400 eight quite new universities were founded.

The *sizes* of new and provincial universities, where known, accentuate the curve. The promotion-rolls of Toulouse and Angers, for instance, added together, give totals of names rising in the following proportions:[96]

$$
\begin{array}{ll}
1362/3 & \times\ 1 \\
1378 & \times 15 \\
1384 & \times 26
\end{array}
$$

Prague, again, shows symptoms of a peak population between *c.* 1390 and 1406.[97] Other hints from different places and of different kinds point the same way. For instance, Miss Campbell reckoned up the totals of extant documents from five French provincial universities. Taken in periods of twelve years they reflect the same asymmetric trough in mid-century:[98]

$$
\begin{array}{ll}
1335\text{--}47 & 134 \\
1348\text{--}60 & 62 \\
1361\text{--}73 & 160
\end{array}
$$

Many unsolved questions hide behind all this arithmetic. But a tentative conclusion suggests itself. A boom in Paris and Oxford seems to have survived, despite a slight fall in numbers in those two universities themselves, by spreading the student-population into new universities. The overall boom was sharply cut short in 1348, to be followed by an almost universal depression. From the late 1360s this was followed by an expansion more pronounced (taking Europe as a whole) than the first, and still vigorous at the beginning of the fifteenth century.

These conjectures relate to the supply of graduates. It is now time to turn to the demand, that is, the number of ecclesiastical 'jobs'.

(b) *The ecclesiastical 'job-structure' in the later middle ages*

This is a bigger subject than universities, as the whole is bigger than a part. Fortunately it is again only trends that have to be discovered. Fortunately too, in view of the marked character of the trends ·found in university population, the establishing of a simple plus-or-minus relation between supply

and demand—all that is needed—calls merely for the identifying of the bare principles on which the church's job-structure
progressed.

The fundamental principle was inertia. It expressed itself
most purely in the keystone of church organization, the
bishopric. New bishoprics could in theory be created. But in the
central and late middle ages few were, outside missionary and
crusading fields. England, northern France, and western
Germany had no new bishoprics between the early twelfth
century and the Reformation.[99] The aggregate population of
these regions probably rose in the same period by over 150 per
cent.[100] The same lesson could largely be learned simply from
the history of church councils. The representation of bishops at
the eight general church councils between 1123 and 1415, boy-
cotting apart, only betrays marked fluctuation in response to
Europe's geographical expansion (between 1179 and 1270), not
her demographic (whose peak was *c.* 1300–48).[101] This con-
servatism in diocesan organization was deep enough to escape
serious debate, until medieval Christendom began trying to
rule itself by council in 1415. Then it was suddenly discovered
that Italy, with her scores of old bishoprics, had far too many
votes in relation to the current balance of power and
population. Rather than change the number of bishoprics the
reformers simply changed the system of voting.

The same inertia touched crucial points of the structure
below bishops. Membership of cathedral chapters, for all its
variations from place to place, varied little in time. Indeed,
after the twelfth century it could show a downward trend,
numbers in some parts being limited by law.[102] The number of
archdeaconries was similarly stagnant. The boundaries of late
medieval archdeaconries–where an archdeacon ruled as a sort
of miniature bishop over a segment of the diocese—have been
found usually to reflect those of Carolingian or Anglo-Saxon
administrative regions. The most obvious likely reason for this is
apparently the correct one. The boundaries were old. Where
their earlier histories are known, they are found to have been
largely fixed by 1100, and wholly—except for the odd episcopal
new broom—by 1200.[103] Below the archdeacon (between him
and the parish priest) the geographical nomenclature of rural
deaneries and 'archpresbyteries' was still establishing itself, it is

true, during the thirteenth century. But this nomenclature too had come to rest by *c.* 1300; and it is anyway doubtful how far these offices, which were often honorary, can be seen as ramifications of episcopal authority.[104] As for the parish itself, on ground level, it was as stagnant geographically as the rest of the edifice. London had as many parishes—about a hundred— in 1500 as in 1066.[105] Stagnation only slightly, if at all, less marked can be hazarded of Milan and Florence, of Paris after *c.* 1200, and of some other large cities.[106] Where high authority was on the spot to provide better for growing towns, it might lift the number of parishes, as at Sens, which had 13 parishes at the beginning of the thirteenth century, 17 at the end.[107] Where not, the old system lasted, oblivious of surrounding change: Nuremberg in 1500 had a population of 20,000 but only its two old parishes (and no bishop).[108] Students of the medieval parish who have made reckonings about its distribution commonly did so until recently on the assumption that it was constant; so little did evidence of change thrust itself on their notice.[109]

Now against all this inertia there were, certainly, some principles of growth. Within the main nodes of authority, responsibility ramified. In the Curia cardinals with their own staffs vindicated independent authority. In all bishoprics bureaucracy tended to grow. The administrative staff of the papal Curia rose from a probable 100–200 at the start of the thirteenth century to a figure nearer 400 or 500 at the time of the Black Death. Nothing we know of big provincial bishoprics assures us they did not obey the same law.[110] Meanwhile at ground level another principle of growth obtained. Gaps left by stagnation in the pattern of official parish churches were filled by a series of decreasing official substitutes: monastic and mendicant churches, and churches founded privately or by confraternities. 'The multiplication of churches and altars' actually became an abuse in some cities, not just to critics of abuses in general,[111] but to authorities who wanted such clergy as there were to enjoy a decent living when there was only so much income to share out.[112]

Inertia at the main points of the structure; some bureaucratic growth within them; and proliferation of non-parish churches at ground level. These, apparently, were the main principles governing the job-structure in the church of the central and late middle ages. From the point of view of graduates it was the first principle, that of inertia, that mattered most; and for the reason just named—the sharing of income. The inert jobs were the richer ones. The old centres of authority, just because they were old, were heirs to the first-comers in Europe's urban development. Despite losses, willed and unwilled, most were substantial landlords, not least in town centres. It was these points of authority which most attracted graduates. Despite the pious wishes of college founders, seeking to give qualified clergy to ordinary parishes, the educated man with a career to make was not primarily interested in the sort of church that pullulated at street-corners, or in poor rural livings—as contemporaries are heard regretting. His eyes were on the higher job-market. And this, though it had its phases of growth, was necessarily limited. It was not like the colonial or crusading frontier, where vigour and enterprise brought proportional reward. It was an enclosure, whose capacity followed rules of its own, and from which even the most brilliant candidate might find himself shut out if numbers happened to have been made up when he arrived.

(c) *The crisis c. 1400*

The crescendo of complaint at 'illiteracy' in the church's high places must be interpreted in the light of these contemporary conditions. The cry for reform in respect of clerical ignorance did not grow louder because the church grew worse. It grew louder because the circles swelled which were professionally sensitive in this particular: namely circles of university men, anxious for a living. Reigning prelates naturally seemed to fall furthest short in the field where graduates excelled. It was thus appropriate that the sharpest criticism of ignorance in the hierarchy should roughly coincide in date with booms in university population: *c.* 1308 and *c.* 1324; and from *c.* 1378 onwards.

These booms were in fact two successively rising stages of one slow one, interrupted by the traumas of plague, war, and inflation in mid-century. Indeed, the slow boom of the fourteenth century was itself the continuation of an even longer process, a process which can be traced continuously from the early thirteenth century. It had begun then with the expansion of the university of Paris. The expansion of the French monarchy was simultaneous. The connection was not lost on contemporaries. By 1300 the university had proved itself to be France's 'secret weapon', and was acknowledged as such by both friends and foes. But their very acknowledgement showed the secret was out: the practical value of universities to both persons and states was now a commonplace—as witnessed by the frequent appeal to 'public and private interest' (*publica et privata res*), in fourteenth-century university foundation privileges.[113]

The result of this leakage was that European universities multiplied. Any prince could found one. The French crown's triumph over Boniface VIII, around 1300, had been in this respect pyrrhic. For in Boniface France had browbeaten Rome's universality in favour of the regionalism of a national state. But this victory for regionalism struck simultaneously at France, who had her own universal institution: the university. In the fourteenth century, as more territorial states appeared, and in their turn began to divest the international church of her power, the university of Paris lost her absolute ascendancy. And the first sufferers were her graduates. We hear the university plead, now, for benefices for her *alumni*: first in single letters, then in long 'rolls'; and from 1378 the prologues to these rolls assume a markedly anxious tone, conscious of rivalry.[114] Paris's plight was only worsened by the fact that her older rivals shared it; for example, her former offshoot Oxford who, conscious in her turn of the new competition, sought in 1322 to take shelter behind Paris's own earthwork of papal privilege— before discovering that the French were largely nationalizing the papacy too.[115] As the fourteenth century passed, for all these pleas and privileges, rivalry from upstarts grew more intense. It came conspicuously, first, from the French provinces, for whose universities the Avignon papacy, overwhelmingly ruled by southern and western French provincials, was a heyday. But rivalry soon swelled from beyond France, above all from the Empire, where rich regional princes were busy creating miniature imitations of the French monarchy, university and all, in the new federal Germany of the Francophile Luxemburgs. Prague, Cologne, and Vienna—to mention only the biggest—were together turning out hundreds of graduates annually by 1400.

The main body of this social *Völkerwanderung* arrived at the church's gate in the epoch of the Great Schism and conciliar movement. The reformer Nicholas of Clamanges, seeking the root cause for the church's divisions in that period, named love of money.[116] Brutal illustrations could be found for his claim. But the quieter dilemma of graduates, seeking means of livelihood suited to their qualifications, was also an illustration. Modern scholars owe to the late E. F. Jacob, Oxford's Chichele professor and fellow of All Souls, a portrayal of the English aspect of this dilemma;—down to the time when, in the depths of Oxford's depression of 1438 (in pity for jobless graduates) Archbishop Chichele founded All Souls College itself.[117] But the dilemma was more than an English one. It was a constant theme in church politics on the continent, as nemesis struck the ladder-climbing element in old universities and new. To the universities of faction-torn France—their own Avignon papacy in jeopardy, and the Roman one lost to the Italians—the conciliar movement offered a chance of a *revanche*. The chance was equally valuable for those late-comers, the universities of the Empire. At the council of Constance in 1415 academic envoys had no sooner met than they fell to discussing the problem of graduates and appointments. Our knowledge of the discussions comes, as it happens, from the envoys of the two universities most conspicuous for recent growth: Vienna and Cologne, now the Empire's two leading universities (Hussite Prague having disgraced itself meanwhile by its own too-precipitate plan for reform). The discussions, it is true, never got anywhere. It was 'very difficult', the Vienna envoy reported, 'to get men of such different classes, traditions, and regions to agree to a common proposal'.[118] But the academic envoys worked up at the council a momentum which they afterwards employed in putting in separate bids with their own princes, meeting varying degrees of success. Experienced old Paris probably got most: making sure in successive French national councils that resolutions always included one reserving a quarter or more of all church benefices to university *alumni*. In the aftermath of the councils, and with the help of secular princes, universities thus won a real political victory within the church.

In practice as in theory, in the church as in more secular fields, the professional intellectuals had in this measure, by the mid-fifteenth century, stormed the controlling citadel.

## (d) *Conclusion*

Virtually unchallenged as masters of debate, written and spoken, fifteenth-century university men faced a temptation common to all possessors of a private weapon: that of using it in a sectional interest. The intellectuals' weapon was more dangerous than most, since it was ideas, and ideas can go on fighting after their first wielders are dead. I am thinking especially of one idea: that of 'Reform'. The idea of Reform need not be the weapon of an interest. But it can be. 'Hang your reforms!' says a sceptic in George Eliot's *Middlemarch*, 'I never hear the word "reform" but it is some trick to put in new men.' Politics is of course full of tricks, including tricks to keep in old men, and any trick the graduates played in the conciliar movement was at least played in a better cause than most. 'The attempt to create in the name of Reform a vested interest for graduates in the more lucrative benefices', a historian of the period has written, 'was . . . perhaps not wholly unlaudable.'[119] That is about it.

But unlaudability begins when a trick, imposing on enough people for long enough, enters the core of religion. I am not talking now about the conciliar movement, which was only one episode; but about the church of the central and late middle ages as a whole. It faced a problem, inborn like an original sin. Masters of reading and writing got from their skill a particular group-interest. So, it is true, did all other trades. But the group-interest of the educated was more dangerous, by reason of the very excellence of their profession. It was not a trade like others; it was a 'mystery' in the old Greek as well as the medieval Latin sense. Particularly in religion, the literate were makers and shapers. For it was chiefly they who fed and interpreted religious tradition; so much so that the word 'clerk' covered both functions. Here was the danger. Religion bound society together. Yet the literates who guarded it were themselves a distinct estate—*studium*. Who should guard the guardians if they slipped? There may have been crude correctives. Peasants who got too critical of academics could always lynch people carrying inkhorns, or at least (a commoner form of inarticulate reaction) remain sullenly indifferent to the clerks' religion. But that is not quite correction. The routine danger remained. It was the danger that influential areas of the establishment might interpret a general religion from a particular point of view: the academic point of view.

What other points of view there were, elsewhere in the establishment, will transpire in Part IV. That Part will consequently illumine this Part, showing the religious peculiarities of the clever *as* peculiarities. But the central peculiarity, by way of summing-up, can be caught at once in a single epitome. The epitome derives from that barometer of medieval mentalities, interpretation of scripture, and concerns Saint Peter. A short while ago we heard the voice of Marsilius of Padua as a radical critic of the church. Marsilius, though far from typical of his age, did speak for a noticeable minority in it—one more noticeable (to judge from the fortunes of his book) in the early fifteenth century.[120] Now Marsilius' *Defender of the Peace* hammered the papacy for wealth, political claims, and secular jurisdiction. The model held up for the popes in these regards was that of the apostles, whose chief, Peter, the popes claimed to represent.[121] But these apostolic sections were separate, in the text of the *Defender*, from those attacking ecclesiastics' lack of learning. It was convenient for its author that they were. For Marsilius would otherwise have brought himself and his readers face-to-face with an unaccommodating tradition. Based on Acts 4:15, Sermon No. 197 by Saint Augustine, and the accepted picture of fishermen, the tradition said Saint Peter and his colleagues were illiterate. As if the first apostles had silently acquired a schooling, Marsilius passed this tradition over. The evangelicals who had taught Marsilius his Bible would not have done.[122] For they belonged to another current of thought—orthodox and unorthodox—which looked askance at universities. But Marsilius' loyalties were on the other side. For all who shared these loyalties the illiteracy of the first apostles posed a problem. We know it was a problem from the ingenuity of the answer scholastics much more orthodox than Marsilius troubled to give it. The Christian message, they said, *had* to come first from the unlearned: for otherwise it might have seemed that learning, rather than divine inspiration, was the source of the message. Once the divine origin of Christianity had been established (as it had been by the late Roman Empire), the teaching of Christianity was best left to the learned—for instance, graduates of the university of Paris.[123]

That may be the right answer. It is not for the historian to say. He can only point out that it happened to grind the axe of those who gave it; and that other evaluations of the learned profession existed—and not only among peasant rioters.

# PART IV

# NOBILITY AND RELIGION

# CHAPTER 13

# Nobility and the Church

> At first, Christ chose poor men. After Pope
> Sylvester's time he endowed his church generously,
> and called in the rich.
>
> Jean Gerson, *De nobilitate* II.
> (*Œuvres Complètes*, ed. Mgr. Glorieux, IX (Paris
> 1973), 485.)

THE subject of the two central sections of this book has been the twin intellectual currents that fed the concept of natural laws: mathematics, and the collection of bookish disciplines which universities existed chiefly to pursue. An attempt has been made to locate these intellectual currents in a social milieu with one general characteristic: that it was drifting towards concentrations of power. Within the drift were to be found many states of mind: raw greed and ambition; and their softer modifications and aliases, down to the state of the man who merely does what is expected of him, and hopes not to be struck in the face for it. But the variations do not spoil the drift.

I now propose to juxtapose this rationalistic culture with another: a culture with a different emphasis, resting chiefly on different social origins, and sharing with the first a control of the commanding heights of the medieval church.

A bridge over into this second culture can be found by the briefest reflection on the ethic of the first. The intellectual élite described in chapters 10 and 11 had an ethic with a number of peculiarities. It put a premium on virtue at the expense of born nobility. It was ready to acknowledge social superiority, so long as that superiority was based on virtue. Finally, both 'virtue' and 'work' were interpreted in ways which reflected the special preoccupations of the culture: 'virtue' with a stress on the virtues of an intellectual; 'work' in a practical context distinct from that of the contemplatives' *opus Dei*.

The appeal of this ethic was strong in some circles. That is shown, if by nothing else, by the large number of manuscripts of ethical works from Stoic origins. But an ethic with these peculiarities could never have had universal appeal. Two groups in particular must have been indifferent to it: born noblemen, whose superiority did not depend on virtue or work; and the stricter monks and ascetics, for whom the first commandment, to love God 'with all thy heart' etc., was normally read as a signpost to their own occupation. From each of these viewpoints, noble and monastic, we happen to know, the scholarly world was often looked on with reserve, sometimes with hostility. The two viewpoints were of course distinct, and mutual tension kept them so. Nevertheless there was an area where they joined. Where they joined, the culture of the intellectual élite was turned inside-out: into a culture neither rationalistic in its religious behaviour, nor in any sense careerist in its social orientation. The purpose of these last four chapters will be to identify this conjunction. It will be found in a relationship between a segment of the medieval upper classes, and ascetic religion. A study of the physiognomy of this rival culture will throw into relief the peculiarities of the rationalistic, and allow, finally, the suggestion of some tentative conclusions.

The ascetic monastic culture was not the same as 'the church'. But there was a relation between the two. Because the subject to be examined is an intrinsically obscure one it will be appropriate to start where the light is brightest: not in the labyrinths of the Christian soul, but in its external symbol, the church. The subject of the present chapter will be, accordingly, 'nobility and the church'.

### I. THE FACTS

No word slips more easily from the tongue of those who discuss medieval history than 'the church'. But what *was* the church, socially speaking? The question deserves a moment's attention. Those who fought; those who worked; those who prayed: the threefold divisions of feudal society are familiar. It was argued in chapter 3, however, that the documents which proclaim these categories must be read 'between the lines'. For in lay society the prerogatives of those who fought were envied by some of those who worked; and defenders of social order used pen and paper to fight back—leaving us, in their propaganda, a picture of misleading symmetry. The same consideration applies to the line between church and laity. A social historian must suspect at the outset schemes which put a gulf between the medieval 'church' and its human environment—whether schemes by contemporaries, whose theories of sun and moon exalted the tonsured clergy as the sole conduits of grace and wisdom; or those post-eighteenth-century schemes which inverted that one by blaming on the same clergy all that was wrong with the age. For the prerogatives of those who prayed were also envied by outsiders. Much church literature is defensive polemic, hardening in our minds a division contemporaries might be too ready to ignore. Socially, intellectually, and even morally the clergy–laity distinction was generally less significant than differences between generations, or of high and low levels in one order. All churchmen were born as laymen. And if it was true (as educationalists knew even then)[1] that the first few years of a child's life were the formative ones, then laity and clergy grew up with the same native emotions.

The familiar distinctions of clergy, nobility, and workers need pushing into the background, then, if any profit is to come of a search for more subtle distinctions and groupings. In particular, in a study of the relation of nobility to church, it is the clergy–laity division that must be held suspect. For the distinction obscures a hard fact: the central fact indeed of the relation. Taking 'the church' in its narrowest sense—as the authorities: that is, bishops and monastic heads—church and nobility were from a sociological angle, in most places and periods of the middle ages, the same. Bishops, abbots, and lay aristocracy, that is to say, were born in substantially the same circumstances.

The identity was widely taken for granted then. By a familiar somersault it grew so strange in the four centuries since the middle ages that by the mid-nineteenth, when scientific history began, it had to be discovered. The act of discovery was done by a German historian Aloys Schulte, whose thesis *The Nobility and the German Church in the Middle Ages* first came out (in German) in

1909.[2] It was a pioneer book. So pioneer was it that it is doubtful if it has even today made its full mark. Untranslated into any other language, Schulte's study remains the acquaintance of a relatively small specialist circle, largely in Germany (though it concerns all of Europe). A résumé of its thesis will be useful. I include in the résumé the nuances added by research since Schulte.[3]

Schulte's message was that high birth was as a broad rule regarded throughout the middle ages as a necessary qualification for high church dignity. Evidence of the application of the rule to bishoprics is found at the dawn of the middle ages in Merovingian Gaul, Lombard Italy, and Anglo-Saxon England; and it would still be thriving, despite setbacks, at the eve of the Reformation in Valois France and the Empire of the early Habsburgs. 'High birth' could be more or less strictly understood. In thirteenth-century England, a place and century which probably found the rule approaching its weakest, no objection was raised to the promotion of the offspring of any prosperous landowner or patrician burgher, with the right qualifications otherwise. Conversely, though, in other places—fifteenth-century Germany being a prime case— the legal tests of nobility could be applied with the utmost strictness, such as in a demand for five generations of pure noble ancestry. The Gregorian reform, which might have been expected to halt this dark-age custom, had the paradoxical effect in some places of actually strengthening it, by supporting provincial dynasties against the throne.[4] For it was in fact only thrones, and those the most aggressive—the Carolingian, the Salian, the Anglo-Norman, and in the thirteenth century the papal—which made any serious inroads on the system; and none of the inroads quite destroyed it.

The noble principle was not attached only to bishoprics: as if their pre-eminence as lords spiritual made high birth an exceptional necessity. Where the provenance of cathedral dignitaries like archdeacons and members of cathedral chapters can be found out, the church hierarchy is found more often than not to reflect lay society, grade by grade; a circumstance which by Innocent III's time was giving the papacy second thoughts' about the legal rights of chapters in electing bishops (for how could such an exclusive electoral body be expected to range freely in its choice of the best man for bishop?). Strong in chapters, the noble principle is also found at work in the cloister. In some Benedictine houses it operated with little variation right through the middle ages. The main reform movements, it is true—it can be shown for Cluny, Hirsau, Cîteaux, and the two great mendicant orders—attacked the principle squarely. But only for a time: all of them—Cluniacs, Hirsauers, Cistercians, Dominicans, and even Franciscans—are to be detected within two or three generations of the reform attending in one way or another to the question of social backgrounds.[5] This pattern of development probably stretched even to less formal communities, like the Lombard Humiliati, and the Brethren of the Common Life.[6] As for communities untouched by radical reform, like certain German *Reichsklöster*, their fastidiousness was such as to have brought their population virtually to nil by the time of the Reformation.

This general preference for born noblemen, and its variations in intensity, are linked as both cause and effect with some familiar trends in social and ecclesiastical politics. But it would be wrong to treat the connection as explicable in familiar political terms. It was not, or not normally, merely a case of the nobility's keeping a stranglehold of church office for private political reasons. These unwritten stipulations—for most of them are unwritten, and research has been based more on practice than on legislation—rested on complex ideological foundations: on concepts both of nobility and of religion inherited from older social situations, largely pre-Christian ones. The ideological foundations can be glimpsed. For, if the customs themselves were unwritten, theologians and canonists set down arguments about them often enough. And although they wrote in different periods and circumstances, the same elements in the argument are there throughout the middle ages. Nothing can serve better to introduce the many-sided question of noble religious proclivities than a review of the arguments for and against upper-class monopoly in church office. For the arguments too were many-sided. It might have been more convenient for students of history if they had not been: if 'the church' could have been put solidly on the side of either the conservative or the egalitarian principle. But the truth of the matter is perhaps more instructive. It is—to name the one fact

that can*not* be disputed—that the church as such accommodated the defence of both principles.

## 2. THE ARGUMENTS: FOR NOBLE PRIVILEGE

Let us then look at the arguments; and first the arguments *for*
a high-class monopoly of church office. The first fact to be
reckoned with was that distinctions of birth obtained in lay
society. Whatever the church might have thought about her
own private constitution, there were fields where she could not
ignore lay social distinctions. In particular there was serfdom.
Respect for this was not just a question of scriptural authority
('slaves, be obedient to your earthly masters' (Eph. 6:5), etc.).
It was a question of diplomacy, in a situation the medieval
church inherited from the late Roman empire. One of the
complex of problems created in Christianity by Constantine's
conversion had been that the church, once a path to the
martyr's arena, had become instead that social ladder whose
medieval traffic occupied us in chapter 9. As Constantine's own
low-born forebears had risen through the army, others now used
baptism and ecclesiastical office. But this social ascent could not
happen without causing offence. Conservative powers saw their
status and servile manpower vanishing. The church, unlike the
army, had to be diplomatic. It could not offer its ladder
indiscriminately. A century after Constantine's conversion
Pope Leo the Great is already heard admitting that slaves
cannot become priests: for this is to steal them from their earthly
masters. 'Soldiers of the Lord [he wrote] must be free from other
claims' (i.e. must be legally free).[7] Leo's stipulation became
standard in subsequent conciliar legislation and was incorporated in the *Corpus Juris Canonici*.[8] As feudalism spread,
with un-freedom stretching in various degrees through much of
society, the stipulation gained wider application. It became one
canonical prop to the claims of Germany's 'free nobility' to
monopoly of church office.[9] Meanwhile the principle behind
Leo's text, if not the text itself, is found fighting manfully in one
situation after another during the middle ages. It did battle in
the late dark age in that controversial affair of pagan slaves
eluding their owners through baptism.[10] It did it again, often, in
the common complaint of the central and late middle ages, that
agrarian bondmen are leaving the farm to seek 'advancement

by clergy'.[11] Where subjection or vassalage was at stake, church recruitment could not in justice simply ignore, as if they were not there, the social distinctions of its host society.

The church must be fair to its neighbours. But the value it set on secular rank did not derive only from this. It had to be fair to itself too. A bishop or abbot was *ex officio* a territorial magnate, head of an organization beset by envious rivals, and generally with business at court. He must hold his own with the lay aristocracy. Where feudal service was due he might have to accompany his contingent to the battlefield. By far the commonest vindication of the noble principle in top church offices was this. 'A noble abbot [monks could argue] will defend us against the counts and magnates. Nay, he will attract the emperor's favour to us. And why? Because he has powerful relatives at court.' That was said not long after Charlemagne's death, in an abbatial election at Fulda.[12] But the same case is heard down the centuries, either directly, or echoed in attempts to refute it. In the mid-thirteenth century one Dominican will be heard beating back the principle on the grounds that 'if some nobles should be made canons to defend the temporal, how much *more* important is it . . . to defend the spiritual'.[13] Another, meanwhile—this time it is the authoritative voice of Aquinas— allows it: it is sometimes better [writes Aquinas] to take 'the less saintly and less learned man . . . on account of his secular power or experience'.[14] The medieval hardiness of this position is betrayed best of all by the courtesy shown it by no less independent a reformer than Gerard Groote, founder of the *Devotio Moderna*.[15]

Practical considerations, whether of diplomacy towards secular rights, or of politics and business, nevertheless only made part of the doctrinal bulwark for the church's preference for nobles. It was not just a matter of the church's material interests. It was a matter of her honour. Pope Leo's letter about ex-serf priests had complained also that they 'polluted' holy orders.[16] That view, which remained as a text in canon law, was given force in the Carolingian period by the practice some lords had of getting serfs ordained and *keeping* them as serfs, waiting at table, etc.[17] The Gregorian reform was launched to scotch that sort of situation. But it did so partly by accepting in effect the converse principle: if a candidate's servile origin polluted the office he undertook, his nobility honoured it.[18] It was true that the primitive church of the first century had managed without noble bishops. But times had changed. Saint Jerome had said so; and times had changed more since his time, as Germanic standards inexorably forced their way into the the church's practice.[19] How this particular Germanic standard forced its way in comes into view in the history of missions. In the face of heathen aristocratic societies, whose chiefs had priestly functions, leaders of Christian missions in the dark ages had to be noble, or be given out as noble, or the mission would fail.[20] This was still true in the twelfth century. About 1120 a hermit called Bernard set out from Germany to convert the heathen of Pomerania. He was ignored. Why? The biographer of his more prudent successor gives a simple answer. The Pomeranians were ruled by a nobility, in whom a barefoot stranger could excite nothing but contempt. The biographer then goes on to describe the successful attempt. It was by an aristocrat, Saint Otto of Bamberg, a born nobleman and now as bishop the greatest magnate of Franconia. He went to Pomerania with an appropriate retinue. *This* language the Pomeranians understood; and they duly embraced Christianity.[21]

The interest recently aroused by 'poverty movements' in twelfth- and thirteenth-century Europe, together with our modern evangelical traditions, may hide from us that many western Christians at the time would have sympathized with the Pomeranians in that story. Saints' biographers, like that one, are among witnesses to the fact. They not seldom start by protesting how unimportant worldly nobility is; but take care to mention that their saint *was* noble, all the same.[22] Even a philosopher like Neckham, otherwise a cudgel of noble pretensions, on noticing this feature of saints' *Lives*, was ready to approve it: nobility of birth made a saint a better advertisement for the values he stood for.[23] Despite all the enthusiasms of the central middle ages, that view would still be staunchly upheld by influential opinion in the fifteenth century: noble birth in its leaders was good for the church's public relations.

But the church's public relations are not a separate part of its activity. Its very elements—the Incarnation, the sacraments, the liturgy, and so on—all have a didactic aspect, inseparable from their nature. So if nobly-born bishops were good for public relations, it was not because they served as an attractive façade, but because their appointment was fitting. It reflected divine order. During one early interlude of non-noble bishops, in France under Robert II, a bishop of the conservative school grumbled at just this: such promotions insulted the divine order.[24] The most voluble exponent of the theme in the twelfth century was the famous Hildegard of Bingen—whose office as head of a Benedictine nunnery gave her some of the sensitivity to social propriety we might associate with the headmistress of a young ladies' academy. Hildegard did not admit non-noble girls to her convent. For

who, unless he courts ruin, puts all his farm-stock into one shed: oxen, asses, sheep, and kids all together? Discretion should similarly be applied in our case. Different classes of people should not be mixed, or they will fall out through conceit and arrogance, and the shame occasioned by their differences. The greatest danger of all is a breakdown in peaceful manners, through mutual back-biting and hatred, when the upper class pounce on the lower, or when the lower is promoted above the higher. God distinguishes people on earth as in heaven, i.e. into angels, archangels, thrones, and so on.[25]

Why should abbesses, alone of God's creatures, make an exception to His Great Chain of Being?

There were in fact a number of reasons why. Hildegard's letter would not have been written if another abbess, in a brand-new Augustinian foundation, had not written earlier, to challenge the aristocratic rules of Bingen. Like most documents on this question Hildegard's letter was a reply. That serves as a reminder that the issue had another side. From the time of the earliest polemic in favour of noble privilege there was an equal and opposite polemical feeling against it. The arguments this polemic employed were esssentially the conservatives' arguments, turned on their heads.

### 3. THE ARGUMENTS: AGAINST NOBLE PRIVILEGE

The first argument that could be turned on its head was the church's misgiving about robbing lay lords of their serfs. There was frequently no cause for anxiety: some lords were positively glad to see their servants take orders—so long as they stayed servants. Setting aside what happened at lower levels of the lay hierarchy, the gladdest secular lords of all to see low-born men promoted to high church office were often centralizing monarchs. If a monarch could not pack the episcopate with men from his own family, he might do better to do away with restrictions on birth altogether, and push for the promotion of his inferior dependants. Henry IV of Germany raised *infimi homines* to bishoprics on this principle.[26] The church's diplomacy towards lay society, in other words, did not necessarily work in favour of reproducing that society's class distinctions. In the right political context it could work the other way.

The same inversion could be made of the second contention: that a nobleman's relations and experience were useful to a church or abbey. They could equally well be a nuisance. The reformed monasteries of the twelfth century tacitly criticized the system of lay 'advocacy', designed to embody these advantages, by siting themselves far from lordly habitations, and discouraging where possible visits from noble well-wishers. Despite his ambivalent reputation in some reforming monastic circles, it is Peter Abelard who has left us the most explicit statement of such reformers' position. In a letter to Éloise at the convent of the Paraclete he advised her to avoid if possible choosing a prioress for her nuns from a noble family:

for this sort easily trust in their birth, and become vainglorious or presumptuous or arrogant. And their appointment is most pernicious of all when they are from the same region. It is to be feared . . . that their crowd of relations will weigh on and unsettle the monastery, so that the prioress, because of her relations, ends up by doing the monastery harm.[27]

When he wrote this the knightly Abelard had himself just narrowly escaped murder, as abbot, by monks of his native Brittany. The claim that high birth buttressed effective monastic rule did not apparently impress him.

The practical argument, then, whether in respect of secular claims, or of the church's own interests, was a two-edged sword. It might militate for noble birth; or equally well against. On the more abstract questions of what was honourable and appropriate, opinions could also be divided. After the millennium all that the church had embraced to capture dark-age minds—power, wealth, military victory: all the desired accoutrements, that is to say, of earthly nobility—came under attack as unchristian. Apostolic reformers, replacing the Old Testament by the New as dominant source of inspiration, expressed the reaction in their lives and preaching. Polemicists meanwhile attacked the claims of nobility at base. Ancient and medieval authorities were heard in chapter 11, exalting the concept of a nobility of virtue as against one of birth. That concept had many functions, of which the boosting of graduates' claims to church office, under the specific form of 'mental nobility', was only one. The concept could also serve reformist Christian ideals. The depreciation of 'carnal' nobility made its assault, in fact, not in a university milieu, but in that of the strictest ascetic monasticism: at Gorze in the late tenth century,[28] and then at the Chartreuse.[29] Against born nobility, the ascetics envisaged a rival notion of nobility of manners, spirit, or soul (even mind: the term comes in here, but only in company). The tradition would culminate in the early fourteenth century, in a full-blown doctrine of 'nobility of soul', elaborated by Eckhart and his school of German mystics.[30] Here as elsewhere they reacted to the dominant traits of the aristocratic church of their native land. But in lesser measure the whole tradition was a reaction. Born nobility, it said, was *not* an appropriate adornment in candidates for church office. It was irrelevant. No Christian should even consider it.

On the place of born nobility in the church there were thus two perennial currents of thought. Some practical factors urged concessions to secular hierarchical views; and loftier reflections, too, suggested that to pick Christ's servants from any other than the highest social class was to treat him unworthily, and to be seen to do so. But both practice and theory could point the other way. Christianity called for a clean break from the world and its distractions and pomps: the church must be—and be seen to be—egalitarian, and free from any criteria so base as a carnal distinction of persons.

It has been normal in Christian history to try to settle debates of this kind by one simple and trustworthy device: appeal to scripture. The medieval debaters of course did so. The baffling character of this particular debate, with its arguments arranged on either side, is revealed nowhere so clearly as in the results of their appeal. It will be fitting to close this summary of medieval polemic on the subject by looking at the lessons it drew from scripture.

The scourges of nobility, naturally, had little difficulty in finding their principal text. 'Brethren,' Saint Paul had written to the first-century Corinthians, 'think what sort of people you are whom God has called . . . few are powerful or highly born. Yet to shame what is strong, God has chosen what the world counts weakness.' [1 Cor. 1 : 26]. A list of medieval divines, from Augustine to Bernard, and on to the Reformation, who appealed to this text in the context of contemporary debate would be a long one.[31] When the church was up against the world's might, in theory or practice, 1 Cor. 1 : 26 was its standard New Testament armour. The text played its part in the ideal of apostolic poverty, and in creating a climate of opinion, orthodox and unorthodox, hostile to noble claims in church. Even a nobleman of exemplary conduct stood to lose by Saint Paul's utterance. For a nobleman, however virtuous, was not what the world counted as weakness. His prerogative stood directly against the tenor of the Gospel; or so it was argued. At the end of the fifteenth century a young cathedral canon would encapsulate this view in a sarcastic *mot*. 'If our Lord and Redeemer were today on earth,' wrote the canon, 'he would himself be turned away from the community of Saint Alban [the main canonical foundation in Mainz], because he was not of knightly origin on both sides, and would therefore endanger the foundation's honour and reputation.'[32] The jest took up a medieval tradition, and in turn fed the Reformation. Erasmus would repeat it.[33]

But *auctoritas habet cereum nasum*: authority has a waxen nose. Zeal for Gospel authority could lead the zealots into inaccuracy. The truth is that Christ would *not* have been turned away from the chapter in Mainz; not, that is, unless the Gospel itself were left unopened. The first chapter of the first Gospel is devoted, not to an account of Christ's nativity or virtues, nor to a statement of general theological principles. It is a list of Christ's earthly ancestors. Christ, it says, was of King David's stock. That was the first thing to be established about him. Medieval minds were on the whole closer than modern ones to this strain in ancient Hebrew thought, with its attention to genealogies. This text was not overlooked in the middle ages. Christianity would indeed have been a difficult religion for the Germanic peoples to assimilate if it had not been agreed, as it was, that Christ and his mother were of the highest birth: 'of royal and free descent' as the great synod of Frankfurt had put it in 794 (freedom in those days being inherited through the mother).[34] It was in the eleventh century, the time of the Hildebrandine reform, that we find that conclusion taken up by commentators on Matthew; not without occasional perplexity, it is true, in view of Saint Paul's own aspersions on genealogies (Tit. 3:9, etc.); but unequivocally.[35] The royal descent of Christ and his mother remained common knowledge. A thirteenth-century preacher could refer to it without risk of being misapprehended.[36] Long after advocates of 'nobility of mind' had started their campaign against all thought of noble birth, the pro-aristocratic school went on drawing attention to Christ's pedigree; royal as it was 'from his grandfathers and great-great-great-grandfathers'.[37] Matthew's genealogy, for all that it included some dubious names, nicely suited the heraldic temperaments of the late middle ages.

Christ's ancestry was complicated by the fact that half his descent was divine, and so not comparable with that of earthly princes. This put all the more weight on the status of the apostles. The Apostolic Poverty movement of the twelfth century saw the apostles as simple fishermen. So some were. But here too scripture allowed other interpretations. Israel, which provided all the main figures in Christ's entourage, was in the first place a race distinguished by birth. Christ more than once stressed that his mission was in the first instance to a race. Within the race—leaving aside the question of such wealthy disciples as Joseph of Arimathaea, Zacchaeus, or the tax-farmer Matthew (whose names came up during medieval disputes on poverty)—the apostle finally chosen to convert outsiders, and to the middle ages the Apostle with a capital 'A', was Paul. Paul said a lot about his weaknesses. But when occasion demanded he did not scruple to stand on his born rank, as free man, as Israelite and Pharisee, and as Roman citizen. Feeble as Saint Paul might subjectively feel himself to be, the social historian is bound to judge that in choosing him God had done the very reverse of picking what was low and despised. He had picked an heir to the highest social distinctions the Jews and Romans admitted. Nor was this fact, any more than the others, lost on scholastics. Paul was a 'noble', no doubt about it.[38]

And that was the state of the question. Should high birth be included among recommendations for church office? Some said yes, some no. In the context of a society where birth counted, medieval churchmen found no avenue of approach to the problem, practical or theoretical, which allowed them to opt definitively for one side; and not even scripture helped them decide. In surviving medieval dispute on the subject, the prize for eloquence should probably be awarded to the anti-noble party. But that was because the more substantial prize, effectiveness in practice, usually went to the conservatives.

Because the debate was equivocal, the hardiness of the noble principle calls for more explanation. Some of the explantion certainly lies in power politics: nobles were masters, by definition; so it was their interpretation of scripture and tradition that counted. But was this the whole answer? It is fair to explore inwards, into souls, as well as outwards into politics. This introduces quite a new series of questions, exploring the problem whether patterns of religious behaviour attached to noblemen as such. The first of these questions is broached in the next chapter.

# CHAPTER 14

# Were Nobles Better Christians?

> The queen filled the convent with girls of the highest
> nobility, not of low birth: for her experience had
> been that a well-born girl rarely or never fell away
> from the virtuous life.
>
> *Annals of Quedlinburg*, 927.
> (*MGH SS* 3, 54.)

LITERATURE in the central middle ages gave patient attention to the problem where 'true nobility' lay. It came down regularly for the answer that nobility lay in virtue, not birth. But that question did not exhaust interest in the subject of nobility and virtue. That one answered, another question called for solution. Less theoretical, and so less ceremoniously treated, it still called up plenty of comment. It was: whether the real, flesh-and-blood nobility, granted it was not *per se* virtuous, was so in fact. As a matter of experience, were nobles inclined to be better or worse Christians?

It will be objected that this is an unchristian question. To make a man's moral state hang from the actions of his ancestors is a primitive doctrine, expressly made out-of-date in the sixth century B.C. by Ezekiel (18:20: the son shall not suffer for the iniquity of the father). To fasten a man's spiritual to his social standing, similarly, is to respect persons. Quite apart from any matter of the church's choice of bishops, Christianity as such (according to Jerome, echoing the epistle of James) 'knows nothing of persons or conditions of men, but considers only souls'.[1] These demurs hold good at one level. But it is not the level at which the following debate will be conducted. The freedom the individual hangs on to regardless of his ancestors or social condition is one of choice. The subject now is not choice, but dispositions. And as matter for theological debate dispositions are respectable. Moral tendencies caused by social status enter the theological arena, in fact, at the same point as those caused by stars: they incline a man to a course of action, but do not compel him to take it. The two sets of dispositions—from nobility and from stars—can actually be found handled side by side, as theologically equivalent, in astrological apologetic.[2] So long as a man's ultimate free choice was safeguarded (the choice of the man inclined to be a drunkard *not* to be, of the naturally mean man to be generous, and so on) the idea was orthodox. Christ himself, after all, had touched on the special difficulties rich men had in getting into heaven. And the peculiar moral problems of the rich, the poor, and dozens of other statuses and situations were familiar territory to medieval moralists.

But there is a stronger objection. It is that our question is repugnant, not now to theology, but to experience. To borrow an unexceptionable generalization from a twelfth-century observer:

it is common knowledge that while good sons are every day born to good parents and bad sons to bad parents, bad sons are equally often born to good parents and good sons to bad parents.[3]

No empirical laws of ethical behaviour, in other words, can be based on birth. 'Thorns and roses grow from the same stem, grain and chaff from the same shoot of corn.'[4] What went for birth went also for social status. 'Some knights are bad, others good' was as far as one thirteenth-century preacher would go towards framing a general law.[5] There were robber-barons and Bluebeards; but also equestrian saints, from Saint George onwards. Dante's *Inferno* was full of the noble and great. But so was his *Paradiso*. From an empirical angle, as well as a theological, there is all this and more to discourage moral generalizing about people born great.

Why none of this constitutes any real objection, however, is that plenty of respectable medieval writers did just this: they generalized about people born great. If satirists took the lead in aspersions on noblemen as a class, theologians were the more ready to explore the moral effects of the noble condition, frequently to its detriment. Generalizations were made, and believed. So the historian is at liberty to make his own—if only by way of reflecting on medieval ones.

And this is just how the present debate must start: by

reflecting on a medieval generalization. In genres of literature most given to the art—broadly, didactic genres—the main drift of generalization is, on the topic of noblemen, in one direction. It is against the noblemen. This drift needs scrutinizing as a preliminary. Otherwise it might be taken at face-value. Then the debate would be closed as soon as opened, and perhaps closed wrongly.

## I. LITERARY ATTACKS ON THE NOBILITY

Fierce criticism of the conduct of nobles, *en bloc*, turns up from authoritative sources throughout the central middle ages. The invective is typified by the following phrases from one of its most voluble exponents, Odo of Cluny, writing *c.* 930:

Nobles applaud themselves for excelling . . . in precisely those particulars which make them worse. The more they excel in them, the warmer is their self-applause . . . Slaves in their own persons to numerous vices, they find pleasure in dominating whichever of their human brethren they can subject. . . . It is the sweat of the poor, anyway, that furnishes those luxuries with which the mighty sate themselves.[6]

The same conclusion is heard century after century. In the early eleventh, Radulf Glaber, the Cluniac historian of Dijon, characterized the nobility of his own day, as a whole, as arrogant and grasping.[7] In the early twelfth, Bernard of Clairvaux wrote to exhort a noblewoman to virtue with the remark that virtue, rare enough anyway, was *especially* rare in the nobility.[8] This was one point in which Peter Abelard apparently agreed with his Cistercian opponent.[9] In the thirteenth century, when records of popular sermons multiply, this view became a commonplace. 'The king of Babylon slew all the nobles of Judah'; yes, says a preacher, that is fulfilled today; the king of Babylon means the devil, who has spiritually killed the nobles of the world.[10] 'They sent me to preach to the poor'; yes, comments another preacher, the poor are mentioned rather than the rich because the poor are more easily converted.[11] A third says nobles should excel in gratitude: 'but they excel in *in*gratitude, both to God and to the subordinates by whose labour they live.'[12] Nor was the theme a prerogative of preachers. In the early fourteenth century John of Jandun the

Paris philosopher adjudged the combination of virtue and
nobility very rare: scarcely a hundred cases altogether could be
found.[13] The literature reviewed in chapter 10 contains more
remarks of this kind.

If so many people in so many centuries arraigned the nobles
of their own day for misconduct, the idea must have struck some
of them that the misconduct was a norm of nature. It did. 'It is
normal, in some people, for nobility of descent to produce
ignobility of mind,' Gregory the Great had written, as only one
of a series of church fathers—including Origen and John
Chrysostom—to coin such general verdicts.[14] These verdicts
found their medieval sympathizers. Odo of Cluny's empirical
criticism of nobles had this dimension: 'Look in all the books of
the ancients,' he urged, 'you will find the more powerful *always*
the more wicked.'[15] 'The wealth a rich man carries on him',
Saint John Gualbert used often to say, in the eleventh century,
'is a great obstacle to his acquiring a humble heart,'[16] 'An
abundance of means to carnal pleasure easily ensnares the rich
and refined man,' wrote a Cistercian in the twelfth.[17] That
thirteenth-century preacher who said the poor were easier to
convert than the rich saw the difference as one in the essence of
things: pride, worldly concerns, and temporal consolations
*normally*, he thought, combined to hamper the rich man's
receptiveness to God's word.[18]

It is true that the literary current these comments represent
was only one of a number of currents. There is a small medieval
literature of flattery—found commonly in dedications and
prefaces. Another school was ready to testify that knights as a
class were brave and chivalrous—or at least had been once. In
the self-conscious and factual moral comment that was written
away from the direct influence of courts, however, the critical
stream was the strong one. Read at its own valuation, and
reinforced by the literature on the nobility of virtue, with which
it merged, it is likely to bias the historian's impression. In league
with other influences, it has in fact probably contributed to
certain sweeping modern judgements of the nobility of this or
that medieval century: 'a brutal military aristocracy', etc.[19]

But under close scrutiny much of this general criticism falls to
pieces. The critics can be shown not fully to have believed what
they said. There is food for reflection already in the fact that,

with three exceptions all the identifiable authors quoted here to illustrate the criticism were themselves of noble, knightly, or patrician birth.[20] (The exceptions are Origen, Peyraut, and John of Jandun; and Origen was *reared* as a patrician.)[21] How such people came to divorce themselves so drastically from their peers will be discussed in the next chapter. Now, it is not the critics' origins that call for examination, but their arguments. They hold revealing contradictions.

Not all the critics are guilty of all the contradictions. Some of the critics just quoted forestall logical objection by contradicting themselves explicitly in other parts of their work.[22] But if the whole tradition of criticism is taken together, including the authors discussed in chapter 10, the same logical flaws occur often enough to be labelled as characteristic hazards—'dispositions' indeed—of the critic of the noble status. The traps into which the guilty critics fell were principally two. The less persistent of the two came about through sheer careless enthusiasm. The nobles are a bad lot, some critics say: and anyway, they add, *they are not really noble*. Half-way through a diatribe on nobility Alexander Neckham explodes: 'but what do these heirs of upstarts think they are doing, claiming to be of noble birth when in fact they are descended from peasants?' And he goes on to tell a tale of the type of *The Princess and the Pea*; acknowledging, that is, that true inborn nobility has some quality about it.[23] The same sort of flaw intrudes into the invective of Jean de Meung. Having insisted on the equality in dignity between a labouring peasant and his noble master, Jean de Meung sneers at some contemporary nobles for staying in the country 'tending ancestral dunghills': as if farmwork were after all *dis*honourable for them.[24] John of Jandun, again, exalted 'nobility of virtue' at the expense of that of birth. Yet in depreciating the latter he exposed his underlying regard for it by grumbling that 'nowadays mere rustics are ennobled'.[25] The idiosyncrasy of each critic's blunder shows that this trait is not among the topoi of the nobility theme. It betrays a state of mind.

The second and more radical internal contradiction in the criticism lies at the latter's logical centre. Anti-noble polemic sometimes said a bad noble was *more* reprehensible than a bad commoner. The reason, when given, was the nobleman had a moral advantage over the commoner: namely the example of

virtuous ancestors. This example should serve at the very least
as a 'bit' (*frenum*) on wrongdoing, and at best as an
inspiration.[26] The nobleman's lapses are therefore less excus-
able. Both elements in the charge are common, the first—the
value of ancestral example—having been admitted by Cicero,
then by Jerome and Boethius, whence it passed into medieval
stock-in-trade.[27] The corollary, that bad nobles are more
reprehensible than ordinary bad people, was put by several of
the more boisterous of the critics already introduced; by none
more boldly, for instance, than Jean de Meung.[28]

To say that bad nobles were worse than other bad people was
rousing invective. In its context however this particular
approach was faulty logic. It made havoc of the notion to which
it was attached, that nobles were usually bad. The least of its
three flaws was that nobles were now allowed an inherited
advantage: example. This undermined the concept of born
nobility as purely carnal. For now a born nobleman had some
*moral* perquisite from his forebears; his abuse of which made him
lower than the low. Secondly, the charge that a bad nobleman
flouted the example of his forebears allowed at least some merit
to the forebears—themselves surely noble. Thirdly (and most
fundamentally): the charge entailed that a nobleman, *if* his will
was not perverse, was better placed than anyone else to achieve
moral excellence.

Far from condemning the nobility as such, then, some of the
fiercest generic criticism of the status was a back-handed
compliment. Bad nobles might be exceptionally reprehensible.
But that was because a well-inclined noble was exceptionally
well placed to be good. It followed that if he *was* well-inclined
a nobleman could reach a pinnacle of excellence. Some
critics betrayed their cause so far as to state that conclusion.
Having patiently explained that nobility of birth is valueless,
and it is only nobility of virtue that counts, they will add
the final *non sequitur* that a man is best of all when he has
both.[29]

The historian who presumes to ask if medieval noblemen
had, as a matter of fact, any generic moral dispositions, comes
up against a strong critical current, then, in a vociferous sector
of his sources. But if he faces the criticism squarely it changes its
character. It reveals a supposition contrary to its overt message.

Wicked noblemen had to be whacked especially hard. But that was partly because more was expected of them.

Better was expected of noblemen. Now that one obstacle has been flattened, an empirical question poses itself. Other than hopeful prejudice, were there the very slightest grounds for this expectation? The question is daunting. Why it is, is that it is about people's souls. Literary sources, we have learned, are not easy to use on a broad question in this field. If souls were institutional history, help might be found from a more objective type of document. But are souls institutional history? Not normally. But there is an exception. One category of soul, for much of the central and late middle ages, came in for the closest human scrutiny souls ever got; and by an institution. The category was not that of noblemen's souls. But if it is agreed for the moment to approach the topic from a new angle, noblemen will soon be found making their way back into view.

## 2. NOBLY-BORN SAINTS

The category was that of saints. The process of testing candidates for inclusion in the liturgy as saints only slowly became formal. The twelfth century in particular saw a standardization in church legal procedure of which this was one aspect. But the elements of the test were there before. Where the task had been ill done, and unqualified saints let through, it was sometimes done again retrospectively. The presence and persistence of a saint's name in the liturgy was meant to be as firm an indication as is likely to be available of distinctive Christian merit on the saint's part, even where little else is known about him.[30]

To effect any major sociological operation on saints would be a task as near impossible as any in historiography. Over 28,000 *Lives* of saints exist in print; while in all the mass of unreliable information they present there is often either next to nothing, or absolutely nothing, reliably told of a saint except his name and sainthood. Slight changes from age to age in the concept of what makes a 'saint' would also imperil such an operation. Fortunately, minor operations on various scales are possible. With appropriate limitations, such a minor one can serve the present purpose. It involves taking a small sample of these

28,000, on as impartial a basis as is consistent with the demand for clear information; and subjecting the sample to a test.[31]

*The Oxford Dictionary of the Christian Church* contains seventy-eight entries under personal names with the prefix 'saint', where the 'saint' in question died between 900 and 1500. With the help of every resource of scholarship—that is, not only the dictionary which establishes the sample—the family backgrounds of some seventy-one of these can be approximately determined—the others being hidden either by the hazy light of legend, or by sheer darkness. These seventy-one backgrounds cannot be categorized precisely. Even in one generation several ways obtained for determining social class, and a writer's choice between them may be partly subjective. The whole six hundred years, on top of that, saw changes in criteria of social distinction, degrees in legal definition of 'nobility', 'freedom', and so on. So it would be dangerous to base an analysis on narrow legal and economic distinctions. But that does not mean there can be *no* distinctions. When Saint Hugh of Cluny's biographer was boasting, *c.* 1120, about the quality of his hero's converts to monasticism, he spoke of 'magnates of divers profession and power'.[32] Such a flexible classification may be stigmatized as too broad to be useful. But the writer thought he meant something when he said it. And it has the merit of straddling all the societies and periods under discussion. His phrase roughly serves as basis for my notion of 'upper-class' in the context of the sample.

A systematic application of this notion of 'upper-class' to the sample shows that of the seventy-one, giving and taking doubtful cases about equally, sixty-two, that is some 87 per cent, were of upper-class birth. A narrowing of the classification to those technically of noble blood lowers the figure to 66 per cent. But that includes families poorer than some of the 21 per cent non-noble magnates. A few of the most celebrated names in the sample—Peter of Tarentaise, Catherine of Siena, and Joan of Arc—lodge confidently among the backgrounds (in all about 12 per cent) undistinguished by exceptional wealth or position. But that category includes some distinctly middle-class families. While at the other end of the scale must be set those saints who, without wearing crowns themselves, belonged to the super-nobility of royal and princely families (at least 11 per cent of the nobles). The sources for these conclusions and the methods by which they are reached can be inspected in Appendix I on pages 405–12

Figures can be liars, in history as outside it. These figures would be no exception if left without comment: without, in particular, three comments. First, as to the exclusions: it could plausibly be contested that the seven names left off the list for lack of evidence are more likely—because notoriety and nobility go together—to have been of low-class than of high-class origin. If that were true, and they were included, the high-class majority might be brought down to under 78 per cent. But an examination of the exclusions will reveal that even that adjustment would be excessive: since the demur is far from applying to all the exclusions.

The second objection applies to kings and queens, who constitute nine of the seventy-one names, or $12\frac{1}{2}$ per cent. Not only do saints of royal rank stand a better chance than others of being put in dictionaries. Before they ever become saints, they enjoy the advantage that their promotion is a political objective for their descendants. Especially from *c.* 1300 canonization became an extremely expensive process. With a national budget behind it the cause of a pious monarch came to the papal Curia uniquely well equipped for a wrangle. For sampling purposes, therefore, the fourteen kings and queens can be banished; which reduces the original upper-class majority from 87 per cent to $85\frac{1}{2}$ per cent.

The same objection does not apply to mere nobles. Neither their canonization nor their inclusion in dictionaries can be directly attributed in a significant degree to dynastic power. (The mere timing of the canonization—too soon or too late—is usually enough to acquit the saint's family of influence in it.) However, a similar objection—our third—does apply to nobles. The preference for nobles as bishops and monks, whatever its motives, eased the path of well-born clerics to positions where party interests could form for their being made 'saints'. The loyalties and revenues of a diocese or religious order were not to be despised—indeed in the late middle ages they came near to being necessary—as accessories in a canonization-process at the Curia.

To translate this consideration into a numerical adjustment

to the 85 per cent (or 78 per cent) would be inappropriate. Whichever way it was done, a big bracket of uncertainty would remain. But the same objection can be tackled another way. A new, smaller sample of saints can be made up on a different basis, in such a way that the objection does not apply. Noble birth, it is agreed, offered a privileged entry to those ecclesiastical positions from which a big proportion of saints was likely to come. But that does not apply to all saints. The sanctity of some rested on work they did after a deliberate rejection of this privilege. One of the dozens of possible examples will illustrate what is meant: that of Aquinas. His high noble birth seemed to mark him as a future abbot of the rich Benedictine monastery of Monte Cassino. He refused this option, and was thrown into the family dungeon for doing so. He managed to escape, and joined the new and still eccentric order of poor preachers. The elements of this story—refusal of privilege, strong family opposition, joining of a strict order—are a commonplace in the literature of reforming orders.[33] The element in question now is the rejection of privileged entry to church office. The group who share this element mostly belong to the definable class of instigators and reformers of monastic and other regular religious movements. No dictionary of this group as such exists. But a historian asked to list, say, twenty of its members, spread over the centuries from the tenth to the fifteenth, and all full 'saints', might produce the following:

> Odo of Cluny
> Gerard of Brogne
> John of Gorze
> Dunstan of Glastonbury
> William of Volpiano
> Romuald of Camaldoli
> Bruno of the Chartreuse
> Robert of Molesme
> Bernard of Clairvaux
> Norbert of Prémontré
> Dominic
> Francis of Assisi
> Clare of Assisi
> Philip Benzi (Servites)

Juliana Falconieri (Mantellites)
Catherine of Siena
Frances of Rome (Oblates of St. Benedict)
Bernardino of Siena (Franciscan Observants)
John Capistrano (Franciscan Observants)
James of the March (Franciscan Observants)

An analysis of the social origins of the saints on this list yields the same result as before. The fathers of thirteen saints on the list were noble, and of four more distinctly upper class by the standards of the societies they lived in. The saints with middling or poor backgrounds were John of Gorze, Catherine of Siena, and James of the March. The upper-class majority is still therefore 85 per cent. References to biographical sources for these saints are in Appendix II on pages 413–15. The list was composed more or less at random, to cover those centuries. Lest bias is thought to have entered, the same Appendix adds some possible replacements. Their class-distribution is much the same.

By themselves, these findings must still be viewed with caution. The study of 'saints' over six centuries embraces too many elastic components to give grounds for the formulation of laws. Among such components would be differing nuances in concepts of sainthood not only from age to age, but from group to group: and even those last twenty saints, though they rejected the privileges offered by their birth, were still canonized by a largely nobly-born hierarchy. The next chapter will return to some of the issues raised by that demur, in discussing spiritual factors which may have contributed to the result just set out. Meanwhile, it is enough just to register that result. In the only gallery of proven Catholic Christian excellence the middle ages furnished, the predominance of upper-class progeny is conspicuous; the more so when it is remembered how small a proportion this class made in the general population.

### 3. THE NOBILITY AND CELIBACY

King David was punished for counting Israel. A historian courts a similar risk, and may perish in the wastes of speculation, in subjecting the Lord's Elect to arithmetic. But there are theologically safer fields for that art. Our investigation now descends into one of them: the nobility as such. This field pays for its safety by being less to the purpose: there can be no guarantees of sanctity here, so no counting of model Christian souls. But counting can, on the other hand, help establish a pattern of noble behaviour, to a degree that requires explaining in religious terms. What remains of this chapter will seek first to establish the pattern; and second, to suggest why non-religious explanations will not suffice for it.

It was shown that a large portion of important church offices were usually reserved for incumbents of noble birth. This had a converse side. A large portion of the nobly-born went into the church. How large was this portion? An attempt to estimate it can begin with that nobility whose church was most markedly aristocratic: the German. Aloys Schulte included this subject in his study of nobility and the German church, mentioned in Chapter 13.[34] From the German free nobility, Schulte picked out twenty-seven dynasties, the size and destinies of whose successive generations could be worked out with a tolerable degree of completeness. His reconstructed genealogies covered just over 2,000 persons, male and female. Schulte asked of his genealogies: how many chose celibate careers? He stressed the elements of uncertainty, even in his limited sample; but also defended the main bias of the result—in that the missing family members (whom he had to be content with inferring, especially on the female side) probably distributed themselves similarly to those in the records. Schulte's result, at all events, was that of the 2,003 noble persons, nearly 557 (28 per cent) are known to have become ecclesiastical celibates, while another 426 (21 per cent) *may* have done so, or lived celibate outside any formal religious status; since only 1,020 (51 per cent) are known to have married.

Schulte's twenty-seven dynasties did not leave him just with those bare proportions. For instance, if the coverage of documents can be trusted, the leaning towards celibacy was stronger among the smaller free nobility, the *Freiherren*, than among princes (the former showing 37 per cent of celibates against 46 per cent definitely married; the latter 21 per cent against 55 per cent). More striking still is the breakaway from celibacy in some idiosyncratic families, especially the four great eastern colonial princely families of the late middle ages: Habsburg, Luxemburg, Bavarian Wittelsbach, and (in less radical degree) Hohenzollern. These appear to have rejected deliberately, here as elsewhere, a medieval and church-oriented tradition. These variations will deserve remembering later, when the psychology behind these figures comes up for attention. All that needs digesting now is the main lesson of Schulte's survey. In so far as his sample is representative, it suggests that at least one child in four, of the German free nobility in the central and late middle ages, entered ecclesiastical service as a celibate.

As a point of reference the minimum estimate—let it be rounded down to 25 per cent—can be held in mind. That, it seems, was roughly the level of the 'human tithe' in Germany. The next question is: how typical was that of the European upper class as a whole? The link between church and aristocracy was even tighter in Germany than elsewhere. That 25 per cent might have been a freak. A similar survey has not been completed for other nobilities. Until it is, the scope for guesswork is too big to permit wide categorical assertions. But a narrow assertion *can* be made: that tentative German estimate of *c.* 25 per cent is far from unparalleled elsewhere.

This can be corroborated by a look at some genealogies from other parts of Europe. It will be recalled from chapter 4 that some noble families remembered whole lists of their relations; and where one of the relations became a clerk and historian, the list might find its way into a chronicle. A genealogy can be analysed, to yield the level of 'human tithe' paid by that family to celibate religion. A genealogy remembered by a cleric might, it is true, be thought biased to include other clerics at the expense of lay kinsmen. But a study of individual genealogies suggests this bias was slight. Where a selective principle can be seen at work, it was a different and stronger one: mere snobbery. A man remembered his important relations, whether in church or laity. The effect of even this bias can be minimized by limiting the analysis to close relations. So long as the genealogist offers some credentials for completeness within the given circle of kinship, and so long as he simultaneously indicates where members of the family were celibate, his record gives us a fair basis for a sample.

I have found three genealogies which fully meet these conditions. The first two have been studied closely from various points of view, though not this, by Professor Georges Duby.[35] They are those of the twelfth-century lords of Bourbourg and of Watterlos in Flanders. The genealogy of the lords of Bourbourg comes in *The History of the Counts of Guines* by Lambert of Ardres.[36] Lambert's heroine in the family appears to have been his contemporary and friend Beatrice; so she can form the datum-point for analysis. Lambert's text permits the identification of nineteen of Beatrice's blood-relations within the second degree (i.e. her grandparents and their descendants, including Beatrice herself). Within this group, three apparently died too soon to pick a career (including doubtful cases as 'half'). Of the sixteen thus remaining, three (19 per cent) were certainly clergy or religious. That excludes Beatrice herself, who was reared in a convent but married when she became an heiress. One maternal aunt (also called Beatrice) deliberately chose to live celibate, as a quasi-religious at home; and ended as effective abbess of the family convent. Inclusion of this aunt (but not of the heroine Beatrice) brings the total of certain professional celibates to 25 per cent. Only ten (63 per cent) of the list certainly married.

The second genealogy I have taken from those studied by Professor Duby is that of the lords of Watterlos, composed by the annalist Lambert of Cambrai as a parade of his distinguished relations.[37] Lambert's text allows us to identify thirty of his relations within the second degree. One died very young. Of the remaining twenty-nine, five (17 per cent) were certainly in religious orders. No woman is mentioned among these religious, although one unnamed paternal aunt is stated to have died unmarried. If she were allowed in as a quasi-religious the total of celibates would rise to over 20 per cent. Only thirteen (40 per cent) are known to have married.

A third genealogy is that inserted by Fra Salimbene of Parma in his chronicle (*c.* 1284).[38] We move from a country nobility to a city patriciate. Its apparent completeness happens to have found some endorsement from a study of Parma archives. Salimbene allows us to identify twenty-one (and a 'half') of his legitimate adult relations within the second degree. Among these are three certain full-time religious (14 per cent).

Beyond these, three more are said to have died as religious, although two of them are known to have married once. Counted as 'halves', these would raise the total religious to 21 per cent. Only 50 per cent of the list are known to have married.

Quite apart from the question of selective memory, genealogies written by medieval clerks about their own families must concern families who gave at least a fraction of their membership to the clergy. As a corrective to this flaw I add a fourth genealogy from non-clerical sources, but otherwise with the same qualifications. It has been reconstructed (by Mlle Higounet-Nadal) from wills and other legal documents relating to the wealthy Giraudoux family of Périgueux (*c.* 1250– *c.* 1350).[39] Excluding shadowy ancestors whose siblings were not recorded (and who would therefore give the analysis a bias *against* celibacy), Mlle Higounet-Nadal's researches identify thirty adult individuals with Giraudox blood. Of these, seven were certainly in religious orders, and one more *possibly* was. If this last lady is counted as 'half', the total of religious celibates once more reaches 25 per cent. Only twelve or thirteen of the list are known to have married.

The four families represented by these genealogies appear to have been in other respects typical upper-class families of their time and place. The two Flemish dynasties provided castellans and *milites*. Each of the two urban families gave their cities holders of high office, as well as rich lawyers or merchants. Where only a sample (second-degree relations) has been taken, again, it does not appear to be markedly exceptional in its own genealogy. Even in the genealogy's less precise regions a scattering of clerks and religious stretches away as far as the eye can see. It is clear there were variations. Even in these small samples one branch of a family can give more than its share of celibates, another less. Other medieval genealogies survive, if with much less compelling degrees of completeness in information, which suggest a lower figure than our 20–25 per cent.[40] Between 900 and 1500, all over Europe, it is inconceivable that the rule should have applied evenly, and places with strong ecclesiastical traditions (like Flanders, Parma, and Périgueux) may have bled their nobility more heavily than colonial areas. When all allowances have been made, however, that estimate of the drainage of upper-class manpower to religious celibacy is arresting. It calls for an explanation.

There is an easy one. An upper-class family would not have been upper-class if it had not had a shrewd appreciation of the accessories to political power. The church was such an accessory, at least where it was well established. The occupation of the local bishopric by a younger brother made at least for a smooth partnership. At most it could serve a dynasty as a ladder. Notorious cases are known from throughout the middle ages of bishops who dismembered ecclesiastical jurisdictions to make independent lordships for their relations. On a more humdrum level, too, canonical and monastic livings served a function essential to a long dynastic ascendancy. They regulated the effective size of each generation by absorbing the surplus: boys for whom no inheritance could be found and who would otherwise quarrel; weaklings unequal to the awesome rigours of soldiering; or girls for whom a dowry could not safely be afforded. These considerations are familiar to all medievalists. They have been referred to so often as to have become axiomatic, abating the need, it would seem, for any further inquiry into the motives for noble interest in the church: it was a political affair.

There can be no question of dismissing these political considerations. Their presence at many times and places is manifest. The only question is, do they account for all of that 20–25 per cent? At the beginning of this chapter I threw doubt on a medieval literary current—the current uniformly critical of the nobility. Now it is a question of throwing doubt on a more recent literary current: one which is content to attribute upper-class interest in religious celibacy to prudential motives.[41] For this too can be shown to have shortcomings; and two in particular.

First, the flow of noblemen and noblewomen into religious celibacy sometimes, without any noticeable change in its character, reached a volume which absolutely precluded its serving a dynastic interest. A few extreme cases will illustrate this. The chronicler and bishop, Thietmar of Merseburg, was one of four brothers, of a count's family at the turn of the millennium, who all became clergy.[42] The Saxon royal dynasty itself—as James Westfall Thompson remarked in discussing this trend to self-extinction in the German nobility—committed dynastic suicide when Henry II's brother became bishop of Augsburg, since Henry died childless.[43] Of men and women related in the second degree to the Westphalian nobleman Hildebrand of Herdersen, in the last decade-and-a-half of the eleventh century, no fewer than sixteen took vows in the new monastic movement at Afflighem.[44] The story of Saint Bernard of Clairvaux—with his five brothers, sister, uncle, and sister-in-law all following him to the cloister—is well known; and was then, to apprehensive parents who did not think such a landslide so rare as to represent no dangerous infection for their own young.[45] The story was essentially repeated, too, in Cappenberg, near Münster, in 1121. Its count, Godfrey, swept his brother, two sisters, and childless wife with him, into monastic life, together with the whole vast family property.[46]

No one will contend that entry to the church on this scale was in the dynasty's interest. All the four non-noble dynasties mentioned became extinct as a result of the mass-entries into religion referred to. Their cases may have been extreme. Some caused astonishment at the time. But other equally extreme cases could be added.[47] Nor does any generic gulf divide such cases from migrations of, say, half the children of a couple into religion, which was positively common. All these migrations, even the partial ones, must furthermore be read in the light of noble demography. To make its survival likely three or four generations ahead a dynasty needed a certain optimum number of children, in the face of the war and disease which might cut off male descendants. Exact estimates of this optimum are impossible for most of the middle ages. So are exact estimates of the size of noble families. But rough estimates have been made, and the impression of the specialists who have made them has *not* been that the nobility consistently maintained the optimum. On the contrary, for quite long periods some nobilities are known to have under-reproduced themselves, and thus tended to extinction. The supposedly providential nobility was not so provident. It was sometimes giving the church children it could ill spare.[48]

The scale of noble entry to the church exceeds what could be accounted for in terms of sound dynastic policy. That is the first feature that eludes prudential explanation. There is a second. A younger son without lands could be placed in a good bishopric, or in a wealthy chapter or monastery, without his being deprived of the service and respect to which his noble birth had accustomed him. He exchanged one form of noble life for another, if usually a more sober and regular one. An un-marriageable daughter, similarly, might find congenial company and curriculum in a noble religious house. But not all well-born arrivals entered the church at this level. Some embraced a religious life whose security and dignity were *not* on a par with that which they left.

Illustration for this contention can be found variously in the literature about monastic and religious movements. Reference was made earlier to the saints who entered religious orders against family opposition: one motive in the opposition sometimes fairly clearly related to the drop in dignity involved.[49] Again, the *Lives* of such saints sometimes record that the noble postulant's entry to a strict order was prefaced by a warning from its abbot or a senior, of the unaccustomed austerities the youth would meet.[50] These cases of a few canonized saints cannot by themselves be held representative. But a wider distribution of the same phenomena will be suggested in chapter 16. And there is another corroborative circumstance, the most telling of all. Since there will not be occasion to speak of it again, a brief consideration of it will be appropriate now.

This circumstance concerns the widespread and often amorphous 'poverty movements' of the twelfth and thirteenth centuries. Their main manifestations, in and out of orthodoxy—the Humiliati, Waldensians, Beguines, and simi-lar women's communities—are agreed to have shared some distinguishing characteristics: simple food and housing; an acknowledgement of the propriety of manual work as a source of income; and sometimes actual financial hardship. But these movements shared one further characteristic: strong partici-pation by persons of upper-class birth. The late Herbert Grundmann dispelled some misunderstanding on this topic. He found, in the 'religious movements' of the twelfth and thirteenth centuries, that the strongest participation generally came from the rich bourgeoisie, nobility, and clergy.[51] That conclusion rested on dozens of immediately contemporary testimonies.

Adherents came 'de nobilioribus, ditioribus et prudentioribus';
they were 'divites et seculares'; 'nobiles et potentes cives'; or at
least 'a mundi negotionibus abstracti'; or (as a mixture)
'nobiles et ignobiles, clerici et laici'; and so on.[52] Inferences
from the movements' rules of life pointed the same way: for
example, the prohibition by the Humiliati (in 1179) of
luxurious clothing, and of the keeping of unnecessary funds
which might be given in alms.[53] Recent research, even where it
has sought to reverse Grundmann's findings, has in effect
usually only confirmed them. This is not to say artisans and
others took no part in religious movements, the 'poverty
movement' included. That is not the issue. The issue is whether
the nobility and upper bourgeoisie did. The evidence is
affirmative. In some groups they played the leading part. And
in most of the lasting religious movements of which we have
evidence they played *some* part; even in heresies, and sects
where other classes may have been preponderant
numerically.[54]

The 'poverty movement' arose partly as a protest against the
upper-class trappings of the existing church. Yet the leading
protesters themselves were more often than not of wealthy
origin. From this angle, then, thesis and antithesis represented
the same phenomenon: an upper-class drift into celibate
religion. The experience of one part of the drift may throw light
on the motives of the others. Worldly prudence, that is to say,
cannot explain *all* the drift. For some of its subjects, at least,
picked forms of religious life of distinctly less worldly appeal
than what lay in their path outside.

The adoption of an ascetic way of life by those who are not
obliged to it has rarely failed to excite a certain wonder among
those who see it. It excited such wonder in the central middle
ages.[55] An acknowledgement that some well-born young people
in the middle ages adopted such a way of life therefore brings
our investigation to the portals of its next question. That
question is: why?

# CHAPTER 15

# The Religious Effects of Noble Condition

The one condition in the whole world to which it
most properly pertains to keep a pure conscience is
the order of chivalry.

Geoffroi de Charny, *Le livre de chevalerie* (1350) (p.
1513.)

SOME nobles were bad, then, some of the time. But not all nobles
were bad all the time; and those who came nearest to saying
they were contradicted themselves. On two separate criteria,
objective figures point another way. They show the nobility
supplied more than its share to the adornments of the medieval
church, triumphant and militant. These figures are the closest
thing to an objective general fact that can be asserted on the
subject; nor are they wholly accounted for by a purely material
view of human motives. They ask for another explanation. Our
next task is to find one, in psychological terms. The result will
only be partial, and an outline. But an outline will suffice for the
purpose: which is to arrive, from the vantage-point of these
religious noblemen, at certain social conclusions about the two
cultures we are comparing.

The explanation unfolds as answer to a double question. Did
noble condition have any effects on a man's moral and religious
attitudes? And if so, what effects? In habitual scholastic fashion
the answering can begin with a statement of the negative view.
There were no effects, some said. Few rounder statements of that
denial were made than by that trumpet of Paris masters-of-arts
in the late thirteenth century, Jean de Meung. This widely-read
poet will serve as an admirable stimulus and butt for the coming
discussion. So I will quote him in full. In the *Romance of the Rose*
Jean de Meung's allegorical Reason insists

> That neither wealth nor reverence, no height
> Of honour, fame or military might
> Nor any other gift from Fortune's source
> (For I make no exceptions) has the force
> To make her favourite *good*, or guarantee
> That he *deserve* such wealth or high degree. (11.6223–8)

Fortune has only one effect on morals: to advertise them.

> But—if a man have in him cruelty,
> Or pride, or other such malignity,
> A great estate will put his faults on show
> Sooner than those of lesser men below. (ll.6231–3)

Even the wide circulation of Jean de Meung's poem, and the fact that it contains much more in this vein, might not entitle this passage to prolonged attention if it represented nothing but itself. But the eclectic poet here again only elaborated an old view, in sharper language than most. His inspiration remained Boethius (*De Consol. Phil.* III, 4); and Boethius' idea wove its way in and out of the whole tradition of anti-noble polemic.[1]

Fortune's gifts have no moral effect; they only display existing virtue or vice. This, then, is the first objection. Let it now be examined. It has flaws. Jean de Meung himself, in writing the lines quoted, was aware others thought differently: for he cited a well-attested popular proverb: 'honours change manners'.[2] It was perhaps dangerous, even for a poet with the realism Jean de Meung often evinced, to take up cudgels against a proverb on a matter of practical psychology. At all events he failed in this case. For if the elements in his declaration are taken one by one and put to empirical test, they reveal the opposite of what he was attempting to say.

The first element to be taken on its own calls up a truism almost too simple to deserve mentioning. It concerns the matter of publicity. No doubt a man *should* behave the same way when he is watched as he does unwatched. But *does* he? And does a caste or class? The medieval nobility for its part enshrined its negative answer in an openly professed ethic: that of honour, and its converse, shame. Despite inroads made by Christian doctrines of conscience, most noblemen still lived in practice largely in a 'shame-culture'. Aquinas, when placing honour at the head of his list of 'external goods', gave as his reason the

observed fact—observed by Aristotle, but wholly endorsed by
Aquinas—that men who have the other goods of life will
sacrifice them to win honour.[3] Conversely, when a proper
nobleman (not a convert to religion) did put pen to paper, he
would back his recommendations with an undisguised appeal to
his reader's sense of public shame: imagine how people will
snub you and cold-shoulder you, he will say, if they associate
your name with cowardice![4] It is true that the public opinion
thus appealed to was often selective. Some nobles at some
periods seem to have taken delight in shocking opinion in classes
below their own. But—quite apart from the question whether
that deviation did not itself testify to a kind of perverse
respect—for most noblemen public opinion at large still meant
something: for two reasons. First: it was normally in a
nobleman's interest not to be hated by his subjects.
(Machiavelli did not invent that axiom: it can be heard quite
distinctly from the knight Philippe de Novare in the thirteenth
century—endorsed by the picturesque reflection that 'a rich
man's belly is as soft as a poor man's, and a dagger goes in as
easily'.)[5] Second: churchmen, for what their words and
sanctions were worth, never ceased to drub into the ears of
secular magnates that their rank imposed on them the duty of
setting a moral example.[6]

Through honour, political interest, and ecclesiastical doctrine, then, a nobleman's moral conduct was influenced by its
very exposure, if by nothing else. Even the Stoical school of
critics can occasionally be heard owning to this. Publicity, they
admitted, did not merely reveal what was already there. It
affected it. In that first particular, therefore, the psychology of
the famous vernacular poet fell short. Let us see if it fell short in
other particulars. Did the gifts of fortune not themselves impart
moral dispositions? Let Jean de Meung enumerate the gifts of
fortune again:

> *richeces* et *reverances,*
> *dignetez, honeurs* et *puissances* (ll. 6223–4)

In denying the power of these gifts to bring a man virtue the
poet was thinking partly of the upstarts of his own day. But the
goods he lists were also roughly what distinguished born
nobility. They can be reduced essentially to three.

(1) The nobleman was at or near the top of a hierarchical political structure. That accounts at once for Jean's *reverances*, *dignetez*, and *honeurs*.

(2) The nobleman was rich in the economic sense: hence Jean's *richeces*.

(3) The nobleman had a military function, which required him from an early age to develop his bodily strength and effectiveness in battle. That was a principal sense in Jean de Meung's day of his word *puissances*.

Now all three of these noble perquisites can be shown to have imparted moral or religious dispositions to their beneficiaries.

The first to admit that they did so were strangely enough the critics of nobility themselves. For it was often stated that all three perquisites imparted *bad* dispositions. *Dignetez* made noblemen proud. For instance, one of the sharpest thirteenth-century critics of nobility was Peyraut. His long disquisition on bad noblemen came in his treatise on vice, and he put it in the chapter on 'pride': a natural association, for which he found precedent in a series of previous writers. *Richeces*, similarly, presented a temptation of their own. One theme in criticism of nobles—Odo of Cluny is again an example, but there are others (including the same Peyraut)—attacked their thoughtless self-indulgence: nobles misspent wealth made by poor men's sweat.[7] As for *puissances*, the nobility's military function was the basis of the most notorious of noble corruptions: bullying brutality. Charges on this last count were the most numerous of all. A veritable dictionary could be compiled of words, less neutral than *puissances*, used by polemicists in this context: *violentia*, *furtum*, *rapina*, *ingiurie*, *Brand*, *Mord*, and so on: of all of which, noble bullies were at some time accused. All three of these charges—pride, reckless self-indulgence, and violence—admitted, sometimes in so many words, that the externals of nobility disposed it to particular sins.

So noble condition was, when it came down to it, admitted to make a difference. And if a difference for the worse, why not for the better? This brighter side of the picture was given less emphasis by didactic and moralist literature, for the obvious reason that it was meant to correct the nobility. So it will be appropriate to make amends now.

Pride, luxury, brutality: a disposition to these three genres of abuse was implicit in noble rank. That was obvious. It was so obvious that even the nobility knew it. This introduces the first of noblemen's special dispositions to virtue, which I shall identify here by way of a prologue to the others. It can be described by the modern psychologist's word 'inhibition'. Students of animal behaviour find that predators, like wolves, have an inhibition restraining them from killing weak members of their own species, like cubs and females.[8] There is an evolutionary reason for this. A predatory species which failed to develop this restraint would destroy itself. Allowance made for the greater complexity of human situations, the analogy is useful in considering the ethics of the military caste in a civilized society. The medieval European aristocracy, for its part, inherited some inhibitions from the historic and even pre-historic past (that against fighting a man of inferior rank had apparently prehistoric roots).[9] It developed others. The inhibitions were repeatedly breached. But they remained a factor in the moral situation. By the time of Saint Louis, if not by that of the first crusade, they were enough of a factor to ensure that a nobleman, just by being that, was hedged in by a substantial ethical code. The code was a back-to-front version of the peculiar corruptions of noblemen just identified. *Richeces*: the wealthy man, *qua* wealthy, must be 'magnificent'; he must spend according to a principle related to his social function, neither exceeding through prodigality nor falling short through meanness, but trampling avarice under foot with a handsome 'liberality' or 'generosity' (the very words originally meant 'free status' and 'high birth'), especially in the matter of alms.[10] *Puissances*: the military man, *qua* military, must channel his strength exclusively to the defence of justice, ecclesiastical and secular, and especially in defence of the weak. *Dignetez* and *honeurs*, finally: a noble's arrogance was curbed not only by ties of obedience to the next man above in the political hierarchy. It was curbed by religion, which demanded some recognition, grudging and minimal though it might be, of the rights of the church. (Magnates who showed none at all usually caused general scandal and horror.) Students of society who like to see human behaviour as an extension of animal could indeed view medieval religion in this light: as the antithesis to noble pride, the elaboration of an upper-class inhibition on self-glorification—an inhibition of the sort wolves have not to eat their young, and with the same function.

We return to our polemical poet:

> richeces et reverances,
> dignetez, honeurs et puissances
> ne nule graces de Fortune,
> car je n'en except nes une,
> de si grant force pas ne sunt
> qu'els facent bons ceus qui les ont (ll. 6223–8)

It is clear that, whatever truth Jean de Meung's words contained, they were not the truth and nothing but the truth. Publicity entailed moral pressures. Rank, wealth, and strength presented moral dangers. And for that very reason, a specifically noble ethic existed to offset those dangers; an ethic which formed at least one factor in a nobleman's moral conduct.

But—matters of honour and inhibition apart—did the externals of nobility dispose their subject to positive virtues or religious qualities? My purpose now is to argue at length that they did. *Dignetez*; *richeces*; *puissances*: the same three externals can be shown, in the right circumstances, to have imparted positive stimuli to religious behaviour. The sarcastic may ask why a fact of such consequence, if it is really so, has not long ago become a commonplace for medieval historians. The answer lies once more in our tripartite division of medieval society. The stimuli I speak of are not classified as 'noble virtues', or listed as such in old codes of chivalry. Why? Because they took young men and women *out* of the ranks of those who fought, into the ranks of those who prayed. They took them out of the compass, that is, of specifically noble literature, into ecclesiastical, which as a rule deliberately underemphasized their class origin. The centre of gravity of our present subject therefore lies in that transition, from one order to another. Now we know that is the place to look for it, and what we are looking for, the search may prove fruitful.

### I. THE VIRTUE OF MAGNANIMITY

*Dignetez, richeces, puissances.* The three constituents of a nobleman's social condition will be taken in order, beginning with the first: the nobleman's honour and political authority.

There is no better-known historian's axiom today than Lord Acton's 'power tends to corrupt'. That axiom echoes one side of a medieval tradition: a side whose aspersions on the noble state have already been heard. But there was another side. In strict theology power could not in itself be evil, or God would not have it. God himself was a political magnate, a *potens*.[11] So power must be good. In human affairs, correspondingly, for all the temptations 'dignities' presented to a nobleman, they must also have their moral advantages. Like Lord Acton, most medieval divines were hesitant to admit this. But the reason for that was historical, not theological.[12] In face of the stubborn barbarian ethic surviving round about them, which saw the quest for glory and power as life's finest occupation, the moralist's first task was to instil humility. It was not for him to encourage self-aggrandizement, which throve so well without any encouraging. The western church, we recall, had taken time to acknowledge with any cordiality that kingship was a God-given institution. In the same way it took time, a slightly longer time, to admit that power could be a stimulus to virtue; and not only time, but painstaking psychology. This last science became a forte of scholasticism near the end of the twelfth century. The particular article of psychology relating to the good effects of power developed especially in the 1240s, when the relevant chapters of Aristotle's *Ethics* found their way into Latin. And it was above all Aquinas' reflections on these chapters and the problems they handled that clinched the issue—at least for one party of theologians. The issue thus clinched can best be understood by a summary of Aquinas' arguments.

The first argument concerned the capacity of the mind to hope. Saint Thomas put his finger on a key feature of this capacity. Hope, he said, is proportional to the means available to achieve it.[13] For instance: a man with troops and martial experience will entertain hope of victory more keenly (other things being equal) than a man without. This rule could be extended. A man with a general abundance of means to action—for example, authority, riches, subordinates, friends, and an appropriate training—is likely to entertain greater hopes in the world of action than a man without.[14] All this, of course, is on condition that other factors are equal. Now one of the factors that may not be equal is free will. This was where virtue came in. A man of abundant means is not only well placed to nourish high hopes. He is, because of that, morally obliged to do so. To fail to do so—to be content with projects appropriate to men less advantageously placed—is a positive disgrace. There was thus, taught Aquinas, a virtue especially appropriate for great men. It was that of imagining and tackling great tasks—tasks whose greatness will test even a great man's capacity. The nearest term we have today for such a virtue might be 'thinking big'. That happens to be almost a translation of the term Aristotle's Greeks had used for it: *megalopsychia*—which became the basis of its Latin name, *magnanimitas*. Today's English word 'magnanimity' normally has the restricted meaning of generosity in matters of justice. But that is a small residue from a long history, in which two grander concepts and scales of value wrestled with each other for rights over the word: popular admiration for worldly achievement, and, by way of reaction, philosophical contempt for it. It was the merit of Aquinas (he would have said: of Christianity itself) to synthesize both traditions into one virtue. The synthesis allowed Christians to approve constructive worldly ambition among persons equipped for it.

As contemporary critics were only too well aware, Aquinas left some awkward questions unanswered. His respect for Aristotle, together with his own psychological realism, led him to endorse the close association of magnanimity with worldly honours and riches—its goal and its means. Equally clearly he endorsed the consequence, or near-consequence, that magnanimity was a virtue exclusive to the world's great. Any affectation of magnanimity by lesser mortals was no virtue at all, he said, but the sin of presumption. As a Christian Aquinas made some effort to get round the moral elitism implicit in this latter position. But the pagan model shines through all the same.[15]

The chief reason Aquinas was content to allow it to do so was that he saw the pagan ethic in a Christian context which transformed it. The transformation was twofold. Its first aspect has not much to do with Aquinas himself, though it is implicit in some of his statements, and was certainly true in his day. It is that in an expressly Christian society honour goes not only to the world-conqueror, but also—and especially—to the saint. Canonization, legend, and pilgrimage could accord to an ascetic hermit a reputation which many an ancient hero might have envied. The ascetic might eschew the honour (though even that was not a foregone conclusion).[16] The honour remained a fact. In practice, as we shall see presently, it opened a Christian outlet for any heroic aspirations there might be in the breasts of youth.

But Aristotle's magnanimity underwent a more explicit baptism, in Aquinas' own moral theology. Aquinas made natural virtues accessories and models for supernatural. He saw *natural* magnanimity—with its consciousness of its gifts, its high aims, its wish to stretch its powers—as a model of a specifically Christian virtue: the theological virtue of hope. Despite its different name, this 'hope' was closely analogous in the supernatural sphere to 'magnanimity' in the natural. The object of supernatural hope, like that of magnanimity, was great and testing. Its means, like those of magnanimity, must themselves be great. The only difference was that now both object and means were God himself.[17]

The details of Aquinas' Christian philosophical structure, together with technical perplexities that arise in it, are matters for academic history. But his treatment of magnanimity has served the present inquiry in three ways. It describes the virtue as understood by Aristotle: Aristotle formed his idea of the virtue largely from popular conceptions, and there is reason to believe that similar popular conceptions underlay the general use of the word in medieval Latin.[18] Secondly, Aquinas makes explicit the association of the virtue with the great: the natural virtue of magnanimity (unlike its supernatural counterpart, hope) was above all an aristocrat's virtue. Thirdly, Aquinas' treatment of the virtue shows, by its very existence and character, that it was possible to conceive a positive connection between Christianity, and a pre-Christian ideal of grandeur.

It only remains to show that this connection was often made in practice, and without some of the fine distinctions Aquinas attached to it. By the time Aquinas was thus circumspectly admitting the virtue of magnanimity into the bosom of theology, medieval chroniclers and biographers had long been using the term 'magnanimous'. They used it roughly in

Aristotle's sense, and in contexts which imply both that this sense was widely accepted, and that 'magnanimity' was unequivocally seen as a virtue.[19] Last but not least: this magnanimity had also acquired occasional religious overtones, but this time without special safeguards or a change of name. Scripture contains a number of passages suggesting there are grades of excellence in virtue. There is the parable of the talents. Then there is the guest at table, who is told, 'friend, come up higher.' Again, in yet a third context, a man who has obeyed all the commandments since youth is told to sell all he has, give to the poor, and follow Christ: all this with the condition 'if thou wilt be perfect'. These and other texts gave vigour to the idea of a ladder, on which different people made their Christian endeavours on a rung appropriate to their particular situation. The idea had other tributaries besides the Gospel. In particular it had long before been fed by neo-Platonism.[20] It also fitted the practice of certain institutions which developed in the medieval church. At the end of the middle ages, backed by yet another Aristotelian term borrowed from epic Greece, the idea of grades of virtue would contribute to the theology of canonization, with its demand for 'heroic virtue'.[21] On a more modest level, meanwhile, it played its part throughout the middle ages in ideas about monasticism and the ascetic life. In playing this part the idea was sometimes more or less consciously linked with that of 'magnanimity'. The magnanimous man thus became the man who boldly attempted the higher grade of virtue. When this link was made, the secular associations of the word 'magnanimity' can occasionally be shown to have survived, including its association with a particular social class.

Much has been written, from the prologue to the *Rule of St. Benedict* onwards, on the perennial analogy between the military and monastic lives, and the notion of *militia Christi*.[22] I shall come back shortly to one practical aspect of this association between soldiery and monasticism. It must be enough to say now that the word *magnanimus* (or *-is*) was commonly used in the central middle ages to denote martial courage, and that this connotation passed over without any noticeable change into monastic usage. Saint John Gualbert, for instance, was *magnanimis* to enter a strict religious order against the wishes of his powerful father.[23] A monk who endures in a strict monastery all his life can be described, similarly, as *magnanimus*.[24] The purely martial aspect of the concept of magnanimity thus became part of the bond that joined the knightly to the monastic life. The virtue the soldier had once used in war he should invoke again in his spiritual battles.

But magnanimity had other secular connotations besides the military. It meant 'thinking big' in general. This general connotation also reappears in a spiritual context. Saint Romuald of Camaldoli as a young nobleman often used to think of doing 'something big' in his life, and it is clear that his biographer later regarded this intention as fulfilled by Romuald's life of strict asceticism.[25] The future Cistercian abbot Henry of Waverley signalled the beginning of his conversion from a life of martial self-aggrandizement by entertaining a hope that he would become famous, not (as he had hoped before) for wealth or prowess, but for miracles.[26] The peculiar spiritual obligations of secular greatness can be displayed in yet other forms. The Cistercian bishop John of Valence had as a young man received an expensive upbringing, and considered at the end he should repay the same 'with usury', with the result that he joined a strict monastic order.[27] Gerald of Aurillac felt, as a count, that he 'was as if on the pinnacle of the world', and thus naturally fixed his gaze on the joys of heaven.[28]

The message of these examples is spelt out boldly by several thirteenth-century preachers. One of Aquinas' fellow-Dominicans, Humbert de Romans, in a treatise for preachers, blamed the nobles of his own day (*c.* 1260) for obsession with business affairs. One of the marks of a truly faithful noble was the virtue 'which consists in this, that a man should set his heart on great things, and scorn the lesser. Yet many [nobles] today do the opposite, as if they were peasants, and with all their energy pursue earthly things which are small, and scorn heavenly things which are great.'[29] The upper-class connotations of spiritual magnanimity are betrayed, similarly, in a short essay on the virtue by yet another Dominican, one who was also, like Humbert, a pastoral theologian: Frère Laurent. In his famous *Somme le Roi*, a compendium of practical ethics, Frère Laurent defined magnanimity as follows:

Magnanimity consists in loftiness, grandeur, and nobility of courage, which makes a man brave as a lion and of great enterprise.[30]

Having thus defined a virtue which might as well be secular as spiritual, Frère Laurent went on to exemplify it in ways almost wholly religious. And he seems still to have in mind people with some claim to worldly greatness:

This is the way chosen by those not content to keep God's commandments, to which they are obliged. They wish to obey his counsels, to which they are not obliged. Thus some leave all they have for God's sake, and abandon themselves to death for his sake in [the crusading kingdom of] Outremer and elsewhere. Some scorn and despise . . . property, friends, their very selves: they become bondmen to others when they were free before, and become poor when they were rich before, or could have been, and opt to suffer great hardship when in the world they had great delight, as many do who enter the religious life. . . . For it is not the habit that makes the monk nor arms the knight, but good hearts and valiant deeds.[31]

The knightly ideal of 'valiant deeds' was spiritualized: it implied now the religious Way of Perfection.

A third expression of this concept in the thirteenth century is to be found in the sermons of Archbishop Federigo Visconti of Pisa (*c.* 1200–77). Federigo was himself a man of high noble birth, and one of the most conspicuous of secular clergy in his day to rival the great mendicants as preacher. In a sermon on Faith, given probably to the clergy in his mercantile city, the archbishop located one quality of faith in its capacity to translate worldly into spiritual prowess:

It is not the devil alone who is conquered by faith. It is the world too. For it is by faith that we recognize God's great generosity and fatherly love towards ourselves; and this recognition directs our hopes to heaven. 'For those who hope in the Lord will renew their strength,' says Isaiah [40:13]. Those who have been strong in winning worldly wealth become strong in scorning it. Those who have been strong in getting, demanding, and hanging on to worldly riches become strong in giving them away. No longer merchants of the world, they become merchants of heaven.[32]

In a few years Giordano of Rivalto, scion of a patrician dynasty of Pisa, would give apt illustration of his compatriot's contention, by entering the Dominican order.

'Magnanimity', then, was a virtue appropriate for the

world's great men. Aristotle had said so, and Aquinas had confirmed his view with only minor adjustments. This view nevertheless clashed with age-old religious objections, sustained by most of Aquinas' predecessors. Aquinas met the difficulty squarely. He annexed to the side of Aristotelian ethics a new set of supernatural counterparts to the natural virtues, banishing Aristotle's invidious elitism. But less systematic and learned writers were content with a clumsier structure. Magnanimity was for them both a secular and a religious virtue. In its religious form it joined itself, easily if not consistently, to ideas of gradation in religious life: the magnanimous man chose the harder and the higher. And one result of this easy elision was that social associations from secular magnanimity fed into its spiritual *Doppelgänger*. Great men of the world, that is to say, were specially bidden to seek spiritual greatness.

*Dignetez:* in considering the positive religious consequence of a nobleman's 'greatness' we have studied a mere concept. In moving to the second element of nobility, *richeces* we move at the same time into another sphere, that of practice. This is perhaps appropriate—wealth being in the Aristotelians' view a tangible sign of 'greatness'. It is at all events necessary. Medieval psychologists never got round to analysing the particular effect of riches which we are now to consider. Yet the effect is nevertheless illustrated repeatedly in practice. In the present discussion of nobility and ascetic religion, a study of the effect is unavoidable: for it represents the very threshold between the two conditions.

### 2. CONVERSION: THE SICK SOUL

To find the threshold we must reflect on one last feature of the doctrine of magnanimity. Magnanimity was a virtue proper not only to the great, but in a unique degree to one age-group among the great. It belonged above all to the young. There were two reasons. The psychological reason was that hope, the substance of magnanimity, involved the future; and youngsters had (or thought they had) a longer future. So they hoped more. The other reason was physiological. Youth had a 'warmer spirit'. Both these points had been put by Aristotle and were developed by his medieval pupils.[33] Writers who spoke thus of the hopes of youth normally meant worldly hopes: the sort of grand ambition shown by those *juvenes* of the chronicles, who frequented tournaments and battlefields.[34] But the hopes of youth could take on a subtler aspect. In real life—if at least a score of biographers can be trusted—youthful hope was not always accommodated by such traditional pursuits. It could burst their bounds, and redirect the warm spirit of youth in a new direction: to religion.

This bursting of the bounds is known now, and was then, as 'conversion'. That word has had several uses. Europe had been converted from paganism to Christianity. Illiterate manual workers in monasteries were often known as *conversi*, originally on the grounds that they were the ones who had not been reared and taught in the monastery. But the conversion a hopeful young man sometimes underwent involved neither changing religions nor, necessarily, changing statuses within the church. It was purely a matter of psychology. His conversion consisted of a change between two mental conditions: from relative indifference to religion, to a consuming preoccupation with it. Even this type of conversion comprised a variety of experiences; but they shared this essence.[35]

Of the varieties of experience subsumed in 'conversion', two will be discussed in this chapter. To denote the first I borrow a term from the modern doyen of the subject, William James. He spoke of the 'Sick Soul'. One genus of 'Sickness of Soul' he found in religious melancholia. One species of that, in turn, was a sense of the 'vanity of mortal things'.[36] This is the species of soul-sickness to be considered now.

### (i) The sick soul described

Soul-sickness, in this sense, can be described as a chronic and radical dissatisfaction with worldly hopes and occupations. One constituent of the sickness is a belief that no improvement in material circumstances can cure it. It is in the nature of this particular sickness that it must affect some kinds of person more than others. It is most truly itself in persons of worldly good fortune: since the better the victim's fortune is, the less reason he has to imagine that an improvement in it will cure him. Similarly, it must be most acute among the young. The hot spirit of youth, with a long life before it, lives in hope. But where there is no good in the world, there can be no hope: no *bonum*, no *bonum futurum*. So the hot spirit of youth feels its plight the more keenly for being unemployable.

Neither this feeling, nor its social idiosyncrasies, were an invention of the middle ages, much less of any later time. They were at least as old as the second century B.C.

I had . . . great possessions of herds and flocks, more than any who had been before me in Jerusalem. I also gathered for myself silver and gold and the treasure of kings and provinces; I got singers, both men and women, and many concubines, man's delight . . . and behold, all was vanity and a striving after wind.

(Eccles. 2 : 7–8, 11)

It does not much matter that Ecclesiastes' classic description of worldly ennui was not really written by a king. The author thought fit to put his words into the mouth of one, and in ascribing the book of Ecclesiastes confidently to Solomon, the middle ages went along with this significant myth. And Solomon was not only a king. He was the son of a king; and Ecclesiastes included in his picture of ennui the problem of the man who inherits great power and wealth: 'for what can the man do who comes after the king? Only what he has already done.' (2 : 12).

To chart the fortunes of that particular scriptural model in the middle ages would no doubt be a rewarding task. But it would be a long one; and it would be a longer one still to review the faint echoes and parallels to it that occur in monastic biography. For Ecclesiastes provided one *locus classicus* for that negative sentiment, a profound indifference to the world, which in a more or less critical form generally prefaced conversion to strict religion. But the medieval Ecclesiastes only concerns us as far as he portrays the negative sentiment. That is, he only concerns us for half of our way. For the full process of conversion ended positively; and there survive quite a number of descriptions from the medieval period itself of the complete process: soul-sickness, discovering its new health.

Two of these descriptions suggest themselves as illustrations. The first was written by Abbot Guibert of Nogent (*c.* 1116) and referred to the case of a youthful contemporary of his own younger days (*c.* 1073). The young man in question was the Picard noble, Everard, hereditary Count of Breteuil near Amiens.

He was in the flower of youth [wrote Guibert]. His personal adornments were of the most pleasing. His family was noble, and he himself marvellously endowed both in looks and other qualities— including all forms of wealth. For a long time his mind, being that of a mortal, was fixed in the pomp of pride. At length however he came to his senses. He turned to reflect on the meanness of the vicious pursuits he had begun to follow in worldly life. He saw his soul was in a miserable state: for his worldly life was leading to nothing but damnation and uncleanness, for himself and others. So he picked a few companions and told them his feelings. With these he would thrash out his thoughts in wide-ranging discussion. Eventually he resolved to manifest in action the fruit of his long deliberations. In league with the companions whom he had secretly persuaded to join him, he slipped away unknown to a faraway part of France, and lived there in deep anonymity, earning his keep by working for a charcoal burner, whose products he and his companions would hawk through country and town. Then, for the first time, he believed himself to possess true riches.[37]

After more adventures Everard and his companions ended as exemplary monks in the abbey of Marmoutier near Tours.

Guibert of Nogent was able in this short description to unite most of the characteristic elements of the soul-sick youth's conversion: youth, wealth, good looks; a period of doubt and revulsion from his way of life; discussion with a few companions; secret departure; a period of monastic experiment, and finally enrolment in a disciplined religious community. For a historian Guibert's account has a further recommendation. Its subject was neither a recognized 'saint' nor a member of one of the famous reforming congregations, such as the Cistercians. Everard's experience, in other words, did not touch merely a small handful of famous pioneers. It stretched away into the coverts of monastic history. Guibert did indeed see Everard's case as remarkable. But that meant it was remarkable for Guibert's experience, which in such matters did not stretch far beyond the region of Laon. Even within that region, he mentioned another closely parallel case some years earlier than Everard's.[38]

Conversions by way of soul-sickness might not be exclusive to canonized saints. But careful biography to some extent was, and their experiences are a degree better authenticated. It happens that the most influential monastic reformer of the twelfth century underwent a similar conversion to Count Everard's. A description of his experience, by a close friend and companion, will serve as a second illustration of the phenomenon. The case is that of Bernard of Clairvaux, recorded by Geoffrey of Chartres about 1160.

At the time of his mother's death Bernard was already becoming his own master in matters of what he did, and how. Now he was singularly gifted. His good looks and fine physique were remarkable. He displayed the most elegant manners. He had an acute mind, and a captivating way of speech. People spoke of him as a youth with high hopes, and as he set foot in the world its paths opened themselves out before him. Life's attractions swam up in all their variety before his eyes. Wherever he looked, high ambition smiled on him. Yet despite all this, the young and happy soul was as if besieged. The habits of his comrades contrasted with his, and their friendship disturbed him. They wished only to make him like themselves. . . . Bernard's thoughts turned therefore progressively towards escape. The world and its Prince seemed to offer him one external prize after another: some now, some to hope for. Yet all of them, he saw, were lies. Vanity of vanities, all was vanity. . . . So, wishing for perfection, he resolved to leave the world, and began to ask where he might most surely and purely find peace for his soul under Christ's yoke.[39]

Differences in emphasis distinguish the two accounts. Bernard's *richeces* consisted more in his prospects than his possessions. His crisis was more solitary. But the core of the two experiences is the same; and even the peculiarities in each account serve our purpose, as guarantees of its freedom from literary topos.

Not all medieval monks had to be 'converted'; either because as youths they had been markedly religious anyway, or because the order they joined had only a feebly religious atmosphere. Of the conversions there were, to the monastic or other kinds of religious life, few accounts survive; and of these accounts, in turn, some emphasize other elements in conversion than a young man's sickness of soul: the influence of a holy man, or of a passage in scripture, or a miraculous experience. There remain a substantial number in which radical ennui, of the sort epitomized in the two narratives quoted, can be detected as starting-point for the conversion. The reference may only consist of a word or two. 'He was tired of the world';[40] 'his love for the world grew cold';[41] 'the world seemed to him vile';[42] 'he could not bear the vexations of the world':[43] these are a handful of typical expressions on these lines, taken from a sample of saints' *Lives* from the tenth to the thirteenth century. Or the reference is longer, very occasionally as long as, or even longer than, those about Everard and Bernard.[44] Again, the symptoms of the sickness vary. The good things of the world of which the young man grows sick can include great learning, or bodily beauty and gifts, as well as or instead of high birth and noble status. Together, these passages, long and short, identify a large, complex, psychological fact, straddling the boundary between the two familiar conditions of medieval society: the secular upper classes (to which all the cases I have cited or referred to belonged),[45] and strict monasticism. It is a large fact, yet one which hides unless diligently looked for.

*(ii) The sick soul and erotic love*

This large fact—conversion—deserves more study than it would be appropriate to give it here. But one facet of it does deserve a moment's more attention. It relates to an aspect of the monastic and ascetic life so far only touched on superficially: celibacy. Every student of medieval history knows that the higher service of religion entailed celibacy; or at least was meant to, and in the central middle ages did among a considerable proportion of persons in orders. But that familiar circumstance hides mysteries. Why should celibacy, then or at any time, be thought an especially holy state? Why did some people feel 'called' to it? Why does it appear to have been so relatively easy for some, so hard for others? One faint ray of light is shed on the mysteries by a consideration about our young nobles' ennui. Or rather, it is shed by three considerations, drawn from three different fields of historical research, and added together.

(a) *Nobles' tendency to under-reproduction*

The first consideration concerns noble demography. I mentioned near the end of the last chapter that nobilities have sometimes tended to under-reproduction: they have reproduced themselves less prolifically than social categories below them, and often less than was necessary to maintain their numbers.[46] So such nobilities have done revolutionaries' work for them, and gradually died out. Information about specifically medieval nobilities and their demography is still too uncertain, and probably always will be, to establish whether this feature was a fixed characteristic of the class as such. A probable demographic boom in the French nobility in the twelfth century—the milieu Everard and Bernard came from—might seem to belie the hypothesis at the outset. But we do not yet know if that boom was greater or less than a boom in lower classes of the population. At all events, a trend to under-reproduction has been established in sections of the medieval German and (most clearly) English nobilities. And that fact by itself is remarkable enough. The class best equipped to rear children, it tells us, often reared fewer than the others. Now celibacy is not the only factor in under-reproduction. Smallness of families and lateness of marriage are others. But celibacy is one. Where it has been possible to isolate celibacy as a factor (as in better-documented modern periods) it appears to have played its full part in the under-reproductive trend. The nobilities affected, in other words, have produced more than their share of lifelong spinsters and bachelors.[47]

Why should they have done? The explanation that jumps first to mind is economic, similar but not identical to that suggested earlier for the related trend of high noble entry to the church. There was only so much wealth, it runs; and a young man only married when a prospect existed of keeping a high social status for himself and his children. Like the other, this explanation certainly goes part of the way. Evidence can be found that this motive operated.[48] But equally surely, like the other, this explanation is only partial, even on the economic side: for why should it only be *noble* youths who want economic assurance before they are married?[49] More important in the present context is a second demur: whether that explanation does not underestimate the strength of sexual and emotional factors.

That query beckons us over into branches of research normally divorced from economics. One relates to celibacy, and the other to the activity it negated.

(b) *'Falling in love' and the noble convert*

First, then, let us cast our eyes back on those descriptions of soul-sickness among youthful converts and—since we live in the twentieth century and are talking of emotion—put a seemingly twentieth-century question. Why could those soul-sick youths not have 'fallen in love' and got married? Every medievalist will understand my caution in calling that a 'seemingly twentieth-century' question. But before tackling it I mean in fact to defend it from a charge of anachronism. An unfortunate side-effect of the persuasive scholarship of the late C. S. Lewis has been its endorsement of the idea that before the twelfth century there was no 'love'—of the sort young people fall in, and get married as a result of.[50] No doubt the idea can be partially sustained by careful definition of terms; and there have been developments and refinements. But the very size of the assertion, in face of the dearth of dark-age evidence, should instil more caution than is sometimes shown in repeating it.[51] The one thing we know for sure about this side of life, before documentation thickens *c.* 1100, is that the human race survived the dark ages. There is next to nothing to identify the emotional concomitants of all that reproduction.

Next to nothing; but not absolutely nothing. It will be worthwhile briefly to mention what there is. In the first place, recent specialist reflections on fragments of early vernacular poetry suggest that girls, who apparently did most of the singing then, *could* love boys and want to marry them, before the twelfth century as after.[52] Again, hagiography, whose very business it was to avoid dilating on such matters, actually tends to confirm that common-sense conclusion. I name only one case among many less striking. The handsome Saint Carthagus (an Irish bishop, †637) achieved his lifelong celibacy only at the cost of rejecting the advances of no fewer than thirty maidens 'who loved him with great carnal love', and whom he repaid by turning them into nuns. (The epithet 'carnal' should not be taken pedantically; ascetics had strict views.)[53] Outside hagiography, in chronicles and histories, individual cases gleam from the darkness before the twelfth century, suggesting the same ingredients were present in love and marriage then as later. Thietmar of Merseburg, for instance, who wrote just after 1000, uses expressions like 'he burned with youthful love for her'; 'the king noticed her fine looks and good reputation' (and wished to marry her); 'he loved his wife while she lived'; and so on.[54] A recent study of marriage-rituals tells roughly the same story. From at least the ninth century the wedding ring is said to be a symbol of *amor*.[55] Our earliest rituals, from the twelfth century, already speak of *amor* and *dilectio* in the solemnization of marriage, with no hint that they are newcomers.[56] A very similar impression, finally, is given by the canon lawyers' use of the term *maritalis affectio*. It had been a Roman Law term, denoting the emotional aspect of a full and satisfactory marriage. The concept had been used freely by early Christian authorities, and the term would be taken up with equal ease when the study of law intensified in the early twelfth century. It was used by Gratian (*c.* 1140) as if it did not need explaining.[57]

Questions about love and marriage in the middle ages, early and late, are deep ones. The only decision that needs taking on them now, however, is the decision to keep an open mind. That done, a certain recurrent feature of conversion-narratives acquires significance. The feature shows little variation between 900 and 1300. It refers to the saint's good physical appearance, and attractiveness to the other sex. This double attribute is certainly not universal. A saint is occasionally expressly said to have had a naturally unimpressive appearance.[58] Nor is it always explicit that where good looks did obtain, they entailed attractiveness to women. But the first attribute is common, and the second commonly enough attached to it, for the feature to be worth identifying.[59] One of the most suggestive episodes involving this feature was told of Count Gerald of Aurillac (†909). Gerald was placed by his good looks and athletic physique, as well as by his rank, in a position where he could satisfy virtually any amorous inclination he had. But he only once strongly felt such inclination, when he was struck by the beauty of a peasant girl and fixed an assignment with her. In the interim he had grave misgivings and prayed for release from the temptation. The answer to his prayer was what seemed to him a marked deterioration in the girl's appearance when she arrived. The saintly nobleman ended by handing the girl back untouched to her father, together with a plot of land, a grant of freedom, and the advice to get his daughter married as soon as possible.[60]

Incidents of this sort are rarely recounted at any length. But bare references to encounters with the opposite sex are not so rare. The early Cistercian abbot Hugh of Marchiennes had contracted a sharp distaste for sexual affairs after a single short surrender to a woman's 'blandishments' at the age of twenty.[61] Roughly the same can be surmised of the more famous Cistercian, Saint Ailred of Rievaulx. We know him to have had one or two lapses from chastity as a youth, and then never again.[62] The absolute 'virginity' of some youthful converts was a rare enough merit to be emphasized by biographers:[63] a fact which suggests that many others who opted for the celibate life did so not without experience of the alternative. Even those converts whose own youthful purity was untarnished need not have been ignorant of the forces that swept round them. Saint Bernard of Clairvaux, whose debonair appearance and manners were attested a moment ago, had narrow 'escapes' as a young man. He once had to leap from his bed, shouting 'burglars!' as a subterfuge, to avoid the uninvited attentions of a vivacious landlady.[64] Such stories are relatively familiar in the *Lives*. The Breton saint, Bishop William of St. Brieuc (†1234) would pay for his good looks with a similar experience (with the same outcome) while still a youth in minor orders.[65] The Spanish Dominican saint Peter Gonzales (†1246), also noted for his fine appearance and manner, twice had to extricate himself from such temptation when already in major orders and a Dominican; and he was far from being the only member of his busy pastoral order to experience such embarrassments.[66]

The convert to religious asceticism can often be shown, then, to have augmented his other advantages with a less pecuniary kind of wealth: personal attractiveness. In so far as this attractiveness was a factor in marriage—and the degree in which it was need not be exactly decided for this to be true—the youth in question did not have to strive to win a partner. There was no shortage. This question of striving and not striving introduces us to a third field of research, instructive in the present connection. It lies as far as possible from saints' *Lives*. It relates, not to the ascetic who embraced lifelong celibacy, but to the lover who did not. The literature of lovers has this advantage, that it gives a more sophisticated picture of the emotions which ascetics were inclined to write off together as 'carnal' love. So let us now look at this literature.

(c) *Love and the unattainable*

Before *c.* 1100 there is not much literary description of erotic love. When such description appears, mainly in courtly literature, the emotion of love is given certain regular attributes. One attribute is that a lady—the literature is usually written from a man's viewpoint—should not be easily attainable. There was an easy way to ensure this. A man should love a lady of higher social class.[67] This theme got a momentum of its own, so that it is hard to tell how far the theme represents fiction and how far fact. But some of it at least was fact. The circumstance has often been remarked on that almost all the southern French troubadours, the fount and origin of the medieval literary preoccupation with love, were of low or modest social origin.[68] They frequented noble courts. It is possible, in other words, that they really did love ladies socially superior to themselves, and spoke for others in the same situation. The possibility has been defended in a suggestion as to the political background of courtly poetry. Troubadour verse came into being, it says, because of the ranked structure of castle society when its lord was absent, on a crusade or other war: a noble woman took her husband's rank, and was now left surrounded by aspiring courtiers to whom social as well as religious taboo made her hard of access.[69]

Love seems to have thriven, then, where attainment of its object was hard. Now this restriction emphatically did not apply to sexual enjoyment as such. Outside courtly love literature there are signs, from the same society and others not very different, of sexual licence at every social level.[70] But what this sexual enjoyment lacked was the quasi-religious status of courtly love. Courtly love promised to purify and satisfy the soul. It shared with Christian theology both these ideals, and a depreciation of merely physical sex. It was thus, as this last was not, a rival to established religious allegiances, and most directly to celibate monasticism.[71]

Why then did some young men choose celibacy instead? Could the reason occasionally have been, in the setting of other factors, the smaller likelihood they enjoyed of finding a partner hard of access? And could this circumstance in turn have contributed to a certain dissatisfaction some of these sensitive young people felt in the sexual encounters they attempted? The answers to these questions would depend on many considerations beyond those adduced here. But if there is one unfamiliar fact that can be confidently asserted, with the aim of setting our questions in lower relief, it is that not everyone saw celibate religion as the perfect state. When Saint Augustine, after his own long pilgrimage into religious celibacy, had said 'our hearts are restless until they rest in Thee' (*Confessions* i, i), he spoke in an immediate sense only for himself. As far as his remark implied even the desirability of celibate service of God, many ordinary people in the central middle ages would not have volunteered it. They thought sex was not only desirable for individual human well-being, but necessary; and that any religious person who thought otherwise had mistaken both human nature and even the meaning of scripture. Evidence of these views, chiefly from refutation, survives from the tenth, eleventh, twelfth, and thirteenth centuries.[72] Few people stuck out firmly for the opposite line by making themselves radical exceptions; and their lives were frequently either ignored, or viewed with wonder.[73] Now it just happens that a significant proportion of these exceptions were well-born. And we are therefore entitled to ask if it was such hearts, particularly, that felt as Augustine did and acted like him.

There is another coincidence that may confirm the suggestion here. Only one major troubadour poet was indisputably of high birth: Count William IX of Poitiers, Duke of Aquitaine (1071–1127). William of Aquitaine's love poetry has a number of peculiarities, besides its early date. One is the relative weakness and lateness of any element of the *femme lointaine* theme. Another, corresponding to that, is the indecent character of some of the poetry: William appears to have been less fastidious in his view of love than other, later (and lower-born) troubadours. A third—and the one that brings him particularly to our attention now—is an element of radical dissatisfaction with love:

> Such has always been my lot
> That I have never and will not
> Ever, enjoy the love I've got;
>    For ever again
> My heart—as love grows hot—
>    Breathes 'all is vain'.[74]

The 'horror' may be recalled which the Cistercian Hugh of Marchiennes had felt after one brief sexual encounter as a youth.[75] Could Duke William's misgiving be the same sentiment, but different in degree, and now, accordingly, in a nobleman who was *not* converted—unless converted (as Professor Nelli has suggested) to a more courtly view of love in his later years?

In the last few pages, speculation apart, evidence has been presented to suggest that the soul-sickness that struck certain wealthy young men was in no measure assuaged by their wealth: but rather exacerbated, as if the vanity of all worldly goods became more obvious as a man was richer in them. Moving nearer the region of conjecture, we saw reason to believe that aristocrats were less likely to marry than their social inferiors. In the light of this circumstance we considered the apparent contradiction, in the case of more than one saintly ascetic, between his rejection of sexual relations, and the abundance of his initial opportunity for them. And we finished by wondering, in the context of the ideal of 'unattainability' propounded by literary exponents of love, whether it was not, here too, the very abundance of a man's opportunity that conditioned his rejection of it.

We turn now to a subject where there is less wondering and more certainty.

### 3. CONVERSION: THE MILITARY LIFE

*Dignitez, richeces*; finally, *puissances*. The third property Jean de Meung assigned to the nobleman could denote 'power' in general, much in the modern sense. But it could also signify physical strength and martial valour. Jean said it was morally neutral. At the risk of shifting attention too much to one side of the word's meaning, I shall throw doubt on this view too. A nobleman was properly a military man. His military function opened the door to both vices and virtues. It could lead to that oppressive violence which critics made the nobility's blackest mark. Conversely, it could be a most powerful stimulus to religion.

The military life was frowned on in some circles because soldiers killed. But there have always been two ways of looking at the soldier's life. The same fact could be read in reverse. It was also soldiers, usually, who *were* killed. While certain strict canonists had long stressed the killing side of soldiery, theorists of Christian knighthood switched the emphasis to the being-killed. Catholic moral doctrine in the west finally come to an accommodation with war in the crusading period, and the resulting ideal dwelt on the crusader's readiness to shed his blood for the faith. The crusader thus became a 'martyr'.[76] Philosophers might point out the nice distinction that real martyrs did not shed others' blood. But the equation held well enough to satisfy those it applied to. It held well enough, too, to spread from crusading to all 'just war'. When chivalry put pen to parchment in the thirteenth and fourteenth centuries, knightly theory will be heard boasting that knighthood is not only legitimate for a Christian, but is actually the highest form of religious life: for it entails every one of the rigours of the life of priest or religious, and adds to them a constant danger of death.[77]

Now danger of death does not always produce the same psychological reactions in everyone. Inexperienced campaigners traditionally underestimated the danger of war until it was upon them.[78] Some others, more experienced, held their lives cheap. But a man who both saw the danger and valued his life needed virtue to face death.[79] The virtue was called by philosophers *fortitudo*, or courage. Both Aristotle and Aquinas located this virtue specifically in the ability to confront death in battle. Other manifestations of *fortitudo* only deserved the name in so far as they approximated to this.[80] Academic philosophy was here describing the first virtue of the practical knightly ethic. Flesh-and-blood knights in the central middle ages thought the same. Men who pretended to knighthood without facing death in battle were looked down on, like the wretched German knights of the late thirteenth century whom an older generation mocked as never having been nearer danger than when 'stewing prunes over a stove'.[81] This central knightly virtue was in fact pre-Christian; and to some extent it was non-Christian. Yet once the knight could claim to be a 'martyr' his fearlessness in battle became cocooned with Christian associations. The knight lived close to death. So, as a Christian, he must surely turn his thoughts constantly to his Saviour. An old crusader will be heard recommending the active military life to youngsters on just these grounds:

When knights and other military men are at war and get into danger they have more fear of the Lord, and are in greater fear of death, than when they are banqueting at home or living in a land at peace.[82]

This was theory. Its blemish as a Christian ethic was that it endorsed the killing of other people, a matter on which the exalters of knighthood were noticeably reticent.[83] But the warrior's proximity to death could breed purer religious feelings: so pure as to remove this blemish, and drive a man out of the military profession altogether. Because he was driven out, we must turn away from military documents for evidence of his sweeping revulsion, and look at spiritual. There, sure enough, the revulsion is to be found: another large fact, hiding behind the assured framework of church history. How large, can be measured from a single circumstance: that a substantial proportion of the main religious movements of the period can trace their historical point of departure to a military man's revulsion from killing.

A substantial proportion: that this is no exaggeration can be shown from a review, category by category, of some known cases of the revulsion. It was first and foremost against war as such. Whatever adjustments theologians might make to accommodate Christianity with war, the facts of war remained bloody, and a few consciences tender: Saint Romuald's, for example. He had as a young man (*c.* 970) been threatened with disinheritance by his father for lack of martial enthusiasm; and what finally decided Romuald to give up war altogether and become, as it proved, founder of the Camoldolensians, was his presence at a battle where his father killed his own cousin.[84] It was about the same time that Saint Bobo of Provence (†986), commander of the Christian side in a critical encounter with local Saracens, had a mysterious spiritual experience in the heat of battle: he vowed if victorious to renounce arms and devote his life to pilgrimage and the care of orphans and widows, which he subsequently did, and became a local legend for doing so.[85] A growing number of such cases are recorded from the eleventh century. Of Herluin, founder of the great monastery of Bec, it is recorded that his world-sickness followed a long and distinguished career as a *miles*;[86] of Saint Hugh of Cluny, that as a youth he had tried to restrain his military peers from rapine;[87] and of Saint Hugh of Grenoble that he and his brothers were encouraged by their parents to a similar restraint.[88] There are more explicit records to knights' revulsion from their profession. Chroniclers who describe the rise of those Clunys of the Black Forest, Hirsau and St. Georgen, suggest that their heavy recruitment from the military classes in the 1070s and 1080s owed much to the latter's disgust with the Investiture wars.[89] About 1120 the same German civil wars gave to the Cistercian order a convert who was younger brother to the Count of Berg. The young Everard had been present at a battle where eight hundred men were said to have been killed: a slaughter which made Everard on his way home resolve to abandon everything and be a monk.[90]

The spread of a strong monasticism during the anarchy of Stephen is a well-known fact of English history. We read it as a case of the church's taking up political lost ground between the two King Henrys. But the wars of the anarchy may, as in Germany, have helped actually to stimulate the monasticism. That they did in some cases is revealed by one of the few individual conversions we know of, that of a monk Henry. He had spent his early life as an exceptionally lawless and bloodthirsty knight. His compunction came gradually, but surely; and he ended as abbot of Tintern and Waverley in turn.[91]

In continental church history there were few more consequential conversions than those of Saint Bernard of Clairvaux in 1111, and of Saint Francis of Assisi in 1205. Bernard's antipathy to the worldliness of the schools, and Francis's antipathy to monetary greed, have often been emphasized. But the fact is that Bernard's long soul-sickness reached its crisis while he was *en route* to join his brothers at a siege, and it was his spiritual experience then that established his resolve to be a monk.[92] And the process of Francis's conversion began, not when he was counting money, but when he was setting off to serve in a Sicilian war.[93] An even more expressly military career broken by conversion was that of the French count who became the Blessed John of Montmirail. One of Philip Augustus' favourite warriors (his valour had saved the king's life in a rout at Gisors in 1198), and a reckless lover of tournaments, John eventually (*c.* 1209) gave up county, castles, and lands to be a Cistercian, and ended as a famous abbot. One day as abbot he asked in a moment of nostalgia to be shown his old weapons and armour. At the sight of them he quickly regretted his surrender to this temptation—'remembering what he had done'.[94]

A warrior's own spontaneous reaction against war was not the only way, however, in which this motive operated. There were others. For instance, the reaction might be that of a man's parents. Saint William of Volpiano, the Cluniac reformer, had no detectable 'conversion'. He had been dedicated to the church by his parents at birth: on a battlefield, as a term of peace in one of Otto the Great's fiercest battles for Lombardy.[95] Some personal reactions to war, too, were less spontaneous than others. A soldier might be coerced, so to speak, into conversion by fear of his own death in battle, as after a wound. This happened to Ingelbert of Clafstert, one of the high noblemen who founded Afflighem, in the late 1070s;[96] to Saint Bernard of Clairvaux's second brother Gerard;[97] and to Bernard of Lippe, co-founder of the Westphalian Cistercian abbey of Marienfeld, in 1197.[98] Nor were women exempt from the shocks caused by men's violence on each other; they may well have felt them more. We know of more than one case of a noblewoman straightaway taking to ascetic religion as a reaction to the news of violent death in her close entourage.[99] Yet other conversions share a military connotation without any direct connection with the battlefield. An example is the conversion of a young Portuguese *c.* 1219, which exudes the military atmosphere of his native land. A vain and self-confident young nobleman, he was shaken out of his worldly preoccupations by the appearance of a spectre, armed from head to foot and mounted on horseback. Both man and horse had the appearance of marble. The spectre shook his spear at the youth and said with terrifying mien, 'change your ways, or I will kill you'. Unlike the future Don Juan in a similar situation, the young man did change his ways, to become the Dominican saint, Giles of Santarem.[100]

The shocks of war, then, could wound the souls of any who came near that occupation: to the extent that they abandoned their way of life for a life of austere repentance. But the proximity of the nobleman to violent death was not only a matter of war. In a nobleman's life war was work. When not at war, he had part-time pursuits, and these normally had a similarly dangerous character. Nobles fought in duels and tournaments. Bad nobles murdered, or turned to gangsterism. Even the good noble was expected to hunt. All these violent and perilous activites could give rise to the sharp reaction which sent a man into ascetic religion. In 978 Peter Orseoli repented of a murder to which he had been accessory in making himself Doge of Venice. He fled to the Catalonian monastery of Cuxa, where he lived in extreme asceticism for nearly twenty years, and was later beatified.[101] A century later the first members of the hermit community at Molesme, precursor of Cîteaux, were two knights who had gone to partake in a tournament, each secretly plotting *en route* to kill the other: when, riding though a glade in a forest, both were struck simultaneously by sudden compunction, so that they confessed, repented, and became hermits in the very glade where they found themselves.[102] Hugh of Cluny's brother was murdered by a man who, similarly, was moved by the forgiving saint's example to repent, and enter Cluny as a monk.[103] Open or veiled references to murders by noblemen are not uncommon in narratives of monastic conversions.[104] Throughout the central middle ages are scattered instances of robber-chieftains who repent and become monks or hermits.[105] The mere proximity to the violent life was enough to provide cogent stimuli to religion in the right minds. The founder of Vallombrosa, John Gualbert, was put on the road to conversion, in about 1031, by an incident in which he forgave the killer of one of his kinsmen.[106]

Where there was no war, and no private sword-play, there was always, finally, hunting. Hunting and religious asceticism play a curious *pas de deux* in sources for monastic history. One reason for their connection was certainly that both took men out to the wilds. Huntsmen were the only people ever likely to discover an unadvertised hermit.[107] Poor monks occasionally found themselves lodged in disused hunting kennels, as at the foundation of Cluny. The young huntsman, riding alone in the solitude, might find there the occasion of his religious conversion—the spiritual call of the desert.[108] But there was another reason why the histories of hunting and asceticism intertwined. Hunting was a bloody and dangerous sport, and keen consciences could be shocked by it into religion. In at least three dark-age legends—those of Hubert, Eustace, and Julian—Christ speaks to the convert-to-be through the mouth or from the horns of a hunted stag. A revulsion from all killing, including the killing of animals, is expressly and dramatically set as the main theme of Julian's conversion. It may also be implied in the other two stag-legends. The fact that hermits and ascetic monks are characteristically portrayed, throughout the middles ages, as on the whole kind to animals, suggests that this motif could not have been foreign to the huntsman's conversion. The three conversions mentioned were of course legendary; and it does not matter now what kernel of reality any of them may have contained. What is more significant is that the three legends were among the most popular of the central middle ages. (They are all in *The Golden Legend.*) That circumstance, together with hints here and there in our more historical saints' *Lives*, suggests that a sudden antipathy to the bloodshed of hunting may occasionally have contributed to a young noble convert's acquired distaste of his social milieu.

But hunting was dangerous not only to the hunted. Like all equitation it was dangerous also to the rider—which is a main reason for its being seen as a noble sport. This danger, too, could have its religious effect. One example of such an effect stands out in monastic history. In 943 or 944 King Edmund of England had disgraced the future Saint Dunstan. Hunting near Cheddar one day the king suddenly found himself hurtling towards the edge of the gorge, over which both stags and dogs in turn disappeared, to fall instantly to their deaths. In the brief moment of crisis, believing his own death imminent, the king thought of only one sin he had committed, that against Dunstan; and swore to make amends if spared. We would of course not have heard the story if he had not been; nor, indeed, if the result of the event had been less momentous. The king returned to inaugurate the refounding of Glastonbury, and with it to launch the tenth-century English reformation. Monastic historians have described the episode as 'a turning-point in the history of religion in England'. Such were the exalted consequences flowing from a few seconds in a huntsman's life.[109]

*Dignitez, richeces, puissances:* in singling out these three perquisites of greatness from the polemic of Jean de Meung, and in treating them as I have done, I may have done injustice to the most widely-read poet of the later middle ages. But the injustice is surely less than he did to his subject. He said such externals made no difference to a man's moral life. The opposite case had been argued. All three, I have suggested, could impart moral or religious dispositions to their possessors. The nobleman was born great. He was equipped for great projects, and so morally bound to undertake them, and not least in the religious sphere: the descendant of heroes must be heroic in religion. Secondly, the nobleman was born rich. The good things of life that other people strove or longed for, he already had. A number of examples suggested that this situation could sometimes be accessory, in an upper-class youth, to the ennui that precipitated religious conversion. Finally, the strength of the nobleman's right arm derived from his military function, a function which never left him. The military life exposed him in an exceptional degree to the danger of violent death.

These three factors, singly or in combination, may be offered in partial explanation of the circumstance sketched in the last chapter: the high participation in ascetic religious movements by persons of upper-class birth. Together with that circumstance, they lend psychological colour to our understanding of the unwritten rule about church appointments, described in chapter 13. The admission of such religious motives does not exclude the more worldly-wise factors sometimes suggested. Different motives could combine, even in the same person, and consciously. The combination doubtless differed from person to person. But the religious considerations just outlined were frequently part of it. Behind the few isolated cases touching well-known names stand regiments of others, more cursorily or elusively recorded.

To say that the high places of the medieval church hierarchy were filled largely by people of upper-class social origin may be to state the obvious. But a second fact is not so obvious. The culture of ascetic monasticism—the culture which directly or indirectly produced most of the canonized saints of the period, and which could contrast, even sharply, with the aristocratic church hierarchy—took its driving force from people of substantially the same social origin. Not only was it so. There were many reasons why it should have been. This is the fact I hope to have established in these three chapters.

But a last question remains. We have watched certain rich young men disappearing through the eye of the needle. But what happened to them, socially speaking, after their conversion? Did the new convert so repudiate his social origin as to join the poor in a 'class struggle'? Or was his conversion from a social point of view of no account, leaving him as a mere religious outrider to the class he had come from? Earlier in this book, in speaking of the culture of intellectuals, I tried to identify that culture's actual emotional relationship with the rest of society. All that remains is to do the same for the culture of the saints.

# CHAPTER 16

# The Saint: the Man without Social Class

> I became all things to all men, that I might by all
> means save some.
>
> St. Paul, 1 Corinthians 1:19.

'LOOK here, upon this picture, and on this. . .'. In parts II and III of this book, on one hand, and in the last three chapters on the other, two cultures have been depicted, set in their social dimension; two cultures which flourished side by side on the commanding heights of the medieval church. The cultures overlapped in terms both of people and of ideas; but their centres of gravity were distinct.

Granted the system of social forces portrayed in part I, both cultures also appear to have been necessary. Each had its function in the life and growth of society, and each projected and employed a perfectly respectable set of human faculties. These functions, like the function of organs in an animal body, nevertheless had an order among themselves. Some organs are more primitive and fundamental to life than others; and health depends on the keeping by each of its place and activity. This notion of order was of course familiar to medieval thought. There was only one worry. How did the notion apply in practice? Who had priority? Popes and emperors, clerks and knights, even—apparently, despite the elusiveness of evidence from illiterate classes—the separate crafts and trades, were ready with their several bids for supremacy.[1] Could men live at all without the peasant's toil? No: then the peasant came first. Yet how could the peasant plough without the blacksmith? So up came the artisan. Or the blacksmith eat without the baker? And so on.

The two cultures studied in this book, rationalistic and monastic, were no exception to this practice. They were not always in dispute. But there was always a degree of tension between them, which when other conditions were right could lead each to put its claim boldly. Certain philosophers were heard in chapter 10, defending the social primacy of those who thought. Ascetic monasticism could make a corresponding claim: the contemplative Mary of Bethany had chosen the better part; and that meant all non-contemplative trades—which is as much as to say everyone else—had chosen the worse.

The revival of ancient disputes would serve little purpose if they represented nothing but dead interests. Some of the tension between rationalistic and contemplative did represent dead sectional interest. But it was not all that. There was real disagreement. Which, intellectual or monk, did the more necessary job? Like the other disagreements—between peasants, knights, and so on—this one implied and ultimately derived from different views about man. The views implied in this case were those which began our inquiry, the 'Greek' and the 'Hebrew'. Where did man fall short? If he fell short only in being ignorant or muddled, then the philosopher was the doctor who could put everything right. But suppose the trouble lay in man's will. A philosopher as such can do little about perverse wills—except possibly his own. Who then was to be the doctor? The answer to that was nothing less than the whole theological apparatus of the medieval church. This apparatus started with divine redemption, and worked down through sacraments and other benefits supposedly conferred by the church on earth. It finished at rock bottom with the standing desirability of civil authority, to hold back the more obviously contagious effects of human perversity.

It was this theological apparatus that gave the ascetic monk his place. By his penances and prayers—which could be viewed from outside as a device for purging his mind of one set of emotions and thoughts, and filling them with another—the monk sought to give flesh-and-blood reality to the church's doctrine of redemption, otherwise mere words. Now it is true that the monk was not the precise counterpart, in his scheme, to the philosopher in the other. The ecclesiastical and philosophical schemes were less symmetrical than I have portrayed them—the ecclesiastical being the more complex and socially-organized. But in one important respect there was a correspondence. Each, philosopher and monk, saw himself as a conduit by which intangible and invisible good flowed down into the everyday world. In the philosopher's case the good was truth, illuminating ignorance. In the monk's it was love, melting sin.

Which was right? Does man's imperfection consist primarily in his ignorance? Or in his perversity of will? If the mere setting forth of arguments could reconcile the two hypotheses to general satisfaction, or convert the world to one or the other, the job would have been done by now. For the ablest minds of the last two or three thousand years have been engaged in it. It is in the context of this debate, nevertheless, that this book has been written. The author of a book of this sort cannot, and perhaps should not, hope to have brought the debate any nearer an end. But no student of history can be denied the ambition of lighting up, if only temporarily, a small corner of such issues. It is with this purpose that I have studied a period when—contrary to one hardy notion about the middle ages—both intellectualist and ascetic views were vigorous. Certain social aspects of the milieux that represented them have been identified. This identification, I hope, has brought the inquiry a step nearer its original aim: that of understanding outlooks according to their social extension.

One step remains to be taken. The world of monks and ascetics has been approached by way of their social origins. To conclude the study of their culture, and the book at the same time, one characteristic will be described which was possessed by this culture at its fullest development. The characteristic has two sides: universality of social sympathy; and universality of social appeal.

This social universality may seem a strange characteristic to attribute to those noble converts, the main carriers of the culture. The class they themselves came from was itself a tiny minority, and they were a tiny minority of the class. On top of that, they lived a peculiar way of life, a perpetual source of wonder to those contemporaries who knew of it, and they lived it largely in private. Their number was certainly much smaller, and their way of life certainly more peculiar, than the numbers and lives of those arithmeticians, grammarians, logicians, and lawyers who bore the rationalistic culture on their backs. In terms of numbers of sins committed, or religious devotions practised, the university 'clerk' was surely nearer the general medieval average than was the ascetic monk. Yet it was the latter who had the universal sympathy and appeal. How can that be?

In the Introduction to this book sources were quoted from different periods of the middle ages to the effect that religious beliefs, misbeliefs, enthusiasms, and vices, often cut across social classes. The rule was not at all absolute. Its purpose in the Introduction was merely to discredit at the outset simple schemes attaching religion to social class. There remains, however—to serve a different purpose now—one instance where the rule *was* virtually absolute. For the rule applied not only to beliefs and vices, but to a certain type of person : namely, the 'saint'. His relationship with others, just as theirs with him, can be shown to have been essentially classless.

This can be shown by reference to two recurring themes in hagiography and related literature. Because the themes are hagiographical, the demur could be raised that they are mere literary stock-in-trade, themselves one more tool of monks' propaganda. The demur can be met. Not only does the hagiography in question come from centuries—the tenth and later—when history was forcing its way palpably into the hagiographic genre. Each of the two themes is represented in too great a variety of ways to reflect mere literary flourish. Many examples, furthermore, carry their own marks of authenticity, in some circumstance or anecdote that seems to reflect real life. Confirmation is available, too, outside hagiography proper. Even if none of these considerations counted, and the evidence were taken at its minimum value, as propaganda, its tribute to the classless ideal would still be a historical fact to be reckoned with.

## I. THE SAINT AS SOCIALLY AMPHIBIOUS

Most of this chapter will be concerned with the first of these two traits. It relates to the saint's face-to-face dealings with his fellow men. One respect in which a saint's biographer saw him as exceptional was, often, that he was what we might call 'socially amphibious'. He could talk to people of different social classes with equal ease, undisturbed by 'class-consciousness'. It is known this was not true of everyone. Earlier we had occasion to speak of elitism among some intellectuals; and it was said there that this elitism merely translated into new terms a more direct class-consciousness operative in the rest of society, clerical and lay. That consciousness consisted of a strong sense of high and low, of who could and could not be spoken to, and with what differentials of respect. What is known in general of medieval life suggests that such consciousness was in one degree or other ubiquitous. Almost everyone had it. It is against that background that the following cases must be seen. They were the exceptions, were described as such and even, occasionally, compared to 'miracles'.[2]

Saint Paul had written to the Corinthians (1 Cor. 1 : 19) : 'To the Jews I became as a Jew, in order to win Jews; to those . . . outside the law I became as one outside the law . . . that I might win those outside the law. To the weak I became weak, that I might win the weak. I became all things to all men, that I might by all means save some.' It was fortunate for the middle ages that Saint Paul had been given to such boasting. They liked models, and in describing his own practice, Paul gave later generations the model of an apostle. The apostle's mission was to all men, and the would-be apostle must acquire the quality of addressing himself to each kind of man appropriately. This quality was not a matter of hypocrisy or play-acting, but a capacity for thinking oneself into the outlook and preoccupations of the person one is talking to. The above passage was expounded in this sense by one of the most experienced pastors of the tenth century, Bishop Atto of Vercelli. Paul, said Atto, 'stooped in humility, taking on mentally the likeness of all men . . . so as to urge them in the way of salvation. . . . This quality of his did not 'involve pretence, such as hypocrites use; nor tricks and deceit; but only kindly fellow-feeling, such as did not emulate the faults of others, but grieved at those faults and sought to heal them'.[3] Saint Paul was in this respect Bishop Atto's ideal apostle: able, as he put in another part of his long Commentary on Paul, to deal equally with every class of person: 'in one way with the great of the world, in another with the middle class, in another with the lowly; in one way, again, with the polished, in another with the rude'.[4]

Saint Paul's claim to have been 'all things to all men' was naturally common knowledge to those who wrote saints' *Lives*; and like Atto they interpreted the claim freely, in terms of the classes and conditions of their own society. It was easy, consequently, for Saint Paul's example to suggest itself to biographers wishing to depict the social adaptability of their subject; and they often did so. The Cistercian bishop, John of Valence (†1145), was 'a knight amongst knights, a simpleton amongst the illiterate, yet no fool when he was among the wise: like Paul, he was all things to all men, so as to win all. . . .'[5] Abbot Stephen of Obazine, similarly, in the same generation, 'so conformed himself to all men that he showed himself weak with the weak, strong with the strong, happy with the happy, and sad with the sad; to the carnal he himself became in a certain manner carnal, while to seekers after glory it was as if he, too, wholeheartedly pursed the same. Thus he fulfilled what the apostle said: I became . . . [etc.].'[6] The capacity to adjust to all human conditions was above all the mark of an able preacher, and it is not surprising to find Saint Paul's boast attached to that notable preacher of early twelfth-century France, Robert of Arbrissel. 'His preaching could not *but* take effect,' wrote his first biographer, Balderic of Dol, 'since, if I may use the phrase, he was "all things to all men". He was gentle with the penitent, severe with the vicious, kindly and approachable with the mournful; a rod to the disrespectful, but a staff to lean on for the old and infirm. . . .'[7] The same Pauline phrase could be used even of a bishop's considerate practice of moderating his austere personal diet at table, to avoid embarrassing guests.[8]

The variety of contexts in which Saint Paul's phrase 'omnibus omnia factus sum' sprang to a writer's mind by itself suggests this was not a case of pure stereotype. The impression is confirmed by the cases where the echo of Saint Paul is at most implicit, and the variety of contexts wider. Adaptability to great and small, that is to say, was independently noticed as a mark of both sainthood in general and individual saints in particular. Of sainthood in general Charlemagne's theologians had once remarked that 'the saints have sometimes the gentleness of does, sometimes the fury of lions; they bear the rod of strong government and the staff that supports the weak'; and a marginal note in the manuscript where that remark appears may even indicate its personal endorsement by Charlemagne.⁹ Translated into an appropriate social language, that generalization would often be exemplified in individual holy men of the central middles ages. Norbert of Magdeburg, for instance—the echo of Saint Paul still just audible—was 'expert among the learned, noble among the noble; yet among the ignoble, a rustic; and among the illiterate, like a fool'.¹⁰ The well-born Cistercian abbot, Hugh of Marchiennes (†1158), was 'the same to great and small—unless it was that the latter often had more freedom with him, spoke with more familiarity, and had his approval more often'.¹¹ Of Hugh of Cluny, friend to princes, his biographer Hildebert explained how he nevertheless 'did not shrink from conversation with anyone at all, or mind what was wrong with them', and instanced poor old men oozing with pus, and lepers 'horrible to behold'.¹² It was once more the preacher whose function was particularly aided by such flexibility, and with the creation of the friars' orders a number of such conspicuously adaptable holy men make their appearance. Salimbene had a good eye for such traits of character. He said of one Franciscan, Henry of Pisa (†c.1250), for whom he had special regard, that 'he could converse well with all sorts of person, coming down and conforming himself to the ways of each: he was liked by his fellow-friars and by seculars—a rare quality'.¹³ Another Franciscan whom Salimbene esteemed highly, Bernabò of Regina (†1285) gave solace to every condition of person: to clergy high and low, knights, and indeed all in need of it: 'He could speak as boys speak, when talking boyishly among themselves; or as women speak among women, chatting about their news.'¹⁴ Other examples are available from the thirteenth century, from this and similar sources.¹⁵

Biographers who wrote of their hero as a saint did so for other reasons than his social amphibiousness. This amphibiousness may, as a matter of theology, actually be an essential ingredient of sanctity. But reference to it in a biography was not essential to a portrait of sainthood: since it is frequently absent. It is not mere hagiographical topos. The examples just given—largely authenticated anyway by their variety of approach and wording—can therefore safely be taken as historical.

These general references to the quality remain a mere handful. A better idea of its distribution can be had if the quality is split into its components. These were basically two. At one end of the scale was 'humility': a virtue derived, the saint himself would have said, from his spending all day mentally in the company of someone much grander and better than himself, viz. Christ. This 'humility' let the holy man, whatever his personal background and status, converse with even the most lowly of other men without embarrassment on either side. At the other end of the scale, meanwhile, yet bound together with 'humility' and from the same source, was the saint's conviction of the dignity of the religion he served: a quality which enabled the saintly *pauper Christi* fearlessly to confront kings if need be. This pair of qualities, taken together, was not seen as at all common in practice, whatever Christian theory might have said. But the saint characteristically had both.

Each can be studied in turn, in its most tractable manifestation. To illustrate humility from saints' *Lives* from the central middle ages presents only one problem: how to select from the mass of material. Humility taken on its own *was* a recognized essential of sainthood, and hagiographers spared no pains to emphasize that their saint had it. For the present purpose one aspect of the theme will suffice to illustrate it. This aspect concerns what was in the middle ages that clear badge of low social rank, menial work.

One fact that cut the converted nobleman from human contact with his inferiors was that he had never done any job which resembled theirs. Even in the field of battle the lives of knight and foot-soldier were different, and the difference was accentuated in peace, where a whole range of necessary but unglamorous tasks—in kitchen, farm, and workshop—lay outside the experience of most persons of rank.[16] All the more surprising was it, then, when the noble convert suddenly decided to try such jobs; and his doing so forms another common theme of the literature.

Again, the theme was not so common nor so uniform as to draw suspicion on itself as stereotype. Suspicion has in fact been expressed about the best-known example of the theme, from the Swabian reform in the early twelfth century. But it may be asked if critics have taken full account of the company in which this example stands. The example comes in the chronicle of Bernold of St. Blasien. Bernold tells how the early converts at nearby Hirsau did menial tasks 'and the nobler they had been in the world, the more contemptible the tasks they wished to do'. Thus ex-marquesses tended pigs; and so on.[17] Now all students of monastic history are aware that menial tasks in monasteries in the central middle ages were commonly done by *conversi* in the economic sense: monastic servants. It is largely that knowledge which has thrown doubt on Bernold's account. It may be right to doubt it. But one thing is certain. Such doubt must contend, not just with one passage in one chronicler, but with well over a dozen passages from other chroniclers and biographers at various times and places, describing the zealous phase of reforming religion.

The authenticity of these passages can be inferred, if from nothing else, from their variety. One former lord, in a reforming Flemish monastery (*c.* 1090), insists, despite the shocked intervention of other monks, on cleaning the latrines—until the abbot firmly orders him to stop.[18] Another, in a Cistercian monastery in France (*c.* 1210), discovers that one of the lower-born monks has done him the service of greasing his boots, and takes 'revenge' by surreptitiously returning the compliment.[19] Others, in various stages of conversion, work for artisans,[20] in the fields,[21] or in the kitchen.[22] One high-born recruit to a new order (*c.* 1219) found in the prospect of such work the very occasion of his conversion. He had seen friars working alongside ordinary building workers in the construction of their own convent, and resolved on the spot to join the order.[23]

It was not the holy man's sweat and labour that lent merit to this acceptance of menial jobs. It was more the humility that the acceptance signified. The great Lanfranc, when prior and schoolmaster at Bec (1045–63), was once riding home from a far part of the Bec estate when his travelling companion heard a 'miaow', which seemed to come from a bundle hanging from the great man's saddle. He must be carrying a cat. 'Why on earth are you carrying a cat?' asked the companion. 'We have a plague of rats and mice', explained Lanfranc, 'and I have fetched the cat to get rid of them.' That a famous prior should stoop to such interests was enough to call up the biographer's wonder: 'behold', he ends, 'the humility to which that great man was ready to lower himself, for God's sake.'[24]

The noble convert's eagerness to embrace menial jobs was

nevertheless more than empty symbol. With his new-found religious outlook he took pleasure in the job, and it grew on him. From Cluniac, Cistercian, and mendicant history come cases of converts who worked in hospitals and—it may be after initial repugnance at the smell, etc.—came to love the work so much that they could hardly be taken away from it.[25] The effect of menial work on a convert's soul is particularly well illustrated in a story preachers used to tell of a 'Count of Poitiers' (probably William II, who had abdicated in 990 to be a monk). William (runs the story) was given at his own request the job of minding first the hens, then the sheep, then the pigs. At each stage he was astonished at the novel pleasure he found in the task. He would watch the hatching of eggs, and see the chicks run after their mother; watch the new-born lamb instantly recognize its mother's bleat and hop towards her; and see each piglet go to its own teat on the sow, in strict order of seniority. He confessed he had never found such delight when at the height of his power— or so the thirteenth-century written tradition of the tale has it.[26]

Some noble converts took on menial occupations. There remained a world of difference between them and real menials; though their frequent use of the title *pauperes Christi* has encouraged confusion on this topic, and perhaps was meant to. What is certain, despite this world of difference, is that the adoption of menial jobs had a social function. It was an efficacious gesture towards the most despised part of the population, to whom these jobs were normally confined.

This social function was most explicit in certain ostentatious acts of self-depreciation. John Pilingotto, a Franciscan tertiary of Urbino (†1304) was an unusually demonstrative saint. Once he chained himself publicly to rails in a public place simply to share the status of criminals normally chained there.[27] The wearing of beggars' clothes by mendicants had a similar implication. As applied to the workers of the world in general, this idea of taking on voluntarily a despised and rejected status is unusually well put in the *Life* of the Cistercian Abbot John of Montmirail (†1217). John's reaction against the veneration paid to him was among the most extreme we have to deal with. It was evinced in deeds as well as words, but some of the latter exactly epitomize the sentiment in question. John's second-in-command in the monastery once asked him what he would be if not a Cistercian. John said a *ribaldus*. The contemporary connotation of that word, a connotation related but not identical to that of its modern descendant, will be clear from the prior's stupefied reaction:

'What! You'd want to belong to the class of men most contemptible to God and men, and be counted as one of them? Would you not then have to behave as they do—swearing and lying, playing dice and gambling, taking a whore round with you, and always getting drunk?'

'On no account,' said John; and he added (to use his own words), 'there are *ribaldi* and *ribaldi*. Many of them have habits very different from those you describe. And after all, look at the jobs they have to do: some have to clean stables, or carry sewage, and humbly submit to doing and carrying all sorts of nasty things, and eat their bread in the sweat of their brow. Their life may be thought degraded and despicable by men. But it is praiseworthy and very precious in God's sight. So why should you be surprised at my saying I wished to be compared to them?'

The prior objected: 'You can be pretty sure they would make life intolerable for you if you did not conform—or rather *de*form—yourself to their revolting habits.'

'To bear whatever injuries they inflicted on me on this account', John declared, 'would be to me a source of the greatest delight.'

Need I say more? [concludes the biographer—who must have heard the story from the prior and doubtless expressed the latter's sentiments]. The degree and quality of this saint's love of humility will be plain to us from these utterances. Let those who will [he challenges] sing the praises of drivers-out of demons, and resuscitators of dead bodies. For my part I praise, and always will, such exceptional humility. That humility now exalts you in joy to the eternal bliss of heaven, O blessed John—you who thus lowered and debased and despised yourself, and so proved yourself a true soldier and perfect imitator of your eternal King.[28]

## 2. THE VIRTUE OF FRANK SPEECH (*parrhesia*)

A true soldier and perfect imitator of Christ had to put himself on a level with the humblest condition of men. But that was not all. Christ, after all, had not merely spoken with the humble. He brought equal ease and independence to his dealings with rulers and chief priests. A capacity to do the same was the second basic component of the saint's social amphibiousness.

For the saint's particular brand of humility did not stop him speaking to kings as an equal, and indeed in some matters as superior. Canonists and philosophers wrote much on the theoretical relation of church and secular lordship. It is easy to forget that in practice, the relation might depend largely on who happened to represent the two powers at a given time; and that this, in turn, involved the unforeseeable interplay of their acts of will. The church view had occasionally to be championed by people who had next to no social or material resources. When it was, the familiar physiognomy of church history could rest on heroic achievements of individual will.

'Heroic achievement' is no exaggeration. That an intelligent and sensitive person, and the same one who chatted to peasants, should speak fearlessly in the face of a show of secular power was not seen as an everyday occurrence. From the moment government became solid enough, and literature precise enough, for record of the phenomenon to be possible, the 'flatterer' became, as we saw in chapter 4, one of the most familiar of all characters in moralists' complaint and satire against courts.[29] The moralists usually wrote at a safe distance. The very ubiquity of flatterers showed how hard it was, close up, to avoid their fault. This difficulty is no extrapolation from modern experience. It was observed then. One of the shrewdest contemporary observers of psychology of whom record survives, and himself an example of social amphibiousness, was the preacher Giordano of Pisa; and he knew of this difficulty.

It is no easy task [he said in a sermon of 1305] to try to reprove a man to his face, and especially if the subject of reproof is a lord. One who attempts this submits himself to unforeseeable dangers. For the human soul is tender, and sensitive, and does not easily take criticism. A man who reproves another must therefore be a man of great virtue and fortitude.[30]

Aristotle, of course, had said the same in his own pre-Christian idiom ('to maintain one's superiority in the presence of notabilities is not easy and . . . is not unbecoming of a gentleman', etc. *Nich. Eth.* IV, 3). In the early middle ages, echoes of the same elementary psychological observation occur in more than one writer;[31] and when virtue and vice became a university subject in the twelfth century, the principle won a place in systematic ethics. 'Frank speaking' became a virtue on its own. It won its place, as it happens, under the disguise of that virtue discussed in the last chapter, magnanimity. Peter Chanter, a Paris theologian writing just before 1200, gave a chapter of his *Verbum Abbreviatum* to 'magnanimity'. But his description of the virtue shows he had his own idea of it, strongly stamped with a notion he must have got from the Bible, of 'frank-speech' (the Greek παρρησία: *parrhesia*). Peter made 'magnanimity' the virtue of those prophets and saints who said (with the apostles in Acts 4:19) 'we cannot but speak of what we have seen and heard'; and who spoke their minds to the great without fear or favour. In the church, said Peter Chanter, this virtue of frank speech 'pertains peculiarly to bishops'.[32]

This was not quite right. In attaching the virtue of frank speech to the office of bishop Peter Chanter was a better canonist than he was a historian. Since the time of Gregory VII (himself a notable example of Peter's view) a few bishops, it is true, had given outstanding illustration of the virtue. This was especially true in England, where a lively crown kept putting church leaders to the test: Becket was for Peter Chanter the very paragon of *parrhesia*, and—so far as it was a question of calm in the face of angry kings—Saints Anselm and Hugh of Lincoln could have gone on the list as well. In France too, in the same post-Gregorian generations, the list could be augmented by more than one bishop, boldly ordering some ruler off church liberties.[33] Even on a list of bishops, though, monastic bishops would be prominent. And it is from the monastic and regular clergy that the more spectacular instances of Christian *parysia* in fact come. Not surprisingly: for bishops usually had an established lordship behind them. Reforming monks or friars started with nothing. Virtue was their only weapon.

How formidably they could deploy this weapon is shown by several examples from the eleventh and twelfth centuries. Romuald of Camaldoli lived on land ruled by the count of Tuscany, Rainald (*c.* 1014–24). The count had murdered a man and married the widow. So Romuald broke off relations, and eventually brought the count to repentance. the noble culprit confessed, according to Romuald's biographer a generation later, that 'neither the emperor [i.e. Henry II] nor any other living mortal can instil as much fear into me as can a glance from Romuald. In his presence I do not know what to say, or how to find excuses to defend myself.'[34] The biographer—it is Peter Damian—goes on to claim that Romuald 'had this grace, by divine gift, that whatever sinners came into his presence—especially the mighty of the world— they were instantly smitten to their very entrails by fear, as if of the judgement of God'.[35]

A second Italian monk whose anger had this supernatural quality was John Gualbert (†1073). 'Father John', wrote his biographer Atto of Pistoia in the next generation, 'was so severe in his reproof of malefactors that the man against whom his indignation was directed thought the anger to be that of earth and heaven, nay of God himself.'[36] Atto's *Life* makes it plain that John made no class-distinctions in picking targets for this formidable temper. The same was true of Stephen of Obazine, the contemporary and tributary of the Cistercian reform. Stephen's natural authority was such as to surround him (according to an anonymous monk of his community who wrote soon after Stephen's death) with an aura of wholesome fear, even when he was in a lighthearted mood.[37] Among Stephen's practices was, when administering punishments within his own community, to start at the top.[38] It was similar with the laity. One story told how Stephen castigated the depredations of a local knight to the latter's face; and the knight 'unable to bear the gaze' of the unarmed, wrinkled little saint, ended by giving up attempts to excuse himself and falling at Stephen's feet.[39]

Besides the variety of its appearances, this motif is lent verisimilitude by the fact that it can attach to characters other than the hero of a *Life*. John of Montimirail, as a famous knight, attended costly and dangerous tournaments. On his way back a 'certain very holy religious canon' would greet him and his retinue with a barrage of irony and invective, about the vanity and bloodshed involved in such pursuits. The canon was probably a Premonstratensian. But he was not an official 'saint', and is otherwise unheard of. It was the knight, John, who became the 'saint'; and partly, no doubt, as a result of these fearless explosions.[40]

Not merely was *parrhesia* not exclusive to bishops. After Peter Chanter's time some of the most characteristic examples of the virtue find it employed *against* bishops. Frank-speaking was part of the armoury particularly of mendicant preachers. The Franciscan Antony of Padua (†1231) put special stress on the value, for preachers, of keeping clear of the favours and bribes by which prelates in his day sought to blunt preachers' criticism of themselves;[41] and Antony himself won a lasting reputation, as preacher, for the impartiality with which he wielded 'the spiritual sword against rich and poor, noble and ignoble'.[42] In the next generation a Franciscan preacher no less formidable than Antony was the Provençal Hugh of Digne (†c. 1254). Hugh twice preached to Pope Innocent IV and his cardinals; and although Pope Innocent had in fact asked Hugh to do so, and expressly given him licence to say whatever he wished, the freedom of Hugh's language on these occasions still caused a shudder within his own order. He had lectured the princes of the church like 'boys gathered for a game' and had them 'trembling like reeds in water'.[43] As for monks in early centuries, so for mendicant preachers in the thirteenth, instances of *parrhesia* could be multiplied; as directed against both ecclesiastical and secular magnates.[44] The most dramatic instance of all is that told by Salimbene about yet a third early prodigy of Franciscan preaching, Bertold of Regensburg (†1272). Bertold and a companion friar were caught by a notorious robber-chief and, having no money for a ransom, were sentenced to death. Meanwhile the robber-chief learned his victim's name, and (one imagines in the spirit of Herod, wanting a miracle) asked the famous preacher for a sermon. Bertold made it a condition that the whole band of malefactors should be assembled to hear the sermon. While the band assembled Bertold's companion sidled over to him, recalled their common sentence of death, and urged 'if ever you gave a good sermon on hellfire and heaven, use your art now!' Bertold's performance exceeded all the companion could have hoped. At the end the whole band was in tears, and made a common resolve to quit its evil way of life. On the ringleader the effect was such that, despite Bertold's caution and without his knowledge, he followed the preacher towards Regensburg; was recognized by a crowd who knew nothing of the brigand's conversion, and hanged on the spot. The story's unedifying end helps warrant its authenticity.[45]

The power to tell home truths to the mighty of the world was, then, a perquisite of sainthood commonly shown in the holy ascetics of the central middle ages. Theology occasionally picked it out, as a virtue corresponding to the biblical and patristic notion of *parrhesia*; and the quality turns up in various guises in the episodes of church literature. Now frank speaking was the most tangible aspect of the saint's indifference to rank, and has been discussed here for that reason. But it was only one aspect. It would not have been a virtue at all if uncombined with others. For it was only *bad* magnates who needed criticism, and the capacity to make friends with magnates who were not bad was just as needful in the saint's repertoire. The characteristic saint could best get his way without being angry. He 'had this divine gift, that his person and conversation were pleasing not only to ordinary people but also to the great; so that he was always both loved and respected by kings'.⁴⁶ Nuances appear in this conversational adaptability of the holy ascetic. A knack attributed to more than one was that of drawing a conversation towards divine subjects, without anyone's noticing.⁴⁷ Freedom from preoccupation with rank could even be expressed by mere silence. John Pilingotto of Urbino, the tertiary Franciscan who chained himself to the railings as a criminal, once caused a stir by a wholly unconscious slight he administered to a local count. The count sought the saint's company, and finding no other means of access, approached him on his way to church one morning, and held his hand. The saint was so rapt that he did not even notice he had a companion, much less one of such eminent rank, and the count had to give up his ambition.⁴⁸

'I became all things to all men, that I might by all means save some.' Like Saint Paul, his most strenuous imitators of the central middle ages were free, in their personal dealings, from the class-consciousness normal around them. When it came to human conversation, the saint talked to rich and poor with equal ease, and could say to each what the occasion demanded. This ideal of social adaptability was not an absolute monopoly of saintly ascetics. The capacity to speak courteously with all social classes was in the thirteenth century included among the essential accomplishments of more than one secular status: of city governor,⁴⁹ knight,⁵⁰ and courtly lover.⁵¹ Occasionally even the scholar can leave behind him a name for social adaptability.⁵² But for constancy and precision the motif as described in literature about religious movements excels its rivals elsewhere. For the saint the quality of social amphibiousness was more than a chance adornment; it reflected the essence of sainthood.

### 3. THE UNIVERSALITY OF THE SAINT'S APPEAL

One last aspect of the saint's catholicity of sympathy has to be considered. The catholicity was reciprocated. If the account in the Book of Acts is to be trusted, Saint Paul did not in the event 'save' all men. But those he did win to his religion belonged to all social conditions. The same can be said of our medieval saints.

This is attested by three circumstances. The first is that the 'man of God' was often said to have had, during his life, a following made up from all ranks. The statement may be implicit, in a whole series of remarks or narratives about the saint's clientele; or explicit, in a simple generalization. For instance, the presence of William of Volpiano (†1031), 'was desired by every order and sex of mankind, like that of one of the Lord's patriarchs or apostles';[53] an assertion confirmed both by William's recorded friendships and (as far as the poor were concerned) the circumstance that a route he was expected to travel on would be lined beforehand by 'a crowd of the poor and sick'.[54] Both the friendships, and the waiting crowds, were similarly recorded of Romuald of Camaldoli;[55] and of Hugh of Cluny a generation later, whose route would be lined by 'a crowd of poor folk',[56] while his counsel was sought (as we know from plenty of other sources besides the *Lives*) 'not only by private persons but by the great ranks of kings, emperors, and bishops, including the bishop of Rome'.[57] To Robert of Arbrissel 'came many people regardless of condition: women, poor, nobles, widows, maidens, old men and young, loose women and those women who spurned the male sex altogether'.[58] If further instances were sought from the thirteenth century, they would be there in narratives about leading mendicants: not only of Francis and Dominic themselves, but of several of the brightest lights among their early disciples.[59]

No occasion finds people quite so ready to praise a man as his death. This was true of medieval holy men, whose funerals commonly called up large gatherings of admirers; and the social promiscuity of these gatherings is the second sign how wide the appeal of such men could be. At the death of Burchard of St. Maur-des-Fossés (*c.* 1015), 'there rose a sudden cry through the city [Paris], through the castles, streets, and squares. Knights, rich men and poor men, old and young, widows and maidens gathered together in common tears and lamentation.'[60] On the death of the Breton hermit William Firmatus (*c.* 1095) three townships disputed possession of the remains; and the winner, Mortain, is said by the *Life* to have used the main force of 'its entire clergy and an innumerable crowd of its people', acting on orders from the count.[61] When bishop Hugh of Grenoble died in 1132, 'innumerable people' came from far and near; 'every age, sex, and condition' offered their devotion.[62] A concourse of this sort is described in exceptional detail by the anonymous biographer of Stephen of Obazine: 'all men, from the least to the greatest' took part; and the individual acts of devotion recorded in the account cover all the social spectrum.[63] These are a sample.[64] Not all hagiographers who describe these posthumous conventions mention their mixed social character. The word-pairs 'rich and poor', 'noble and ignoble', are sometimes omitted, in favour of others, like 'young and old', 'men and women', and so on. But that variation betrays nothing more than a writer's idea of what constituted a mixed crowd; and even when generalizations about rich and poor, etc., are missed out, single incidents can reveal that both rich and poor were in fact present at the funeral gathering.

The third.measure of a saint's universality of appeal lies in his posthumous miracles. At the end of each *Life* is commonly affixed a collection of cures and other miracles, worked at the saint's tomb or at the invocation of his name. Among aspects of these collections which lend themselves to analysis is the class-distribution of the miracles' beneficiaries. That distribution suggests the social areas where devotion for the saint was felt. No extensive breakdown of this aspect of miracle-collections has yet been published, but the preliminary analyses which have been, point in one direction. They suggest a wide class-distribution of the miracles.[65] A not untypical case might find some 10–20 per cent of beneficiaries in the upper classes of nobles, knights, and high lay officials; 20–40 per cent in the clergy or a religious order; and 40–70 per cent either of unspecified class or expressly assigned to peasantry or artisanry.[66] Variations certainly occur, and are instructive. Some saintly monks appealed predominantly to monks of their own order. A few saints had a popular clientele rising to 90 per cent or even 100 per cent of the total.[67] But the differences are usually of degree. Taken as a whole, the population of the posthumous hagiographic miracle-collections is notable for its mixed character.

### 4. CONCLUSION

In this concluding chapter a single characteristic has been picked out, recurrent in portraits of saintly ascetics in the central middle ages. From the point of view of mere mortal historians sainthood remains a complex subject. Many nuances and corollaries have gone unmentioned. What has been mentioned, however, is enough to complete the pattern established in the larger inquiry.

It is time to draw the strands of this pattern together. Behind the monolithic appearance of the medieval church was a variety of traditions, both co-operating and competing. This book has been concerned to bring one, especially, out of the shadows, and to locate it socially. The central two parts of the book examined from this angle the two main rationalizing currents, mathematical and literary; and related them to a broad category of people, who can be characterized as those with careers to make. Part IV has tried to put that discovery in relief, by studying the religious behaviour of a contrasting category: of that fraction of the upper class which, rejecting all their status offered them, underwent religious conversion. This category became the driving force of the monastic-ascetic culture, which provided the church with the majority of its canonized saints. From the point of view of their social relations, and disregarding the question of their origins, these saints had a striking quality. It was a quality observed to a large extent independently, and always with wonder, by the saints' biographers. They were classless. Preoccupied, apparently, with supernatural thoughts which impelled them to a love of human beings as such, they were indifferent in their sympathies and social dealings to the 'class' of the persons they spoke to; and this universality of sympathy was answered by the mixed character of a saint's corpus of admirers.

Without embroilment in demographers' disputes it can roughly be estimated that for every saint, later to be canonized, living in western Europe in (say) 1200, there existed something in the order of a million other people. If the number of canonized saints was augmented, as it has been in this survey, by every identifiable kind of *proxime accessit*, the augmented army would still remain a minute proportion of the population. This book has been about society, not a freakish minority. So it may fairly be asked how our findings on the minority serve to illumine the larger questions of social relationships.

There are two answers. The first lies in what may be termed the direct moral influence of sainthood. It was part of the essence of sanctity that it should seek to communicate itself: *omne bonum diffusivum sui*. Social amphibiousness was one consequence of this. And the amphibiousness was also part of the holiness communicated: a saint's entourage, too, forgot its social differences. To assure ourselves of this in the field of society as a whole it may be enough just to recall those funerals. While there is in general plenty of evidence of inter-class hatred here and there in the central middle ages, it does just happen that scarcely any of that evidence refers to these particular gatherings. The socially-mixed crowds at saints' funerals apparently forgot any class war they had.[68] If the quest for assurance is narrowed to the monastic entourage, the contagious effect of a saint's amphibiousness is attested more directly. In 1128 or 1129 a Jew from Cologne visited the new Premonstratensian community at Cappenburg in Westphalia, founded by a converted count in close co-operation with Saint Norbert. The Jew noticed that men of different conditions lived in pious simplicity together, 'educated and uneducated, healthy and sick, noble and ignoble'.[69] So impressed was he by the spectacle that it contributed to his conversion to Christianity soon afterwards. A similar sight precipitated the conversion to celibate religion of the Blessed Giles of Santarem in *c.* 1220.[70] Under Hugh of Cluny, with his careful regulation of attitudes among the men of different social origins he had to deal with, Isaiah's prophecy was fulfilled, and 'the wolf dwelt with the lamb, and the leopard lay down with the kid'.[71] In the course of the middle ages similar affirmations were made of several communities in more or less close contact with reformers: those of John Gualbert in the eleventh;[72] those of Dominic's disciples in the early thirteenth.[73] None of this evidence belies the social complications of monastic life in more humdrum conditions, away from the influence of heroic sanctity. Emotionally classless communities were the exception even in monastic history—despite the prescriptions of St. Benedict's Rule.[74] But the exceptions do not lose illustrative value for that. They suggest a diffusive effect in the saintly quality under discussion.

The second reason why the saintly minority is worth the social historian's attention is an intellectual one. The medieval church claimed authority to teach on fundamental questions about God's relationship with the world. The doctrines to which the church lent this authority were derived (at least it was claimed they were) from scripture. But scripture's nose was as waxen as that of any other authority, and could be bent variously. No single device for meeting this difficulty has ever won universal and lasting assent. But medieval churchmen, for all their differences over detail, did agree on certain principles in the matter. One of the principles was that uttered *c.* 1200 by Alexander of Ashby, the Nottinghamshire canon, and quoted in the Introduction. I quote his words again:

I think they only purely and rightly understand the holy writings who by the purity of their life keep close to that spirit by which the scripture was composed and expounded.[75]

Alexander himself had experience of the two cultures we have considered, intellectual and monastic. His remark was written in the conceptual language of the first. But it was a recommendation of the second. Those who prayed, Alexander thought, *understood* better. The remark expressed a view held by very many medieval divines; and it helps explain the significance in social history of the small saintly minority. Whatever other contribution they may have made to the life round them, they also made this: that they nourished and preserved certain attitudes. Right or wrong, the attitudes might have disappeared if the saints had not lived as they did.

The attitudes comprised a special view of God's relation with nature. It was a view which accommodated miracles: those done and foretold in the Gospel, plus a greater or lesser number of others done since (its defenders seldom argued the toss on particular recent miracles, at least not on rationalistic grounds); and it was in general ready to interpret the turn of events in terms of God's will. It was with this view that the partial rationalism of the central and late middle ages was in tension.

We—people living in the last quarter of the twentieth century—are not called on to judge between these views, miraculous and rationalistic, once and for all. The validity of any such judgement would presuppose a wisdom even the more philosophical of us only try to climb towards; and it is not clear any human being has ever quite got there. But most of us will be ready to welcome a ray of light on the next step up; and that is what this essay on medieval history has been meant to provide. In our scientifically triumphant but humanly restive century, many people have looked with the same unease as the poet Eliot on the 'broken images' of past religions; images representing, with varying degrees of aesthetic appeal, the foci and cohesive power of dead societies. Some of the societies were quite unlike ours. Medieval Christian society, on the other hand, is our own ancestor. It has bequeathed to us many images, broken and unbroken. And among the broken ones is a view of nature which admits—interleaved with those natural laws which we see day after day bring our jet aircraft safely down on their radar tracks—the direct concern and intervention of the old God of Jacob.

The breaking of this particular image is the work of triumphant reason, a reason in whose language most of us do our public thinking. This book has been conceived in that language: as a study of facts, and drawing of inferences. In the context of the self-contained dialectic of medieval society, the facts have distinguished the social centres-of-gravity behind two views of nature, one more self-consciously rationalist than the other. It may or may not be commonplace that reason, thus beating the bounds of its own province, should discover something to make it stop and question itself. It has certainly done so here. For what it has found, to all appearances, is that of the two views, it was the *less* self-consciously rational that rested on the fuller human experience.

# APPENDIX I

# A sample list of medieval 'saints' (900–1500), with notes on their social origins

Source: *The Oxford Dictionary of the Christian Church*, ed. F. L. Cross (Oxford 1957[1]), abbreviated below as *ODCC*. The list includes all personages there dubbed 'saint', who (*a*) operated mainly in the Latin-speaking half of Christendom, (*b*) died between the years 900 and 1500, and (*c*) about whom appropriate details are known. Those otherwise qualified but failing to meet requirement (*c*) are listed at the end.

Reliable information on the saint's social background can often be had from the same dictionary, and from other standard works of reference. The most informative of the latter in each individual case is noted with one of the following abbreviations:

| | |
|---|---|
| *ADB* | *Allgemeine Deutsche Biographie* |
| *DNB* | *Dictionary of National Biography* |
| *NCE* | *New Catholic Encyclopedia* |

Doubtful cases are referred to other secondary and primary sources. For references to *Vitae* see the main bibliography on pp. 420–1.

Even where the wealth and legal status of a family are thus discovered, the subtlety of social distinctions in any milieu lends a degree of arbitrariness to any system of classification. Five categories have suggested themselves, of which only the first two are innocent of problems. 'Noble' here envisages those of whom the (often loose) medieval usage would have employed the words *nobilis* or *generosus*. The concept includes the *miles* in the sense of an economically self-supporting equestrian 'knight', though not in the broader sense sometimes used in war of all fighting men (cf. M. H. Keen, *The Laws of War in the Late Middle Ages*, London 1965, 254–7: 'The Peerage of Soldiers'). The words 'wealthy', 'middle-class', and 'poor' are all notoriously difficult to define without any reliance on the subjective judgement in which they commonly originate. I have sought by various means to reduce this reliance and its effect on the objectivity of the final arithmetic. But a few disputable cases are bound to remain; and I can only hope the reader who scrutinizes these cases—identified by parentheses—will concede that the benefit of any doubt has as often been awarded in one direction as in the other.

Geographical indications have been added where they may help the envisaging of a social class.

The categories are:

R       reigning king or queen
N*      of royal or ducal family
N       noble
W       born into a family of either free landowners or prominent bourgeois
MP      born into a family undistinguished by exceptional wealth or social position
( )     Parentheses denote a conjectural element in the assignation to a category

(W)     Abbo of Fleury (*c.* 945–1004)
        '[parentes] . . . non vana tumens et nobilitate superbus alebat sanguis, sed tamen avis atavisque derivata eos honestabat libertas . . .' *Vita*, 388D–9A.

W       Ailred of Rievaulx (1109–67)
        'His family were well-to-do, well-connected, and prominent in the neighbourhood of Durham and Hexham', F. M. Powicke, *Ailred of Rievaulx and his Biographer* (Manchester 1922), 30.

N       Albert the Great (*c.* 1200–80)
        Son of a count in Swabia.

N       Alphege, Archbishop of Canterbury (954–1012)
        Noble; abandoned an estate to enter a monastery. *DNB*, under 'Aelfheah'.

N       Anselm, Archbishop of Canterbury (1033–1109)
        'Decayed nobility', owning land, related to the powerful counts of Savoy. R. W. Southern, *Saint Anselm and his Biographer* (Cambridge 1963), 7–10.

N       Anselm, Bishop of Lucca (*c.* 1036–86)
        Milanese nobility; nephew to Pope Alexander II.

W       Antonino, Bishop of Florence (1389–1459)
        His father was a leading member of the Florentine guild of notaries, three times its 'proconsul' (an office with pre-

cedence directly after the priors of the commune). The father
left a small country property. R. Morcay, *S. Antonin* (Paris
1914), 13–15.

N  Antony of Padua (1195–1231)
    Lisbon nobility.

N  Becket, Thomas (*c.* 1118–70)
    D. Knowles, *Thomas Becket* (London 1970), 3–4, emphasizes
    the knightly character of Thomas's rearing: Thomas's father
    was a Norman, a generation away from the Conquest, and
    entertained high nobility in his London house.

N  Bernard of Clairvaux (1090–1153)
    Burgundian nobility.

W  Bernardino of Siena (1380–1444)
    Bernardino's father, a member of 'the distinguished family of
    the Albizzeschi' (Moorman, *Franciscan Order*, 374), was a
    provincial governor for the commune of Siena.

N  Bonaventura (1221–74)
    His father practised as a physician, but was of noble birth
    (Moorman, *Franciscan Order*, 140). For the 'extremely high'
    rates of pay for doctors in thirteenth- and fourteenth-century
    Italy, see Luzzatto, 130.

N  Bridget of Sweden (*c.* 1303–73)
    Her father was one of the wealthiest landowners of Sweden,
    and a provincial governor.

N*  Bruno, Archbishop of Cologne (925–65)
    Brother of Emperor Otto the Great.

N  Bruno the Carthusian (*c.* 1032–1101)

N  Cantilupe, Thomas de, Bishop of Hereford (*c.* 1218–82)
    Buckinghamshire nobility.

MP  Catherine of Siena (1333/47–80)
    Daughter of Sienese dyer. *NCE* describes her mother as a
    'housewife', an appellation justified, perhaps, by the sole fact
    of Catherine's being her mother's twenty-third daughter.
    But dyers in fourteenth-century Tuscany were not pro-
    letarian, rather 'small masters whose business required some
    capital' (R. de Roover, 'Labour Conditions in Florence *c.*
    1400', *Florentine Studies*, ed. N. Rubinstein (London 1968),
    302). Their restive condition was not inconsistent with noble
    lineage (G. A. Brucker, 'The Ciompi Revolution', ibid. 322
    and note).

MP  Pope Celestine V (*c.* 1215–96)
    The hermit Pietro Morrone, of S. Italian peasant stock.

N   Clare of Assisi (1194–1253)
    From a noble family of Assisi. *NCE.*

N   Dominic (1170–1221)
    M. H. Vicaire (*Hist. de S. Dominique*, I, 50–4, 365–72), having
    upbraided previous biographers for inattention to the
    matter, argues for 'une réelle probabilité' that Dominic's
    parents belonged to two of Spain's highest dynasties.

N*  Dunstan (*c.* 909–88)
    Related to the West Saxon royal house.

W   Edmund Rich, Archbishop of Canterbury (*c.* 1170/85–1240)
    'There is no reason to doubt that the name "Rich" signified
    the reputation which Edmund's father had obtained among
    his less prosperous neighbours', C. H. Lawrence, *St. Edmund
    of Abingdon* (Oxford 1960), 109; and 106–10; and cf. P. H.
    Reaney, *A Dictionary of English Surnames* (1958), at 'Rich'.

R   Edward ('the Martyr') (*c.* 963–78)

R   Edward the Confessor (1003–66)

R   Elizabeth of Hungary (1207–31)

N   Elmo (= Peter Gonzales, O.P., *c.* 1190–1246, according to
    *ODCC*)
    The identification is disputed. But Saint Peter Gonzales was
    in any case of noble birth. *NCE.*

N   Ethelwold, Bishop of Winchester (*c.* 908–84) *DNB.*

N   Frances of Rome (1384–1440)
    Roman nobility. Delaruelle–Labande–Ourliac, 1156–9.

W   Francis of Assisi (1181/2–1226)
    Son of a rich cloth merchant.

(P) Fulbert, Bishop of Chartres (*c.* 960–1028)
    Probably of poor and non-noble parentage, in N. France.
    *NCE*, against *ODCC.*

(N) Gilbert of Sempringham (*c.* 1083–1189)
    Son of a Norman knight and an Englishwoman. His father
    held three manors. *DNB.*

N   Giovanni Capistrano (1386–1456)
    Son of a German knight who had settled in the Abruzzi after
    fighting in the Regno. *NCE* ('John').

N   Gotthard, Bishop of Hildesheim (†1038)

N    Hildegard, Abbess of Bingen (1098–1179)
From an unknown noble family of Böckelheim in the Palatinate.

N    Hugh, Abbot of Cluny (1024–1109)
(Eldest) son of a Burgundian count. N. Hunt, *Cluny under Saint Hugh* (London 1967), 26.

(N)    Hugh, Bishop of Grenoble (1052–1132)
'parentes ... secundum saeculi dignitatem non infimos' (*Vita*, i, 764A). The biographer further reveals that Hugh's father and brothers were *milites* by profession.

N    Hugh, Bishop of Lincoln (1140–1200)
His father was lord of Avalon, near Dijon.

(N)    Hyacinth (1185–1257)
Of noble Polish parentage, according to a traditional account.

W    Ivo, Bishop of Chartres (*c.* 1040–1116)
His parents were 'peut-être de familles nobles; en tout cas, ils étaient propriétaires d'un domaine assez vaste' (J. Leclercq, Introduction to Ivo's *Correspondance*, I (Paris 1949), viii).

P    Joan of Arc (1412–31)

N    John Gualbert, Abbot of Vallombrosa (*c.* 990–1073)

R    Ladislaus, King of Hungary (1040–95)

N    Pope Leo IX (1002–54)
Nobility of Alsace.

R    Louis IX, King of France (1214–70)

(W)    Malachy, Archbishop of Armagh (1094–1148)
His brother was also a bishop, and their father was given by the contemporary *Annals of the Four Masters* the somewhat mysterious description, 'Armachiae et totius occidentalis Europae lector primarius'. *DNB*.

R    Margaret, Queen of Scotland (*c.* 1045–1093)

(N)    Mechthild of Magdeburg (*c.* 1210–*c.* 1280)
*NCE*.

N    Norbert, founder of Prémontré (*c.* 1080–1134)
(Younger) son of a nobleman of Xanten.

N*    Odilo, Abbot of Cluny (*c.* 962–1048)
Auvergne nobility (*NCE*). For the *princely* character of Odilo's family and connections, see J. Hourlier, *S. Odilon* (Louvain 1964), 28–30.

N    Odo, Abbot of Cluny (879–942)
     There is no doubt that Odo was noble. That his family was
     *pre-eminent* among the nobility south of the Loire is argued by
     J. Wollasch, *Neue Forschungen über Cluny und die Cluniacenser*
     (ed. G. Tellenbach, Freiburg/B 1959), 120–42 and 49–87.

(N)  Odo, Archbishop of Canterbury (Archbishop 942–59)
     According to an early tradition, son of a Danish soldier,
     adopted—after being punished by his father for attending a
     Christian church—by an English nobleman. *DNB*.
     Compare 'Oswald' below.

R    Olaf, king of Norway (995–1030)

N    Osmund, Bishop of Salisbury (†1099)
     Son of a Norman count.

(N)  Oswald, Archbishop of York (972–92)
     Nephew through his father to Saint Odo of Canterbury; also
     related to archbishop Oskytel of York and to Abbot Turketyl
     of Bedford. Oswald effected his reform of the monastery at
     Winchester by (with his uncle Odo's help) *buying* the
     monastery. *DNB*.

N    Otto, Bishop of Bamberg (1062/3–1139)
     His parents were of the free nobility, though not very
     wealthy. *ADB*.

(MP) Peter Damian (1007–72)
     The young Peter Damian worked as a swineherd. But this
     was a disgrace imposed on him by brothers jealous of their
     inheritance. The excellence of his education at all levels
     confirms the impression that his family had substance. *NCE*
     and *Vita*.

(W)  Peter Nolasco, founder of Mercedarians (*c.* 1189–*c.* 1256)
     Despite confusion and legend, it seems likely that he was of
     merchant family, and faintly possible that he was of knightly.
     *NCE*.

MP   Peter, Bishop of Tarentaise (1102–74)
     Of poor peasant stock in the Dauphiné; became a Cistercian.
     *NCE*.

(W)  Raymond Nonnatus (*c.* 1204–40)
     Was in a position to ransom slaves in N. Africa.

W    Richard, Bishop of Chichester (1197–1253)
     His father probably held a knight's fee from the bishop of
     Worcester; Richard rejected a project for his marriage with a
     certain *nobilis domina*. E. F. Jacob, 'St. Richard of

Chichester', *Journal of Ecclesiastical History*, 7 (1956), 174–88; 176.

N(*)  Romuald, founder of Camaldoli (*c.* 950–1027)
An early tradition makes his father a kinsman of the dukes of Ravenna. *NCE.*

R  Stephen, king of Hungary (975–1038)

(W)  Stephen Harding († 1134)
*DNB.*

N  Thomas Aquinas

MP  Vicelin, Bishop of Oldenburg (*c.* 1090–1154)
'parentibus morum magis honestate quam carnis et sanguinis nobilitate adornatis'. Helmold, *Chronica Slavorum* I, c. 42 (ed. B. Schmeidler, *SS\** 1937, p. 84.17–18).

(MP)  Vincent Ferrer (*c.* 1350–1419)
(Fourth) child of citizens of Valencia, to both of whom early Dominican *Lives* ascribe nobility, making Vincent's mother the daughter of a naval captain (A. Teoli, *Storia della Vita e del culto di S. Vincenzo Ferrerio* (Rome 1735), 1). Modern scholars prefer a more middle-class ascription. A doubtful case. *NCE.*

R  Wenceslas, ruler of Bohemia (*c.* 907–29)

N  William, Bishop of York (bishop 1142–54)
His father was treasurer to King Henry I and possibly (in a late tradition) related to Roger II of Sicily. *DNB.*

(W)  Wolfgang, Bishop of Regensburg (*c.* 924–94)
His parents were free; and though not noble were wealthy enough to get their son a good education. *ADB.*

MP  Wulfric of Haselbury († 1154)
'de mediocri Anglorum gente' (*Vita*, c. 1, p. 13). As a young priest Wulfric hunted, and had new silver coins in his purse to give to a beggar (ibid). But Wulfric had never possessed his own chain mail, apparently (c. 9, p. 22). He was served by a *puer* as hermit (c. 3, p. 17 and *passim*).

(W)  Wulfstan, Bishop of Worcester (*c.* 1109–95)
*DNB.*

| *Totals* | R | | | 9 |
|---|---|---|---|---|
| | N* | 3 | (+1) | 4 |
| | N | 28 | (+6) | 34 |
| | W | 8 | (+7) | 15 |
| | MP | 5 | (+4) | 9 |

*Exclusions*

The decision on what constitutes uncertainty must itself sometimes be uncertain. Grounds for it are added in each doubtful case.

Gertrude 'the Great' (1256–*c*. 1302)

Pope Gregory VII (pope 1073–85)
The frequent and confident assertion that this pope was of low birth rests on quicksand. G. Marchetti-Longhi, 'Ricerche sulla famiglia di Gregorio VII', *Studi Gregoriani* (ed. G. Borino, Rome 1947–61), II, 287–333 contrives a case for a high aristocratic origin. P. E. Schramm, reviewing the same in *Göttingischer gelehrte Anzeigen*, 207 (1953), 67–70 throws doubt on that particular connection, but fails to improve the argument for low birth. (The expression *vir de plebe*, used of Gregory VII by a correspondent, is no more than a flattering allusion to King David, cf. Psalm 89:19.)

John Nepomuk (*c*. 1340–93)
Cf. P. de Vooght, *Hussiana* (Louvain 1960), 414–21.

Peter Martyr (1205–52)
Cf. A. F. Dondaine, 'S. Pierre Martyr', *Archivum Fratrum Praedicatorum*, 23 (1953), 70.

Sebaldus (eleventh century?)

Simon Stock (*c*. 1165–1265)
Cf. D. Knowles, *The Religious Orders in England* (Cambridge 1948), 197.

William of Norwich (1132–44)
I am conscious of possible injustice in excluding this twelve-year-old saint and martyr, since the legend clearly makes him a tanner's apprentice; but I follow the consensus of historians in regarding the whole account as 'open to much suspicion' (*ODCC*).

*Total:* 7.

# APPENDIX II

# *A sample list of instigators and reformers of monastic and other regular religious movements, with notes on their social origins*

(*For abbreviations see Appendix I*)

N  Odo, Abbot of Cluny (Appendix I)

N*  Gerard, founder of Brogne (*c.* 880–959)
Related on his father's side to the Austrasian ducal house; Gerard's maternal uncle was bishop of Liège. E. Sackur, *Die Cluniacenser* (Halle 1892–4), I, 121–2.

MP  John, Abbot of Gorze (*c.* 915–74)
His father was an elderly peasant who had made himself very rich by a lifetime's hard work; his young mother was of 'liberioris generis'. Sackur, I, 146, and *Vita.*

N*  Dunstan of Glastonbury (Appendix I)

N  William of Dijon and Fécamp (962–1031)
Related through his mother to the Italian royal house of Ivrea, in whose service his father Robert of Volpiano was *miles.* Sackur, I, 257–8; II, 1–3.

N*  Romuald of Camaldoli (Appendix I)

N  Bruno of the Chartreuse (Appendix I)

W  Robert of Molesme (*c.* 1027–1111)
His parents 'secundum saeculi dignitatem clari ... rerum vero copia, quibus temporaliter abundabant ...'. *Vita.*

N  Bernard of Clairvaux (Appendix I)

N  Norbert of Prémontré (Appendix I)

N  Dominic (Appendix I)

W  Francis (Appendix I)

N   Clare (Appendix I)

(N)  Philip Benzi (1235–85)
     See *ODCC*, under 'Servites'. The Benzi were among noble
     families reduced to the rank of *popolani* by the commune of
     Florence in 1343. Villani, XII, c. 23.

W   Juliana Falconieri (1270–1341)
     See *ODCC*, under 'Servites'. The Falconieri were 'una
     possente casa di popolo' in 1300. Villani, VIII, c. 39 (cf. VIII,
     c. 1).

MP  Catherine of Siena (Appendix I)
     Her dubious title to appear on this list rests on her having
     inspired an enthusiastic group of mystics, which however
     never became an order.

N   Frances of Rome (Appendix I)

W   Bernardino of Siena (Appendix I)

N   John Capistrano (Appendix I: 'Giovanni')

MP  James of the March (*c.* 1394–1476)
     Of distinctly poor background. He tended sheep as a boy,
     and there was no money for his education. Moorman,
     *Franciscan Order*, 376–7.

Totals   N*              3
         N      9(+1)    10
         W               4
         MP              3
                        ───
                         20

Supplementary list

N   Ethelwold (Appendix I, and Knowles, *Monastic Order*, 39)

N   John Gualbert of Vallombrosa (Appendix I)

N   Herluin of (*c.* 995–1078) Bec (see Knowles, *Monastic Order*, 89).

N   Robert of Chaise Dieu (†1067)
     Ibid. 197. Robert was from the family of the counts of
     Aurillac.

N   Stephen of Muret (*c.* 1045–1124)
     See *ODCC*, under 'Grandmont'. Stephen's father was
     'nobilissimus'. *Vita*, i, p. 105.

MP  Blessed Robert of Arbrissel (†1117)
     See *ODCC*, under 'Fontevrault'. The *Vita* gives no hint that
     his parents had an unusual social status: i, 1046D–47A.

(W)  Stephen Harding (Appendix I)

MP  Stephen of Obazine (*c.* 1100–59)

'parentibus inter suos honestis. ... Qui ... parentes nec nimium locupletes, nec admodum pauperes, sufficientia vite satis habebant et per cetera quoque bona probabiles ...' *Vita*, I, i, p. 42.

(N)  Gilbert of Sempringham (Appendix I)

Except in the case of Robert of Arbrissel, I have avoided here those reformers and founders whose title to the prefix 'saint' is in doubt. But for Mary of Oignies and other inspirers of the early Beguine movement, see McDonnell, *Beguines*, 97, and for Diana of Andalò and the first Dominican nuns see Grundmann, *Religiöse Bewegungen*, 213 nn. 30 and 31. Hersinde, Robert of Arbrissel's first woman counterpart, had 'scorned nobility' to take up her job at Fontevrault (*Vita*, iv, 1054C).

# Bibliography

## I. MANUSCRIPT SOURCES

*Florence*
Biblioteca Medicea-Laurenziana    MS. Conv. soppr. 548
     MS. Plut. 33 sin. 1
Biblioteca Nazionale    MS. Conv. soppr. J. 10.35
     MS. XXXV 222

*London*
British Library    MS. Cotton Domitian 1

*Rome*
Vatican Library    MS. Latin 760

*Vienna*
Klosterneuburg Stiftsbibliothek    MS. 902


## II. PRINTED SOURCES

### 1. *Collections and Periodicals with abbreviated titles*

*AASS*    *Acta Sanctorum.*
*AHDLMA*    *Archives d'histoire doctrinale et littéraire du moyen âge.*
*Annales ESC*    *Annales—Économies—Sociétés—Civilisations.*
*CS*    Camden Society
*EHD*    *English Historical Documents*, ed. D. C. Douglas (Vol. I, ed. D. Whitelock, London 1968).
Mansi    J. D. Mansi, *Sacra conciliorum collectio* (Paris–Leipzig 1902–13).
*MGH*    *Monumenta Germaniae Historica.*
Sections *BDK*    *Briefe der deutschen Kaiserzeit.*
     *QGG*    *Quellen zur Geistesgeschichte des Mittelalters.*
     *SS*    *Scriptores rerum germanicarum.*
     *SS\**    *Scriptores rerum germanicarum in usum scholarum separatim editae.*
     *SSRM*    *Scriptores rerum merovingicarum.*

Muratori[1]  L. A. Muratori, *Rerum Italicarum*
*Scriptores* (Milan 1723–51).

*PL*  A. Migne, *Patrologia Latina* (*PL*
22.593A = Vol. 22, column 593, top
quarter).

*RS*  Rolls Series.

2. *Primary sources*

(a) *General*

AELFRIC, *Colloquy*, ed. G. N. Garmonsway (*Methuen's old English*
*Library*, London 1965[2]).

ALBERTANO OF BRESCIA ( = Albertanus Judex), *Liber de amore et*
*dilectione proximi*, printed with the same author's *Opus de loquendi ac*
*tacendi modo* (Cuneo 1507), fos. 25$^{ra}$–62$^{va}$.

—— *Ars loquendi et tacendi*, ed. Thor Sundby, in the latter's *Brunetto*
*Latino's Levnet og Skrifter* (Copenhagen 1869), xciii–cxix.

ALEXANDER OF ROES, *Memoriale*; *Noticia Seculi*; *Pavo*; in his *Schriften*,
ed. H. Grundmann and H. Heimpel (*MGH, Staatschriften des*
*späteren Mittelalters*, I (i), Stuttgart 1958).

AQUINAS, THOMAS, *Summa Theologica* (3 vols., Turin–Rome 1952–6);
*Summa Contra Gentiles* (Turin 1935).

ATTO OF VERCELLI, *Epistolae*; *Expositio in epistolas S. Pauli*; *Sermones*; in
*PL* 134.95–124; 125–834; 833–60.

BEDE, *Historia Ecclesiastica*; in *Bedae Opera Historica*, ed. C. Plummer, 2
vols. bound as one (Oxford 1896).

BACON: see ROGER BACON.

BENVENUTO DA IMOLA ( = Benvenuto de Rambaldis), *Comentum super*
*Dantis Aldigherii Comoediam, nunc primum integre in lucem editum*, ed.
J. P. Lacaita, 5 vols. (Florence 1887).

BONVESINO DELLA RIVA ( = Bonvicinus de Rippa), *De magnalibus urbis*
*Mediolani*, ed. F. Novati (*Bullettino dell'Istituto Storico Italiano*, 20,
Rome 1898), 61–182.

BRUNETTO LATINI: see LATINI.

BUBNOV, N., *Gerberti ... Opera Mathematica* (Berlin 1899).

CECCO OF ASCOLI ( = Francesco Stabili), *L'Acerba*, ed. A. Crespi
(Ascoli 1927).

CHARNY, GEOFFROI DE, *Livre de Chevalerie*, ed. K. De Lettenhove in the
same editor's *Œuvres de Froissart*, vol. I, parts 2 and 3 (Brussels
1873), 462–533.

*Chartularium Universitatis Parisiensis*, ed. H. Denifle and E. Chatelain, 4
vols. (Paris 1889–97).

*Corpus Juris Canonici*: see FRIEDBURG.

418     *Bibliography*

Dubois, Pierre, *De recuperatione Terrae Sanctae*, ed. Ch. V. Langlois (*Collection de textes pour servir à l'étude et à l'enseignement de l'histoire*, Paris 1891).

Faral, E., *Les arts poétiques du xii^e et du xiii^e siècle; recherches et documents sur la technique littéraire du moyen âge* (Paris 1924).

Fibonacci: see Leonardo.

Friedberg, Aemilius, ed., *Corpus Juris Canonici*, 2 vols. (Leipzig 1879).

Gerbert: see Bubnov, Olleris, Weigle.

Giordano of Rivalto (=of Pisa), *Prediche inedite*, ed. E. Narduci (Bologna 1867).

—— *Sermons on the Creed* (abbreviated as *Credo*), in Florence, Bibl. Naz., MS. XXXV, 222.

Henry of Ghent (=Henricus a Gandavo), *Summae quaestionum ordinariarum* (Paris 1520; r.p. *Franciscan Institute Publications, Text Series*, 1, 2 vols. St. Bonaventure–Louvain–Paderborn 1953).

Hugo of Trimberg, *Der Renner*, ed. G. Ehrismann, 4 vols. (Tübingen 1909).

Humbert de Romans (=Humbertus de Romanis), *De modo prompte cudendi sermones*, in M. de la Bigne, ed., *Maxima Bibliotheca Veterum Patrum* (Lyons 1677), Vol. 25, cols. 456E–567F.

Humbert of Silva Candida, *Adversus Simoniacos* (*MGH, Libelli de Lite*, 1) 95–253.

Jean de Meung, (continuation of Guillaume de Lorris's) *Le Roman de la Rose*, ed. F. Lecoy (*Les classiques français du moyen âge*, 3 vols., Paris 1968).

John of Jandun, *De laudibus Parisius*, in A. J. V. Le Roux de Lincy and L. M. Tisserand, *Histoire générale de Paris: Paris et ses historiens au xiv^e et xv^e siècles* (Paris 1867), 32–78.

John of Salisbury, *Metalogicon*, ed. C. C. J. Webb (Oxford 1909).

—— *Policraticus*, ed. C. C. J. Webb, 2 vols. (Oxford 1909).

Lampert of Hersfeld, *Annales*, in his *Opera*, ed. O. Holder-Egger (*MGH SS\**, Hanover 1894).

*Latin Poems commonly attributed to Walter Mapes, The*, ed. T. Wright (Camden Society, London 1841).

Latini, Brunetto, *Li livres dou Tresor*, ed. F. J. Carmody (*University of California Publications in Modern Philology*, 22, Berkeley 1948).

Leonardo of Pisa (=Leonardo Fibonacci, Leonardo Pisano), *Liber Abaci*, ed. B. Boncompagni (Rome 1857).

'Le livre des secrets aux philosophes, ou Dialogue de Placide et Timeo', excerpted by E. Renan, *Histoire littéraire de la France*, 30 (Paris 1888), 568–95.

*Liber Abaci*: see Leonardo.

LIZÉRAND, G., ed., *Le dossier de l'affaire des Templiers* (*Les classiques de l'histoire de France au moyen âge*, Paris 1964).

*Mir. S. Fidis* ( = *Liber miraculorum sancte Fidis*) ed. A. Bouillet (*Collection de Textes pour servir à l'étude et à l'enseignement de l'histoire*, Paris 1897).

*Moralium dogma philosophorum des Guillaume de Conches, Das*, ed. J. Holmberg (Uppsala 1929).

NECKHAM, ALEXANDER, *De naturis rerum*, ed. T. Wright, (*RS* 34, London 1863).

ODO OF CLUNY, *Collationes* (*PL* 133.517–638). See also *V. S. Geraldi* in section (b) below.

ODO RIGORD, *Regestrum Visitationum archiepiscopi Rothomagensis*, ed. Th. Bonnin (Rouen 1852). The letters a–d refer to quarters of the page, in downward series. Reference may also be made to the English translation by S. M. Brown (Columbia University Press, New York 1964).

OLLERIS, A., *Œuvres de Gerbert* (Paris 1867).

PETER THE PAINTER ( = Petrus Pictor), *Carmina*, ed. L. van Acker (*Corpus Christianorum, Continuatio Mediaevalis*, 25, Turnholt 1972).

PEYRAUT, GUILLAUME ( = Guilelmus Peraldus), *Summae Virtutum ac Vitiorum*, 2 vols. bound as one (Antwerp 1587). Numbers denote respectively: volume, tract, part, chapter. Folio-numbers can also be used to refer to the edition of Antwerp 1588.

PHILIPPE DE BEAUMANOIR, *Coutumes de Beauvaisis*, ed. A. Salmon (*Collection de textes pour servir à l'étude et à l'enseignement de l'histoire*), 2 vols. (Paris 1899).

PHILIPPE DE NOVARE ( = de Navarre), *Les quatre ages de l'homme*, ed. M. de Fréville (*Société des anciens textes français*, Paris 1888).

RADULF GLABER ( = Rodulphus Glaber), *Historiarum libri quinque*, ed. M. Prou (Paris 1886). Cf. *V. S. Guil. Divion.* in section (b) below.

RATHERIUS OF VERONA, *Praeloquia*; *De contemptu canonum*; *Sermones*; in *PL* 136.145–344; 485–522; 689–758.

RICHER, *Historiarum libri quatuor*, ed. G. Waitz (*MGH SS\**, Hanover 1877).

ROGER BACON, *Opus Mains*, ed. J. H. Bridges, 3 vols. (Oxford 1902).

SALIMBENE DE ADAM, *Cronica*, ed. G. Scàlia, 2 vols. (*Scrittori d'Italia* 232–3, Bari, 1966).

*Secretum Secretorum*, ed. R. Steele, in *Opera hactenus inedita Rogeri Baconi, Fasc. V* (Oxford 1920), 1–175 (Bacon's Latin text), 176–283 (English version of eastern Arabic text).

[SIDRACH] *La fontaine de toutes sciences du philosophe Sidrach*, excerpted by E. Renan and G. Paris in *Histoire littéraire de la France*, 31 (Paris 1888), 285–318.

SEXTUS AMARCIUS, *Sermones*, ed. K. Manitius (*MGH, QGG*6, Weimar 1969).

STEPHEN OF BOURBON, *Anecdotes historiques*, ed. A. Lecoy de la Marche (Paris 1877).

SUGER, *Vita Ludovici Grossi Regis*, ed. H. Waquet (*Les classiques de l'histoire de France au moyen âge*, Paris 1929).

SYMON DE PHARES, *Recueil des plus célèbres astrologues et des quelques hommes doctes écrit sous le règne de Charles VIII*, ed. E. Wickersheimer (Paris 1929). The letters a–d refer to quarters of the page, in downward series.

THEOPHILUS, *De diversis artibus*, ed. C. R. Dodwell (*Nelson's Medieval Texts*, London–Edinburgh 1961).

THIETMAR OF MERSEBURG, *Chronicon*, ed. R. Holtzmann (*MGH SS*\*, Berlin–Zurich 1955).

THOMASIN OF ZIRCLARIA, *Der welhische Gast*, ed. H. Rückert (Quedlinburg–Leipzig 1852).

VEGETIUS (=Flavus Vegetius Renatus) *Epitoma rei militari*, ed. C. Lang (*Bibliotheca Teubneriana*, Leipzig 1872; r.p. Stuttgart 1967).

VILLANI, GIOVANNI, *Cronica*, ed. A. Racheli (Trieste 1857).

WALTER MAP, *De nugis curialium distinctiones quinque*, ed. T. Wright (*CS*, London 1850).

—— See also *Latin Poems*.

WEIGLE, F., *Briefsammlung Gerberts* (*MGH BDK* 2, Weimar 1966).

(b) *Saints' Lives*

*V.S.* = *Vita sancti*, *V.B.* = *Vita beati*. The author's name, where known, is in parentheses.

*V.S. Abbonis abbatis Floriacensis* (Aimoin), *PL* 139.387–414.

*V.S. Adalberti episcopi Pragensis* (John Canaparius), *MGH SS* IV. 581–95.

*V. Ailredi* (= *The Life of Ailred of Rievaulx by Walter Daniel*) ed. F. M. Powicke (*Medieval Texts*, London–Edinburgh 1950).

*V. P[rima] S. Bernardi abbatis Clarevallensis* (William of St. Thierry and others), *PL* 186.226–466.

*V.S. Bernardi Tironensis* (Gaufridus Grossus), *PL* 172.1367–1446.

*V. D[omini] Burchardi venerabilis comitis* (Odo of Les Fossés), *PL* 143.847–62.

*V.B. Egidii de Santarem* (Andreas Resendius O.P.), *AASS* May III (1680), 402–35.

*V.S. Geraldi Auriliacensis comitis* (Odo of Cluny), *PL* 133.639–704.

*V.S. Guilelmi archiepiscopi Bituricensis*, *AASS* Jan. 1 (1643), 627–39.

*V.S. Guilielmi episcopi confessoris Brioci in Britannia Armorica* (Godefridus Calvus), *AASS* July VII (1731), 122–7.

*V.S. Guillelmi abbatis Divionensis* (Radulf Glaber), *PL* 142.698–720; page-numbers in parentheses refer to the edition by N. Bulst, *Deutsches Archiv*, 30 (1974), 450–87.

*V.S. Guilelmi Firmati* (Stephen, Bishop of Rennes), *AASS* April III (1675), 334–341.

*V.S. Herluini ... fundatoris Beccensis coenobii* (Gilbert Crispin), *PL* 150, 697–712.

*V.S. Hugonis Cluniacensis* (Hildebert of Le Mans), *PL* 159.856–906.

*V.S. Hugonis episcopi Gratianopolitani* (Guigo, Prior of the Chartreuse), *PL* 153.759–84.

*M[agna] V.S. Hugonis Lincolniensis* (Adam of Eynsham) ( = *The Life of St. Hugh of Lincoln*) ed. D. L. Douie and H. Farmer (*Medieval Texts*, London–Edinburgh 1961).

*V. Hugonis abbatis Marchianensis* ( = Marchiennes), in E. Martène and U. Durand, *Thesaurus Novus Anecdotorum*, III (Paris 1717), 1709–36.

*V.B. Jacobi Certaldensis* (Raphael Maphaeus), *AASS* April III (1675), 153–6.

*V. Joannis abbatis Gorziensis* (John of St. Arnulf), *PL* 137.239–310.

*V.S. Joannis Gualberti* (Atto of Pistoia), *PL* 146.667–706; (Andreas), ibid., cols. 765–812.

*V.B. Johannis de Monte-Mirabili*, *AASS* Sept. VIII (1762), 218–35.

*V.B. Johannis Pilingotti*, *AASS* June I (1685), 148–55.

*V.S. Johannis Valentinensis episcopi* (Magister Giraudus), in E. Martène and U. Durand, *Thesaurus Novus Anecdotorum*, III (Paris 1717), 1693–1702.

*V.B. Lanfranci Cantuariensium archiepiscopi* (Milo), *PL* 150.29–58.

*V.S. Maioli* (Cyrus), *PL* 137.715–78.

*V.S. Norberti* (B), *AASS* June VI (1685), 810–58.

*V.S. Odilonis Cluniacensis abbatis* (Jotsald), *PL* 142.897–940.

*V.S. Odonis abbatis Cluniacensis* (John of Salerno), *PL* 133.43–86.

*V.B. Petri Damiani* (John of Fonte Avellana), *PL* 144.113–80.

*V.S. Petri Gonzales* (Stephanus Sampaynus, O.P.), *AASS* April II (1675), 389–99.

*V.B. Roberti de Arbrissello* (Baldric, Bishop of Dol), *PL* 162.1017–58.

*V.S. Roberti abbatis Molesmensis*, *PL* 157.1269–94.

*V.S. Romualdi* (Peter Damian), *PL* 144.953–1008.

*V.B. Roberti Salentii* (a Celestine monk), *AASS* July IV (1725), 495–509.

*V.S. Stephani Obazinensis* ( = Vie de saint Étienne d'Obazine), ed. M. Aubrun (*Publications de l'Institut d'Études du Massif Central, Fasc.* VI, Clermont–Ferrand 1970).

*V.B. Wulfrici anachoretae Haselbergiae* (John, Abbot of Ford), ed. M. Bell (*Somerset Record Society*, 47, 1933).

3. *Secondary Sources*

*Adel und Kirche: Gerd Tellenbach zum 65. Geburtstag dargebracht von Freunden und Schulern.* Herausgegeben von Josef Fleckenstein und Karl Schmid (Freiburg 1968).

ANTON, H. H., *Fürstenspiegel und Herrscherethos in der Karolingerzeit* (*Bonner historische Forschungen*, 32, Bonn 1968).

BALDWIN, J. W., *Masters, Princes and Merchants: the social views of Peter the Chanter and his circle*, 2 vols. (Princeton 1970).

BARON, H., *The Crisis of the Early Italian Renaissance* (Princeton 1966²).

BISCHOFF, B., *Mittelalterliche Studien* (collected essays, 2 vols., Stuttgart 1966–7).

BLOOMFIELD, M. W., *The Seven Deadly Sins: An Introduction to the History of a Religious Concept, with special reference to medieval English literature* (Michigan 1952).

BOLIN, S., 'Mohammed, Charlemagne and Rurik', *Scandinavian Economic History Review*, 1 (1953), 5–39.

BOSHOF, E., *Erzbischof Agobard von Lyon, Leben und Werk* (*Kölner historische Abhandlungen*, 17, Cologne 1969).

BOSL, K., *Die Reichsministerialität der Salier und Staufer* (*Schriften der MGH*, 10, Stuttgart 1950).

—— *Frühformen der Gesellschaft im mittelalterlichen Europa* (collected essays) (Munich 1964).

—— 'Über soziale Mobilität in der mittelalterlichen "Gesellschaft"', *Frühformen*, 156–79.

CAMPBELL, A. M., *The Black Death and Men of Learning* (New York 1931).

CANTOR, M., *Vorlesungen über die Geschichte der Mathematik*, I (Leipzig 1894²), II (Leipzig 1900).

COULTON, G. G., *Five Centuries of Religion*, I (Cambridge 1923), II (Cambridge 1927).

CURTIUS, E. R., *Europäische Literatur und lateinisches Mittelalter* (Berne 1948).

—— 'Zur Literarästhetik des Mittelalters, II', *Zeitschrift für romanische Philologie*, 58 (1938), 129–232.

DASBERG, LEA, *Untersuchungen über die Entwertung des Judenstatus im 11. Jh.* (*École pratique des hautes études, Sorbonne, VIᵉ Section: Sciences économiques et sociales. Etudes Juives*, 11, Paris 1965).

DAVIDSOHN, R., *Geschichte von Florenz*, Vol. IV, pt. 3 (Berlin 1927).

DELARUELLE, E., LABANDE, E.-R., and OURLIAC, P., *L'Église au temps du Grand Schisme et de la crise conciliaire* (*Histoire de l'Église*, 14, Paris 1964).

DE ROOVER, R., 'The Development of Accounting Prior to Luca Pacioli', in A. C. Littleton and B. S. Yamey, eds., *Studies in the History of Accounting* (London 1956), 114–74.

DOEHAERD, R., *La haut moyen âge occidental: Économies et sociétés (Nouvelle Clio*, 14, Paris 1971).

DRESDNER, A., *Kultur- und Sittengeschichte der italienischen Geistlichkeit im 10. und 11. Jh.* (Breslau 1890).

DUBY, G., *Hommes et Structures du moyen âge: Recueil d'articles (École pratique des hautes études, VI^e Section: Le savoir historique*, 1, Paris 1973).

—— 'Les "jeunes" dans la société aristocratique dans la France du Nord-Ouest au xii^e siècle', *Hommes et Structures*, 213–26.

—— 'Remarques sur la littérature généalogique en France aux xi^e et xii^e siècles', *Hommes et Structures*, 287–98.

—— 'La noblesse dans la France médiévale. Une enquête a poursuivre', *Hommes et Structures*, 145–66.

—— *Rural Economy and Country Life in the Medieval West* (London 1968).

—— *La société aux xi^e et xii^e siècles dans la région mâconnaise (Bibliothèque générale de l'école pratique des hautes études, VI^e Section*, Paris 1953). Page-numbers in parentheses refer to the re-issue in (Paris) 1971.

—— 'Structures de parenté et noblesse dans la France du Nord aux xi^e et xii^e siècles', *Hommes et Structures*, 267–86.

*Espaces et Réseaux*: see LOMBARD.

FOSSIER, R., *La terre et les hommes en Picardie jusqu'à la fin du xiii^e siècle*, 2 vols. (Paris–Louvain 1968).

FOURNIAL, E., *Histoire monétaire de l'occident médiéval* (Paris 1970).

*Frühformen der Gesellschaft*: see BOSL.

GALBRAITH, V. H., 'The Literacy of the Medieval English Kings', (*Raleigh Lecture on History*), *Proceedings of the British Academy*, 21 (1935), 201–38.

GAUTHIER, R. A., *Magnanimité: L'Idéal de la grandeur dans la philosophie païenne et dans la théologie chrétienne (Bibliothèque Thomiste*, 28, Paris 1951).

GIEYSZTOR, A., 'Les Structures économiques en pays slaves à l'aube du moyen âge jusqu'au xi^e siècle et l'échange monétaire', *Moneta e Scambi*, 455–84.

GOETZ, M. P., *The Concept of Nobility in German Didactic Literature of the Thirteenth Century (Catholic University of America: Studies in German*, 5, Washington 1935).

GRAUS, F., 'Die Gewalt bei den Anfängen des Feudalismus und die "Gefangenenbefreiungen" der Merowingischen Hagiographie', *Jahrbuch für Wirtschaftsgeschichte*, 1961 (East Berlin), 61–156.

GRAUS, F., *Volk, Herrscher und Heiliger im Reich der Merowinger.* (*Tschechoslowakische Akademie der wissenschaften*, Prague 1965).

GRIERSON, P., 'Money and Coinage under Charlemagne', in H. Beumann, ed., *Karl der Grosse* (Dusseldorf 1965), I, 501–36.

GRUNDMANN, H., 'Adelsbekehrungen im Hochmittelalter', *Adel und Kirche*, 325–45. Reprinted (with the original page-numbers supplied) in the author's *Gesammelte Aufsätze*, I, *Schriften der MGH*, Vol. 25, 1 (Stuttgart 1976), 125–49.

—— '*Litteratus-illitteratus*: Der Wandel einer Bildungsnorm vom Altertum zum Mittelalter', *Archiv für Kulturgeschichte*, 40 (1958), 1–65.

—— *Reliogiöse Bewegungen im Mittelalter. Untersuchungen über die geschichtlichen Zusammenhänge zwischen der Ketzerei, den Bettelorden und der religiösen Frauenbewegung im 12. und 13. Jh. und über die geschichtlichen Grundlagen der deutschen Mystik* (Hildesheim 1961²).

—— '*Sacerdotium—Regnum—Studium*: Zur Wertung der Wissenschaft im 13. Jh.', *Archiv für Kulturgeschichte*, 34 (1951), 5–21.

—— 'Vom Ursprung der Universität im Mittelalter', *Berichte über die Verhandlungen der sächsischen Akademie der Wissenschaften zu Leipzig, Philologisch-historische Klasse*, Band 103, Heft 2 (Berlin 1957).

HARTNER, W., 'Zahlen und Zahlensysteme bei Primitiv-und Hochkulturvölkern', in the same author's collected essays, *Oriens-Occidens* (Hildesheim 1968), 57–116.

Heitmann, K., *Fortuna und Virtus: eine Studie zu Petrarchas Lebensweisheit* (*Studi Italiani*, 1, Cologne 1958).

HILL, G. F., *The Development of Arabic Numerals in Europe, Exhibited in Sixty-Four Tables* (Oxford 1915).

*Hommes et Structures*: see DUBY.

HYDE, J. K., *Padua in the Age of Dante* (Manchester 1966).

JONES, C. W., *Bedae Opera de Temporibus* (Cambridge, Mass. 1943).

KATZENELLENBOGEN, A., *Allegories of the Virtues and Vices in Mediaeval Art* (New York 1964²).

KIBRE, P., *Scholarly Privileges in the Middle Ages* (*Medieval Academy of America*, London, England 1961).

KNOWLES, D., *The Monastic Order in England* (Cambridge 1949).

LANGLOIS, C. V., *La vie en France au moyen âge, de la fin du xii^e au milieu du xiv^e siècle, d'après des moralistes du temps*, II (Paris 1925).

LATOUCHE, R., *The Birth of Western Economy* (London 1961).

LECOY DE LA MARCHE, A., *La chaire française au moyen âge* (Paris 1886²).

LEHMANN, P., *Die Parodie im Mittelalter* (Stuttgart 1963²).

LEWIS, P. S., *Later Medieval France* (London 1968).

LITTLE, L. K., 'Pride Goes before Avarice: Social Change and the Vices in Latin Christendom', *American Historical Review*, 76 (1971), 16–49.

LOMBARD, M., *Espaces et Réseaux du haut moyen âge (École pratique des hautes études—Sorbonne: VI<sup>e</sup> Section: Sciences économiques et sociales: Le savoir historique*, 2, Paris 1972), collected essays.

—— *L'Islam dans sa première grandeur (viii<sup>e</sup>–xi<sup>e</sup> siècle)* (Paris 1971).

—— 'L'or musulman du vii<sup>e</sup> au xi<sup>e</sup> siècle. Les bases monétaires d'une suprématie économique', in *Espaces et Réseaux*, 7–29.

LOPEZ, R. S., 'An Aristocracy of Money in the Early Middle Ages', *Speculum*, 28 (1953), 1–43.

LOTTIN, O., *Psychologie et Morale aux xii<sup>e</sup> et xiii<sup>e</sup> siècles*, 5 vols. (Louvain–Gembloux 1942–60).

LUZZATTO, G., *An Economic History of Italy* (London 1968²).

McDONNELL, E. W., *The Beguines and Beghards in Medieval Culture* (Rutgers 1954).

MAGNOU-NORTIER, E., *La société laïque et l'Église dans la province ecclésiastique de Narbonne (zone cispyrénéenne) de la fin du viii<sup>e</sup> à la fin du xi<sup>e</sup> siècle (Publications de l'Université de Toulouse–Le Mirail*, Series A, Vol. 20, Toulouse 1974).

MARTINI, F., *Das Bauerntum im deutschen Schrifttum von den Anfängen bis zum 16 Jh.. (Deutsche Vierteljahrschrift für Literar- und Geistesgesch. Buchreihe* 27, Halle 1944).

*Mittelalterliche Studien*: see BISCHOFF.

*Moneta e Scambi nell'Alto Medioevo (Settimane di Studio del Centro Italiano di Studi sull'Alto Medioevo* 8, Spoleto 1961).

MOORMAN, J. R. H., *A History of the Franciscan Order* (Oxford 1968).

MURRAY, A., 'Piety and Impiety in Thirteenth-Century Italy', in G. J. Cuming and Derek Baker, eds., *Popular Belief and Practice (Studies in Church History*, 8, Cambridge 1972).

—— 'Religion among the Poor in Thirteenth-Century France: the Testimony of Humbert de Romans', *Traditio*, 30 (1974), 285–324.

MUSSET, L., 'A-t-il existé en Normandie au xi<sup>e</sup> siècle une aristocratie d'argent?', *Annales de Normandie*, 9 (1959), 285–99.

NELLI, R., *L'Érotique des troubadours (Bibliothèque méridionale*, 2me séries, Vol. 38, Toulouse 1963).

PARÉ, G., BRUNET, A., and TREMBLAY, P., *La renaissance du xii<sup>e</sup> siècle: Les écoles et l'enseignement* (Paris–Ottawa 1933).

PLESNER, J., *L'émigration de la campagne à la ville libre de Florence au xiii<sup>e</sup> siècle* (Copenhagen 1934), 74–5.

PLUMMER: see BEDE (above, p. 417).

RABY, F. J. E., *A History of Secular Latin Poetry in the Middle Ages*, 2 vols. (Oxford 1957²).

RASHDALL, H., *The Universities of Europe in the Middle Ages*, new edn. ed. F. M. Powicke and A. B. Emden, 3 vols. (Oxford 1936).

ROOVER, de: see DE ROOVER.

RUNCIMAN, S., *A History of the Crusades*, 3 vols. (Cambridge 1951).
SAWYER, P., *The Age of the Vikings* (London 1971²).
SCHEVILL, F., *Medieval and Renaissance Florence* (New York 1961) ( = a revised edition of *A History of Florence*, New York 1936).
SCHMUGGE, L., *Johannes von Jandun (Pariser Historische Studien*, 5, Stuttgart 1966).
SCHREINER, K., *Sozial- und standesgeschichtliche Untersuchungen zu den Benediktinerkonventen im ostlichen Schwarzwald (Veröffentlichungen der Kommission für geschichtliche Landeskunde in Baden-Württemberg, Reihe B, Forschungen, 31. Band*, Stuttgart 1964).
SCHULTE, A., *Der Adel und die deutsche Kirche im Mittelalter: Studien zur Sozial-, Rechts- und Kirchegeschichte* (Darmstadt 1922²; r.p. Stuttgart 1958).
SMITH, D. E., *History of Mathematics*, 2 vols. (New York 1953).
—— and Karpinski, L. C., *The Hindu–Arabic Numerals* (Boston– London 1911).
SOUTHERN, R. W., *The Making of the Middle Ages* (London 1953).
THOMPSON, J. W., *The Literacy of the Laity in the Middle Ages* (University of California 1915; r.p. New York 1960).
THORNDIKE, L., *A History of Magic and Experimental Science*, II (New York 1923).
VAN LUYN, P., 'Les *milites* dans la France du xiᵉ siècle: examen des sources narratives', *Le Moyen Âge*, 77 (1971), 5–51, 193–258.
VAN STEENBERGHEN, F., *Aristotle in the West: The Origins of Latin Aristotelianism* (Louvain 1955).
—— *La Philosophie au xiiiᵉ siècle (Centre de Wulf-Mansion: Philosophes médiévaux*, 9, Louvain 1966).
VERLINDEN, C., *L'esclavage dans l'Europe médiévale*, I (no more published) (Bruges 1955).
VICAIRE, M. H., *Histoire de Saint Dominique*, 2 vols. (Paris 1957).
VIOLANTE, C., *La società milanese nell'età precomunale (Istituto italiano per gli studi storici in Napoli*, Bari 1953).
VON MARTIN, A., *Coluccio Salutati* (Leipzig/Berlin 1916).
WERNER, K. F., 'Untersuchungen zur Frühzeit des französischen Fürstentums (9.–10.Jh.)', *Die Welt als Geschichte* (Stuttgart) Part I: Vol. 18 (1958), 256–89; Part II: Vol. 19 (1959), 146–93; Part III: Vol. 20 (1960), 87–119.
WHITE, L., *Medieval Technology and Social Change* (Oxford 1962).
YUNCK, J. A., *The Lineage of Lady Meed (Publications in Mediaeval Studies*, 17, Notre Dame 1963).

# Notes

1. INTRODUCTION

1. D. J. de Solla Price, *Little Science, Big Science* (New York 1963), 8–14, 92–3.
2. I hope to deal more fully in a separate book with the main subject discussed in this section, viz. partial or total disbelief in miracle. The footnotes to this section point only to a few illustrative sources. Bibliographies to some of the older literature (before 1928) can be found through Coulton, *Five Centuries*, II, 70–6; Von Martin, *Coluccio Salutati*, 42–4; R. Limmer, *Bildungszustände und Bildungsideen des 13. Jhs.* (Munich 1928), 130–1.
3. Van Steenberghen, *Philosophie*, 394–400.
4. For two bold rationalists cf. L. Schmugge, *Joh. von Jandun*, and n. 8 below (Peter of Abano).
5. R. F. Seybolt, 'Fifteenth-Century editions of the *Legenda Aurea*', *Speculum*, 21 (1946), 327–8.
6. General survey: R. Aigrain, *L'hagiographie, ses sources, ses méthodes, son histoire* (Paris 1953).
7. R. C. Finucane, 'The Use and Abuse of Medieval Miracles', *History*, 60 (1975), 1–10, esp. p. 10; and Idem, *Miracles and Pilgrims* (London 1977), 73–4.
8. B. Nardi, *Saggi sull'aristotelismo padovano* (Padua 1958), 19–74, esp. pp. 22–3, 43 (on Peter of Abano, whose innocence is unproven); and cf. the grudging remark of Jean de Meung, 18439–40.
9. The kernel of the argument is in Augustine, *De vera religione*, xxv, 47 and *Retractationes*, I, 13, 7; and is developed by numerous medieval writers, e.g. Aelfric, *Sermones catholici*, *Sermo xxi*: In Ascensione Domini (ed. B. Thorpe, London 1844, I, pp. 304–5); Radulf Glaber, *Hist.* v, c. 1 (§10, p. 121).
10. These arguments are taken from Peter Damian, *De divina omnipotentia*, c. 11 (*PL* 145.611D–614C).
11. The raw material for this interpretation, though not the interpretation itself, can be found in R. C. van Caenegem, *The Birth of the English Common Law* (Cambridge 1973), 62–74; and in P. Brown, 'Society and the Supernatural: a Medieval Change', *Daedalus: Proceedings of the American Academy of Arts and Sciences*, 104 (1975) pp. 133–51.
12. See below pp. 200–1.
13. J. A. Weisheipl, *The Development of Physical Theory in the Middle Ages* (London 1959), 52, 55–7, 73, 84.
14. H. Günter, *Psychologie de la légende* (Paris 1954), 17–18; F. Graus, *Volk, Herrscher und Heiliger im Reich der Merowinger* (Prague 1965), 451–5.
15. *Chart. Univ. Par.* I, pp. 543–55 §§152, 174; cf. §§3, 48, 50, 56, 180, 190.
16. S. Guerchberg, 'The Controversy over the Alleged Sowers of the Black Death in the Contemporary Treatises on Plague', in S. Thrupp, ed., *Change in Medieval Society* (London 1965), 208–24.
17. A. Van Hove, *La doctrine du miracle chez St Thomas et son accord avec les principes de la recherche scientifique* (Louvain 1927).
18. H. de Lubac, *Surnaturel. Études historiques* (Paris 1946), 398.
19. William of Auvergne, *De fide*, c. 2 §4 (*Opera Omnia*, Venice 1591, 8F); repeated (without acknowledgement) by Bernardino of Siena, *Sermo* 27, a. 3, c. 4 (*Opera Omnia*, ed. J. Delahaye, Venice 1745, I, p. 122).

20. Franco Sacchetti, *Sposizione di Vangeli*, II (*Opere*, ed. A. Chiari, Bari 1936–8, I, p. 119, lines 3–7). Further examples in Murray, 'Piety and Impiety', 95–6.
21. *V.S. Norberti* (B), 824F.
22. Alexander of Ashby, quoted by R. W. Hunt, 'English Learning in the Late Twelfth Century', in R. W. Southern, ed., *Essays in Medieval History* (London 1968), 106–28; p. 115. Aquinas' treatment of the relationship of sin and error is discussed in detail by Lottin, *Psychologie et Morale*, III, 651–66.
23. e,g. H. Grundmann's treatment of Zanoni in the former's *Religiöse Bewegungen*, 157–69; cf. 520–4.
24. e.g. G. Koch, *Frauenfrage und Ketzertum im Mittelalter* (East Berlin 1962) : compare the insistence that heretics won allegiance among 'manual workers' and 'lower classes', with the contrary or inconclusive data in the notes, on pp. 71–2, 74, 83, 158, etc. On 'double' history : B. Croce, *History as the Story of Liberty* (London 1941), 22.
25. *Contra insulsam vulgi opinionem*, c. 1 (*PL* 104.147A).
26. Atto of Vercelli, *Epist.* 5 (*PL* 134.110B).
27. Ratherius of Verona, *De cont. can.*, c. 6 (*PL* 136.494BC).
28. *Hist.* III, 1 (§2, p. 52) ; IV, 6 (§18, p. 106) ; cf. III, 8 (§26, p. 74) ; IV, 5 (§2, p. 105) and (§14, p. 108).
29. Salimbene, 745.1–4.
30. Villani, VII, c. 155.
31. Alexander of Roes, *Noticia Seculi*, §19, p. 166.13–15.
32. Salimbene, 675.8–676.1.
33. e.g. *Chart. Univ. Par.* III, p. 24 §1218 (attachment to university sermons) ; p. 514 §1569 (to doctrine of Immaculate Conception of B.V.M.) ; Koch (as in n. 24) p. 45 n. 77; p. 65, p. 161 (for class-universality of some heresies) ; Humbert de Romans, *De modo prompte cudendi sermones*, II, c. 52, col. 539H (for class-universality of some convivial customs).
34. Salimbene, 866.24–8.
35. Stephen of Bourbon, *Anecdotes historiques*, ed. A. Lecoy de la Marche (Paris 1877), §229, p. 197.
36. Jean de Meung, 11157–70, 11177–88 (though it is true that in this, as in the last, example, the upper and clerical classes take the brunt of the criticism).
37. *B. Version*, Passus x.75–6 (ed. W. W. Skeat, Oxford 1886, I, p. 290).
38. *V.S. Geraldi Auril.*, 692C, 696B ; Thomas of Chantimpré, *Bonum universale de apibus*, II, i, 8 (edition of Douai 1605, p. 114) ; Frère Laurent, *Somme le Roi*, chapter on Avarice (edition by Bérard, Paris c. 1493, fo. 13v) ; *Annales S. Iustinae Patavini*, year 1260, *SS* 19, 179; Charny, 479c. See below, c. 16 pp. 399–402.
39. See Plate III (a).
40. *Mor. dogma philos.*, p. 77 (thirteenth-century prologue).
41. Stuttgart 1932, translation London 1941.
42. Leipzig–Berlin 1916.
43. London 1963.
44. Princeton 1966[2].
45. p. 419. Further comment on the passage: N. Rubinstein, 'Florentine Constitutionalism and Medici Ascendancy in the Fifteenth Century', in N. Rubinstein, ed., *Florentine Studies* (London 1968), 442–62 ; p. 447. A similar view is quoted from Buonaccorso by Baron, *Crisis of the Early Italian Renaissance*, 420–1 ; cf. 408. Cardinal D'Ailly meanwhile applied the concept to the church in *Tractatus de reformatione*, quoted by Lewis, *Later Medieval France*, 296. For the situation in earlier centuries see chapters 10 and 12 below.

2. MONEY

1. Ed. C. Johnson (*Medieval Texts*, London 1956, 4–5. C. Johnson's translation, compressed).
2. M. M. Postan, 'The Rise of a Money Economy', in E. M. Carus-Wilson, ed., *Essays in Economic History*, I (London 1954), 1–12.
3. For a theory of money not so tailor-made: G. Crowther, *An Outline of Money* (London 1948²), 1–21; and W. T. Newlyn, *Theory of Money* (Oxford 1962). The following section may also be compared and contrasted with K. Marx, *Capital*, Vol. I, part 1.
4. A warning against the inferring of commerce: P. Grierson, 'Commerce in the Dark Ages; a Critique of the Evidence', *Trans. Royal Hist. Soc.* (5th series, 1959), 123–40.
5. Doehaerd, *Haut moyen âge*, 226–7.
6. Latouche, *Birth of Western Economy*, 160–1.
7. A point stressed by C. Cipolla, 'Appunti per una nuova storia della moneta nell'alto medioevo', *Moneta e Scambi*, 619–25, esp. 623–4; and *illustrated* (if Professor Gieysztor's hypothesis is correct) by A. Gieysztor, 'Les structures économiques en pays slaves à l'aube du m.â. jusqu'au xiᵉ siècle et l'échange monétaire', *Moneta e Scambi*, 455–84, esp. 477–9.
8. Fournial, *Hist. monétaire*, 58 for the lower figure; Lopez, 'Aristocracy of Money', 17–19 for the higher.
9. Laws prescribing that the buyer of a horse etc. must know the vendor: Latouche, 162 (Charlemagne); *EHD* I.382, 399 (= Athelstan, Laws at Grately, §§10, 24; Edgar, Code at 'Wihtbordestan', §7).
10. Gieysztor, 482.
11. Against Fournial, 71, who repeats the axiom of a chronic early medieval 'disette de numéraire'. For a story of silver talents melted into ornaments see pp. 34–5 below.
12. Lopez, 'Aristocracy of Money', 17–18.
13. M. M. Postan, 'Economic Relations between Eastern and Western Europe', in G. Barraclough, ed., *Eastern and Western Europe in the Middle Ages* (London 1970), 125–74; p. 126.
14. Southern, *Making of the Middle Ages*, 41–2; quoted with approval by Grierson, 'Commerce in the Dark Ages' (as in n. 4), 126–7.
15. Local: Duby, *Soc. . . . mâconnaise*, 34 (51–2). Long-distance: Gieysztor, esp. 477–8.
16. J. Werner, 'Fernhandel und Naturalwirtschaft im östlichen Merowingerreich nach archäologischen und numismatischen Zeugnissen', *Moneta e Scambi*, 557–618, esp. 590–3. For England see note 101 below.
17. P. Grierson, 'Money and Coinage under Charlemagne', in H. Beumann, ed., *Karl der Grosse* (Dusseldorf 1965), I, 501–36; p. 501.
18. Cf. D. M. Metcalf, 'Analyses of the Metal Contents of Medieval Coins', in E. T. Hall and D. M. Metcalf, eds., *Methods of Chemical and Metallurgical Investigation of Ancient Coinage* (*Royal Numismatic Soc. Special Publications*, 8, London 1972), 383–434; pp. 406–7.
19. Duby, *Soc. . . . mâconnaise*, 33 (51), and Fournial, 71–2 (with other examples).
20. Lopez, 'Aristocracy of Money', 25.
21. Grierson, 'Money and Coinage', 535 (= St. Gallen, in the year 836).
22. Violante, *Soc. milanese*, 39 (= Farfa, in the year 799).
23. Ibid. 231–2; and the same author's 'Les prêts sur gage foncier dans la vie économique et sociale de Milan au xiᵉ siècle', *Cahiers de civilisation médiévale*, 5 (1962), 147–68, 437–59. Roman Law made the validity of a lease dependent on the payment of a money rent—a recipe for collusive make-believe; Doehaerd, 141.
24. e.g. Violante, *Soc. milanese*, 80; Duby, *Soc. . . . mâconnaise*, 312 (249).
25. P. Grierson, 'Le sou d'or d'Uzès', *Le Moyen Âge*, 60 (1954), 293–309.

430 *Notes, Chapter 2 Money*

26. Duby, *Soc. ... mâconnaise*, 357 (281).
27. Werner (as in n. 16), 590–4; Fournial, 71–2; further examples of the use of scales are mentioned by Professors Yanin and Valdeavellano in their contributions to *Moneta e Scambi*, 495, 228–9.
28. *Praeloquia*, I, c. 17 (*PL* 136.179A).
29. F. Vercauteren, 'Monnaie et circulation monétaire en Belgique et dans le Nord de la France du vi$^e$ au xi$^e$ siècle', *Moneta e Scambi*, 279–311; p. 299 n. 44bis (=act of Count Arnulf I, dated 928–34).
30. Doehaerd, 286.
31. *V.S. Maioli* (Cyrus), III, c. 4 (*PL* 137.767C); Radulf Glaber, *Hist.* I, c. 4 (§9, p. 11). Duby, *Soc. ... mâconnaise*, sees Cluny as even more moneyless than it was, through omission of Cyrus' account. Date (927): E. Sackur, *Die Cluniacenser* (Halle 1892–4), I, 228–9; cf. II, 337–41 (on Cyrus).
32. *V.S. Maioli* (Cyrus), III, c. 7 (col. 769B).
33. Radulf Glaber, *Hist.* IV, c. 7 (§22, p. 110).
34. H. Pirenne, *Mahomet et Charlemagne* (Paris 1937); A. F. Havighurst, ed., *The Pirenne Thesis* (Boston 1958) (a guide to the discussion). Homogeneity of the period stressed by Doehaerd, 348, 350–2.
35. Doehaerd, 284–7, 309; Vercauteren (as in n. 29), 285–6, 296, 310.
36. J. F. Verbruggen, 'L'armée et la stratégie de Charlemagne', in *Karl der Grosse* (as in n. 17), I, 420–36; pp. 435–6.
37. Doehaerd, 222, 226; G. Luzzatto, 'Economia naturale ed economia monetaria nell'alto medioevo', *Moneta e Scambi*, 15–32.
38. Latouche, 158–60, 240–4; Doehaerd, 260–3.
39. Latouche, 170–2; Doehaerd, 220–36.
40. Grierson, 'Money and Coinage', 535–6.
41. Fournial, 40–1; R. S. Lopez, 'Moneta e monetieri nell'Italia barbarica', *Moneta e Scambi*, 57–88; 71–4, 80; cf. 137–41; and 52–3, 149–52, 155, and 737 (remarks by various contributors). On the problem of wear: C. C. Patterson, 'Dwindling Stocks of Silver, and their relevance to studies of the metal contents of silver coinage', in Hall and Metcalf, *Methods of Chemical ... Investigation* (as in n. 18), 149–52.
42. Grierson, 'Money and Coinage', 535 (=Council of Frankfurt §5; *MGH Leges in folio*, I, p. 72.39–46); cf. Aachen capitularies, addenda for *missi* §18 (*MGH Leges in folio*, I, p. 213. 30–5); and Doehaerd, 312–13.
43. III Edgar 8; V Ethelred 26.1; Canute 8 (*EHD* I, 397, 408, 420).
44. Doehaerd, 211–13.
45. Latouche, 147; Professor Latouche's source, A. Blanchet, *Manuel de numismatique française*, I (Paris 1912), 337 gives no primary authority for his assertion that silver-mines were worked in Bohemia in Carolingian times.
46. *Vita Karoli*, §13 (*SS\**, Leipzig 1911, p. 16.11–12).
47. Grierson, 'Money and Coinage'; Doehaerd, 309–11.
48. Latouche, 172.
49. Lombard, *L'Islam*, 183.
50. Ibid. 10, 21, 23 (wheat); 23, 183 (linen); 84, 90, 164 (rice); 23, 29, 90, 167 (sugar); 90, 124, 167 (oranges); 44, 166–7 (dates).
51. Ibid. 121, 130.
52. The debate to 1955: F. J. Himly, 'Y-a-t-il emprise musulmane sur l'économie des états européens du viii$^e$ au x$^e$ siècles? Une discussion de temoignages', *Schweizerische Zeitschrift für Geschichte*, 5 (1955), 31–81. A more recent judgement: Doehaerd, 314–19. Both authors are sceptical of significant influence from Islam.
53. Industrial revolution: Lombard, *L'Islam*, 14, 27, 30, 35, 84, 90, 164 (irrigation and canals); 23–4, 67–9, 84 (ship-building); 47, 74, 124, 127 (building); these are in

addition to the new crops and manufactures already cited. Other factors in
demand and supply of slaves: ibid. 20, 27, 40, 60, 83, and esp. 194–7. For mines,
see below pp. 43, 47. The European slave trade for the Spanish market is described
by C. Verlinden, *L'esclavage dans l'Europe médiévale*, I (no more published) (Bruges
1955), 181–247; and for the Iranian market by S. Bolin, 'Mohammed,
Charlemagne and Rurik', *Scandinavian Economic Hist. Review*, 1 (1953), 5–39; pp.
26–33.

54. Ship-building and timber supply are the subjects of two papers by Maurice
Lombard now in his *Espaces et Réseaux*, 107–51, 153–76; summarised in *L'Islam*, as
in last note (for ship-building), and 25, 172–81 (timber). The European
abundance of timber is surveyed by C. Higounet, 'Les forêts de l'Europe
occidentale du vᵉ au xiᵉ siècle', in *Agricoltura e mondo rurale in occidente nell'alto
medioevo (Settimana di studio ... XIII, Spoleto 1966), 343–98.

55. Lombard, *L'Islam*, 178–81.

56. Lombard 'La chasse et les produits de la chasse dans le monde musulman: viiiᵉ–xiᵉ
siècles', now in his *Espaces et Réseaux*, 177–204.

57. Lombard, *L'Islam*, 231; P. H. Sawyer, *The Age of the Vikings* (London 1971²), 88–
90; Bolin (as in n. 53), 19–21.

58. Sawyer, 181–2.

59. Ibid. 194.

60. Verlinden, 211–13.

61. That the northern trade was conducted by Rus, Rhadanite Jews etc., not by
Muslims, is the uniform impression given by Arab travellers' descriptions,
assembled by R. Hennig, 'Der nordeuropäische Pelzhandel in den älteren
Perioden der Geschichte', *Vierteljahrschrift für Sozial- und Wirtschaftsgesch.* 23
(1930), 1–25; pp. 14–20; cf. Bolin (as in n. 53), 23, 34.

62. Bolin, 25–6.

63. Sawyer, 87–8.

64. Gieysztor, 474–6, 480.

65. Argued ibid. 477–9.

66. V. L. Yanin, 'Les problemes généraux de l'échange monétaire russe aux ixᵉ–xiiᵉ
siècles', *Moneta e Scambi*, 485–505; 486–7; Sawyer, *Vikings*, 108–16.

67. Doehaerd, 288; Verlinden (as in n. 53), 219.

68. Gieysztor, 458–9.

69. See below, p. 52.

70. Sawyer, *Vikings*, 188–9.

71. Cf. the poem introducing Bk. II of Thietmar of Merseburg's chronicle (p. 37.34).

72. Ibid., Bks. I and II *passim: pecunia, praedia, premia, exuviae, tributum*, etc. e.g. Miesko
of Poland's *tributum*, Bk. II, c. 29 (p. 75.29–30).

73. Cf. D. M. Metcalf (as in n. 18); and, more particularly, in the same volume,
H. McKerrell and R. B. K. Stevenson, 'Some Analysis of Anglo-Saxon and
Associated Oriental Silver Coinage', pp. 195–209.

74. Lombard, *L'Islam*, 57–71, 123 (delay in west); 55, 85, 213 (refugees).

75. Ibid. 88–90; 144–6; 141 and 237.

76. Ibid. 118, 142–6; 23 and 138.

77. Bolin, 14–19.

78. Lombard, *L'Islam*, 116–17.

79. Bolin, 36–9; Yanin (as in n. 66), 494–8; Gieysztor, 476–7; Sawyer, *Vikings*, 107–
18.

80. Bolin, 22.

81. Lombard, 'L'or musulman du viiᵉ au xiᵉ siècle. Les bases monétaires d'une
suprématie économique', now in his *Espaces et réseaux*, 7–29.

82. D. Obolensky, *The Byzantine Commonwealth* (London 1971), 71.
83. Violante, *Soc. milanese*, 38–40; Lombard, 'L'or musulman', 27–8.
84. Violante, *Soc. milanese*, 31, n. 125; approved by Doehaerd, 318.
85. Boshof, *Agobard*, 109–12; Verlinden, 216–18.
86. Verlinden, 218–24; Lombard, *L'Islam*, 197–9.
87. Venice: Verlinden, 222; Violante, 31–4. 'Sclavus': Violante, 31 n. 125.
88. Fournial, 73–7. But Dr. Fournial's general conclusion is the opposite to mine.
89. e.g. *Mir. S. Fidis*, 239 (*aureos denarios*); also 22, 58, 239, 247, 263 (*aurei*); 133 (*manco*); 207, 240 (*bizantis, -us*); *V.S. Romualdi*, 990C (*aureum*); *V.S. Hugonis Clun.* (Hildebert), 863B, 882D (*aureos*).
90. A point stressed by D. M. Metcalf, 'How large was the Anglo-Saxon currency?', *Economic Hist. Review*, 18 (1965), 475–82; pp. 475–6.
91. Verlinden, 214.
92. Lombard, *L'Islam*, 194.
93. Ibid. Cf. Verlinden, 218.
94. Doehaerd, 280.
95. Verlinden, 212–14.
96. Lombard, 'L'or musulman', 155.
97. The pattern of Otto I's relationships with the East and with Italy are described in two papers in the *Festschrift der Jahrtausendfeier der Kaiserkrönung Ottos des Grossen* (*Mitt. des osterreichischen Inst. für Geschichtsforschung, Ergänzungsband 20*, Graz-Cologne 1962), pt. I: E. Dupré Theseider, 'Otto I und Italien', pp. 53–69, and H. F. Schmid, 'Otto I und der Osten', pp. 70–106. The languages and Slavonic mistress: Schmid, 78–80. The origin of Otto's family and its struggle with Mainz are recounted by Thietmar of Merseburg, *Chronicon*, Bk. I, esp. pp. 8–12. Bk. II indicates the eastern origin of part of Otto's wealth: pp. 37.32, 74, 29–30 and 76.30; cf. pp. 56.13 and 82.9–10 (Byzantium); p. 48.13 (Magyars), and 37.34 (Danes); as also the southern origin of another part; pp. 56.7–8; 58.14. D. Claude, *Gesch. des Erzbistums Magdeburg bis in das 12. Jh.* I (*Mitteldeutsche Forschungen, Band 67/I*, Cologne–Vienna 1972), besides giving further indications of the local flow of money (esp. pp. 52, 55), describes the protest from Mainz about the power of the emperor's money (pp. 66–8). The use of 'money-fiefs or something very like them' for military purposes is described by K. Leyser, 'Henry I and the beginnings of the Saxon Empire', *English Hist. Review*, 83 (1968), 1–32; p. 14.
98. Cf. Liutprand of Cremona, *Antapodosis*, v, c. 13, in J. Becker, ed., *Liudprandi Opera*, (SS* 41, 1915), pp. 136.25–137.3: [in 942] 'Rex Hugo ... nuntios suos regi Ottoni dirigit ... auri argentique copiam ... promittens. Quibus rex ... "gazas a se mihi promissas non solum non suscipio, verum meam illi libentissime tribuo ..."'.
99. Latouche, 255.
100. Discovery of Rammelsberg: Sigebert of Gembloux, *Chronica* (year 968), ed. L. C. Bethmann (*SS* 6, Hanover 1844), p. 351.22–3: '... industria sua ...'. For other traditions see editor's note to Widukind, *Rerum gestarum Saxonicarum*, III, c. 63 (SS*, Hanover 1935, p. 138 n. 2).
101. P. Grierson, 'La fonction sociale de la monnaie en Angleterre aux vii^e–viii^e siècles', *Moneta e Scambi*, 341–62.
102. Mints: R. H. M. Dolley and D. M. Metcalf, 'The Reform of the English Coinage under Eadgar', in R. H. M. Dolley, ed., *Anglo-Saxon Coins* (London 1961), 136–68, esp. 147. Few hoards: Sawyer, *Vikings*, 98. Legislative evidence: the same author's 'The Wealth of England in the Eleventh Century', *Trans. Royal Hist. Soc.* 15 (1965), 145–64, esp. pp. 148–9, and cf. n. 43 above. Analysis: D. M. Metcalf (as in n. 18), 413–18 (inconclusive); 409–10 (Rammelsberg provenance possible).
103. Vercauteren (as in n. 29), 308.
104. Gieysztor, 476; Sawyer, *Vikings*, 116.

105. e.g. in J. Bernard's contribution to C. M. Cipolla, ed., *Fontana Economic History of Europe, I: The Middle Ages* (London 1972), 274; and Latouche, 174.
106. Verlinden, 218–21.
107. Doehaerd, 91–3 (press-gangs); 93, 185 (bans on export); cf. 189, Index ('Esclaves'), and 254–8, 280, 285, 290 (internal European slave-trade).
108. L. White, *Medieval Technology and Social Change* (Oxford 1962), 80–4, 110.
109. R. S. Lopez, 'Aux origines du capitalisme gênois', *Annales d'hist. économique et sociale*, 9 (1937), 429–54; pp. 445–51.
110. Cf. Peter Damian, *Contra philargyriam*, vi (*PL* 145.538D); and Otto of Freising, *Chronica*, VII, c. 23 (p. 347.5–6).
111. G. Duby, 'Le budget de l'abbaye de Cluny entre 1080 et 1155', in his *Hommes et structures*, 61–82; p. 67. Cf. *Mir. S. Fidis*, 183b (share of Saracen spoil to Conques); 53c, and 14n (sharp rise in gifts after 982), 54bc (mostly gold); etc. Islamic wealth recurs as a 'marvel' motif in the Chansons de Gestes; A. Dickman, *Le surnaturel dans les Chansons de Gestes* (Paris 1926), 84, 92–4, 100.
112. An attempt to explain it has been made by D. Herlihy, 'The Agrarian Revolution in Southern France and Italy, 801–1150', *Speculum*, 33 (1958), 23–41.
113. P. Schmid, 'Die Entstehung des Marseiller Kirchenstaats', *Archiv für Urkundenforschung*, 10 (1928), 176–207: p. 176 (monastery a ruin *c.* 1000 largely through Saracen raids); pp. 87–206 (ruled *c.* 140 monasteries and cells in 24 dioceses *c.* 1079).
114. Musset, 'Aristocratie d'Argent', 286.
115. Ibid. 287.
116. Latouche, 257.
117. Duby, *Soc. ... mâconnaise*, 332–6 (263–6).
118. Violante, *Soc. milanese*, 42; Du Cange, *Glossarium*, VI, p. 239 (for second example, dated 752). Ibid. for numerous further examples.
119. The distribution of examples in the standard large dictionaries gives some idea of the development. For the German word, see R. Ris, *Das Adjektiv reich im mittelalterlichen Deutsch: Geschichte, semantische Struktur, Stilistik (Quellen und Forschungen, Neue Folge*, 40, Berlin 1971). In all cases the two meanings run side by side for centuries longer in the case of *pecunia* and *feoh*.

3. AVARICE

1. See n. 87 below.
2. Building: Duby, *Soc. ... mâconnaise*, 353–5 (278–80); travel: ibid. 350, 363 (276, 283–4); more generally ibid. 348–63 (275–86).
3. J. Huizinga, *The Waning of the Middle Ages* (London 1924), 18–20; M. W. Bloomfield, *The Seven Deadly Sins* (Michigan 1952), esp. 95; L. K. Little, 'Pride Goes Before Avarice: Social Change and the Vices in Latin Christendom', *American Historical Review*, 76 (1971), 16–49. My quarrels with Professor Little's illuminating and well-documented article are (1) his confusion of the question of a sin's psychological primacy with that of its social prevalence (see n. 62 below); and (2) the relative cursoriness of his study of tenth-century evidence (see pp. 77–9 below). On the subsidiary matter of simony see n. 8 below. For my debts to Professor Little see especially pp. 79–80 below.
4. A. Murray, 'Money and Robbers, 900–1100', *Journal of Medieval History*, 4 (1978), pp. 55–94.
5. Ibid., pp. 59–63.
6. Ibid., pp. 68–83.
7. Ibid., pp. 83–9.
8. Gregory's multiple definition: *Hom. in Evang.* I, c. 4 (*PL* 76. 1091–2); adopted or echoed by eleventh-century theologians: cf. A. Dresdner, *Kultur- und Sittengesch. der*

*italienischen Geistlichkeit im 10. und 11. Jh.* (Breslau 1890), 34, 36; Gregory's definition would be put in Gratian's *Decretum*, I, q. 1, c. 114 (Friedberg, 402–3). Unlike Professor Little (p. 21) I regard the repetition of Gregory's definition as largely a formality, belied by usage.

9. Dresdner, 61, 59; other examples ibid. 48, 59–61, 63, 65, 69.
10. Dresdner, 32, and Sextus Amarcius, *Sermones*, I, 35 (for 'chests'); Dresdner, 64, 61 (*monetarii, pretium*). For close association of simony with *pecunia* see also Dresdner, 34–5 (*pretium, pecunias*), 67 (*a negotiatoribus ad vendendum*). Other texts pointing the same way include: Humbert of Silva Candida, *Adv. Simoniacos*, II, c. 17 (pp. 158–9: simonists are closely compared with *negotiatores*); and John of Salisbury, *Policraticus*, VII, c. 17 (Vol. II, p. 163, lines 5–23, esp. lines 10–15: among ways of entering office, that *Simone ducente* is exclusively linked with *divitiae* and *pecuniae*). Groundwork and further references in J. Leclercq, 'Simoniaca heresis' (*Studi Gregoriani*, I, Rome 1947), 523–30. The question of the monetary character of simony deserves fuller treatment.
11. For the following: C. Violante, 'I vescovi dell'Italia centro-settentrionale e lo sviluppo dell'economia monetaria', in the same author's collected *Studi sulla Cristianità Medioevale* (Milan 1972), 325–47, esp. 334–44.
12. Dresdner, 48–9.
13. Ibid. (three instances; the oblique reference quoted by Dresdner on p. 32 should be added). Simony and avarice are conspicuously absent in certain passages where Ratherius criticizes the clergy, e.g. *PL* 136.506B–7A, 409B, 417C, 419C, 697D, 717CD. Migne's editors found 'mulierositas' the 'maximus ... abusus ... clericorum' of Ratherius' milieu, ibid., col. 102C.
14. *Hist.* II, c. 6 (§10 p. 37) and V, c. 5 (§25 p. 134).
15. *Adv. Simoniacos*, III, c. 21 (p. 225.4–6).
16. Dresdner, 68–72.
17. *Adv. Simoniacos*, III, c. 7 (p. 206.6–15).
18. *V.S. Joh. Gualb.* (Atto), c. 1 (*PL* 146.671D); cf. c. 37 (col. 683C): 'eodem tempore, quo Simoniaca haeresis per Tusciam pullulabat' (referring to mid-century).
19. *Hist.* V, c. 5 (§26 pp. 134–5).
20. C. Erdmann, 'Endkaiserglaube und Kreuzzugsgedanke im elften Jh.' *Zeitschrift für Kirchengesch.*, 51 (1932), 384–414; p. 397 (quotation); pp. 394–5 and 401–2 (dating). The words about selling consecrations ('et vendent suas sacrationes ...') were additions of 1084–6 to a sibylline text of 1002–39: that addition itself teaches a lesson.
21. Cf. Dresdner, 32–3.
22. 'Bertold', *Chronica* (*SS* 5, p. 274).
23. *Annales*, 132.29–133.11.
24. Ibid. 241.2–4.
25. *Reg.* I, 35 (p. 56.14 and .19–20).
26. *Sermones*, I, i (pp. 51–3) and III, vii, lines 882–911 (pp. 173–5).
27. Duby, *Soc. ... mâconnaise*, 30 (49).
28. Lea Dasberg, *Untersuchungen über die Entwertung des Judenstatus im 11. Jh.* (*École pratique des hautes études, Sorbonne, VIᵉ Section: Etudes Juives*, 11, Paris 1965).
29. S. Runciman, *A History of the Crusades*, I (Cambridge 1951), 135.
30. Dasberg, 91–100.
31. Dasberg, 101–11.
32. Dasberg, 50–72 (alliance with king); 138–42 (royal promotions to episcopate); 115–73 (Gregorian–Cluniac scheme).
33. *Hist.* III, c. 6 (pp. 68–71).
34. *Sermones*, I, ii, lines 84–8 (p. 55) (bias in execution of law); III, vii, lines 882 (p. 173) and 887 (p. 174) (bishops). Pogrom in Speyer: Runciman, I, 137–41. It is Sextus

Amarcius' remarks on Jews which strongly suggest the poem was written *before* the pogrom. (I have argued both for this dating, and for the topicality of Sextus Amarcius' poem, in *Erasmus*, 28 (1976), 110–14.)

35. Runciman, I, 137. The simonistic relation of bishop and king would obtain for each of the last three bishops of Speyer in the eleventh century: J. Fleckenstein, 'Heinrich IV und der deutsche Episkopat', *Adel und Kirche* (= Fs. G. Tellenbach) (Freiburg 1968), 221–36; p. 228; Gregory VII, *Reg.* v, 18 (p. 381); so is unaffected by the dating of Sextus Amarcius' poem.

36. *Epist.* iv, 36 (*PL* 189.366–8); 'Sarracensis deteriores' (col. 367A); the opposite view from Alexander II: Runciman, I, 135; and cf. *Mir. S. Fidis*, 247–8.

37. Duby, *Soc.* . . . *mâconnaise*, 486 (369), and idem, 'Le budget de l'abbaye de Cluny entre 1080 et 1155: Économie domaniale et économie monétaire', in the same author's *Hommes et Structures* (Paris 1973), 61–82; pawning of gold etc. from sacristy to Mâcon Jews: p. 76.

38. Bernard of Clairvaux, *Epist.* 163 (*PL* 182.567C); quoted with further examples by L. K. Little, The Function of the Jews in the Commercial Revolution', *Povertà e Ricchezza nella spiritualità dei secoli xi e xii* (*Convegni del Centro di Studi sulla spiritualità mediovale*, 8, Todi 1969), 273–87; p. 284.

39. R. M. Thomson, ed., *Tractatus Garsiae* (*Textus Minores*, 46, Leiden 1973), 18.72–82; 20.116–22.120; 20.131–4; 28.232–6.

40. P. Kehr, 'Das Papsttum und die Königreiche von Aragon und Kastille', *Abhandlungen der preussischen Akademie der Wissenschaften, Phil.-hist. Klasse* (1928), 27–36; p. 35; and more generally J. F. Rivera Recio, *La iglesia de Toledo en el siglo xii*, I (Rome 1966), 133–51, 375–8.

41. J. A. Yunck, *The Lineage of Lady Meed* (*Publications in Mediaeval Studies*, 17, Notre Dame 1963), 31–40 (the emergence of the satire in the eleventh century). F. J. E. Raby, *A History of Secular Latin Poetry in the Middle Ages* (Oxford 1957²), I, 317–37 (Hildebert and Marbod).

42. Poem 38 (*PL* 171.1727B–D): 'Princeps, praelatus, monachi, populique senatus, / Clericus et miles, mulier, sexusque viriles, / Nummo laetantur, jussisque suis famulantur. / Omnis ei plaudit. Si quid jubet impiger audit. / Quod placet impletur, quod displicet hoc prohibetur. / Cum nummus loquitur, cunctorum vox sepelitur.' Cf. Poem 39 (cols. 1728A–C).

43. L. van Acker, ed., *Petri Pictoris Carmina* (*Corpus Christianorum, Continuatio Mediaevalis*, 25, Turnholt 1972), *Carmen* 13 (pp. 101–2) lines 27–30: 'Ad dominam pulchram veniat formosus adulter, / Si nichil attulerit, pellitur a thalamo; / Introeat turpis, nummo comitante beato: / Invenit absque mora cuncta parata sibi.'

44. Ibid. (p. 102), lines 39–44: 'Divitis ad clausam portam si tristis egenus / Pulsat, amore Dei non aperitur ei; / At si denarius pulsaverit, huic aperitur, / Exclusoque Deo clauditur ille domo. / Hospite de tali iocundior est domus omnis, / Hoc quicumque caret hospite vilis erit.'

45. Yunck, 206–7, 211–15, 279, 282.

46. See below, pp. 222–3.

47. Walter Map, *De nugis curialium*, ii, c. 17; ed. T. Wright (Camden Society, London 1850), 87. Cf. Yunck, 93, 109.

48. p. 93; on the lack of living money-satire before about 1100 cf. pp. 31–40.

49. p. 322.

50. *Fecunda ratis*, ed. E. Voigt (Halle 1889), lines 1601–2 (p. 198): 'Hinc indefensam pepulit cum vecte Sophiam, / Precipitem trudens, moribundam ad rudera stravit.' Quoted by Yunck, 62–3.

51. *Carmina* (as in n. 43), *Carmen* 3 (p. 49).

52. Yunck, 181; for the social context of this hurt self-interest compare pp. 303–12 below.

53. P. Lehmann, *Die Parodie im Mittelalter* (Stuttgart 1963²), 74–5, 83.
54. Ibid. 261 (*Geldevangelium*); 183–8, 251–2.
55. Ibid. 190–202 ('Passions' and 'Catechisms'); 257 ('Book of the Generation of Jesus Christ').
56. Yunck, 175, 255–6, 279 and n. 86, 308 and nn. 13 and 14.
57. Yunck, 207, etc.
58. See below, pp. 81–2.
59. The main theme of *Tractatus Garsiae* (n. 39 above); and cf. Yunck, 256 (John Bromyard's *Crux*).
60. (As in n. 43), lines 32–8: 'Et tenet imperium cum Iove denarius. / Factus uterque deus magno veneratur ab orbe, / Plus tamen alter agit, cum sit uterque deus. / Nam quod nec tonitrus nec fulmina flectere possunt, / Flectit denarius et facit esse suum. / Iupiter offensus non omnes vindicat iras, / Offensas nummus vindicat innumeras.'
61. See n. 3 above.
62. Against Little, 'Pride Goes Before Avarice', 39 ('a change in the notion of chief vice, then, clearly took place'); and even against the more cautious Bloomfield (p. 95) who stresses the inconclusiveness of the evidence. But is the evidence really so inconclusive, when not only Aquinas (Bloomfield, 87–8), but apparently *all* the penitential theologians of the thirteenth century (Bloomfield, 123–32) upheld the hegemony of pride, established by Gregory the Great? It may be remarked that of the two thirteenth-century writers whom Bloomfield adduces as breaking the rule, one was a canonist (Henry of Ostia: Bloomfield, 82) and the other in effect a popular writer (Latini, see below, p. 123: Bloomfield, 90). Professor Little's most cogent document for the primacy of avarice is similarly didactic: visual art (see below, pp. 79–80), i.e. the exceptions occur in what can be termed applied (as against pure) psychology.

Dante was a model of clear-headedness in keeping the psychological and social questions distinct. He found more people in hell for avarice than for any other sin (*Inferno*, VII, 25), yet allowed that fact to interfere in not the slightest degree with the psychological scheme which framed his poem.

63. *Adv. Simoniacos*, III, c. 29 (p. 235.43); c. 33 (pp. 241–3); c. 37 (p. 245.28–32). Humbert echoes Jer. 6:13 (see below, p. 79 at n. 81) in III, c. 5 (p. 204.45).
64. *PL* 145.529–44, cf. cols. 455–64, 463–72; N.B. passages at 455C, 463B, and tell-tale biblical quotations at 531D and 532B (the latter being Jer. 6:13, on which see below, p. 79 at n. 81).
65. *Reg.*, 647 (= Index at Philippians 2:21 (six references)); also for Hildebert of Tours, cf. *De nummo* (*PL* 171.1402C). Gregory VII nowhere quotes Jer. 6:13.
66. Cf. Little, 'Pride Goes Before Avarice', 20–22.
67. Odo of Cluny, *Collat.*, II, 3 (col. 550D).
68. e.g. Ratherius, *Praeloquia*, I, 5 (col. 160: greed of merchants); and Atto of Vercelli, *Expos. in epist. Pauli*, Col. 3:5 (*PL* 134.631D–2A: avarice and idolatry as the worst sins: a theme occasioned by the text).
69. The works are: Odo, *Collationes* (*PL* 133.517–638), *V.S. Geraldi* (ibid. 639–704); Atto, *Epistolae* (*PL* 134.95–123), *Expositio in epistolas Pauli* (ibid. 125–834), *Sermones* (ibid. 833–60); Ratherius, *De contemptu canonum* (*PL* 136.485–522), *Sermones*, (ibid. 689–732); (Ratherius' *Praeloquia* (ibid. 146–344) have been used for positive but not negative evidence).
70. Odo: *PL* 133.539CD, 540D, 544AB, (549C), 553C, 660B, 688D, 690A, etc.; as 'idolatry' (cf. Col. 3:5) 562C, 590A, 609A; 'Mammon' 580B; hope in *pecunia* 670B; simony 574A, 590D ff.; avarice as one of current evils 539CD, 550C, 550D–551A, 565D ff.

Atto: *PL* 134.117C, 336C, 340C, 685A ff. (as *radix omnium malorum*), 826D–7A, 834A, cf. 841C (*lucrum*); and see n. 68 above.

Ratherius: *PL* 136.698D, 716C, 712B; for Ratherius' relative silence on simony see n. 13 above.
71. Doubtful cases are that from Atto quoted in n. 68 (under St. Paul's influence); and Odo, *V.S. Geraldi*, II, 34 (*PL* 133.690A), where avarice might be read as on a par with lust and pride, among sins it was Gerald's triumph to have conquered.
72. *Sermo* 39 (*PL* 136.712B).
73. *De cont. can.* §10 (*PL* 136.499A).
74. *Sermo* 3 (*PL* 134.837CD). For a gauge of Atto's priorities cf. *Epist.* 9 (*PL* 134.115D–9B): priests' usury and avarice are in one place denounced (col. 117B), but the letter's bias gives priority to incontinence, in one place explicitly (col. 116A).
75. *Collat.* I, 11 (*PL* 133.528A).
76. *Collat.* II, 33 (ibid. 578A). Note the absence of avarice (or simony) also at cols. 531B, 543C, 554A; its humble place at 584B; blame for prodigality at 548BC, 549CD, 613D; and the brevity of the section on monastic poverty at 583AB.
77. *PL* 134.684AB.
78. *De cont. can.* §4 (*PL* 136.591B–D).
79. *Collat.* III, 22 (*PL* 133.606D).
80. Ibid. c. 32 (col. 615D: Simon Magus, appearing for the only time in *Collat.*, is made the occasion for an admonition to repent—since even *he* was urged to repent; with no word here on simony); ibid. II, 35 (col. 543D: 'cogitationes divitum' in Job 12:5); ibid. II, 38 (col. 545A: 'calix aureus Babylon' in Jer. 51:7).
81. *Collat.* II, 42 (col. 588B: apparently compounding Isa. 56:11 with Jer. 6:13: the compound has the effect of limiting the force of the latter text to the clergy). Cf. nn. 63 and 64 above, n. 86 below, and Murray, 'Piety and Impiety', 90.
82. Little, 'Pride Goes Before Avarice', 24–5.
83. The respective sets of figures reached by Professor Little (who insists on their approximate character) are: Pride: 5, 5, 5, 20, 20; Avarice: 1, 2, 10, 28, 30.
84. *Hist.* II, c. 6 (§10 p. 37).
85. Duby, *Soc. ... mâconnaise*, 335 n. 1 (266 n. 13).
86. *V.S. Hugonis Grat.*, c. 5 (*PL* 153.776BC: quoting Jer. 6:13 in full).
87. Sextus Amarcius, *Sermones*, I, i, heading (p. 51) '... de virtutibus patrum et posteriorum viciis' (the theme of the whole poem); Hildebert, *De nummo* (*PL* 171.1403C): 'Servit avaritiae sed *in hoc aevo* scelus omne'.
88. *De quarta vigilia noctis* (*MGH LL* 3, 505–25); P. Classen, *Gerhoch von Reichersberg (1093–1169)* (Wiesbaden 1960), 292–8, 426–7, and esp. 295. Quoted by Little, 'Pride Goes Before Avarice', 22–3.

4. AMBITION

1. *Epist.* I, vi, 37.
2. *Carmina misc.*, 50 (*PL* 171.1404C).
3. *De dominus vobiscum*, line 56 (p. 51).
4. Poem 38 (*PL* 171.1727B): 'mutat honores'.
5. Line 2 (*Latin Poems*, 223).
6. Yunck, 274 f., 215 f.; for thirteenth-century examples cf. pp. 15, 213.
7. Yunck, 256, and 257 n. 44; for age of material, G. R. Owst, *Literature and Pulpit in Medieval England* (Oxford 1966²), 224.
8. Cf. R. Lennard, *Rural England 1086–1135* (Oxford 1959), 392 n. 1; Violante, *Soc. milanese*, 159; Duby, *Soc. ... mâconnaise*, 359 f. (282), but compare 337 (267) for peasant traders; for the remarkable case of 'Stabilis' in Andreas of Fleury, *Mir. S. Benedicti*, VI, 2, cf. Van Luyn, 228–9 and Coulton, *Five Centuries*, I, 239; *Mir. S. Fidis*, 63. In the last case the loss was miraculous. The bias of sources of course leans

heavily towards the inclusion of serfs, etc. who got caught. For a redress of the balance, see next note.

9. Peasant-pioneers: Violante, *Soc. milanese*, 78–84; Duby, *Soc. ... mâconnaise*, 13, 302–4 (35–6, 242–4); Bosl, 'Soziale Mobilität', 176 etc. Smiths: Fossier, *Picardie*, 370–7, and index under *Fèvre*; for the grandson of an early blacksmith achieving nobility, Plesner, *Émigration ... à ... Florence*, 74–5; and for a tale which may have a similar reality behind it, Hyde, *Padua*, 72. Millers: Fossier, *Picardie*, 387– 9, and index under *Meunier*. The precocity of these particular smiths and millers is clear from the more general picture of village artisans in Duby, *Rural Economy*, 154; there, the artisans' emergence as business men on their own account is associated mainly with the thirteenth and later centuries. But it is inconceivable that all lords should have kept an equally strict grip on their technical staff.

10. Violante, *Soc. milanese*, 49–70; Duby, *Soc. ... mâconnaise*, 407–8 (314–15) (swift turnover among the *meliores et ditiores* burghers until the end of the twelfth century); cf. Langlois, *Vie*, 66 (quoting *La Bible Guiot*, written *c.* 1205–9: heirs of usurers invariably fall after second or third generation).

11. Violante, *Soc. milanese*, 64, quoting Landulf Senior, *Hist. Mediolanensis*, II, c. 32 (on Aribert).

12. Petrus Pictor, *De denario*, lines 5–18 (p. 101).

13. *Germania*, 44, 2; cf. E. A. Thompson, *The Early Germans* (Oxford 1965), 10.

14. Pages 120–1 below. The circle drawn on p. 84 is described on p. 126.8–15 of the Latin text, and pp. 226–7 of the translation of the Arabic. See Plate II and legend.

15. *De nugis*, I, c. 1, pp. 1–2. I have compressed in translation.

16. Bosl, 'Soziale Mobilität', 161–5; I have added 'vassal' from F. L. Ganshof, *Feudalism* (London 1964³), 5, and 'Ritter' from Van Luyn, 5–6.

17. A. L. Poole, *Obligations of Society in the Twelfth and Thirteenth Centuries* (Oxford 1946), 66; and 57–76 *passim*.

18. R. S. Lopez, 'Aux origines du capitalisme génois', *Annales d'hist. économique et sociale*, 9 (1937), 429–52; p. 438.

19. Duby, *Soc. ... mâconnaise*, 381–96 (297–307); 516 (390), 582 (436–7); (the burghers) 409 (316).

20. Magnou-Nortier, 242–52.

21. Musset, 'Aristocratie d'argent'.

22. *EHD* I, 432 § 2; § 6 gives the exception, the overseas merchant: because he was too often away to qualify for a seat in the king's hall?

23. Bosl, 'Soziale Mobilität', 158–69, and literature cited.

24. Lopez, 'Aristocracy of Money', esp. 36–40.

25. Atto of Vercelli, *Epist.* 9 (*c.* 950?) (*PL* 134.116D–117B); Violante, *Soc. milanese*, 161.

26. Violante, *Soc. milanese*, 143.

27. *Adv. Simoniacos*, III, c. 20 (p. 224.40–2).

28. Ibid., lines 43–9. For the meaning of words: J. D. A. Ogilvy, 'Mimi, scurrae, histriones', *Speculum*, 38 (1963), 603–19; and (for *gnatonicus*) Webb's note to John of Salisbury, *Policraticus*, Vol. II, p. 80. In *Adv. Simoniacos*, III, c. 23 (p. 224.11–12) Humbert sees the promotion of noblemen to church office as the creditable exception; while earlier, in II, c. 34 (p. 183, 15–22) he has argued that nobles who *are* simonists can at least plead they are using their own money, not wasting that of the church (cf. p. 323 below for polemic on this).

29. *Adv. Simoniacos*, III, c. 40 (p. 248.32–4): '... mediocris potentiae laicos ...'.

30. *Contra clericos aulicos* (*PL* 145.463B).

31. Ibid. (*col.* 464B). Peter echoes here, without naming it, a decretal of Celestine I, *Epist.* 2, c. 4, cf. Friedburg, I, 231. Humbert also quoted the text as of topical interest in *Adv. Simoniacos*, III, c. 5 (p. 204.31–45).

32. 'Bertold', *Annales*, year 1069 (*SS* 5, 274). Cf. J. Fleckenstein, 'Heinrich IV. und der deutsche Episkopat in den Anfängen des Investiturstreites', *Adel und Kirche*, 221–6 for the background.

33. Letter to Anti-king Hermann (1082–5) (*MGH BDK* 5, 42.27–9): 'vel vana considerabatur nobilitas vel divitiarum irrempebat copiositas'.

34. *Sermones*, I, lines 32–9 (p. 52).

35. Ibid. III, lines 882–7 (pp. 173–4): '... (line 883) plerumque rudes sublimant et viciosos / Ordinibus, stulte vitantes quęrere, num sit / Servus, quem sacrant, aut liber, sobrius aut non ...'.

36. Cf. Fleckenstein (as in n. 32).

37. For genealogies and their problems: Duby, 'Litt. généalogique'; cf. Duby, 'Noblesse'; and K. Hauck, 'Haus- und Sippengebundene Literatur mittelalterlicher Adelsgeschlechter, von Adelssatiren des 11. und 12. Jhs. aus erläutert', *Mitt. des österreichischen Inst. für Geschichtsforschung*, 62 (1954), 121–45.

38. Almost the whole of what follows is based on K. F. Werner, 'Untersuchungen zur Frühzeit des französischen Furstentums (9.–10.Jh.)', *Die Welt als Geschichte*, Vols. 18–20 (Stuttgart 1958–60). I shall quote this below according to the three separate 'Parts', not the sections with Roman numerals in the article. For the modern historiography, Part III (Vol. 20), 118–19; for a more recent instance: R. S. Lopez, *La Naissance de l'Europe* (Paris 1962), 156. For the origin of the house of Blois and of some smaller neighbouring dynasties, see also J. Boussard, 'L'origine des familles seigneuriales dans la région de la Loire moyenne', *Cahiers de civilisation médiévale*, 5 (1962), 303–22; and for that of the house of Guisnes, Duby, 'Structures de parenté et noblesse dans la France du Nord aux xi^e et xii^e siècles', *Hommes et Structures*, 267–85. An admirable guide to the sources and general physiognomy of the subject is now J. Martindale, 'The French Aristocracy in the Early Middle Ages', *Past and Present*, 75 (May 1977), 5–45. (This article appeared after this chapter was written, though without making me wish to revise my views).

39. Werner, Part III (Vol. 20), 116–18; Boussard, 308–9; Duby, 'Structures', 280.

40. Ibid., Part I (Vol. 18), 256–64; Part II (Vol. 19), 185–9; Part III (Vol. 20), 115–19.

41. Ibid. 117; and L. Halphen and R. Poupardin, eds., *Chroniques des comtes d'Anjou et des seigneurs d'Amboise* (Paris 1913), 24–7; for the vogue: B. Smalley, 'Sallust in the Middle Ages', in R. R. Bolgar, ed., *Classical Influences on European Culture A.D. 500–1500* (Cambridge 1971), 165–75.

42. Duby, 'Litt. généalogique', 296–7. But the clearest case of an upstart ancestor's passage from epic to chronicle is one not mentioned by Duby or Werner. The *Chanson de Geste Hugues Capet* makes its hero the son of butcher's daughter. Villani (IV, c. 4) takes up roughly this suggestion as serious history (without indicating its source).

43. Bosl, '*Potens* und *Pauper*', *Frühformen der Gesellschaft*, 105–34; G. Duby, 'Les laïcs et la paix de Dieu', *Hommes et Structures*, 227–40, esp. 232–3; and comment by L. Prosdocimi in *I laici nella 'societas Christiana'* (*Misc. del Centro di Studi Medioevali*, V, Milan 1968), 463. The survival of the principle described by Tacitus (*Germania*, c. 7) is documented by K. Bosl in an article whose title consists of the Latin sentence quoted, in *Frühformen der Gesellschaft*, 62–73.

44. Fossier, *Picardie*, 534–41; Duby, *Soc. ... mâconnaise*, 230–45, 316–35; Van Luyn, 19–42, 193–205. The degree of mixture varied, as did the dominance of one group. Bosl, *Reichsministerialität*, 138–9 describes an extreme separation, and dominance of ministerial *milites*.

45. *Hist. Aecclesiastica*, VI, c. 2 (ed. M. Chibnall, *Oxford Medieval Texts*, Vol. III, Oxford 1972, p. 216). Cf. Duby, 'Les "jeunes"'.

46. Van Luyn, 216–26; P. Bonenfant and G. Despy, 'La noblesse en Brabant aux xii^e

et xiii^e siècles: quelques sondages', *Le Moyen Âge*, 64 (1958), 27–66; p. 36 (dating the merger *c.* 1200).

47. Magnou-Nortier, 241, 253–4; Violante, *Soc. milanese*, 162 (*valvassores* cut themselves a place between those above and below them); Van Luyn, 215–17 and Table 8; Fossier, *Picardie*, 539 (a *miles optimus* in 1089); Werner, Part II (Vol. 19), pp. 183–5 (clear distinction between upper and lower nobility strong after *c.* 1050); Bosl, *Reichsministerialität*, 91 (high *ministeriales* name themselves after their fortified residences, from *c.* 1100 onwards).

48. I, c. 10 (*PL* 136.168C).

49. Werner, Part II (Vol. 19), p. 186, sees the passage about the dynasty as indicating a fast rate of change relative to that in France. A translation of the passage will be found in R. S. Lopez, *The Tenth Century* (New York 1959), 34.

50. Cols. 168C, 169B ('factum sit, infectum sit, narratum est ...' etc.); for the likelihood that Ratherius refers to his own career in the longer passage see editors' note 56.

51. John of Jandun, *Questiones bonae fortunae* (*c.* 1315–20): 'hodie etiam vere rustici nobilitantur'; quoted by Schmugge, *Joh. von Jandun*, 79.

52. *V.S. Guil. Divion.*, c. 2 col. 703B (463); N. Bulst, *Untersuchungen zu den Klosterreformen Wilhelms von Dijon (962–1031) (Pariser hist. Studien*, 11, Bonn 1973), 22–3. Dr. Bulst makes Vibo (the grandfather) 'noble' on the single basis of Radulf Glaber's *militari industria clarus*; but it is at least clear that he *became* rich (*locupletatus*) in Italy.

53. Violante, *Soc. milanese*, 48; Lopez, 'Aristocracy of Money', 15–16, 36–9.

54. V. Fumagalli, *Le origini di una grande dinastia feudale Adalberto-Atto di Canossa* (Tübingen 1971), 27–9, 50–2, 74–7 (summaries).

55. Ibid. 57, 62, 68 (Framsit, etc.) I intentionally ignore S. Italy, whose nearness to rich Islam may have had a disturbing effect on social ranks: the Frank Hildemar, living in Civitate *c.* 850, emphatically distinguished between 'the rich' and 'nobles' in his comment on the Benedictine Rule, *c.* 59 (and c. 2), quoted by Schulte, 84 n. 1, and Schreiner, 119–20.

56. See n. 22 above.

57. Magnou-Nortier, 242; Duby, *Soc. ... mâconnaise, 342 (270) (burgenses* as recognizable social group 1060–75); P. Bonnassie, *La Catalogne du milieu du x^e à la fin du xi^e siècle* (Toulouse 1975), 492–500.

58. See n. 43 above, for polarity. *Mediocres*, etc.: Atto of Vercelli, *Expos. in epist. Pauli*, Col. 4 (*PL* 134.639D); Bosl, '*Potens* und *Pauper*', 125–6, 133; Magnou-Nortier, 241–2, esp. p. 242 n. 167; J. Martindale (as in n. 38 above), 6, 15, 22. For three examples from *before* c. 960, ibid. 13 and p. 33.

59. *Carmen ad Robertum regem* (*PL* 141.773–86); summarized in lines 297–8 (cols. 781–2); J. Le Goff, 'Note sur la société tripartie: idéologie monarchique et renouveau économique dans la Chrétienté du ix^e au xii^e siècle', in T. Manteuffel and A. Gieysztor, eds., *L'Europe aux ix^e–xi^e siècles: Aux origines des États nationaux* (Warsaw 1968), 63–71; p. 64 for Adalbero's text; pp. 63–4 for the claims of Alfred and Abbo of Fleury to have preceded him. This article is a fund of both bibliography and ideas (but not the present idea) on the 'three orders'.

60. As in R. S. Lopez, *La Naissance de l'Europe* (Paris 1962), 156.

61. Violante, *Soc. milanese*, 163.

62. pp. 41–2.

63. *De diversis ordinibus hominum*, lines 221–4, *Latin Poems*, 235: 'Pauper mavult hodie terram circuire, / quam mercedem capiens gregem custodire; / non est elemosina tali subvenire, / non vult servire, malit namque fame perire'.

64. *Des todes gehugede*, quoted by Martini, *Bauerntum*, 30.

65. Quoted by Langlois, *Vie*, 44 ( = *Li proverbe au vilain* No. 193) : 'Ne cuit pas que Dieu vueille / Que povres s'enorgueille; / Mais chascuns endroit soi / Esgart selonc, son estre; / Car ne pueent pas estre / Tuit ne conte ne roi'.
66. Cf. Lopez, *Naissance* (as in n. 60), 155.
67. Duby, *Soc.* .... *mâconnaise*, 577–83 (433–7) ; Bonenfant and Despy (as in n. 46), 49–60; Bosl, *Reichsministerialität*, 602–19; Plesner, *Émigration* . . . *à* . . . *Florence*, 85–6, 128–53; etc. For the penetration of *ministeriales* etc. to noble monopolies in the church, Schulte, 67, 62–4, and *Nachtrag* ( = supplementary pages at the end of the same volume), 7–9.
68. Line 8436 (developed in lines 8653–7).
69. *Credo*, fo. 160: 'tutto lo studio delle genti e d'ongne gente è pur di salire e di montare in altura e come posse essere grande al mondo questo è tutto lo studio delle genti'; and *Prediche inedite* (ed. Narducci), 51: 'tutte le brighe e mali che nascono, si è perche l'uomo esce di schiera [etc.]'.
70. For what follows: H. R. Patch, *The Goddess Fortuna in Medieval Literature* (Harvard 1927), and F. P. Pickering, *Literature and Art in the Middle Ages* (London 1970), 200–16.
71. Patch, 164–7; Pickering, 202, 214; for the classical and early medieval wheel/sphere: Patch, 147–8; Pickering, 214; and below, Plate III(b).
72. Patch, 48.
73. Patch, 112; Pickering, 216 (referring to MS. Corpus Christi College Cambridge 66, fo. 66). See also below, Plate IV.
74. Patch, 67–8.
75. Pickering, 213 for comment.
76. Pickering, 213.
77. White, *Medieval Technology*, 110 (mentioning this drawing).
78. Goetz, 76 (quoting *Bescheidenheit*, 117, 26 f.).
79. *Mir. S. Fidis*, 63.
80. *V.S. Hugonis Clun.* (Hildebert), 875B.
81. *V.S. Guil. Firm.* (†1095), 340AB.
82. *V.S. Joh -Valent.*, 1696E.
83. Langlois, *Vie*, 36, 42; for a comparable view from *La Bible Guiot* see n. 10 above.
84. Jean de Meung, lines 11407–60.
85. Plague: Violante, *Soc. milanese*, 144–5; hazards of family size: D. Herlihy, 'Three Patterns of Social Mobility in Medieval History', *Journal of Interdisciplinary History*, 3 (1973), 623–47; lover's heart: Nelli, *Érotique*, 295; for some of the practical results of which, see Bosl, *Reichsministerialität*, 67–70, 78; Van Luyn, 211; Duby, 'Les "jeunes" '; Duby, 'Structures' 276, 281; Boussard (as in n. 38), 316–17; etc., and for a cautionary note: Werner, Part II (Vol. 19), 178.
86. John of Salisbury, *Policraticus*, VII, c. 19 (Vol. II, p. 170.19–21).
87. Gauthier, *Magnanimité*, 239–368.
88. See pp. 78–9 above, and 436 n. 69.
89. *PL* 133.545A, 613B, 650C are all I have noted.
90. Cols. 584D, 610B, 613C, etc. Compare also B. H. Rosenwein and L. K. Little, 'Social Meaning in the Monastic and Mendicant Spiritualities', *Past and Present*, 63 (1974), 4–32, pp. 5–16, for passages on upper-class violence.
91. *Collat.* II, c. 21 (col. 567B): 'Quanto autem quique pauperiores sunt, tanto in illam abominationem [ = superbiam] rarius incurrunt'; not, I think, neutralized by I, c. 13 (col. 528D) 'superbia vero et luxuria ... in ipsis mendicis et pauperrimis ... vigere solent', since the reference to class in the latter passage is subsidiary to an abstract ethical argument.
92. Not at all in the Letters or Sermons; once in *Expos. in epist. Pauli ad Corinth. I and II* (at col. 387C); and twice in the long *Expos. in epist. Pauli ad Hebraeos* (754A and

830BC). *Aemulare, -atio* is commoner, but usually used in the sense of the emulating of good works (386BC, 345BC, 455B, 471A, 790B). For *elatio* and *superbia* see esp. 311A. Atto misses opportunities to dilate on social ambition at cols. 354C, 474B, 523C, 593B, 633D.

93. *Sermo* 3 (col. 837D) : '... Et licet de superioribus quoquo modo se excusent, vitiis, his [ = superstitionum] tamen prosternuntur jaculis.'

94. *Epist.* 9 (col. 116D–17A) ; echoed in *Expos. in epist. Pauli ad Hebraeos*, at Hebr. 5:4 (col. 754A; and cf. 830BC).

95. *De cont. can.* I, c. 22 (*PL* 136.511C).

96. Esp. in *Sermones*, 24–5 (col. 703B–D).

97. Dresdner, 50 (quoting *SS* 12.198).

98. Dresdner, 59; cf. 52.

99. Humbert, *Adv. Simoniacos*, III, c. 33 (241.1–3) ; II, c. 20 (163.9–11) ; II, 35 (183.41) ; III, 37 (245.23–30). For Peter Damian's mingling of the two subjects, see any of the works mentioned in the next two notes.

100. *Contra philargyriam*, vi (*PL* 145.537D).

101. *De fuga dignitatum* (*PL* 145.455–63), esp. i, col. 457B; *Contra clericos aulicos* (cols. 463–72), esp. i, col. 467A, and *proemium*, col. 463B.

102. *Quaest. naturales*, ed. M. Müller (*Beiträge zur Gesch. der Philosophie und Theologie des Mittelalters*, 31, *Heft* 2, Münster i.W. 1934), p. 1, line 9.

103. *De excidio*, line 17 (p. 81).

104. Lines 298–300 (*Latin Poems*, 14–15).

105. e.g. *Latin Poems*, 106–7, 152–9, 160.12, 188.27.

106. VII, c. 17 (Vol. II, p. 162.11–15).

107. VII, c. 19 (Vol. II, p. 172.12–22); cf. c. 18 (p. 166.5–9).

108. VII, c. 19 (Vol. II, p. 179.9–12). Between pages 160 and 181 the word *ambitio* (with *ambire* etc.) occurs twenty-seven times.

109. VII, cc. 18, 21.

110. *Policraticus*, VII, c. 17 (Vol. II, p. 162.18–24) and v, c. 1 (Vol. I, pp. 281–2) ; on the trend: Gauthier, *Magnanimité*, 239–368. Cf. also Bernard of Clairvaux, *Sermo de conversione ad clericos*, c. 19 (*PL* 182.852AB): 'Nemo enim magis iram meretur, quam amicum simulans inimicus [ = ambitious *clergy*]'.

111. Cf. *Policraticus*, where *avaritia* etc. is frequently mentioned in the chapters on ambition; *V.S. Wulfrici*, 32, 47; *Mor. dogma philos.* 31.10–25; and for the influence of this last work (in this particular) in art, R. Tuve, 'Notes on the Virtues and Vices', *Journal of the Warburg and Courtauld Institutes*, 26 (1963), 264–303; 290–3. Cf. Plate I below.

112. e.g. the unedited sermons of 1 and 24 June 1305 by Giordano of Pisa, in *Credo*, fo. 158^v: 'Non studiano le genti in altro oggi senon immontare in richezze temporali ...'; and fo. 160^v (as quoted in n. 69 above). Those of Giordano's sermons edited by Narducci contain similar expressions, e.g. pp. 51–2, 129. Archbishop Federigo Visconti of Pisa (†1277) was only a degree less explicit; MS. Florence, Laur. Plut. 33 sin. 1, fo. 20^va: '... carnales, cupidi et ambitiosi ...'; fo. 28^rb: '... avarus ambitiosus ...'; fo. 89^rb: 'concupiscentia versatur supra delitias, divitias, honores'; etc. (On these latter sermons: J. B. Schneyer, 'Das Predigtwirken des Erzbischofs Friedrich Visconti von Pisa (1254–77), auf Grund der Rubriken des Cod. Florenz, Laur. Plut. 33. sin. 1', *Recherches de théologie ancienne et médiévale*, 32 (1965), 307–32.)

113. Cf. Plates I(c) and IV.

114. *Adv. Simoniacos*, III, c. 20 (p. 224.11–13).

115. Dresdner, 52 (quoting *PL* 149.467C).

116. *Contra clericos aulicos*, ii (*PL* 145.467B, 466A).

117. Ibid. ii and iii (cols. 468D, 465B, 465D, 466D, etc.).

118. *Contra philargyriam*, vi (*PL* 145.537D).
119. *Policraticus*, VII, c. 19 (Vol. II, p. 180.15) and c. 17 (p. 162.17–23).
120. VII, c. 17 (p. 162.15–18).
121. *De nugis, Dist.* IV, *prol.* (p. 138).
122. Ibid., *Dist.* III, *prol.* (p. 107) 'operum immensitae defessi'.
123. *De fuga dignitatum*, i (*PL* 145.457B).
124. *Policraticus*, VII, c. 19 (Vol. II, pp. 179.20–180.12).
125. As in n. 120.
126. *De nugis, Dist.* IV, *epilogus* (pp. 140 f.).
127. F. Pollock and F. W. Maitland, *The History of English Law before the Time of Edward I* (Cambridge 1898²), 146: 'multis vigiliis excogitatum'.
128. Coulton, *Five Centuries*, I, 240 (from *Mir. S. Benedicti*); for the growing testimony to the problem *c.* 1200: B. Geremek, *La salariat dans l'artisanat parisien aux xii^e–xv^e siècles* (Paris 1968), 78–85, 106–10; B. Harvey, 'Work and *Festa Ferianda* in Medieval England', *Journal of Ecclesiastical History*, 23 (1972), 289–308.
129. *V.S. Steph. Obaz.*, i, 15 (p. 68.37–8; p. 66.30–4); and cf. last sentence of Bk. ii (p. 188.45): 'Urget enim tempus ...'.
130. *V.B. Wulfrici*, c. 96 (p. 121).
131. Durand of Osca, *Liber Antihaeresis*, ed. G. Gonnet, (*Enchiridion fontium Valdensium*, I, Torre Pelice 1958), 42, 44.
132. Villani, IV, c. 131: 'non ardivano d'andare innanzi col loro stuolo, e ritrarresi della impresa non pareva loro onore al grande spendio e apparecchiamento ch'aveano fatto.' The word 'ritrarresi' might be translated 'withdraw'; but a time-element seems justified by the preceding phrase. For the 'time' problem in the later middle ages: J. Le Goff, 'Le temps du travail dans la "crise" du xiv^e siècle: du temps médiéval au temps moderne', *Le Moyen Âge*, 69 (1963), 597–613; and E. P. Thompson, 'Time, Work-Discipline and Industrial Capitalism', *Past and Present*, 38 (1968), 56–97; p. 56.
133. *De nugis, Dist.* I, c. 1 (pp. 1–2).
134. *Coutumes de Beauvaisis*, ed. A. Salmon (Paris 1899), I, p. 26; cf. pp. 122–3 below.
135. Quoted in (this) translation by R. W. Southern, 'King Henry I', in idem, *Medieval Humanism* (Oxford 1970), 206–33; pp. 220–1.
136. *De palpone et assentatore* (*c.* 1220), *Latin Poems*, 114, lines 271–4.
137. Ibid. 118, lines 411–14; 119, lines 425–6 and 445–6.
138. And has long done so: Curtius, *Eur. Lit.* 523.
139. *De avaritia et luxuria mundi, Latin Poems*, 164, lines 53–6: '... neque conscientia teste gloriari / noverunt praeter laudem nullius avari'.

5 . REASON AND POWER

1. *Hist. littéraire de la France*, 30 (Paris 1888), 573.
2. *Opus Maius*, I 399; on fascination in general (but guarded about this particular story), 398–400; cf. Thorndike, *History of Magic*, II, 665; the story of the camel and the notion there implied were condemend by the Bishop of Paris in 1277, *Chart. Univ. Par.*, I, p. 540, c. 112.
3. Ed. C. R. Dodwell (Edinburgh 1961); authorship and date ibid. xviii–xliv and B. Bischoff, 'Die Überlieferung des Theophilus-Rugerus nach den ältesten Handschriften', *Mittelalterliche Studien*, II (Stuttgart 1967), 175–82.
4. III, prol., p. 64 '... toto mentis conamine ...'.
5. I, prol., pp. 2, 4.
6. III, prol., pp. 62–3; cf. p. xx and Lottin, *Psychologie et Morale*, III, 326–456.
7. I, 9 (ed. C. H. Buttimer, Washington 1939, 17.7–18).

8. Albertano de Brescia, *De amore et dilectione proximi*, III, 2 (Cuneo 1507, fo. 54$^{vb}$) quoting 'Pamphilus'.
9. Cf. Thorndike, *History of Magic*, II, 654–5 (= *Epist. de secretis operibus*).
10. *Picatrix*, ed. E. Garin, *Medioevo e Rinascimento* (Bari 1954), 175. Cf. T. Gregory, 'L'Idea di Natura nella Filosofia medioevale prima dell'ingresso della fisica di Aristotele', in *La Filosofia della Natura nel Medioevo* (= *Atti del terzo congresso internazionale di filosofia medioevale*, Milan 1966), 27–65; p. 57. On *Picatrix*, cf. W. Hartner, 'Notes on Picatrix', *Oriens-Occidens* (Hildesheim 1968), 415–28.
11. Cf.. Thorndike, *History of Magic*, II, 280 (= *Liber sacratus/Salomonis*).
12. Ibid. 279–89, 751–812, 229–45, etc.
13. Cf. Peter Abelard, *Ethics*, ed. D. E. Luscombe (Oxford 1971), 36.18 f., for a statement of this common doctrine.
14. *Philosophia*, ed. K. Sudhoff, *Archiv für die Gesch. der Naturwissenschaften und der Technik*, VIII (1918), 6–40; p. 34, quoted by T. Gregory (as in n. 10), p. 56.
15. Ibid. n. 86, and for Daniel's sources R. Lemay, *Abu Ma'shar and Latin Aristotelianism in the Twelfth Century* (Beirut 1962), 313–41.
16. Bernard Silvester, *Experimentarius*, ed. B. Savorelli, in *Rivista Critica di Storia della Filosofia*, 14 (1959), 283–342; p. 317; cf. translator Philip's additions to the *Secretum Secretorum* (n. 38 below), 61.30–1.
17. Ibid. 61.30–1; in full in Jean de Meung, lines 17549–67; cf. T. Gregory, 56–7.
18. Thorndike, *History of Magic*, II, 585, 700.
19. *Hom. in Evang.* II, 35 (*PL* 76.1259BC).
20. e.g. Bernard Silvester (as in n. 16), 317.
21. Albertano, *De amore*, III (fo. 58$^{vb}$).
22. Salimbene, 345.20; cf. 541.23–5, 906.21–3, 937.1–2 (citing Gregory's authority only).
23. Campbell, *Black Death*, 112.
24. Cf. *S. Bonifacii Vita altera*, ed. W. Levison (*SS** Hanover 1920), 75–6; also Hugo of Trimberg, lines 21367–71: 'Und möhten si des wazzers fluz, / Der wolken guz, des luftes duz, / Der sterne glast, der sunnen schin / Enthaben und vor uns sperren in, / Si têtenz gerne.'
25. Saint Augustine, *De civ. Dei*, v, 1. The mathematics behind astrological schemes of history is expounded in a paper by J. D. North, 'Astrology and the fortunes of churches', to be published in the Proceedings of the Second International Colloquium in Ecclesiastical History (held in Oxford, 22–9 September 1974).
26. A. Momigliano, 'Pagan and Christian Historiography in the Fourth Century A.D.', in A. Momigliano, ed., *The Conflict between Paganism and Christianity in the Fourth Century* (Oxford 1963), 72–99, esp. 82–7, with references to the vast bibliography on this and related topics. The idea was easily available to the middle ages through Saint Augustine, *De civ. Dei*, v, 21 etc., and more elaborately in Orosius.
27. *Liber Hermetis Mercurii Triplicis de VI rerum principiis*, ed. Th. Silverstein, in *AHDLMA*, 30 (1955), 217–301; pp. 289–91; the key passage is quoted by T. Gregory (as in n. 10), 54.
28. *De naturis rerum*, II, c. 174 (p. 308).
29. John of Salisbury, *Metalogicon*, VI, ii, 593a (II, p. 9.15–27).
30. *Tetralogus* (1041), ed. H. Bresslau (Hanover 1915³), 77, quoted by Raby, *Secular Latin Poetry*, 395: 'Moribus his dudum vivebat, Roma decenter, / his studiis tantos potuit vincire tyrannos.'
31. Thomasin of Zirclaria, lines 9229–38.
32. H. Kehrer, *Die heiligen drei Könige in Literatur und Kunst*, 2 vols. (Leipzig 1908) mentions references in Tertullian and Caesarius of Arles, but finds no serious literary tradition until the tenth century. The first artistic representation of the

'kings' was in 976, in Basil II's 'menology'; cf. E. Mâle, *Religious Art in France: Thirteenth Century* (London 1913; r.p. as *The Gothic Image* 1961), 213 n. 2. After exploration of more elusive texts, the impression is confirmed by B. Bischoff, 'Wendepunkte in der Gesch. der lateinischen Exegese im Frühmittelalter', *Mittelalterliche Studien*, I, 205–73, 224–7.

33. Note the *non*-intellectual implication of the names assigned for the three Magi in eighth- and ninth-century exegesis: Humilis, Fidelis, Misericors, etc. Ibid. 226, 231.
34. Thomasin of Zirclaria, lines 9223–8.
35. Anton, *Fürstenspiegel*, 51–2, 256–7.
36. Thorndike, *History of Magic*, II, 279–89 for this and other Solomonic literature.
37. Walter of Châtillon, *Alexandreid* (1178–82), I (*PL* 209.465–6), stresses the decisive influence of Aristotle on the future conqueror (lines 41–3). The intellectual (as against moral) character of this influence is indicated by Roger Bacon, *Opus Maius* (*c.* 1266), I, pp. 291, 390, 393 (cf. Thorndike, *History of Magic*, II, 647; but Roger's view was not unique). Alexander is made a model of gratitude for his instruction in *Le livre des secrets aux philosophes* (*c.* 1300) (see n. 1 above), p. 575. The slightly earlier 'Sidrach' (1243) closely associates Greek power and Greek science (p. 306) '. . . [li Grigois] seront en leur tens la plus puissant gent du monde, et saront presque tout l'art d'astronomie . . . [and when they fall] n'aront en eulz pooir et perdront leur sens'. Compare also G. Cary, *The Medieval Alexander* (Cambridge 1956), 105–10.
38. History of Arabic versions: M. Manzalaoui, 'The Pseudo-Aristotelian *Kitāb Sirr al-Asrār*: Facts and Problems', *Oriens*, 23–4 (1974), 147–257. European diffusion: R. Steele, introduction to his edition in *Opera hactenus inedita Rogeri Baconi*, Fasc. V (Oxford 1920), p. xxvi; Thorndike, *History of Magic*, II, 267 n. 3; A. H. Gilbert, 'Notes on the Influence of the *Secretum Secretorum*', *Speculum*, 3 (1928), 84–98; Cary (as in last note), xxi–xxvi; N. Orme, *English Schools in the Middle Ages* (London 1973), 22–3. Albertano of Brescia quotes the *Secretum* in *De amore et dilectione proximi*, II, fo. 47^ra. My explanation of the appeal of the *Secretum* is in opposition to Cary's (p. xxvi). I have not had the opportunity to consult Dr. Manzalaoui's (largely unpublished) work on the European influence of the *Secretum*; see Manzalaoui, 252–3, items 164–8.
39. p. 45.13–19 (cf. p. 182).
40. pp. 141–3 (cf. pp. 237–8).
41. Manzalaoui (as in n. 38), 176–9, 196–201.
42. Introduction by A. Salmon to his edition (Paris 1899), I, p. xxix.
43. I, pp. 16–27.
44. Introduction by F. J. Carmody to his edition, *Li livres dou Tresor* (Berkeley and Los Angeles 1948), pp. lv–lvii.
45. III, c. 75, pp. 393–4. A particular application of this advice: III, c. 100, p. 419.30–2 (how the podestà should stir up martial feeling among the people if necessary by causing his horse to whinny and neigh).
46. Cf. Salimbene, 136–239 (year 1239), esp. 209.7–8 and 173.10–11, where Salimbene puts *intellectus* and *sapientia* respectively first and most elaborately among the three qualities needed in a bishop. In the elaboration of *sapientia* (173–7) Salimbene draws nearly 50 per cent of his citations from the Wisdom books, and 57 per cent from 'Solomon'. Contrast the seventeen qualities for bishops in *MGH Poetae*, II, 355, lines 71–6, where only *sapientia radix* (line 72) and *doctrina* (line 74) speak for the mind.
47. Cf. the summaries by L. K. Born, 'The Perfect Prince: A Study in Thirteenth- and Fourteenth-Century Ideals', *Speculum*, 3 (1928), 470–504; especially the stress on prudence in Peyraut (pp. 485–6) and Egidius Colonna (pp. 489–90), and the thirty-two chapters on wisdom in *Speculum Dominarum* (p. 494).

48. *De naturis rerum*, II, c. 174 (p. 308).

49. VI, c. 2 (Vol. II, pp. 8–11).

50. *Epist.* xvi (to Philip, Count of Flanders, †1191) (*PL* 203.149A) '... militiam ordinant ...'.

51. *Opus Maius*, Bk I, 1 (Vol. I, p. 1) '... per virtutem sapientiae reprimi, ut melius a finibus Ecclesiae longius pellantur quam per effusionem sanguinis.' Bk. VI, 3rd prerogative (Vol. II, p. 217) 'Et contra inimicos rei publicae adinvenerunt magnas artes, ut sine ferro, et absque eo quo tangerent aliquem, destruerant omnes resistentes.' The military intention of the first passage is doubtful, but of the second, not.

52. The state of research on subjects discussed in the following five paragraphs is summarized with full bibliography by P. Le Gentil, 'A propos de *La Chanson de Roland et la tradition épique des Francs* de Ramon Menendez Pidal', *Cahiers de civilisation médiévale*, 5 (1962), 323–33.

53. Davidsohn, *Gesch. v. Florenz*, IV, i, p. 40 for the fashion in Italy *c.* 1300.

54. For the following: Curtius, 'Literarästhetik', esp. 224–9; and more concisely in *Eur. Lit.* 181–2; for possible criticism of Curtius' view, Le Gentil (as in n. 52), 328 n. 28.

55. R. Kaske, '*Sapientia et Fortitudo* as the controlling theme of Beowulf', *Studies in Philology*, 55 (1958), 423–57, r.p. in L. E. Nicholson, ed., *An Anthology of Beowulf Criticism* (Notre Dame 1963), 269–310.

56. P. Van Luyn, 'Les *milites* dans la France du xi^e siècle: examen des sources narratives', *Le Moyen Âge*, 77 (1971), 236.

57. 14 per cent of total. *Nobilis* and *fortis* follow closely behind, then (down to 7 per cent) *strenuus*, etc.

58. John of Marmoutier, *Historia Gaufredi*, year 1147, in L. Halphen and R. Poupardin, eds., *Chroniques des comtes d'Anjou et des seigneurs d'Amboise* (Paris 1913), 218.

59. Ibid., p. 212. Cf. Thompson, *Literacy*, 159–60; and A. L. Poole, *From Domesday Book to Magna Carta* (Oxford 1951), 243.

60. Ed. C. Lang (Leipzig 1885, r.p. 1967); English translation in T. R. Phillips, *The Roots of Strategy* (London 1943). The editors' sceptical footnote in the edition of John of Marmoutier's account cited above neglects the use of augmented texts of Vegetius. See M. Jähns, *Gesch. der Kriegswissenschaften vornehmlich in Deutschland* (*Gesch. der Wissenschaften in Deutschland*, 21, Munich and Leipzig 1889), II, 187.

61. 80.3–10; 95.10; 104.13–15; 111.2–3; 113.16–114.11; 232 ('providus').

62. e.g. 25.2–5; 97.1–4; and especially 110.8–12.

63. Jähns, II, 190.

64. Esp. Bk. III, cc. 9 (pp. 86–9) and 11 (pp. 93.18–94.4); also among the *regulae* at the end of Bk. III, pp. 121.5–7, 125.5–8. On the background cf. Jähns, II, 115; also *Secretum*, 154.22–31 (and 249).

65. Curtius, 'Literarästhetik', 205–8; cf. the distribution of the phrases 'in arte duelli nimium gnari', 'pugnae doctior usus', 'artibus instructi Franci, bellare periti', etc. Cf. F. Irsigler, *Untersuchungen zur Gesch. des frühfränkischen Adels* (Bonn 1969), 246 n. 168; and for such terms in Vegetius. C. Lang's index under *doct-* and *campidoct-*.

66. Jähns, I, 120; Thompson, *Literacy*, 44 n. 56; 48 n. 84. R. R. Bolgar, *The Classical Heritage and its Beneficiaries* (Cambridge 1954), 126 includes Vegetius among authors studied by Sedulius Scotus. A folded MS. of Vegetius Bks. 1 & 11 (for carrying in the pocket) survives in Wolfenbüttel Cod. Lat. 84; cf. B. Bischoff, 'Über gefaltete Handschriften, vornehmlich hagiographischen Inhalts' (*Mittelalterliche Studien*, I) 98 and cf. 93–100 for the meaning of the fold.

67. Phillips, in the Introduction to his translation (see n. 60) tells us that Vegetius was a favourite author of Fulk Nerra, and that later both Henry II and Cœur de Lion

carried a copy everywhere in their campaigns (pp. 35–6). I have searched for, but failed to find, contemporary authority for these assertions.

68. Thompson, *Literacy*, 143 (for the count's copy); Philip of Harvengt, *Epist.* xvii (*PL* 203.151D–156D), cf. n. 50 above; for John of Salisbury's admiration, see the two *inches* of references to him in C. C. J. Webb's index to his edition of *Policraticus*.

69. Jähns, I, 120–1; C. Lang, in the preface to his edition (pp. xxiii–xlviii) actually identifies over 130, excluding translations, excerpts, etc.

70. Jähns, II, 188–212; cf. III, 347–56 for adaptations of Vegetius by Christine de Pisan and other fifteenth-century strategists. For preachers' references to Vegetius see G. R. Owst, *Literature and Pulpit in Medieval England* (Oxford 1961²) 181, 552, 559.

71. Davidsohn, *Gesch. v. Florenz*, IV, i, p. 40.

72. Cf. R. Steele, introduction to *Secretum*, xxii–xxvi.

73. Lawsuits: *V.S. Steph. Obaz.*, pp. 116–22 (date 1141–7); *Chronicle of Battle Abbey*, transl. M. A. Lower (London 1851), pp. 185–96. Commerce: see pp. 87–90 above on ecclesiastical *ministeriales*.

74. The main positions in the debate are given by M.-D. Chenu, *La théologie au douzième siècle* (Paris 1966²), 62–89. Matthew Paris begins his great chronicle with some scathing references to the anti-history party; ed. H. R. Luard (*RS* 1880), I, p. 1.

75. *Hist. Novorum* (*c.* 1100), ed. M. Rule (*RS* 1884), 1.

76. *Chronica* (1143–6), ed. M. Chibnall (*SS*\* 1912), 1.10–14.

77. *Hist. Pontificalis* (1164), ed. M. Chibnall (*Nelson's Medieval Texts* 1956), 2.

78. Alexander of Roes, *Memoriale* (1281), 104.4–10.

79. Philippe de Novare, p. 13 '... eux faire apanre les estoires ... qui lor porroient avoir grant mestier, se il les retiennent'.

80. Gerald of Wales, *De instructione principum*, I, 11, ed. J. S. Brewer (in *Opera*, VIII, *RS* 21, 1891) 42–3; quoted by Galbraith, 'Literacy', 213, cf. 202.

81. *De inventione*, II, liii; cf. E. Wind, *Pagan Mysteries in the Renaissance* (Harmondsworth 1967²), 260 and n. 2: though this was not a 'scholastic commonplace' until early in Albert's century.

82. *De virtutibus et de vitiis et donis spiritus sancti* (*c.* 1160), ed. Lottin, *Psychologie et Morale*, VI, 27–92; pp. 51.4–52.3. Cf. Aquinas, *ST* II (ii), q. 47, a.1 *resp.*

83. Cf. Curtius, *Eur. Lit.* 479.

84. Cf. Aquinas, *ST* II (ii) q.49 a.6; Peyraut, *Summae*, I, iii, pt. 2, c. 2 (fo. 101ʳᵃ).

85. F. Graus, 'Die Gewalt bei den Anfängen des Feudalismus und die "Gefangenenbefreiungen" der Merowingischen Hagiographie', *Jahrbuch für Wirtschaftsgesch.*, 1961 (East Berlin), 61–156; pp. 132–3.

86. Gauthier, *Magnanimité*, 119–61 analyses the dependence of Cicero and Seneca on Chrysippus, Panetius, Hecato, and Posidonius. The two principal channels for these ethical ideas were Saint Martin of Braga, *Formula honestae vitae*, ed. C. W. Barlow, *Martini Episcopi Bracarensis Opera Omnia* (New Haven, Conn. 1950), 236–50 (closely dependent on Seneca's lost *De officiis*); and the *Moralium dogma philosophorum* (equally dependent on Cicero's *De officiis*, in its turn an adaptation of Panetius' περὶ τοῦ καθήκοντος and of a work by Posidonius). Professor Barlow's list of MSS. of the *Formula honestae vitae* exceeds 635, including translations and adaptations; all but *c.* 20 are from the twelfth century and later (ed. cit., pp. 231–2). Miss Tuve (art. cit. in n. 89 below, p. 268) identifies 90 MSS. of the *Mor. dogma phil.* On the role of prudence in Cicero and Seneca see also Heitmann, 98–120.

87. Lottin, *Psychologie et Morale*, III, 255–78, esp. 255, 257, 259.

88. Translation of *Nichomachean Ethics*: D. A. Callus, in the collection edited by himself, *Robert Grosseteste* (Oxford 1955), 62–5. Impact of the work on scholastic views of prudence: Lottin, *Psychologie et Morale*, III, 271–8 (exceptional position of Albert, p. 276). Common background to Aristotle and the Stoics; Gauthier, *Magnanimité*, 144–56.

89. R. Tuve, 'Notes on the Virtues and Vices', *Journal of the Warburg and Courtauld Institutes*, 26 (1963), 264–303; and 27 (1964) 62–72; with an extra MS. illumination for prudence on p. 286.
90. Lottin, III, 265 (for *electio* as key act of prudence in Albert), and generally 265–78. Questions of 'intellectualist' tendencies in Albert's and Aquinas' ethics: Lottin, III, 539–75, 651–66. The contrast between the two Dominican masters on one hand, and Bonaventura and Franciscans on the other, is noted 276 n. 2 and 539 n. 2.
91. Luke 16:8 and Matt. 11:25. Cf. examples from Wyclif's Bible in J. A. H. Murray, ed., *A New English Dictionary*, VII (ii) (Oxford 1909), 1533 f.
92. Augustine, *De Trinitate*, XIV, c. 9 §12 (*Corp. Christ. Ser. Lat.* 50A (1968), 439.39 f.): 'prudentia in praecavendis insidiis'. Peter Lombard's treatment of prudence contents itself with citing this definition, *Libri Quatuor Sententiarum III, dist.* 33 (Quaracchi, 1916, p. 697). Cf. Lottin, III, 255.
93. *Collat.* I, xxv (*PL* 133.537A).
94. Cf. Salimbene, 561–3 *passim* and 699.19–20 (synonymous with *malitia*).
95. Quoted by N. Tommaseo, *Dizionario della Lingua Italiana*, III (Turin–Naples–Rome 1871), p. 1310 (from *Canz.* 8, 2, pt. ii): 'prudente, cioè savio, vuol dire quasi per certo vedente; ch'egli è si avveduto, ch'e' prevede gli' incerti avvenimenti.' Another example of the *providentia* meaning at top of p. 1311.
96. Ibid., p. 1311.
97. Quoted by Fréd. Godefroy, *Dictionnaire de l'Ancienne Langue Française*, X (Paris 1902), p. 441A (from *Charles V*, I, 22): 'en hautece de lecture ne parleure, et prudent pollicie en toutes choses generaument'. Other similar examples ibid.
98. An example in W. von Wartburg, *Französisches Etymologisches Wörterbuch*, IX (Basel 1959), p. 490 §2 late.
99. Tommaseo (as in n. 95), 1310. Cf. Aquinas, *ST* II (ii), q. 47, a. 13.
100. Cf. *Mor. dogma philos.* 68.5–6: 'melior est enim gloria divitiis, vectigalia urbana rusticis'; repeated by Brunetto Latini, *Tresors*, 304.10–11. A more direct counsel in Albertano, *De amore et dilectione proximi*, fo. 54$^{vb}$ (in the context of the four moral virtues, and of *ratio* in particular): 'Divitie vel opes ut dixi sunt diligendae. Multo fortius artes quibus divitie vel opes acquiruntur diligere debes.'
101. p. 241.38–41; cf. Albertano, *Ars. loq. et tac.*, p. cvii.
102. Matt. 10:16; *De instructione principum*, I, 11 (as in n. 80), 39–42.
103. *Anglo-Saxon version of Boethius' Consolation of Philosophy*, XVI §1, ed. W. J. Sedgefield (Oxford 1899), 35.13–21: 'Leorniað forðaem wisdom, & þonne ge hine geleornod haebben, ne foryhycgað hine þonne. Þonne secge ic eow buton aelcum tweon þ ge magon þurh hine becuman to anwealde, þeah ge no þaes anwealdes ne wilnigan.' A penetrating improvisation on *De consolatione philosophiae*, II, c. 6, lines 11–14 (Loeb edition 1973, pp. 208–10, lines 11–14), where virtue is rarely rewarded, and that incidentally.

## 6. THE DARK AGE OF EUROPEAN ARITHMETIC

1. G. Paré, A. Brunet, P. Tremblay, *La renaissance du xii$^e$ siècle* (Paris–Ottawa 1933), 99; although the word 'quadrivium' in this sense appears already in Boethius, *De arithmetica*, I, 1 (*PL* 58.1079D, 1081D).
2. *Il Saggiatore* (Florence 1842), 171. For this and similar remarks from Roger Bacon, etc., cf. J. A. Weisheipl, *The Development of Physical Theory in the Middle Ages* (London 1959), 52, 55–7, 73, 84.
3. Cf. M. Cantor, *Vorlesungen über die Geschichte der Mathematik*, I (Leipzig 1894²), 4; C. Lévi-Strauss, *The Savage Mind* (London 1962), 6; and above all the thorough and perceptive paper by W. Hartner, 'Zahlen und Zahlensysteme bei Primitiv- und

Hochkulturvolkern', now in the author's collected essays *Oriens-Occidens* (Hildesheim 1968), 57–116.

4.  Cf. Boethius, *De arithmetica*, I, I (*PL* 58.1082BC) and p. 204 below.

5.  *Germania*, cc. 5, 11, 13, 15, 26; hundreds and fines in c. 12.

6.  Cf. *Widsith*, line 91 (ed. R. W. Chambers (Cambridge 1912), 217).

7.  M. F. Woepcke, 'Mémoire sur la propagation des chiffres indiens', *Journal Asiatique*, 6ᵉ série, I (Paris 1863), 234–8 on the *gobar* ('dust') numerals; and the (inconclusive) discussion by D. E. Smith and L. C. Karpinski, *The Hindu–Arabic Numerals* (Boston–London 1911), 63–70.

8.  See n. 64 below, Plate V, and the epigraph to this chapter on p. 141.

9.  *Propositiones Alcuini*, Nos. 46, 41 (see below, nn. 62 and 63). Since the problems concern both camels and a variety of Gallic creatures (including bishops) they are unlikely to have a common origin, *pace* Cantor, I, 786.

10.  *Hist. Francorum*, IV, 32; Thompson, *Literacy*, 21 n. 71. This and the case of Otto III (below, p. 160) are the only references specifically to arithmetic in Thompson's book.

11.  Augustine, *De doctrina christiana*, II §§62–5 (*Corp. Script. Ser. Lat.* 80, pp. 51.20–53.2); Alcuin, *Epist.* 148 (*MGH Epist.* IV, p. 239.32).

12.  The story is told by C. W. Jones in the introduction to his edition of *Bedae Opera de Temporibus* (Cambridge, Mass. 1943), 6–111.

13.  Jones (as in last note), 73 n. 3, for the earlier limit; Cantor, *Vorlesungen*, I, 816 for the later.

14.  Jones, 64–5.

15.  Jones, 112.

16.  *Hist. Eccl.* III, 25 (ed. C. Plummer (Oxford 1896), I, 182). References to Plummer's editorial matter in this work will be indicated in the following footnotes as 'Plummer'.

17.  Ibid. The monks were Ronan (I, p. 181), Romanus (181–2), Wilfrid (182), and Agilbert (184; cf. note to 'domum rediit', II, p. 192).

18.  Ibid. (I, 183–9). I admit the danger of relying literally on Bede's account (cf. Plummer's note to 'judaizante ...' II, 190). But the contrast between the two arguments as he states them is so stark as to suggest that such a contrast was there in the tradition he drew from.

19.  Ibid. (I, 185–7).

20.  Ibid. (I, 187).

21.  Ibid., *passim* and n. to 'Anatolius', II, 191. Cf. W. Levison, 'Bede as Historian', in A. H. Thompson, ed., *Bede* (Oxford 1935), 112.

22.  *Hist. Eccl.* V, 21 (I, 341). That Bede himself should have composed this letter for the abbot makes no difference here (cf. II, 332).

23.  For Christian refugees from Syria and Egypt see the six references collected by P. Chavanis, 'Ethnic Changes in the Byzantine Empire in the Seventh Century', *Dumbarton Oaks Papers*, 13 (1959), 28 n. 25. The precise dates and destinations of these journeys are unspecified, but the designation of the 'Greek' empire in most of them would of course include Italy. Refugees from these areas would have been drawn from the Greek-speaking upper class. Christian allegiance among subject populations in north Africa, at least, was frail: R. G. Goodchild, 'Byzantines, Berbers and Arabs in Seventh-Century Libya', *Antiquity*, 41 (1967), 114–24. Bede (*Hist. Eccl.* IV, 1; vol. I, pp. 201–4) tells of the difficulty there was in finding a head for the English church, and of the previous status of Theodore: 'sufficiens ... in possessione hominum propriorum'; cf. the reference to 'suis' in Canterbury (p. 204).

24.  *Hist. Eccl.* IV, 2 (I, 204–5) and note II, 205.

25.  Ibid. IV, 1 (I, 202–3).

26. *Epist. ad Leutherium* (*MGH Auctores Antiquissimi*, 15,477, lines 12–18). Aldhelm's editor R. Ehwald dates the letter 671 (474, n. 1). Aldhelm was making the most of his difficulties in order to excuse himself for not spending Christmas with his correspondent.

27. Cf. A. F. Leach, *The Schools of Medieval England* (London 1915), 37–41.

28. *Epist. ad Leutherium* (pp. 477.18–478.2).

29. Numbers above fifteen occur in lines 1498, 1769, 1829, 2195, 2209, 2278, 2361, 2733, 2994, 3042, 3050 (ed. A. J. Wyatt and R. W. Chambers, Cambridge 1968). A logarithmic graph of the numbers of ten and over in *Beowulf* has this shape:

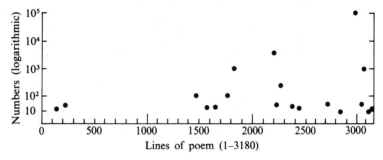

Graph to show distribution of numbers of ten and above in Beowulf.

Literary reasons for these variations have been suggested, but need not be exclusive, even if proven. Cf. D. G. Calder, 'Setting and Ethos: The Pattern of Measure and Limit in Beowulf', *Studies in Philology*, 69 (1972), 21–37.

30. W. Levison, *England and the Continent in the Eighth Century* (Oxford 1946), 83–4; 265–79.

31. H. Focillon, *The Year 1000* (New York 1969), 39–72.

32. Levison, 'Bede as Historian' (as in n. 21), 148–51; Jones (as in n. 12), 140–61 (133 MSS. of *De temporum ratione*); 164–7 (67 MSS. of *De temporibus*), etc.

33. Quoted by Plummer, I, xxxix, n. 2 from Marianus Scotus, Florence of Worcester, and an anonymous MS. in Rouen (MS. 1470).

34. Levison, 'Bede as Historian', 112; Jones, 114–22.

35. C. Jenkins, 'Bede as Exegete and Theologian', in *Bede* (as in n. 21), §3 pp. 173–80; Plummer, I, lix–lxi, n. 8.

36. Plummer, I, lvi, n. 3 and xl–xli, n. 5.

37. *Hist. Eccl.* IV, 2 (p. 205).

38. Alcuin, *De pontificibus et sanctis ecclesiae Eboracensis carmen*, ll. 1445–6, in J. Raine, ed., *The Historians of the Church of York and its Archbishops* (*RS* 71, 1879–94), I, 392.

39. Alcuin, *Epist.* 140 (*MGH Epist.* IV, p. 239.28–31): 'Obprobrium est grande, ut dimittamus eas [=artes mathematicas] perire diebus nostris …'.

40. Plummer, II, 205.

41. *Vita Karoli Magni*, c. 25 (*MGH\** 1911, p. 30, lines 15–18).

42. Alcuin, *Epist.* 262 (*MGH Epist.* IV, p. 420.9–12).

43. *Admonitio generalis*, §72 (*MGH Leges in quarto*, II, i, p. 60).

44. Cf. the word 'computus' in the index of *MGH Leges in quarto*, II, ii, p. 598 for the main references.

45. *Epist.* 148 (*MGH Epist.* IV, p. 239.33–4).

46. J. Boussard, *The Civilisation of Charlemagne* (London 1968), 130.

47. *PL* 107.670–728.

48. Cantor, *Vorlesungen*, I, 791–2.
49. *PL* 107.671B.
50. See pp. 148, 151 above.
51. *Epist. tertia ad Einhardum* (May 836); ed. L. Levillain (Paris 1964), I, 46–8: 'In Victorii quoque calculum ... ingredi cupio.' Earlier in the same letter pp. 44–6 Lupus betrays he has just begun to read Boethius' *De arithmetica*. For Victorius, see below, p. 156. The copy of Victorius Lupus asked for may be Bern Stadtbibliothek MS. 250; cf. the exhibition-catalogue *Karl der Grosse* (Aachen 1965), 222.
52. *Commonitorium cuiusque episcopi (PL* 99.1380A): 'compotum si non maiorem, saltem minorem, id est epactas, concurrentes, regularesque terminos ...' Cf. Jones, 75 n. 3; and (for the rigmarole) pp. 31, 81, 106–7.
53. Cf. *MGH Leges in quarto*, II, i, 234–5 and 109–11.
54. *PL* 101.1143–60. Cantor, *Vorlesungen*, I, 784–8.
55. *Epist.* 262 (*MGH Epist.* IV, p. 239.34) '... reprehendunt haec scire studentes'.
56. *De clericorum institutione*, III, c. 22 (*PL* 107.399B and 400D).
57. *De arithmetica, praefatio (PL* 58.1079A): 'ea quae ex Graecarum opulentia litterarum, in Romanae orationis thesaurum sumpta conveximus ...'.
58. *De officiis*, I, 6, 19. Cf. *Mor. dogma philos.*, 11. 15–19 (adding 'abacus' to the condemned list).
59. *De arithmetica* (col. 1080A): 'Experiare igitur licet quantum nobis in hoc studio longis tractus otiis labor adjecerit; (1080B): 'Quod nobis quantis vigiliis ac sudore constiterit, facile sobrius lector agnoscet'; (1080C): 'laboris mei primitias ... consecrabis'.
60. R. L. Poole, *Medieval Reckonings of Time* (Helps for Students of History, London 1913), 24.
61. Cf. Turchillus, *Regunculae super abacum*, ed. E. Narducci (as at p. 454 n. 16 below), 137, line 4: 'In multiplicatione et divisione constat hec scientia'; and Bodleian MS. Selden supra 25, fo. 112ʳ ( = treatise on abacus) quoted by C. H. Haskins, *Studies in the History of Medieval Science* (Cambridge 1927), 332 n. 45: 'Huius artis tota pene utilitas in multiplicacione ac divisione constat.'
62. *PL* 101.1157AB (No. XLI).
63. Ibid., col. 1148BC (No. XIII).
64. Cantor, *Vorlesungen*, I, 778–80, 791. B. Bischoff, 'Wendepunkte in der Geschichte der lateinischen Exegese im Frühmittelalter', in the same author's *Mittelalterliche Studien*, I, 223, thinks it probable that Bede pioneered the use of this system in the West. But he surely overlooks the greater likelihood that we are in the presence of a tradition passed by unwritten, demonstrative teaching. See the quotation from Martianus Capella in the next note, and also the persuasive argument of E. Alföldi-Rosenbaum, 'The Finger Calculus in Antiquity and in the Middle Ages. Studies on Roman Game Counters I', *Frühmittelalterliche Studien*, 5 (Berlin–New York 1971), 1–9; and in general, D. E. Smith, *History of Mathematics* (New York 1953), II, 200. The system would have served, at the very least, as an international number-language (as Arabic numerals do now). That the system continued in use late in the middle ages, is suggested by the following phrase in a sermon by Archbishop Federigo Visconti of Pisa (†1277): '... unde in algorismo sive in aubaco transitur in numero centenario de leva in dextram ...' (Sermon *Pueri Hebreorum*; MS. Florence, Laur. Plut. 33 sin. 1, fo. 36ᵛᵃ).
65. Martianus Capella, *Arithmetica* ( = extract from *Satyricon*); ed. E. Narducci, 'Intorno ad un comento inedito di Remigio d'Auxerre al "Satyricon" di Marziano Capella e ad altri comenti al medesimo "Satyricon"', *Bullettino di Bibliografia e Storia delle Scienze Matematiche e Fisiche*, ed. B. Boncompagni, 15 (Rome 1882), 505–80; p. 570, lines 21–3: 'Solus mihi [ =Arithmeticae] numerus approbatur qui digitis cohercetur. alias quaedam brachiorum contorta saltatio sit.' Compare Abbo of

Fleury's comment: *In calculum Victorii commentarium* (ed. N. Bubnov, *Gerberti* ... *Opera Mathematica*, Berlin 1899, 199–203), p. 202, lines 3–9: 'Arithmetica Martiani profitetur, quod sibi solus numerus approbatur, qui digitis cohercetur; alias, inquit, quaedam brachiorum distorta saltatio fit, quippe dum propter $\overline{XC}$ [ = 900,000] sinistrum femur sinistra manu ita comprehendimus, ut pollicem ad inguina vertamus, atque pro decies centenis milibus ambas sibi invicem manus complicamus saltatricum gesticulationem aliquo modo imitamur.' The highest order expressed on hands alone was 9,000 cf. Bede, *De Temporum Ratione*, c. 1, ed. C. W. Jones (as in n. 12) p. 180.49; Rabanus Maurus, *De Computo*, c. 6 (*PL* 107.673D–4A); Smith (as in n. 64), II, 198–201.

66. G. Friedlein, 'Victorii Calculus ...', *Bull. di Bibl. e Storia delle Scienze Mat. e Fisiche*, 4 (1871), 443–63. For remarks on small groups of errors, especially among fractions see pp. 443–4.

67. Cantor, *Vorlesungen*, I, 791–7.

68. Cantor, *Vorlesungen*, I, 796–7: a German 'times-table' with Teutonic words. A. F. Leach, *The Schools of Medieval England* (London 1915), 95, refers to the 'gerym' in the list of books of a certain 'Athelstane' in MS. Cott. Dom. I, fo. 55ᵛ; but another part of this MS. is our witness that the abacus was *not* known (see below p. 454 n. 11).

69. For the effect of legend, compare Richer's 'etiam in mathesi ... studuit' (*Hist.* III, c. 43; *SS*\* 1877 p. 100) with the later Hugh of Flavigny's plain 'in mathesi studuit' (*Chronicon Virdunense*, c. 1; *SS* VIII, p. 367). William of Malmesbury spoke of Gerbert as 'abacum certe primus a Sarracenis rapiens' (*De rebus gestis regum Anglorum*, II, c. 167, ed. W. Stubbs, *RS* 1887, Vol. I, p. 194.14–15) and was echoed by later authors. But Cantor, *Vorlesungen*, 797–824, scotches both errors in this story. Near-contemporary sources on Gerbert are printed by N. Bubnov, *Gerberti* ... *Opera Mathematica* (Berlin 1899), 376–92.

70. Cf. the materials in Bubnov (as in last note). The letters are translated, with comment and bibliography by H. P. Lattin, *The Letters of Gerbert* (Columbia U.P. 1961).

71. *Hist.* III, c. 44 (*SS*\* 1877, p. 100); c. 49 (p. 102).

72. *Fragmentum de norma rationis abaci* (ed. Bubnov, p. 23, lines 13–14): 'ipsa norma rationis aut neglecta aut funditus ignorata'.

73. Franco of Liège, *De quadratura circuli*, ed. Winterburg (*Abhandlungen zur Gesch. der Mathematik*, 4, Leipzig 1882), 135–90; p. 143: 'dubitationem ... tantum ut in ea [ = quadratura circuli] omnes italie gallie atque germanie defecerint sapientes'.

74. Richer, *Hist.* III, c. 43 (p. 100): 'etiam in mathesi plurimum et efficaciter studuit'.

75. Ibid., c. 44, line 1 (p. 100).

76. *Regulae de numerorum abaci rationibus, praefatio*, ed. Bubnov, p. 6, lines 3–5 ( = Lattin, 45): 'Vis amicitiae pene impossibilia redigit ad possibilia. Nam quomodo rationes numerorum abaci explicare contenderemus, nisi te adhortante, o mi dulce solamen laborum, Constantine?'

77. *Hist.* III, c. 45 (p. 101): 'in brevi admodum profecit'.

78. Ibid. 'G[erannus] vero, cum mathesi operam daret, artis difficultate victus, a musica reiectus est'.

79. Ibid., c. 49 (p. 102): 'Qui labor ei in mathematicis impensus sit'; c. 50 (p. 102): 'Ratio vero astronomiae quanto sudore collecta sit ... Quae cum pene intellectibilis sit ...'; c. 54 (p. 104) 'In geometria vero non minor in docendo labor expensus est.

80. William of Malmesbury (as in n. 69 above): 'Abacum ... rapiens, regulas dedit, quae a sudantibus abacistas vix intelliguntur'; echoed by Albericus de Tribus Fontanis, *Chronicon* (*SS* 23, p. 775) by way of Guido of Chalons; cf. Bubnov (as in the same note), p. 387, lines 20–2 and p. 392, lines 15–17 (and n. 83).

81. Abbo of Fleury, *In calculum Victorii commentarium* (ed. Bubnov, p. 203, lines 4–7): '...

Qui serit in lacrimis . . .'. This phrase may have been falsely attributed to Abbo. It occurs in only one of the MSS., and that from the twelfth century. Contrast Abbo's wish to learn more astronomy than he was able, in *V.S. Abbonis*, c. 3 (*PL* 139.390C, and Bubnov, 197 n. 1.). But someone, if not Abbo, thought the phrase applicable. For Bernelinus, see the preface to his *Liber Abaci*, ed. A. Olleris, *Œuvres de Gerbert* (Paris 1867), 257–400; p. 357: 'Parturiunt montes . . . [etc.]'.

82. Namely Constantine of Fleury, Archbishop Adalbero of Rheims, Remi of Trier (who pestered Gerbert three times for a 'sphere') and Brother Adam—though nothing shows the last was assiduous.

83. *Gesta episcoporum Halberstadensium* (year 1002) (*SS* 23, p. 89.40–45), echoing Thietmar of Merseburg, *Chronicon*, VI, c. 61 (*SS\** 1955, p. 392.14–22). Cf. Bubnov, p. 391, lines 27–8.

84. *Gesta episc. Halberstadensium* (as in last note). For Gerbert's dubious reputation in legend, Southern, *Making of the Middle Ages*, 201.

85. Abbo studied music 'occulte propter invidos' (loc. cit. in n. 81 above). Bernelinus (loc. cit. in the same note) wrote: 'Ad hoc etiam accedit quorumdam improbitas qui nihil recipiendum autumant nisi quod sacraverit Libitina, quique quod assequi nolunt venenose dente . . . lacerare non omittunt. Quos equidem existimo . . . invidiae livore ignota blasphemare.'

86. See n. 69 above.

87. Richer, *Hist.* III, cc. 43–4 (pp. 100–1).

88. Ibid., cc. 44–5 (pp. 100–1).

89. Preface to *Regulae de numerorum abaci rationibus* (Bubnov, 6); for the date see also Lattin (as in n. 70), p. 46.

90. The letters are collected in Bubnov, 99–106.

91. *V. Joannis abb. Gorz.*, c. 136 (*PL* 137.310BC).

92. Richer, *Hist.* III, c. 44 (p. 100).

93. Ibid.: 'ut iuvenem retineret nullumque regrediendi aditum ei ullo modo preberet'.

94. Thompson, *Literacy*, 83.

95. Printed in F. Weigle's edition of Gerbert's letters (*MGH, BDK* 2 (1966)), p. 222, esp. lines 10–12; and by Olleris (as in n. 81), and Lattin, 295.

96. Cf. Cantor, *Vorlesungen*, I, 805–6: the tutor was Bernward of Hildesheim.

7. THE EMERGENCE OF THE ARITHMETICAL MENTALITY

1. G. F. Hill, *The Development of Arabic Numerals in Europe, Exhibited in Sixty-Four Tables* (Oxford 1915), Table I, No. 1.

2. Richer, *Hist.* III, cc. 50–4 (pp. 102–4); note especially the phrase in c. 51 (p. 103): 'Cuius instrumenti ratio in tantum valuit, ut . . . circulos visibus inexpertos scientiae daret atque alta memoria reconderet'. Gerbert's letters to Remi of Trier and Brother Adam touch on mathematical instruments; Weigle, pp. 162.1; 179.10; 180.26; 190.17.

3. Cf. Smith, *History of Mathematics*, II, 137, quoting Maximus Planudes (*c.* 1340) on 'galley' division: 'The necessity for erasing certain numbers and writing others in their places gives rise to much confusion where ink is used, but on the sand table it is easy to erase numbers with the fingers and to write others in their places.' The same would apply to slate (see p. 172 below). The abacus shared with the slate and sand table the quality of being infinitely re-usable.

4. Smith, II, 177–92; J. M. Pullan, *The History of the Abacus* (London 1968). The latter work is weak on the specifically medieval phase of the instrument's history, but clear in explaining its principles of operation.

5. See p. 156 above, and n. 65. The passage from Abbo continues: 'ubi infinita numerorum congeries perpenditur, quae a philosophis repudiatur, qui finitae quantitatis multitudinem scientia comprehendere gaudent'.

6. Weigle, *Briefsammlung Gerberts*, p. 217.7–8; contrast Juvenal, *Satura*, x: 'Felix ... qui ... suos iam dextra computat annos' (meaning a man over a hundred), quoted by Smith, II, 197; and the phrase used by Federigo Visconti, quoted on p. 451 n. 64 above.

7. Hermannus Contractus, *Tract on the Abacus*, quoted by Cantor, *Vorlesungen*, I, 831 n. 3.

8. Bernelinus, *Liber Abaci* (Olleris, 257–400; p. 359).

9. Text in Bubnov, 6–22.

10. Remigius of Auxerre, *Commentum super Arithmeticam Martiani Capellae*, ed. E. Narducci (as on p. 451 n. 65 above), 572, lines 13–16. Remigius uses the imperfect tense. Later he says mysteriously 'una quaeque ars suum abacum habebat' (p. 576, line 15). Compare Smith, II, 177–8. Richer regarded the abacus as an introduction to *geometry*, *Hist.* III, c. 54 (p. 104).

11. British Library MS. Cott. Dom. I. fo. 37ᵛ, line 23: 'Abbacus. Id est tabula pictoria.' This entry comes in a 'glossary of difficult words' (fos. 37ᵛ–38ᵛ) whose script suggests it belongs to the late tenth century.

12. *Fragmentum de norma rationis abaci*, ed. Bubnov, p. 23, lines 13–14.

13. Cantor, *Vorlesungen*, I, 801–2 (Walter of Speyer); Bubnov, 197–203, esp. 197–8, n. 1 (Abbo).

14. See p. 452 n. 80 above.

15. C. H. Haskins, 'The Abacus and the Exchequer', in the same author's collected *Studies in the History of Mediaeval Science* (Cambridge 1927), 327–35.

16. E. Narducci, 'Intorno a due trattati inediti d'abaco contenuti in due codici vaticani del secolo XII', *Bull. di Bibl. e Storia della Scienze Mat. e Fisiche* (ed. B. Boncompagni, 15, Rome 1882), 111–62; p. 111.

17. Olleris, 311–48.

18. Pullan (as in n. 4), 71–87.

19. Adelard of Bath, *Regulae abaci* (ed. B. Boncompagni, 'Intorno ad uno scritto inedito di Adelardo di Bath intitolato "Regulae Abaci"', *Bull. di Bibl. e Storia della Scienze Mat. e Fisiche*, ed. B. Boncompagni, 14, Rome 1881, 1–134); p. 91.7–9: 'ut ea quae magistro suo pitagora docente audierant, oculis subjecta retinerent, et firmius custodirent'.

20. Leonardo Pisano, *Liber Abaci*, ed. B. Buoncompagni (Rome 1857), p. 1: 'quod scientia per practicam versa in habitum, memoria et intellectus adeo concordent cum manibus et figuris, quod quasi uno impulsu et anelitu in uno et eodem instanti circa idem per omnia naturaliter consonent ...'.

21. See n. 3 above.

22. D. E. Smith and L. C. Karpinski, *The Hindu–Arabic Numerals* (Boston–London 1911), 137 n. 1, quote Prosdocimo de' Beldomandi (†1428): 'si in aliquo calculo astroloico error contigisset, calculatorem operationem suam a capite incipere oportebat, dato quod error suus adhuc satis propinquus existeret; et hoc propter figuras in sua operatione deletas.' Prosdocimo was criticizing certain methods in algorism, not the abacus; but the principle is identical.

23. Pullan (as in n. 4), 17–20, 51–5.

24. Smith, II, 188, quoting Palegrave (1530): 'I shall reken it syxe tymes by aulgorisme or you can caste it ones by counters.'

25. Smith and Karpinski, 120. The rendering 'O' Creat' may nevertheless be a gratuitous compliment to Ireland: *ocreatus* means 'booted'.

26. Bibliography: Florian Cajori, *A History of Mathematical Notations* (La Salle. Ill. 1928), II, 45–70. Smith and Karpinski, op. cit., have written the classic short essay on the subject.
27. See n. 1.
28. Hill, Table III, Nos. 6, 14.
29. Hill, p. 20.
30. B. Bischoff, 'Die sogenannten "griechischen" und "chaldäischen" Zahlzeichen des abendländischen Mittelalters', in the same author's collected *Mittelalterliche Studien*, I, 67–73.
31. See below, pp. 170–2.
32. Hilary Jenkinson, 'The Use of Arabic and Roman Numerals in English Archives', *Antiquaries Journal*, 6 (1926), 263–75; Pullan, 40–8.
33. R. de Roover, 'The Development of Accounting Prior to Luca Pacioli', in A. C. Littleton and B. S. Yamey, eds., *Studies in the History of Accounting* (London 1956), 114–74; pp. 123–31 on Florentine accounting. D. J. Struik, *A Concise History of Mathematics* (London 1954), 105 n. 1, records Mrs. F. E. Roover's findings about the Medici accounts in particular.
34. Villani, XI, c. 94; later evidence in L. C. Karpinski, *The History of Arithmetic* (New York 1925), 170–3; though the studies of commercial accountancy and dictamen were merged, then as now, in business schools on the fringe of Oxford university from the thirteenth century, N. Orme, *English Schools in the Middle Ages* (London 1973), 70–9, esp. 75–7.
35. A. Ghiardi, ed., *Statuti della Università e Studio Fiorentino, 1387* (Florence 1881), *Rubrica 22* (p. 31): '[Massarius] scribat [ = in Libro rationum Universitatis] manu propria. Si scribere non posset, tunc duobus ad minus scholaribus adhibitis subrogare possit.'
36. Florence Edler de Roover, *Glossary of Medieval Italian Terms of Business* (Cambridge, Mass. 1934), 18 (earliest example: *abbachista* (1341)); Narducci, 'Intorno a due trattati ...' (as in n. 16), 131. These authorities give enough instances to soften the contrary implication in the passage referred to from Villani in the last note, '... i fanciulli, che stavano ad apparare *l'abbaco e algorisimo* in sei scuole, ...'.
37. R. de Roover, Plate V and pp. 139–40.
38. G. C. Marri, ed., *Statuti dell'Arte del Cambio di Firenze, 1299–1316 (Fonti sulle Corporazioni medioevali* IV, Florence 1955), 72–3. Cf. statutes of 1300 (§100), 1313 (§93), and 136 (§94). The clause banning the use of Arabic numerals is in all cases preceded immediately by one prescribing the restitution of usurious gains. In translating the clause I have divided it into paragraphs.
39. H. Denifle, 'Die Constitutionen der Juristen-Universität Paduas von 1331', *Archiv für Literatur- und Kirchengeschichte des Mittelalters*, 6 (Freiburg-im-Breisgau 1892), 309–562; p. 453, lines 25–8 ( =§16): 'Ponat eciam in libro venali extrinsecus et in evidenti loco et claris litteris nom per zyphras [variants: zephytas, zephiras] nomen venditoris cum ipsius congnomine et precium libri ...' The fine for a breach of the law is 20 *solidi*. Cf. p. 454.34–5. An almost identical prescription appears in the university statutes of Bologna and Florence. See C. Malagola, *Statuti della Università e dei Collegi dello Studio Bolognese* (Bologna 1888); Statute of 1317–47, *Rubrica 30* (pp. 28–9); Statute of 1432, *Rubrica 30* (pp. 87–8): this Rubric was among those left intact by the confirmation of 1459. See also A. Ghiardi, (as in n. 35), *Rubrica 34* (pp. 41–2).
40. Cf. Hill, Table IV, No. 1 (beginning of thirteenth century); Table VI, No. 1; etc. The earliest of Hill's examples of *dates* in Arabic is a note recording the date of the purchase of a book in 1246; Table III, No. 4. The curious erudition of stationers is perhaps also testified by the occasional use of 'Chaldean' numerals for foliation; cf.

B. Bischoff, 'Die sogenannten "griechischen" und "chaldäischen" Zahlzeichen' (as in n. 30 above), p. 71 (No. 6, and remarks on Bodleian MS. Lyell empt. 5).

41. Printed by J. O. Halliwell, *Rara Arithmetica* (London 1841²), who gives an indication (Introduction, pp. v–vi) of the very large number of MSS. of both Sacrobosco and the Song of Algorism. On their popularity see also Karpinski, *The History of Arithmetic* (New York 1925), 54–5.

42. Cf. the passage quoted by Smith and Karpinski (as in n. 22) from Prosdocimo de' Beldomandi. Smith, *History of Mathematics*, II, 179, reads this evidence upside-down, as indicating the beginning of the use of the slate. But a careful reading of it suggests on the contrary that the slate had long been in use, and was indeed beginning its slow journey to the scrap-heap. Prosdocimo writes: 'Inveni in quam pluribus libris algorismi nuncupatis mores circa numeros operandi satis varios atque diversos, qui licet boni existerent atque veri erant, tamen fastidiosi, tum propter ipsarum regularum multitudinem, tum etiam propter ipsarum operationem probationes, utrum ại bone fuerint vel ne [there follows the passage quoted above, n. 22]. *Indigebat* etiam calculator *semper* aliquo lapide vel sibi conformi, super quo scribere atque faciliter delere posset figuras cum quibus operabatur in calculo suo. Et quia haec omnia satis fastidiosa atque laboriosa mihi visa sunt, disposui libellum edere in quo omnia ista abicerentur.' My italics. Prosdocimo died in 1428; his book was printed in 1483.

43. Villani, xi, c. 94.

44. R. de Roover, 165.

45. See n. 34 above.

46. Gautier de Conci, *Les Miracles de Nostre Dame*, ed. V. F. Koenig (Geneva 1955–), Bk. I, Mir. 10, lines 138–40 (Vol. I, p. 59), Bk. II, Mir. 32, lines 224–7 (Vol. IV, pp. 426–7). Other French examples in A. Tobler and E. Lommatzsch, *Altfranzösisches Wörterbuch*, I (Berlin 1925), 669. Cf. *Richard the Redeless*, Passus IV, lines 53–4, ed. W. W. Skeat, *Piers the Plowman* ... (Oxford 1886), I, p. 627, with note in II, p. 303; and *King Lear*, Act I, scene 4 (Fool).

47. Cf. C. H. Haskins, 'Adelard of Bath', in his *Studies* (as in n. 15), 20–42; Cantor, *Vorlesungen*, I, 849–50.

48. Ed. B. Boncompagni (Rome 1857).

49. Ibid., p. 1: '... ut ... gens latina de cetero, sicut hactenus, absque illa [ = hac scientia] minime inveniatur'.

50. Smith, I, 215 n. 5.

51. *Liber Abaci*, p. 1: '... ex proprio sensu quedam addens ...' (against Cantor, *Vorlesungen*, II, 31 and n. 3).

52. This occurs in Leonardo's shorter book *Flos*, printed in Volume II of Boncompagni's edition of *Liber Abaci*, pp. 227–52. Cf. Cantor, *Vorlesungen*, II, 40–7, and (for a modern mathematician's appreciation), H. Eves, *An Introduction to the History of Mathematics* (New York 1969³), 209–28.

53. Cf. the Introduction to *Flos* (p. 227): '... questionum ... plurium que subtilius quam in libro maiori de numero, quem composui, sunt solute ...'. But not all shared this opinion: cf. ibid., p. 247, where an intimate friend of the author apparently 'fortiora pabula in libro meo numeri apposita pavescebat ...'.

54. The following remarks are based on *c.* 30 *Vitae* written between *c.* 900 and *c.* 1300, included among the *Vitae* listed in the bibliography (q.v. for abbreviations). Notably numberless *Vitae* from each of the four centuries include: *V.S. Geraldi* (no number above 7 except for small sums of money); *V.S. Romualdi* (year-periods, no date of birth or death); *V.B. Roberti de Arbr.* (no cardinal number above 4); *V.B. Joh. de Monte Mir.* (no date of birth or death).

55. e.g. (day of death) *V.S. Hugonis Clun.* (Hildebert); (gifts) *V.S. Burchardi*.

56. Especially in *V.B. Roberti Salent., passim.* (e.g. 500 genuflexions per day, c. 2 §19 (p. 498AB)); also *V.S. Hugonis Grat.*, c. 6 (col. 780D).

57. W. von den Steinen, 'Heilige als Hagiographen', *Historische Zeitschrift*, 143 (1930), 229–56, reprinted in the same author's *Menschen im Mittelalter* (Berne–Munich 1967), 7–31.

58. Ed. C. R. Dodwell (London 1961). On the book's origin see B. Bischoff, 'Die Überlieferung des Theophilus Rugerus nach den ältsten Handschriften', revised in *Mittelalterliche Studien*, II, 175–82.

59. p. 56.

60. Feet and fingers, *passim.* Half a thumb-length, p. 107; as thick as a straw, p. 79; a handsbreadth, pp. 49, 59, 79, 95; as thick as an arm, p. 59.

61. *Mir. S. Fidis*, 54.1–4: 'tabula aurea, non minus quam septem pedibus digitisque duobus in longitudine habens, non illis geometricalibus, sed ut utraque manu protensa rustici solent metiri duobus pollicibus junctis'.

62. pp. 158 f.; compare pp. 17, 23, 28, 124, 180, etc. for (less baffling) fractions in the mixing of metals.

63. Ed. H. Waquet (Paris 1964).

64. c. 1 (p. 8), c. 28 (p. 224).

65. pp. 60, 132, 140, 156 (*quamplures*); pp. 22, 24, 48, 160, 174 (similar words); p. 224 (locusts).

66. c. 33 (p. 276). 100 knights are beheaded in c. 9 (p. 50), and a request is put 100 times in c. 5 (p. 26).

67. Cf. editor's introduction pp. xv–xvi. 'Aliquot dies', 'aliquot annos', 'alio tempore' are frequent expressions, cf. pp. 118, 254, 316, etc.

68. *Hist. Calamitatum*, ed. J. Monfrin (Paris 1962).

69. p. 86, line 830 ('pluribus... convocatis' to judge Abelard at St.-Denis); p. 82, line 666 ('tanta scolarium multitudo' gathered at Abelard's hermitage); p. 67, lines 137–8 ('aliquos ... discipulos' of William of Champeaux who left him for Abelard). How many assailants were involved in the assault on Abelard? Cf. p. 79, lines 578–88.

70. p. 63, lines 9–10 ('ab urbe Namnetica ... octo credo miliariis remotum'; N.B. 'credo').

71. pp. 89, line 941, and 91, line 996.

72. e.g. another dateless autobiography: Hermannus quondam Judaeus, *Opusculum de conversione sua*, ed. G. Niemeyer (*MGH QGG* 1963); cf. editor's remark on p. 32.

73. *Mor. dogma philos.*, ll. 15–19 (abacus); Brunetto Latini, *Tresors*, II, c. 69, p. 247.38–9 (augorisme). Note that Latini (*c.* 1268) renders the *abacus* of *Mor. dogma philos.* as *augorisme*. The *Moralium* was composed in the second quarter of the twelfth century.

74. *Dist.* 37, esp. c. 10, in Friedburg, I, 138. Comments emphasize the point: cf. J. W. Baldwin, *Masters, Princes and Merchants* (Princeton 1970), I, 79; O. Lottin, *Psychologie et Morale*, III, 46 n. 3; Raymond of Peñaforte, *Summa de Poenitentia*, Bk. I, c. *de sortilegis et divinis* § 5 (ed. of Rome 1603, p. 106). Lingering associations with superstition played some part in setting theologians against the *quadrivium*. But only a small part. See, e.g., Henry of Ghent, *Summae*, a. XI, q. vii (fo. 83$^{rM}$), where it is specifically the *measuring* of the sun, etc., that is rejected.

75. P. Vinogradoff, *Roman Law in Mediaeval Europe* (Oxford 1929), 60–1.

76. *V.S. Steph. Obaz.* 134, lines 21–44; compare 146, lines 36–8; and 180, lines 35–43.

77. *V. Joannis abb. Gorz.*, c. 9, col. 247B; Lizérand, *Templiers*, 188; *Chart. Univ. Par.* III, p. 132 §1307; p. 413 §1521 (iii). The practice was common in court proceedings of the late middle ages.

78. Ed. J. C. Robertson, *Materials for the History of Thomas Becket*, III (*RS* 1877), 2–13: churches, p. 3; contingent, p. 4.

79. *De laudibus Parisius*, ed. A. J. V. Le Roux de Lincy and L. M. Tisserand, *Hist. générale de Paris* (Paris 1867), 32–78; p. 32.
80. Ibid., pp. 40, 42, 44.
81. Ibid., p. 52.
82. Sir James Ramsay, 'Chroniclers' Estimates of Numbers and Official Records', *Engl. Hist. Review* 18 (1903), 625–9; 'The Strength of English Armies in the Middle Ages', ibid. 29 (1914), 221–7.
83. Ramsay (1903), p. 626.
84. Ibid. 626–7.
85. Ramsay (1914), 22–3; cf. (for Bannockburn), G. W. S. Barrow, *Robert Bruce* (London 1965) 293–9, and, in general, M. Prestwich, *War, Politics and Finance under Edward I* (London 1972), esp. 108–13.
86. V. H. Galbraith, *The Making of Domesday Book* (Oxford 1961), 144; and, for later use of Domesday figures, 189.
87. Ed. G. D. G. Hall (*Nelson's Medieval Texts*, London 1965), 82.
88. Fossier, *Picardie*, I, 258–9.
89. F. Lot and R. Fawtier, *Hist. des Institutions françaises au m.â., II: Institutions monarchiques* (Paris 1958), 159.
90. Especially later in the work. Cf. the edition of G. Scalia (Bari 1966), 924.2–3, 929.5.
91. Ibid. 49.23–7; 705.2–5; 706.29–707.5; 710.26–711.7; 726.15–17; 727.14–19; 737.11–13; 729.3–8; also 46.4–6.
92. Ibid. 466.7; 634.6–7; 717.2.
93. The possible exception: ibid. 677.23–30.
94. Ibid. 779.22–8.
95. Ed. F. Novati, in *Bullettino dell'Istituto Storico Italiano per il Medio Evo*, 20 (Rome 1898), 61–176; statistics are most dense between pp. 67 and 116.
96. Most figures for food are between pp. 97 and 112.
97. p. 100.3–4: 'sicut cum quibusdam ex carnificibus diligenter examinavi'; cf. p. 100.16–17: 'sicut ipsi pescatores, veritate rey dilligenter examinata, manifeste fatentur'; p. 105.1–2: 'ab eis qui rei veritatem se sire pro certo testantur vere sum doctus'. Bonvesino refers to his own industry in the preface, p. 62.3–5: 'cum ingenti dilligentia et multo labore deliberate investigata'. The passive mood is often used, suggesting he may have had assistants, e.g. p. 69.4–5: 'murus ... diligentissime mensuratus'. Bonvesino more than once refers to governmental accounting: 1,200 *modii* of flour are eaten each day, 'cuius rei veritatém sic esse certificant qui solent bladi triti a molandinis tributa exigere' (p. 85.4–5); 'sicut ex libris comunis habetur' (= 300 ovens, pp. 88.4–5); 'ut ab illis qui sallis tributa pro comuni exigere solent, diligenter examinatum est' (p. 112.21–3). The mere fact that 'exempts' (i.e. church institutions) are treated separately—e.g. concerning ovens, p. 88.4–7—points to tax-documents as Bonvesino's sources. For the excellence of Caravalle monastic accounts, cf. pp. 96–7. An 'account' is however expressly mentioned only once, in relation to wine, p. 97.22–3: 'ut asserunt qui veritatem se fatentur perpendere, *ratione* dilligenter examinata'. Bonvesino occasionally excuses his failure to count an item; pp. 84.15, 79.2–3, 84.15, and especially 174.4–7.
98. Positive appreciation (with biography etc.): Angelo Monteverdi, 'Due cronisti milanesi dei tempo viscontei—Bonvesin de la Riva e Galvano de la Fiamma', *Cultura Neolatini* (*Boll. dell'Istituto di Lingue e Letterature Romanze*, Univ. di Roma), 4, 5 (1944–5), 5–20; and the same author's contribution to *Storia di Milano* (Treccani degli Alfieri, Milan 1954), IV, pp. 393–430.
99. pp. 62.18–63.8.
100. An inaccurate summary of Bonvesino's statistics by Galvaneo della Fiamma

(writing *c.* 1330–40) is found in the latter's *Manipulus Florum*, cc. 236–7, Muratori[1], XI, 711B–714B.
101. XII, c. 46.
102. XI, cc. 91–4.
103. A. Frugoni, 'G. Villani "Cronica" XI, 94', *Bullettino dell'Istututo Storico Italiano per il Medio Evo*, 77 (Rome 1965), 229–55.
104. Cf. G. Celoria, 'Sull' eclissi solare totale del 3 giugno 1239', *Memorie del reale Istituto Lombardo di scienze e lettere, classe di scienze matematiche e naturali*, 13 (Milan 1977), 275–300, quoting Ristoro d'Arezzo, [*Libro*] *della composizione del mondo*, I, c. 16. On Ristoro: H. R. Jauss, ed., *Grundriss der romanischen Literatur des Mittelalters*, VI, ii (Heidelberg 1970), No. 3459. I have not had the opportunity to consult the edition of Ristoro's book by A. Morino (Accademia della Crusca, Florence 1977).
105. *Civilization of the Renaissance*, Pt. I, c. 7, (tr. S. G. C. Middlemore, London 1929, 90–3); the speech is in M. Sanudo, *Vite de' Duchi*, in Muratori[1], XXII.958–60.
106. R. de Roover, 129.
107. Hyde, *Padua*, 65, n. 3; R. Davidsohn, *Gesch. von Florenz*, IV, pt. 3 (Berlin 1927), 75.
108. (As in n. 95 above), p. 91.14–15.
109. C. M. Ady, *Pius II* (London 1913), 13.
110. E. H. Gombrich, 'The Early Medici as Patrons of Art: A Survey of Primary Sources', in E. F. Jacob, ed., *Italian Renaissance Studies* (London 1960), 279–311; p. 299; cf. p. 285 for Lorenzo's careful accounting of money given for 'buildings, charities and taxes'.

## 8. MEN AND MATHEMATICS

1. S. Bochner, *The Role of Mathematics in the Rise of Science* (Princeton 1966), 113; compare 39.
2. See p. 155.
3. Cantor, *Vorlesungen*, I, 796–7.
4. B. Bischoff, 'Wendepunkte in der Gesch. der lateinischen Exegese im Frühmittelalter' (*Mittelalterliche Studien*, I), 205–73; p. 208.
5. Idem, 'Das griechische Element in der abendländischen Bildung des Mittelalters', ibid. II, 246–75; pp. 264–5; compare pp. 251–2, 257–8, 260.
6. R. de Roover, 118.
7. Ibid., for the peculiarity, 137–9, 155, 170.
8. Bk. II, c. 13; ed. C. Johnson (*Nelson's Medieval Classics*, London 1950), 108.
9. A. Nagl, 'Das Quadripartitum des Ioannes de Muris und das praktische Rechnen im 14. Jh.', *Abhandlungen zur Gesch. der Mathematik*, 5 (Leipzig 1890), 137–40.
10. *Liber Abaci*, 203, 182, 152, 274.
11. Peyraut, *Summae*, I, iii, pt. 3, c. 6 (edition of Antwerp 1587, fo. 142r): 'tale enim est ac si ille cui debentur marcae auri et argenti, reciperet pro eis fabas vel lapillulos quibus facta est computatio: plus enim est faba una respectu marcae argenti quam tribulatio praesens respectu poenae futurae'.
12. Many examples in Dresdner, 48, 59–63, 65, 69.
13. Yunck, 316 n. 20.
14. *Liber Abaci*, 1.
15. Ibid.
16. The three: Smith and Karpinski, 131.
17. For the diffusion of Sacrobosco and the *Song of Algorism* see p. 456 n. 41 above. Bernelinus' eleventh-century *Liber Abaci*, unlike its thirteenth-century namesake a practical treatise on the abacus, survives in some seventeen MSS. (Olleris, 245, 269–84); the contrast is all the more striking when we reflect on how much easier it was in Leonardo's time to have books copied.

18. H. Jenkinson 'The Use of Arabic and Roman Numerals' (as on p. 455 n. 32). In the sixteenth century nearly half of known algorisms are still in Latin, Karpinski, *The History of Arithmetic* (New York 1925), 71–2.
19. See p. 169 above.
20. pp. 160, 186, 273.
21. *Prediche inedite*, ed. E. Narducci, 133. (For 'ragionare' see below, pp. 205–6.)
22. E. Fiumi, 'L'imposta diretta nei comuni medioevali della Toscana', *Studi in onore di A. Sapori*, I (Milan 1962), 329–53.
23. Summary in D. Waley, *Italian City Republics* (London 1969), 77, 79.
24. F. Lot and R. Fawtier, *Hist. des institutions françaises au m.â.*, II (Paris 1958), 159.
25. Pullan (as on p. 453 n. 4), 71–4.
26. 'Million': Smith, II, 80–2. Marco Polo's sobriquet 'Il Milione' appeared in 1305.
27. e.g. *V. S. Steph. Obaz.*, 134. 33–44 (the counting of daily consumption and expenses was left strictly to God); 180. 39–43 (St. Stephen supervised scrupulously all quantities used in the kitchen); 146. 36–8 (God punished the measuring of grain in the grain-store).
28. Bonvesino, 96–7; cf. 75. 8–10 and note.
29. Although there are still a few serious lapses later, e.g. 458b, 468d (Rocher-le-Mortain 1263 and St. Victor-en-Caux 1263). The amount of the Visitor's procuration is more often given after 1254 than before (pp. 205a and following).
30. R. de Roover, 167.
31. See p. 169 above.
32. Cf. R. E. Latham, ed., *Revised Medieval Latin Word-List* (London 1965), 245, and compare xxi-xxiii for sources.
33. B. H. Slicher van Bath, *The Agrarian History of Western Europe*, A.D. *500–1850*, (London 1963), 77–82; G. A. Brucker, *Renaissance Florence* (New York 1969), 52 (and Dante, *Par.* XVI, 48).
34. The situation is reviewed by H. E. Hallam, 'Some Thirteenth-Century Censuses', *Economic Hist. Rev.* 10 (1957–8), 340–61.
35. A. Frugoni, 'G. Villani, "Cronica" XI, 94', *Bull. del Ist. Stor. Ital. per il m.e.*, 77 (1965), 235 n. 1 (a census ordered in 1285). Cf. Bonvesino, 73.1–2, 85.6–86.4, 169.3–170.6, 172.4–5 and 15–18, 175.4,8,24. Milan put more military reliance on its nobility, and therefore had less reason than Florence to count every able-bodied citizen. Padua's earliest detailed census, in 1320, was almost certainly military in purpose: Hyde, *Padua*, 34–7.
36. III, c. 15 (pp. 99.12–100.10).
37. See above, p. 130.
38. E. Ruffini Avondo, *I sistemi di deliberazione collectiva nel medioevo italiano* (Turin 1927), esp. 34–6.
39. Ibid. 24–8; cf. Andrea Dandolo, *Chronicon*, x, c. 1 (Muratori[1] XII. 506D).
40. C. J. Hefele and J. Leclercq, *Hist. des conciles*, V(ii) (Paris 1907), 1087–8.
41. Ruffini Avondo, 58–9, 40–53.
42. C. Malagola, ed., *Statuti della Università e dei Collegi . . . dello Studio Bolognese* (Bologna 1888), *Rubrica* 6 (p. 10).
43. G. R. Galbraith, *The Constitution of the Dominican Order* (Manchester 1925), 14, 21, 29, 33 (background in other religious orders); 46–7, 64–5, 103, 110, 113–14, 136, 158, 182–9 (Dominicans and majority voting, with scrutiny from 1281 (p. 113); p. 5 (possible influence on English parliament). For the late maturity of strict majority rule in England, see Sir G. Edwards, 'The Emergence of Majority Rule in English Parliamentary Elections', *Trans. Royal Hist. Soc.*, 5th ser., 14 (1964), 175–96; and 'The Emergence of Majority Rule in the Procedure of the House of Commons', ibid. 15 (1965), 165–87.
44. Herodotus, II, c. 109; Gerbert, *Geometria*, prologue (*PL* 139.92B–93A).

45. O. von Simson, *The Gothic Cathedral* (New York 1962²), 21–58.
46. Ibid. 176
47. Short history: F. Saxl, 'The Revival of Late Antique Astrology', first published in 1936 and reprinted in Saxl's collected essays, *A Heritage of Images* (Harmondsworth 1970), 27–41. Short technical exposition: W. Hartner, 'The Mercury Horoscope of Marcantonio Michiel of Venice', first published in 1955 and reprinted in Hartner's collected essays, *Oriens-Occidens* (Hildesheim 1968), 440–495, esp. 442–57. Bibliography: J. D. North, *Richard of Wallingford* (Oxford 1976), III, 292–300.
48. Cf. Hill, Table II, No. 5; Table V, Nos. 1 and 2; Table VI, No. 6, etc.
49. See p. 454 n. 22 above.
50. Salimbene, 515.11–23.
51. Symon de Phares, *Recueil des plus célèbres astrologues et des quelques hommes doctes écrit sous le regne de Charles VIII*, ed. E. Wickersheimer (Paris 1929), 250c (Henry Seldem), 242d (Denis Plusdoré): compare 220d (Berthelemy de Morbecha), 244a (Meletun de Russis), 253d (Rolland Scriptoris); and further 224c (Symon de Bussy); 230d (Nicolas de Paganico), 245c (Jehan Furois), 255d (Jaques de Villette), and 259 (Jehen Colleman).
52. Cantor, *Vorlesungen*, I, 829 n. 1.
53. Hartner, 'Zahlen', 86–7, and on the mental structures involved, 86–94.
54. *De arithmetica*, preface *(PL* 58.1079B).
55. e.g. Rabanus Maurus, *De clericorum institutione*, III, c. 22 *(PL* 107.399A); Gerbert, *De geometria*, prologue *(PL* 139.93A).
56. *Metalogicon*, II, c. 13, tr. D. McGarry (Gloucester, Mass. 1971), 105. Compare also IV, c. 6.
57. Rabanus Maurus, op. cit. (col. 399B).
58. H. J. R. Murray, *A History of Chess* (Oxford 1913), 402–10 (spread *c.* 1000); 411 (Roman Law); 431, 440, 447, 499 (allowed by other authorities, as an exception to games in general).
59. Ibid. 501–2.
60. Ibid. 217–18.
61. F. N. David and M. G. Kendall, 'Studies in the History of Probability and Statistics II: The Beginnings of Probability Calculus', *Biometrika*, 43 (1956), 1–14, esp. 4–6; r.p. in E. S. Pearson and M. G. Kendall, ed., *Studies in the History of Statistics and Probability* (London 1970), 19–34.
62. Florence Edler de Roover, *Glossary of Medieval Italian Terms of Business* (Cambridge, Mass. 1934), 235–8.
63. E. Mâle, *The Gothic Image* (London 1961⁴), 84 nn. 2, 4.
64. See the note by Jerome Taylor to Hugh of St. Victor, *Didascalicon*, II, c. 7 in his (Taylor's) translation of that work (Columbia University Press, New York 1968²), 201n.40.
65. See pp. 113–16. For others' recognition of the role of mathematics in science see A. C. Crombie, 'Quantification in Medieval Physics', in S. Thrupp, ed., *Change in Medieval Society* (London 1965), 188–207, esp. 188–93.
66. See p. 458 n. 87 and p. 456 n. 43 above for the two named examples.
67. p. 237; compare p. 142 and Bacon's approving note.
68. *Coutumes de Beauvaisis*, 25.
69. R. de Roover, 139–40, 167.
70. F. Schevill, *Medieval and Renaissance Florence*, 143.
71. P. Hunter Blair, *The World of Bede* (London 1970), 3–5; C. H. Haskins, 'Adelard of Bath', in the same author's *Studies in the History of Mediaeval Science* (Cambridge 1927), 20–42, pp. 33–4; for Leonardo see p. 192 above; E. S. Duckett, *Alcuin* (New York 1951), 15; *Chronicle of Aurillac* (as in *PL* 141.50, n. 97); for the case of Gregory VII see p. 412 below; and for that of Urban IV, p. 290 below.

72. Symon de Phares, 219b, 220d, 224c, 242d, 250c, 253d.
73. Symon de Phares, 1.
74. pp. 193 (Vincent de Chartres)–269. I exclude 29 names from the count as anachronisms (e.g. Pachomius), repetitions (e.g. Raymond Lull, Peter of Abano), mere names (e.g. those on pp. 198–9 and 234), or irrelevancies (i.e. the author himself; non-Christians).
75. The grandees are: popes, 1 (Sixtus IV; Petrus Hispanus is not *said* by Symon to have been a pope); kings or emperors, 4; cardinals, 3; dukes etc., 1; archbishops or bishops, 6 (excluding any expressly said to have been in service); others, 4 (first president of *parlement;* a counsellor of *parlement;* an English captain; a canon); total, 19.
76. 'Expressly said': i.e. 'pensionaire de' (pp. 226c, 231c, 241d, 245d, 254d, 262b); 'stipendié' (pp. 202a, 206c, 219d, 223c, 259b, 264c, 268a); 'de la retinue de' (256a); 'son [medecin et] astrologien' (256c, 261d, 269c); 'baillé à' (238c); 'moult famillier à' (236a); 'appellé par' (235d); 'au service de' (233a). 'Clearly implied' denotes that an astrologer is said to have predicted 'to king A event B', or 'made C for king A', as if the astrologer was or wished to be in the pay of the magnate in question. Astrologers used for diplomatic missions are included here.
    The two categories 'expressly said' and 'clearly implied' account in about equal proportions for the 156 names I have counted under 'service'.
77. The bulk of the 157 names of astrologers *not* said to have been in service is accounted for by two categories: (1) religious orders, namely (in descending order of frequency): Franciscans, Benedictines, Dominicans, Carmelites, Augustinians; and (2) citizens of free towns: Florence, Milan, Venice, Rome, Cremona, Pavia, Piacenza, Bruges, Ghent, Ypres, Basle, Geneva, Constance, Lyons, Orleans, Montpellier. Doctors and teachers of medicine are conspicuous in the second category, e.g. 207c, 208c, 243d.
78. e.g. Arnold of Villanuova, Petrarch, Petrus Hispanus, Sacrobosco, Jean Petit, Henry Seldem. The large number of Symon de Phares' astrologers in court service was noticed by Miss A. M. Campbell, *Black Death*, 127–8. Her discovery that the percentage of courtiers among astrologers rose in the second half of the fourteenth century may, however, only reflect the fact that there were more courts.
79. Piere l'Aragonais, 206b; (Jacques d'Illiers, 207b); Jehan de Palusach, 211b; (Jacques d'Orleans, 211b); Lothar de Blois, 215a; Anda[l]lo le Gen[nev]ois, 217b, 225c; Eustace de Bon Vueil, 224df; Symond de Perre Couverte, 235d; Nicolle d'Amendel, 237b; (Espinel de la Mirandolle, 237d); Jean de Preaux, 242c; Jehan de Bregy, 254df; (Johanin de Werdemberg, 264a). Parentheses indicate that Symon de Phares' description gives little ground for supposing mathematical expertise.
80. Martin l'Escoissois, Patrice Beriulz, Michel Scotus; Edoart Wihrell; Jacques Bollenc, Yves Dariam; Guidon de Caillac; Michel le Gascon.
81. Johannes de Bechaz, 202c.
82. Taddeus Florentinus; Simon de Pavie, 264d. The dominant source of both fortunes was plainly the practice of medicine.
83. 268b.
84. 86b: Hermes Trimegistus.
85. 3b, 11d; compare 13b: 'plus que bergiers ignorans la science de l'astrologie . . .'

### 9. THE UNIVERSITY LADDER

1. See pp. 63–4, 67 above.
2. See p. 479 n. 18 below.

3. The picture of early medieval lay literacy in this paragraph is based mainly on J. W. Thompson, *The Literacy of the Laity in the Middle Ages* (University of California 1915, r.p. New York 1960) and P. Riché, 'Recherches sur l'instruction des laïcs du ix<sup>e</sup> au xii<sup>e</sup> siècle', *Cahiers de civilisation médiévale*, 4 (1962), 175–82.

4. Gregory VII, *Reg.* IX, 2, p. 571.8.

5. Ibid., lines 10–11.

6. See the two cases cited on p. 447 n. 73 above.

7. Mansi XXII, 228, c. 18; cf. 999, c. 11 (year 1215). The significance of this decree is depreciated by Gaines Post, 'Alexander III, the *Licentia Docendi* and the Rise of the Universities', *Anniversary Essays* [for. C. H. Haskins] (Boston–New York 1929), 255–77; but inconclusively, and without reference to the positive testimony of Alexander of Ashby (*c.* 1200), on whom see R. W. Hunt, 'English Learning in the Late Twelfth Century', now in R. W. Southern, ed., *Essays in Medieval History* (London 1968), 106–7. On the decree see also G. Paré, A. Brunet, P. Tremblay, *La renaissance de xii<sup>e</sup> siècle—Les écoles et l'enseignement*, 81–2.

8. *Capitulare ecclesiasticum*, c. 71 (year 789), *MGH Leges in Folio, I, 65.5–6;* Notker Balbulus, *Gesta Karoli Magni*, c. 3, ed. H. F. Haefele, *SS\** 1959, p. 4.2–5; Asser, *De rebus gestis Aelfredi*, ed. W. H. Stevenson (Oxford 1959), § 75, ll. 14, 18–21; § 102, ll. 18–19; Schreiner, 16.

9. *Vita. S. Guil. Divion.*, c. 14 (*PL* 142,709D–10A); *Vita S. Ottonis Babenbergensis, SS* 12, p. 889. 46–9.

10. Rashdall, III, 404–14.

11. Long before: *Capitulare Francofurtense*, c. 29 (year 794), *MGH Leges in Folio,* I, 74.15–16; Bede, *Hist. Eccl.*, IV, 21 (vol. I, 254, lines 16–21); Long after: Campbell, 151–2 (Cambridge), 154 (Oxford); W. Vischer, *Gesch. der Universität Basel* (Basel 18–60), 272: 'ut . . . beneficia . . . consequi possint', and 277: 'cupientes ecclesie que viris litteratis permaxime noscitur indigere . . . promovere'. For Paris in its heyday: Lecoy, *Chaire*, 85 and 451.

12. See p. 310 below.

13. Franciscus Diago, *Vita venerabilis Humberti de Romanis*, in M. de la Bigne, ed., *Maxima bibliotheca veterum patrum* (Lyon 1677), XXV, col. 421GH; a similar account in Jordan of Saxony, *Vitas Fratrum*, IV, c. 11 § 2, p. 172.

14. Thegan, *Vita Ludovici Pii*, c. 20 (*SS* II 595.28–30, 40–4).

15. Asser, *De rebus gestis Alfredi* (as in n. 8 above), §106, lines 30–46.

16. *EHD* I.432 § 7(= Stubbs SC 89).

17. Ratherius of Verona, *De cont. can.* § 22 (*PL* 136.511C).

18. *PL* 182.852–3.

19. *Policraticus*, VII, c. 15 (Vol. II, p. 156.21–7).

20. *De nugis*, I, c. 10 (p. 9).

21. Lines 17877–88; quoted by Goetz, 54.

22. Philippe de Novare, I §15 (pp. 10–11).

23. J. Plesner, *L'émigration . . . à . . . Florence*, 146–8.

24. Hyde, *Padua*, 154–75, esp. 169–70.

25. e.g. ibid. 117–18. Many thirteenth-century Italian communes would yield examples. (Albertano of Brescia, whom we have met in this book, was one.)

26. Duby, *Soc. . . . Mâconnaise* 582 (436–7).

27. T. H. Aston, 'Oxford's Medieval Alumni', *Past and Present*, 74 (Feb. 1977), 3–40; pp. 27–31.

28. Yunck, 145 nn. 27, 29.

29. Lines 9151–60. Cf. Dante, *Par.* IX, 133–5 (a century later).

30. Adam of Perseigne, *Epist.* 24 (*PL* 211.667D).

31. *De recup. Ter. Sanct.*, § 29 (p. 23 and n.).

32. *De laud. Par.* I, c. 3 (p. 40). On the vexed question when Paris itself admitted legal studies, Rashdall, III, 322–3 n. 3.
33. *Adv. Simoniacos,* III, c. 20 (p. 224.45 and 47).
34. Stephen Langton, quoted by J. W. Baldwin, *Masters, Princes and Merchants,* II, p. 58 n. 141; cf. I p. 85.
35. Langton, ibid.
36. Alan of Lille, *Textes inédits,* ed. M.-T. d'Alverny (Paris 1965), 274.
37. Latin proverb quoted by Yunck, 145 n. 29.
38. Mansi, XXI, 438D, 459B, 1179B.
39. Yunck, 145, n. 29.
40. Luzzatto, 130.
41. Schulte, 63–4.
42. Campbell, 22–3.
43. As in n. 36.
44. Langton, as in n. 34.
45. L. Thorndike, *Michael Scot* (London 1965), p. 3 (Thorndike's translation).
46. Jacques de Vitry, in Lecoy de la Marche, *Chaire,* 401.
47. Gillebertus, in Yunck, 145.
48. Robert de Courson, in Baldwin, *Masters,* II, p. 89.
49. MS. Klosterneuburg 902, fo. 198ᵛ ['Von den reichen phaffen']: 'si lernt seu [ = unsers herren wart] aussen und lesent seu da durch daz/[fo. 199ʳ] si do von gelobt werden, daz man gesprechen mug: der ist ein guet phaff, der ist ein gueten chirchen wol wert. Durch disen ruem behaltent seu unsers herren wart di er gesprochen hat.'
50. G. Marlot, *Histoire de la ville, cité et université de Reims* (Reims 1846), III, 809 (text); cf. G. Sievert, 'Das Vorleben des Papstes Urban IV', *Römische Quartalschrift für christliche Alterthumskunde und für Kirchengeschichte,* 10 (1896), 451–505.
51. Philippe wrote *Des quatre tenz d'aage d'ome* when he was seventy. The date of his birth is unknown. He died between 1261 and 1264.
52. Quoted by M. Spinka, *John Hus' Concept of the Church* (Princeton 1966), 9.
53. Ibid. 274, 284, 296–7.
54. Hugo of Trimberg, *Der Renner,* 17551–8.
55. Henry of Ghent, *Summae,* a.11, q.5 (fo. lxxx *verso* NOP). For the long debate, cf. Gaines Post, Kimon Giocarinis, and Richard Kay, 'The Medieval Heritage of a Humanistic Ideal: *Scientia Donum Dei est, unde vendi non potest*', *Traditio,* 11(1955), 195–234; Baldwin, *Masters,* 126–8.
56. *Hist. Calamitatum,* p. 70, line 250.
57. *V.S. Petri Dam.,* 117C.
58. *Vitas Fratrum,* p. 174, line 4; cf. p. 484 n. 45 below, and Vicaire, *S. Dominique,* 155–7 etc.
59. Luzzatto, 131.
60. Schulte, 244.
61. Richer, *Hist.* III, c. 45 (p. 101).
62. Violante, *Soc. milanese,* 189.
63. Schulte, 70–3.
64. Schreiner, 93–4, 98, 107; L. Génicot, 'Haut clergé et noblesse dans le diocèse de Liège', (in *Adel und Kirche*), 249 n. 18; P. S. Lewis, *Later Medieval France,* 296.
65. Robert of Courson, in Baldwin, *Masters,* II, 89 n. 92.
66. (As in n. 49) fo. 199ʳ : '. . . di lernt durch nicht anders denn daz si maister werden genant und zu hoehern dingen choemen von irr maisterschaft. Do von gewinnent si auch nymmer chain rue von irr chunst als wie, wenn si so vil gelernent mit arbait daz si den stuel besitzent der maisterschaft—und daz auch si di andern lernen schullen—so trachtent si tag und nacht do nach und gedenkent wie si newler vinden

und seltsaeme di var ungehoert sey und wie si gotez taugen mit rede zerloesen, und wie si ein igleich dinch daz got beschaffen hat mit warten eruaechten und ergunten. Mit solt an/[fo. 199ᵛ] dingen marternt si sich staetichleich, nur durch uppigem ruem ...'

67. Stephen of Bourbon, *Anecdotes historiques*, ed. A. Lecoy de la Marche (Paris 1877), 212.
68. *De rebus a se gestis*, II, c. 1, ed. J. S. Brewer (in *Opera*, I, *RS* 21, 1861), 45–6.
69. Gregory of Tours, *De sancto Patroclo*, c. 1 (*MGH SSRM* I(ii), 702, lines 29–31): quoted by Thompson, *Literacy*, 22 n. 78.
70. Ademar of Chabannes, *Epist. de apostolatu S. Martialis* (*PL* 141.107BC).
71. Ibid. (108C–109A).
72. J. Spottiswoode, *History of the Church of Scotland* (1668), 44. I owe this anecdote to Dr. Marinell Ash.
73. Salimbene, 344.28–30; cf. 805.9–10 ('... sagacissimus ... ultra modum baroniçabat').
74. Lines 12320–6.
75. II, c. 155 (pp. 246–7); cf. c. 173 (p. 283) and c. 174 (p. 311) for similar judgements.

## 10. THE INTELLECTUAL ÉLITE

1. Albertano of Brescia, *De amore*, fo. 34ᵛᵃ. I quote Albertano as spokesman for medieval moralists with strong Stoic imprint.
2. Also noticed as anticipating the Renaissance by Curtius, *Eur. Lit.* 477.
3. Especially if he had before him Ps. 14:1, or other biblical references to fools (mostly in the Wisdom books). Among writers *c.* 900–*c.* 1100, the trait is particularly strong in Ratherius of Verona (*PL* 136.487A, 490B, 492A etc.), while noticeably weak, on the other hand, in hagiographers. For the frequency of the term after *c.* 1300: J. Lefebvre, *Les fols et la folie* (Paris 1968), 16–19 with further bibliography.
4. Cf. T. Gregory, *Anima Mundi* (Florence 1955), 233; also 203 n. 3, 242, and p. 466 n. 19 below.
5. *De eodem et diverso*, ed. C. Bäumker (*Beiträge zur Geschichte der Philosophie und Theologie des Mittelalters*, Münster-in-W. 1903), 7.6–10. Quoted by Thorndike, *History of Magic*, II, 26.
6. Van Steenberghen, *Aristotle in the West*, 168 quotes the passage and comments: '... an annoyance that had been too long pent up breaks forth with a violence of expression that surprises us today'.
7. *SCG* III, 65(end) and 69; cf. É. Gilson, 'Pourquoi S. Thomas a critiqué S. Augustin' *AHDLMA* 1(1926), 5–127, esp. 8–13.
8. K. Michalski, *La philosophie au xivᵉ siècle* (collected essays) (Frankfurt 1969), 7, quoting *De corpore Christi*.
9. Peter of Abano, *Conciliator* (1303), *diff.* IX (Venice 1526), fo. 14E.
10. Symon de Phares, 3, 11; 1, 13; 201, 208, etc. Cf. Philip of Tripoli's interpolations (c. 1200) to the astrological parts of the *Secretum*, on 'insipientes ... et alii non minus stulti' who attack the science (p. 271, lines 3 and 7).
11. *Livre des secrets*, 569.
12. Lecoy de la Marche, *Chaire*, 452.
13. Cf. Ducange, *Glossarium*, VII, 244–5; cf. Duby, *Soc.* ... *mâconnaise*, 249 (208).
14. Violante, *Soc. milanese*, 163; Salimbene, 725.22.
15. Salimbene, 136.31 (etc.).
16. Peyraut *Summae*, II, vi, pt. 3, c. 29 (fo. 138ʳᵃ).

17. J. Le Goff, 'Les paysans et le monde rural dans la littérature du haut moyen âge (V<sup>e</sup>–VI<sup>e</sup> siècles)', in *Agricoltura e mondo rurale in occidente nell'alto medioevo* (Spoleto Congress, 13 (1966), 723–41, 759–70) with bibliography.
18. Violante, *Soc. milanese*, 151.
19. T. Gregory, *Anima Mundi*, 237–8; cf. 238 n. 2 and 106 n. 1.
20. Philip of Harvengt, *Epist.* 16 (*PL* 203.149C); cf. *Epist.* 17 (152B); these letters are quoted and are discussed by Thompson, *Literacy*, 139–43.
21. Andreas Capellanus, *De Amore*, 1, c. 11, ed. E. Trojel (Havniae [= Copenhagen] 1892) 235: 'naturaliter sicut equus et mulus ad Veneris opera promoventur, quemadmodum impetus eis naturae demonstrat.'
22. 'Ganymed and Helena', ed. W. Wattenbach, *Zeitschrift für deutsches Altertum*, 18 (new series 6, Berlin 1875) pp. 124–36; p. 131, strophe 34.
23. Salimbene, 820.3–4.
24. A few examples: Aelfric, *Colloquy*, 41; Peter the Venerable, *Epist.* IV, 36 (*PL* '89.367D f.); Humbert de Romans, *De modo prompte cudendi sermones*, 1, c. 72 (591G) and c. 78 (495B); Honorius, *Elucidarium*, as in Martini, *Bauerntum*, 30 n. 29.
25. Lehmann, *Parodie*, 76, 80–1.
26. Ibid. 57, 76–7, 197–8 (and—undatable—257).
27. Bibliography: Martini, *Bauerntum*, 35–6 n. 6; also Lehmann, *Parodie*, 76 n. 2 and Le Goff, 'Les paysans . . .' (as in n. 17), 733–4 n. 33.
28. *Par.* xvi, 55–6 and 63.
29. *De remediis*, II, c. 59 (Cologne 1628, pp. 518–19); distribution: Heitmann, *Fortuna und Virtus*, 11–13, and C. N. J. Mann, 'Petrarch and the Transmission of Classical Elements', in R. R. Bolgar, ed., *Classical Influences in European Culture A.D. 500–1500* (Cambridge 1971), 217–24; 217 (over 200 MSS.).
30. See below pp. 263–5.
31. Stressed by Martini, *Bauerntum*, 35–6.
32. Lehmann, *Parodie*, 198.
33. Lefebvre (as in n. 3), 51–4.
34. Ibid. 47–70.
35. Thorndike, *History of Magic*, 190 (and 636).
36. William of Auvergne, *De fide*, c. 2 § 3 (*Opera Omnia*, Venice 1591, 8F).
37. See p. 233.
38. T. Gregory, *Anima Mundi* (Florence 1955), 203, n. 3, 242; Thorndike, *History of Magic*, 634–6.
39. p. 192 (cf. p. 258).
40. pp. 396.4–7; 426.16–19.
41. p. 70.17–20 (= *De off.* III, 6, 29); on the term *utile* see also F. Irsigler, *Untersuchungen zur Gesch. des frühfränkischen Adels* (Bonn 1969), 240–1.
42. Heitmann *Fortuna und Virtus*, 241–3.
43. Lines 9504–16; cf. 7957 ff., 11239 ff.; on thirteenth-century expressions of the view that wealth is conducive to virtue: H. Baron, 'Franciscan Poverty and Civic Wealth as Factors in the Rise of Humanistic Thought', *Speculum*, 13 (1938), 1–37; and my 'Piety and Impiety', 91.
44. No. 162 'O consocii . . .' (ed. A. Hilka and O. Schumann, Vol I, Fasc. 2, Heidelberg 1961, p. 272.5–6).
45. *De consol. phil.* II, v, prose (Loeb edn., p. 204, lines 85–8).
46. Nicholas of Clairvaux, quoted by Thompson, *Literacy*, 162 n. 155.
47. II, vi, iii, c. 7, fo. 118<sup>va</sup>.
48. Heitmann, 118 and n. 156; A. von Martin, *Coluccio Salutati* (Leipzig–Berlin 1916), 107; for an extreme case *c.* 1500, see p. 280 below.
49. *Opera omnia* (Venice 1591), 628RH–629LA; William's astrological position is examined (in other respects than this) by M. Schmaus, 'Das Gesetz der Sterne:

Ein Kapitel aus der Theologie des Wilhelm von Auvergne', *Speculum Historiale* (Fs. Joh. Spörl) (Freiburg–Munich 1965), 51–7.

50. *ST* I, q. 115, a. 4 *ad tertium;* for a similar view in Roger Bacon, cf. Thorndike, *History of Magic*, 671; John of Jandun thought the multitude as such prone to evil, Schmugge, 68 and 75.

51. *Chronica majora*, year 1251, ed. H. R. Luard (*RS* 57), v (London 1880), 249–51).

52. G. G. Coulton, *Social Life in Britain from the Conquest to the Reformation* (Cambridge 1919), 56; N. Orme, *English Schools in the Middle Ages* (London 1973), 192–3.

53. *Chart. Univ. Par.* III, pp. 53–4 §1238.

54. Cf. ibid., p. 152 §1324 (year 1364); p. 197 §1366 (year 1371); and especially p. 303 §1465 n. 6 (years 1382–3). Another possible candidate is the Prague revolt of 1422; F. Graus, *Struktur und Geschichte. Drei Volksaufstände im mittelalterlichen Prag* (Sigmaringen 1971), 71–2, 77; although the peculiar circumstances of this Taborite attack on the university cast doubt on its title to be called 'anti-intellectual'.

55. Saint Martin of Braga, *Formula honestae vitae* (also commonly known as *De quatuor virtutibus cardinalibus*), § 6 (ed. C. W. Barlow, *Martini Episcopi Bracarensis Opera Omnia*, New Haven, Conn. 1950, 247.4–248.11). On the distribution of this work see p. 447 n. 86 above. My translation is from the French version by Brunetto Latini, *Tresors*, 248.11–13.

56. II, c. 27 (Vol. I, p. 143); for the diviners cf. II, c. 28 (Vol. I, p. 165.2–6).

57. Morning sermon of 7 Dec. 1304, in D. M. Manni, ed., *Prediche del B. Giordano da Rivalto* (Florence 1739), p. 19 (right-hand column).

58. *De gestis pontificum anglorum*, ed. N. E. S. A. Hamilton, *RS* 52 (1870), 259–60, notes. The book may have been Julius Firmicus' *Matheseos*. On William's revisions, cf. pp. xviii–xx.

59. Ptolemy of Lucca, *Annales*, year 1276 (ed. B. Schmeidler (*SS\** 1955), 184.22 ff.); and idem, *Hist. Eccles.*, cc. 21 and 24 (Muratori¹ XI, 1176D and 1178BC).

60. Martin of Troppau, *Chronicon: Continuatio Brabantina*, SS 24, p. 263.40: '... a clerico suo quasi dementi perfossus periit'.

61. *De gestis pontificum anglorum*, p. 394; and *De gestis regum anglorum*, ed. W. Stubbs, *RS* 90 (1887), I, 131–2.

62. Cf. ibid., p. cxliv, 5th line from bottom (='Letter to Peter').

63. *V.S. Abbonis*, c. 20 (*PL* 139.410D): 'quasdam computi ratiunculas dictitans'; and c. 3 (col. 390C): 'occulte propter invidos'.

64. Cf. Campbell, *Black Death*, 26–8 (Al Khatib, murdered in 1374).

65. *Gemma ecclesiastica*, I, c. 51, ed. J. S. Brewer (in *Opera*, II, *RS* 21, 1862), 149.

66. Cf. *V.S. Abbonis*, 397B; Symon de Phares, 211, 215.

67. Villani, IX, 136.

68. *Decameron*, Day VI, Novella 9.

69. Dino Compagni, *Cronica*, I, c. 20.

70. Dietrich of Niem, *Historiae*, I (*De Schismate*) c. 1 (Strasbourg 1609, p. 2). For a self-made intellectual who sought to *end* the Great Schism, and had a similar reputation—as 'presumptieux et orgueilleux'—see Symon de Phares, 248 (on Gerson).

71. Preface to A. Garreau, *S. Albert le Grand* (Paris 1932), 15–16, quoted twice by Van Steenberghen, *Aristotle in the West*, 169–70, and *La Philosophie au xiii^e siècle* (Louvain–Paris 1966), 277.

72. Radulf Glaber, *Hist.* III, c. 7 (*PL* 142.657D); Anna Comnena, *Alexiad*, x, transl. E. R. A. Sewter (Harmondsworth 1969), 325–6; but for a generally more favourable view of France by one near-neighbour in the eleventh and twelfth centuries see R. W. Southern, 'England's First Entry into Europe', in the same author's *Medieval Humanism* (Oxford 1970), 135–57 *passim*.

73. Alexander of Roes, *Noticia Seculi*, 160.9–10; 161.7–8 etc.
74. p. 950.4–7.
75. A. Corvi, *Il processo di Bonifacio VIII* (Rome 1940), 152.
76. VIII, c. 55.
77. *De laud. Par.* II, c. 5 (p. 56, line 1); cf. Peyraut, II, vi, pt. 2, c. 4 (fo. 102ʳ): '. . . ut iam non reputetur superbia peccatum'.
78. Lines 6622–5.
79. F. M. Pelzel, ed., *Lebensgeschichte des . . . Königs Wenceslaus* (Prague–Leipzig 1788–90), II, *Urkundenbuch*, No. xxxiii, pp. 53–4: 'ne . . . Gallicorum decipiaris astutiis. . . . Sentiat turba . . . quid inter eorum mollitiem intersit et fortitudinem Germanorum'.
80. Cf. E. Renan in *Hist. littéraire de la France*, 31 (Paris 1888), 285–318.
81. pp. 304–5.
82. p. 306.
83. p. 304; that printed editions add 'and the English' to certain of these passages does not lessen the force of the argument: the two nations were by then tarred with the same brush.
84. pp. 304, 307.
85. *De recup. Ter. Sanct.* p. 139.
86. Quoted ibid. 129, note.
87. *De laud. Par.* II, c. 8 (p. 60, lines 4–5).
88. Cf. *De recup. Ter Sanct.*, p. 99 n. 1.
89. Morning sermon of 3 March 1306, *Quaresimale Fiorentino*, ed. C. Delcorno (Florence 1974), 160.13–161.4.
90. Benvenuto da Imola, III, p. 530.
91. Cf. Dino Compagni, I, cc. 1 and 2; II, c. 2 etc; Villani, VI, cc. 65, 78, etc.
92. Davidsohn, *Gesch. v. Florenz*, IV (3), p. 68, quoting Remigio de' Girolami.
93. H. Baron, *The Crisis of the Early Italian Renaissance*, 179–81.
94. Quoted (in English) by I. Origo, *The World of San Bernardino* (London 1963), 183.
95. e.g. Ademar, *Epist. de apostolatu S. Martialis* (*c*. 1030) (*PL* 141.107D): 'in Langobardia, ubi ego plus didici, est fons sapientiae'.
96. *De proprietatibus rerum*, XV, c. 169 (edition of Frankfurt, 1601, p. 712).
97. *Noticia Seculi*, 160.4.
98. Salimbene, 788.10.
99. *Purgatorio*, VI, 137.
100. Davidsohn, *Gesch. v. Florenz*, IV (1), 51.
101. D. Hay, 'Italy and Barbarian Europe', in E. F. Jacob, ed., *Italian Renaissance Studies* (London 1960), 48–68; 57.
102. E. Mollat, *Les papes d'Avignon* (1949⁹), 328; cf. Bernard Gui's similar usage in 1317: D. M. Bueno de Mesquita, *Giangaleazzo Visconti* (Cambridge 1941), 5 n. 3.
103. D. Hay (as in n. 101), pp. 55–6.
104. Quoted by C. T. Davis, 'Education in Dante's Florence', *Speculum*, 40 (1965), 415–35; 431. An exception is made for Bede, Michael Scot, and Albert the Great.
105. Villani, I, c. 47.
106. Continuation of Aquinas' *De regimine principum*, quoted by N. Rubinstein, 'Marsilius of Padua and Italian Political Thought of his Time', in J. Hale, R. Highfield, and B. Smalley, *Europe in the Late Middle Ages* (London 1965), 44–75; 55.

11. THE ASSAULT ON THE CITADEL: THEORY

1. The condemned doctrines: *Chart. Univ. Par.* I, pp. 543–58 §473, clauses 144, 154, 211, etc. Siger studied from his writings: Van Steenberghen, *Philosophie*, 373–402;

but N.B. his oral teaching, 435. See p. 471 n. 60 below for Siger's place in the thought of Dante.

2. Heitmann, *Fortuna und Virtus*, 126–7.

3. Bull of condemnation in T. Netter, *Fasciculi Zizaniorum*, ed. W. W. Shirley, *RS* 5 (1858), 242–4; see first paragraph, p. 242.

4. *Chart. Univ. Par.* III, pp. 486–533 §§1557–83; summary, pp. 486–7.

5. Philip of Harvengt, *De institutione clericorum*, IV, c. 110 (*PL* 203.816B): 'Loquendi usus obtinuit ut quem viderimus litteratum statim clericum nominemus... Se quis igitur litteratum militem idiotae presbytero conferat... affirmabit eumdem militem meliorem presbytero clericum esse, quia scilicet miles legit, intelligit, dictat, versificatur et inter clericos linguam latinam proferens soloecismi nescius approbatur, presbyter vero non solum nescit orationem grammaticam irreprehensibiliter informare sed forte nec completorium solus regulariter cantitare.' Quoted by P. Riché, 'Recherches sur l'instruction des laïcs du ix^e au xii^e siècle', *Cahiers de civilisation médiévale*, 4 (1962), 175–82; p. 181 n. 55.

6. Rashdall, III, 394–5; and cf. the *Apocalypsis Goliae* (line 329): 'Hic generosior tonsuram despicit' (*Latin Poems*, 16).

7. Kibre, *Scholarly Privileges*, 142–3.

8. H. Grundmann, 'Vom Ursprung der Universität im Mittelalter', *Berichte über die Verhandlungen der sächsischen Akademie der Wissenschaften zu Leipzig, Phil-hist. Kl.* 103 (2) (Berlin 1957), 27.

9. Ibid. 29–30.

10. Ibid. 27–8.

11. *Epist.* 18 (*PL* 203.158D).

12. *Art.* 7, q. 6 (fos. 81^r–82^r).

13. II, vi, pt. 3, c. 7 (fo. 118^v); cf. pp. 274–5 below.

14. J. Leclercq, 'Le magistère du prédicateur au XIII^e siècle', *AHDLMA* 15 (1946), 105–47; pp. 109–11.

15. L. Thorndike, *Michael Scot* (London–Edinburgh 1965), 1.

16. Ibid. 3.

17. E. Renan and G [aston] P [aris], 'La fontaine de toutes sciences du philosophe Sidrach', *Hist. litt. de la France* 31 (1888), 285–318; p. 297. Distribution: 286, 314–17.

18. L. Schmugge, *Joh. von Jandun*, 15–16, 21–3, 42.

19. *De laud. Par.* I, c. 2 (p. 40, lines 14–15).

20. Schmugge, 68, 75, 100.

21. Ibid. 73.

22. Ibid. 54. The text in MS. Vat. lat. 760 runs (fo. 99^vb): 'Sunt enim quidam qui non utuntur nisi sensu et ymaginatione vel si utuntur aliis virtutibus hoc est ita modicum quod debet quasi pro nihilo reputari, sicut homines volgares et rustici valde ignorantes qui non cognoscunt nisi sensibilia communia et propria, et parum aut nihil distinguunt de formis substantiatis [?]... Alii vero transcendunt sensibilia et ymaginativa et distinguunt intenciones non substantiatas a substantialibus communibus et propriis ut bonitatem, maliciam, paternitatem, filiacionem, adoracionem, pavorem et huiusmodi.'

23. Ibid.: 'Infimos quidem intelligo homines pure practicos qui modicum aut nihil speculationis [?] attingunt, cuiusmodi sunt mercatores, artifices plurimi. Et si audeo dicere fere omnes juriste huius temporis de quibus alias etc. Excellentissimos intelligo methaphisicos qui pertingunt ad considerare quidditates formarum abstractarum etc. et ipsius dei summi quoquomodo mediocres infimos propinq-/ [fo. 100^ra ] uiores intelligo salva reverencia ipsorum mathematicos qui considerant numeros et magnitudines et perfectibilia et sunt sensibilia saltem per se communia. In hoc enim excedunt infimos quia probationes magnitudinis et numerorum

cogitabiles magis denunciant certissime et pulcherrime de eis. Sed alios mediocres intelligo perfectiores et excellentes naturales qui proprietates non substantiatas eliciunt ex sensatis per suam bonam congnitionem et discutiunt magnas ambiguitates de rebus naturalibus ut sciunt experti. Verum praesens [?] est quod quilibet istorum ordinum seu graduum habet plurimam latitudinem et diversitatem secundum diversas complexiones individuales, omnes tamen possunt rationabiliter reduci ad istos iiii$^{or}$ gradus; et gradus quidem infimus est graduum [!] plurimorum, gradus autem supremus est praecipuorum seu maxime notorum, gradus medius propinquus infimo est omnium sapientium, sed propinquus summo est plurimum [?] sapientum, et istos gradus vocat Commentator virtutes quibus diversificantur homines, et dictae sunt in Thopicis, id est sunt insinuati hoc modo predicto.'

24. Ibid. (fo. 100$^{ra}$ continuing): 'diversitas autem istorum graduum potest reduci ad unitatem virtutis cognative, nam qui habent ipsam infimam sunt infimi, et qui optimam sunt excellentissimi, mediter sunt mediocres modo predicto.'

25. *Exhortatio virginitatis*, I, 1 §3 (*PL* 16.352A).

26. *Sermo* 117 §12 (*PL* 39.1981A). This and the Ambrosian phrase are quoted by Schreiner, *Untersuchungen*, 19 n. 53.

27. III, 6, line 1.

28. How formidable, can be gauged from the caches of examples found in the following works, on which my own general remarks are based. (1) E. R. Curtius, *Eur. Gesch.* 186–7; (2) idem, 'Zur Literarästhetik', II, p. 213; (3) (apropos of Dante, *Convivio*, IV) A. Gaspary, *Gesch. der italienischen Literatur* (2 volumes, Berlin 1885, 1888), I, p. 518 n. 1; for a wider secondary bibliography on the background to Dante's views, see (4) C. T. Davis, 'Il buon tempo antico', in N. Rubinstein, ed., *Florentine Studies* (London 1968), 45–69; p. 63 n. 3; (5) E. Faral, *Les arts poétiques*, 116 §27 presents Juvenal's line as a topos taught by Matthew of Vendôme's *Ars versificatoria;* with a success to be judged from the examples assembled by (6) E. Langlois, ed., *Le Roman de la Rose* (*Soc. des anciens textes français*), IV (1892), 317–19 [ = notes to various lines between 18595 and 18616 in the same edition] with another example in (7) idem, *Les mss du Roman de la Rose* (1910), 93–4. Alcuin's early adoption of the theme is discussed by (8) H. H. Anton, *Fürstenspiegel*, 45, 85 ff. and esp. n. 81. German examples from the central middle ages can be found in (9) Martini, *Bauerntum*, 38–9 n. 19; and (as part of a larger cache of examples) in (10) A. Hilka, O. Schumann, W. Meyers, eds., *Carmina Burana* (2 volumes, Heidelberg 1930/41 and 1961), II (i), p. 11. Three more vernacular references in (11) H. R. Jauss, ed., *Grundriss der romanischen Literatur des Mittelalters VI: La littérature didactique, allégorique et satirique*, Vol. I (Heidelberg 1968), 88. I know of only one thorough attempt to relate this theme to a particular historical context before the time of Dante, namely (12) H. Köhler, 'Zur Diskussion der Adelsfrage bei den Trobadors', *Medium Aevum Vivum* (Fs. W. Bulst) (Heidelberg 1960), 161–78.

29. The three examples respectively in Schulte, 90 n. 1; Jacques de Vitry, *Hist. occidentalis*, c. 31 (ed. J. F. Hinnebusch, Fribourg 1972, 156, lines 10–11); W. Sievert 'Das Vorleben des Papstes Urban IV' (as on p. 464 n. 50), 453.

30. Anton, *Fürstenspiegel*, 45 n. 3; Schulte, 298.

31. See item (6) in n. 28 above.

32. Curtius, *Eur. Gesch.* 187.

33. Köhler, 'Zur Diskussion der Adelsfrage', 172, 177–8.

34. As in n. 28, item (10); Vol. I (i), p. 9, lines 1–8 (21 complete or partial MSS. listed); see also Vol. II (i), p. 11.

35. I take this as implied by Gregory VII's objection to a marriage between cousins, in *Reg.* II, 3 (p. 127.18–20): 'Ex hoc enim nobilitas generis valde corrumpitur, cum proles non de legitima coniugii permixtione generatur.'

36. *Cronica*, I, 8.
37. A. Dondaine, 'Guillaume Peyraut. Vie et oeuvres', *Archivum Fratrum Praedicatorum*, 18 (1948), 162–236. I quote the *Summa* in the edition of Antwerp 1587. The passages on noble claims to church office are summarized by Schreiner, *Untersuchungen*, 63–6.
38. II ( = *Summa viciorum*), vi, pt. 3, c. 18 §8 (fo. 137$^{va}$) (citing Origen).
39. Ibid.
40. e.g. ibid., c. 28 §1 (fo. 137$^{ra}$); though the expression *nobilitas animi* also occurs, cf. c. 29 (fo. 137$^{vb}$) etc.
41. Ibid., c. 30 §1 (fo. 139$^{ra}$).
42. Ibid., at the 2nd 'perversity'; compare the 6th *causa* (fo. 139$^{va}$): 'nullam autem sapientiam, nullam aliam gratiam nobilitati carnis adaequant'.
43. Equality: c. 6 (fo. 114$^{va}$); c. 28 § 2 (fo. 137$^{ra}$) and §10 (fo. 137 $^{vab}$); No intellectual pride: c. 4 (fos. 112$^{vb}$–113$^{va}$); c. 7 §§4 and 5 (fos. 118$^{rab}$); c. 34 §1 (fo. 143$^{rb \cdot va}$).
44. Lines 18577–88.
45. Lines 18841–7.
46. Cf. the invective of *Faux Semblant* against the orders of which he is supposed to be a parody, lines 11287 ff.
47. Lines 18585–8.
48. Lines 18840–54; cf. 18766, 18880.
49. Lines 18588, 18636, 18857.
50. Lines 18799–800, 18682–3.
51. Lines 5771–8.
52. Line 18653.
53. Lines 18605–28.
54. Lines 18697–9.
55. Lines 18720–4.
56. Line 18713.
57. Ed. E. Moore and P. Toynbee, *Le opere di Dante Alighieri* (Oxford 1924$^4$), 293–338; see n. 28 above, item (4) for bibliography.
58. Bk. IV, c. 17 (p. 320. 77–84).
59. Ibid. (p. 319.21–2); contrast *Nich. Eth.* VI, cc. 5, 8, 12; on the scholastics' problem with prudence, see Lottin, III, 255–78.
60. *Dante et la Philosophie* (1953$^2$), esp. 13–14 (philosophers are few); 120–1, 160, 270 (philosophy is free from theology); 143–51, 180–90 (and from the empire); and index p. 337. The faint traces of 'Averroism' in Dante are nowhere thrown better into relief than in B. Nardi's attempt to defend, by comparison with Dante, the doubtful orthodoxy of Peter of Abano: *Saggi sull'Aristotelismo Padovano* (Florence 1958), 19–74; e.g. 31, 33. For Dante's view of Siger see Gilson (as above), 256–79, and index p. 338.
61. Ed. A. Crespi (Ascoli 1927), under Cecco's full name of Francesco Stabili, with a long historical introduction.
62. C. 12, 'Della Nobiltà' (pp. 213–19), esp. lines 1418–20 (p. 213), 1430–2 (p. 214), and 1505–7 (pp. 218–19). Cecco minces his words more than these isolated passages would suggest, but not enough to repel the charge of determinism, then or now.
63. C. 12, lines 1436–8 (p. 214).
64. C. 7, 'Della Prudenza', lines 1153, 1171, 1180–1 (pp. 197–9).
65. Lines 1153–64 (pp. 197–8).
66. Line 1167 (p. 198). The *seconda stella* is Mercury, on whose achievements see J. Seznec, *The Survival of the Pagan Gods* (New York 1961), 15.
67. X, c. 40.
68. Von Martin, *Coluccio Salutati*, 93–113.
69. Analysed in this regard by H. Baron, *The Crisis of the Early Italian Renaissance*, 419–23.

70. Ed. S. Grande, in *La Giapigia* ... *di* ... *galateo* (3 volumes, Lecce 1867–8), I, 171–91.
71. p. 173.

12. THE ASSAULT ON THE CITADEL: PRACTICE

1. P. Champion, ed., *Procès de condamnation de Jeanne d'Arc*, I (Paris 1920), 12: 'Et pource qu'il nous appartient singulièrement, selon nostre profession, extirper telles iniquitez manifestes, mesmement quant nostre foy catholique est en ce touchée, nous ne povons ou fait d'icelle dissimuler la longue retardacion de justice qui doit desplaire à chacun bon chrestien ...'
2. G. A. Brucker, *Florentine Politics and Society 1343–1378* (Princeton 1962), 28, 33–40, 44–5, 53; for the same in France, Lewis, *Later Medieval France*, 174, 176, 246–7.
3. Duby, *Soc.* ... *mâconnaise*, 582 (436–7); see p. 222 above.
4. Lewis, *Later Medieval France*, 177. For critics of ambition in law schools see above, pp. 222–4.
5. *Chart. Univ. Par.* III, p. 324 §1486.
6. H. Grundmann, 'Sacerdotium-Regnum-Studium: Zur Wertung der Wissenschaft im 13. Jahrhundert', *Archiv für Kulturgeschichte*, 34 (1951), 5–21, esp. 14–15.
7. *Chart. Univ. Par.* III, p. 111 §1293 (year 1364); and pp. 303–4 §1465 (year 1382): 'non obstantibus quibusdam altercationibus prehabitis inter dictum rectorem et episcopum ... in omnibus mater nostra Universitas in comparatione ad episcopum ... obtinuit principatum' (p. 303).
8. pp. 338–9 §1500; pp. 340–419 §§1504–22; pp. 484–6 §§1585–6.
9. e.g. p. 341 §1504. History of the clause (from its appearance *c.* 1256): H. Rashdall, *The Universities of Europe in the Middle Ages*, new edition, ed. F. M. Powicke and A. B. Emden (Oxford 1936), I, pp. 328–32; P. Kibre, 'Academic Oaths at the University of Paris', in *Essays in Medieval Life and Thought* ... *in honor of Austin Patterson Evans* (Columbia University Press, New York 1955), 123–37.
10. pp. 478–9 §1548 (year 1388).
11. p. 348 §§1509–10 (*relatio*).
12. p. 367 §1512 (year 1385); cf. pp. 394–5 §1516; on the contest concerning oaths to the chancellor: p. 409 §1520, cap. 34 and pp. 480–1. §1550.
13. p. 35 §1223: 'uniuscujusque conscientie relinquentes ...' Further battles for jurisdiction: pp. 230–1 §1410; p. 298 §1457; p. 428 §1528; etc.
14. John of Jandun, *De laud. Par.*, pp. 34, 36; for a similar usage in Oxford (in the fifteenth century), E. F. Jacob, *Essays in the Conciliar Epoch* (Manchester 1963³), 215 n. 1. The earlier part of the story is in Paré–Brunet–Tremblay, and Van Steenberghen, *Aristotle in the West*.
15. H. Denifle, *Die Entstehung der Universitäten des Mittelalters bis 1400* (Berlin 1885), I, 106–32; discussed with the old heat by Rashdall, I, 331 n.
16. *Chart. Univ. Par.* II, p. 184 § 728a; III, pp. 53 and 54 §1238; p. 144 §1319; p. 445 §1537.
17. Van Steenberghen, *Aristotle in the West*, 162–7; *Chart. Univ. Par.* III, p. 145 §1319.
18. Based on Denifle (as in n. 15), 123–4, and the successive *rotuli* printed in *Chart. Univ. Par.* III and IV. Compare Campbell, *Black Death*, 166, with only negligible differences.
19. Van Steenberghen, *Aristotle in the West*, 82, and 66–88.
20. e.g. *Chart. Univ. Par.* III, p. 44 §1233; p. 144 §1319, cap. 10.
21. The sum allowed by the Servites in Florence for a student's return journey to Paris in 1363 was equal to about half his annual food-and-clothing allowance; *Chart. Univ. Par.* III, p. 103 §1278, cap. 2.

22. Rashdall, I, 318–20; and cf. the *rotuli* in the Cartulary.
23. G. Sievert, 'Das Vorleben des Papstes Urban IV', *Römische Quartalschrift für christliche Alterthumskunde und für Kirchengeschichte*, 10 (1896), 451–505.
24. J. Heidemann, *Papst Clemens IV. Eine Monographie. I Teil: Das Vorleben des Papstes und seine Legationsregister Kirchengeschichtliche Studien VI Heft 4*, (Münster-in-Westphalien 1903), 83–7.
25. For what follows: Alexander of Roes, *Memoriale de praerogativa Romani imperii; Noticia Seculi;* and *Pavo;* in his collected *Schriften*, ed. H. Grundmann and H. Heimpel, (*MGH Staatsschriften des späteren Mittelalters* I, 1, Stuttgart 1958), respectively pp. 91–148; pp. 149–71; and pp. 172–91. See also H. Heimpel, 'Alexander von Roes und das deutsche Selbstbewusstsein des 13. Jahrhunderts', *Archiv für Kulturgeschichte*, 26 (1935–6), 19–60; and Grundmann, 'Sacerdotium' (as in n. 6), esp. pp. 5–9.
26. *Memoriale*, 108.3 ('circumspectus, vigilans') and 126.7–8 ('tamquam perspicatiores').
27. Ibid. 126.10–11.
28. e.g. 'prudentia' is assigned as national characteristic to the Italians, *Noticia*, 160.4.
29. Cf. *Schriften*, 38–87 (editors' introduction).
30. *Sermo de informatione episcoporum (PL* 139.174C); the only example in the relevant section of Dresdner, 31–81. The sermon is attributed to Gerbert of Aurillac.
31. Bk. III, c. 20 (*MGH Libelli de Lite*, I, p. 224.42).
32. Esp. *Contra inscitiam et incuriam clericorum (Opusculum* 26) (*PL* 145.497–504; see esp. col. 499A): 'Cum . . . per sacerdotium vecordium imperitiam plebs indocta depereat, par fuerat ut episcopalis gravitas a talium se promotione suspenderet.' But most of the work is about *incuria*.
33. Compare also Langlois, *Vie*, 40 (*Li proverbe au vilain*) and Baldwin, 113 (Thomas of Chobham).
34. And note the moderate tone of those passages where he comes nearest to making such a complaint, *Reg.* IX, 2 (p. 571.5–11) and VI, 5b (p. 402.24–8).
35. Cf. Mansi, XXI, 355, 385, 417, 439, 453, 487, 507, 523, 843, 1147, 1167; XXII, 119, 139, 141. The second Lateran Council, in 1139, attacked hereditary ecclesiastical appointments in favour of 'honestas, *sapientes*, et religiosas personas' (Mansi, XXI, 530D), echoing councils in Clermont in 1130 (ibid. 439D), Pisa in 1134 (ibid. 490: 'sed qui *prudentia* et merito vitae clarescant'), and London in 1138 (ibid. 522AB). Otherwise the councils indicated, from 1116 to 1176, include nothing on this subject among recorded canons. Some actually denounce the pursuit of (medical and legal) learning by religious; see above p. 224, at n. 38.
36. I base this remark on the useful, if misleadingly named, collection by T. Wright, *The Political Songs commonly attributed to Walter Mapes (CS*, London 1841). The only clear exception belongs, remarkably enough, to a *monastic* context: ignorant deacons are promoted ('isti penitus carent scientia' etc., *De malis monachorum*, lines 89–100, p. 190). I do not accept *Apocalypsis Goliae episcopi*, lines 331–2 (p. 16), as an exception: 'librans libros' refers only to clerics' abandoning all pretence at clerical life. Doubtful cases are *De ruina Romae*, line 106 (p. 220), and *De diversis ordinibus*, line 49 (p. 230). Of course there is plenty on the theme that scholars without money are barred from promotion; but that is different.
37. Cf. W. L. Wakefield and A. P. Evans, *Heresies of the High Middle Ages* (New York-London 1969). In the 190 pages of documents in this collection covering the period before 1216, only one-utterance attributed to a heretic could be construed as a charge of poor education in a churchman; and a careful reading of the whole account will discredit even that construction (p. 113, and cf. esp. p. 114: the churchman accused was for one thing the famous scholar Hildebert of Lavardin, then Bishop of Le Mans).

38. *Sermones dominicales et in solemnitatibus*, ed. Fr. Locatelli (Padua 1895), 36–7, 278–84, 315–17, 343–59.
39. Th. Bonnin, *Regestrum Visitationum archepiscopi Rothogamensis* (Rouen 1852), i–ii. Examinations: 159cd, 173d, 332cd, 395d, and cf. 350d; idiots and alcoholics: 111d, 132d, 353c, 384d, 564d; 'simplicity': 403a, cf. 491d; ignorance on a particular matter: 514a, 501c, 245a; *insufficientia litterarum:* 491d.
40. cc. 3, 18 (Mansi, XXII, 218–19, 227–8). Cf p. 218 above.
41. cc. 10, 11, 27, 30 (Mansi, XXII, 998, 999, 1015, 1018). The phrases quoted are from cc. 30 and 27 respectively.
42. O. Dobiache-Rojdestvensky, *La vie paroissiale en France au xiiie siècle* (Paris 1911), 153–7 (nine or ten instances).
43. Unless *prudentia* is so understood. *Ibid.* 153, from E. Martène and U. Durand, *Thesaurus Novus Anecdotorum*, IV (Paris 1717), 717AB.
44. J. Scammell, 'The Rural chapter in England from the eleventh to the fourteenth century', *Engl. Hist. Review*, 86 (1961), 1–21; p. 14.
45. *Summae*, II, vi, pt. 3 c. 30 (fo. 139$^{ra}$). See above pp. 274–5.
46. *De modo prompte cudendi sermones*, II, c. 2 (*Bibl. max. veterum patrum*, Lyons 1677, 508C); F. Heintke, *Humbert von Romans* (*Historische Studien*, 222, Berlin 1933), 40.
47. Sermons *Qui bene praesunt*, *In lingua agnoscitur sapientia*, and *Justus si morte*; MS. Florence, Laur. Plut. 33 sin. 1, fos. 10$^{va}$–11$^{ra}$, 16$^{rb}$, 101$^{va}$. It is in the first of these passages that Visconti urges his parish priest to put learning first: 'Studeamus ergo karissimi sic habere predicta tria, scilicet opus, scientiam et zelum; et precipue scientiam . . . quia quilibet vestrum opus et zelum potest de facili optinere, set scientiam propter defectum pecunie et librorum ad eundum Bononiam diceret se de facili habere non posse, cum non habeatur hodie scientia nisi per doctrinam . . .' (fo. 11$^{ra}$).
48. *Cronica*, 247.7–10; cf. 757.31–758.1.
49. G. R. Owst, *Preaching in Medieval England* (Cambridge 1926), chapters 1 and 6. A brief treatment of the same topic is given by N. Orme, *English Schools in the Middle Ages* (London 1973), 13–14.
50. G. Lizérand, ed., *Le dossier de l'affaire des Templiers* (Paris 1964²), 84–101. The four quotations are respectively from pp. 86, 86–8, 90–2, and 86. Dubois rests his last contention on a dubious 'decretal'. Cf. Gregory IX, *Decretalium*, Lib. III, v. cap. 29 (ed. A. Friedburg, *Corpus Juris Canonici*, II, 478), which has a much more moderate sense.
51. II, xx, 13; ed. C. W. Previté-Orton (Cambridge 1928), 325.28–326.2.
52. II, xxiv, 6, p. 371.13–17.
53. Ibid., cap. 9, p. 372.28–9 (pope), p. 373.3–4 (cardinals); cap. 5, p. 370.20–2 (bishops); cap. 2, p. 369.5–10 (chapters); cap. 6, p. 371.1 (abbots etc.); cap. 10, p. 373.10–12 (highest to lowest).
54. *Chart. Univ. Par.* III, pp. 223–7 §1406 (year 1375): '. . . multum . . . miratus . . . quod nunquam audierat . . . de premissis' (21 Sept., p. 226).
55. G. B. Ladner, *The Idea of Reform* (Cambridge, Mass. 1959), 39–48, esp. 41–2, traces the hesitant entry of the words *reformare, -atio*, etc. into Christian Latin (e.g. into some Vulgate versions of St. Paul). But the words remain relatively rare in St. Augustine (cf. pp. 153–283, esp. 198), and a glance at Dr. Ladner's index-entry on p. 541 will confirm that the idea which we today designate as 'reform' did not necessarily go under that name in early centuries. The same lesson can be read in the fact that Pope Gregory VII's letters do not contain the word 'reform'.
56. Delaruelle–Labande–Ourliac, 146 n. 40.
57. Lewis, *Later Medieval France*, 294.
58. *Tractatus de materia concilii*, ed. F. Oakley, *The Political Thought of Pierre d'Ailly* (New Haven 1964), 244–349; p. 336 (cf. p. 330, quoted by Lewis, 294).

59. *Chart. Univ. Par.* IV, p. 185 §1891 (June–August 1410): 'paucis litteratis ...'; and p. 217 §1932 (17 Sept. 1411): 'coquus, dapifer ...'.
60. H. Kaminsky, 'The Politics of France's Subtraction of Obedience to the Church' (*Proceedings of the American Philosophical Society*, 115, No. 5, Philadelphia 1971), 366–97; p. 397 n. 180 (quoting P. Leroy in 1406: 'Il y eut plus de notables hommes, et de clers pourveus, qu'il n'y avoit eu par devant la sustraxion.').
61. Delaruelle–Labande–Ourliac, 210.
62. Ibid. 239 n. 10.
63. M. Spinka, *John Hus' Concept of the Church* (Princeton 1966), 296–7; cf. 272,285 (also 310, 314).
64. Stephen of Bourbon *Anecdotes Historiques*, ed. A. Lecoy de la Marche (Paris 1877), 185–6; Schulte, 282–3 (a subdeacon cannot read the Epistle).
65. P. Adam, *La vie paroissiale en France au XIV^e siècle* (Paris 1964), 148. In part-vindication of the remarks in the next paragraph, I note in passing that the original title of Abbé Adam's work (as a thesis) was '*La décadence* de la vie paroissiale [etc.]'.
66. Sources: *Calendar of Entries in the Papal Registers relating to Great Britain and Ireland* (1893–); K. A. Fink, *Das Vatikanische Archiv* (Rome 1951²); *Ross Fund Report on sources for medieval Scottish history in Vatican Archives*, by Ian B. Cowan [duplicated] (Glasgow University 1967 and 1968).
67. *V.S. Guil. Divion.*, c. 14 (*PL* 142.709D; I have ignored the *difficilior lectio* by N. Bulst in *Deutsches Archiv*, 30 (1974) 472).
68. H. Grundmann, '*Litteratus-illitteratus*' 1–65; and idem, 'Vom Ursprung der Universität im Mittelalter'. The change was noticed by V. H. Galbraith, 'The Literacy of the Medieval English Kings', *Proc. British Acad.* 21 (1935), 201–38; pp. 203–4; and has recently been documented at an earlier stage by P. Riché, 'Recherches sur l'instruction des laïcs du IX^e au XII^e siècle', *Cahiers de civilisation médiévale*, 4 (1962), 175–82, pp. 180–1.
69. *Chart. Univ. Par.* III, p. 463 §1542.
70. Ibid., p. 41 §1230.
71. To judge from the documents in G. Lizérand's *Dossier* (see n. 50). The invasion of regulars at Oxford is particularly well brought out in the figures provided by T. H. Aston, 'Oxford's Medieval Alumni', *Past and Present*, 74 (Feb. 1977), 3–40; p. 17. (Regulars formed nearly a quarter of recorded alumni between *c.* 1280 and *c.* 1420.)
72. Prices: L. Febvre and H. J. Martin, *L'apparition du livre* (Paris 1971²), 20–1. Early manufacture and use: D. Hunter, *Papermaking: The History and Technology of an Ancient Craft* (London 1957²), 473–6; and J. Stiennon, *Paléographie du moyen âge* (Paris 1973), 156–8.
73. G. H. Putnam, *Books and Their Makers in the Middle Ages* (New York–London 1896), 264–6.
74. Putnam, 242.
75. Stiennon, 112–24.
76. Stiennon, 127. Not all abbreviations *succeeded* in saving time and space (ibid. 125). But that need not rebut the usual assumption that the bulk of them were meant to.
77. Putnam, 271–2.
78. Putnam, 233 (citing Richard Aungerville, *Philobiblion*); and generally on MS. trade, 225–75.
79. J. Larner, *Culture and Society in Italy 1290–1420* (1971), 161; on the speedy familiarity with the new invention cf. L. Thorndike, *History of Magic*, I, 859. I owe to Dr. Larner the stimulus which led to the above investigations about paper.
80. Bibliography and summary to 1936: Rashdall, III, 325–38. Cf. n. 85 below.

81. Rashdall, III, 330 ff. 335, 337; more signs (in subdivision of buildings, etc.) in S. Roux, 'L'Habitat urbain au moyen âge: le quartier de l'Université à Paris' (*Annales ESC* 24 (1969), 1196–219, esp. pp. 1198, 1202: 3rd storey built *ad opus scolarium* in 1279).
82. Dates: of Black Death, P. Ziegler, *The Black Death* (Harmondsworth 1969), 79; of long vacation, Rashdall, I, 489. Slightness of effect: Campbell, *Black Death*, 166; cf. Roux (as in last note) p. 1198 (entry of 1348); *Chart. Univ. Par.* III, p. 60 §1241: 'multitudinem studentium [=Augustinian hermits] Parisiensium' (1358).
83. Ibid., p. 106 §§1282–5.
84. 'Multitudes': ibid., p. 189d §1358 (year 1369); and pp. 409–10 §1520 cc. 32 and 35 (year 1384). 'Thousands': ibid., p. 504 and n. 6 §1564 (year 1388). Class of 100 despite ban on attendance, ibid., p. 434 §1430 (year 1386); of up to 300, ibid., p. 472 §1546 (year 1396); of 250, ibid., p. 427 §1528 (year 1386: 250 francs collected; at 1 franc per scholar, cf. p. 472). Other signs of pressure, ibid., p. 317 §1481 (year 1383), and p. 538 §1588 (year 1383); cf. Roux, 1202–3, 1218.
85. Estimates of absolute numbers: Rashdall, III, 326–8, 331–3. For references to the foundation of colleges and halls in what follows I rely chiefly on Rashdall, III, 169–235, and W. A. Pantin, 'The Halls and Schools of Medieval Oxford: an Attempt at Reconstruction', in *Oxford Essays presented to Daniel Callus* (Oxford 1964), 31–100. The problem on which conjectures are offered in this paragraph awaits the outcome of research still in progress when this book goes to press. See Aston (as in n. 71 above) especially pp. 6–8 (promising a further article on both absolute numbers and trends). The line of argument pursued here, and especially on pp. 309–12 below, nevertheless receives provisional corroboration (as concerns Oxford) from Mr. Aston's tentative remarks, ibid., p. 32: '. . by way of a provisional conclusion, it looks not improbable that Oxford's alumni did find the going harder . . .'.
86. *Medieval Oxford* (Oxford 1936), 109; *Survey of Oxford*, I (Oxford Historical Society, new series, 14, Oxford 1960), 69. Salter's reading of at least one of these cases, that in the Oriel records for 1303, is nevertheless open to challenge; a fact pointed out to me by Dr. Janet Cooper, Assistant Editor of the Victoria County History of Oxfordshire (in a letter of 21 April 1977).
87. i.e. a rise from 3 to 15, paying rental to the Hospital of St. John the Baptist. (Dr. Janet Cooper, ibid.).
88. Rashdall, III, 328 n. 3.
89. Salter, *Survey*, I, NE 34, NE 55 (as examples).
90. Rashdall, III, 326; Campbell, *Black Death*, 160.
91. G. E. Lytle, 'Patronage Patterns and Oxford Colleges *c.* 1350– *c.* 1530', in L. Stone, ed., *The University in Society*, I (Princeton-London 1974), III–49; p. 126 (with further references).
92. Other possible signs: (1) it apparently cost 50 per cent more to hire a cheap room in a Hall in 1407 than in 1382, if we may judge from the admittedly fragmentary surviving figures, given in Pantin (as in n. 85), 58, 79–80; (2) the rent of a shop owned by the university rose over twofold between 1366 and 1426; Salter, *Survey of Oxford*, I, NE, No. 1. (I have in general kept off the treacherous ground of rents. But these two cases elude some, at least, of the objections which bedevil the wider demographic argument from rent-levels).
93. E. F. Jacob, 'English University Clerks in the Later Middle Ages, pt. i', in *idem*, *Essays in the Conciliar Epoch* (Manchester 1963²), 207–22.
94. p. 146, cf. pp. 158, 162, 169.
95. pp. 162–3.
96. Based on figures in Rashdall, III, 336 n.
97. Rashdall, II, 217. M. Spinka, *John Hus* (Princeton 1968), 5–6.

98. Campbell, 168.
99. Westermanns, *Grosser Atlas zur Weltgeschichte* (Berlin 1969), 88–9; for bibliography, H. Jedin and others, ed., *Atlas zur Kirchengeschichte* (Freiburg 1970), p. 55*.
100. B. H. Slicher van Bath, *The Agrarian History of Western Europe*, A.D. *500–1850* (London 1963), 80.
101. The approximate range of contemporary estimates is given in the following table, compiled (except where otherwise stated) from C.-J. Hefele and H. Leclercq, *Histoire des Conciles*, V–VII (Paris 1912–16). I put the first two in parentheses as the least reliable.

| | |
|---|---|
| (1123:300–500 | Vol. V (i), p. 631.) |
| (1139:500–600 | Ibid., pp. 721 and 722 n. 1.) |
| 1179:300–400 | Vol. V (ii), p. 1087. |
| 1215:400 | A. Luchaire *Le concile du Latéran et la Réforme de l'Église* (Paris 1908), 8–13. |
| 1245:150 | H. Jedin and others, *Handbook of Church History*, IV (Freiburg–Montreal 1969) p. 196. |
| 1270:300–500 | Vol. VI (i), p. 169. |
| 1311:300 | Vol. VI (ii), p. 645. |
| 1415:200 | Vol. VII(i), pp. 195–6 n. 3. |

102. G. Le Bras, *Les Institutions de la Chrétienté médiévale*, A. Fliche and V. Martin, *Histoire de l'Église*, 12 Paris 1964²), 378 n. 4; K. Edwards, *The English Secular Cathedrals in the Middle Ages* (Manchester 1949), 33–4 ('generally the number of prebendaries in the English chapters remained practically unchanged throughout the middle ages'). A nicely-documented example: D. M. Owen, *Church and Society in Medieval Lincolnshire* (Lincoln 1971), 37–43.
103. A. Hamilton Thompson, 'Diocesan Organization in the Middle Ages', *Proc. British Acad.* 29 (1943), 153–94; esp. pp. 159–67, 173–4, 177; Cf. J. Scammell, 'The Rural Chapter in England from the Eleventh to the Fourteenth Century', *Engl. Hist. Rev.* 86 (1971), 1–21; esp. pp. 7, 20.
104. Hamilton Thompson (as in last note) esp. pp. 177–84 (areas), 184–94 (status and function).
105. C. N. L. Brooke and G. Keir, *London 800–1216: The Shaping of a City* (London 1974), 122–47.
106. A. Visconti, *Storia di Milano* (Milan 1937), 49–50; J. Plesner, *L'émigration . . . à . . . Florence*, viii, 162–5; J. Gaudemet, 'La paroisse', in F. Lot and R. Fawtier, *Hist. des institutions françaises au moyen âge*, III (Paris 1962), 197–219, esp. 199–203 (Paris).
107. Gaudemet (as in last note), 197.
108. G. Strauss, *Nuremberg in the Sixteenth Century* (New York 1966), 37–8, 47.
109. e.g. J. R. H. Moorman, *Church Life in Thirteenth-Century England* (Cambridge 1945), 4. The 'freezing' of the parish system in the twelfth century is remarked on, with exceptions, by C. N. L. Brooke, 'The Missionary at Home: the Church in the Towns 1000–1250', in G. J. Cuming, ed., *The Mission of the Church and the Propagation of the Faith* (*Studies in Church History*, 6, Cambridge 1970), 59–83; p. 72.
110. *Handbook of Church History* (as in n. 101), IV, 261 (cardinals); 30–1 and 262–3 (Curia); with literature.
111. J. A. Jungmann, *The Mass of the Roman Rite* (New York 1950), I, 131 and n. 24; Gerald of Wales, *Gemma ecclesiastica*, ed. J. S. Brewer (in *Opera*, II, *RS* 21, 1862); cf. Intr. xxxi–ii.
112. G. R. Galbraith, *The Constitution of the Dominican Order* (Manchester 1925), 78–81; J. Le Goff, 'Ordres mendiants et urbanisation dans la France médiévale., *Annales ESC* 25 (1970), 924–46; esp. 930–2.

113. J. Krcmar, *The Prague Universities, compiled according to the sources and records* (Prague 1934), 5 ( = bull of Clement VI, 25 Jan. 1347) ; J. F. Hautz, *Geschichte der Universität Heidelberg* (Mannheim 1862–4), II, 313 (year 1385) ; B. Stübel, *Urkundebuch der Universität Leipzig* (Leipzig 1879), 5, line 17 (year 1409). (These three texts are related.) The double concept behind the phrase is already present in Frederick II's seminal charter for Naples university in 1224 (as in H. Rüthing, *Die mittelalterliche Universität Historische Texte, Mittelalter*, 16, Göttingen 1973, p. 49) ; and is echoed in many late-medieval university foundation documents.

114. *Chart. Univ. Par.* III, p. 245 §1428 'ut primam et primogenitam studiorum . . .' etc. Note that this was the one request on the roll to lack Clement VII's *concessum*.

115. *Chart. Univ. Par.* II, p. 269 §818 ; Rashdall, I, 555 n. 1 ; Lytle (as in n. 91 above), 127–33.

116. Quoted by L. Pastor, *The History of the Popes* (London 1938⁶), I, 146, with other contemporary examples of the view.

117. As in n. 93 above ; and the same author's *Archbishop Henry Chichele* (London 1967), 73–86. The important role of colleges in general in meeting what he calls the 'crisis of patronage' in these decades, is admirably depicted by Lytle (as in n. 91 above).

118. F. Firnhaber, 'Petrus von Pulka, Abgesandt der Wiener Universität am Concilium zu Constance', *Archiv für österreichische Geschichtsquellen*, 15 (1856), 57, lines 12–14. Cf. the Cologne letters in E. Martène and U. Durand, *Thesaurus Novus Anecdotorum* (Paris 1717), II, cols. 1611–99 *passim* ; and the summary of a Cologne sermon, expressing the university's intention of exploiting the disgrace of Prague, in R. Swanson, 'The University of Cologne and the Great Schism', *Journal of Ecclesiastical History*, 28 (1977), 1–15 ; p. 11. An illuminating treatment of this subject is that of M. Harvey, 'English Views on the Reform to be undertaken in the General Councils (1400–18) with special reference to the proposals made by Richard Ullerston' (unpublished Oxford D. Phil. thesis, 1964), esp. 188–94.

119. Lewis, *Later Medieval France*, 296.

120. G. de Lagarde, *La naissance de l'esprit laïque au declin du moyen âge*, II (Vienna–Paris 1934), 303–30.

121. See the exceptionally long index-entry under 'Peter, Saint' in Previté-Orton's edition (as in n. 51), 506.

122. De Lagarde, II, 118–38 ; de Lagarde notices other differences between Marsilius and the Waldensians but not this.

123. Henry of Ghent, *Summae*, a. 11, q. vi (fos 81ʳ–82ʳ). Cf above, p. 265 ; and more generally, R. Guelluy, 'La place des théologiens dans l'Église et la société médiévales', *Misc. . . . Albert de Meyer* (Louvain–Brussels 1946), 571–89.

## 13. NOBILITY AND THE CHURCH

1. Vincent of Beauvais, *De eruditione filiorum nobilium*, c. 1, ed. A. Steiner (Cambridge, Mass. 1938), 7 f. (lines 65–92).

2. A. Schulte, *Der Adel und die deutsche Kirche im Mittelalter: Studien zur Sozial-, Rechts- und Kirchengeschichte* (Darmstadt 1909¹ ; 1922², r.p. Stuttgart 1958).

3. The best general survey of theory and law, especially in monasteries : K. Shreiner, *Sozial- und standesgeschichtliche Untersuchungen zu den Benediktinerkonventen im östlichen Schwarzwald*, 1–139. Bibliography and summary for the secular church in Germany : L. Santifaller, *Zur Geschichte des ottonisch-salischen Reichskirchensystems* (Sb. Wien 229, Band 1, *Abhandlung*, Vienna 1964), 123–57. Reflections on the situation in N. France : L. Génicot, 'Aristocratie et dignités ecclésiastiques en Picardie aux xiiᵉ et xiiiᵉ siècles', *Revue d'hist. ecclésiastique*, 67 (1972), 436–42. The references in the following footnotes will provide a further entrée to the large literature.

4. L. Génicot, 'Haut clergé et noblesse dans le diocèse de Liège du xi$^e$ au xv$^e$ siècle', *Adel und Kirche*, 237–58.

5. Cluny: J. Fechter, *Cluny, Adel und Volk*. *Studien über das Verhältnis des Klosters zu den Ständen (910–1156)* (Tübingen 1966), 1–15; Hirsau: Schreiner, 58; Cistercians (La Ferté): Duby, *Soc.* . . . *mâconnaise*, 380 (297); Dominicans (Strasbourg): Schulte, 245; Franciscans: Moorman, *Franciscan Order*, 352, 362.

6. Humiliati (Milan): Galvaneus della Flamma, *Manipulus Florum*, c. 327 (Muratori[1] 11.712E)—albeit an unreliable source, see pp. 458–9 nn. 98, 100 above; Brethren of the Common Life: Schreiner, 70 n. 90; for Beguines, H. Grundmann, *Religiöse Bewegungen im Mittelalter*, 348 n. 49.

7. Schreiner, 20 (= *PL* 54.611A).

8. Ed. A. Friedburg (Graz 1872), I, 214 (=Gratian, *Decretum*, I, liv, 21). For the perennial vigour of the clause in dark-age legislation, see F. Graus, 'Die Gewalt bei den Anfängen des Feudalismus und die "Gefangenenbefreiungen" der Merowingischen Hagiographie', *Jahrbuch für Wirtschaftsgeschichte*, 1961 (Berlin), 90.

9. Schulte, 75–82.

10. Boshof, *Agobard*, 109–12.

11. See above pp. 220, 245.

12. Schreiner, 17 (referring to *SS* 15, 224.24–7).

13. Peyrant, *Summae*, II, vi, pt. 3, c. 30 (fo. 139$^{ra}$); cf. Schreiner, 65.

14. *ST* II, 2, q. 100, a. 3; Schreiner, 68.

15. Schreiner, 68–70.

16. *PL* 54.611A: 'Duplex itaque in hac parte reatus est, quod et sacrum ministerium talis consortii vilitate polluitur, et dominorum . . . jura solvuntur'. (This part is not in the *Corpus Juris Canonici*.)

17. Boshof, *Agobard*, 75–81.

18. Gregory VII himself occasionally set aside episcopal candidates of noble birth, if otherwise ill-qualified; but an examination of his words on these occasions shows he was far from riding roughshod over the principle that high birth was in itself a recommendation. See his *Registrum* IV, 4, 5 (esp. p. 301.26–7); IX, 2 (p. 571.6 and 16–23); VIII, 21 (p. 562.11–14). He can even stipulate that (Norwegian) candidates for instruction in Rome *must* be noble: VI, 13 (p. 416.37–8).

19. Schreiner, 20 (= Jerome, *Epist.* 66 §4, *PL* 22.640–1).

20. Argued by K. Bosl, 'Der "Adelsheilige": Idealtypus und Wirklichkeit, Gesellschaft und Kultur im Merowingerzeitlichen Bayern', *Speculum Historiale* (Fs. J. Spörl) (Freiburg–Munich 1965).

21. Schreiner, 96 n. 25 (= *SS* 12.841–5).

22. e.g. *V.S. Odilonis, praefatio* (898BC); *V.S. Hugonis Grat., prologus* and c. 1 (763C, 764A–5B).

23. *De naturis rerum*, II, c. 155 (pp. 243–4).

24. Adalbero of Laon, *Carmen ad Robertum regem*, esp. lines 36 ff. (*PL* 141.773–86; cols. 773–4); cf. Schulte, 73; Schreiner, 20–1.

25. Schulte, 226–7.

26. J. Fleckenstein, 'Heinrich IV. und der deutsche Episkopat in den Anfängen des Investiturstreites', *Adel und Kirche*, 221–36.

27. *Epist.* 8 (*PL* 178.269CD); Schulte, 234.

28. John of St. Arnulf, *V. Joannis abb. Gorz., prologus* (*PL* 137.245C–6D). This is the first appearance of the term 'nobilitas carnis' I have found in Schreiner (cf. 46–7), though the term itself is certainly older.

29. *V.S. Hugonis Grat., prologus* (763D).

30. E. Benz, 'Über den Adel in der deutschen Mystik', *Deutsche Vierteljahrschrift für Literaturwissenschaft und Geistesgeschichte*, 14 (Halle 1936), 505–35. The term 'nobilitas animi' was used by Peyraut, II, vi, pt. 2, c. 29 (fos. 137$^{vb}$–8$^{vb}$).
31. Cf. Schreiner, 17, 19, 20, 46, 64, 127, 129.
32. Schulte, 248–9.
33. Ibid.
34. Schreiner, 97 n. 28, with other Carolingian examples.
35. Cf. Bruno of Segni and Rupert of Deutz, in their Commentaries on Matthew (*PL* 165.73A and *PL* 167.1337A–D respectively). The theme is missed by the following commentators on the same passage: Rabanus Maurus (*PL* 107.727–48); Walafrid Strabo (*PL* 114.863–4); Paschasius Radbertus (*PL* 120.45–6); Peter Damian (*PL* 145.891–4); and Anselm of Laon (*PL* 162.1227–53, with a hint of the theme at 1247D).
36. Lecoy de la Marche, *Chaire*, 438–9 (= Giles of Orleans, 1273). Cf. Thomas of Chantimpré, *Bonum universale de apibus* (c. 1260), I, vii, 2 (edition of Douai 1605, p. 25) [ = Christ and the Baptist].
37. Jean Gerson, *Tractatus de Nobilitate*, II, in *Œuvres Complètes*, ed. Mgr. Glorieux, IX (Paris 1973), 487; cf. Schreiner, 97; and (for Dame Juliana Berners's endorsement), E. Prestage, ed., *Chivalry* (London 1928), 214.
38. Henry of Ghent, *Summae*, a. 11, q. 6 (fo. 81$^r$, top).

14. WERE NOBLES BETTER CHRISTIANS?

1. Quoted by Humbert de Romans, *De modo prompte cudendi sermones*, I, c. 81 (496D); I have failed to locate this phrase in Jerome, to whom he ascribes it, but Jerome expresses similar sentiments in *Epist.* 60 § 8 (*PL* 22.593A).
2. Cecco of Ascoli, *L'Acerba*, c. 12, esp. lines 1415–32 (pp. 213–15).
3. *V.S. Hugonis Grat., prologus* (763C).
4. Peyraut, *Summae*, II, vi, pt. 3, c. 18 (fo. 137$^{rb}$).
5. Humbert de Romans, *De modo prompte cudendi sermones*, II, c. 83 (559A).
6. *Collat.* III, c. 30 (613A–C).
7. *Hist.* IV, c. 5 (679BC).
8. *Epist.* 113, *ad Sophiam virginem* (*PL* 182.256C): 'virtus paucorum ... praesertim nobilium'.
9. See p. 326 above; and cf. Abelard's *Ethics* (ed. D. E. Luscombe, Oxford 1971), 78–81.
10. Humbert de Romans, I, c. 80 (495G); cf. Jer. 39:6.
11. Jacobus a Varagine, *Sermones dominicales, 1st in Advent*, MS. Florence, Bibl. Naz. *Conv. soppr.* J. 10.35, fo. 13$^v$: 'Evangelizare pauperibus misit me [Luke 4:18]. Fit aut[?] pocius mentio de pauperibus quam de divitibus quia pauperes facilius convertuntur ...'
12. Peyraut, *Summae*, II, vi, pt. 3, c. 29 (fo. 138$^{rb}$).
13. L. Schmugge, *Joh. von Jandun*, 79, quoting *Questiones de bona fortuna*: 'nobilitas et virtus in paucis, nobiles nam et boni nusquam centum'.
14. *Dialogus*, II, c. 23 (*PL* 66.178AB): 'sed sicut nonnullis solet nobilitas generis parere ignobilitatem mentis'; cf. Schreiner, 19 and nn. 54–5; 20 and n. 56.
15. As in n. 6 (613C).
16. *Vita*, c. 17 (678A).
17. *V. Hugonis abb. March.*, c. 4 (1714A).
18. As in n. 11. The passage continues: '[convertuntur] quia diviti[bu]s superbia est annexa secundum Gregorium / [fo. 14$^r$] tumor mentis est obstaculum virtutis [*Mor.* 23, c. 17; *PL* 16.269: '...veritatis'], tum quia cor divitis est plenum sollicitudinis

seculi que suffocant verbum dei tum etiam quia divites habent consolationes
temporales et ideo parvipendunt spirituales'.

19. e.g. C. Morris, *The Discovery of the Individual* (London 1972), 31 ( = tenth century) ;
cf. F. Graus, 'Gewalt', 70: '...nur zu often glich ihre Herrschaft einer nackten
Tyrannai' (seventh and eighth centuries).

20. See Appendix I (for Odo, John Gualbert, and Bernard) and the reference-works
mentioned there (for the others).

21. Ibid. (for Origen) ; A. Dondaine, 'Guillaume Peyraut. Vie et œuvres', *Archivum
Fratrum Praedicatorum*, 18 (Rome 1948), 168–9: all we know about Peyraut's birth is
that it took place *c*. 1200 in the village of Peyraud. For John, see Schmugge, *Joh. von
Jandun*, 4.

22. e.g. Odo, *Collat.* I, c. 13 (528D) : pride among the very poor; Humbert de Romans
as in n. 5, and I, c. 82 (496GF).

23. *De naturis rerum*, II, c. 155, p. 244: 'Sed quid est quod novorum successores nobilibus
orti natalibus perhibentur, cum eorum praedecessores abjectissime fuerint
conditionis?'

24. Line 18724.

25. Quoted by Schmugge, *Joh. von Jandun*, 79. Another illustration of this theme:
Ratherius of Verona, *Praeloquia*, I, c. 10 (*PL* 186.166.C–8A).

26. Peyraut, *Summa*, II, vi, pt. 3, c. 28 § 9 (fo. 137^vb^) ; cf. John of Jandun (Schmugge,
79) : 'licet aliquis a senioribus suorum progenitorum habeat fortem inclinationem
ad virtutem ...'.

27. Cicero, *De off.* I, 33–4, 121 ; Boethius, *De consol. phil.* III, 6 (prose). The passage from
Cicero is quoted in the *Mor. dogma philos* (see p. 447 n. 86 above), p. 55.9–11. For
quotations and echoes of Boethius: Schreiner, 121 (Stephen of Paris (†1142), in a
commentary on the Rule of Saint Benedict) ; 126 (John of Castl (*c*. 1400)) ; 105
(Aenius Silvius, *De ritu ... Germaniae*). Peyraut (as in the last note) paraphrases
Boethius, but ascribes the words to Jerome.

28. Lines 18795–6. Cf. Sallust, *Bellum Jugurth.* 85, 22–3; *Mor. dogma philos.* 54.14–15
(quoting Sallust) ; Thomasin, 3863–72 ; Nicholas of Siegen (1456), Schreiner, 104.

29. Cecco of Ascoli, p. 212, lines 1433–8; cf. Hugo von Trimberg, 1431–2 ; Jean de
Meung, 18590–2, 18601–4 ; an element of the same contradiction is present in the
hagiographical motif, 'nobilis genere, sed nobilior fide' (on whose diffusion see
W. Levison in *SSRM* 7.312 n. 4).

30. E. W. Kemp, *Canonization and Authority in the Western Church* (Oxford 1948).

31. I am aware of the ambitious survey by K. and C. H. George, 'Roman Catholic
Sainthood and Social Status : a Statistical and Analytical Study', *Journal of Religion*,
35 (Chicago 1955), 85–98; but also of the strictures on it by F. Graus, 'Gewalt', 87,
and *Volk*, 363. A delicate and learned assessment of problems of method in this field
of research is that by Pierre Delooz, 'Pour une étude sociologique de la sainteté
canonisée dans l'Église catholique', *Archives de sociologie des religions*, 13 (Clermont-
Ferrand 1962), 17–43.

32. *V.S. Hugonis Clun.* (Gilo). An entrée to the problems of definition can be had
through Duby, *Soc. ... mâconnaise*. 230–45 (191–201) ; more generally, the same
author's 'Noblesse'; and for Italy, E. Cristiani, *Nobiltà e Popolo nel Comune di Pisa*
(Naples 1962), 72–8.

33. e.g. *V.S. Romualdi*, 957BC, 961AB, 988C ; *V.S. Joh. Gualb.*, 647B ; *V.S. Hugonis Clun.*
(Hildebert), 860A, 861A, 894B ; *V.Hugonis abb. March.*, 1716AB ; *V.S. Joh. Piling.*
150A–E; etc.

34. Schulte, 261–93.

35. See especially his 'Structures de parenté' and 'Remarques sur la littérature
généalogique' in *Hommes et Structures*, 267–85, 287–98.

36. *SS* 24 ; see pp. 592–3, 604, 620–1, 637–9.

37. *Annales Cameracenses*, year 1108, *SS* 16.511–12.
38. *Cronica*, 52–4, 75–8 and see Index, 1214. Ferd. Bernini, 'Il parentado e l'ambiente familiare del cronista Frate Salimbene da Parma secondo nuovi documenti', *Archivum Franciscanum Historicum*, 28 (1935), 345–73 prints this remarkable genealogy (pp. 359–61) and goes some way to confirm its credit from documents. The one misrepresentation of which the same documents tend to convict Salimbene is that of exaggerating the rank of certain ancestors: none can be proved to have been a 'lord'; though there is no doubt the family had a notable position in the city (pp. 357–8).
39. A. Higounet-Nadal, 'Une famille de marchands de Périgueux aux XIVᵉ siècle: les Giraudoux', *Annales ESC* 20 (1965), 110–33; see especially 112–13, 115–17, 120–2.
40. In addition to the genealogies mentioned in the second of Professor Duby's articles (as in n. 35 above), cf. W. Dugdale, *Monasticon Anglicanum*, V (London 1925), 376–84, esp. 377–82 (Courtenays and connections); and two genealogies reconstructed from the exceptionally well preserved early notarial registers of Genoa: *Cesare Imperiale, Jacopo d'Oria e i suoi Annali* (Venice 1930), 342 (with further references); and R. S. Lopez, *Benedetto Zaccaria, Ammiraglio e mercante* (Messina–Milan 1933), 280. See also: D. O. Hughes, 'Urban Growth and Family Structure in Medieval Genoa', *Past and Present*, 66 (1975), 3–28, esp. 7n. and 27n. But family acts may ignore some entries to religion (Higounet-Nadal (as in last note), 116), just as monastic records may ignore those families or branches less inclined to celibate careers.
41. e.g. Duby, *Soc. . . . mâconnaise*, 9(33): 'la restriction au mariage n'est qu'un réflexe de défense qu'impose l'exiguité des ressources. Dès que l'on se sent assez riche pour s'établir sans perdre son rang, on se marie . . .'.
42. Schulte, 263.
43. *Feudal Germany* (Chicago 1928), 11.
44. Cf. p. 378 below: Ingelbert was Hildebrand's brother.
45. W. W. Williams, *St. Bernard of Clairvaux* (Manchester 1935), 11, 29–30.
46. Grundmann, 'Adelsbekehrungen im Hochmittelalter', *Adel und Kirche*, 325–45; pp. 338–41.
47. Schulte, 263–5; Fechter, 6 (×2), 7, 9 (×2), 10 (×2), 11, 12 (×3): a total of eleven examples in which two or more members of one family enter Cluny. I include one (p. 12) where a lord took his whole family into the cloister; but exclude another (ibid.) where a count took thirty of 'his knights' the same way.
48. Schulte, 250–93; K. B. McFarlane, *The Nobility of Later Medieval England* (Oxford 1973), 142–67; T. H. Hollingsworth, 'The Demography of the British Peerage' [= 1550–1924], *Population Studies*, 18, No. 2 (London 1964); for the more baffling data from early medieval France, P. Feuchère, 'La noblesse du nord de la France', *Annales ESC*, 6 (1951), 306–18, esp. 311–17; L. Génicot, 'La noblesse au moyen âge dans l'ancienne "Francie"', ibid. 17 (1962), 1–22, esp. 13; J. C. Russell, 'Aspects démographiques des débuts de la féodalité', ibid. 20 (1965), 1118–27 esp. 1122–4; and the studies of G. Duby already cited, esp. *Soc. . . . mâconnaise*, 8–9 (32–3) and *Hommes et Structures*, 415. These works suggest a boom in noble fertility in northern France (only), in the twelfth century. For further guidance to the growing literature on this testing subject see D. O. Hughes (as in n. 40) esp. 3–5nn. Emily R. Coleman, 'Medieval Marriage Characteristics', *Journal of Interdisciplinary History*, 2 (1971–2), 205–19 and D. Herlihy, 'Three Patterns of Social Mobility in Medieval History', ibid. 3 (1973), 623–47 present evidence to suggest that in the lower ranks of society the number of children per family rose proportionately to wealth; but that trend cannot be extrapolated upwards to the knightly and noble classes. I draw attention to signs of noble under-reproduction in the eleventh-century French *Mir. S. Fidis* (where it is naturally presented as divine punishment), pp. 56d–7; 145a; 157d–8; 238a; 245c.

49. e.g. *V.B. Joh. de Monte Mir.*, 228BC, 229A; Salimbene, 56.1–2; Coulton, *Five Centuries*, I, 33. In the second and third cases the continuance of the dynasty was also involved.
50. *V.S. Romualdi* (concerning ex-Doge Peter Orseoli), 963A; *V.S. Joh. Gualb.*, 673C; *V.S. Hugonis Clun.* (Hildebert) (concerning ex-count Guido), 885D; *Magna V.S. Hugonis Linc.*, I, c. 7, pp. 23–4. Cf. Coulton, *Five Centuries*, I, 350 for the Cistercians' adoption of this practice.
51. Grundmann, *Religiöse Bewegungen*, 167.
52. Ibid. 160, 164–5. The third and fourth of the phrases quoted refer to Humiliati, the rest to Franciscans. Grundmann's section on this subject (157–69) also deals with Waldensians. See also pp. 17, 21, 49, 184, 188–94. Grundmann's findings have been extended e.g. by McDonnell, *Beguines*, 81–100; and by B. Bolton, '*Mulieres Sanctae*', *Studies in Church Hist.* 10 (Oxford 1973), 77–95, esp. 85, 93.
53. Grundmann, *Religiöse Bewegungen*, 168–70.
54. G. Koch, *Frauenfrage und Ketzertum im Mittelalter* (East Berlin 1962), 21–30 (esp. p. 26 on position of lower nobility among women-Cathars), 61, 147, etc.
55. See below, p. 486 n. 73.

15. THE RELIGIOUS EFFECTS OF NOBLE CONDITION

1. Robert de Blois, *Beaudois*, intr. v. 43: 'Li nons ne fait pas la proëce' (in E. Langlois ed., *Le Roman de la Rose*, IV (Paris 1892) 317); Freidank, *Bescheidenheit* 93, 18 f. (in Goetz, *Nobility*, 81); Dante, *Convivio*, IV, 10: '(divizie) non possono causare nobilitade'; etc. Morals are only publicized by high status: Juvenal, *Sat.* VIII, 140; Matthew of Vendôme (in Faral, 116 § 28).
2. Line 6247 (and note). The proverb is quoted by J. Morawski, *Proverbes français* (Paris 1925), No. 850 as: 'Honnors meuent et varient les mors.'
3. *ST* II(i), 2.2.3; cf. *Nich. Eth.* IV, 3 (1123a); Gauthier, *Magnanimité*, 78–82, 335–8.
4. Charny, 485.
5. Philippe de Novare, II § 40 (pp. 24–5).
6. Bibliography: F. Irsigler, *Untersuchungen zur Gesch. des frühfränkischen Adels* (Rheinisches Archiv, 70, Bonn, 1969), 233. Some early examples: Anton, *Fürstenspiegel*, 60, 74, 83–5, 104. The moral onus of public position: Cicero, *De off.* II, 44; a passage (significantly?) ignored in *Mor. dogma phil.* but echoed elsewhere, e.g. Hugo of Trimberg, 561–4.
7. *Collat.* III, c. 30, 613A and C; Peyraut, *Summae*, II, vi, pt. 3, cc. 8–22 (fos. 118ᵛ–133ʳ).
8. K. Lorenz, *King Solomon's Ring* c. 12 (London 1952), 181–99.
9. H. C. Lea, *The Wager of Battle*, r.p. in idem, *Superstition and Force* (Philadelphia 1892⁴), 122, 140–1; M. H. Keen, *The Laws of War in the Late Middle Ages* (London 1965), 255 n. 3.
10. For the trampling, see Plate VIII.
11. *V.S. Geraldi Aur.*, 668A.
12. The following is based on the magisterial doctrinal history by R. A. Gauthier, O.P., *Magnanimité: L'idéal de la grandeur dans la philosophie païenne et dans la théologie chrétienne (Bibliothèque Thomiste*, 28, Paris 1951).
13. *ST* II(i), 40.5 *resp.*
14. *ST* II(ii), 129, 6–8. Analysis in Gauthier, 318–68.
15. *ST* II(ii), 129.3, ad 2: 'actus magnanimitatis non competit cuilibet virtuoso, sed solum magnis'. Gauthier, 351–4 (and 114–16 for Aristotle).
16. Gauthier, 337.
17. Gauthier, 338–46.

18. Cf. Gauthier, 251–7.
19. Ibid.
20. R. Hofmann, *Die heroische Tugend. Geschichte und Inhalt eines theologischen Begriffs (Münchner Studien zur historischen Theologie, Heft* 12, Munich 1935), 17–29.
21. Ibid. 3–17 (Aristotle), 30–133 (slow adoption by scholastics), 152–65 (in canonization, *c.* 1600).
22. Recent references in Van Luyn, '*Milites*', 15.
23. *V.S. Joh. Gualb.* (Andreas), 769A.
24. *V.S. Joh. Gualb.* (Atto), 677A; cf. *V.S. Bernardi Tiron.*, 1428C.
25. *V.S. Romualdi*, 955B; cf. 964B: 'si quis ... magnum ... inciperet ... longanimiter perseveraret' (on the shifting relation between long- and magn-animity, and its model in the *Life of Saint Antony*, cf. Gauthier, 212–18, esp. 216–17).
26. *V.B. Wulfrici*, 68–73, esp. 71–2.
27. *V.S. Joh. Valent.*, 1693CD.
28. *V.S. Geraldi Aur.*, 669C.
29. *De modo prompte cudendi sermones*, 497B.
30. Text printed by Gauthier, 293.
31. Ibid. 294.
32. MS. Florence Laur. Plut. 33 sin. 1, fo. 3$^{ra}$ cf. p. 442 n. 112 above). Another example: Peter Chanter, *Verbum Abbreviatum*, c. 123 (*PL* 205.317C): '... ingenous animos et magnos faciunt otium et quies pusillos...'.
33. Aristotle, *Rhet.* II, xii, 3; Aquinas, *ST* II(i), 40.6; cf. Philippe de Novare, II, §§ 33, 34, 52 (pp. 21–2, 31).
34. Whose problems and ambitions are depicted by G. Duby, 'Les "jeunes" dans la société aristocratique dans la France du Nord-Ouest au xii$^e$ siècle', *Hommes et Structures*, 213–25.
35. Contemporary usage in this sense (from 10th to 13th centuries): *V.S. Romualdi*, 961A, 998D, 986; *V.S. Joh. Gualb.*, 673C; *V.S. Steph. Obaz.*, 86–8; *V.S. Petri Gonz.*, 392C: 'conversus ... in Deum, quem in clericali sanctissimoque statu pristino oblivioni quodammodo tradiderat, et in alterum transmutatus novum hominem'.
36. *Varieties of Religious Experience* (London 1902), Lectures VI and VII, esp. pp. 149–57, 161. The 'sociological' comments on this complaint are my own; though it is fair to observe that James's one example of it was a count—if scarcely a young one (Tolstoy).
37. *De Vita Sua*, I, c. 9 (*PL* 156.850D–51A; ed. G. Bourgin, in the series *Collection de textes pour servir à l'étude et l'enseignement d'histoire*, Paris 1907, 24–5). The essence of the story is confirmed in a deed of 1073; H. Grundmann, 'Adelsbekehrungen', 326 n. 4.
38. Ibid. (851B; ed. Bourgin, 25): 'Teudebaldus, quem sanctum hodie universi agnominant...' For a certain provincialism in Guibert's appreciation of contemporary religious movements, contrast this remark with his designation of Saint Bruno the Carthusian as 'quidam in urbe Remensi vir', ibid., c. 11 (853B; ed. Bourgin, 30).
39. *V.P. S. Bernardi Clar.*, I, c. 3 §§ 6, 8 (*PL* 185.230B, 231B).
40. *V.S. Geraldi Aur.*, 670C.
41. *V.S. Herluini*, 698C.
42. *V. Hugonis abb. March.*, 1714E f.
43. *V.S. Guil. Bitur.* (B), 636C.
44. e.g. *V.B. Joh. de Monte Mir.*, 221–5 *passim*.
45. And I have omitted, though psychologically in the same category, cases of wealthy and successful scholars, e.g. *V.S. Petri Dam.*, cc. 2 and 4 (117C f., 119C f.); *Vitas Fratrum*, IV, c. 8 (p. 168) (=Roland of Cremona).
46. Pages 346–7 above, and 482 n. 48.

47. Hollingsworth (as ibid.), 19–20.

48. As the devil was aware in tempting the Blessed Peter Crisei of Foligno (†1323) to get married. He promised this Franciscan tertiary such wealth that if he had fifty sons 'quilibet militari [more] poterit vivere', *Vita*, c. ii § 12 *AASS* July IV (1725), 667E.

49. For the caution of artisans: Hughes (as on p. 482 n. 40), 22–6.

50. *The Allegory of Love* (Oxford 1936), 1–23.

51. e.g. in the otherwise percipient article by E. R. Coleman, 'Medieval Marriage Characteristics', *Journal of Interdisciplinary History*, 2 (1971–2), 205–19; p. 212.

52. J. Coppin, *Amour et mariage dans la littérature française du Nord au moyen âge* (Paris 1961), 1–22, esp. 7–9; the literature reviewed in this connection by R. Nelli, *L'Érotique des troubadours* (Toulouse 1963), 11 n. 1, 21–3, 24–6, 29–40 seems to me not to back his firmly negative conclusion; indeed the lovely tenth-century *Invitatio Amicae* ( = *Carmina Cantabrigiensia* 27) (ed. W. Bulst, Heidelberg 1950, pp. 52–4) does the opposite.

53. *V.S. Carthagi*, xi, in *Vitae Sanctorum Hiberniae*, ed. C. Plummer (Oxford 1910), I, p. 173; this and another example in Graus, *Volk*, 465.

54. p. 8.22; 42.30; 60.14–15. Cf. pp. 42.18–19; 74.32–3; 92.20–2, etc.

55. J.-B. Molin and P. Mutembe, *Le rituel du mariage en France du xii^e au xvi^e siècle (Théologie historique*, 26, Paris 1973), 159, 172–3, cf. 168: Isidore on connection of fourth finger of left hand with the heart.

56. Ibid. 56, 201; later or undatable examples on pp. 117, 153 n. 69, 183, 192.

57. J. T. Noonan, 'Marital Affection in the Canonists', *Studia Gratiana*, 12 (1967), 481–509; cf. Thietmar of Merseburg, 74.32–3 ( = *conjugalis amor, c.* 1000).

58. *V.S. Steph. Obaz.*, 172 (c. 50, lines 2–5).

59. Good-looking converts, other than those mentioned in the text of this and the next paragraph: *V.S. Joh. Gualb.*, 673CD (cf. 672A: 'charus'); *V.S. Hugonis Clun.* (Hildebert), 863A, 864BC; *V.S. Hugonis Grat.*, 765B; *V.S. Steph. Obaz.*, 110 (c. 11, line 14) ( = Raynald, fifth abbot of Cîteaux (†1150)); *V.B. Wulfrici*, 17bc; *V.B. Joh. de Monte Mir.*, 219C ('corporis probitate'); *V.B. Jacobi Certaldi*, 153D. Graus, *Volk*, 463–8 lists dark-age examples, though the element of topos in descriptions from those centuries (sixth to tenth) is probably too strong (see ibid. 468) to allow general historical conclusions to be drawn from them.

60. *V.S. Geraldi Aur.*, 648B–9B: note the verbal allusion to the love of Dido (*Aeneid*, IV, 2); looks and physique, 650C, 641A.

61. *V. Hugonis abb. March.*, 1714A.

62. *V.S. Ailredi*, 75–6 (cf. F. M. Powicke's remarks ibid. lxxxiii).

63. e.g. ibid. lxxxii (Waldef); and *V.S. Geraldi Aur.*, 649A; *V. Hugonis abb. March.*, 1714AB ('mirabile temporibus nostris'); *V.S. Guil. Bitur.* (B), 636B; *V.S. Guil. S. Brioci*, 122D; *Vitas Fratrum*, IV, c. 7 (p. 165), c. 25 §9 (p. 228) ( = Isnard).

64. *V.P.S. Bernardi Clar.*, I, c. 3 § 7 (*PL* 185.230D–1B).

65. *V.S. Guil. S. Brioci*, 122DE.

66. *V.S. Petri Gonz.*, 393E, 394E; and *Vitas Fratrum*, IV, c. 4 § 2 (p. 159). The latter source mentions a similar case with a second 'fratrem quendam decorum corpore' (§ 1, p. 158). For the Dominican problem in general (and Saint Dominic's awareness of it), see Grundmann, *Religiöse Bewegungen*, 214–52.

67. Nelli, 139–43, 164, 244. A typical expression of the sentiment: Adam de la Halle, *Chanson* 15 (ed. J. H. Marshall (Manchester 1971), 67–8).

68. Nelli, 160; Coppin (as in n. 52), 37. The 'ministerial' status of most *Minnesinger* has been remarked by A. Borst, 'Das Rittertum im Hochmittelalter', *Saeculum*, 10 (1959), 213–31; 226.

69. Nelli, 295.

70. Murray, 'Religion among the Poor', 314–17 for a mere fragment of the evidence.

71. Nelli, passim, esp. 247–59.
72. Ratherius of Verona, *De cont. can.*, I § 8 (496C); *Discordia* § 1 (619B); cf. Atto of Vercelli, *Expos. in Epist. Pauli, in I Cor.* 7 (350BC) and Peter Damian, *Lib. Gomorr.* (*PL* 145. 159–90) passim (e.g. 183B: autoerotism seen as *debitum naturae* in a story); Guibert of Nogent, *De virginitate*, c. 1 (*PL* 156.580D–1A); Peyraut, *Summa Vitiorum*, III, pts. v and vi (fos. 21$^{ra}$–24$^{ra}$); *Chart. Univ. Par.*, I, p. 553 esp. cc. 168 and 169.
73. Ignored: see sources named in last footnote. Wonder: *V.S. Odonis Clun.*, 71A ('nunquam memini tales viros vidisse'); Murray, 'Piety and Impiety', 106 nn. 4 and 5; Moorman, *Franciscan Order*, 12.
74. *Chanson* VII, str. iii (ed. A. Jeanroy, Paris 1964, 17). For William's peculiarities, and Professor Nelli's thesis of his development, cf. Nelli, 79–104.
75. *V. Hugonis abb. March.*, 1714A: '... in seipsum reversus, mox conceptam foeditatem exhorruit, ...'. See above, p. 371.
76. C. Erdmann, *Die Entstehung des Kreuzzugsgedankens* (Stuttgart 1935); on such 'martyrs' esp. 317.
77. Cf. esp. Charny, 510–13, 519, 522–4.
78. Vegetius, III, c. 12 (p. 95.9); and III, c. 10 (p. 91.12–15); on medieval endorsements see p. 129 above; also Latini, *Tresors*, II, c. 95 § 12 (line 100), p. 278; Philippe de Novare, II § 52 (p. 31); Charny, 472, 504, 516.
79. As observed by Aristotle, *Nich. Eth.* III, 9.
80. Ibid. 6; *ST* II(ii), q. 123, a. 4.
81. A. Borst (as in n. 68 above), 230.
82. Philippe de Novare, II § 76 (p. 44).
83. Even Charny never mentions it, though he urges 'cruel revenge' in one place (p. 489, cf. 491). Philippe de Novare is silent on this side of the knightly life, but has less reason to speak of it.
84. *V.S. Romualdi*, c. 1, 955CD.
85. *V.S. Bobonis* (†986), *AASS* May v (1685), 184–91. Almost the whole *Vita* is devoted to this one episode.
86. *V.S. Herluini*, 698C.
87. *V.S. Hugonis Clun.* (Hildebert), 860C, cf. 894B.
88. *V.S. Hugonis Grat.*, 764C.
89. *Vita Theogeri* (year 1084) (*SS* 12, 452.28–32); *Casus monasterii Petrishusensis*, II, c. 48 (*SS* 20.648.24–9); *Hist. Hirsaugiensis monasterii*, c. 3 (*SS* 14.256.44–50); Bernold, *Chronicon* (year 1083) (*SS* 5.439.20–4); Schreiner, 31 n. 130.
90. Grundmann, 'Adelsbekehrungen', 341–2.
91. *V.B. Wulfrici*, 89–71.
92. *V.P.S. Bernardi Clar.*, I, c. 3 § 9 (232A).
93. *Legenda Maior* (Bonaventura), c. 1 § 3; cf. Moorman, *Franciscan Order*, 4–5.
94. *V.B. Joh. de Monte Mir.*, esp. 225A, 219DE; the nostalgia, 224B.
95. *V.S. Guil. Divion.*, § 2, 703B–4A.
96. *Chronicon Affligemense*, § 14, 826B. Cf. Grundmann 'Adelsbekehrungen', 337–8.
97. *V.P.S. Bernardi, Clar.*, I, c. 3 §§ 11, 12 (233A–4C).
98. Grundmann, 'Adelsbekehrungen', 332.
99. G. Koch, *Frauenfrage und Ketzertum* (E. Berlin 1962), 32 (the wife of a baron joins the 'Patarines' on the death of a viscount who loves her). The German women's mystical movement owed much to the widowing of upper-class women by crusades, and one of its chief monuments, Eckhart's *Book of Divine Comfort*, is said to have been written for Agnes of Hungary after the assassination of her husband Albert of Habsburg: J. Quint, intr. to his selection, *Meister Eckehart, Deutsche Predigten und Tractate* (Munich 1965), 7. In the last case of judicial combat in the registers of the French *parlement* (1386), the wife of the victor entered a convent

from remorse at his having killed a man later proved innocent—at least according to the Chronicler of St. Denis: Lea, *Wager of Battle* (as on p. 483 n. 9 above), 230.

100. *V.B. Egid. Sant.*, §3, *AASS* May III (1680), 405F–406A.
101. *V.S. Romualdi*, 960B.
102. *V.S. Roberti*, c. 1 §4 1272B–D.
103. *V.S. Hugonis Clun.* (Hildebert), 882AB.
104. Veiled: e.g. *V.S. Romualdi*, 975CD; (and 965D–6A: 'sublimi culmine terrenae potestatis erectus, sed multis . . . peccatorum molibus aggravatus').
105. Grundmann, 'Adelsbekehrungen', esp. 330–2. Cf. H. Günter, *Psychologie de la Légende* (Paris 1954), 159–60, giving five further examples between the dates 900 and 1500.
106. *V.S. Joh. Gualb.* (Atto), 672CD; that the victim was John's own brother, as commonly asserted, appears to have been a late addition, derived from Peter Damian's account of what may well be yet a further case, see editors' remarks, ibid. 710–11. Another similar case (thirteenth century; the conversion of Loth, O. P.): Davidsohn, *Gesch. v. Florenz*, IV, pt. iii, p. 40, and n. 6.
107. e.g. the Legend of St. Giles in *The Golden Legend*; History of the Foundation of Le Dale (Derbyshire), Dugdale, *Monasticon*, VI (London 1830), 893R.
108. *V.S. Romualdi*, 956A (concerning Romuald himself).
109. W. Stubbs, ed., *Memorials of St. Dunstan* (*RS* 63, London 1874), 24; cf. Knowles, *Monastic Order* 38.

16. THE SAINT: THE MAN WITHOUT SOCIAL CLASS

1. Ch. Oulmont, *Les débats du clerc et du chevalier* (Paris 1911); for claims to supremacy by the poor in general, see N. Cohn, *The Pursuit of the Millennium* (London 1957[1]), cc. 2 and 3, pp. 31, 45, 53–4, 71; and for those by separate crafts, Aelfric, *Colloquy*.
2. Humility better than miracle: (*V.S. Romualdi*, 976D–977A); *V.S. Hugonis Clun.* (Hildebert), 886D–887A; *V.S. Bernardi Tiron.*, 1443AB; *V.B. Joh. de Monte Mir.*, 228F–229A see p. 393 below.
3. Atto of Vercelli, *Expos. in Epist. Pauli, in I Cor.* 9 (369D–70A).
4. Ibid., *in Col.* 4:5–6 (639CD).
5. *V.S. Joh. Valent.*, 1696E.
6. *V.S. Steph. Obaz.*, 130.25–132.30.
7. *V.B. Roberti de Arbr.*, 1053A.
8. *M.V.S. Hugonis Linc.*, III, c. 13 (Vol. I, p. 125).
9. W. von den Steinen, 'Randbemerkungen Karls des Grossen: eine Selbstanzeige', in the same author's *Menschen im Mittelalter* (Berne–Munich 1967), 33.
10. *V.S. Norberti* (B), 808F.
11. *V. Hugonis abb. March.*, 1727A.
12. *V.S. Hugonis Clun.* (Hildebert), 863C; ('omnibus omnia . . .', 885B).
13. Salimbene, 262.19–22.
14. Ibid. 864.3–9.
15. Salimbene, 447.27–33 (John of Parma); 362.22 ('omnibus omnia . . .'); Visconti, Sermon *Legatus fidelis*, MS. Florence, Laur. Plut. 33 sin. 1, fo. 88[ra]: (of the Franciscan legate Mansueto) 'cum ejus bonitas sit nota omnibus hominibus cognoscentibus eum . . . cum clerici et layci, masculi et femine, senes et juvenes per vicos et plateos pronuntient eum sanctum.' Dark-age examples of the same motif: Arbeo, *V.S. Haimhrammi*, ed. B. Krusch (*SS\** 1920), 37.15–22; Bede, *Hist. Eccl.*, III, c. 17 (I, 161) (Aidan); *V.S. Bonifacii*, c. 3, ed. W. Levison (*SS\** 1905), 12.15–23 (Willibaldus); *V.S. Wynnebaldi*, *SS* 15(1), p. 110.11–15, 34–7 (Hugeburcus).
16. e.g. *Mir. S. Fidis*, 95d (a knight in disguise is discovered because he cannot use a spade).

17. Year 1083, *SS* V,°439.24–32. Doubted by Schreiner, *Untersuchungen*, 41–4 (but not by Schulte, 144–9).
18. *Chronicon Afflighemense*, c. 15 (*PL* 166.827AB).
19. *V.S. Joh. de Monte Mir.*, 227DF.
20. Work for charcoal-burner, see above, p. 365; building-work: *V.S. Joh. de Monte Mir.*, 228A.
21. *V.S. Adalberti* (Canaparius), 585.17–19; *V.P.S. Bernardi Clar.*, § 10, 232D (=Bernhard's brother Guido).
22. *V.S. Ethelwoldi* (Wulfstan), c. 9, p. 39; *V.S. Steph. Obaz.*, 56; *M.V.S. Hugonis Linc.*, IV, c. 10 (Vol. II, p. 50); general services: *V.D. Burchardi*, 859CD; list of jobs: *V.S. Romualdi*, 976D–977A.
23. *V.B. Egid. Sant.*, 406B.
24. *V.B. Lanfranci*, 32D f.
25. e.g. *V.S. Hugonis Clun.*, 863CD f.; *V.B. Joh. de Monte Mir.*, 219–20; *V.B. Egid. Sant.*, 407C.
26. Stephen of Bourbon, *Anecdotes historiques*, ed. A. Lecoy de la Marche (Paris 1877), 187.
27. *V.B. Joh. Piling.*, 151CD.
28. *V.B. Joh. de Monte Mir.*, 228F–9A.
29. See pp. 108–9 above.
30. Morning sermon of 1 June 1305, *Credo*, fo. 158ʳ. The sermon refers to the courage of John the Baptist and other 'sancti che riprendeano i sengori & non curavan la faccia loro'; the preacher's text is John 16:8–11.
31. e.g. Odo of Cluny, *Collat.* III, c. 24 (607D f.); cf. also c. 13 (600AB); and Atto of Vercelli, *Epist.* 9 (117B).
32. c. 123 (*PL* 205.316B–18A). See Gauthier, *Magnanimité*, 243–4 for the analysis and background of this chapter; and on the same concept in Nicholas of Hanapes, O.P. (†1291), ibid. 242 n. 2.
33. e.g. *V.S. Hugonis Grat.*, 773C. These remarks and the following examples concern only the period *c.* 900–*c.* 1300. For a dark-age version of 'frank-speaking' see Graus, *Volk*, 382, and notes 470–1.
34. *V.S. Romualdi*, 990BC.
35. Ibid. 990C–991A.
36. *V.S. Joh. Gualb.*, 777AB.
37. *V.S. Steph. Obaz.*, 174.18 f.
38. Ibid. 176.29–32.
39. Ibid. 124.14–34.
40. *V.B. Joh. de Monte Mir.*, 219DE.
41. *Sermones dominicales et in solemnitatibus*, ed. Fr. Locatelli (Padua 1895–1903), 213b–214a.
42. Albertino de Verona O.F.M. (*flor.* 1249–50), *Sermones in festis sanctorum necnon in maioribus solemnitatibus coram populo habendi*, MS. Florence, Bibl. laur., Conv. soppr. 548, fo. 55ᵛᵃ: 'recto tramite incedebat feriens equaliter gladio spirituali divites pauperes nobiles et ignobiles.'
43. Salimbene, 324.29–33.
44. e.g. *V.S. Petr. Gonz.*, 392F; *V.B. Roberti Salent.*, 504F.
45. Salimbene, 816.10–819.5.
46. *V.S. Geraldi Aur.*, 659D–660A.
47. e.g. *V.B. Egid. Sant.*, 407D; *V.S. Petr. Gonz.*, 392F.
48. *V.B. Joh. Piling.*, 150E.
49. Brunetto Latini, *Tresors*, III, c. 94 (p. 416.14–16). This and the next two references are offered as mere examples.
50. Philippe de Novare, III § 104 (pp. 57–8).

51. Guillaume de Lorris, *Le Roman de la Rose*, ed. F. Lecoy (Paris 1968), lines 2087–9.
52. The only striking example I have met is the physician Peter of Spain, as pope John XXI; cf. Ptolemy of Lucca O.P. (†1327), *Hist. Ecclesiastica*, XXIII, c. 24 (Muratori¹, XI, 1178BC). A hostile source, Ptolemy cites as Pope John's one virtue that even the most humble man could expect a welcome audience from him, but (N.B.) 'dummodo esset Literatus' (1178C). Cf. p. 248 above. The Renaissance humanist Cardinal Giulio Cesarini (†1444) was noted for social amphibiousness; L. Pastor, *The History of the Popes*, I (London 1938⁶), 268–9.
53. *V.S. Guil. Divion.*, c. 26, col. 718B (ed. Bulst, pp. 484–5).
54. Ibid.
55. *V.S. Romualdi*, 995A.
56. *V.S. Hugonis Clun.*, 863B.
57. Ibid. 903D.
58. *V.B. Roberti de Arbr.*, 1053B.
59. J. H. Albanes, *La vie de Sainte Douceline* (Marseilles 1879), 218, 220 (Hugh and Douceline of Digne); cf. *V.B. Joh. de Monte Mir.*, 223C.
60. *V.D. Burchardi*, 860A.
61. *V.S. Guil. Firm.*, 340D.
62. *V.S. Hugonis Grat.*, 784B.
63. *V.S. Steph. Obaz.*, 206 § 7, lines 2–4; and *passim* 200–14.
64. See also *V.S. Bernardi Tiron.*, 1439A.
65. Bibliography, and discussion of these collections, in R. C. Finucane, 'The Use and Abuse of Medieval Miracles', *History*, 60 (1975), 1–10.
66. Examples: *V.S. Joh. Gualb.*, 703–6: noble, knightly, or other high laity, 5; clergy or religious, 10; nondescript or poor, 6 (= 23 per cent, 48 per cent, 29 per cent). *V.S. Hugonis Clun.*, 891–4: 2½—8—3 (= 18 per cent, 60 per cent, 22 per cent). *V.S. Joh. Valent.*, 1698–1700: 3—1—7 (= 27 per cent, 9 per cent, 64 per cent). *V.B. Roberti Salent.*, 507–9: 3—5—24 (= 9 per cent, 16 per cent, 75 per cent). The analysis of beneficiaries of Simon de Montfort's posthumous miracles in J. C. Russell, 'The Canonisation of Opposition to the King in Angevin England', *Anniversary Essays* [for C. H. Haskins] (Boston–New York 1929), 279–90; pp. 286–7, yields approximately 10 per cent, 20 per cent, 70 per cent in the three categories. Mr. Finucane tells me he shares my general impression, though he stresses that among significant variations are differences in the *type* of miracle (especially cures) recorded for the different social classes.
67. e.g. *V.S. Joh. Piling.*, 153C–155D: 1 priest, 8 nondescript (= 12 per cent, 88 per cent); *V.B. Jacobi Cert.*, 154DE: 5 nondescript (= 100 per cent).
68. See the accounts referred to in notes 60–64 above. The sources cited by Mr. Finucane (as in n. 65, p. 1, n. 8), on the Becket cult, have not changed my impression.
69. Hermannus quondam Judaeus, *De conversione sua*, c. 6, ed. G. Niemeyer (*SS QGG* 4 (1963), 88.23–89.15); Grundmann, 'Adelsbekehrungen', 340.
70. *V.B. Egid. Sant.*, 406B.
71. *V.S. Hugonis Clun.*, 885B.
72. *V.S. Joh. Gualb.*, 773C (and 678A).
73. Under Jacobino of Reggio, O.P. (†1233): Salimbene, 103.4–8, cf. lines 15–17.
74. On whose initiative in this regard, and its appeal to some dark-age reformers, see the perceptive lecture by H.M.R.E. Mayr-Harting, *The Venerable Bede, the Rule of St. Benedict, and Social Class* (Jarrow 1976).
75. See p. 428 n. 22 above.

# Index

*Numbers in parentheses, where they do not refer to related notes, indicate references of secondary importance*

MAP 1. Europe and her neighbours *c*. 800–*c*

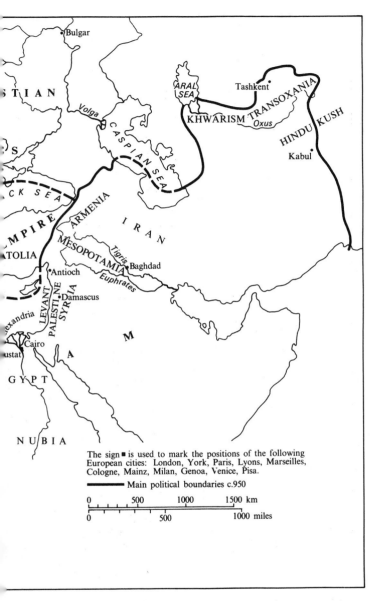

Bulgar

ARAL
SEA

Tashkent

TRANSOXANIA

KHWARISM

Oxus

HINDU KUSH

Kabul

STIAN

Volga

CASPIAN SEA

S

CK SEA

EMPIRE

ARMENIA

IRAN

TOLIA

MESOPOTAMIA

Tigris

Baghdad

Antioch

Euphrates

LEVANT

PALESTINE

SYRIA

Damascus

Alexandria

Cairo

ustat

M

A

GYPT

NUBIA

The sign ■ is used to mark the positions of the following
European cities: London, York, Paris, Lyons, Marseilles,
Cologne, Mainz, Milan, Genoa, Venice, Pisa.

━━━━━ Main political boundaries c.950

| 0 | 500 | 1000 | 1500 km |

| 0 | 500 | 1000 miles |

·oo (showing places mentioned in chapter I)

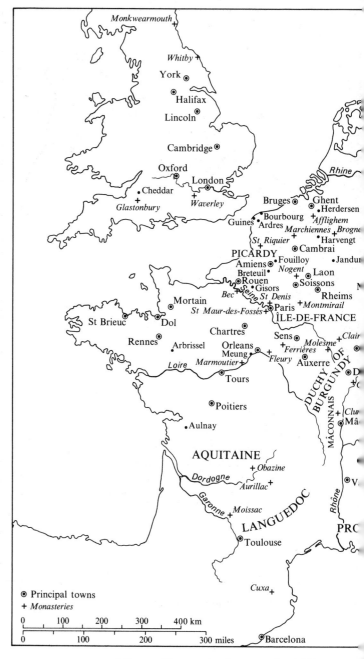

Monkwearmouth +

Whitby +

York ◉

Halifax ◉

Lincoln ◉

Cambridge ◉

Oxford ◉  London ◉

•Cheddar +

Glastonbury +  Waverley +

Rhine

Bruges ◉  Ghent ◉
•Herdersen
Bourbourg +  *Afflighem*
Guines •  Ardres  Marchiennes +  Brogne
*St Riquier* +  •Harvengt
◉ Cambrai

PICARDY  •Fouilloy  •Jandur
Amiens ◉  *Nogent*
Breteuil •  +  Laon
◉ Rouen  •Gisors  ◉ Soissons
*Bec*  *Seine*  St Denis  Rheims
Mortain ◉  St Maur-des-Fossés +  ◉ Paris  +*Montmirail*
St Brieuc ◉  Dol ◉  ÎLE-DE-FRANCE

Rennes ◉  Chartres ◉  Sens ◉  *Molesme* •  *Clair*
•Arbrissel  Orleans ◉  +  *Ferrières*
Meung •  +  *Fleury*  Auxerre ◉  ◉
*Loire*  *Marmoutier* +  ◉ D
◉ Tours  +◉

◉ Poitiers  + *Clu*
◉ Mâ

•Aulnay

AQUITAINE
+*Obazine*
*Dordogne*  +  ◉ V
*Aurillac* +
*Garonne*  •Moissac  *Rhône*
LANGUEDOC  PRC
◉ Toulouse

◉ Principal towns
+ *Monasteries*
*Cuxa* +
0    100    200    300    400 km

0        100        200        300 miles  ◉ Barcelona

MAP 2. Europe in the central middle ages (

POMERANIA

LIPPE
+ Marienfeld
◉ Münster
+ Cappenberg

◉ Magdeburg

Elbe

Elbe

ogne
◉
ix

BERG    + Hersfeld

◉ Mainz    Fulda +

+ Bingen

FRANCONIA    ◉ Bamberg
            ◉ Nuremberg
◉ Speyer        Regensburg
            ◉
+ Hirsau    Danube    ◉ Freising
rze                ◉ Augsburg

St Blasien    + Reichenau
res    +    ◉
    Constance

◉ Prague

Vienna
◉

Milan    Padua
Vercelli ◉    ◉
ble ◉ Pavia    ◉ Venice
Volpiano ◉ ◉ Cremona
    Parma ◉    Po
Genoa    Bologna ◉    ◉ Ravenna
◉
e
•
ICE    Pistoia    Camaldoli    Urbino
    Pisa ◉ ◉ Prato    ++    ◉
    Florence    Vallombrosa
        ◉    • Arezzo
        Siena

TUSCANY

• Tivoli
◉ Rome

+ Monte Cassino

ving places mentioned in chapters 2–16)